Landscaping With Perennials

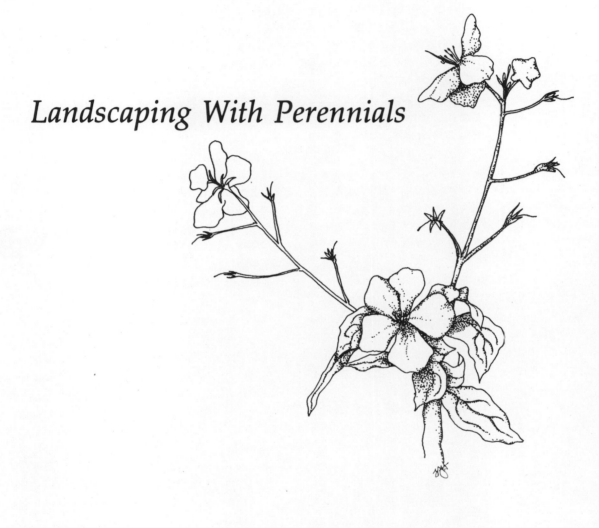

Landscaping With Perennials

by
Emily Brown

Illustrated by
Leslie J. Haning
and
Rachel Gage

TIMBER PRESS
Portland, Oregon

ISBN 0-88192-063-0

Printed in Hong Kong
Book design: Sandra Mattielli

TIMBER PRESS, INC.
9999 SW Wilshire
Portland, Oregon 97225

Contents

Acknowledgments

The encounter with an enthusiast, a one or two hour touching of minds with a gardener who has grown a plant I liked or has liked a plant I have grown—of what inestimable value that unplanned, inconsequential exchange. It is impossible to estimate the enrichment or to approximate the number of people or minutes. But I keep harking back to those encounters and envy those who easily keep a journal. When summing up all the gifts of knowledge from many over a long life, I was sad to have forgotten some names. Since I am now saying, "Thank you, thank you" to some whose names I do remember, I must hope those with whom I spent little, or much, time looking at plants will realize that I say thank you to all of you with true sincerity.

Some of the ones I do remember or have their names in letters and jottings were all contributary donors to my accumulating knowledge to a greater or less degree. Since the influence of a few was very important especially in the beginning, I will list their names with the briefest notes as to their field.

I will append a list of just the major reference books which I use constantly. The journals of the various societies are continual reference sources.

Lappula

Mai Arbegast	Useless to race her in saying, "Look at this". What a seeing-eye!
Ernesta Ballard	A first class horticulturist. I followed her on a number of expeditions.
Keith Bixford	His knowledge of an approach to readers through clarity of sentence, paragraph and chapter structure is very valuable.
Margaret K. Brown	Her skills and kindness in imparting her knowledge was the springboard of her sister-in-law's search for design principles and plants of merit.
Thomas D. Church	Everybody's ideal teacher and doer of garden design.
Elizabeth de Forest	Her appreciation of plants and her ability to communicate about them was remarkable.
Carl English	His interest, investigation and production of unusual plants was an inspiration.
Harold Hillier	A close tie to a knowledgeable Britisher is a prerequisite in a life of studying plants.
Barbara Joe Hoshizaki	An authority on ferns who communicates her enthusiasm in person even more than in her writings.

1

Gerda Isenberg	Also an authority on ferns, growing many choice types in her nursery. Her first love, Western Natives, she will share with anyone fortunate enough to know her.
Elizabeth McClintock	A friend and mentor who can make taxonomy seem necessary, attractive and even easy.
Sydney Mitchell	An immigrant to the West Coast who was able to show to others what he found special in "Your California Garden and Mine". He gave me some of my first South Africans.
Edith North	How many plants we investigated together. Her garden has a few unique perennials some which we planted years ago.
Victor Reiter	He keeps on divulging information about more Rock Garden plants from his beautiful and extensive collection. Many hours have I spent fruitfully in his garden.
Lester Rowntree	Sitting with her under a tree in her rookery in the Carmel Highlands, one could talk or look across to China.
William Schmidt	What a doer, his fingers in many pies outside his chosen specialties. He is not far away although he now lives in Arizona.
"Peg" Stebbins	With Margaret Truax taught me the A-Z of gardening.
Pete Sugiwara	A nursery man of note; a skillful grower of trees big and trees bonsai and plants in between with the true Japanese outlook on nature.
Betty White	A dear friend with whom I spent happy hours on exciting adventures. She had the best double perennial border I have known at first hand.

A number of photographs were taken by me but I wish to thank the following for permission to use some of their superb photographs.

Chris Andrews; C. A.
Keith Bickford; K. B.
Ted Cardoza; T. C.
Dick Dunmire; D. D.
Lucy Erickson; L. E.
Harland Hand; H. H.
Louise and Lent Hooker; L. L. H.
Lynn Hunton; L. H.
Kathryn Mathewson; K. M.
Richard Turner; R. T.
Josephine Zeitlin; J. Z.
George Waters; G. W.
Barbara Worl; B. W.

Cyclamen

Bibliography

Mary Bartlett	*Gentians*	Henry Inn	*Chinese Houses & Gardens*
G. Beck	*Fritillaries*	Gertrude Jekyll	*Woods & Garden etc.*
Alan Bloom	*Plantman's Progress*	Hartmann & Kester	*Plant Propagation*
Hal Borland	*A Countryman's Flowers*	Loraine Kuck	*The World of the Japanese Garden*
Thomas D. Church	*Gardens are for People* *Your Private World etc.*	Elizabeth Lawrence	*The Little Bulbs* *Gardens in Winter*
H. K. Davidson	*The Art of the Zen Garden*	Brian Mathew	*Dwarf Bulbs*
F. Gordon Foster	*Ferns to Know & Grow*	Mildred Mathias, Ed.	*Flowering Plants in the Landscape*
H. Lincoln Foster	*Rock Gardening*	Gay Nightingale	*Growing Cyclamen*
Ira N. Gabrielson	*Western American Alpines*	Mitsumura Suilo Shoin, Ed.	*Invitation to Japan*
H. G. Hillier	*Hillier's Manual*	Graham Stuart Thomas	*Plants for Ground Cover* *Perennial Garden Plants*
Barbara Joe Hoshizaki	*Fern Grower's Manual*		
Joseph Hudak	*Gardening with Perennials* *Perennials for Your Garden*	Roger Twain	*Earthly Pleasures*
		Woodcock and Coutts	*Lilies*
Will Ingwersen	*Alpine Garden Plants*		

Hortus III

Encyclopedias of the New York Botanical Garden, The Royal Horticultural Society,
The American Horticultural Society

W. Keble Martin	*The Concise British Flora in Colour*
A. B. Graf	*Exotica: Pictorial Encyclopedia of Exotic Plants*

Reasons For Gardening

Why do people make a garden?

Plants are alive and give a sense of grace and beauty to both the homesite and its occupants. A garden is a living testimonial to man's relation to nature. In a garden and gardening we both acknowledge and assert our place in and oneness with the natural order. The garden provides contrast to the humdrum and demanding affairs of life. A place to find peace in time of turmoil; a relief from sorrow; a place for reflection and personal integration; the site for enjoying the pleasure of friends; and a triumph of our aesthetic senses and the joy of being alive. A garden will do all these things and more.

A garden will add more to our lives if well planned. It must compliment our living quarters; it must not be an extraneous adjunct to the building. It may camouflage the nature of the building, but it should do so with some finesse. Some buildings are just enclosures in which to eat, sleep and watch television. The inhabitants and the public probably thoroughly dislike the appearance. Sometimes buildings which are really quite horrible looking can be improved by a garden; a garden can half-hide the building or be so pleasing in character that one can avoid looking at or seeing the building. The building can be given a face-lift such that its plant clothing and ornaments demand most of the attention. Commonly, plants used to disguise an ugly structure are not much more than utilitarian screens; they need to be attractive as well as efficient screens, however. A garden should certainly be related to the building whether to hide it; to provide distraction; or to harmonize with it. In any case you will do a better job if the garden has a harmonious life of its own.

Many people like a feeling of privacy. A fence or a wall is often the most successful and the most attractive way to enclose the yard. Most hedges are just a barrier and not a very solid one. However, a hedge along the streetside can do more than simply provide privacy. It can also possess artistic values.

What do people want to see as they approach the building? Men seem to crave a bit of lawn—a green carpet. Women care more about a bit of color or rather "instant color". As if green were not a color! To cater to this craving for color, nurserymen advertise "instant color". Their gullible customers flock in to buy Pansies, Petunias, Marigolds, Impatience, and other plants in full bloom, mostly annuals. (Hopefully, there seems to be a swing toward perennials.) If the plants, awash with color, recover from being transplanted when past the peak of their vigor, they will give color, but only for a spell. Bedding plants have little structure; their function is to produce a momentary swatch or strip of "color", the brighter, the denser, the better. (I apologize to the Snapdragon, the *Lobelia* and the like; their faces have shape and character when you look closely.) This kind of planting is only incidental to the architecture of the garden; it plays the part of gingerbread used as trim on the eaves of the house or the lace at the hem of a petticoat. Do you think I am saying that a garden should have no color? No indeed, and later I will describe many perennials chosen for color. We shall try to make some gay compositions.

You have more or less decided that there are good reasons to make a garden. Do you think it is a good idea to make a better than average one? You will have greater success and enjoyment if you have a plan.

How to go about making this plan? First, visit every garden you possibly can—in all seasons. Consider your general impression, the overall appearance of the landscape design. After enjoying the flowers and the color, seek out the details which make up the complete picture. Look at the form, the mass which the foliage makes, its density and its manner of branching. Then try to see how the individual leaf shapes play a part. Develop your "seeing-eye" and make an inventory of landscaping ideas which you can later use in your own garden. Associating and integrating a variety of elements takes careful planning and doing. Is this an art which can be studied and learned? If you will but develop a seeing-eye you will soon come to recognize the different forms and the relationships between them. When you like a landscape which you encounter, always ask yourself "why?" Take the time to analyze your reasons. After a time, these exercises will not only become a habit but will develop your sense of how to combine plants in a fitting and pleasing manner. Meanwhile, there is no better place than here to admit that some combinations which turn out to be smashing are the result of mostly happenstance—and perhaps the general tendency on the part of growing plants to associate with each other in an appealing and admirable community.

How about just going to nurseries? There are salesmen who will tell you what to buy; there is often a "landscaper" who will come to your home and make a plan. It is better for you to make your own plan unless, of course, you have already engaged an independent landscape architect to make it for you. But have a plan one way or another. One day you will have the urge to fill up the garden with plants and have only to go and buy them. When you are selecting plants at the nursery without a plan, you will be led to the plants which are just old enough to have arrived at their season of bloom. You should look rather for those containers in which the leaves are just emerging and which may stand in some neglected corner or you may pass some containers with old basal rosettes which bravely persist in spite of lack of care. Even the nurserymen must be busy bringing the flowering plants to the foreground and trying to sell them. They must hope a knowledgeable client or two will discover the unusual perennial temporarily in a corner.

At no season will the basal leaves or the stem leaves look their best in a gallon can; you should have an idea how the plant will grow when you have had it at home awhile and next year and the year after. A large percentage of perennials attain their greatest value in their third year.

If you have become convinced that there are reasons to make a garden, what do you do about this urge to make a garden in a hurry? The planning and the preparation are a delightful pastime. You can gather perennials you see and like—some of those you have discovered when visiting gardens. Try to have a holding place where these can be nurtured while your plan is in progress. You have started with a plan based on principles of form. You will no doubt modify and augment as your ideas and tastes change but your additions and changes will conform to your first plan when you have made a good one.

Start first with your background plants, the bones of your garden must set the stage. Research plant materials every way you can through Societies, Arboretums and literature. Meanwhile, this is such an enjoyable occupation that you need be in no hurry to complete your project. There is trememdous satisfaction in the careful process of building your garden. It does not need to be an artistic masterpiece; nevertheless, perfection should be your goal. You will improve the details as the months, seasons, years pass and the work this entails will give you joy more than you can imagine. The garden is almost as close to the earth as we can get and we need this place of renewal to enrich our too ordinary and stressful lives.

Nothing is earned, everything is grace,
    and yet, and yet
Work as hard as you can.

From *Road of the Heart Cave* by Geoffrey Brown Thrown to the Winds Press 1984

Compatibility

In these chapters I want to stir your imagination to the exciting possibilities for landscaping by pointing to the garden use of many perennials. Perennials combine well with all manner of plants—shrubs, trees, bulbs; herbs, succulents, ferns and grasses. They work as well with those non-plant elements so necessary to a well conceived landscape—pavement, walls, rocks and water. In addition, while I will certainly deal with the common perennials, I want to introduce you to the satisfaction and design potential of many of the less commonly used species and their cultivars. They can greatly expand your horizon of perennials and broaden the palette you use in creating unusual and gratifying landscapes.

Before proceeding, something should be said about general "tone" or "style". The garden should be of a type which especially appeals to its owner and, moreover, goes with the building and countryside which I hope appeal to the owner. Everyone has values, perhaps not always acknowledged, which influence their likes and dislikes. If you have a choice of the building in which you live, other than whether it is the most reasonable, you probably have some ideas of the style you like. If you lean toward "colonial", you probably would not look at "modern". Or the expression, "modified modern" may describe a style which appeals to you. The modification is not a question of degree only; it is a question of what it leans to: are its modifications the result of leaning toward a little French influence, or Spanish or English or Dutch or Japanese? The expression "contemporary" covers a multitude of sins—not necessarily sins since the style of any age can be directed by artistic principles. Contemporary—of the last half of the 20th century—usually means, among other things, simplicity vs. complexity and low stature vs. tall. It means incorporating the values of light and shade and the resultant shadows. There is also a "feel" of a particular style which is impossible to define.

Style is affected by the climate of the place. Walls are thicker, doors are narrower in windy, cold climates. In a warm climate, the building will have a closer connection with the outdoors and its architecture will be modified by the number and shapes of its doors and its outdoor rooms.

Do you have to live in a big city? Even apartment houses have personalities. Perhaps you choose one that has a style not so contemporary that you cannot tell whether you like it or not. At least you will look to see if it has balconies.

When you can retire, your new abode will be chosen for comfort first, but for a style somehow suitable to the geography in which it is situated. Certainly, if you have chosen a countrified area, or some other area with felicitous climate you may be able to find a cottage. You may move to Arizona for reasons of health but probably also do so because the aspect of nature there appeals to you. The building you choose will probably be of a Spanish type. If you are planning to live in an area with many trees, you may seek a building made of wood to create a harmony between setting and building.

A cottage or house in the Victorian style will have a particular flavor which should be reflected in the garden. If you found a house with Tudor architecture, you might landscape with plants which were popular at the time. If the environment and the building influence the design of the garden, as they properly should, they all come back to your personality and what you like best in and for your surroundings.

Let us put you on the couch for a bit. How do you react to size—large or small? To position and order—do you like shoes in pairs placed in a row and forks with forks and knives with knives in the drawers? Do you prefer sturdiness to delicacy? What about color—do you like a kaleidoscope of color or only two colors combined and, perhaps those in pale shades? Do you prefer the traditional or to experiment with the unusual? A careful analysis of your likes and dislikes will give you the guides you need in deciding what kind of garden you will like.

Do you want a formal garden? An informal one? Formal and informal have gradations between very formal and not at all formal. Do you like best a garden apparently quite without any plan?

It is usually assumed that a plan with straight lines is the chief ingredient of formality. This is not necessarily so, since many very formal gardens use curved lines. But there is order in a formal garden. The lines have a definite proportion to the setting and a relation to each other. There is a sense of balance and symmetry. The bounds and divisions need not be geometric. So it is with a plant; if it is clipped, it certainly has a feeling of formality, but if it is naturally geometric in shape it need not be used just in a formal setting.

A "natural" garden is clearly a type of an informal garden. It certainly should not, however, be construed as a garden without plan; the lines do not just proceed at random. The plants are not without arrangement; they are not placed just wherever there is a hole. But the plan is simple; it has no manufactured features; its lines follow the topography of the ground and the form and style of any buildings upon it.

This concept is not the same as a "wild garden". In a wild garden a more casual plan is followed. The plants in a wild garden are the more rough and unsophisticated species which usually originate from fields, hills and mountains; they are often called "field flowers". Or their habitat may be a meadow, or a glade or a foothill. They need not be planted in a jumble; in the wild most of them will be found growing in drifts. The best guide for a wild garden plan is to try to imitate nature. Few of us have room for a wild garden since the concept only makes its point if there is a combination of a number of species, more than one of each and all of them requiring roughly identical conditions.

But we all have room for a "natural garden". The principle which determines its successful realization is easily formulated. Do not manipulate. Let the manner in which the paths go and the beds lie be simply the easiest way. As you see it is fundamentally the form of the garden which determines whether or not it is natural. However, the choice of plant material, especially perennials, will be modified. You will not necessarily choose "wild flowers", but if you do, they will not be the coarser more "weedy" type grown in the wild garden; they will be rather well-behaved types which associate well with other normally cultivated types. You will choose, from the cultivated types, subjects which are not very exotic looking. You will not plant orchids in a bed with daisies. You will use species with a shape which fits with the shapes of their neighbors. You may shear for health's sake but you will never clip.

If the natural garden is only one type of the informal garden, what other forms may the informal garden take? An informal garden may have a manufactured form; the shape of its spaces and its contours may depart from the way the land lies. The result must not appear too ordered, too regular, too even. The plants which you choose may be as elegant as you please; only do not place them in the manner of a museum display. Stay away from pairs, straight rows, geometric shapes and symmetry.

Well, a formal garden. It is apt to depend upon pairs and rows and geometry and symmetry. I have said a formal garden may have curves upon which an informal garden depends heavily. But the curves are long and flowing and are usually related to another feature which repeats the form. The lines of a formal garden cannot just wander; they must appear to have a purpose as they curve or follow a straight line. The formal garden must be neat—not that an informal garden should not be neat also—but a tidy neatness. The plants used in a formal garden are various; one does not need to stick to Boxwood, Italian Cypress and Tuberous Begonias. Plants do have personalities; one senses that some are more formal than others. But the form of the plant in a formal garden is firm rather than drooping; cascaders and trailers can play a part in a formal garden only if there is a wall. The branching habit should be regular rather than random. The texture should be firm rather than flimsy. The pattern of the leaves may be quite intricate but the pattern should appear to be "formally" sculpted.

Do you prefer an informal garden? A formal garden? A wild garden?

A simple garden depends on the use of a limited number of species. The design is uncomplicated. The plants can be unusual, outstanding species with definite personalities but the few selected must all be related to each other and to the site. A simple garden may be developed in a very small front yard or in an arboretum. Sometimes it is wise to make a garden for a public building "simple". Only a few species used in quantity will have an effect of dignity. They should be chosen for dignity not severity; some perennials do have a dignified character. You should appraise them for such a characteristic. One or two examples come to mind: Hellebores or *Astilbes* in the shade and *Pelargoniums* or Peonies in the sun.

The "elegant" garden will no doubt be a minigarden. It will be created by someone who likes plants with an elegant personality—such as orchids. Some plants seem elegant merely because they are either hard to grow or rare. A terrace will have an elegant look rather than a simple look if the pots contain unusual and/or striking rather than ordinary plants.

A "homely" garden is simply an informal or natural garden with emphasis on the well-known, familiar species. A homely garden must have a design but it is carried out with perennials which are more "everyday" than exotic and which are arranged in a fashion not too orderly or precise.

Let us pin down a few characteristics in perennials which make them good choices for these various types of garden. The most important consideration in selecting a perennial is how well it suits its site which depends to a great extent on its personality. Several traits contribute to the personality—its manner of growing, its habit, its shape, its size, its texture, and the simplicity or intricacy of its parts.

Let us examine a few of the traits which make up personality. Graceful: this term is used to describe a plant with either arching branches or nicely spaced branches. A few flower stems are called "wands" which obviously implies a slender curving stem. Graceful perennials go well with graceful shrubs and trees.

Delicate or dainty are words used to describe various perennials. Usually dainty perennials go better with each other than with coarse or rough perennials. You will see such perennials as *Dicentra, Corydalis* and surely some of the ferns described by these terms.

Rigorous or sturdy describe a character opposite from delicate. Sometimes perennials with these attributes are called "masculine". Masculine and feminine are known to mix well, at least sometimes.

"Coarse" is a term given to the foliage of certain perennials, usually those which are tall or wide or both. The characteristic usually refers to the texture of the leaf which is often hairy. Woodiness in the structure contributes to coarseness, also. Subshrubs add materially to a combination of perennials: use the woodier ones with the coarser perennials.

"Huge": pure size—the big plant goes best with other strong growers and in a big space. A huge perennial can serve in place of a large shrub or one may be used to act as a focal point.

It is not all that easy to define what elements establish the personality of a plant. It is, however, quite definite in a large majority. Which to select for which purposes?

Libertia

Section I: The Materials

Aster

1. Form of the Plant

Remember, flowers have a fleeting existence; the garden will be there well before and after the height of bloom. So, most of the year, the color and especially the form of the foliage will provide you with all elements of your landscape design.

Many perennials are herbaceous, many others are semi-herbaceous in temperate climates, that is, most of the above ground foliage dies back in the fall but basal leaves in the form of rosettes or tufts remain the year around. In a mixed planting there will be some evergreen perennials. On the other hand, you can expect some bare ground during the non-growing period but this time-span is short because new growth starts in a temperate zone so early in certain species that there seems hardly more than a pause. Leaves will begin to emerge when it is still technically winter. Often the embryo leaves will be furled together and the visual effect will be a pointed cone, attractive in shape and pleasing in its promise of an entirely unexpected maturity. (See later examples.)

New leaves start to grow from above ground parts of the plant. Many of these leaves will grow on their own stems and live their lives as independent foliage. According to season, flower stems will start growth from crowns and may or may not be decorated with leaves. (The flower stem without leaves is called a stalk.) Those leaves on the flowering stems may be quite different in shape from the strictly foliage leaves. But there will be some common characteristics—some feature of the form or the texture. The flower stem leaves may be few or many; they usually decrease in size as the height of the stem increases. The persistent rosette of certain perennials, having looked sufficient unto itself for several months, pushes forth from its center the nascent flower now only in tight green bud.

Meanwhile the evergreen plants begin to put on new leaves, either early or late. Sometimes the new leaves just mix with the old leaves. A combination of young and old is often attractive; sometimes the new leaf coming from the same node pushes the old leaf off. Some just drop. In the case of clumping, perennials, evergreen or herbaceous like *Moraea, Agapanthus, Hemerocallis, Diplarrhena, Astartea* and *Libertia,* new leaves come up between the old blades and more often than not the oldest (marred or dead), must be cut out.

All this growth of foliage takes place on plants of different shape; the shape is determined by the habit of growth. Let us survey several and various habits and give a few examples of each. Look again for the emergent leaves of herbaceous perennials and at the form of nascent foliage as it first pushes from the soil. I have called it a pointed cone but it is more than a cone; the tight wrapping of the leaves gives it special texture as well as contour, it is etched by their edges. Amazing examples are *Trillium, Cynoglossum grande, Baptisia, Hosta, Polygonatum, Eucomis.* In the latter the new leaves burst from the top of the bulb. The cone of *Hedychium* is crimson, as the new foliage

Agapanthus

Baptisia

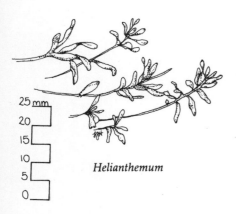

Helianthemum

Helleborus

Pulmonaria

erupts from the nodes of the rhizome. Look at the emerging stem of a *Polygonatum;* all the intricate parts are wrapped around each other forming a slender column. Leaves may be pressed together like an accordian instead of being wrapped; one cannot believe the big leaves of *Rodgersia* can be compressed so neatly and safely.

Next, examine carpets and mats. Some will keep growing new leaves throughout the year. There is a maximum refreshment time around Spring when the days lengthen and the nights are warmer. At the same time stems of spreaders lengthen. Real cascaders include *Helianthemum* and certain *Hypericum.*

I will mention a few mats and include some which will trail somewhat. *Thymus, Blechnum, Arabis, Armeria, Erinus, Rubus, Tanakaea, Campanula* spp in variety, *Raoulia glabra,* the mound which looks like a sheep's back—asleep on an Australian hillside. A little higher are the foliage mats of *Primula, Achillea, Aster, Solidago, Adenothera,* and other *Campanulas.* These mats are often made up of a type of growth called a tuft: the divisions in the mat, made by the tufts, can often be easily seen. *Geum* makes a beautiful mat, slowly, especially the uncommon sp *G. georgenberg.*

You will probably grow, to combine with your perennials, a few subshrubs, some evergreen, some prostrate. They will be given a fresh look with the new foliage of February and March: e.g. *Putoria, Jasminum parkeri, Leptospermum, Genista.*

Many perennials grow both foliage and flowers from a central crown. As the plant increases in width, new crowns may be made, (either from below ground or from a rooting stem), e.g. *Primulas.* Occasionally the foliage grows spokewise from the crown; this habit is evident in *Helleborus niger* and *Pulmonaria augustifolia.* The stems of *Pulmonaria* usually are close to the ground, with the leaves in an overlapping pattern.

Let us think now of perennials which grow from that special formation called a rosette. Some rosettes make a pattern flat upon the soil. (As the flower stems grow, this basal foliage often is hidden.) The big rosette of *Verbascum chaixii* is almost covered by the upper leafage while the plant is in bloom. The rosette of some rock garden plants, like *Ramonda* is always visible. The rosettes of succulent families are their claim to fame; *Crassula* and *Echeveria* make perfect rosettes. The rosettes of *Sedums* are often tight and tiny. Look for rosettes in a number of perennials, e.g. *Digitalis lutea,* some *Veronicas, Hutchinsia, Haberlae, Saxifraga.* Some *Saxifragas* have a pronounced rosette as *Saxifraga umbrosa* var. *primuloides nana.* Some *Aquilegias* have a beautiful rosette when young.

As you may recall, there is usually a difference in the form of basal and stem leaves. The foliage on the flowering stems often contributes another detail to the form of the plant. The total form is determined by the stem/leaf/flower/combination. Look at a plant of *Aster frikartii;* it has quite a spread because of its branching habit. Then look at the wide expanse of a plant of *Gypsophila;* all from a single root many, many branchlets are manufactured.

Let us move to a large section of perennials which grow in "clumps". Clumps seems an ugly word but it has come to mean several stems from a crown. You will find that many clumps grow from a rhizome. The great majority have blade-shaped leaves of various forms which give each plant a distinctive look. An erect, stiff blade will result in a clump quite different from the clump formed by soft, bending leaves which make a fanning or spreading mass. The first type is represented by *Iris siberica,* the second by *Iris douglasii.* When a plant has a few rather than many leaves and they fan in a curving manner, the clump looks rather like a fountain. The leaves of *Hesperaloe* curve in a pronounced manner. *Arthropodium cirrhatum,* New Zealand Rock Lily, makes a fuller fountain.

Soft leaves, not blade-shaped, grow in clumps also. Sometimes when the foliage is only partially mature, the clump has the look of a bubbling fountain. The clusters of foliage of *Thalictrum* may be fluffy or quite delineated according to the species; *Foeniculum* looks almost foamy especially in its bronze form. *Paeonia* is more open—the pattern of its individual leaves can be clearly seen but it is still full and flowing, a soft clump.

. A quite different habit of foliage is less common; leaves of some genera make a distinct fan. You will find this fanning arrangement of the leaves in several bulbous and rhizomous perennials. Some examples are *Babiana, Iris* and *Neomarica.* A plant of *Neomarica* will appear to be espaliered when the winged flowering stems angle away from foliage stems.

Another habit which is sculptural is the tiered form. This is to be found in many *Salvias* and in *Ballota nigra.* It is a spectacular feature of *Phlomis* and *Paris.* It is at the time when the latter two are in flower that the tiered effect is accentuated. Tiered leaves give foliage a distinct character; this is noticeable even in the smaller genera like *Galium*.

Just a few more plant habits to mention, and I will let you find the examples. Stems may arch, may trail, may drape, may even loll and in each case the look is different. Plants with some of these habits are suitable for slopes, edges, top of walls and those places where the stems can sprawl or hang.

Habits may be dense, open, horizontal or erect. Plants may form a mound, a cushion or a colony. The habits vary enough but in almost every instance the character of the leaves which clothe the stem is basic to the total personality. Since it would be impossible to categorize the habits of all the perennials you will want to grow let us turn to the form of the leaf.

Echeveria

Galium

Iris

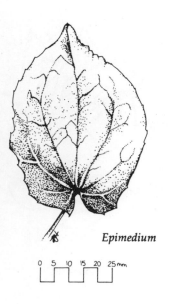

Epimedium

0 5 10 15 20 25mm

2. Form of the Leaf

Aspidistra

Of those circles which are intricate, most are modified by what happens on the edges or on the surface, e.g. some spp. of *Ligularia*. Modifications occur sometimes at the point of attachment to the stem; this variation in the outline may not be noticeable at first glance. Occasionally, they result in a slight twist to the leaf. You will see an example in the drawing of an *Aspidistra* leaf.

Some leaves which have a rounded look are more oval upon examination; there are quantities of true ovals, slender or broad or in between shape. Of course, in drawing the outline of any leaf, one does not use a drawing aid, such as a compass. However, some are close to a geometric oval, e.g. the leaflet of one sp. of *Epimedium*. But, this oval, as many others comes to a point at the tip and tapers at the base. Naturally, the many leaves which end in a point would be regarded as less geometric than those which are egg-shaped, or just oval.

A blade-shaped leaf which is wide through the center portion gives the appearance of being oval, e.g. *Eucomis, Canna, Aspidistra*. The base of the leaf of *Aspidistra* is rolled into a sort of funnel.

Leaves as they spread from their stems at the base may have rounded portions and those which continue to a point are usually called "heart-shaped". The heart may be a traditional Valentine heart or a human heart with sides uneven: *Brunnera, Cyclamen, Epimedium* (another), *Asarum, Eryngium, Maianthemum* and some *Campanulas*.

Another variation with a descriptive appellation is kidney-shaped: e.g. another *Asarum*, some *Violas*, some *Ligularias, Boykinia jamesii*, and some *Alchemillas*.

A spoon-shaped leaf really looks like a spoon. It is not a common shape but I think of an example: *Globularia meridionalis*; many small, slender spoons radiate from the crown.

"Hastate" is rather a technical term referring to a form that is like the head of an arrow. Such a shape might be called triangular. The most typical example is the leaf of *Arum*. You will also notice this shape in the many small leaves of some *Salvias*. Others with leaves nearly triangular are: *Veronica grandis* var. *holophylla, Eryngium alpinum, Tiarella, Pelargonium* 'Ninon'.

Leaves are often lobed, either with shallow lobes or deep lobes: e.g. *Hepatica, Francoa, Vancouveria, Aconitum*, some spp. of *Pelargonium*, and a sp. of *Erodium*, *E. pelargonifolium*. Some others which are more deeply lobed are: *Acanthus, Geranium, Rupicapnos*.

The shapes of leaves are various, mostly miraculous. Besides shape, several other qualities have a part in the character of the leaf and what it contributes to the garden. Size, of course—a very large leaf is said to be bold. Substance—a very thick leaf is forceful, adds a note of stability. Texture—quite a different effect is made by a glossy

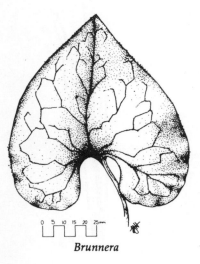

0 5 10 15 20 25mm

Brunnera

leaf than by a velvety leaf. These habitual qualities are noted in the Plant Descriptions whenever they are definite enough to be significant.

Form of foliage in all its great variety contributes most to the design of mixed plantings. Let us look at some shapes.

To start with the circle, circles are more than just round. A round leaf is sometimes notched on its edges or perhaps curled throughout. There is the large round leaf which grows on its own stem or the small round leaf which combines with others to create its special pattern on its branching stem. Some leaves have fairly long stems; some lie close to the ground virtually stemless. To name a few circles: *Bergenia, Pelargonium hortorum, Tropaeolium, Mentha requienii, Begonia, Hosta, Gunnera, Alchemilla, Origanum, Hydrocotyle.*

"Indented" is a term you will meet in descriptions of the edges of leaves. There is a difference in looks between toothed and indented a little and indented a lot. The leaves of certain genera are indented moderately: e.g. *Alchemilla* and *Saxifraga.*

A still more general term is "cut". When cut deeply a leaf becomes divided. Never is a leaf cut in straight lines; mostly beautiful patterns are made. Just a few of many as examples: *Angelica, Romneya, Cynara, Aralia, Argemone, Artemisia, Astrantia.* When very finely cut, the leaf is described as "lacy": e.g. *Astilbe, Filipendula, Thalictrum, Anemone, Achillea, Pulsatilla, Gonospermum.*

A leaf may be divided "palmately" or "pinnately". In the latter, the segments are narrower. In the overall view of mixed foliage, the effect of different kinds of divided leaves is similar. Compare *Dicentra, Polemonium, Paeonia.*

Many perennials have very small leaves placed in a crowded manner on their stems. Those leaves which are thick give the plant a different appearance than those which are thin: e.g. *Dianthus* (some spp.) *Edraianthus, Lithodora, Erinus, Houstonia, Tanacetum* and *Bauera,* a subshrub with tiny leaves. Some leaves are so narrow that they look needle-like, notably some spp. of *Calluna* and *Erica.*

Small leaves sometimes wrap the stem. When they overlap each other, the word "imbricated" is used to describe this shingle effect. The dwarf spp. of *Teucrium* offer the best examples.

Above we noticed leaves with decorated edges. They may be notched as in *Veronica armena* and *Geranium andressi;* they may be toothed or scalloped e.g. *Asarina, Achillea umbellata, Phacelia bolanderi.*

When wavy-edged, the waviness can be slight or marked. When exceptionally wavy, they become frilled as in *Teucrium scorodonia* and *Geum georgenberg;* or crinkled as in a cv. of *Ligularia* or *Rubus calycinoides.* The extreme of crinkled encompasses the whole leaf.

You have seen that the edge of the leaf can be trimmed with curling hairs, delightful, especially noticeable in *Hesperaloe.* On the other hand, the edge may be smooth and "entire". In all probability, there are more entire leaves than there are notched, toothed, crimped and wavy added altogether.

When the edge of the leaf is smooth, the face (technically the blade) may be decorated. It may be creased or pleated: e.g. *Pleione, Tigridia, Avena sterilis.* The midrib, and the veins, may be enlarged and seem to protrude above the surface. Often their color is lighter or darker than the color of the leaf proper. When the ribs are quite prominent, various distinguishing patterns are created, for example in *Watsonia marginata,* (which also has edge detail). Vein pattern is best exemplified by the fancy-leaved *Begonias.*

Occasionally it is easier to describe the form of a leaf by comparing it to the shape of the leaf of a well-known genus. Therefore the leaves of *Abutilon* sp., *Veronica* sp., and *Tiarella* sp. are called "maple-like". The species name of a *Thalictrum* is *aquilegifolium,* by which we know that the leaf is "columbine-like".

The largest group of all the categories is the sword-shape or blade-shape. The variations are legion. Most of the time the edges are entire but they may be undulate or trimmed or ribbed. The design is different in each genus, if only imperceptibly. Since there are too many to cover adequately, I will give only a few descriptions.

Sword-shape is obviously pointed. It would have some width and some length and some firmness. Strap-shape is narrow and is the same width for most of its length. Blade-shape, like a knife can be rounded or pointed. Needle-shape is very narrow indeed. A little wider might be called pencil-shaped. A leaf which is rounded rather than flat is found in some of the smaller bulbous plants. The small-&-round is best exemplified by *Narcissus bulbicodium.*

Arum

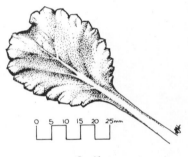

Saxifraga

Cynara

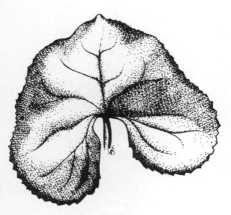

Ligularia

In general, the Narcissi have leaves with rather soft substance; the leaves may be called sword or strap but they are apt to flop, looking like neither. The leaves of a number of bulbous or cormous plants, however, are firm. Observe the decorative foliage of *Iris siberica*. Less erect but not really floppy are the leaves of *Scilla* and *Camassia*. I have mentioned a fan-shaped habit of growth and the pleating of some leaves, both of which are found in *Babiana* leaves, for example. The leaves of several other bulbous or cormous perennials are still more slender than the leaves of *Babiana*. The upright form and the blade-shape adds to the pattern of mixed foliage, to be found in other low-growing spp. e.g. *Liriope, Ophiopogon, Sisyrhincium,* and several grasses for instance the unusual Japanese Blood Grass, *Imperata, and Miscanthus sacchariflorus*. These more or less dwarfs are placed in the foreground or on the edge of planting, effectively.

As we have seen, many or several blade-shaped leaves growing together make a series of vertical lines; the manner in which the leaves grow together has been touched upon in the section on habit of growth. All the resulting clumps are important in garden design. The height of the leaves will usually be lower than that of the flowers in the blooming period and will attain the maximum of the season's growth after the bloom is finished. Perhaps the largest and most handsome sword is that of *Watsonia undulata*.

The sword and blade and strap shapes tall or short, wide or slender provide the backbone of a mixed planting through most of the year.

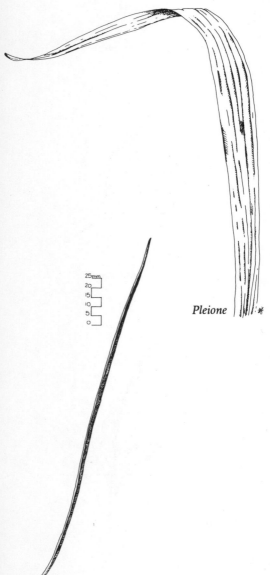

Pleione

Narcissus

Dicentra

3. Color of Foliage

Green foliage—so many shades of green—do they all go together; well, yes, if mixed with a seeing-eye. Some plants have two or more shades in their leaves—the new lighter, brighter than the old. Can you imagine your surprise if these two clashed; they won't, but if you place plants with different shades of green in proximity, there may be an inharmonious effect. For example, a yellow-green looks sickly beside a blue-green.

Shades of Green

Light green: Leaves of a light green color are apt to be thin rather than thick; the light shows through. Maiden-hair Fern is an example; some others are *Polemonium* spp., *Dicentra* spp., *Thalictrum* spp. Plant descriptions often read "fernlike foliage" which usually indicates a translucent leaf. Sometimes it refers to the leaf placement, when the leaflets are evenly spaced on either side of a midrib—like a frond's placement. This particular arrangement of leaflets is called fern-like even when the color is not light green.

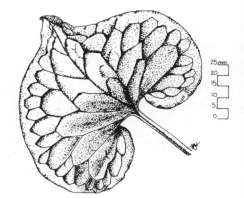

Asarum

Light green is very useful as a brightener when combined with other greens. It is decidedly brightening when it is the color of new leaves against the background of last year's darker green. I have cited the examples of *Epimedium* spp. which all display this characteristic in earliest spring to a marked degree.

Medium green: Medium green is found in the great majority of perennials. It is, however, variable. If the leaf is smooth and waxy, like the leaf of some *Gaultherias* (e.g. *G. procumbens*), the green will be bright even though the hue is dark. *Asarum* is glossy; the intricate pattern of veinage adds to the sheen.

The surface of a leaf may be crinkled as in *Francoa*. This unevenness will modify the shade of green. Some leaves are rough (rugose) which makes the color duller. Of course, hairs of various kinds and colors make a great difference in color.

Medium green, because it is so common in perennials, will be the predominant color in most plantings and set the basic tone. Light greens, dark greens and the less common colors are used to break the monotony of regularity in plantings.

Look for color on the backs of leaves, usually white or silver, but sometimes a shade of red or purplish. When the leaves twist a bit in the breeze they add color to the design. Brown, most outstanding in ferns, adds a rich note.

Dark green: Very dark green, usually seen in leaves which are shiny, is most useful in nearly any planting. It accentuates greenness. It contributes strength to the composition and is a substantial color to which to tie all others. It is very useful as a transition color. Put a dark green between a yellow-green and a bluish-green. Or place it as a background for plants with variegated leaves to "set them off". I have extolled the darkest Hellebore, *Helleborus foetidus,* and the color of its foliage is one of the reasons.

Francoa

Romneya

Paeonia

Salvia

Fragaria chiloensis is one of the darkest green and glossiest ground covers. I do not know a perennial with darker green leaves than *Angelica pachycarpa*; it looks like highly polished wax. *Clivia* has a darker hue than most plants with sword-shaped leaves; again, partly due to the glossy surface. The leaves are a deeper green than, for instance *Agapanthus*.

I have used examples of genera, but species of the same genus differ just as markedly. The crinkled leaves of the common Foxglove rosette, *Digitalis purpurea*, are of a somewhat dull color, but *Digitalis lutea* has dark green leaves and they are shiny. I obviously am talking about basal leaves which are out of sight only during the short blooming period. Their quantity of green is sometimes the reason for their selection. Stem leaves are usually less evident but there is a bonus when they are a good green.

Yellowish: The color green differs according to its composition. There is yellowish-green. *Euphorbias* have yellowish foliage, the yellow heightened by the flower color. *Chamaemelum* is always yellowish but more so in the hotter, drier months. *Selaginella* is yellow-green even in the shade. There are shrubs with yellowish hue, notably *Euonymus* or *Abutilon*. Perennials with yellow-green foliage should be planted in their vicinity.

Bluish: There is bluish-green. Sometimes you will not see the blue in a dark green, such as in *Rosmarinus officinalis* 'Tuscany Blue' or *Helleborus foetidus*, until you put it next to a yellow-green. The foliage of *Romneya* spp. is an example of a light green with a bluish tinge.

Bronze: Bronze is a fine color to use in foliage designs. A green may be shaded bronze, especially in new or young leaves. Once in a while the bronze is so dark that it hides the green. The foliage of some cultivars of *Canna* looks pure bronze. Perhaps the deepest bronze can be seen in the dark cv. of a *Foeniculum*. Try Fennel next to a grey such as Lambs' Ears; it is an interesting shocker. Many spp. have leaves which produce a bronze tint as they age and their juices are dried by the sun. Most are beautiful when they take on these tints, which we usually associate with fall. In truth, however, bronze tints are most commonly found in new leaves, many of which are generously tinted bronze or copper. Notice the early spring leaves of *Epimedium* and *Paeonia*.

Red: Red is common in foliage either as a shading on the tips of the leaves or occasionally on an entire leaf. Usually red is associated with a new leaf or a dying leaf. (That very accommodating shrub, *Loropetalum*, has single red leaves scattered throughout its many evergreen ones in the fall.) There are a few perennials with dark red leaves, e.g. *Lobelia cardinalis* and *L. tupa*. Just one plant of such a strong color looks like an odd introduction but a group adds depth of color to a planting.

Purple: Purple ranges from a faint tint in green to a nearly plum hue in which the purple obliterates the green. Usually one finds the deeper purples in cvs. Breeders have developed several cvs. from *Tradescantia officinalis* which provide a useful deep note. An annual *Salvia, S. officinalis* 'Purpurea' is grown just for its purple foliage. The deepest purple note looks black. The best example is *Ophiopogon nigricans* (see new name). It is much too small to make any kind of a statement but unusual enough to be photographed repeatedly. Alternate names for this *Ophiopogon* are *O. planiscarpus* 'Nigrescens' and *O. planiscarpus* 'Kokurga'. This is *O. arabicus* (of gardens).

Some of the greys are tinted with purple. That wonderful trailing *Sedum, S. sieboldii*, quite grey in winter, becomes almost lavender in summer. The small trailing *Kalanchoe, K. fedtschenkoi*, is very changeable; a cv. called 'Silver Cloud' assumes in maturity a color like that of a summer thundercloud. Greys have various tints according to exposure as well as season. *Salvia apiana* has a very pronounced lavender caste in the heat of summer. The most astounding example of lavender and purple in foliage is a cv. of *Athyrium, A. nipponicum (A. goeringianum, A. japonicum)* 'Pictum'. The coloration is most noticeable in the newer leaves—shades of green and pink with the lavender. The coloring of this beautiful, herbaceous fern is classed as variegation, but it is a blending of several hues.

Pinkish: New foliage sometimes has a pinkish tint rather than a purple. The silky leaves of *Convolvulus cneorum* have a pink blush when new.

Grey: Grey foliage. Use a great deal of grey in your compositions unless you are presently (you may change your mind) one of those people who can't abide grey.

Of course, you can plant a whole garden with different shades of grey; they all seem to blend but do they really? The blue-greys look better with each other; some shades look better in proximity to green than others depending on the shade of green.

Grey is often produced by hairs on the back and/or on both sides of the leaf. Hairs differ not only in color but in substance. The texture accentuates the greyness. When the hairs are quite long the texture is velvety. Two velvety examples are *Stachys lanata*, and *Salvia argentea*, the one with big basal leaves. One grey is yellowish, the other bluish. *Artemisia pycnocephala* has very fuzzy hairs; the hairs are in length between the other two but they are extra thick and close; the leaves stay grey in the hot sun of summer because they are so well protected.

   Artemisias are a varied source of grey; there are dwarf, medium and large species. Some of the low ones are very silky. Some of the tall ones have this texture also. A cv. might be especially pleasing for its grey color and for its finely cut leaves, as well as for its texture. One of these desirable cvs. is *A. absinthium* 'Lambrook Silver'. Foliage can be grey without being hairy. One of the best examples is *Calocephalus brownii*; it is a brittle subshrub, stems and leaves all white-grey, hairless and quite impervious to the effects of weather.

   Well-known grey plants. Several spp. have been called "Dusty Miller", and to add to the confusion, different spp. are given that common, if meaningless, name in different areas. If you should unwisely ask for a plant by that name, you might get one of the *Artemisias* or the grey form of *Santolina* or the plant now known as *Senecio cineraria*. The latter "Dusty Miller", well known for its decorative leaves, indented in most intricate fashion, is today mostly grown as an annual. Young plants look fresh and neat. Because of their small size when young, they are useful as "plants in a row". I have seen this *Senecio* planted as an edger in the panels along Park Avenue in New York. Several other Senecios are decidedly grey.

   Combinations: Now how do we mix colors to create fine garden effects with them. Perennials of various colors of green are very serviceable in a mixed planting. One can act as a buffer between yellowish foliage and blue-grey foliage; or if its shade of grey does not associate well with yellow-green, I suggest that you place a dark green foliaged plant between the yellow-green and the grey. Let me give you just one example; you have planted a group of *Euphorbia*; its yellowish foliage is heightened by the greenish-yellow of its flowers; the *Artemisia* I gave as an example of grey would look better if you placed a drift of dark *Helleborus foetidus* between them. It is like three people walking down a beach; the two on the outside have little in common, have never liked each other; the one in the middle likes them both and brings them together by the threads he has to each. Now don't be afraid to use grey with most greens. Sometimes a strong, bold insertion of greyish-green is just what is needed to produce either a change from the monotony of one color or a transition with a cooling effect. And besides, grey may act, as well, as a foil for warring bright colors of flowers.

   Variegation: You should look first at the design of variegation; do you like spots or do you prefer stripes? When the leaf has a lighter colored edge, I like this edge to be more even than jagged. And, besides a clear line, I like a clear color, whether yellow or white. *Pelargonium hortorum*, garden Geranium, has many patterns but its shadings are typically in bands.

   Variegated foliage relieves an expanse of the darker greens as grey does. The cream coloring makes the composition more lively. Place it in front of either pale or dark-green foliage; it is better, however, against a green which has the basic color in the variegation. Some solidly green leaves are definitely tinged with yellow and make the best background for perennials with yellowish variegation. By the same reasoning, it follows that you plant a sport of some species which has whiter variegation with either a shrub with whitish variegation or with a shrub with blue in its green rather than yellow. One perennial, *Iris pallida*, has two forms, one with white stripes and one with yellow.

   Special places for perennials with variegated foliage are, for example, in part shade, the spots where sunlight melds into shade, and in front of very dense or dark foliage. In such cases the design of the variegation shows up well and the light color brightens the scene. For such a purpose, two good examples are the striped cvs. of *Liriope* and a slender grass with white edges, *Acorus gramineus* 'Variegatus'.

   Why does the color of foliage matter? Think of green, straight green, all of the same hue and value. While green is the basic color of foliage and without it floral arrangements are tiresome and often harsh, by the same token a single shade of green quickly becomes monotonous and says little.

   Look at the natural landscape. Nature is awash with a variety of greens, reds, greys, purples. Can we do any less than try to match the splendid creation of nature?

Artemisia

Senecio

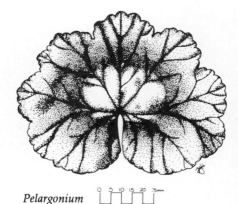

Pelargonium

To do so we must learn to recognize the many variations in color—again, the "seeing eye". With a "seeing eye" organize your landscape to include and integrate compatible examples.

There is too much variability of sites and personal preferences to talk about all the excellent ways of organizing sound foliage displays. Let us look at one type by way of example

Mats

Foliage color is very evident and important in plants which are used in mats. Mats differ remarkably in appearance; they differ not only because of the differing forms of leaf and habit which we have already discussed, but also because of color variations. The color of the foliage is thoroughly displayed. A mat may be all one color or a tapestry of colors derived from the innumerable shades derived from the use of different species. One could easily create a patterned mat just with the genus *Thymus*. *T. herba-barona* is a dark green; *T. v.* 'Argenteus' and *T. lanuginosus* are two shades of grey; *T. drucii* is a medium green. Such a show of mixed greens and textures is delightful on a slope.

Another variegated single genus mat can be made with a collection of *Potentillas; P. cinerea, P. verna, P. cerastoides,* each has foliage of a different shade of green. But a bank of a single genus is only one of many ways in which tapestries can be made with mats. See Layout 14. Here you will see a carpet on a flat area made up of some 20 different kinds of mats. I have used mats as an example of a type of plant in which the foliage plays an especially noteworthy role but you will discover plants with other habits in which the leaf color and texture make equally important contributions to garden design.

Ferns

The character of fern fronds varies a great deal; other colors may be blended with the green, as grey, gold, lavender, and brown; and textures may be thick, even leathery, in which case the green is dark in contrast to the light translucent green of a fern like *Adiantum pedatum.* Ferns and their varying colors of green are indispensable in a shady garden not only for their intricate and different forms but for their major contribution to the basic array of green.

A collection of ferns can be a much more simple affair than the word "fernery" implies. However, if you like ferns, and so collect, you will have lots more than a few species. Foliage color can make the difference between an exciting and a dull collection; for instance, the Holly Fern, *Cyrtomium,* unfern-like with its entire solid thick leaves but a great addition of dark green to a mixed planting. *Phyllitis,* Hart's Tongue, is also dark. *Pellaea andromidaefolia,* Coffee Fern, is a soft grey. It is not too difficult to glimpse the gold on the backs of *Pityrogramma,* Gold-back Fern. *Pteris quadriaurita* has a variegated form 'Argyraea' called Silver Fern.

Some ferns are two-toned with the newer fronds lighter and brighter. The most important color in ferns is brown, many shades of strong brown; most spores are brown and their individual placement on the frond determines how much the brown is in evidence. Numerous spores produce a very rich look. Combine ferns with perennials; their color and form mixes with all other colors and forms, adding versatility and delighting the eye. See p. 47.

Rotate

Campanulate

4. Form of the Flower

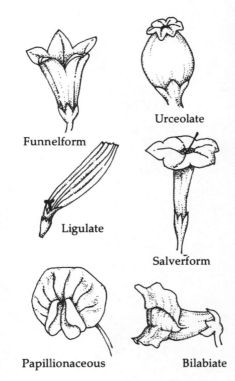
Funnelform

Urceolate

Ligulate

Salverform

Papillionaceous

Bilabiate

Single Flower

The flowers do arrive in due time. Some stay from youth to old age, most only at their best for a few weeks. Unless you have planned for a special event, like a wedding reception, different species will not be in bloom at once. But the flowering periods will overlap each other to some extent. Only during that more or less short visit might the importance of color in flowers take precedence over the form of the flower and the habit of the plant. The size and shape of the plant which the bloom adorns may often be determined by the habit of the branching stems. The habit of the flower itself, its poise together with its form completes the total personality.

It is desirable to have several forms all contributing to the pattern of the garden. You may be attracted particularly to one form, such as the daisy, but a planting only of daisies becomes boring and meaningless. In any composition, a diversity of flowers is more interesting and, after all, our objective is to consider the ways in which perennials may be used in combination to create pleasing and satisfying landscape design. So forsake monomanical obsession with the daisy form; use it extensively if you like it, but not to the exclusion of other forms, many of which will give your entire planting a finer appearance and feeling.

Before beginning to give examples of these various forms, two characteristics which affect the appearance of the flower should be described.

The first is a formation called a bract. In common parlance the words bract and calyx are used without distinction. Both these auxiliary parts of the flower may be present (not both enlarged in any one species). If the flower should have all three the order would be: petals, calyx, bracts. The parts of the bract are usually greenish and leaf-like but often are so like petals that the nonbotanist cannot tell the difference. When the bracts look like petals, they are often as decorative; sometimes they may be large and even brightly colored; in these instances, the petals are normally insignificant or absent. One outstanding example is *Eryngium,* with a distinctive ruffled collar of bracts, called "piccadill" by Thomas. This collar is very prickly indeed and handsome; the flower itself is cone-shaped. *E. zabelii* is a name which covers a group of hybrids; selections have been made for cones particularly cone-shaped and for fancy collars. A bract is a much reduced leaf associated with flowers. You will see the phrase "involucre of bracts" the circle or collar. And a panicle may be "bracted". The circle of bracts can be usually found at the base of the flower stalk of a flower cluster or the flower stalk. It is below the calyx.

The calyx is the outer whorl of floral envelopes, with separated or united sepals. This is another auxiliary part of the flower, technically a modified leaf. The sepals, however, can be petal-like and have as interesting form and color as any petals. Two

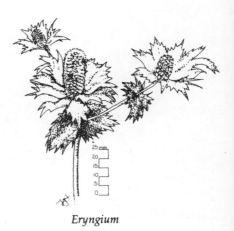
Eryngium

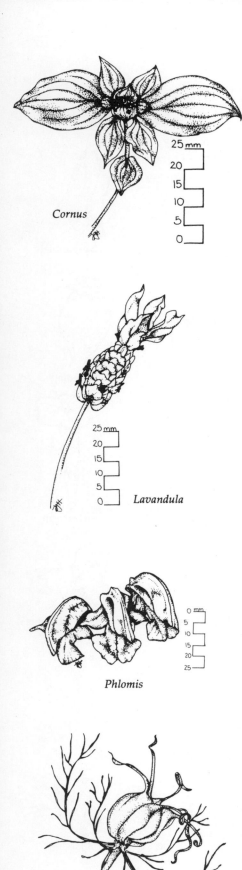

Cornus

Lavandula

Phlomis

Nigella

outstanding examples are: *Cornus* and *Arum*. In quite a number of genera, the bracts and calyces are prominent and the real flowers seem tiny. Think of *Limonium* spp., *Goniolimon* (related), and *Lavandula stoechas*. *Origanum hybridum* has tassels made of calyces.

Let us turn to the second variation, called "petaloids". A petaloid is a modified petal, a part not yet quite become a petal. It occurs in the center of the flower, at the base around the clusters of syle-plus-stamens and although about the same color as the petals, the petaloids are smaller and have usually a twisted form. They look like a ruffle; the flower which they adorn has a distinctive look. The flower is on the way to becoming a double form but this abortive mutation is often very attractive, (or it may look messy).

A few garden *Chrysanthemums,* having already undergone a change in petal from simple to the fancy kind called "spoon", develop a small frilly collar around the center. It makes the flower not only different but dressy. *Paeonia* has been bred for centuries, mostly toward doubleness. If the flower has a mass of narrow, petal-like structures in the center, it is called semi-double. Once in a while, this mass is in the nascent stage; the reproductive organs are in full view but around them there is a curly ruff of petaloids. You will like a cultivar with this feature. Herbaceous Peonies are an excellent choice for a forward bay in a shrubbery border, in a prominent position where their special character will show off.

Let us look again at a flower with no petals; look more closely this time. Sepals, the parts of the calyx look often so like petals, no less colorful, no less well-formed, no less handsome, that they are not recognized at a distance. A flower may have both; when the petals are prominent, the sepals may be unnoticed. To find them look on the backside of the flower. Often the calyx will change color and become enlarged after the petals drop. It is now quite visible and often interesting looking: you can see where its position is on the stem. *Phlomis* has calyces arranged in whorls, three or four tiers of them. (Please see the drawing of the inflorescence.)

The seed may be developing within divisions of the calyx; the vesicles may be hidden or clearly displayed. They may have an intricate design. Some annuals or perennials with decorative seed vesicles are: *Silene, Nigella, Salvia, Ballota, Phlomis, Helleborus.* Some are pods as in *Fibigia.* Some split open and show the seed within. The arrangement in whorls is a complicated design often attractive as well as interesting.

Certain perennials have seed heads of beauty made up of whirls of winged seeds. A few are worth growing for the seed heads alone: e.g. *Clematis, Pulsatilla.*

The berries of a perennial are sometimes more interesting than the flower. Occasionally, the closed vesicle looks like a berry. The berries of *Dianella* are both green (unripe) and vibrant bluish purple. The delicate flower spray of *Libertia ixioides* develops into a graceful stem with oval greenish fruits on the tips of the branchlets. The different spp. of *Actaea* might be grown just for the unique berries.

Certainly, the common *Iris, I. foetidissima,* with quite dull flowers is often grown for its bright-orange winter berries. *Belamcanda*'s pods open to show jet-black seeds which give the genus the name Blackberry Lily.

If you like to make arrangements with dried material, you will plant some perennials mainly for the lovely shapes and muted colors after the plant has seemed to die. *Fibigia,* noted above, has perhaps the most velvety pod of any—a string of flattened ovals grey and hairy.

Most interesting designs can be found in the grasses, dry or fresh. *Uniola,* for instance, is very graceful; it is a translucent green and turns to lovely shades of cream, beige and light-brown. I will give you a list of decorative grasses hoping you will research them and choose a few to plant. Meanwhile, watch the fields for intriguing forms. You will surely find one called Rattlesnake Grass, *Briza maxima,* an annual which selfsows.

It is difficult to say, when considering the single flower which form is the most common and, of course, which form is the most attractive. Let us look at a few shapes. I admit that the circle is represented by a great number. The members of this group conform to the round shape in two manners. One is the daisy-form, made up of two kinds of flowers. The other is a form in which only a few petals, 3–7, radiate around a center. The center now instead of being made up of flowers, contains the reproductive organs and is small in relation to the circle of petals. The round form is duplicated and emphasized by this secondary circle. The round flowers of *Potentilla, Silene, Phlox* etc. are wheel-like with small hubs to the wheel. Sometimes there is a ring of brighter color near the center which makes a second circle; (Potentilla) sometimes there is a ring of a different color around the rim. Sometimes the perfect circle is broken by uneven petals.

Daisies require some more attention since they differ more than one supposes. A flower is classified partly by number of petals. Its appearance and character are affected strongly not only by number of petals but in the manner in which they are attached and the angles in which they are arranged. *Gerbera* is perhaps a typical daisy but it is a gorgeous one mostly because of the curving and spacing of the petals.

The direction of the parts of the flower changes as the flower opens. The flower which is a ball in bud, becomes a cup and finally perhaps a saucer. When fully mature, you will see most clearly these differences in placement of the parts. There are both basic and trivial differences in the manner in which the parts are put together. Some petals are narrow at their base; they are placed close together but show spaces between them, e.g. *Oxalis* sp. On the contrary, petals may overlap at their place of attachment and then there will only be spaces at the circumference.

In some cases, a tube made up of bases of petals rolled together or pressed close together rise from a central point at the top of the stem. This tube may hide the reproductive organs and may or may not be covered with the calyx or bracts: e.g. *Dianthus, Silene, Salvia* and many other genera.

At the top of the tube, you will find the petals flaring in a regular or irregular circle as in *Zauschneria.* On the contrary some flowers are all tube; the petals will bulge only a little and when young perhaps finish in a point. In the maturing flower, the tip opens a little with the edges of the petals forming a ruching; as the tip opens more, the stigma lengthens and looks like a elongated clapper for the narrow bell: e.g.*Veltheimia.*

In some species the petals are all alike. Irregularity is interesting. A number of species of the genus *Viola* have a decided personality created by the inequality of the petals, the two upper ones being smaller, narrower and quite erect. The outline resulting from this arrangement is more oval than round. There are many species in which two sets of petals quite diverse in shape are combined, making diversified forms—their description to be postponed.

Globes are definitely round. In certain species of some genera, the globe is so obvious that the common name takes notice: e.g. *Trollius,* Globe Flower, *Echinops,* Globe Thistle, *Calochortus,* Globe Lily. The flowers of double *Ranunculus,* in youth, make perfect globes.

Many buds, as noted above, are quite round, some more round than others. A few flowers look like buds because they are closed bells and some closed bells never open. Closed bells are very common in ERICACEAE: *Erica, Calluna, Gaultheria, Cassiope, Arctostaphylos.* Look at the fat, closed bells hanging from the stem of *Convallaria,* Lily-of-the-Valley. From a distance, we cannot differentiate between a closed bell and a berry or similar fruit. A minute frill may be found at the tip of the closed bell while the berry may have a bead on its tip.

You will find more open bells than closed bells. Let us see how the bell-shape can vary. The traditional bell is found mostly on spike-like inflorescences and there it is displayed as it should be—hanging. *Campanula* is Bellflower and flowers with all sorts of bells (and less often with stars). Some of its bells are on their own stems. The bell of one species is so opened that it looks more like a saucer and it no longer hangs. A true bell is found in *C. persicifolia, C. barbata,* and many more spp. and cvs. The bells of *Adenothera* are as like the traditional bell as those of *Campanula.*

The tubular form was given some attention above. It looks often like a slender trumpet. Some genera have an inflorescence with both buds in the shape of tubes and open flowers in the shape of trumpets. The trumpet is a lovely form. Again this shape has many variations. There is the slender, straight trumpet of *Cyrtanthus,* which only flares at the very end. There is the wide spreading trumpet of some of the daffodils (but daffodil trumpets have a collar of sepals of greater or less importance to set off the trumpet). The trumpets of *Gladiolus* may be wide and heavy or slender and delicate, i.e. *G. tristus* var. *concolor.* A beautiful species of *Gladiolus,* once called *Acidanthera,* is not coarse but graceful. Trumpets of various shapes will be seen in *Salvia jurisicii, Salvia patens, Alstroemeria,* and *Incarvillea.* Think of the various trumpets of *Gentiana,* a few "closed" and some gently flaring. *Dodecatheon* is called rightly Shooting Star. The recurved petals are turned sharply back to expose what is called the "pointel" which indeed comes to a sharp point. An odd and bright "ring" of color accentuates the form

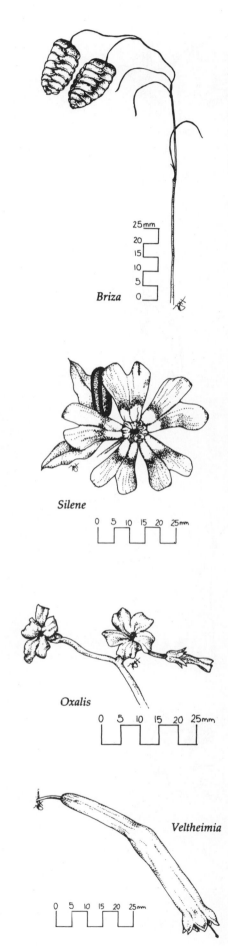

Briza

25mm
20
15
10
5
0

Silene

0 5 10 15 20 25mm

Oxalis

0 5 10 15 20 25mm

Veltheimia

0 5 10 15 20 25mm

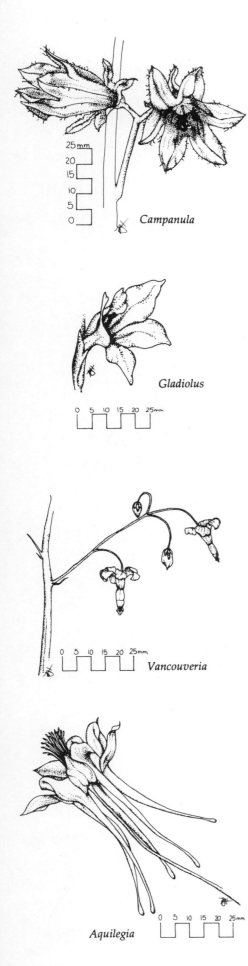

Campanula

Gladiolus

Vancouveria

Aquilegia

of this projection.

Erythroniums vary greatly in shape; a common shape is a bell. If you are a collector of *Erythroniums,* you will find a species with recurved petals.

An amazing shape is seen when petals are "recurved". You will find often that there are two sets of petals or rather two parts to the flower. Petals which are recurved, turn backwards from a central portion which is comprised of parts in a distinctive arrangement. *Narcissus* is probably the most simple. It is the trumpet which is left facing forward, no ordinary trumpet but one with shapely lines. The base petals (sepals) grow sharply back in the opposite directions; when planted in a group, these flying parts of each flower face to the same direction, to the same point of the compass; or should I say fall away from the same point? The flaring trumpet of *C.* × *hascombensis* is long and narrow, the flare sculptured and clear lavender.

Vancouveria is called Inside-out-flower. Its cousin *Epimedium* goes also sometimes by this common name, but the recurved feature is more evident in *Vancouveria.* The flowers are very small but the odd form can be easily noticed because the pedicels hold the blossoms away from the main stalk making them look like parasols. The stems lift the flowers above the foliage mass where they do a ballet. Cyclamen is a genus of many species. In some the recurved feature is more prominent.

If this form seems extraordinarily inventive to you, you will find the complicated details of many two-lipped flowers a still greater marvel. You take for granted perhaps the form of the Snapdragon and the Bearded Iris. And you have noted the slender shape of *Zauschneria* when you have seen it visited by hummingbirds. The two-lipped form is very practical, offering perches for birds and insects. Often their platform is protected from intruders or perhaps from weather by a curved roof over the landing pad. The beard at the entrance to the tube is not only directional but functional, a steadying mat for small feet. Perhaps orchids have the most complicated details. More mundane perennials should also be investigated for their clever contrivances. *Asarina* is close to the Snapdragon in shape; its upper lip is quite pronounced.

Sometimes the upper portion of the flower is so dominant that it is called a "hood". *Aconitum* is the best example. "Pouch" is another term applied to the petals of the upper portion of two-lipped flowers as in *Iris, Asarina* and *Antirrhinum.* Examine the flower forms of *Linaria, Salvia, Dicentra* and *Penstemon* and you will find other pouches. Perhaps the pouch of *Calceolaria* is the most pronounced.

Mimulus has a face sometimes called a "monkey face". The upper lips of two-lipped flowers serve a purpose. In the process, they often hide the reproductive organs. When stamens and/or pistils protrude another detail is added to the design. The intricate and beautiful arrangement of these parts is on display, of course in open flowers. One of the most extraordinary is *Eucharis.*

In the encyclopedic descriptions, you will often see the phrase "protruding stemens" or "exerted stamens". The stamens in some examples are usually numerous and brushlike and give a frilly look to the flower. Perhaps the genus in which this feature is most common is *Hypericum. Dictamnus* is also an outstanding example.

Look now at the back of the flower instead of the front. The flowers of certain genera have spurs and when a genus is bred for finer flowers, an endeavor is made to lengthen the spurs. This is the case in *Aquilegia.* Species of *Linaria* may have spurs of less length but they are prominent. Within the spur is a nectary, sometimes hard to reach except with an efficient probe.

I have only set out some of the more obvious instances in the form of a flower which required imagination. A hand lens should be a permanent member of your handbag collection. What you will see will astonish you!

Inflorescense

Let us examine the shape of flowers in which each species is determined to develop in its blooming period. Probably, if you took a count, you would find that an inflorescence of some kind is more common in perennials than a single flower on its own stem.

The term "spray" has significance for all gardeners. It is more than a "bunch" and more stretched out and uneven than a "head". Spray is not a horticultural or a botanical word; it is used loosely to designate a cluster of flowering stems. Let us get technical for a moment and define some terms which describe a special arrangement of flowers on their stems in order to show that different types of branching result in different botanical forms.

Raceme: A raceme is "an unbranched, elongated, indeterminate inflorescence with pedicelled flower." What does this look like? Since the flowers have stems they stand away from the stem to some extent and since there are no branches the shape is more or less narrow. It need not be erect.

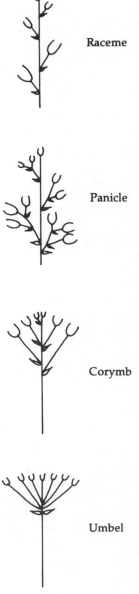

Raceme

Panicle: An indeterminate branching inflorescense the branching usually ending in racemes or corymbs. Now we have a more complicated form.

Corymb: The branching is regular, the topmost branch being central and higher. There is a picture of this and other flower forms on page 1210 of *Hortus III*. There you will find other terms used to describe the various ways in which a variety of plants carry their flowers.

Cyme: The head is like a corymb only its central flower blooms first. There is a "helicord cyme".

Panicle

Umbel: The branching is so arranged that each branch reaches a similar level forming a flat top. An umbel is a type of inflorescence which is a common example of the disc shape. We will find it in a number of perennials, e.g. *Asclepias, Filipendula, Angelica, Foeniculum*. And there are modified flattops in which the branching is less precise. Either way it is a form we will select to make a decided contribution to the composition.

Corymb

We will look at some spray-like clusters which have less rigid rules than the botanical terms prescribe. Spray-like inflorescences are often bending. Sometimes the flowers are openly spaced; on the other hand, flowers may be closely packed along the branches. Some species, of certain genera in which the normal inflorescence is a spike, have a curving inflorescence which looks to us more like a spray. Take a look at several *Penstemon. Penstemon digitalis* has upright stems quite erect but the tubular flowers hanging at irregular intervals from the branches make a soft, quite informal appearance. How about *Penstemon heterophyllus* var. *purdyii*? The flowers grow out of the stems in spike-like regularity but it might be said that the curves of the stems produce a form more like a spray than a spike.

Umbel

The long wand-like stem of *Gaura* could be called a spray. The small, dainty, pinkish-white flowers are arranged on short branches at the tips of four-foot stems. Perhaps it is the light grace of the plant which makes one call it a spray. *Linaria* has this effect also, not the stiff 'Canon Went' but the species which branches so casually, the tips decorated with flowers of the odd shape which gives it the name "Three-Birds Flying".

Goldenrod has sprays of quite another type; crowded with flowers, the stems bend and angle from the overladened tips.

Spray-like stems may be found in *Heuchera, Francoa, Astilbe* and *Filipendula*. The inflorescences appear spray-like because of their branching and because their flowers are small, often dainty, sometimes "fluffy". You may describe both a single flower and an inflorescence with quite nontechnical words, like "fluffy", "dainty", even "foamy". You may invent some of your own descriptive words. However, all would agree that "column" is an apt term which covers the form of many species. In garden parlance most columnar perennials are "spikes" of some kind.

The column is a form without which the world is unthinkable. Columns take all sorts of forms or character, thick or thin, even or tapering, soft or strong. But all variations depend upon the vertical line. The columnar stem is extended by the inflorescence; the top of the flower spike may be rounded or pointed. Sometimes there are caps of various shapes on these columns. The caps are sometimes called caps (headdress) in another sense. Perhaps the most curious one is the pineapple-looking top above the flower spike of *Eucomis*. Columns may be described as "spires" or "pyramids" and these words suggest definite images. The fullest pyramid is made by *Scilla peruviana*. Terms are added such as "erect" or "dense". Some spikes are naturally stiff and the landscape plan may call for such a decidedly vertical line. An erect column may be made more stiff by staking and trimming. A tall, thick column may be referred to as a "tower", e.g. *Campanula pyramidalis* and *Eremurus* hybrids.

Eucomis

The personality of the spike is somewhat determined by the manner in which the flowers are attached to the main stem. They may be close together or somewhat separated, they may hang or face forward; they may surround the stem or fall only in

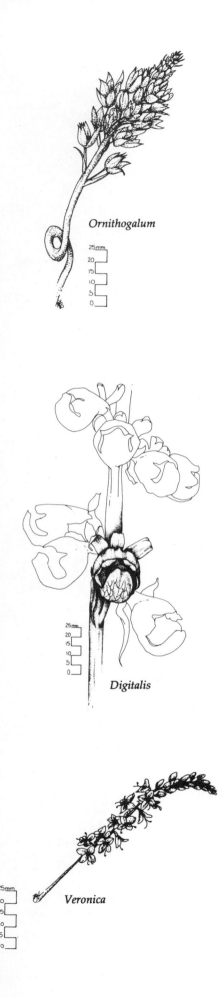

Ornithogalum

25mm
20
15
10
5
0

Digitalis

25mm
20
15
10
5
0

Veronica

25mm
20
15
10
5
0

one direction. Compare *Ornithogalum, Digitalis, Delphinium*. The flowers may overlap. They may hug the main stem when they have very short stems of their own. You may like to use the proper word for these individual stems, i.e. "pedicel". The pedicels may be short or long or of different lengths; they may be firm or wiry or drooping. Can you see that the looks of spikes will vary tremendously? You will find a distinctive spike occasionally which is malleable and bends and curves. You might apply descriptive words like plume or wand to such an inflorescence. A plume is softer than a wand, and a wand is narrower. Both are tall and thin and the opposite of stiff.

Spike includes both those erect and stiff and those looser and bending; we can easily find extreme examples of both. The tall, straight spike is represented first in our minds by *Delphinium, Digitalis,* and *Alcea (Althaea)* which you would include often in the higher ranks of perennial plantings which have depth. A plant with the name of "poker" is obviously an example of a stiff form. When Red-Hot Poker was planted in the old days, not only was it chosen for height, but for a strong vertical line. There are presently cultivars of *Kniphofia;* the dwarfer forms are only two feet tall. A clump will produce a number of stems and the parallel columns produce rockets of color. The poker is made up of many drooping tubular flowers packed around the top 12 inches of the stem.

The look of the spike differs according to how the flowers face, all one way, *Salvia guaranitica,* all around as in *Dictamnus.* The look is quite different when the flowers overlap. The look of the spike differs according to the timetables of the flowers' openings. The upper flowers usually open after the lower ones, (note exceptions). If the buds at the top are slow to open, the spike will come to a point. The time in which most flower spikes open their flowers all at once is very fleeting. The following spikes look pointed: *Hesperaloe, Penstemon, Ornithogalum thyrsoides.* Other *Ornithogalums* look quite different. The dainty spike of *Tiarella* has a point when the tip is still in bud.

The spikes of some genera have only a few flowers and usually scattered; this produces a loose, open appearance. Two examples are *Pasithea* and *Anthericum.*

The typical look of the spike is, however full. *Physostegia* is a curious perennial called "Obedient Plant." If a pedicel is bent in a new direction, it remains in that position. How many would have to be bent to change the appearance of the spike? Breeding has brought about variations. P.'Vivid' has been described as "stumpy" while P.'Summer Snow' "tapers". Both look best in a drift of several stems.

The spikes of Foxglove vary in shape as well as in height. The column of *Digitalis mertonensis,* with big, fat flowers is fatter than the column of *Digitalis ferruginea,* which is slender and taller, sometimes 6 feet.

When most of the flowers are concentrated toward the top of the main stem, the form becomes a cylindrical head. Some cultivars of *Phlox* will be more cylindrical than others. The best representatives are 'Fujiyama' and a form of *Phlox maculata* named 'Alpha'.

A quite different effect is produced by the spike form in some *Veronicas.* The flowering portion of the stem is long and the taper is exaggerated; it is erect but not always stiff. I think we can guess what "spicata" means without knowing any Latin; *Veronica spicata* has been a popular species in gardens for as long as I can remember; 'Crater Lake Blue', ten inches tall, is a well known cultivar. 'Barcarole', rose-pink and about the same height, is less well known; now there are new names and the group is often listed as "*Veronica* hybrids" and in each the habit will be somewhat different.

Now, one which not only tapers but curves a bit is *Veronica virginica* 'Alba'; the buds at the tip are slow to open. The spikes seem to wave in groups like a ballet chorus.

The cv. 'Red Fox' is not very common in western North America, but is worth seeking for its tall tapering spikes. One I like very much is 'Shirley Blue', very floriferous and good for the center of the bed since the spike is two-thirds the height of the taller *Veronicas.*

One cv., 'East Freisland' has a tall, narrow column. *V. grandis* var. *holophylla,* 24 inches tall before the flowering part begins has a spike wider than the tapering kinds; another uncommon species which I particularly like is *V. incana;* it has narrow spikes six inches long at the tops of the stems sometimes two feet tall. These stems grow in a decided arch which creates a distinctly curving spike—this sp. is best on the front edge of the border.

Veronica species and cultivars range in height from four inches to four feet. The spike form is characteristic in even the smallest kind.

Cimicifuga is for late summer with tall spikes on four-foot stems. Depending on species, they will be erect or somewhat curving. The stems of *C. cordifolia* branch but the spikes on the side stems are as upright as the center ones. The more curving stems are noted for their grace and have been called "wands". They make an open mass of creamy white, very conspicuous in semi-shade. There is a cultivar, 'White Pearl', described as "pokery" and "dainty" because of its tiny ivory flowers; the stems are very graceful.

You have not seen an out-of-the-ordinary spike, I am sure, to equal that of *Primula vialii*; the shape is curious, it is fat at the bottom and densely clothed with lavender flowers up to a small sharply pointed tip which is crimson; the contrast in color makes the shape appear very different. (The flowers open from the bottom up.) The spikes of this odd Primrose look best in a crowded group; the upward thrust is very erect but the blooms are of different heights, resulting in an attractive irregular pattern.

The arrangement of the parts of the *Primula* flower is very precise. The arrangement of petals and bracts of other flowers produces a different look. Look at the interrupted spike of *Phlomis*. In each tier, the whorl seems to have a casual arrangement of its parts.

The spikes of three plants have similar shapes. *Thermopsis, Baptisia* and *Lupinus arboreus*, shrubby perennials, have flowers with a Lupine-like structure. They may be grown as neighbors if you want to emphasize the particularly soft, erect form of their spikes.

Thermopsis caroliniana, Carolina Lupine, is an herbaceous perennial which must build its bushy clump in a hurry in order to make a shrublet four feet tall by summer; it often has a minor early blooming period when it is half mature size. When at its full height, there are many erect ten-inch spikes packed with yellow pea-like flowers. Place several plants in a group so they can lean against each other.

Baptisia has a woody base but is herbaceous in the practical sense because its four or five-foot stems are cut to the ground in autumn. After the leafy shrub has developed, a number of spikes are formed among the branches and reaching above them. The spikes about 18 inches tall are erect but do not give an appearance of stiffness. The individual flowers are dense all around the stem, of soft texture and of the typical shape of LEGUMINOSAE, the pea family. The upper lip of this two-lipped flower is closed and distinctly rounded.

The Lupine which seems particularly close to *Baptisia* in form is the Bush Lupine, *Lupinus arboreus*, native in the Western U.S. Its spikes likewise grow upright among the leafy branches. The spikes of hybrid Lupine are fuller and fatter.

One must examine the Bush-Lupine and *Thermopsis* side by side to discover the difference. Hybrid Lupine produces a mass of handsome, fat spikes on low stems from a base of distinctive foliage.

Snapdragons have been greatly improved in behavior by the breeders and are now available with shorter stature and brilliant, vibrantly colored spikes, and a longer period of bloom.

There are many more spikes, large and small, and with variable characteristics. *Verbascum*, Mullein, is straight and strong. All species are not as huge as the tallest. The spikes have many open flowers which taper to a point of unopen buds. *Verbascum chaixii* is a fairly tall species. The color provided by *V. chaixii* continues for many weeks since the main spike is cut back when spent and numerous lesser side branches repeat the show.

Verbascum phoeniceum, the Purple Mullein from east Europe, has many slender spikes sometimes only two feet high.

Verbascum virgatum is another of garden size. The tip, still in bud, bows its head to seemingly signify a temporary drowsiness; then the buds awake and the tip becomes erect; the lower flowers are meanwhile mostly still alert. Other plants share *Verbascum*'s behavior at the top of the spike, notably *Bulbinella, Euphorbia,* and *Digitalis lutea*.

There is a cross between *Verbascum* and *Celsia, Celsioverbascum*. The slender spikes are only moderately tall and each flower has the typical "face". Numerous stems stand erect from a clump of narrow, greyish leaves.

Flowers may be arranged in heads instead of sprays or spikes. Looking at some heads, it is difficult to discern the individual flowers. Mostly they are packed closely together and are sometimes almost small enough to require that hand lens. The heads

Lupinus

Phlomis

Verbascum

may be domed or they may be flat-topped, or in between. The head of *Scilla peruviana* is triangular—a pyramid. The heads of *Achillea* are on the flat side, but the old-fashioned big one is so flat that it is described as a platter or plate. *Daucus*, Queen Ann's Lace has a flat head made up of many small flowers. A cushion has a rounded top, and pincushion is an apt name for some of the *Scabiosas*.

A massed ball of flowers often looks like a single flower. The circumference is round. Look closely to see the divisions; often other parts are to be discovered between the actual flowers, bracts, stamens, pistils, etc. The heads of *Alliums* are usually dense; what is more round than Drumstick Allium, *Allium giganteum*.

The heads of Eupatorium are dense, made up of many fuzzy flowers. In *E. rugosum,* the fluffy heads are somewhat flattened.

The daisy form is found in the many spp. of the Composite family. The shapes are various; *Asters* don't all look alike. One *Aster* looks like *Erigeron*.

Think of the heads of *Euphorbia, Alstroemeria, Ornithogalum arabicum, Bergenia, Agapanthus, Campanula glomerata.* They are all different but all with the individual flowers somewhat separated, enough anyway to be recognized as single flowers. The overall shape of the head is round but not flat and often not perfectly round; it may be conical or oval. Each is round enough to be an expression of the circular form.

In the chapter on Form of the Plant, an interesting habit was described, that of the stem producing leaves and/or flowers in tiers. Here are two examples in which the flowers are surrounding the stem and at more than one level, *Phlomis* and *Ballota*.

The forms which I have attempted to define cannot really be pigeon-holed. Each species shape is individual but some can be likened to others because of similarities.

You have seen that the shapes of flowers are wonderfully different, each kind and even each individual with a pattern unlike any other. You have looked at a number of ways in which the flowers are displayed on their stems, even though only a few variations of the many inflorescence have been described. The perennial plant with all its characteristics fully developed will almost never be available for its site in the garden, (unless it can be transferred from a container in which it has already reached maturity). As in people, the aspects of personality are made increasingly manifest with age. A seedling or even a division from a clump may look unprepossessing and lacking in character. An herbaceous perennial in whatever stage it is planted, develops over several months in its first year, the shape ever changing. Several years must pass before the majority of perennials show their real personality clearly. For example, if you plant a Scabiosa and it looks spindly you will say, "When will it branch out? Will it truly become a bushy plant with multiple stems and many flowers?" It will look better next year and still better the year after. In some genera, a very leafy plant will develop in the second year; in some others, the fully mature plant will wait for the third year. Meanwhile, look even in the first year, its emerging leaves, perhaps few and small but promising that this will be a plant with decorative form and foliage which in maturity will give value to this present "stick" and all through those months while the flowers are not on stage. Here again is the basic principle, the whole plant is important, with the leaves and habit of growth the predominant ingredients.

Do the individual variations make any difference in the overall design? Each of the smallest lines in a drawing affect the total composition and so will these small differences in the form of the flower, as well as in the form of the foliage, affect the garden composition.

Aster 0 5 10 15 20 25mm

5. Color of the Flower

Earlier I offered two or three sentences about selection of flowers for color. I now want to enlarge on these principles.

The first and by all means the most important principle is simply that you select as your dominant flower colors the one or two which particularly appeal to you. Most of us have a favorite color or two or three which go together; we choose, possibly only unconsciously, these colors when we select our clothes or paint for the house or fabric for the furniture—or the flowers in our gardens. A color scheme with a certain shade predominating comes about naturally in most gardens because the owner likes it better than others.

Some people change their color of choice according to season. If so, in spring, a major part of the border will be yellow; the reasons are three: first, the owner likes yellow; second, yellow seems to be a bright herald of spring; and third, yellow colors are available in the market; there are more flowers with yellow color in the spring than at any other time. Instinctive feelings play a part, such as a need for something especially bright and cheerful after dark days of winter.

Lavender might predominate in the fall because much autumn bloom is lavender. Lavender could be a major color in all seasons. But lavender need not be dreary. A predominant lavender can be sparked with purple, red, or magenta as will be evident in the following paragraphs.

If you would favor blue, you are in trouble; there is very little true-blue in flowers. But there is no need to stick to actual blue; blue shades are found in many lavenders, violets, mauves and purple. Innumerable spp. listed in the horticultural books and catalogues are called "blue"; however, the tone of most of these plants is a lavender-blue and looks just like some shade of lavender when compared with flowers admittedly lavender or violet or light purple. Your palette can contain all the bluish tones as well as the few real blues. Use flowers with a blue cast to accentuate the predominance of blue. Use the true blues in as great quantitiy as your design permits. Your garden will then appear definitely bluish.

Commonly you will meet blue associates by their common or cv. names which contain the word "blue", e.g. 'Bluebell', 'Blue Chips', 'Blue Giant', 'Blue Charm', 'Blue Perfection', and 'Hyacinth Blue'. But recall my earlier advice—many of these descriptions are approximations of blue so let us start with a few species which if not blue are almost blue.

The palest blue is to be found in the shrub called *Plumbago* and the perennial best known for this color is *Linum*. The blue of *Linum perenne* might be called "washed out", a more complimentary adjective would be "pastel". There is a tiny *Veronica, V. repens,* with flowers of very light blue. Of course, these pale blues go well with other pastels such as pink and lavender; they are not very noticeable if there are much

Delphinium

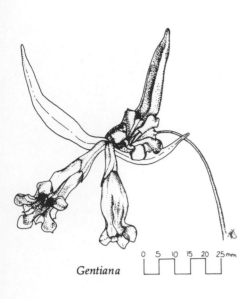

Gentiana

0 5 10 15 20 25mm

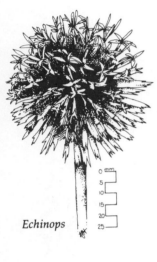

Echinops

0 mm
5
10
15
20
25

Astilbe

brighter colors in their vicinity. But their "blueness" can be augmented as suggested by adding other and warmer blue.

At the other end of the range is intense blue. The most notable example is *Anchusa*. This easy perennial, common name Alkanet, *A. azurea* 'Little John', is so very bright and deep that the colors of medium blue—or medium lavender—may look paler than they really are beside it. Another example of intense blue is *Veronica* 'Blue Charm'; however, its blue in real life is less blue than in the colored picture in a catalogue. Closer to blue is the color of *Ceratostigma plumbaginoides* (*Plumbago carpentae*). Its blue is a strong hue as well as clear. *Phlox divaricata* is a blue-blue, together with spp. of *Myosotis, Cynoglossum, Parochetus, Gentiana, Salvia*. If there is a wide expanse of a lighter color, the intense spot will act as an accent or if the areas are about equal, the two will make an attractive combination. It is best not to use a small area of a lesser blue with a solid patch of the strong color; the lighter one will look insignificant. Bright, deep blue will attract contented bees and hummingbirds.

Spp. with medium blue color are rare but perennials called "blue" abound and should be grown in combination with pale blue and intense blue. Use the bluest of several kinds of *Iris,* and the metallic blue of *Echinops* and the cornflower blue of *Catananche caerulea* and some *Aquilegias* and some *Campanulas*. See the list of blues in the Appendix.

This brings us to the second principle of combining colors: when two or more shades are used together be sure the proportion of one is in relation to the others—to compliment rather than detract.

The placing of a dark or deep or strong or bright color is important.

The principle of careful combining of several shades applies especially to lavender, since there are such a number of flowers of a lavender hue with varying intensities. The lavenders which are most intense may be dark enough to be called "deep" purple like the newer cvs. of hybrid *Penstemon*. This is a splendid shade to be used where you need a vivid exclamation point. This darkest color is strong as well as deep.

There are some lavenders which are intense and bright rather than deep. These usually have considerable red in their tone. They may be called purple or be labelled magenta. Cultivar names are uncertain guides, with the exceptions 'Purpurea' and 'Atropurpurea', the meanings "purple" and very "dark purple". Whatever, the bright and deep colors are very useful in giving a mixture "punch". It is important to place some of the intense colors in the foreground as well as in the mid- and back-sections. Two strong purples are found in *Astilbe chinense* 'Pumila' and *Fritillaria persica* 'Adiyaman'.

Stokesia laevis 'Blue Danube', *Platycodon grandiflorus* 'Double Blue' and the cvs. of *Primula* hybrids have been given names indicating blue, but none is anywhere near blue. They are usually the colors called "violet" or "lilac", which are different shades of lavender to different people.

If you think you do not like the color lavender, look about for a bit before excluding lavender from your garden. You will, I opine, find that it is very difficult to get along without since there are so many flowers with excellent form with this color. You will have to make your decision in the end by trial and error.

At one time I tried to avoid plants with magenta flowers because magenta was my least favorite color. Gradually it became evident that this is another color which contributes to brightness in a combination. *Physostegia* 'Vivid', pink but magenta-pink, is very vivid indeed. The best example is the mounding geranium, *Geranium incanum* with many single flowers of clear bright pinkish-magenta. *Liatris* is a must if a blue tone of magenta is needed. Of course, magenta goes well with all lavenders and blues.

Some pinks go well with the lavender/magenta/purple shades. Pinks go with reds. This combination was thought daring only a few decades ago. Pinks are quite easy to differentiate and their descriptive names are appropriate: "apple-blossom pink", "peach-pink", "shell-pink", "dawn-pink" (these four are pastels); and then "shocking-pink", "striking-pink", "phlox-pink" (these three are bright). Some pinks are called "salmon-pink"; they contain some yellow; others with the name "apricot-pink" contain more yellow. There are some attractive yellowish pinks in cvs. of *Dianthus:* one is called 'Doris', one 'Helen'. The pinks with a yellow tone naturally go best with yellow flowers. Pinks with a blue tone are sometimes called "orchid" (some Peonies are orchid pink). "Rose" is between pink and red and is bluish. These go best with lavender and blue.

Reds may be strongly bluish or strongly yellowish. Words used for red are "crimson" and "scarlet" (these colors are brilliant, as in *Monarda* 'Cambridge Scarlet'); others are "ruby-red", "cardinal-red" (*Lobelia cardinales*), "cherry-red" and "raspberry-red" (these are more or less what they sound like). "Blood-red" is not a blue red, it is used to describe a clear red. "Coral-red" (*Heuchera* 'Matin Bells') has the most yellow in it. *Astilbe* × *arendsii* 'Fanal' is called a deep garnet. "Turkey-red" (the annual bedding *Salvia*), is the strongest and most harsh. "Rose-red" or "rosy-red", has blue in it; e.g. *Lythrum* cv. and some cvs. of "red" *Asters*. This is quite close sometimes to magenta. The red cvs. of hardy *Phlox* are of different tones. 'Sandra' is called "brilliant scarlet-orange".

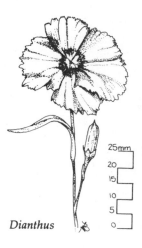

Dianthus

Let us go in the other direction to orange. Perhaps you do not like orange in the garden; that is no doubt because you find some shades of orange too harsh. There is a scarlet-orange, however, which blends in a vivid composition with red. Look carefully at *Geum* in order to choose the orange you like best. *Trollius* can be either orange or yellow. "Coppery-orange" can be seen in *Asclepias tuberosa* and *Helenium* 'Coppelia'. And a tawny orange is muted rather than harsh. This color goes very well with blues and lavenders. "Tangerine" is a name I use for a pleasing tone of orange. A soft orange, a burnt orange, is versatile. It adds to yellows and goes wonderfully well with lavender, e.g. *Papaver atlantica*. *Telephium* (*Sedum*) has a cv. called 'Autumn Joy'; the color changes as the plant ages and becomes finally a unique orange.

Think of all the tones in yellow. The most useful are "soft-yellow", "lemon-yellow", and "primrose-yellow". "Ming-yellow" seems just right in certain combinations. There is "sulphur-yellow"; *Euphorbia polychroma*, Cushion Spurge, is sulphur-yellow. I like least "golden-yellow" or "gold" which is often strong and brassy; a very strong yellow, such as that of *Trollius* or common *Coreopsis* looks best with plenty of the dark green of foliage to cool it. "Butter-yellow" is softer, e.g. *Ranunculus* spp. "Greenish-yellow" can be called "chartreuse". Some Hellebores are chartreuse; there are cvs. of several genera which have been developed to display the yellows containing this mixture of green, e.g. *Nicotiana*.

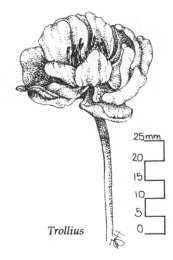

Trollius

There is very little greenish-blue in flowers. When there is, the plant is very much admired because its color is unusual and outstanding. I think of *Puya*. "Turquoise" is a good name for this rare color.

There are a few flowers really green; the greenest is perhaps the annual Bells of Ireland. Pale green can be found in the seed receptacles of several perennials, notably the various spp. of *Helleborus*, *Libertia*, and *Iris*. Flower arrangers like to use several kinds of flowers after they have gone to seed; receptacles are often a fine shade of green, as well as grey, yellow, red, purple.

In the garden the introduction of a color which is out-of-the-ordinary acts either as a blender or as an accent.

All these colors look quite different when the petals are shaded or when they are decorated with freckles, spots, dots, stripes, feathering or any kind of tracery. A mottled design changes the basic color or so it seems. When you use many of these mixed colors, use some clear undiluted colors also to establish a base and a quieting agent.

Of course this is one of the reasons we use white. There is "blue-white" and "snow-white" and ivory and several shades of cream; any and all whites must be added in quantity to our compositions.

White gardens have often been described both in England and in America. A white garden has the added value of being more visible at night.

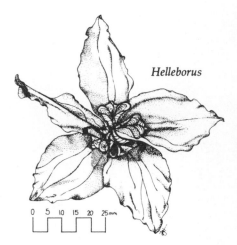

Helleborus

Muted colors are frequently used instead of white for this blending purpose. Several have been given names which describe them rather well, for instance, "dusty-rose", "ashes of roses", "warm beige", "dusty-mauve". Mauve is the name of a color which is understood differently by different people but all would think of it as muted. These muted colors are often made up of two colors both of which can be detected.

When flowers are planted near each other which have the color of one or both of the component colors of the antecedents used in the breeding, a pleasing connection is discovered—a kind of echo. Many of these blendings of forbears produce colors more often pale than strong; they are found in hybrids and the cvs. of hybrids. They might be the result of a mutation which was not quite complete or a hybrid in which the characteristics did not fully meld. Look for these cvs.; they are not just novelties; they have a special value in a mixed planting. Examples: Many garden *Chrysanthemums* are two-toned or two-shaded and softly muted. *Nicotiana*, *Aquilegia*, and *Mimulus*, as

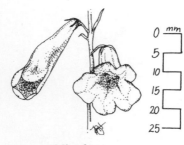

Mimulus

Penstemon

examples, have been bred to produce wonderful unusual colors—two-shaded and also softly muted—some of them hard to describe. They are all exceptionally useful for tying basic colors together.

MIXTURES

I have reviewed the colors which can be used as predominating colors. You must use with them colors which combine well. In what quantity? I have indicated that the dark or bright be used in a smaller proportion (say 10%). I have never seen an all red bed or an all magenta bed, with one exception—and it was not very restful. Travellers and soldiers have admired the Flander's fields with quantities of red poppies. But they have the grasses to cool them and besides they are not orange-red—they are cerise. It is good to add a bit of cerise—say 10% to a composition of blue and lavender. Blue and lavender can be as much as 70% when it is chosen as the dominant color. Ten percent is a fairly close estimate for pink unless you like pink very much: then it could be 30%. You could turn your figures around and allow it 70% and then it would be the dominant color—with others subservient to it.

Orange cannot be used in any great amount unless the flowers have hues to which to tie. These could be copper-bronze, apricot, reds with no blue in them and some yellows. With plenty of these associating colors, the orange could be 20%. A large percent of orange would contribute an effect of brilliance but would require the companionship of good foliage.

And yellow? Strong yellow functions like orange. Use it in small quantities as an accent. Pale yellow serves as a cooler and a melder as does white. Together with cream or ivory, it could be 50% of any scheme, or even predominant. Soft yellow is warm as well as restful. A very small patch of it placed among bright and deep colors is apt to be lost. Make the patch big enough so that the color does not disappear against foliage or sky.

So we come to an assessment of the percentage of white. I could answer "quite a lot" but you would still say "how much?" If I must be more definite I would say at least 20%. However, if you look at your color combination and you find it is lacking somehow in satisfaction and serenity—it is probably because there is a need for more white or cream or green or other quiet colors, e.g. grey, in the foliage.

This is our aim—to tie together the parts within the planting and then tie the whole to the site. As always we must look at the background planting. Suppose one of the shrubs is *Pittosporum crassifolium,* our combination should have something with grey foliage and some bright colors. Suppose on the other hand that one of the shrubs is *Pittosporum tobira* 'Variegatum', now we should use something grey again but we should pick up the variegation with white or cream. Suppose we have *Pittosporum undulatum,* we need a perennial with dark green foliage and some flowers with a yellow on the pale side. Suppose the path is brick, our edging plants should reflect the color—an odd pleasing color. Suppose the path is gravel, hopefully a color of stone with warm tones in it (as brown), then we use a perennial with a foliage of special grey like that of *Androsace tomentosum* and with flowers pale yellow or mauve or yellow-pink. Combinations innumerable: all we need is a decision as to whether they really enhance our ideal of the design.

An example: A room done in grey and pink leads by "French doors" into a narrow courtyard. The little patio can be seen from any part of the room. Let us carry out the two-toned scheme in the garden adding only white as cooler and blender. The color grey is easy because the leaves of our choices of plants will be grey and supply this basic color; many lovely grey foliage plants are available in all sizes. This color scheme can be attractive in itself as well as serve the purpose of connecting the garden closely with the house interior decoration.

Good true pink is more difficult to find in suitable perennials. But the larger plants may have pink blossoms. Vines will make the vertical lines. One can be a white Trumpet Vine with a pink blush in the base of the trumpet. Another is a pink *Wisteria* trained on a trellis. There is a wall on which to espalier and decorate with vines; a pink Dogwood can be the central trained figure with hybrid *Clematis* in both white and pink. In the beds annuals may be combined with perennials; in a small garden only a few spp. are required. Separate colors of Stock and Larkspur, from seed, will provide the tallest heights. In the narrow beds of this garden the range goes from low to medium since it is not practical to cover a full range of heights. *Dianthus* may be planted in quantity, for picking and for fragrance as well as for the shades of pink. Dwarf pink roses should be used for accents along the edges. *Linaria* 'Canon Went' is a most valuable perennial providing soft grey leaves and spikes of pink over many weeks. This *Linaria* seeds itself readily (as do the others) but the seedlings are not too difficult to pull. Those *Linaria* plants over two years old which become too dense and too wide can be removed in favor of younger ones. The owner must work to keep this little gem of a garden manicured.

This sample color scheme is a very simple one although the plan may be somewhat difficult to carry out because of the strictures on flower color.

More usual color schemes will give more leeway in selection of plants; other criteria besides color will be important. Foliage will be various shades of green as well as the predominant grey of the above sample.

To find the color which you need, you may only have to choose a different sp. of the same genus. You like the character of the *Linaria* in the sample scheme; a *Linaria* called Three Birds Flying contributes to another color scheme entirely. For many perennials there are two seasons with quite different color contributions. For instance, *Zauschneria* is grey for most of the year and then, when in flower, a brilliant scarlet. *Hesperaloe* is bronze in its foliage season; then its bloom is a startling mixture of yellow to apricot to crimson.

In Chapter 18, please find several layouts for your consideration; they have been planned for many combinations of various flower colors as well as for the forms of flower and leaf and branch which produce the foundation of our designs.

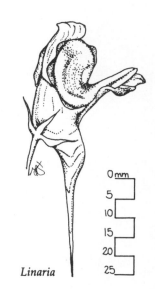

Linaria

Zauschneria

6. Hybridization

Celsioverbascum (Bi-generic cross)

Kniphofia (More dwarf)

What ideals do the hybridizers have in mind when they marry two different species. The offspring will be various and perhaps numerous, all different. The parents were chosen for certain admired characteristics. Will the children have a mixture of characteristics in which those outstanding traits of one or both parents will predominate? The breeders compare carefully all the offspring and select one or more which seems to have acquired a good gene or two from each parent. The selection is thereafter propagated. The hoped for quality may turn out to be rather weak in the hybrids' offspring. If so the progeny may be recrossed. The hybrid is now crossed with one of the original "type" species, the desired quality of which was not strongly enough emphasized in the first lot of infants. The crossing can be repeated continually with these same originators. Or new parents may be introduced.

You will see new species names like "hybridum"; you can guess that this is a name for a group which has been bred from several parents occasionally some of them unknown. Or a descendant may be given a more indicative name which sometimes is related to the name of the hybridizers. Sometimes a hybrid is indicated by the sign "X" but this sign need not be used. Sometimes a hybrid becomes so established in the plant world that it is listed along with the spp. with only its hyb. status in fine print in the literature. When a descendant is a member of a "strain", developed from crossing with several parents, a name will be given the strain. (Double quotes are used for strains.)

Species within a genus are crossed. Genera are sometimes crossed but not easily. This **"bi-generic" cross** is an unusual accomplishment and the offspring is prized. Besides, the characteristics sought may have been, to some extent at least, achieved.

What do these hybridizers seek? Of course sometimes the cross turns out an odd combination which they did not at all expect or foresee, and the progeny may be interesting and unique. But they do have specific aims; many results turn out as they expect. The spp. of some genera cross-pollenize with ease. There will occur a breed of natural hybrids. Sometimes like a species they will breed true from seed. In this case, they select a superior natural hybrid. Unpollinated seed is germinated to obtain seedlings of the natural cross, or the plant may be propagated vegetatively to assure getting a replica.

But man wants a hand in the direction to be taken by the progeny. Will it be better or just different? The goals are several, some with decided benefits to gardens.

A change in size is sought. Seldom do the breeders aim for a taller plant; often they wish to encourage a tendency in the other direction. The more dwarf plants are more useful in small gardens.

A habit of density is encouraged. The more branches, more closely packed to produce a compact plant. You have seen often a cv. name 'Compactum'.

The most important work on the foliage is to increase resistance to disease. For instance, mildew is less prevalent in Snapdragons and Michaelmas daisy, today. Sometimes tolerance of cold can be increased.

A great deal of attention is given the flower.

An obvious change is in the number of petals. A selection may be double or semidouble. A group of aborted petals (petaloids) may make a rim around the center. Sometimes the petaloids make the flower look cluttered or they may be a welcome decoration. A greater number of petals changes the overall shape.

We have only to look at the wide variation in number and shape of petals in hybrid chrysanthemums and peonies to wonder at the development of unusual forms.

The single flower has an advantage however. The reproductive centers, often marvelous and beautiful, are better seen when petals do not crowd them. The single flower may be less flamboyant but its design is more evident and frequently more attractive.

Gerbera (Improved)

Form of the individual parts may be improved somewhat. The hybrid may have a more slender trumpet than that of the type or the cup-shape may become deeper or shallower. A detail of the flower may be emphasized. Notches in the petals may be accentuated becoming more noticeable. Spurs may be lengthened; think of the hybrids of Long-Spurred *Aquilegia*. In these cultivars of Columbine, the shape of the flower has changed sometimes to show to advantage the spacing of the petals. On the other hand, the very plumpness of one of the species Columbines will have its own charm.

The number of flowers which a plant may produce can be increased. The characteristic is called "floriferous". This is important in a fruiting plant. An apple may improve in quantity as well as quality.

The breeders labor for color year after year. Usually they aim toward greater brilliance. But they go a long way with pale colors also. Do you remember how hard the seedsmen worked to obtain a "white" marigold? Some aim only for achievement's or novelty's sake. Color is often tied to size as in the case of *Gerbera,* the best hybrids having become mammoth and colorful as well. Some species have modifications of the flower color caused by spots, stripes and lines. By selection the progeny may have more intricate patterns. Think of *Helleborus orientalis;* this hellebore does its own work of hybridizing. Every year we see new patterns occurring on some of the flowers.

The leaf may also have a pattern of stripes, bands or spots. This is called "variegation", and is a natural mutation which can be somewhat accentuated. We gardeners can increase the production of variegated leaves by constantly removing whatever all-green ones grow. Once in a while there is a leaf which is a sport, all white or all cream, an "albino". But I know no way of inducing these greenless leaves to appear. If you have a plant with very nice variegation the pattern is just as attractive whether you feed or starve but enough moisture must be provided to keep the plant healthy.

Veronica 'Red Fox' (Brilliant)

To return to a flower and its color, there is another development besides increase in color intensity and the addition of decorative details. Species with flowers of two quite different colors can be hybridized. The results may be several different color blends of the two colors in the parents. When all the seedlings bloom the best blends are selected and given cv. status; lovely muted shades quite new to the world of flower color sometimes occur. It is instructive to plant these odd tones and shades in the same bed with the true species which were used in the breeding—a demonstration of the wonders of horticulture.

What about the true species? What have they to recommend them? Besides, are the new colors always better? A species with a simple basic natural colored flower should not be discarded in favor of its fancier progeny. It sometimes happens that the mutations become so popular that the type species are no longer grown and it sometimes happens that the parents are no longer to be found in the wild. What if the cvs. are better in every way? Some cvs. are so good that they are patented. (No other breeder can try the same cross without permission.) If you propagate by cuttings your new plant will not deviate or throwback but you are honor-bound to propagate that patented cv. only for yourself. (The reasons are commercial of course.)

So the cv. is superior and admired and protected. Is it such an improvement that we do not care about the true species anymore? Well, there are drawbacks to artificial breeding. Flowers may not last as long. The life of the plant may be curtailed

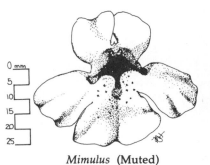

Mimulus (Muted)

Trillium (Natural)

especially if it is a result of recrossing. And its powers of reproduction may be diminished. Plants can be overbred.

Is there some useful or handsome element in the stock, the species in the wild, from which the variations sprung? Perhaps a unique detail of the natural personality may have been forgotten. With population coming under increased pressure and strain, it becomes more important not to lose the forbears of our cultivated forms.

Especially, we must save the endangered species—the true native types. We can carry them on in our gardens in case their native habitats should be destroyed. You will be able to find specialists who are with great care raising these rare and often exquisite species. Besides, there is an intrinsic value in a plant born in its natural place, in its original form. Its generations have been unchanged except perhaps by the activities of bee or bird or chipmunk and their personality has remained little touched by winds or weather.

A partial list of unusual spp., strains or cultivars to look for in the catalogues or seed lists

Acaena novae-zelandiae
Achillea 'Maynard's Gold' (*A. tomentosa*)
Agapanthus praecox 'Blue Baby'
Alstroemeria "Dr. Salter's hybs."
Antirrhinum "Madam Butterfly" F. 1 hybs. 'Wonder', 'Little Darling' etc.
Aquilegia & *A. prenaica* hybs. "Dwarf Fairyland", "Music", 'Maxistar', 'Ministar'
Aster 'Lucida'
Asteriscus maritimus
Aubrieta novalis 'Blue'
Campanula fragilis 'Jewel'
Celsia arcturus
Celsioverbascum 'Golden Wings' (*C. acaulis* × *V. phoenicium*)
Cosmos 'Sea Shells' (Fluted petals) *C. bipinnatus* 'Candy striped'
Dianthus 'Bambina'
Digitalis 'Temple Bells'

Eustoma grandiflora F. 1 hyb
Genista villarsii
Gerbera 'Black Heart', 'Happipot' & 'Frisbee' a selection of 'Happipot'
Gypsophila elegans 'Giant White'
Iris sintenisii
Kniphofia "Miniature hybs."
Lupinus "Band of Nobles"
Mimulus cupreus cvs.
Papaver 'Danebrog'
Papaver nudicaule "Oregon Rainbows"
Pelargonium hortorum 'Wilhelm Lanscuth'
Primula acaulis F. 1 hyb. 'Blue Jeans'
Pulsatilla regeliana
Scabiosa alpina
Teucrium 'Moe's Gold'
Thalictrum stanieki
Tropaeolum 'Peach Melba' 'Spitfire' etc.
Vaccinium darrowii 'John Blue'
Watsonia meriana

7. Directions

You are convinced you want to find a place in your garden for a combination of perennials. How much space do you need? Very little: you can discard some plants not now giving full value for the room they take up. The latitude is almost limitless when you decide to select just a corner, a bay, a strip. If you wish to have a "border" your space can be anywhere from ten to one hundred feet and its depth can be two to twenty feet. If you can only build a short border, you will have fewer different kinds of plants. If you have a narrow border, you may want to confine your selections to provide for only two heights, low and medium or medium and high, which two depends largely on the background. If your border will be over five feet in depth, you may want to incorporate shrubs or subshrubs. If you will need extra color for a season, you may want to incorporate annuals.

There are several criteria which will limit your choices of plants besides size. If your border will be near a tree like Eucalyptus, its inhabitants must not only be drought resistant but tough. If it will be near any kind of tree, the health of your selections will depend on how much water and food the tree demands how much shade it casts and when and what effect the tree's type of root growth will have on the well-being of the roots of the perennials in its vicinity. Will your border be in the path of the prevailing wind; what will you choose to plant which does not suffer from being battered about? Perhaps you can include in your plan some wind protection, to allow a greater choice.

How many perennial plants can you crowd into either a small or large space, naturally all depends on the type of perennial. You will acquire your plants in various stages of maturity, as first transplants, or the next size up or perhaps a year old in a one gallon container. All will multiply in size when planted in the ground; it is useful to know how much and how fast. What is the plant's eventual width? Some will keep on spreading horizontally until they touch the neighboring plant; then stems will overlap and finally climb into each other's lap. How wide will an individual become which has no obstruction in its way? The whole class of spreaders, by underground roots or by overground stems, will widen indefinitely. The average non-spreader will at least triple in size. Width can, of course, be modified by division. It is helpful, however, to have a certain percentage of perennials the growth of which is somewhat predictable.

The dictionaries and catalogues seldom give the width of a plant. The English writers will often give a measurement of width. How well and wide will the plant grow for you? Height as well as width must necessarily be an approximation. In the Plant Descriptions in this book, I have often given maximum measurements by using the phrase "to" three feet; someone has seen that species that high or wide; if one were to use the phrase "usually" two feet, one would have to add where and how.

And when? You have seen that some perennials just keep on getting bigger, especially wider. Will you be learning about width in maturity when you read a measurement? If a plant will reach its best size only at the end of its third year, will you plant only two of a kind instead of six? Will you be patient about those with a moderate growth rate? You can look forward to the need for division in more cases than not and some will need division in the third year and some in the fifth. Of course the dwarfs in each genus will not require division that soon—perhaps never.

You might be tempted to plant too close so that the border will look full right away. If you can't resist the temptation, you will have to remove and replace the first year. You can forstall replacing if you can decide to leave space for growth. A rule of thumb? Leave 6 inches for those you believe are upright growers and restrained growers, leave 12 inches for those which promise to become wider. You should leave more space between drifts than between plants. Somebody said, "A community of plants comfortably adjusted to one another, cooperating instead of co-elbowing."

You are limited in what you select by several factors: amount of sun, amount of light, amount of rainfall, your kind of soil and the temperature of your region. I do not say "zone" because the boundaries of zones are so imperfectly drawn. States and counties may have various temperatures within them. Six miles away a plant may die whereas it receives only a little frost damage in your garden. In both gardens the tops, the new foliage, may burn but in the first much more severely. The years differ greatly. Plants suffer from prolonged cold, repeated cold, sudden cold. There seems to be no discernible cycle except that in a temperate climate a "big freeze" seems to occur every 50 to 60 years. The gardeners of California or West Coast U.S. are cautious after one of those years or even a winter with more than average cold but more chances are taken as the memory fades.

We cannot be oblivious of the conditions which influence temperature in our region. How much altitude is involved? A lot higher will be colder but a little higher will be warmer. Plants in Bogota nearer the equator but at the top of a mountain live in the same conditions of temperature as the midwest coast of the U.S. Plants in any one garden will be in greater danger in the depressions and low spots. Is your garden south or west facing; if so, it will be warmer. If you live near an ocean, you will have less cold especially if your piece of ocean has a warm current running near your shore. How much stress have your plants been under? Have they been battered by wind or are their roots exposed? We used to hear experts say, "Hold off watering your tender plants in the fall, or feeding, so that they will not have new growth when the frosts come." If you allow your plants to become poorly, they will not stand anything including frost. On the whole a healthy plant will not be as much hurt by the elements as a sick one.

How can the situations in your garden be modified in order to assist plants in resisting the effects of cold. Site your tender species in a warm spot, not in a gully or in a draft. Against a warm wall is a good place (watch that they do not dry out there). Protection overhead can make a big difference, boughs, a roof, eaves. The "overhang" made by architects for people, is a great boon for plants. You may have a greenhouse or a lath house. You will have at least a storage place for the plants you have to "lift". Shelves against the house covered with a pitched roof will winter over a number of semi-tender plants. Mulching for winter is a cold-climate practice useful for other climates also. What was the condition of your soil when you introduced a tender perennial to your garden? Drainage is most important since plants do not like wet feet and will be less able to stand cold. Noted above was the caution against letting a plant get sickly. What is the condition of your plant? Is it too old or is it too young?

Has it had a chance to become acclimatized? Getting used to a new climate is possible for many plants provided the adjustment is made little by little. So, you have made your plan to include some perennials known to be questionably hardy. Can you leave the spaces empty for the months it takes to accustom your plant to the special atmosphere where it will lead the rest of its life? If you must fill its space, put in a non-greedy temporary plant. But do include in your total list of plants some borderline cases. How many depends on how courageous you are.

You will see in the Plant Descriptions some phrases. When the perennial is hardy, there will be nothing said. When it is less than hardy, you will see "semi-hardy", when it is more tender than that you will see "semi-tender", and truly tender you will see "tender". This means really tender—it will not stand frost at all. But even so, don't necessarily cross it out, for you may be able to acclimatize even a perennial from a

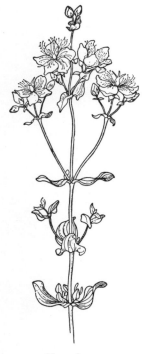

Hypericum

tropical climate. In the literature you will see other phrases, "not reliably hardy", "somewhat tender", "protect", "some species more than others" and all will be influenced by the garden from which the author writes. Don't rely on any one opinion. You have one easy way to be safe. Grow all plants which are not reliably hardy in containers; move all to protection during all the winter months or just during a cold "spell".

This thought brings us back to where we started: how much space is needed and how many plants. You may become a pot addict. You will then very likely build on to your house all sorts of structures for plants.

I have included in the Plant Descriptions many species, some of which I have not grown and a few of which I have not seen. How to interpret the information in the Plant Descriptions? Each genus follows the same outline of facts. After the botanical name, in parenthesis, a former name or synonym then the family name and then the common name, if any. The next line defines the region of origin, often useful if you know your geography well enough to imagine the conditions under which the native species are born. The description of the genus follows three headings: 1) Evergreen or herbaceous, the general appearance and personality, the dimensions, and the highlights of foliage and flower characteristics; 2) Points for culture when pertinent, in order of exposure, soil, moisture, drainage, fertilizer, hardiness if questionable, and propagation; and 3) Special attributes, items of history, reference of note, use. There are several Plant Descriptions, some for the subject matter of a given chapter, one for plants best for the shade or semi-shade and one list called General, mostly for sun or part-sun. Occasionally, there seemed reason to chop up a genus, especially when its many species vary in character and use. There are cross references, and lists of special categories in the Appendix.

The nomenclature mostly follows *Hortus III,* except in those cases where work on the taxonomy has been published since the date of *Hortus* or where some genus or species was not included, notably plants native in regions still being explored or documented. The spellings? Alternatives are not given but you will know of some. Modern cultivars? Names are different in every region where they are introduced; it was impossible to state: "Doris" of Delaware is just the same to all intents and purposes as "Edith" of Fresno. Sometimes you will find a German or a French name, usually easy to translate. Often, there are just too many cultivars all equally good perhaps and, in any case, it would be impossible to weed out the duplicates. Consider that the cultivars named are just examples.

Abbreviations. Not many. I wanted to put "fl." for flower and "lf." for leaf, etc. but it all began to read too much like telegraphy. The countries are given with initials, but not following the modern telephone book. When there were many countries of origin, the word "widespread" was used. The abbreviations of terms will be easy to understand.

ABBREVIATIONS
Text

genus = gen.	double = dble.
variety = var.	illustration = ill.
cultivar(s) = cv(s).	chapter = Chap.
species = sp. (singular), spp. (plural)	states = old U.S. Post Office abbrevia-
medium = med.	tions

Plant Lists and Plant Descriptions,

and = &	ground cover = g.c.	numerous = num.	southwest = S.W.
annual = ann.	hardy = hdy.	opposite = opp.	subspecies = subsp., subspp.
biennial = bien.	herbaceous = herb.	perennial(s) = per(s).	temperate = temp.
central = cent.	hybrid(s) = hyb(s).	related = rel.	terminate = term.
culture = cult.	inch(es) = in.	rock garden = r.g.	tropical = trop.
east, eastern = E.	month(s) = mo(s).	several = sev.	west, western = W.
especially = esp.	mountain(s) = mtn(s).	semihardy = semihdy.	Width, wide = w.
evergreen = evgrn.	north = N.	similar = sim.	
excellent = excel.	North America = N. Am.	south = S.	
fertile = fert.	northeast = N.E.	South America = S. Am.	
foot, feet = ft.	northwest = N.W.	southeast = S.E.	

Athyrium

0   15   30   45   60   75 mm

Section II: The Sites

8. The Woodland, Shady Places and the Rock Garden

It is easier to visualize the use of plants which prefer shade in a setting in which the shade is produced by trees. But there is also shade produced by buildings and walls. The latter is usually deep shade or part time shade most of the day but no shade at all in the parts of the day when the arc of the sun brings it around a corner. This is all to the good if the sun is mild; it may be dangerous if it is scorching. If you have any sheltered situation, you will have no difficulty in selecting appropriate plants for your shady or part-shady site from those plants to be discussed specifically for a situation under trees.

You hear warnings about the heat of the mid-day sun. Another difficult situation is in semi-shade and occurs when shade exists until say to four p.m. Then the sun brings around the heat of the late day to the inhabitants of the shady place. In the long days of a hot, dry summer, this can be a wilting and a punishing sun. Best to plant a tree as a partial screen before next summer.

Clivia

There are, of course, two types of trees; if you have deciduous trees, your shade will be deep when the trees are in full leaf and quite broken when the canopy is made up of but twigs and branches. If your trees are evergreen, your shade will be more or less constant throughout the year although again the sun's arc throughout the day will bring about nuances in the amount of shade in a given area. The type of foliage, the type of branching and the pruning of the trees will have a great effect on the density of the shade. Two telling phrases are "filtered shade" and "dappled shade". Most plants, even those which prefer shade, do best when there is a bit of light. Some light will penetrate the shade if the branches of the trees are high. If there are openings between the branches, light will enter the place below them intermittently, in different amounts as the sun "moves". But there will be light on cloudy days also. Many plants look well and behave well in the partial shade brought about by openings to the sky, through the branches of trees. (You may read the expression "high shade"). *Clivia* likes the cool of shade but needs light to bloom.

A slightly different situation is created by one tree as against several trees. Suppose in both cases the boughs are high and open; in the midst of the several trees there will be less light since less can come in from the sides. However, the trees in a grove can be thinned as well as pruned. The distance between the trunks can be enlarged as well as the distance between the boughs. If planted with some space between them so that the foliage does not completely mesh in the canopy, there will be shafts of light or that treasured filtered light. In the case of evergreen trees, the amount will be fairly predictable taking into account other sources of shade which affect the

45

situation part of the day or part of the year. Another tree or other trees, some distance from the site to be planted, may shorten the day and the total hours of light because they cut off the sun either in its rising or setting. This curtain may also be advantageous if it blocks a prevailing wind. A windbreak is a major function, of course, of any trees in your garden. The mini-climates which develop either by design or chance have an inestimable influence on the growth of the plants you select.

I have called this chapter "The Woodland" hoping you may have room for trees rather than just one tree. A "grove" might be the term which you would more likely have in mind for your group of trees. Certainly "woodland" connotes at least several trees mostly of the same kind, creating therefore the same kind of shade and dictating the same kind of plants. These plants and the soil which they prefer is called "woodsy". You have no doubt an intuitive sense of a woodsy type of foliage and hopefully you will enlarge your image while looking at some possibilities to be suggested. You will say that you have a small garden and so it is not possible to have a woodland unless perhaps you can turn the whole yard into a planting of trees. I will describe a proper woodland because we might as well imagine an ideal situation and besides there are so many delightful perennials to plant beneath trees that we might as well conjure up a site big enough to hold a fair percentage of their number. Meanwhile, we will not forget the bed on the north side of the house; in some of the Plant Descriptions you will find many which would suit either situation.

Digitalis

In any case, let us try to envision a garden under trees which will be beautiful to walk through and perhaps even sit in. Perhaps you do not care about a show for viewing; perhaps you live where the seasonal growth of perennials is spread out over many months of the year. When there is seemingly no growth, there is often basal foliage. People say to me, "I would like to come see your garden; when is your garden at its best?" And I answer with something vague like, "Well it depends." Every year my garden diary, sketchy as it is, reveals wide variations in the timing of the blooming especially of woodsy plants. We cannot know all the circumstances which alter the behavior of plants or their subtle inner workings. We do not need all happenings to be dated. I have learned not to take seriously the times of flowering given in the literature and I have learned to rely on no one year's experience to establish a firm pattern. So, the utmost pleasure can be derived from watching for the early growth of perennials and delighting in the surprise when the expected date is not yet due. Curiously, one or two plants of a group will shoot up stems and blossom well ahead of the siblings. I call these "heralds" and they communicate an urgency and a promise inherent in nature.

These apparently out of season plants are sometimes right on season because you have acquired another species or cultivar which has a natural quite different blooming period. A few genera contain species which spread their growing periods throughout the year. *Cyclamen* is the most striking example; all in the same garden, you may plant fall, winter, spring and summer blooming species. Certainly, there is no other plant as appropriate as *Cyclamen* for a planting under high branched trees. When not in flower, the many short stalked leaves of various shapes and with various markings make fascinating patterns on the floor. In the Woodland Plant Descriptions you will find several listed more or less in sequence according to season but you must expect them to vary in their timing for you. The year is apt to begin with *C. orbiculatum* or *C. coum*, or *C. atkinsii*. The most dwarf species, as *C. ibericum* and *C. cilicum* 'Nanum' do not form their buds until early spring. I plant the dwarfs in shallow boxes and sit the box on a tree stump. This raised position is more secure, more visible and allows one to smell any subtle fragrance more easily. Some *Cyclamen* are more evergreen than others. I recommend to you a book, *Growing Cyclamen* by Gay Nightingale, which gives both illuminating descriptions and botanical differences.

Cyclamen is the prime example of the value of marked foliage for a shady setting. Interesting mottling is noticeable throughout the year. (Some species have leaves of unmottled green.) Let us look at some other genera which decorate the floor of a woodland with leaves variously patterned.

Oxalis, O. oregana, the Redwood Sorrel, has attractive leaf markings and grows in a billowy mound. Too bad it is so vigorous; it is hard to control. It wanders underground, its red stems sometimes coming up a foot away from the main patch. Nothing delicate should be near its possible path. But if your grove is comprised of Redwood it is a natural. The encyclopedia calls it "robust".

Quite opposite in character, not rapacious at all in habit is a species of *Tiarella, T.*

Cyclamen

wherryi. It grows in contained rosettes multiplying with constraint. The leaves have faint traceries of darker color which follow the outline of the leaf. There is a vestige of basal foliage throughout the winter in temperate climates and a renewal when spring growth begins. Many short, slender, fluffy spikes rise above the leaves later on and stay a while. *Tiarella* grown in quantity makes a unique contribution in form and color to a woodland carpet.

Hepaticas have a two-toned pattern. The combination is subtle since it is the back of the leaves which has the darker purplish tone. But the leaves do not lie flat on the ground; some turn away from the center of the rounded clump and thereby show the second tone.

A variegated *Trillium, T. luteum,* is quite dwarf and shy; it comes up every year but does not increase its small patch in my garden. Its mottling is yellowish and in a scattered pattern; the color seems to announce the color of the small future flower. It is an oddity pleasing to meet on the floor of the woods. The three parted leaf is a miniature of the larger species.

More variegation will be treated later. Marking and shading is either a special case of variegation or is a happening in its own right.

All ferns are appropriate in woodland but those with a blend of color make a unique contribution. *Osmunda regalis,* Royal Fern or Flowering Fern, is a stalwart fern. The fertile part of a frond has sporangia (the sheath which clothes the spores) clustered on the branching midrib; these clusters look like sprays of flowers. The rich brown has a coppery tone. This fern has the appearance of a plant bridging the ages; it is in fact a representative of an intermediate group between primitive families and highly evolved families. I like it for its look of antiquity and for its inventive ingenuity in providing for future generations.

The most amazing color scheme is to be found in the herbaceous fern from Japan, *Athyrium nipponicum* 'Pictum' (see synonyms). Soft grey and green and blue-green are painted with various shades of lavender. The color varies between youth and age and also according to amount of light. One day in spring, tightly curled, purplish fronds will emerge—more of them than last year—and very soon a splashing fountain of broad graceful fronds will have developed to flow over a space 30 inches wide. Just one plant is enough to provide a beautiful accent. The roots will grow from divisions, however, and it is good to repeat the feature nearby.

Tiarella

If most ferns are less fantastic in their coloring, they all give a two-toned effect due to the highlighting of the very bright green of the very new fronds. Maidenhair and Five-finger will have several shades when lush with fronds of several ages. As early as February in California, the new fronds of some small ferns have a look of exceeding delicacy; they glimmer as a ray of light reaches them. Poking forth from rocks, *Polypodium californicum,* which is called Disappearing Fern, is a surprise but it retreats after too short a time. A native of the eastern U.S., *P. polypodioides* is called Resurrection Fern, attractive, leathery and given to appearing suddenly.

Look for genera in which the new fronds have a pinkish caste in their new copper or bronze fronds. *Blechnum brasiliense* is tender but *Dryopteris erythrosora,* Autumn Fern, is hardy. A number of species of *Adiantum* are hardy. When the new fronds have special color or texture, some of last year's fronds even though not damaged or faded, should be removed to offer a better view. Some ferns have intricate patterns of spores; it is possible to expose those fronds with handsome spore designs by somewhat thinning the thick clumps. But talk about fern color should not detract from the basic value of ferns, the wonderful and varied shapes and textures. Maidenhair has been noted for its fresh green; the design of its many small circles trimming its wiry stems would be reason enough for giving it a place in a woodland. New clusters of Maidenhair appear unexpectedly in odd places. One plant is attractive in company with other woodsy genera like *Pulsatilla* and *Uvularia* or several plants can be grown together to form a lacey mass in a shady corridor. Some ferns can be utilized as ground covers. Two excellent for this purpose, creating a mat, are *Blechnum penna-marina* and *Azederach officinale.* Bronze tips on new fronds add to the design.

One of the aspects of ferns we have touched upon is the shimmery quality. Let us look at some other plants with glossy leaf surfaces which catch the flickerings of light penetrating the tree canopy. *Tanakaea radicans* is a quite dwarf clumping species with an incredible sheen in its foliage. You will see a sketch on p. 80 since it is an example of a habit of growth; low, evergreen tufting, with good behavior and charm. The leaves are not more than two inches long and come to a point, just barely fringed on the edges;

Adiantum

Gaultheria

Bergenia

Pulsatilla

creamy white flowers on less than one foot scapes make a muted display; there are no petals, the five calyx lobes are greenish, and there are ten stamens.

The most glossy perennial is certainly *Galax*. The leaves of *Galax* are leathery and sculptural; they probably cannot be surpassed in symmetry. A few other perennials have to some extent this patent-leather look, notably *Shortia galicifolia* and one of the uncommon Saxifrages, *S. fortunei* 'Rubrifolia'. The glossiness is brought to our attention in these three plants, because they are examples of perennials with foliage of an unusual color; these have leaves of bright red or reddish bronze which shines equally with the green. *Gaultheria procumbens* also has bronze new leaves and is only a little less glossy. Under dense trees this *Gaultheria* will grow into a wide mat, producing its starry white flowers and crimson berries in only a little light. The leathery leaves are so numerous that they partially hide flowers and fruit. *Metrosideros carmineus*, the trailing kind of *Metrosideros*, with a shiny leaf is an extraordinary foliage plant. The leaves are round, tiny, placed in opposite positions on the main slender stems and delicate side stems. It makes a beautiful pattern, especially when it drapes itself across a lichen-covered flat rock. The stems lie flat except the tips which seem to reach up for light, causing the stems to rise a bit to show a muted rose-color on the backside.

A much larger plant, *Bergenia*, is noted for its gloss. The big shiny leathery leaves are diminished in number in the winter although not much in size. The raindrops sit upon them and shimmer in the last bit of light.

A number of other perennials have the glossy leaves which you will surely find an asset in shade or semi-shade. You will come upon others described in the Plant Descriptions.

Another attribute which makes a plant good for woodland is delicacy. I suppose this is due to contrast—the small and light textured as against the weight and strength of the trunks of the trees. Earlier we discovered delicacy in a number of ferns. Some other examples with this character are *Astilbe, Thalictrum, Corydalis, Dicentra*. The foliage of these has a light substance. The leaves are either many and small or intricately divided.

The foliage of *Pulsatilla* is pinnately divided, soft and delicate. The flower then adds to that quality by its personality, especially when it has acquired its seed. Wood *Anemones* have a fluffy seed head also and a leaf with a similar pattern.

Delicacy can be achieved by just smallness. Some of the woodland carpets have tiny leaves. *Campanula cocklearifolia* has upright stems only one or two inches high and leaves tiny, not much bigger than a pin head and shiny: look closely and you will see that they are spoon-shaped. *Mentha requienii* is flatter and even smaller. The foliage of the dwarfs of *Potentilla, Hypericum* and *Galium* is relatively small and that of *Gentiana* not much larger. Use enough of whatever carpets you choose for the woodland floor so that the particular aspect of a personality is made evident.

Some perennials good for shady places are not only small but also restrained; they will not make a mat or a carpet. One must be pleased to see appear just one or two plants of a choice species, not hidden by the stems of neighbors. In some gardens the plants of *Cornus canadensis* will be few and far between, quite unlike the carpet they make at home. That tiny dwarf variegated *Arabis* I have recommended to you hardly enlarges itself but lies flat and neat against the earth almost as if it were wearing camouflage.

Let us turn to a few perennials of a larger size, famous for form and texture. *Pulmonaria* spreads horizontally and its leaves make a pattern because of the manner of their placement. Their surface is more or less rough. The roughest surface is found in *Brunnera* with a leaf of good size and pleasing shape. *Omphalodes* is almost as rough but with leaves one quarter the size of those of *Brunnera*. Since both have forget-me-not like flowers, they make good companions.

Hellebores are good companions for any and all perennials partial to shade. *H. niger* has a fascinating shiny leaf, like dark precious leather. The stems flare out from the crown making an asymmetrical pattern of segments. Then the perfect flower stands upright in the center, its waxiness a large part of its beauty. Several other Hellebores are easier to grow. The foliage of *H. foetidus* is extraordinary; it makes a 2-foot high ground cover of deeply incised dark-green shiny leaves. The Corsican Hellebore stands taller than the others and the flowers with seed developing have an extraordinary attractive form. The leaves of *H. orientalis* are shiny with large segments and leathery texture—forming full clumps. In earliest spring the flowers rise above the foliage in sheets of color. An alluring picture of color is to be seen when this Hellebore and *Epimedium* are planted in combination. The *H. orientalis* is a cultivar with flowers of deepest rose; the *Epimedium* is in winter costume—deepest reddish bronze.

All the *Epimediums* are admirable perennials. If you have room acquire every species you can find. *Epimedium pinnatum* var. *colchicum* may be your favorite at the moment because of its outstanding season of fall color but you will like also the fresh-apple-green new leaves of many of the other species. One species (E. grandiflorum 'White Queen') makes a wide sheet of ferny foliage, the small white flowers showing just above. The dainty leaves persist through mild winters but if the foliage stems are cut back, the spring green will be fresher and fuller. The leaves of *Epimedium* vary not only in size but in shape; see the chapter on leaf form for a sketch of a human heart and a Valentine heart. As for flowers, you may have yellow or white or a coral-orange—more rare. The flowers, sometimes inside-out, dance and add to the attractive foliage.

A cousin, the Western U.S. native, *Vancouveria*, makes a nice combination with *Epimedium*. At first glance, the foliage and flowers seem much alike. A planting close together makes a conversation piece. The leaves of *Vancouveria* grow on thin wiry stems which gives a graceful lilt to their posture. The foliage of *Vancouveria* is darker than that of *Epimedium* and usually smaller and, grows on shorter, more procumbent stems. *Vancouveria* is a natural under redwoods—from whence it comes.

I grow *Dodecatheon*, Shooting Star, near its cousins, *Vancouveria* and *Epimedium*, because all three have flowers with bent-back petals, suggesting the descriptive term "inside-out". Both the Eastern and Western species need some light; the Western species does best and spreads well on a quite sunny crown of a hill. Look for other flowers with this bent-back design. See the drawing of dwarf *Narcissus* on p. 134. Sometimes it is the sepals instead of the petals which are bent back; no matter, both give a look of flight.

While speaking of flowers, let us look at several which compliment a setting in dappled shade. Racemes or sprays of small flowers go well with small patterns of light and shade. The smallest flowers imaginable may be found in the dainty columns of *Saxifraga umbrosa* and *Heuchera micrantha*, or *H. tiarelloides*. The blossoms are almost invisible until a breath of air moves the stem a little. Investigate these other three genera: *Boykinia, Patrinia, Actaea.* Their effect is muted.

Plants with much larger flowers may be used for accents. Set off in an open space, some flowers on tallish stems and with unusual form draw the eye. *Trillium* and Lilies and so-called Lilies are natural inclusions. On the ground floor, smaller flowers with strong colors will be visible through openings between the larger plants. Dwarf Primrose is an obvious example; but do not overlook other Primroses with paler colors: *P. rupicola* is soft yellow. Even a small bright patch attracts attention and makes you want to go to look more closely. *Erinus* will suddenly cover its miniature mat with bright pink and the flowers of an *Hypericum* will open all at once in bright yellow. The foliage of both is decorative for months.

Deep and bright colors are important, but white, or cream most of all. Typical plants for a shady setting are *Aruncus* and *Cimicifuga*. Both are herbaceous but develop into quite large plants with handsome foliage before blooming time. There is a very tall *Thalictrum*—some consider it weedy—which reaches up through the branches of any closeby tree, such as a Dogwood. It has a fluffy mass of leafy stems while growing. The flowers are small but numerous stamens flicker in the light which comes through the upper canopy of leaves. Much nearer the ground, in a glade, the flower of *Anthericum* will open; the slender strap-shape basal foliage will have been barely visible, through the early spring. Later the stalk rises to carry only a few trumpets no wider than an inch which glisten white against the dark background. You may choose to have two or three plants but even just one makes a choice picture.

Less white, more greenish are the flowers of *Polygonatum*. The older the plant, the taller and the more bells hanging from the underside of the curving stem. True Solomon Seal and its siblings and relatives are naturals for any space under trees. They look well under a cultivar of a Maple, perhaps because of the contrast between the smooth oval leaflet of the perennial and the much cut leaf of the Maple. Creamy white and off-white do a like job of lighting up the shade. Just two examples: *Eucomis* and *Penstemon.* The progress of the foliage growth of *Eucomis* is intriguing to watch; there is a drawing in Form of the Flower on p. 27. The *Penstemon* would be the delicate species *P. digitalis,* the one with a graceful, open loose spike. See p. 34. There are many others

Helleborus

Heuchera

Cimicifuga

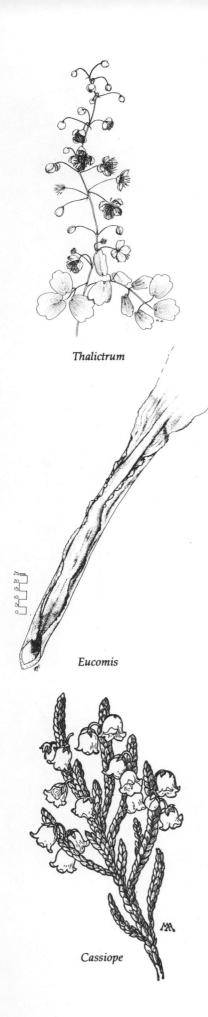

Thalictrum

Eucomis

Cassiope

with attractive foliage and whitish flowers, some which bloom early and some which bloom late.

Perhaps the best source of white for a woodland, subtle rather than flashy, is from evergreen perennials with variegated leaves. The white or cream stripes show up well in the shade or semi-shade. (See the list of plants with variegated leaves.) Be sure to include in your planting the variegated forms of *Liriope*, a Wallflower—*Cheiranthus linifolius*, a Grass—*Arrhenantherum elatius*, and the lovely cultivars of *Polygonatum* and *Uvularia*.

Do you feel the need for grey foliage in the shade? You will find some perennials with matting or trailing habit which are good for forward positions. The following have greyish leaves: *Pterocephalus parnassii* (with many furry seed heads as well), *Raoulia australis* with no discernible flower and relying on the artistry of its delicate foliage; two other carpeters are *Acaena* and *Laurentia fluviatilis*. The greyest leaves may be found in the lovely sprawler, *Androsace lanuginosa*, (best with ample light).

Foliage with unusual color is valuable also, like the beige of *Arthropodium candidum* or the almost black of the *Ophiopogon planiscapus* 'Nigrescens' (See containers); neither color stands out from a distance but both are a nice surprise on a close look. The foliage of *Maclaeya* is two-toned. The color on the backside is soft grey-beige and is visible whenever the leaf is not full-face. The form of this plant is superb. The pale beige of fluffy seed heads adds a muted odd note; they may come late to the color scheme of the woodland but are none the less a part of the composition. The seed heads of *Pulsatilla* follow the flowers quickly and stay awhile until the wings of the seed are ready to carry them away. You will think of *Clematis* immediately when anyone says "fluffy seed heads". *C. integrifolia* will grow in part shade.

Let us leave color now, in foliage, in flower and in seed and turn to some further shapes created by various woodland plants.

Many leaves have blade, strap or sword shapes. You will find that you want to combine with low growers some perennials with a definite upthrust and a strong personality. The leaves of *Clivia* have very good texture as well as form; this plant is a must for the shade in temperate zones. *Arthropodium cirrhatum* from New Zealand has handsome evergreen leaves, but is questionably hardy. The leaves of *Eucomis* are attractive, early and late. Do you live in too cold a climate for these borderline species? Your leaf canopy if you have evergreen trees will afford considerable protection. However, you must look for some hardier perennials with sword shapes. Consider the many *Irises*; if you have a damp enough place you can grow *I. ensata*. You can grow any *Iris* native in your area; in California, I grow quantities of the *Irises* native to the U.S. West Coast. There are a number of foreigners from far places as Africa and Australasia. Try some after checking as much as possible their hardiness; some may acclimatize in your protected spots.

There are clump formers one or two of which will make important contributions to the foliage design. *Aristea, Bulbinella,* and *Libertia* each has a different form. Look for *L. ixioides,* narrow blade-shaped leaves in a small flaring clump. You will find other suggestions in Form of Foliage.

I have left out so many perennials which would be candidates for any shady area and especially for those where the roof is tree tops. In two or three layouts you will find a few not included here.

And look among the subshrubs for some species you will want to incorporate. *Zenobia pulverulenta,* really a shrub, is small and slow growing and deciduous from the East U.S.; it has a perfect personality for woodland. A few examples of dwarf shrubs are *Daphne cneorum, Pieris japonica* 'Pigmaea', *Cyathodes* sp., *Cassiope* sp. *Whipplea modesta* is a West Coast sprawler; its branches like a log over which to tumble.

Logs have a part to play in an extensive woodland. Still more important are rocks. In natural woods, you will very often find rocks cropping up among the tree-trunks. Even a single tree looks more established with a rock or two beneath it. If you do not have a natural outcrop, you must find or even buy some and actually plant them. Put together shapes and sizes and colors which go well together and go well with the plants in their vicinity. A setting of rocks and stones, contributes to the welfare of all kinds of plants not just alpines; deep root-runs and perfect drainage are two most important benefits. Sometimes rocks may be used more for landscaping purposes than for cultural advantage; they associate harmoniously with plants; the texture of these two fruits of the earth seem related. Some rocks lie absolutely flat on the ground and have a tray function instead of a propping function. The ones which prop act also as a backdrop. The rocks with mounding shapes should go down well below the surface and extend above for 10 to 20 inches; one or two might stand higher. So much the better if they have lichen growing on them. Again, pay heed to the color of your rocks so that they bring out colors in your foliage design.

Several rocks have a copper tone in their makeup. Several plants are displayed especially well against a rock in which the grey is predominant. *Phyllodoce empetriformis*, Mountain Heath, enjoys the firm surface to lean against. New stems arise above the rock, curving a bit but then becoming erect reaching for the light; the tips are very slender ending in a point. The color of the young, fresh, tiny leaves is white-grey at the tips and blue-grey below. Several small subshrubs enjoy rocks and frequently use them for support. The dwarf forms of Heath and Heather are naturals. Two which were mentioned above have characteristics which conjure rocks, *Cassiope* with its imbricated foliage and *Cyathodes* with its thin and wiry stems.

Let us look at some of the smaller perennials to plant with rocks. Dwarf species may be found in several genera in which most species are standard size, e.g. *Globularia, Scabiosa, Statice*. In your search, you will discover at least one "little one" in genera in which you have previously known only the larger most common species: e.g. *Alchemilla, Astilbe, Campanula, Erysimum, Dianthus, Gentianella, Gypsophila, Haberlea, Helichrysum, Hypericum, Potentilla, Saxifraga, Scabiosa, Thalictrum, Thymus*. As you see by the alphabetical order, I went fishing for these genera not bothering to hook every one I came to. There are many more. Violets, fairly small to begin with, have some choice species smaller than others: *Viola alpina* var. *charophylloides*, from Korea, can be found.

Campanula

Some species of *Androsace* are four inches high but there are also some only two inches high, e.g. *Androsace pyrenaica*. A species of *Arabis* is named *A. androsacea* and is only one inch high. *Asperula bryoides* var. *olympica* is a one inch silver cushion. *Bellium bellidioides* is bigger but not very big as daisies go, perhaps the littlest unless *Bellium minutum* is smaller. *Dryas octopetala*, called Alpine Avena and *Cortusa matthioli* var. *pekinensis* are examples of dwarf plants for the collector. If you get started with dwarfs, you will no doubt become addicted.

You might become addicted to rock gardening also. A proper rock garden is a special accomplishment. One has to resist any attempt to mimic Matterhorn or to construct a miniature Andes; the best rock garden writers are firm in their writings that we do not attempt to "emulate mountain scenery". But if you do not get the urge to construct a true mini-rock garden, I encourage you to build a simple garden with rocks. In this chapter we have been concerned with plants to grow in a woodland and I tried to entice you into the fringes of the rock-gardening field by recommending that you select rocks as carefully as you select normal and dwarf species to make a pleasing composition in a shady garden.

Scabiosa

You can make a mini-rock garden in the sun, of course, as well as in the shade. Perhaps you are not yet such an afficianado that you are ready to build a scree but you are able and eager to try to approximate the environment of a rock garden perhaps only because you have become enamoured of some of the typical rock garden plants. Go to a meeting of the Rock Garden Society, where plants are displayed and there is hardly any chance that you will not be hooked. Some of the temperamental ones you acquire may be enticed into staying alive. On the whole, the requirements seem easier to achieve in a garden with shade. It is easier to maintain the sponginess of the soil, the humidity in the air and the excellence of the drainage in a situation under trees.

In any case read the rock garden books and the alpine books, always written by someone truly enthusiastic. One of my favorite books on rock gardening, *Rock Gardens* by A. Edwards, will give you a number of suggestions both negative and positive. One of the most useful is to acclimatize a difficult species in several steps. By acclimatizing the author means adjusting the plant to the specific conditions of all kinds in your garden—soil, wind, light, not just climate. For example, when a plant arrives, having been most carefully wrapped and packed, it usually looks very healthy and vigorous indeed. You are bound to be tempted to immediately pop it into the place waiting for it, already prepared with pebbles and humus a foot or more deep. But resist the temptation. Introduce it to its new world, little by little, first in a container and in a place sheltered from the weather. Then perhaps in six to eight weeks move it gradually into a more exposed position. If it is known to be really temperamental, plant it out now into a trial bed with a growing medium made partly of your soil and partly with those

Dryas

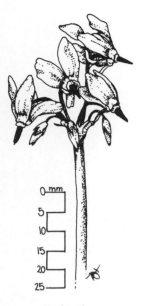

Dodecatheon

Maianthemum

ingredients in which it had been grown for the start of its life before it came to you. Some genera are quite temperamental at first and then settle down. For instance, *Dodecatheon* may sulk, may even remain out of sight for 2 or 3 years; suddenly, you have the start of a stand.

Plants are like people in this regard; both can accustom themselves to an imperfect or different environment and can change inherited or habitual preferences if not rushed. Will your imported plants flourish in maturity and old age especially under trees which have priority on the water and the nutrition? Will enough be left to nourish the small perennials? Often one must be satisfied with much less than optimum performance. But a good start makes a tremendous difference. I try to buy two plants of a species new to me and of uncertain adaptability; one I take some chances with, the other I coddle at least for the first year. As for the years to come, the more demanding are given more attention. I used to put ice on the ground around cold climate perennials like Lily-of-the-Valley once a week; now I am content with a few flowers instead of many. Is *Maianthemum* a satisfactory substitute? As for hot climate perennials, I am satisfied with a reduced copy of a plant which is a gorgeous bush in Hawaii.

The smallest plants require the most careful watching. A newly planted small individual may dry out without being noticed. Then it is gone.

Tiny plants are interesting to those who are curious. You may become fascinated with the details of a plant which seem to be especially well delineated in a dwarf. There are two reasons for this: first one has to look more closely to see any bud or flower at all—sometimes one must use a hand lens; second, characteristics like tracery on a petal or projection of the cluster of stamens are often actually bigger in proportion to the whole flower. On a leaf, the veins may seem more pronounced or the minute teeth on the edges deeper and more pointed. "Dwarf" is a term used to define size in comparison to the plant's relatives; it means that the dimensions of the plant are smaller than those of other members or the genus. Even when you see the varietal name "nanum" you do not necessarily have a tiny plant. Often, however, one or more species or cultivars of a genus will be truly "nanum", or "minimum" or "minutum" and these will be desirable for your special places in a woodland or in a shady garden. There are coves in the shade garden where you can grow a single plant of one of these true dwarfs to act as a show piece or if the selection seems to grace the spot you can add next year a companion or two.

The perennials described in this chapter are only samplings; you will find a number of other suggestions in the list of plants for a rock garden and in one or two of the lists for the layouts. You do not need a stand of redwoods, or a group of maples or a grove of olives; you can have a mini-woodland with two or three trees and some ground to plant between them. You may think that I harp upon shade overmuch. Yes, sun is useful for growth, but too much sun is drying and scorching; even a perennial which prefers sun, although it may have fewer flowers, will be safer and in better health most of the time in filtered sun. In any case, let us welcome a shady place rather than deplore it. Apologies to you gardeners who do not have a ray of sun because of buildings or fog or too many trees.

Hardiness: When hardy, I have said nothing about hardiness. I have used semi-hardy to indicate that a plant is less than perfectly hardy. This plant needs protection against frosts to survive. I have used tender to indicate that the plant will not tolerate *any* frost. I have used semi-tender to mean that a plant may survive a short period of frost but not prolonged frost or often repeated frost. This plant may lose its above ground portions but its roots may survive if mulch is used to protect the root area.

Explanation of the order: When there are varying heights in a genus, the spp. are often described in groups, Tall, Medium and Low. When the spp. are divided according to use, sometimes a group will appear under one heading and sometimes another group under a different heading. When there are two or more entries under different headings of various spp. a general plant description will occur under only one of the headings but reference to the list which includes the plant is included.

The spp. are not listed alphabetically. One sp. follows another because it is related or similar in appearance. One sp. may follow another because it has a similar habit. Occasionally the better known spp. are described first and spp. hard to find are given at the end of the spp. descriptions of the genus. Very often a dwarf sp. will come at the end both because it is smaller and because it is more uncommon. Occasionally the spp. will be arranged one below the other because I like the second better. You will have to judge from the text whether I like it equally well. I put them this way so that you might better see relationships horticulturally. When you wish to find a certain sp. in the descriptions, you may find its position in the text by means of the alphabetical index. Please do not read the descriptions of the spp. as if the whole were a jumble.

Hybrids: When a cv. name follows directly after the genus name, no name has been given to the hybrid and the parentage of the cross may not have been recorded.

PERENNIALS FOR THE WOODLAND

Acaena	Dampiera	Paris
Aconitum	Daphne	Pasithea
Actaea	Dicentra	Patrinia
Adiantum	Digitalis	Pellaea
Adonis	Disporum	Phlox
Amsonia	Dodecatheon	Phyllodoce
Andromeda	Draba	Pieris
Androsace	Edraianthus	Podophyllum
Anemone	Elmera	Polemonium
Anemonella	Epigaea	Polygonatum
Anemonopsis	Epimedium	Potentilla
Angelica	Erica	Primula
Aquilegia	Erythronium	Pterocephalus
Aralia	Eucomis	Pulmonaria
Arthropodium	Eupatorium	Pulsatilla
Arum	Francoa	Ramonda
Aruncus	Fritillaria	Raoulia
Asarum	Galax	Reineckea
Asperula	Galium	Rhodohypoxis
Aspidistra	Gaultheria	Rodgersia
Astilbe	Gentiana	Rupicapnos
Astrantia	Gillenia	Sanguinaria
Athyrium	Globularia	Sanguisorba
Bergenia	Helleborus	Saxifraga
Blechnum	Hepatica	Schizostylis
Boykinia	Hypericum	Selaginella
Brunnera	Iris	Shortia
Calluna	Lapeirousia	Stylophorum
Calochortus	Laurentia	Synthyris
Cassiope	Lilium	Tanakaea
Ceratostigma	Liriope	Tellima
Ceterach	Lithodora	Thalictrum
Cimicifuga	Maianthemum	Tiarella
Claytonia	Mertensia	Tigridia
Clintonia	Metrosideros	Tradescantia
Coptis	Mitchella	Trillium
Cornus	Mitella	Trollius
Corydalis	Omphalodes	Uvularia
Cotula	Ophiopogon	Vaccinium
Cyathodes	Osmunda	Vancouveria
Cyclamen	Oxalis	Whipplea
Cynoglossum	Pachysandra	

Sun

Acaena	Gladiolus		
Acantholimum	Gypsophila		
Achillea	Hebe		
Acorus	Helianthemum		
Aethionema	Helichrysum		
Alchemilla	Hypericum		
Allium	Iberis		
Alopecurus	Iris		
Alyssum	Jasione		
Anacyclus	Lavandula		
Anaphalis	Leucanthemum		
Anchusa	Leutkea		
Androcymbium	Lewisia		
Androsace	Linaria		
Antennaria	Lithodora		
Antirrhinum	Lithospermum		
Aphylanthes	Morisia		
Aquilegia	Narcissus		
Arabis	Neomaxica		
Arcteria	Nierembergia		
Arenaria	Onosma		
Armeria	Oenothera		
Artemisia	Origanum		
Asarina	Ourisia		
Astilbe	Papaver		
Aubrieta	Paradisea		
Aurinia	Paronychia		
Bellium	Penstemon		
Bloomeria	Phlox		
Boykinia	Physoplexus		
Brodiaea	Phyteuma		
Calceolaria	Potentilla		
Calochortus	Pterocephalus		
Campanula	Rosmarinus		
Carex	Salix		
Cheiranthus	Saponaria		
Chrysogonum	Satureja		
Chrysopsis	Scabiosa		
Clematis	Scilla		
Codonopsis	Scutellaria		
Cyananthus	Sedum		
Daphne	Semiaquilegia		
Dianthus	Sempervivum		
Diascia	Silene		
Douglasia	Sisyrinchium		
Draba	Soldanella		
Dryas	Statice		
Edraianthus	Stylophorum		
Eranthus	Tanacetum		
Erinus	Thymus		
Erodium	Tropaeoleum		
Erysimum	Tulipa		
Geissorhiza	Verbascum		
Geranium	Veronica		
Geum	Woodsia		

Shade

Aceranthus	Polygonatum
Adiantum	Polypodium
Andromeda	Primula
Anemone	Pulsatilla
Anemonella	Ramonda
Asperula	Ranunculus
Astilbe	Raoulia
Campanula	Rhodohypoxis
Cardamine	Sanguinaria
Cassiope	Saxifraga
Ceratostigma	Schizocodon
Claytonia	Scleranthus
Coptis	Selaginella
Cornus	Semiaquilegia
Cortusa	Shortia
Corydalis	Soldanella
Cyclamen	Stylophorum
Cymbalaria	Tanakaea
Dampieri	Tellima
Dicentra	Thalictrum
Diphylleia	Tiarella
Dodecatheon	Tolmeia
Epigaea	Trachelium
Epimedium	Tricyrtis
Ficus	Trillium
Fritillaria	Trollius
Galax	Uvularia
Gaultheria	Vaccinium
Gentiana	Vancouveria
Globularia	Viola
Haberlea	Wahlenbergia
Hepatica	
Heuchera	
Hosta	
Houstonia	
Hutchinsia	
Jeffersonia	
Leiophyllum	
Lewisia	
Linnaea	
Lobelia	
Maianthemum	
Meconopsis	
Mitchella	
Mitella	
Myosotis	
Omphalodes	
Ophiopogon	
Parochetus	
Phlox	
Phyllodoce	
Platycodon	
Pleione	
Polemonium	
Polygala	

Acaena: ROSACEAE.

Mtns. of S. hemis., N. Zealand.

Evgrn. R.g. & g.c. Low & spreading. Leaves small, indented, lying close on ground-hugging stems.

Sun or ½ shade. Warmth. Good drainage. Division.

Best in foreground; associate with rocks. A pattern created by leaf form & placement on branching stems; attractive against a surface of woodsy earth. Grow low spp. 2–3 in. tall & 2 ft. w. in a situation where a flat tracery is needed as a feature. Combine with it a genus having members of a like personality, as *Mitella* or *Laurentia*, & add as contrast perennials with somewhat more erect habit but with small stature.

A. inermis, A. microphylla: Small, bronze-green.

A. fissitipula, A. buchananii: N. Zealand. Grey-green & silky.

A. pinnatifida: Hairy beneath, erect scapes to 1 ft.

Aconitum: RANUNCULACEAE. Monkshood, Helmet Flower, Wolf's Bane.

Eur., Brit., Asia.

Herb. Roots, seeds & probably leaves poisonous. Erect stems over 2 ft. tall even in areas where growth is less than maximum at maturity. Sev. stems in a clump create a mass of glossy dark green. 1–2 ft. w. Leaves many, shiny, with an incised pattern. Hood shape outstanding feature of the flower. Fall bloom.

½ to full shade as well as sun. Soil moist. Division.

Growth often starts as early as Feb. Bloom in fall. In spite of height use toward the foreground in order to have full view of foliage. Another glossy sp. should be planted in proximity to repeat the glitter, as *Asarum.*

A. napellus: Many forms including a hyb. *A.* × *bicolor.* To 6 ft. Stems at 3 ft. may need support. Lustrous foliage. Hooded flowers on branching spikes, blue to purple, autumn.

A. carmichaelii (*A. fischeri* of gardens): To 6 ft. Where does it grow that tall? Dark green, glossy, deeply-cut leaves. Flowers light wedgewood-blue to violet-blue. Very handsome as an accompaniment to glossy-leaved shrubs.

A. septemtrionale 'Ivorine': White; type sp. yellow or flesh-pink.

A. sparksii: The one called Monk's Cap instead of Monkshood.

A. anthora, A. columbianum, A. ferox, A. lamackii, etc. listed in the seed exchange of American Rock Garden Society.

Actaea: RANUNCULACEAE. Cohosh, Necklace Weed, Baneberry.

Eur., Asia & N. Am.

Deciduous. Clump forming. 2–3 ft. × 1–2 ft. w. Open branching structure. Compound leaves, light texture.

Shade. Soil loose, moist. Cuttings.

Best in moist woodland. Poisonous berries, either scarlet, white or black. Birds avoid. Plant with *Patrinia* or *Boykinia* to make a solid group of compatible subjects of sim. height. Summer bloom.

A. spicata: Herb Christopher. Bush 2–2 ft. Leaves ferny green. Flowers small, fluffy in sprays. Berries black & shining.

A. pachypoda. var. *alba* Doll's Eyes, White Baneberry of E. N. Am. woods. Leaves dissected. Flowers white on stems sometimes to 3 ft. Berries like white beads.

A. rubra var. *arguta:* W. N. Am. Red spherical berries.

A. triplinervis: Dense clumps. To 1½ ft. Leaves grey-felted; 3-veined. *A. t.* 'Summer Snow': dwarfer; flowers whiter.

Adiantum: POLYPODIACEAE. Maidenhair Fern.

Worldwide.

Rhizomous crowns with extremely delicate fronds. This as well as tougher more sturdy ferns are decorative in varied arrangement—in a long solid line or in a deep & wide group or in twos or threes or even singly. Maidenhair blends well with *Vancouveria, Epimedium, Astilbe* & naturally other ferns. Leaf pattern produces a round look. Clumps 1½ × 1 ft.

Only 2 are hardy.

A. pedatum: Five-finger Fern, toughest.

A. venustum: With bronzy pink new fronds.

Sev. are semi-tender.

A. raddianum 'Variegatum': One of the cvs. for a container, another *A. r.* 'Gracillimum'.

A. hispidulum: Rosy Maidenhair. Small. Easy. Semi-hdy. Low to high light.

Adonis: RANUNCULACEAE. Pheasant's Eye.

Eur. & Far East.

Herb. Low spreader. 1½ × 1½ ft. Leaves in narrow segments, pinnate, toothed, ferny. In propitious climates, leaves soon after emerging make a full carpet & bright yellow flowers are harbingers of spring.

Part shade. Soil moist. Division.

Flowers solitary, terminal. Blooms early spring.

A. amurensis: China, Japan. Woodlands of E. U.S. Earliest to bloom.

A. vernalis: Spring Adonis. Early buttercup-like flowers. Dormant in summer.

Amsonia: APOCYNACEAE. Blue Star.

Wet woodlands & riverbanks of N. Am.

Herb. Clump forming. A somewhat solid look as a result of its numerous branches. Leaves elliptic to ovate, soft on erect stems. In temperate climates, plant in warmest site.

Sun or ½ shade. Soil moist & fert. Division. Cuttings.

Calyx lobes & stamens in fives. Unprepossessing without suitable culture.

A. tabernaemontana: 2 ft. × 18 in. Suffruticose in warm climates. Flowers soft, starry, of a blue described as "pale blue" or "periwinkle blue", in flattish or pyramidal clusters.

Aconitum

Actaea

Adiantum

Anemone

Bloom spring & summer. Excel. in New Orleans. *A. t.* var. *salicifolia*: Erect, leaves willow-like.

Androsace: PRIMULACEAE. Rock Jasmine. Temp. N. Am., Asia, Eur.

Evgrn. Many thin stems make a carpet about 1 ft. wide. Stems lie together in neat formation creating a mat a few inches in height. At least one sp. very small. Rosettes. Leaves numerous, often superimposed.

Partial shade where summers are hot. Soil open; sandy with stone chips. Perfect drainage; both air & moisture must pass freely through med. Cuttings. Seed.

Bloom spring through fall. Low g.c. or for scree r.g. The more alpine, the more difficult.

A. lanuginosa: Himalayas. Trailing, not rooting, many silvery hairy ovate leaves. Flowers ¼ in., lilac-pink with yellow center in umbels from the leaf axils. May be the easiest.

A. l. var. *leichlinii*: A form with white flowers & yellow eyes which change to red.

A. primuloides, A. primuloides var. *chumbyi* & *A. sarmentosa*: Stoloniferous, forming low mats. For r.g., in dry walls & as g.c. From mtns., accommodating. Flowers pink on 2 to 4 in. flowering stalks.

A. chamaejasme: Stoloniferous. Rosettes. Flowers in umbels 2–8 flowered having scapes to 5 in. Flowers white to ½ in. across. Throat yellow, then red. Bloom June. Type sp. of a group from mtns. of N. hemis. Difficult alpine. For specialist.

A. villosa: From high mtns. of Eur. & Asia. Rosettes. Leaves thickly clothed with silvery hairs. Very small flowers, white or rose with reddish yellow eye. Bloom May. Difficult alpine.

A. pyrenaica: Densely tufted. Leaves close, linear, to ⅛ in. Ciliate, green at first becoming brownish red. Flowers white with yellowish eye. Summer bloom.

A. vandelli: Tiny. 1 in. high, 2 in. spread. Gravel & leaf-mold. Snails. For trough or alpine house.

Anemone: RANUNCULACEAE. Windflower. India, N. Am., China, Eur.

Herb. & tubers. 150 spp. Delicate. Leaves lobed & indented.

Excel. seed heads. Petal-like sepals known as tepals.

Sun & part shade. Soil, well-drained, gritty, organic matter, loose texture. Water in growing season. Dead head. Roots multiply. Divide just before foliage dies down. All dislike wind.

Woodsy spp. go well with *Astilbe, Epimedium, Vancouveria,* & Ferns. Bloom summer & fall.

Anemones fall into 3 groups as garden plants.

The hyb. *Anemone*, sometimes called Poppy Anemone. This is the cut flower of early spring found at the florist's in cheerful bunches & therefore best named Florist's Anemones.

A. coronaria, A. hortensis & *A. pavonina*: Closely allied spp., forbears of strains. Sun. These *Anemones* grow from a curious irregular, knobby, tuberous root, planted 2 in. deep, in the fall. Leaves, parsley-like, as

early as Jan. In warm climates, roots left in the ground. Flowers pink, purple, scarlet, "blue", with dark centers. Some cvs. e.g.: 'His Excellency', single crimson; 'Mr. Fokker', single blue; 'The Admiral', deep pink, semi-dble; 'The Bride', single white; 'Sylphide', single mauve. Leaves to 8 in., flowers to 12 in.

Strains sold for the garden are "de Caen", "St. Bavo", "St. Bridget", "Au Creagh Castle".

The Japanese *Anemone*: Sev. spp. from 2–5 ft. tall, as are hybs. & cvs., some grouped under H. × *hybrida*. Since they are invasive, the Japanese *Anemones* have been listed in "The Site for a Large Perennial".

The wood *Anemones*: Differing spp. 5 × 12–18 in. Some have a more dwarf habit than others.

A. pulsatilla: Those with "pasque flower relationship" mostly from lower altitudes than others which are high alpines, have been segregated as a separate genus—*Pulsatilla*.

A. nemerosa: European Wood Anemone. 6–12 in. high; somewhat cupped, drooping blooms with 5, 6, 7, up to 12 petal-like sepals typically white suffused with pink or purple, sometimes blue or purple. Cvs. & varieties e.g.: *A. n.* var. *allenii*, the sturdiest, *A. n.* var. *robinsoniana, A. n.* 'Blue Beauty', *A. n.* 'Blue Bonnet', *A. n.* 'Vestal', *A. n.* 'Leeds Variety'.

A. palens: To 8 in. Leaves basal after flowers, palmately 3 cleft; involucral leaves, divided into many linear lobes. Middle segment sessile. Flowers solitary to 3 in. across. Sepals blue-violet, hairy on exterior. Fruit styles 2 in. long.

A. blanda: This sp. & *A. apennina* are dwarf. Encourage the growth of a number of plants in a selected area in order to repeat the dainty & delightful form of the flower.

A. sylvestris: The Snowdrop.

Anemonella: RANUNCULACEAE. Rue-Anemone.

Woodlands E. U.S.

Tuberous roots. Differs little (botanically) from *Anemone*. Leaves indented, delicate. Bloom spring.

Shade. Leaf compost. Tolerant as to soil. Some moisture.

Easy from seed & transplants readily. On stems 6–9 in.

A. thalictroides: Leaves sim. to those of *Thalictrum*. Sepals 5–10, white to pale purplish pink, to 1 in. across. Dble. as well as single.

Anemonopsis: RANUNCULACEAE. (Anemopsis)

Mtn. woods of Japan.

Herb. Underground rhizome. One sp. Leaves lobed.

Part shade. Deep, fert., light, porous soil with organic matter, with some moisture. Division or seed.

Might be found in the catalogue of a specialist.

A. macrophylla: False Anemone. Looks like a small version of *Anemone japonica*; to 3 ft. × 18 in. w. Leaves divided, often 3 times, coarsely toothed, hairless; multiple, compound. Flowers nodding, half open. Bloom July. Sepals, 7–10, lilac or light

Anemonopsis

purple, outer ones purple on outside.

Angelica: UMBELLIFERA.

N. hemis. & N. Zealand.

Herb. Foliage withstands rain & cold. Leaves with deep indentation. A decorative sp. of the genus, the sp. described below, has great style; look of glossy leather evident in shade. Excel. cut as foliage for arrangements. Sheen can be seen from a distance.

Ample water. Grow seed each year. In moist shade, improved growth.

Most spp. need a wide space, 2–3 ft.

A. pachycarpa: Leaves handsome—shiny, leathery, pinnate, deeply cut. Growth low & restrained; basal leaves to 2 ft. across with sev. at the crown.

Aquilegia: See genus description under General Plant Description.

Herb. Some spp. will do well in open shade. Bloom spring & summer.

A. glandulosa, A. jucunda & A. siberica: From Siberia, 1–2 ft. The first bright blue with short incurved spurs; the second white, smaller & with broader petals; the third close to *A. flabellata.*

A. flabellata: Twice divided basal leaves form tufts with attractive patterns. Flowers lilac-blue (or white), upper flowers open first. Spurs curved & coiled inward. Needs sun part of the day.

A. ecalcarata: From China. Foliage clump dense. Wine to rich purple & with spurs nearly lacking. A genus name, *Semiaquilegia,* where the sp. "ecalcarata" was formerly classified has been discontinued.

A. saximontana: From Colo., U.S., an alpine gem.

A. spp.: Of Alpines, probably all difficult except for specialists.

Arthropodium: LILIACEAE. New Zealand Rock Lily.

N. Zealand.

Evgrn. Clump, more or less fountain-like. Mature plant with 12 or more narrow, oval leaves to 18 in. A blue-green look, with firm texture & arching form. Leaves only a little shorter than flower stalks. Strong accent plant.

Sun or part shade. Soil sandy with organic content. Good drainage. Keep a bit drier in winter; it withstands U.S. W. Coast winter rainy season. Fertilize spring & fall. Snails & slugs. Semi-tender; areas with mild winters only; hardy in Seattle, Wash., U.S. Division. Slow growing but long-lived.

Fine in containers. Will cut. Resistant to salt spray & sea wind.

A. cirrhatum: Clump to 3 × 2 ft. Leaves blue-green, long-oval. Flowers creamy white with yellow stamens. Panicles above leaves, late spring. Combat snails.

A. candidum: Dwarf to 14 × 8 in. with beige-brown linear, delicate leaves. Needs an open space in order to view unusual foliage.

Arum: ARACEAE. Arum Lily.

Eur.

Herb. Notable for hastate leaves. Hooded spathes. Spreads.

Shade & ½ shade. Soil moist. Control. Division.

Foliage desirable for arrangers, long-lasting if submerged in very cold water. Width of each spear-shaped leaf to 6 in. Flowers pick, also. Orange fruits decorative. Strong below ground life while dormant. Above ground growth in fall or winter. Covers 1 ft. or more.

A. italicum: S. Eur., Canary Islands. Includes cv. 'Marmoratum' (of gardens), marbled along the veins with grey & 'Pictum' (of gardens) marbled with grey & cream throughout. Leaves narrow, spear-shaped. Appear in autumn. Roots travel during summer. Berries: orange-red, summer into winter, after leaves have disappeared. Not much liked by birds & animals. Popular easy sp.

A. maculatum: Cuckoopint, Lords and Ladies or Adam and Eve. Similar to *A. italicum* but blooms earlier.

A. palaestinum: Black Calla. Grown for bizarre flower, almost black.

A. proboscideum: Mouse Lily. Appenines. Green all winter. Shade; soil moist, leafy. "Nose" applies when the plant is just out of the ground. Oddity.

Aruncus: ROSACEAE. Goatsbeard.

From rich, moist woods of N. hemis., including Japan.

Herb. Massive clump. Leaves broad, fern-like. Tall slender curving stems. Full mound 6 × 4 ft. at maturity, and in propitious climate. Improves annually. Although herb., produces shrub-like structure by midsummer.

Shady & cool. Cut to the ground each year. Division of root.

Front of shrubbery or fringes of woodland. Flowers in "plumes".

A. dioicus (A. sylvester or *Spiraea aruncus):* Shrubby, leafy plant to 4 ft. across & as tall. Leaves ferny on graceful stems; flowers creamy, arching plumes. Male plumes have many stamens, showier, look more like "beards". Female develop seed heads which are used dried. Somewhat like *Astilbe.*

A. kneiffii (A. dioicus 'Kneiffii'): To 18 in. Leaves dark & ferny. Very narrow irregularly shaped leaflets.

A. astilboides: About ¼ the size of *A. dioicus.* Leaves finely divided—threadlike; flowers white early summer.

A. plumosus var. *glasnevin:* Dwarfer & neater with erect plumes (England).

A. aethusifolius: Very dwarf indeed. Seek from specialist. Grow in a container.

Asarum: ARISTOLOCHIACEAE. Wild Ginger or Birthwort.

N. Am., Quebec to Ark.; Eur.

Evgrn. The Wild Gingers are hardy at least to N.Y. City but may loose leaves in late winter. For moist situations; make clean-looking carpets to 6 × 18 in. Leaves heart-or kidney-shaped. Thick texture. Some green, some mottled.

Rich, moist soil with ample humus. Fertilize in spring. Topdress in colder climates. Groom. Division.

Overlapping leaves produce a thick deep mat.

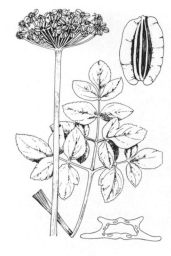

Angelica

Aquilegia

Arum

Asarum

Asperula

Astilbe

Foliage cuts well esp. for edge of vase. Dense in the garden; leaves overlapping in neat formation hide curious purplish flowers. Bloom July.

A. canadense: Snakeroot. Canada. Indians used for stomach disorders. Leaves heart-shaped, grey-green.

A. caudatum: W. U.S. forests. Deciduous in harsh climates. Leaves glossy, kidney-shaped on trailing stems. Flowers interesting but hidden under leaves.

A. hartwegii: Marbled with silver.

A. shuttleworthii: From rich woods of Va. to Ala., U.S. Leaves either green or mottled.

A. europeum: Called "Wild Ginger" because both rhizome & leaves aromatic. Leaves heart-shaped to 3 in., very glossy.

Asperula: RUBIACEAE. Woodruff.
Eur., Asia, Aust.
Semi-evgrn. Small leaves in fairly thick mats; some cut, some linear.
Shade or ½ shade. Soil loose. Division.
R.g. or g.c. or trough. Small, low plants 6 × 6 in. soon hidden by aggressive subjects. There are dwarf garden hybs., very desirable.

A. odorata = Galium odorata

A. nitida: Compact cushion. Erect stems. Leaves in whorls, 4, linear, ending in white points. Flowers few, pink, in clusters. Delicate look.

A. bryoides var. *olympica:* Esp. for trough. Gritty soil.

Astilbe: SAXIFRAGACEAE. False Goatsbeard.
E. N. Am., China, Korea, Japan.
Herb. Fernlike foliage. Numerous, much cut leaves on upright stalks form dense, feathery clumps. Most decorative plant for woodland, wide drifts in shady borders or edging beds or for streamside. Long life of the foliage each season & very long-lived plant.
Shade & sun but only where sun is not hot. Soil, moisture-retentive but not a bog nor clay. Accepts acidity. Fertilizer beneficial. Division.
Delicate looking. Flowers long-lasting in the garden, but only 2 days when cut. Buds do not open in water but keep if picked just after buds have opened. Flowers are small in tapering panicles; on stems 1 to 4 ft. tall, have a fluffy look. Clumps gradually increase in size, even to 3 ft. in width. Leaves may be cut back in fall or left until spring. Leaves fern-like on brittle stems, many (firm, no staking needed). *Astilbe* looks well with Ferns, *Aruncus, Tiarella, Cimicifuga,* etc.

A. × *arendsii* hybrids (*A. chinensis* var. *davidii, A. astilboides, A. japonica, A. thunbergii;* all contributed): Tall garden hybs. to 4 × 2–3 ft. w., late spring & early to late summer. Leaves bright green, dark green, dark coppery green. Leaves start growth in Feb. All early leaves, bronze or copper. Brownish tints in older but still young leaves in most of the colors. Cvs. e.g.:"Fanal', deep crimson; 'Bridal Veil', white; 'Peach', or 'Peach Blossom'; others 'Crispa', 'Deutschland'.

A. dwarf garden hyb: *A.* × *arendsii* recrossed with *A. simplicifolia:* Leaves & flowers (with 8 in. plumes) sim. to those of tall kinds.

A. chinensis (A. sinensis): Sometimes 3 ft. tall. Flowers white, pink or purple flushed. Summer.

A. c. var. *pumila:* Half as tall; colonizes. Flowers in dense clusters, mauve-pink. One cv., 'Gnome'. Flowers showy, pyramidal.

A. 'Snowdrift': Shown at Chelsea Flower Show & admired.

A. biternata (like Goats Beard) & *A.* × 'Gloria Suberba': Seeds available.

A. taquetii 'Superba': Aug. More tolerant of sun. Flowers rosy purple on mahogony stems. Full, with slender tips.

Astrantia: UMBELLIFERAE.
Eur., Caucasus.
Herb. Distinctive. Short-lived. Leafy basal tufts produce only a few flower stalks. Stems with sev. flowering side branches. Flowers have a frilled look.
Sun or part shade. Soil loose with leafmould or compost; moist not wet. Division. Seed.
Ruff of petal-like buff-colored bracts. These bracts have green veins and have a fluffy fanciful look. Plant in open glade to show form. 2 × 1 ft. Not often cultivated in the U.S. Bloom May & June.

A. major: Robust, best known. Clump forming to 3 ft. Leaves (basal) divided, lanceolate, 2–3 ft. Flowers tiny in an umbel, greenish white sometimes pinkish or purplish. Colored bracts important. *A. m.* 'Shaggy': Bracts whiter & larger.

A. maxima: Leaves trifoliate, middle lobe free or nearly, or 5–7 parted. Leafy collar of bracts fringed with hair-like teeth beneath the light central umbel of tiny flowers.

A. bierbersteinii: Caucasus. To 1 ft. Leaves with smaller, blunter lobes.

Athyrium: ASPIDIACEAE.
Am., Eur., Asia, far north & also tropics.
Herb. Fern. Many spp. Fronds of various shapes & colors.
Shade. Soil moist, loose. Division.
Amazing display of curving graceful fronds.

A. nipponicum var. *pictum (A. goeringianum* var. *pictum)* (or 'Pictum'): Japan & Taiwan. Large, 2 × 3 ft. wide. Very graceful. Many arching fronds, 1–2 ft. long, doubly pinnate & toothed. Sev. shades, the youngest, the most lavender. Spore cases in herringbone pattern.

Bergenia: SAXIFRAGACEAE. (*Saxifraga, Megasea*—outmoded names)
Asia.
Herb., or evgrn. in mild climates. Some more hdy. than others, & some prefer more moisture than others. A number of spp. & many hybs.; spp. cross easily; any plant seen in a garden or on sale quite likely to be a hyb. or a form. Bold foliage effects. A masculine & sophisticated look. Thick rhizomes. Lengthen to make a drift 3–6 ft. wide. Leaves large, undivided, thick, glossy. Round, oval; smooth edged or curly edged. On firm stems which carry them at angles producing a wavy effect.
Light shade. Soil deep, fert., never completely dry. Use top dressing of good soil in spring.

Paris polyphylla is almost all green. When standing free in an opening in a woodland, one cannot fail to recognize it. What a fantastic architectural and mechanical contrivance! E.B.

Eryngium amethystinum, an old timer in big perennial borders and admired for its steel blue color is now often used to take the place of a shrub. *E. proteiflorum,* a species all silver instead of steel, needs a large space also. It is chosen mainly for its flaring rosette; plant it near a path for a close view. *E. yuccifolia* has an equally outstanding rosette. E.B.

A wide bed borders a path. Large forms break the flow of herbaceous perennials with strong evergreen punctuation. Clumps of sword-shaped leaves are good for this function. *Diplarrhena* is a genus which is stronger and neater than many others. You can see the stalks of its spent flowers which though lovely are second in importance to the form created by its vertical lines. E.B.

This dainty S. Afr. *Gladiolus, G. tristus* var. *concolor,* seeds itself widely in the garden. Here is a stray which shows the form of the spike better than would a picture of a cluster of flowering stems. The choice spp. of this genus have an undisputed role in the garden. E.B.

SOME OUT-OF-THE ORDINARY SPECIES

Kangaroo Paw has an amazing shape when seen close-up. (Drawing in the chapter on Form of Flower.) Here the photograph was taken far enough away to see the branching habit. The branches stand apart from each other as if to display the artistic form. E.B.

Alstroemeria is a genus with most attractive flowers, of varied shapes. This species, *A. pelegrina*, looks the most like an orchid. It is the most difficult, perhaps best in a container. E.B.

Hesperaloe parviflora: Outstanding richness of texture is apparent in the buds as well as in the open flowers. The flowers open successively on a 3 ft. curving stem over many weeks, midsummer onwards. Basal narrow leaves are bronzy-green and handsome. E.B.

The genus *Oenothera* is composed by reputation of a number of spp. which only open their blooms in the evening. Here is an exception, one which keeps the several flowers in their cluster open through the day. A soft but bright yellow for many weeks. E.B.

SOME ODDITIES

Combat snails. Groom. Division. Divide before g.c. looks poorly.

Blooms in winter—often an additional season. Flowers in clusters on erect stems. Both leaves & flowers excel. for flower arranging. Large scale g.c. or rocky slopes. Can spread to form a wide expanse of glossy, fairly low foliage or the clump may be confined by cutting away the travelling rhizomes.

B. crassifolia & *B. cordifolia*: Similar, vigorous to 1½ ft., the first with leaves mahogany tinted in winter, more oval than those of the second & rounded to wedge-shape at their bases; the second, quite round with heart-shaped bases, edges crinkled & usually constantly green. Flowers mostly magenta but those of *B. cordifolia* may also be mauve, pink or white.

B. c. var. *purpurea*: Reddish, thick leaves. Flowers deep purplish red. Other differences may be noticed by comparison, i.e. shape of flowers & position of flower clusters on their stout stalks. When drawing the finger & thumb up a leaf-blade, a sound occurs—suggested to E.A. Bowles the name "Pig-squeak".

B. purpurescens: Leaves elliptic to 10 in. long, upper surfaces convex, more or less shaded purplish red. Flowers sometimes dark purplish red, sometimes pink; larger & later in opening than *B. crassifolia*. Sev. other names which are applied to plants of this sp. are only garden names.

B. stracheyi: Less tall, to 9 in., more compact than most; leaves on short stems grow in thick masses. Flowers clear pink or greenish white, partially hidden. (One of best for picking) Not hdy. north of S. New England, U.S.

B. × *schmidtii*: *B. crassifolia* × *B. ciliata* var. *ligulata*: Flowers in graceful sprays of clear pink with rosy red calyces. Bloom early.

Hybrid *Bergenias*: Many. Must be obtained from special sources. Outstanding cvs., e.g.:

'Abendglut' ('Evening Glow'): Flowers rosy red.

'Ballawley': Leaves less leathery than many other cvs.; liver-colored in winter. Flowers bright crimson on red stems.

'Sunningdale': Leaves red-brown in winter; deep reddish pink heads.

'Silberlicht' ('Silverlight'): Leaves deep burnished tones with mahogony-red reverses; flowers white with dark centers; petals pinkish tinge in age.

Blechnum: BLECHNACEAE. Deer Fern.
Worldwide but chiefly S. hemis.
Evgrn. Fern. About 200 spp. of varied shapes & sizes. Many other spp. valuable besides sp. described here. G.c., some traffic. Tolerant.
Looks best when grown in fert., moist soil.

B. penna-marina: Australasia. Few-branching rhizomes. Makes a carpet. Stalks to 1 ft. Blades, linear, pinnately lobed, about ½ in. wide. Dense. 6 ft. w. Invasive. Division.

B. spicant: Larger in every way. Handsome.

Boykinia: SAXIFRAGACEAE.
E. Asia, N. Am., mostly W. U.S., Japan.
Herb. Rhizomes. Airy personality. Thin but numerous branches on bushy plant to 2 ft.

tall in more or less open formation to 18 in. wide. Leaves mostly kidney-shaped, lobed & toothed. Flowers very small in branching clusters. Easy to establish as background plant in small woods. Dormant but a short time. Bloom summer.

½ shade or ½ sun. Soil moist. Semi-hdy. Cut back. Division.

Resembles *Heuchera*. Plant with Ferns, *Corydalis*, *Patrinia* & *Dicentra*. Layout 3. Good in moist r.g.

B. jamesii; Colorado Rockies. Habitat humus-filled crevices. Leaves kidney-shaped. Flowers cherry-red.

B. major: Native of moist places in U.S. forests. Flowers small, densely crowded.

B. elata: Moist shady places, Wash. to Calif., U.S. 9–24 in. tall; erect stems very slender. Leaves with bristly pointed teeth.

B. aconitifolia: E. U.S. Leaves kidney-shaped, 5–7 lobed.

B. tellinioides: Japan. Leaves with shallow lobes peltate. Uncommon.

Brunnera: (Anchusa) BORAGINACEAE.
W. Caucasus.
Herb. Leaves heart-shaped to 8 in. across on short pedicels, rough, numerous, close to the ground. Younger leaves smaller replicas of those full grown. Progressive but not overly rampant appearance. May spread out-of-bounds but not difficult to dig. Keep to 4 ft. w.

Half or full shade. Good drainage. Soil moist. Cut off spent leaves. Tolerates neglect but handsome only if healthy. Division.

Good in the foreground or in open bays in a woodland. Plant with *Omphalodes* for comparison. Lasts cut if conditioned. Leaves said to look like those of *Mertensia* but texture unique.

B. macrophylla: (Macrophylla = large-lvd.) Leaves rough, even prickly to touch, heart-shaped, dull green. Stems bearing leaves elongate to make minimum spread of foliage 18 × 18 in. Some cvs. have spots of silvery grey; other rare cvs. are variegated with creamy white. In Feb. new foliage will begin to thrust from the ground. Flowers tiny, in clusters resembling Forget-Me-Nots but looser. To 18 in. Vivid blue. Late spring.

Calochortus: LILIACEAE. Fairy Lantern, Globe Lily, Golden Lantern, Mariposa Tulip, Cat's Ear.
N. Am., Calif., Mexico, Middle East.
For descriptions of the best methods of growing *Calochortus* see *Dwarf Bulbs* by Bryan Mathew. Lovely pictures.
Best alternative—climb a high mountain in W. N. Am. at the right week of the year & look between cracks in the granite rocks, or walk through untravelled woods or meadows at lower altitudes & peer into the duff under trees. You may find exquisite lantern, globe or cup-shaped flowers on 6–12 ft. stems.
Endangered spp.: *Calochortus clavatus* subsp. *recurvifolius*, *C. coeruleus* var. *westonii*, *C. dunnii*, *C. greenei*, *C. longebarbatus*, *C. obispoensis*, *C. persistens*, *C. striatus*, *C. tiburonensis*.
Threatened spp.: *Calochortus catalinae*, *C. excavatus*, *C. palmeri*, *C. pulchellus*.

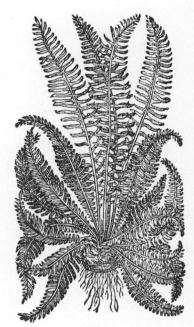

Blechnum

Calochortus

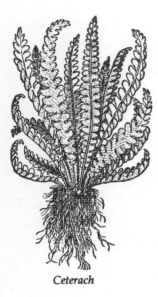

Ceterach

Claytonia

Clintonia

Cassiope: ERICACEAE. White Heather. NE. Asia, Japan, Ala. See drawing p. 50.

Evgrn. Creeping & carpeting or prostrate subshrubs. Leaves opposite, scale-like, overlapping or linear, spreading in 4 ranks. A tight precise look but not at all stiff.

Part shade. Soil moist, loose, acid. Drainage. Cuttings.

Use with dwarf *Pieris, Calluna, Pimelea.*

C. lycopoidioides: Prostrate, wide-spreading stems. Flowers small. Bloom in April & May.

Ceratostigma: PLUMBAGINACEAE. Leadwort. India & China.

Herb. & shrubby. Leaves small, spoon-shaped, darker on the backsides, hairy or bristly. Flowers usually excel. blue.

Sun or partial shade. The g.c. will flourish in more shade than the shrubs. All need fert. well-drained soil, never very dry. Semi-hdy. or semi-tender. Division or cuttings.

The g.c. may be easily contained. For borders & edgings. Since space is empty while plant is dormant, interweave with evgrn. companions. Or row planting to create a ribbon look can be planned for mos. of growth. Fullness of foliage & flowers increases well into fall.

C. plumbaginoides (Plumbago larpentae): China. Spreader by underground, slender rhizomes. To 1 ft. tall. Width may be controlled. Many much-branched, hairy stems. Leaves less than 2 in. long, close to stems, bronze & reddish in fall. Flowers bristly heads on leafy shoots. New flowers appear daily in Sept., Oct. Really blue, though not as blue as the color of the shrubby kinds. Shear to the ground for winter. *C. abyssinicus:* Leaves more rugose. Flowers as pale blue as *Plumbago.* Good in a pot.

C. willmottiana & *C. griffithii:* The first hdy. in Washington D.C., U.S., the second more tender. The blue of the second is deeper, sometimes called cobalt-blue. Twiggy bushlets to 3 × 2 ft. wide with a bronzy look & a rough texture; can be treated as herb. per. or pruned only for shaping. Leaves turn.

Ceterach: ASPLENIACEAE. Spleenwort. Arabia.

Evgrn. Looks something like *Blechnum penna-marina.* Tight growth not more than 6 in. above ground level. The fronds are at angles, crowding each other.

Sun or part shade. Soil open—gritty, peaty, with lime or gypsum. Water. Division.

Excel. in a vertical site. See Layout 5.

C. officinarum: Cracks of old walls with lime, mortar. Fissures of rocks. To 6 in. Stalks to 3 in.; blades cut almost to midrib. Lobes broad, blunt.

Cimicifuga: RANUNCULACEAE. Bugbane. N. Am., Siberia, Russia, Far East, Japan.

Herb. One sp. with aromatic leaves: used to drive away bugs. Leaves may be broad or ferny. One sp. has tall flaring branches with curved, swaying stems. Another is more erect. All 4–6 × 2 ft. w. Bloom summer & fall.

Shade & ½ sun. Cool, moist, acid. No support needed. Division.

Affinity with *Actaea.* This genus is both graceful & elegant. Position so that whole plant can be seen; with small shrubs & ferns. See Layout 9. Flower spikes are sometimes called "bottle-brush-like".

C. dahurica: Far East. Rare. More widely branched than others.

C. foetida: Very rare. Center spike arches like a shepherd's crook. Fragrance like waterlily. Mtns. to 5 ft. Leaflets lobed, almost round.

C. americana: Summer Cohosh. N. Am., Blue Ridge Mtns.

C. cordifolia: N. Am. Leaves dark, broad. Flowers creamy green from brown buds.

C. racemosa: Snakeroot. E. No. Am. Broad clump; leaves divided. Flowers on branching stems to 5 ft.; wand-like spikes, fluffy white plumes, summer, early. Somewhat moist woods.

C. ramosa: Quite different—blooms Oct.; to 7 ft.; side shoots of plumes open after the main branch. Whiter white.

C. simplex: Bugbane & Kamchatka. Russia to Japan. Leaves small & much divided. Wands to 4 ft. Cvs. excel., e.g. 'White Pearl'—superior.

Claytonia: PORTULACACEAE. Spring-beauty. Mostly W. N. Am. & S. Am., Aust. & N. Zealand.

Herb. Tuber. Small, succulent. Stems 12 in.; flowers small as many as 15 in a raceme. Will establish only in suitable climates. Some roots long; hard to transplant.

Shade & semi-shade. Soil moist, deep. Division.

The sparse short linear basal leaves usually short-lived.

C. virginica: Nova Scotia to La. & Tex., N. Am. To 1 ft., damp woods. Basal leaves, when present to 5 in. long, grass-like, fleshy. Stem leaves opposite usually one pair only. An ethereal look. Flowers in racemes to 6 in., white tinged with pink.

C. megarhiza: High mtns. of W. N. Am., Wash. to N. Mex. Basal leaves blunt to 6 in., spatulate. Flowers in dense racemes white or light pink. For the alpine house.

Clintonia (Dowingia): LILIACEAE. Queen Cup, Bluebead or Brides Bouquet. E. & W. N. Am.

Herb. In nature, often found in rock crevices in cool, moist woods; from a creeping rhizome. Sometimes grows as an annual. Small bell-like flowers in clusters at top of stems, 1–2 ft.

Shade. Soil decomposed organic material. Moisture. Imitate habitat. Division of root. Or seed. Increase slow.

For rich, damp r.g. or bogs. Named for de Witt Clinton. Has a quiet look but distinguished.

C. borealis: Leaves thin, glossy, green, said to look like leaves of Lily-of-the-Valley. Spreads to 1 ft. or more. New growth early spring; bloom May & June. To 18 in. high. Flowers in clusters, fragrant, nodding, green-yellow with protruding stamens. Berry, oval, deep blue.

C. andrewsiana: Calif., U.S. Flowers small, carmine, bell-like. The 3 outer segments broad, rich carmine-rose; the inner segments narrow & paler with a creamy central vein. Berry violet-blue.

C. uniflora: From W. N. Am. woods. Less imposing but pleasing.

C. umbellata: Speckled Clintonia. Flowers white, more spreading, to 6 flowers in umbels, fragrant.

Coptis: RANUNCULACEAE. Goldthread. N. Atlantic.
Evgrn. Slow spreading carpeter. Less than 8 in. both in height & width.
Shade. Soil loose, moist. Add peat & sand. Division.
Site near a tree stump or rock in cool position. Greek koptein = to cut—divided foliage.

C. groenlandica (*C. trifolia* var. *groenlandica*): Greenland & E. N. Am. To 6 in. Leaves shining with 3 leaflets. Flowers, spreading buttercups, white, ½ in. across.

Cornus: CORNACEAE. Dogwood, Cornel, Cornelian Cherry.
N. hemis.
Evgrn. & herb. One herb. per. sp. a dwarf. Dogwood = dagwood or dagger wood, because daggers for skewering meat were made from some of the woods of the arboreal spp. Many fine trees & shrubs; the most useful shrubs to combine with pers. are the small colored stemmed spp. as *C. alba* & *C. seticea.* Creek Dogwood is especially appropriate as background in moist woods. Only the carpeter will be described.
Shade. Soil moist & fert., full of duff. Division.
The herb. per. dwarf sp. can form a thick drift more than 3 ft. wide.

C. canadensis: Bunchberry. Moist, acid woodlands & bogs from Greenland to N. Am.; Ala., N.J., mtns. of W. Va., Minn., Calif.; & E. Asia. A dwarf in true sense (not just smaller in comparison). Mats of tiny rhizomes with erect stems no taller than 8 in. Leaves miniature—From the upper whorl a solitary flower—a minute cluster with 4½ in. bracts, white, spreading. Bloom in spring. Berries red.
Evgrn. or herb. Shade. Cool position. Soil as much like a decayed log as possible. Deep. Roots very tough; can push around obstacles underground to come up where they wish. A modicum of moisture should always be present.
This sp. flourishes in Canada but not necessarily at high altitudes; choose a place in r.g. or woods to imitate the natural habitat & cherish any response. Fascinating to discover the replica of the arboreal forms. Grow with restrained & choice genera & spp., e.g. *Epigaea, Gentiana, Trillium.*

Cortusa: Primulaceae Cent. Eur. to n. Asia Related to primrose. About 8 spp. hairy herbs. Similar culture.

C. matthioli var. *pekinensis:* For damp woods Geranium-like leaves 8 inch scapes. Flowers intense crimson.

Corydalis: (PAPAVERACEAE) FUMARIACEAE. N. hemis. (1 in E. Afr.)

Herb. 300 spp. Ferny foliaged. Short rhizomes, fibrous roots, tubers. 1–2 ft. w. Basal & stem leaves pinnately divided. Feathery look. Flowers in dense short spikes. Flowers with only one spur. Bloom April & May & Feb. Dainty plants with lacy appearance.
Shade. Soil sandy. Moisture. Drainage. Pull young volunteers of invasive kinds. Foliage of some kinds dies down at beginning of summer. Seed.
To at least one writer, *Corydalis* seems "trivial", but specialists seek the rarer kinds for alpine greenhouses. Greek korydallis = the lark; the flowering spur suggests the spur of a bird. Mostly for r.g. & walls. A few— tender. The following hardy except those from China.

C. lutea & *C. ochroleuca:* Europe & Britain. Sim. except yellow of the first golden & of the second pale to almost white. To 1 ft. Leaves numerous, triangular with 2 to 3 div.; 3 to 4 in. long. Flowers short-spurred in racemes. Heads tiny, snapdragon-shaped. Sprout with frequency in the lap of a *Polemonium* or leaning against a *Dicentra* but extras are easily pulled. Filmy, lacy, ferny; blends with woodland plants.

C. scouleri: NW. N. Am. Vigorous questing rootstock. Use by itself or with other strong spreaders.

C. saxicola (*C. thalictrifolia*) & *C. cheilanthifolia:* China. Less hdy. than most. Rootstock woody, spreading. For moist woodland. To 1½ ft. Leaves pinnate. Flowers with short, blunt spurs in *C. saxicola* & straight ascending spurs in *C. cheilanthifolia.*

C. wilsonii: A dwarf for a sheltered spot in a rich scree mixture. Leaves blue-green. This sp. & others from Asia not yet commonly in cultivation. Seed slow to germinate esp. if not fresh.

C. cashmeriana: Himalayas. More tender than the above. Short-lived. Leaves bright green, 3 times divided. Flowers blue in raceme-like clusters. Typical genus color yellow.

Cyathodes: EPICRIDACEAE.
S. hemis. equivalents of the HEATH family of the N. hemis.
Evgrn. Two prostrate spp. combine well with members of HEATH family & with woodland perennials like *Cassiope.* Bracts overlap on the stalks. Flowers small, bell-shaped.
Sun or partial shade. Loose soil with acidity. Shear to shape. Slow growing. Cuttings.
Find in specialty nurseries. Fruit a berry-like drupe.

C. colensoi: Is the stronger, to 6 ft. wide.

C. empetriformis: To 2 ft. wide. Flowers tiny in very small racemes. Fruits reddish to ⅛ in. long.

Cyclamen: PRIMULACEAE. Sowbread.
S. Eur., N. Afr., Greek Islands, Iran, Israel.
Corm. See monographs on *Cyclamen,* for instance, *Growing Cyclamen* by Gay Nightingale.
The florist's *Cyclamen* used widely for containers, originally derived from *C. persicum,* developed by selection over many years. Use in containers for a colorful fall

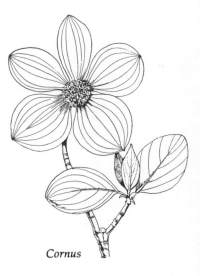

Cornus

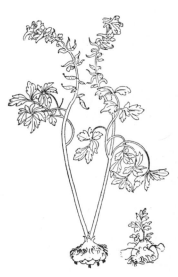

Corydalis

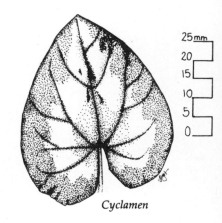

25 mm
20
15
10
5
0

Cyclamen

Cynoglossum

Dicentra

display, from pink to red & white.

Sev. spp. make excel. woodland plants for any of 3 seasons, each with unique characteristics. They vary in size, color of flower, design of leaf. Hdy & non-hdy. Flowering stalks spiral at fruiting time. *Cyclamen* also grows well in low pots or shallow boxes. Unique shape & texture of foliage; marbling in pleasing rather than confused pattern. Needs an exclusive site wherein features can be displayed. Many spp. natural for a woodland.

Part shade or shade. Light through high branches beneficial. Soil containing leafmold, shredded bark, etc. Since the stems, as well as the crown, dislike a great deal of moisture, use large pebbles or small rocks over the soil surface adjacent to corms. Drainage essential. Add coarse sand, grit & crushed limestone for best medium. When planting, cover corms with ½ in. of mix. Topdress with fertilizer incorporated in mix annually at beginning of growing season of each sp. Don't cultivate in vicinity of corms. Mice & chipmunks eat immature corms. Protect any choice drift with hardware cloth. Aphids, mites & thrips may attack but mostly the florists' kind. Cool, humid conditions; mist in hot weather. Let dry out somewhat while dormant (see notes under description of spp.). Cormlets. Spread 2–3 ft.

Plant smaller kinds in r.g. or shaded plant houses.

C. hederaefolium (C. neapolitanum): S. Eur. & naturalized in W. Am. Probably best known & easiest. Flattish corms rooting from top. Leaves, more or less the shape of *Hedera helix,* English Ivy, richly patterned with silver. Flowers rose-pink, deeper-colored or white in throat on 3 in. stems. The white form lovely in a rock wall. Fall bloom.

C. purpurascens (C. europaeum): Patate Della Madonna. Eur., Carpathians & Yugoslavia. Easy. Large flattened corms root from all parts. Leaves kidney to heart-shaped, basal lobes touching, faintly marbled.

C. p. var. *viridifolium:* Plain green leaves.

C. p. var. *album:* White form. Fall bloom. Flowers fragrant. Dry out only a little.

C. cilicicum: Sicily. Leaves roundish heart-shaped, short basal lobes overlap. Upper sides marked with silvery zone. Flowers pale pink with darker blotches at the bottom, pointed petals. Fall bloom.

C. coum (C. hyemale, C. ibericum) & *C. atkinsii,* a superior variant. Balkan Peninsula, Turkey, Syria. Spherical to flattish corms rooting from below their middles & underneath. Leaves kidney-to heart-shaped, lobeless, toothless, quite leathery in comparison, appear before or with blooms; marked or plain green. Flowers pink, magenta-pink, or white, with purple blotch at the bottom marked with 2 white or pink spots. Tips of petals rounded; constricted throats. Flower & leaf stems creep underground before emerging. Bloom winter or earliest spring. Does not need a rest period in summer. Less prolific than some others. Treasure it.

C. coum var. *atkinsii album:* Blooms a little later. Charming.

C. orbiculatum: Flowering nearer winter than spring.

C. cyprium: Neat clumping, white, March. Only for specialists.

C. repandum: S. Eur. Naturalizes in slight shade in a mild area. Flattish, hairy corms rooting only from their bottoms. Leaves heart-shaped, dark green but reddish on the backside, gap between basal lobes, margins, shallow-lobed. Flowers March, pink, deepening at throat; or white. Fragrant.

For those who seek white, here are some of the *Cyclamen* with white forms: *C. creticum, C. balearicum, C. hederaefolium, C. purpurascens, C. cilicicum, C. repandum* & the florist's hybs.

Cynoglossum: BORAGINACEAE. Hound's Tongue, Chinese-Forget-Me-Not, Wild-Comfrey.

Eur., Asia, N. Am.

Herb. Mostly ann. & bien. Upright stems. Leaves rough. Flowers scorpioid in branching sprays. Grow with *Omphalodes* and *Myosotis* for affiliation. All 3 truly blue. Look well in solid row or drift.

Part shade. Deep fert. soil of average moisture. Seed. Some spp. self-seed.

Greek: kyon = a dog, glossa = a tongue; refers to rough leaves of some spp.

C. nervosum: Himalayas. Per., to 3 × 2 ft.; stems branching & hairy. Leaves to 10 in. long below & becoming smaller above, oblong, somewhat hairy. Stems may flop if plant overfed. Flowers in clusters, Forget-Me-Not-like & blue. Early summer.

C. amabile: Chinese Forget-Me-Not. A bien. to grow as an ann. Stems usually branchless. Plant in a dense row esp. against a wall.

C. grande: N. Am., Calif. to Wash. To 3 ft. Leaves mostly basal, to 8 in. long. Slightly hairy above, densely hairy underneath. Flowers in panicles widely-branched; hairy calyces; corollas, bright blue, ½ in. by ½ in.; crests in their throats. Spring. Hard to tame.

Dampiera: GOODENIACEAE.

W. Aust.

Evgrn. 35 spp. of herbs & shrubs. One sp. a shrub introduced to England by Captain Dampier R. N. One sp., a low herb, introduced to U.S. by U. of C., Santa Cruz, Calif. Rare in cultivation. Auricled corolla lobes, tubes split. Flowers purple to blue.

½ shade. Semi-tender. Seed?

D. brownii: Tall shrub, mostly hairy. Leaves oval, wavy toothed. Flowers purple from axils. Clothed with dark hairs. July.

D. diversifolia: Evgrn., low, best for r.g. or select site for contained g.c. to 1 ft.w. Flowers dark bright blue. Bloom summer.

Dicentra: FUMARIACEAE. Bleeding Heart, Dutchman's Breeches, Squirrel-Corn, Golden Eardrops, Steer's Head.

N. Am., E. Asia.

Herb. Mostly from open or lightly shaded fringes of woodlands. Foliage dainty, much dissected, making a ferny hummock. Flowers in sprays, drooping, quite like lockets.

Part shade or part sun. Soil loose. Some moisture. Division. Seed.

Greek: dis = twice, kentron = spur. The outer segments of the flower have spurs.

D. spectabilis: Korea, China, E. Siberia. Bushy to 2 ft. × 18 in. Leaves to 1 ft., divided, cleft & toothed. Flowers many, hanging on curved stems. Rose-pink to rosy red, rarely white, heart-shaped, the outer petals like a pouch, the 2 white inner petals protruding from the base. Spring blooming.

D. eximia, D. formosa & *D. formosa* var. *oregana:* N. Am. All 3 closely related. Finely divided, ferny leaves. Flowers of *D. eximia* narrow esp. just before outer petals bend outward. Cvs. e.g. *D. e.* 'Snow Drift'. *D. formosa* broader at this point & the inner petals less visible. Flowers red to pink.

D. formosa: Western Bleeding Heart, & its relatives may be used in beds & r.g. as well as in woodland. 1½ ft. × 2 ft. In partial shade, in somewhat moist, rich soil. All kinds good for picking. The white forms of normally pink varieties are weaker & more difficult to keep growing.

D. formosa var. *oregana:* Found only in a small area near the border of Calif. & Oreg. in N. Am. Differs in size—it is smaller; differs in leaves—they are definitely glaucus; & in flowers—they are creamy yellow, inner petals pink-tipped.

D. nevadensis: Often considered a variety of *D. formosa.* Leaves narrower, more sharply toothed; flowers smaller.

D. cucullaria: Duchman's Breeches. NE. & NW. N. Am. Blooms in early spring & dies back completely by summer. Clusters of very small, grain-like, white tubers are easy to lose if the soil is disturbed. To 1 ft. tall. Leaves triangular, divided, making a most attractive pattern. Flowers white-tinged-pink & tipped yellow, hang 4–10 from the stem & do look like "pant's legs". Not easy, except in suitable climates.

D. canadensis: Leaves handsomely cut & flowers with very short spurs.

D. spectabilis: Lady's Locket, Lyre Flower, Lady-in-the-Bath & Our Lady-in-a-Boat. Leaves die down; best in woodland plantings where empty spaces seem natural as the seasons change. (Turn the open flower upside down & part the petals to see the tub or boat.)

There are cvs.: 'Adrian Bloom', 'Paramount', both carmine-crimson; 'Alba' & 'Silver Smith', white & dainty; & 'Bountiful', plum-crimson. *Dicentras* are sometimes grown in pans in an alpine house.

Digitalis: SCROPHULARIACEAE. Foxglove. Eur., Asia & N. Afr.

Herb. Sometimes basal leaves evgrn. Mostly crowded rosettes. Tall & med. erect spikes. Various habits: some exceedingly slender, some with flowers turning all in one direction from stems. Prime examples of the vertical line. Bien. usually easy from seed; sow in mid-spring. The hybs. quite true from seed.

Part sun & part shade. Soil, deep, loose, moist not wet. While developing, young plants need ample water & weekly dilute food. Transplant rosette carefully—with a large ball of roots; dividing hybs. every year is beneficial.

Use tall kinds together with shrubbery as well as in borders & cutting gardens. Use lower kinds in mixed per. plantings & lowest in r.g. Bloom spring & summer.

D. purpurea: Common Foxglove. Bien. Sometimes blooms first year & sometimes as well in third year. To 7 ft. tall. Basal leaves in crowded rosettes. Flowers in one-sided racemes, 2 ft. (plus) tall; flowers diminishing in size upward. Flowers various colors & shapes. Summer, long season.

D. grandiflora (syn. *D. ambigua*), *D. lutea* & *D. laevigata:* Per. Stems 1–3 ft. tall. Flowers pale yellow. The first: flowers 2 in. long, narrowly bell-shaped; the second: flowers to 1 in. long, many, calyces hairy; the third: flowers more globose, the yellow marked with purple-brown. Bell partly closed; edge somewhat notched.

D. lutea var. *australis:* Sim. but differs in that the raceme is cylindrical rather than one-sided.

D. ferruginea: Rusty Foxglove. S. cent. Eur. & W. Asia. Bien. or per. 1–6 ft. tall. Very slender stems, upper ⅓ in a crowded spike. Clump 2 ft. w. Flowers less than 1 in. long, yellowish marked with rusty red or reddish brown, with darker veins. Center lobe of lower lip longer than others. Fascinating faces. Bloom July & Aug.

D. × mertonensis, D. purpurea × D. grandiflora: Quite short stems to 2 ft. from compact rosettes. Clump 1 ft. w. Fat flowers in wide spikes; May & June; copper-colored.

Disporum: LILIACEAE. Fairy Bells. N. Am., E. Asia.

Herb. Related to *Polygonatum* & resembling *Uvalaria.* Combine with these two & *Trillium* & Lilies. Underground stems. Rhizomes. Leaves light green on arching stems.

Shade. Soil moist & full of organic matter. Mulch. Water in dry periods. As growth starts, give dilute application of complete fertilizer. Division.

Best in open woods but a patch can be, in time, developed in a shady site beneath a tree with non-rapacious roots.

D. smithii: W. N. Am. Moist woods. Bushy clumps. Wirey branched stems. To 1 ft. or 3 ft., more often 1 ft. Leaves oval to 5 in. Flowers cylindrical, tubular bells, greenish white to 1 in. long, often in clusters. Fruits pale orange to red.

D. hookeri: ("Fairy Bells" applied to this sp.) Flowers white, ½ in. long. Often solitary or in twos or threes. Berries scarlet. The flower shape is likened to that of a top (narrowed at the base). See *D.h.* var. *oreganum.*

D. parvifolium: Probably a natural hyb. between *D. smithii* & *D. hookeri.* Hardly taller than 1 ft. Leaves 1 in. in length; flowers ½ in. long, cylinders.

D. sessile: Japan, China; woods & foothills. Flowers tubular, pendulous, to 1 in.

D. sessile var. *variegatum:* Leaves light green streaked & edged with white. Smaller than the sp. Flowers like the sp. but greenish, the tubes flaring lightly to show the tips of the stamens.

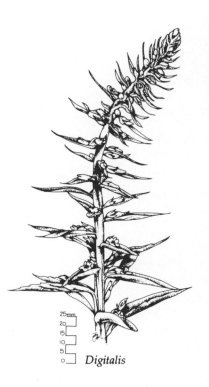

25mm
20
15
10
5
0

Digitalis

Disporum

Dodecatheon

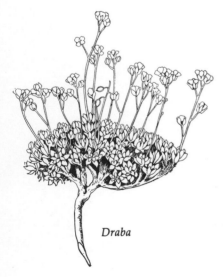

Draba

Dodecatheon: PRIMULACEAE. Shooting Star, American Cowslip, Bird's Bill, Sailor Cap, Mosquito-bills.

S. Alaska to Mex., mostly W. & Arctic N. Am. & E. N. Am.

Herb. A catalogue of a "rare plant" nursery in NW. N. Am. lists 11 different offerings. There is a note "shipped in spring only". Several might be successful in a woodland setting, in humusy soil, somewhat acid, & never completely dry. Those from high altitudes are short-lived in the lowlands. They are ideal, however, for a r.g. The stems may be 1–2 ft. They look well in a group, the flowers like a flight of small colorful birds. Spread to 3 ft. The flower of Shooting Star has an interesting design. The petals are reflexed like those of a *Cyclamen*. Stamens are bright orange. Around the "pointel" is a ring of yellow. In umbels 3–25 flowers.

Part shade. Shortly after early spring flowering, the plants wither. While they are dormant, soil must not be disturbed. The mulch, placed for their benefit during their growth, helps to mark their site. Keep thoroughly moist during the time the foliage is dying. Division.

A thoroughly piquant flower on a slender stem. Bloom spring.

D. meadia: E. N. Am., dry woodlands & prairies. Best known. Some spp. have rice-grain bulblets among the roots; this does not. Leaves to 8 in. long, more or less oblong, tinged with red at base. Stalks 8 in. to 2 ft. Flowers 1 in., few to many in umbels, erect in bud, then hanging, usually lavender. A white flowered one, *D. m.* var. *album* & a red *D. m.* var. *splendidum.*

D. pulchellum: Moist cliffs & riverbanks of both E. & W. N. Am., sim. to *D. meadia* & also without rice-grain bulblets. Lacks the red shading at the base of the leaf, smaller, blooming 2 weeks later.

D. p. var. *watsonii:* From high altitudes; this is the smallest of the genus. *D. p.* var. *album.*

D. alpinum: Wet places, high altitudes, NW. states of U.S. Flowering stalks to 5 in.; flowers with whitish base, yellow zone, dark purple band.

D. jeffreyi: Wet soils, N. Am.; Mont. to Calif. & Alaska. Flowers purplish to pinkish. This is probably the tallest western kind, sometimes to 2 ft. It is appropriate for a streamside.

D. hendersonii: N. Am., Calif. to Brit. Col. One of those which produce rice-grain bulblets. To 16 in. tall. Leaves rather spoon-shaped to 6 in. long. Stems reddish. Magenta to deep lavender, in umbels of 3–17. There is a diminutive form, only 3 in. tall.

D. hendersonii var. *album:* Rare. Clear white. To 6 in.

D. dentatum: White; to 6 in.; crinkled leaves.

D. pauciflorum: Blooms as early as Feb. 'Red Wings', a cv. by Carl English. Thrives under cultivation.

D. clevelandii subsp. *patulum:* (D. patulum) From hot open places. Creamy white, brown "bill".

Draba: CRUCIFERAE.

Mtns. & arctic regions of N. hemis.

Evgrn. Some choice. Mostly for r.g. or trough. Some perishable. Alpines must be protected from an excess of winter wet.

Part shade. Soil, gritty, light, open, not very lean. Excel. drainage. Best site for most spp. is crevices in a rock slope. Division: remove rosettes to replant in Aug.

Investigate other choice spp., as *D. glacialis, D. hispanica* with white flowers. Bloom spring.

D. aizoides: Dense cushions of stiff, bristly rosettes on stems to 4 in. Flowers 4-petalled, yellow, small.

D. lasiocarpa: Makes a cushion. More tolerant of sun, heat, humidity than most.

Edraianthus: CAMPANULACEAE.

Italy to the Caucasus.

Herb. Low, compact. Tufted. Leaves narrow, grassy, elongate, linear. Flowers clustered or solitary.

Sun & part shade. Soil, porous, gritty, lean. Seed. Very wet soil in winter is disastrous.

Greek hedraios = sitting, anthos = a flower (some kinds stalkless). Sev. spp. esp. for r.g. Those with solitary flowers look like *Wahlenbergia*, a close relative. Flower stems "lop" on the ground.

E. dalmaticus: Leaves broad, linear without teeth. Flowers 6 to 8, funnel-shaped.

E. tenuifolius: Leaves to 6 in., hairy & bristly. Flowers in clusters, violet-blue with a white base, narrowly bell-shaped: the petals ribbed.

E. graminifolius: Grassy. Tufted, compact. Flower, a bell. Cluster headed.

E. pumilio: Recommended by Harold Hillier. Low dense cushion. Flowers stalkless, violet.

Elmera: SAXIFRAGACEAE.

U.S., Wash., subalpine & alpine altitudes.

Evgrn. Closely related to *Heuchera* & *Tellima*. Leaves mostly basal, reniform, long petioled.

Shade. Soil loose. Division.

Woods. Excel. in large troughs.

E. racemosa (Heuchera racemosa): Basal leaves. Long stalked, kidney-shaped, double-toothed. To 10 in. Flowers greenish yellow loosely arranged in racemes. Triangular sepals. Five small, white 3 to 7-cleft petals.

Epigaea: ERICACEAE. Trailing-Arbutus or Mayflower.

E. N. Am. & Japan.

Partly evgrn. Leaves small, oval, rough, numerous on woody stems in a dense mat. Native habitat disappearing. Difficult to establish. Spread when thriving to 2 ft.

Open shade. Soil, gravelly, sandy, acid. Rotted logs a good situation. Mulch; light protection with cover in dry weather. Seed. Propagation difficult.

Greek: epi = upon, gaea = the earth; alludes to low, trailing habit. Flower a small trumpet in clusters nearly hidden by foliage.

E. repens: In poor, acid soil, N. Am. from Mass. to Ohio, Ga. & Tenn. Some people think Mayflower refers to the ship which brought the pilgrims to New England—more probably the name came from May, the season of bloom. Famous for fragrance. Housing development could eradicate it.

Does not transplant. Easy from seed; 3 yrs. to flowering. Does not thrive in Calif. probably because plants cannot survive dehydration at any time. Leaves oval, to 3 in., fringed with bristly hairs. Flowers nearly pink, stalkless in clusters amongst the foliage.

E. asiatica: Supposed to be easier to grow but questionable with inauspicious conditions as dry air & inconsistent moisture at roots & natural duff in the ground. Prostrate shrub with ascending branches. Leaves many & leathery; normally evgrn. Calyx lobes somewhat longer than those of *E. repens.* Flowers nearly white to deep pink, with leafy bracts in tight clusters towards ends of branches.

Epimedium: BERBERIDACEAE. Barrenwort or Inside-Out-Flower.

China, Japan, Manchuria, Algeria, Asia Minor, SE. Eur., N. Afr.

Partially evgrn. Related to *Vancouveria* of N. Am. Both are sometimes called "Inside-Out-Flower" because the petals of most spp. face backwards. The flower has been likened to a miniature *Aquilegia,* Columbine but it looks most like the flower of a *Dodecatheon,* Shooting Star. Even without flowers, this genus would be grown for its often evgrn., compound heart-shaped leaves. The leaflets may be as many as 9, often only 5. New leaves have most delicate texture & beautiful fresh tints; autumn leaves may have shadings from russet to gold. Foliage stems bend horizontally. 9–18 in. tall. Bloom spring & summer.

In general, *Epimedium* prefers shade. It does best in a cool situation with friable damp soil. Spreads 2–3 ft. Division.

Those spp. which spread by energetic rhizomes make the most dense cover but clumping spp. planted 1 ft. apart soon close ranks as the tufts multiply. There is no other lovelier g.c. for shade. The foliage varies as to variety & as to season but is very attractive at all times. Stems with spent leaves are mostly hidden by new growth. (Foliage is absent only for a short time after being cut back.) All bloom in early spring. There are a number of spp. & hybs. from which to choose, unless one wishes to have them all. The flowers of some kinds have spurs & some do not. Here follows a sampling.

E. pinnatum var. *colchicum:* "Turns" best in W. Coast N. Am. gardens. Flowers large, yellow, spurless. Used more than once as a parent.

E. × *perralchicum:* *E.p.c.* × *E. perralderanum.* Foliage good; flowers yellow. 1 ft. tall.

E. × *warleyensis:* With *E.p.c.* as one parent, raised in Miss Willmott's garden. Leaves rather small. Flowers somewhat smaller than average, truly orange. Uncommon.

E. × *versicolor* 'Sulphureum' & *E.* × *versicolor* 'Neosulphureum': 2 pale yellow clones whereas other clones have other colors resulting from crossing *E.p.c.* with *E. grandiflorum.*

E. grandiflorum (*E. macranthum*): Bishop's Hat. Japan & Manchuria. Leaves with leaflets having heart-shaped bases, becoming ovate-triangular, spiny-edged, about 2 in. long. The leaf may be 4 times thrice-divided. Flowers in sprays, white to light purple, with long-spurred petals, to 2 in. wide. 'Rose Queen', the best known cv., with light crimson flowers, the spurs tipped with white. *E. g.* var. *album* or 'White Queen', all white.

E. alpinum: A common sp. from N. Cent. Italy to Albania. Several heart-shaped leaflets, pale, veined & flushed copper-red when young. Flowers small, dark red with bright yellow spurs.

E. pubigerum: Evgrn. In clumps. Tiny white flowers above mound. *Tiarella* like.

E. × *cantabrigiensis:* Restrained flowers, winter. Parents in question. Good cross, whatever.

E. acuminatum: Mt. Omei, Holy Mtn. of China. Sepals white, petals wine. Spurs incurved.

E. 'Okuda Form': Flowers white. Highly regarded.

Erica: ERICACEAE. Heath or Bell-heather.

Eur., N. & S. Afr., islands of the Atlantic.

Evgrn. Not a heather which is *Calluna.* In Heath, the corolla is bigger & showier than the calyx. Leaves of *Erica* most commonly in whorls. *Ericas* have needle-like leaves & flowers bell-shaped, usually nodding. Spring & summer.

Sun & part shade. Needs drainage. Soil friable. Add sand. Mulch when planting & keep surrounding area mulched always. Cuttings.

There are many heaths, the lower, smaller kinds excel. to combine with perennials. Spp. could be included in subshrubs. The dwarfs are esp. appropriate for r.g. or for pots & troughs. Name of genus comes from Greek "Erieke" & Latin "Erice" meaning Broom or Heath.

E. carnea (*E. herbacea*): Spring Heather, Snow Heather. Mtn. woods & stony slopes, Europe. Evgrn. Leafy mound to 3 ft. wide with more or less procumbent & spreading branches. Flowers urn-shaped in 1-sided racemes. Horticultural varieties with red, pink or white flowers. A favorite cv. is 'Springwood White', or 'Sherwood'. Other cvs. e.g.: 'Coccinea', 'Gracilis', 'Praecox', 'Alba'. Main season of bloom winter into spring; second lighter blooming when plants are sheared following the first display.

E. erigena 'W. T. Rackcliff': Excel. shape. A dwarf. Grows well in a container.

Erinus: SCROPHULARACEAE.

Mtns. of E. Eur. & N. Afr.

Evgrn.

Part shade. Excel. drainage. Seed. Division.

E. alpinus: Tufted to 6 in. Leaves spatulate, coarsely toothed, lobes notched. Flowers purple to ½ in., in racemes to 2¼ in.

Erythronium: LILIACEAE. Avalanche Lily, Trout Lily, Fawn Lily, Lamb-Tongue, Adder's Tongue, Glacier Lily, Dog's Tooth-Violet.

One sp. in Eur. & Asia, the remainder in N. Am., mostly in the West.

Bulb. Exception to the rule not to describe bulbous plants. Found from sea level to

Epimedium

0 5 10 15 20 25mm

Erica

0 mm
5
10
15
20
25

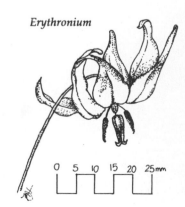

Erythronium

0 5 10 15 20 25mm

7500 ft. often in oak, pine, fir, redwood or maple woods, sometimes near streams, occasionally near snow-line & rarely in open meadows or on open slopes. Some are not too difficult to grow in cultivation & a few not only thrive but multiply. Spread to 2 ft. They are all so very beautiful that it is hard to decide which to try. Perhaps the easiest should be selected first. Some of the common names indicate the shape or mottling of the leaves & sometimes the location of the native habitat. Dog's Tooth-Violet describes the shape of the corm. Bloom, spring.

Light shade. Cool. Good drainage. Read Mathew for special advice. One warning: When corms are dug, transport them in damp peat or moss to keep them from drying out completely. Select & prepare the place for a permanent colony before arrival of a shipment. Discover as much as possible about the native habitat. In general, attempt to naturalize under non-thirsty trees & shrubs & accompany with dwarf plants of a woodland nature. Keep somewhat drier in summer. Control snails.

Details make appreciable difference in the character of one sp. or another. (Mention could be made of appendages at the base of the petals; the anthers & the stigma may be of distinctive shape or color.) Certain familiar characteristics: 2 opposite leaves at ground level; leafless scape; flowers (1–5) with reflexed petals often 2-toned, nodding, lily-like, arranged in attractive fashion.

E. dens-canis: Only sp. from Eur. & Asia. Leaves heavily mottled. Flowers of a Japanese variety of this sp., large, deep violet.

E. californicum: N. Am., Calif. woods to 3000 ft. Leaves dark, mottled. Flowers cream with orange-brown markings; 1 to sev. on stalks to 1 ft.

E. citrinum: N. Am., Siskyou Mtns. Sim. to *E. californicum.* Flowers cream with yellow center.

E. helenae: N. Am., Central Coast Range of Calif. On C.N.P.S. list of "rare plants". Flowers cream, center darker & more defined than those of *E. californicum.*

E. howellii: N. Am., SW. Ore. Almost identical to *E. citrinum.*

E. oregonum: N. Am., woods of Ore., Wash. & Vancouver Island. Leaves mottled; flowers 1 to 5, cream, yellowish center outlined with zig-zag marks of yellowish brown.

E. revolutum: N. Am., near streams & swamps in woods from Canada to Calif. Leaves mottled; flowers deep rose but otherwise sim. to *E. oregonum.* Perhaps the easiest. A cv., 'Johnstonii' is reported to be very fine. Rose-pink with white centers.

E. tuolumnensis: N. Am., in gritty, humusy clay under oak & yellow pine, at 1500 ft., in Tuolumne Co., Calif. Easy also. Flowers well when established. Leaves green—bright yellow-green; flowers yellow with a greenish center. Inner petals eared. Cvs. e.g. 'Pagoda', 'Kondo'.

E. grandiflorum: N. Am. mtns. Leaves plain green; flowers golden yellow, with a streak of green on outside of petals, pale center. 1 to sev. blooms on stalks 6–12 in. Inner petals eared.

E. montanum: Avalanche Lily. N. Am., mtn. peaks, Wash. & Oreg. Leaves plain green; flowers pure white with orange bases to the petals. Untamable.

E. americanum: N. Am., Nova Scotia to Fla. To 8 in. Leaves mottled. Flowers yellow.

E. multiscapoideum: Look for this & its variety. Produces stolons. Leaves heavily mottled. Flowers big with recurved petals. Color white or greenish white with a yellowish center.

Eucomis: LILIACEAE. Pineapple Lily. Natal, Transvaal, S. Afr. See drawing p. 27. Bulb. Curious. Its tuft like that of a Pineapple. Leaves a pointed oval, 3 or 4 forming a flaring tuft from top of the bulb. Flowers in an unusually thick spike, the shape a column, trimmed at its top with a leafy rosette of bracts; like a top-knot. Bloom spring & summer. Unique. Fine addition to a woodland planting.

Sun or part shade. Extra water when the leaves are fully grown. Soil porous; drainage essential. Feed at least annually & at regular intervals when grown in pots. Airy conditions essential. Semi-hardy but successful in N.Y. in a protected place & covered in winter. Plant bulbs with top below the surface 4 in.; in temperate climates, the bulb may be placed so that the top is just at soil surface. Foliage dies in the fall, must be cut back; new growth begins in Feb. Plant sev. bulbs in a group to 2 ft. w. for accent among soft-leaved perennials as *Astilbe, Erysimum.*

Greek: eukomes = beautiful headed; alludes to tuft of bracts. Plants look well, massed in the garden & sev. to a pot but when they become crowded, should be divided after the foliage dies down in late fall. The 2 ft. stems with upper 1 ft. forming a column of densely packed flowers are good for picking.

E. bicolor: 1–2 ft. Leaves 2 ft. long by 3 in. wide, arch as they enlarge, in age sometimes becoming horizontal. Flowering stalk 2 ft., the stem mottled with red at its base & its top portion closely packed with very small lily flowers, to form a cylinder 3 in. across. This sp. with stalks of the individual blooms longer than those of other kinds, has an appearance more uneven & more "frilly".

E. comosa (E. punctata): Common Pineapple Flower. To 3 ft. Leaves 2 ft. long by often 3 in. broad, of firm texture, somewhat spotted with purple on the undersides. The many flowers are tightly packed & outward facing on stout stalks spotted purple at the base. The tuft of bracts at the top is stiffly upright. The maturing seed pods are wine colored; columns still handsome when flowers have lost their petals.

E. undulata (E. autumnalis): To 2 ft. Leaves with very waxy margins, all green, channeled. Flowers green or whitish with petals to ½ in., with flowering stalks very short, forming a dense column. Typical tuft of bracts at the top.

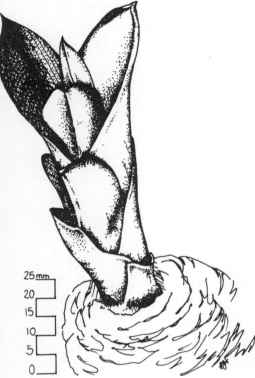

Eucomis

25 mm
20
15
10
5
0

Eupatorium: COMPOSITAE. Mist Flower, Boneset, Snakeroot, Joe Pye Weed. N. Am.

Herb. Closely related to *Ageratum.* Flowering heads made up of all disk-type florets crowded in rounded or panicled clusters. A fluffy look.

½ sun or ½ shade. Soil ordinary but moisture retentive. Cuttings. Seed.

E. coelestina: Mist Flower. From moist meadows, woodlands & stream banks. Tolerant of drier situations. To 3 ft. Leaves mostly opposite & petioled. Flowers bluish. Color is not a true blue. Spring but often 2 seasons, including fall.

E. perfoliatum, Common Boneset, *E. sessilifolium,* Upland Boneset, & *E. rugosum* (*E. urticaefolium, E. ageratoides*), White Snake Root, are hdy. perennials usually with white flowers. The latter to 3 ft., has broad dense clusters quite white. Partial shade. (*E. album,* also white).

E. maculatum, E. dubium, & *E. purpureum:* All called Joe Pye Weed. Coarse, sometimes to 10 ft. *E. purpureum,* the most adaptable to open woodlands with less moisture. Best planted among shrubs.

E. sordidum: One of sev. spp. from Mexico & W. Indies & S. Am., not hdy. in the north. *E. atrorubens* may be grown only in a container but *E. sordidum* is safe outdoors in Calif. Leaves unusual, veined & toothed, the young shoots covered with tawny to reddish, wooly hairs. Flowers in clusters 3½ in. across, violet, fragrant.

Francoa: SAXIFRAGACEAE. Bridal Wreath. Chile.

Evgrn. Tender. Foliage in open clumps, to 2 ft. wide. Leaves wavy, crinkled, leathery, shiny, a texture which gives them style. Flowers in slender, curving, soft spikes. Bloom July.

Part shade. Med. soil. Water & fertilize for best growth. Division. Full foliage rosettes will root easily, sometimes in water.

Flower stems graceful usually sev. to a clump.

F. sonchifolia, & *F. ramosa:* Similar spp. To 2 ft. tall. Part shade. Edging, shrubbery. Flowers fairly close along a slender stem each an open trumpet of delicate texture. White or pale pink.

Fritillaria: LILIACEAE. Fritillary. Near & Middle East, U.S.S.R., Mediterranean region & W. N. Am.

Bulb. Exception to exclusion rule. Stem leaves linear & narrow-oval, often curved, some ending with a sharp point. Sometimes whorled. The stems of most spp. less than 2 ft. with the exception of the tall & strong *F. imperialis.* Bloom spring.

Sun & part shade. Soil acid. Site woodsy. Imitate habitat.

Many spp., sev. rare in cultivation. Those described here from W. N. Am. difficult but some possible to tame. Flower an unusual bell of contrasting colors sometimes speckled; the clapper often evident. The tall spp. where successful grown in a group 3 ft. w.

F. imperialis: The Crown Imperial. To 4 ft. Basal leaves whorled, broad, glossy, green. Flowers, the most common color brick-red. Spring. Excel. drainage. Temperamental. Successful plants of tall spp. are majestic. *F. i.* 'Aurora', *F. i.* var. *lutea, F. i.* var. *maxima.*

F. persica, to 3 ft., *F. pyrenaica* to 1½ ft., *F. verticillata* to 2 ft.: Japan. *F. v.* var. *thunbergii:* With narrow bells.

F. meleagris: Snake's Head Fritillary, Guinea Hen Flower, Checkered Lily. To 1½ ft. The British native; well known.

F. m. 'Alba', *F. m.* 'Artemis', *F. m.* 'Pomona', *F. m.* 'Purpurea'. Cvs. grown in climates where *F. meleagris* thrives.

The following all W. N. Am.: (except the last)

F. nigra, F. atropurpurea, F. lanceolata: All checkered. 1–4 ft. *F. lanceolata* common at sea level & up to 5400 ft. esp. Santa Cruz Mtns. & flanking hills. Shallow cups, 1 in., creamy olive blotched with maroon; dangle.

F. brandegei: Yellow Pine Bell. From 3000 ft., S. Sierra Nevada, N. Am. (The pine is yellow, not the flower.) Stem 1 ft. to 3 ft. Leaves in whorls on upper stem. Flowers, 4 to 12 nodding bells, pink & purple.

F. purdyi, F. roderickii, F. falcata, & *F. glauca:* Siskiyou Lily. From serpentine ridges. Variable. Leaves clustered mostly at base. Stems 6–12 in. Flowers semi-nodding, mauve-white flecked with chocolate.

F. pluriflora: Pink Fritillary or Adobe Lily. Open sun, heavy clay in habitat. To 12 in. Leaves mostly near base of stem. Flower color, mauve-pink.

F. striata: From adobe soil. Leaves alternate, glaucus. Stem 10–15 in. Flowers 2, 3 & occasionally more; white, pink or mauve sometimes striped red. Very sweet scented.

F. pudica: Yellow Fritillary or Johnny Jump Up. Wide field of distribution; variety of situations. 3–12 in. Leaves few, scattered, lanceolate. Flowers: generally 1 but sometimes 2 or 3 nodding bells, deep-yellow turning to brick-red with age. (One form with brown blotch.)

F. recurva: Scarlet Fritillary. Found up to 5000 ft. in clay soil on edge of thickets, sometimes in light grassy gravel, sometimes near running water. Stem 10–24 in. Leaves in whorls or opposite, linear. Flowers 1–4 or more tubular nodding bells, bright scarlet, flecked with orange, often edged with orange. Better after a forest fire. Plenty of water in growing season, none through long summer months.

F. liliaceae: The White Lily or Fragrant Lily. Near Pacific Ocean. Leaves in a close rosette at base of stem. 9 in. tall. 1–3 semi-pendant dainty bells. Creamy white with faint green streaks. When grown in containers, use deepest available; when grown in woods, site where light comes through the branches. Protect. Endangered. Not in the trade. Possible from seed.

F. biflora: Black Fritillary or Mission Bells. S. Calif., U.S. Full sun, open fields at low elevation up to 3250 ft. Leaves near base of stem to 2 in. long & 1 in. wide in clusters; rest of stem bare. Flowers 1–7 semi-nodding bells,

Eupatorium

Francoa

Fritillaria

Galium

Gaultheria

Gentiana

dark purple-brown, veined with red & green. Disagreeable smell. Greenish band on each segment. *F. b.* var. *meziana:* Dark. One of the easiest.

F. dasyphylla: To 6 in. Flower outsides dull wine-purple, insides yellow. Rare.

F. × *pallidiflora:* U.S.S.R. to 9000 ft. Very adaptable to outdoor cultivation in Britain & N. Am.; available from a specialist. 6–20 in. Leaves broad, lanceolate, grey. Flowers 1 to 4 pendant, pale yellow spotted reddish inside. Bell has a squared appearance. Best view from a position flat on the ground.

Galax: DIAPENSIACEAE. Wand Flower.
E. N. Am.

Evgrn. Only 1 sp. Leaves with long stalks, circular to heart-shaped. Exceedingly glossy. Dense clumps & colonies in auspicious climates. Not easily pleased. Only lasts one year in the wet winters & dry summers of mid-Pacific Coast, U.S.

Shade. Soil acid & humusy. To 1 ft. w. where it thrives. Division.

Arrangers admire greatly the waxy leaves. The foliage stays fresh many days when cut. Flowers slender spires to 6 in., early summer. Full spreading mat in auspicious climate.

G. urceolata (G. aphylla): Leaves bronze, turning brilliant red. Flowers delicate wands, small, white.

Galium: RUBIACEAE. Bedstraw or Sweet Woodruff.
Eur., Asia, N. Afr., N. Am.

A g.c. comfortable if not stylish. Less than 3 in. tall. Spreads 6 ft. or more.

Shade or ½ shade. Soil porous. Shear. Division.

G. odoratum (Asperula odorata): Light shade. Leaves indented, lacy pattern; on erect stems about 4 in. Flowers May. Shear. Control.

G. molluga: Sometimes naturalized in U.S.

Gaultheria: ERICACEAE.
Japan; W. China; N. Am., wet woodlands & bogs, Newfoundland to N.C.

Evgrn. Mostly somewhat woody. Leaves usually leathery, rough, generally small, oval, closely placed on spreading stems. Clusters of bells on numerous stems, the bells mostly closed. Bloom spring.

Shade or ½ shade. Soil, moist, acid, loose. Semi-hdy. Many spp. Division.

Prefer a cool climate with moisture in the air. Wide g.c., to 3 ft. leafy, quite tight.

G. shallon: A large shrub. Sprays of closed bells.

G. hispidula: The Creeping Snowberry. Carpets on moist duff. Fruit white.

G. nummularioides: Himalayas. Hdy. to Pa., U.S. Prostrate to 1 ft. tall. Fruit blue-black.

G. ovatifolia: Fruits scarlet. Easier than some others.

G. humifusa: To 4 in. Fruit red. Dense mats hard to establish.

G. procumbens: Checkerberry or Wintergreen. E. N. Am. Fruit scarlet. To 8 in. OK in drier, but not less acid, soil. Flowers barrel-shaped. Spreads widely. Easy.

Gentiana: GENTIANACEAE.
Alpine & cool-climate areas of many continents.

Evgrn. or herb. Mostly difficult. Leaves usually small & tightly packed often deep green & shiny. Look for emerging foliage, rolled together becoming a point. Use with restrained growers so that crowns will remain clear. Summer bloom. Some trumpets open, some closed, bell-shaped or flaring. Most of the blues intense. "Gentian blue", the name of a color.

Part sun, part shade. Moisture. Soil loose, fert. Division.

Use with rocks or in special foreground spaces. 1 ft. w. Some spp. amenable to cultivation. Mostly the spp. of mtn. derivation confirm demanding reputation.

G. acaulis & the *G. acaulis* complex (several sim. spp.): Dwarf alpines. Upturned trumpets. Blue-shaded in throats, on 6 in. stems.

G. a. var. *clusii:* Deep, true blue. One flower at a time. Early.

G. farreri: Type in a group with *G. ornata* & *G. sino-ornata,* Autumn Gentian. Upturned trumpets. Stems like spokes of a wheel from the crown. Dislike heavy rain. Hybs.

G. dahurica: To 1 ft. erect or procumbent. Flowers funnel-form, white-spotted, in leaf axils.

G. septemfida, G. lagodechiana & a hyb.—*G. hascombensis:* W. Asia. Sun or shade. Bell-shaped at tips of rather lax 1 ft. stems. Summer. Easier than many others. *G. septemfida,* floriferous in Victor Reiter's San Francisco garden.

G. asclepiadea & *G. a.* var. *alba:* Willow Gentian. Eur. Damp soils. Clumps of arching stems to 1½ ft. Trumpets in pairs, in axils of upper leaves. Easy. Improves.

G. newberryi: Alpine Gentian. N. Am.; mtns. of Calif., S. Ore., & W. Nev. 2–4 in. Solitary on leafy stems. Outside blue with brown stripes; inside, white. Probably not in the trade.

G. andrewsii: E. N. Am. Type of the group called "Bottle Gentian" & easiest of that group. Soil moist, slightly acid; sun & part shade.

G. lutea: Butterwort, the gentian root of commerce. 1½–6 ft. Most ungentian-like. Flowers in whorls in stiff spires, golden yellow.

G. autumnalis: Pine Barrens Gentian. Rare native of sandhills of East Coast of the U.S.

G. verna: Grow in a box or trough. 3 parts grit, 1 part leafmould, handful dried manure, lacing of bonemeal. Insert leafmould in pencil shaped holes to replace humus in compost lost through shrinkage. Protect from excessive wet.

G. veitchiorea: Go to Tibet to see.

Gillenia: ROSACEAE. Bowman's Root.
Upland woods E. N. Am.

Herb. Wiry reddish stems, sparsely leaved. Shade or ½ shade. Soil with humus. Seed. Division. Appropriate for woods. Becomes tall and wide.

G. trifoliata: Deciduous to 2 ft. Flowers in loose showers, with 5 petals to ½ in. long, white or pink.

Globularia: GLOBULARIACEAE.
Eur.
Evgrn. & herb. Dwarf kinds are prostrate "subshrubs" to 4 in. tall × 1 ft. w. Leaves are numerous to 1 in. & vary in shape; some are definitely spoon-shaped.

Sun & part shade. Good soil improves performance. Division.

Small spp. of distinction. Both form of the plant & form of the leaf out-of-the-ordinary. The leaves often flare abruptly from the crown. The flower is a rounded cushion, fluffy with prominent stamens. Summer & fall.

G. cordifolia: G. c. var. *bellidifolia* (syn. *G. meriodionalis*). Leaves form dense mats. Flowers appearing "fluffy" in "globes" ½ in. across; deep bluish lavender.

G. c. var. *alba* & *G. c.* var. *rosea:* Very nice in a decorative box.

G. meridionalis (G. bellidifolia): Italy. Differs from *G. repens* in being of more open growth with more vigorous leaves & heads, long peduncled. Outer bracts, calyx lobes as long as tube. Note confusion in nomenclature.

G. repens, G. cerastioides, G. trichosantha, G. incanescens: All worth seeking.

G. vulgaris & *G. aphyllanthus:* Herb. To 1 ft. Leaves elliptic to 1¼ in. long, notched & pointed, from basal rosettes.

Haberlea: GESNERIACEAE.
Balkans.
1 or 2 sp., tufted herbs. Related to *Ramonda.* Leaves in a rosette.

Shade. Soil, rich, with leafmould. Well-drained. Division.

Shady nook in a r.g. or in alpine house. Less than 1 ft. w.

H. ferdinandi-coburgi: Leaves notched or toothed in open rosette. Flowers umbellate, 5 lobed, tubular, 3 or 4 on a scape. 2 shades of lilac, throat hairy-white, spotted yellow. Bloom April.

Hacquetia: UMBELLIFERAE.
Cent. Eur.
Only 1 sp., a mtn. plant of the carrot family.
Part shade. Soil rather heavy. Resents root disturbance, care needed to transplant. Seed.

Good in r.g. Bloom April.

H. epipactus: Low, 6–9 in. × 6–9 in. w., clump-forming, tufted. Foliage fresh green, all-basal with trifoliate leaflets, deeply cleft & toothed. Flowers tiny, in umbels, button-shaped, yellow with ruff of yellow-green leafy bracts. Late winter to spring. Plant early fall. Divide with care. Also grows from ripe seeds.

Helleborus: RANUNCULACEAE. Hellebore, Christmas-Rose, Lenten-Rose, Bear's Foot.
Eur. & Asia.
Mostly evgrn. To 3 × 2 ft. Noted for excel. foliage & winter bloom. Shade. Control snails & slugs. Semi-hdy. Division. All spp. are perfect woodland plants. The more leafy spp. create a fine background for almost a complete list of plants used for shady places. The leaf is handlike. Sepals of the flowers form cups or saucers,—a rounded outline. The texture of the flower is thick, often leathery. Attractive in bud. Interesting center lobe seen when flower fully open. Decorative when flower forming seed.

H. niger: Christmas-Rose. Woods & thickets of European Alps. Rhizomous. Leaves few, flaring from the crown, deeply divided into 7–9 narrowly-obovate toothed leaflets; leathery, dark green. Flowers in bud white, 1–2 to a stem, opening to cup-form, then showing golden stamens; flattening to shallow saucers, meanwhile changing to rose & finally green. Bloom mostly Dec., Jan., Feb. Hard & slow to grow.

H. n. var. *macranthus (H. n.* var. *altifolius, H. macranthus):* Italy & Yugoslavia. Leaves narrower. Flowers with narrower sepals, often pink tinted.

Cvs. selected mostly for size & whiteness of flower; e.g. 'Praecox', 'Maximum', 'Major'. Garden variants, some with deep rose-pink outsides. 'White Magic', a hyb. found in New Zealand, more luxuriant and perhaps easier.

H. orientalis: The Lenten Rose. Greece & Asia Minor. Most common. Rhizomes much branched. Broad clumps. Evgrn. but older leaves often damaged by insects; remove in fall & throughout the year, to make room for new. Leaves long-stalked, 5 to 11, with double-toothed, broad leaflets. Leathery. Flowers saucer-shaped, somewhat nodding, 2 in. or more across, often 3 or 4 together on flowering stalk; greenish cream, fading to yellow-green or purplish green. Variations named, *H. o.* var. *albus* & *H. o.* var. *atropurpureus.* In the garden, pink, plum, rose-purple & maroon, some decorated with spots & streaks in the inside. Cross-pollinate readily. Bloom begins Feb., mostly March & April. Control snails & slugs; most important for this sp.

H. foetidus: Bear's Foot, Stinking Hellebore, sometimes Green Hellebore. Without rhizomes. A grouping produces a solid sea of ferny, black-green, to 24 in. tall. Leaves pedate, 7 to 11 narrowly-lanceolate leaflets. Shiny, somewhat leathery; excel. for arrangements, only keeping if submerged overnight. Long-lived in the garden. Foliage clusters top stout stems. Flowers in clusters, small rounded bells, green often edged maroon. Jan.–March. Cut flower stems all the way to the ground when they have passed their prime. Poisonous to eat (& maybe to touch). When crushed, the stem exudes an unpleasant odor (which soon disappears). Watch for seedlings.

H. lividus: Majorca. Tender. 3 leaflets. Flowers pinkish green, flat, fragrant.

H. l. var. *corsicus (H. corsicus):* To 3 ft. Sev. stems to a clump need support (with other plants or encircling hoop). Leaves large, 3 leaflets, saw-edged, form a palm 6 in. across, light green modified by bluish grey. Flowers cup-shaped, yellow-green, massed in a tight cluster on flowering stems. March to May. Attractive after they have gone to seed.

H. hybrids between *H. lividus* & *H. l.* var. *corsicus: H. × sternii* or *H. × baueri:* More hdy. than *H. lividus.* The rosy tone maintained.

0 5 10 15 20 25mm

Globularia

Helleborus

Hepatica

Heuchera

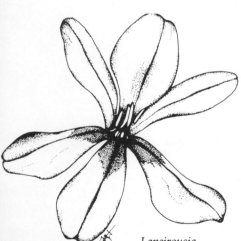

Lapeirousia

H. multifidus var. *viridis*: Leaves divided to base. Each erect leaf topped by big ruff of deeply divided leaflets. Flowers nodding, yellow-green, early spring. Rare.

H. viridis var. *istriacus*: Coarser. To 1 ft. tall. Leaves palmate, divided half way. Flowers bowls, to 2 in., green, with grey sheen in winter. Rare.

H. nigricors: *H. niger* × *H. lividus* var. *corsicus* (England, 1920s). Of good repute.

H. macranthus: *H. angustifolia* × *H. niger* var. *angustifolia*: Italy to Greece. Resembles *H. niger*. More robust. Leaves ashy grey-green. Flowers white, rarely rose-tinged. Winter.

H. purpurescens: One of sev. deciduous spp. Seek 'Pluto' & 'Ballard's Black'.

Hepatica: RANUNCULACEAE. Liverleaf. N. Am., Eur., temp. Asia.

Herb. or semi-evgrn. Basal tufts of evgrn. 3–7 lobed leaves; often with purplish undersides. The form of the lobe is distinctive in some spp. stubby or blunted. A young leaf arising from a young plant is curious & noticeable. Flowers solitary on slender stalks; to 6 in.; no petals but the calyx colorful, blue-lavender, pink or white. Bloom Mar. & April.

Shade or ½ shade. Soil moist, loose. Spreads to 2 ft. under excel. culture. All except *H. americana (H. triloba)* prefer limey soil. May be potted & forced. Division.

The involucre & the stamens prominent. (No petals)

H. acutiloba: N. Am., Quebec to Mo. A low per. for woodland. Blue-lavender, pink or white.

H. americana (H. triloba): Only sp. to tolerate acid soil.

H. media: Hyb. between 2 European spp. Not common in the trade.

Heuchera: SAXIFRAGACEAE. Alum Root, Coral Bells. N. Am.

Evgrn. 70 spp. Related to *Tolmeia* & *Tiarella*. To 3 ft., more often 2 ft. Width 1 ft. Thick clumps of heart-shaped hairy leaves. Shade. Ordinary cult. Division.

Leaves in a dense, decorative, flaring, often glistening rosette. Well behaved before, during & after bloom. Bloom summer; dainty spires.

H. sanguinea: Coral Bells. SW. U.S. To 1½ ft. Leaves nearly round to kidney-shaped, 2 in. across, forming mounds. Flowers bell-shaped, small, in branched panicles, top of slender stems. Scarlet. Cvs. of varying colors, including chartreuse. Great improvements in cvs. in size & texture.

H. micrantha: W. U.S. Crosses with *H. sanguinea*; see above. Leaves grey marbled. Flowers pinkish white on stems to 3 ft.

H. maxima: Channel Islands off Calif., U.S. Leaves, stems & flowers covered with velvety hairs. Basal leaves round-cordate to 7 in. across.

H. cylindrica var. *alpina*: (The var. more dwarf) Leaves heart-to-round-shaped, deeply lobed. Flowers ivory-green, spike-like.

H. × *chiqui*: *H. cylindrica* × *H. sanguinea*: A successful cross.

H. × *brizoides*: Flowers larger on taller stems, pink, coral, crimson. Looser clusters. Cvs.:

e.g. *H. 'Rosamundi'*.

H. tiarelloides: *H.* × *brizoides* × *Tiarella cordifolia*. Bigeneric hyb. of *Heuchera* & *Tiarella*. Slowly spreading evgrn. g.c. Good basal foliage. Flowers on stems to 18 in.; pink to red or salmon; with 8 stamens. May onward. The hybs. need shade & moisture.

H. t. var. *alba*: The white form harder to find. Pleasing.

× *Heucherella tiarelloides* forma 'Baldaccii': *H.* × *brizoides* × *Tiarella cordifolia*: (The same bigeneric hyb. as above.) Excel. results from this cross. Salmon-pink bells. Don't allow to dry out in summer.

× *Heucherella alba* 'Bridget Bloom': A fine cv. from the cross. Good basal foliage. Flowers many, clear pink. May & later.

Iris: For genus description, see General Plant List.

Some spp. for woodlands are: N. Am. Pacific Coast Irises, such as *I. innominata*, *I. douglasiana*, *I. longipetala*, *I. macrosiphon*, *I. munzii*, *I. purdyi*, *I. tenax*, *I. hartwegii*, *I. bracteata*.

Kirengeshoma palmata: See Bogs Plant Descriptions.

A distinctive herb. shrublet for damp woods. Form & color of foliage exquisite. Flowers unique. Choice & slow.

Lapeirousia (Lapeyrousia): IRIDACEAE. Mostly S. Afr.

Herb. To 1 ft. Mostly tender. Safe in Seattle, Wash. Or, greenhouse. Or r.g. in warm climates. Leaves narrow sword-shape shorter than flower stalks; med. green. Flower spike more or less Gladiola-like.

Part shade. Soil cool, moist. Multiplies. Spreads widely.

A small persistent per. looking as if it should grow from a bulb. Bloom spring, summer & fall.

L. laxa: (*Lapeirousia cruenta*, *Anomatheca cruenta*): Hardiest. Stems 9–12 in., wiry. Leaves erect near the base forming a fan. Flowers a flaring tube, to 6 in. A "pointed star", segments to ½ in., pink to "carmine-crimson" with deeper markings in the throat, on the 3 lower petals. Descriptions vary: one says "blackish blotch", another "dots". Bloom begins in May in southern part of the West Coast in the U.S., i.e. Santa Barbara, later farther north, June–Aug. or Aug.–Sept. A drying out period is said to be beneficial; in open woodlands, however, roots thrive & increase with year-round moisture. A scattering of plants may spread widely.

Rare white form. Both the colored & the white varieties bright as they appear sometimes in mid path in open woodland. Allow to roam.

Laurentia (Isotoma): LOBELIACEAE. Americas, Mediterranean, Afr., Aust.

Herb. Will spread to form a flat carpet. Leaves small, roundish, bluish green. Slender stems, quite limp, with many nodes.

Shade & ½ sun. Soil med., some water all year. No trimming. Cover when young, rabbits & mice like foliage. Division.

Prostrate. Spreads widely by flat stems rooting at nodes. Allow to creep in woodland paths.

Delicate. G.c.

L. fluviatilis: Leaves ovate, form a carpet of bluish green. Flowers pale blue. Summer. See Layout 14.

Lilium: LILIACEAE. Lily.
Widespread in N. hemis.

Bulb. A few must be included since some are esp. suitable for a woodland. Many spp. hybs. & cvs. See Container Plant List.

Sun & ½ shade. Soil with sand & organic matter. Excel. drainage. Top dress. Fertilize before & after flowers. No wind. Protect from pests & diseases. *Botrytis elliptica* attacks those with less than perfect environment; stagnant wet air encourages *Botrytis.* Wire baskets to foil mice, etc.

Select from the catalogues & books on lilies for those kinds which will best perform for you, using the following checkpoints: 1) Fragrance, 2) Shape, 3) Color, 4) Use, 5) Time of bloom. Plant in borders, allowing to remain. Or plant in pots. Spring & summer. Some spp. require less light than others; choose for woods adaptable spp.

Especially good in woods: *L. pardalinum, L. parvum, L. humboldtii.*

L. pardalinum: Leopard Lily. Calif., U.S. June, July. To 8 ft. Flowers recurved, bright crimson, lighter in center, brown spotted.

L. parvum: Small Tiger Lily or Sierra Lily. Cent. Calif. & Ore., U.S. Rhizomous. Along streams & in wet meadows. To 5 ft. Leaves whorled, to 5 in. Flowers campanulate, few to many in a raceme.

L. p. forma *crocatum:* Flowers orange to bright scarlet to dark red, spotted purplish brown.

L. humboldtii: Sierra Nevada. To 6 ft. June, July. Flowers nodding, recurved, orange with large maroon dot.

L. formosanum var. *wilsonii:* To 6 ft. Oct.–Nov. Plant 6 in. deep. Long trumpets.

L. martagon & Martagon hybs.: To 5 ft. June. Flowers recurved, pendant. All colors—deep wine-purple, yellow, orange, lilac, tangerine & mahogany. 'Album', pure white. A parent, *L. hansonii,* resistant to virus.

Liriope: LILIACEAE. Lilyturf.
E. Asia.

Evgrn. Tufted. Spreading. 1 ft. × 1½ ft. Leaves short, narrow blades, mostly dark green, shiny. Flowers small in congested spikes. Summer & fall bloom.

Mostly shade. Moist & good soil. Control spread. Groom. Semi-hdy; they need sheltered sites in cooler climate. Division.

Good for strips, edgings & woodland g.c. See *Ophiopogon* of similar aspect.

L. muscari: Big Blue Lilyturf. "Big Blue" is only big in comparison to some other spp.

Cvs. e.g. *L. m.* 'Curly Twist' & *L. m.* 'Monroe White' (*L. m.* 'Monroe no. 1'). The breeding has produced bigger & brighter flowers.

L. m. var. *variegata:* Young leaves margined with yellow.

L. m. 'Silver Banded': Compact with leaves edged with yellow.

L. m. 'Silvery Midget': White margins.

L. m. 'Silvery Sunproof': Stripes. To 18 in. Flowers of the variegated forms are on short stalks often hidden by foliage.

L. spicata: Creeping Lilyturf. China & Japan. Questing rhizomes. Leaves thin enough to be mowed. Flowers whitish; fruits black.

Lithodora & *Lithospermum:* BORAGINACEAE.
Open rocky places in S. & W. Eur.

Low spreading evgrn. plants 8 × 18 in. with dark green crinkled foliage. Listed together since the layman is naturally confused. R.g. ½ shade. Soil moist, fert. loose. No lime. Drainage. Cuttings.

Restrained. Flowers of *Lithodora* really blue. Bloom May & June.

Lithodora diffusa (*Lithospermum diffusum, L. prostratum*): Prostrate. To 12 in. Leaves narrow, evgrn., hairy. Flowers tubular, brilliant blue, striped with reddish violet. May & June. Loose, well-drained acid soil. May rot from too much water overhead. Very floriferous. Foliage small & crinkled in a dark green mat.

Lithospermum: Puccoon. Flowers yellow, orange or sometimes white.

L. ochroleuceum: Erect to 18". Flowers pale yellow, June. All those plants with blue flowers which belonged to *Lithospermum* are now assigned to other genera.

L. canescens & *L. incisum* natives of N. Am. sometimes seen.

Macleaya (*Bocconia*): PAPAVERACEAE.
Plume Poppy.
China, Japan

See General Plant Descriptions. Abbreviated description here. Herb. Erect stems to 7 ft. No staking. Leaves rounded, large lobed of uniquely beautiful form. Excel. with shrubs in filtered shade. Beautiful in Minnesota. Spreads to 3 ft.

M. microcarpa: Erroneous name *Bocconia cordata.* From running rootstocks. Numerous leafy stems make a colony where site and soil are conducive to growth. Flowers in branching plumes, summer. Buff or flesh tinted, soft in texture as well as color. A cv. with deeper coppery buff color.

M. cordata: Sim. to *M. microcarpa.* Root rather compact. Flowers more white.

Mertensia: BORAGINACEAE. Bluebells, Virginia Bluebells or Virginia Cowslip.
No. hemis., ½ in N. Am.

Herb. Bloom in spring, plentiful in a good site. Tubular flowers in sprays, blue with pink overtones. Whole plant dies down in mid-summer.

Partial shade. Soil loose, moist with humus. Division.

G.c. For cool woodlands only. A planting in good health looks very lush. 1–3 ft. w.

M. virginiana: Goes dormant in summer. Appears again early spring. Leaves greyish. Flowers blue-violet in arching sprays, placed along one side of stem. Nodding, bell-shaped, in bud stage pink. 'Rubra', a pink cv.; also *M. v.* var. *alba.*

M. paniculata: Bushy sprawler to 2 ft. Smaller bells than those of the above sp. but profuse. "Delft blue". If cut back in spring, another flowering season may occur.

M. ciliata: N. Am., Rocky Mtns. To 2 ft. Flowers

Lilium

Lithospermum

Mertensia

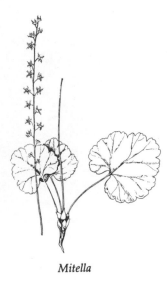

Mitella

Omphalodes

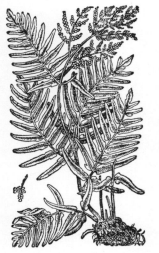

Osmunda

in spring, light blue with pink buds. Fringed.

M. maritima: Oyster Plant. N. Eur. & Brit. Light blue, narrow bells in summer. Needs rough soil & sun.

Metrosideros: MYRTACEAE.
N. Zealand.
Evgrn. Trees & shrubs, subshrubs & mounder, & trailer. The trailing subshrub looks unlike the familiar tree.
Shade. Soil moist & fert. Semi-hdy. No trimming necessary.
Thin stems of the trailers will cascade over a rock. To 2 ft.

M. perforatus (M. scandens) & *M. carmineus:* Trailing stems. Leaves boxwood-like, those of the second more leathery. Bloom cannot be predicted. Without bloom plant very decorative. Flowers with stamens to ½ in. long, pink or white in lateral clusters below leaves. (The foliage of these 2 spp. often thought to be the immature stage of the arboreal sp., *M. tomentosus*).

Mitchella: RUBIACEAE. Partridge-Berry, Twin-Berry, Squaw-Berry.
N. Am., Japan.
Evgrn. A flat creeper; restrained. Leaves very small & thin, close to stems, make a tracery over the earth. To 1 ft. w.
Shade. Duff. Feed to enlarge. Division.
An unsubstantial look.

M. repens: Nova Scotia to Mexico. Stems trail & hug ground, rooting at nodes. Leaves opposite, shiny, nearly round. Flowers small, fragrant, white, pink in bud & in the throat. In pairs, in spring, from axils, near tips. Berries bright scarlet, if developed, remain through winter.

Mitella: SAXIFRAGACEAE. Bishops's Cap or Mitrewort.
N. Am., & E. Asia.
Herb. Horizontal rootstocks. To 1 ft. w. Foliage good texture. Leaves cordate or lobed. Flowers small, often inconspicuous.
Shade. Moist soil full of organic matter. Division.
G.c. Less showy than *Heuchera*, more like *Tiarella*. Dainty. Combine with these spp. & some of the Saxifrages. Uncommon.

M. diphylla, to 1½ ft., & *M. nuda,* to 8 in.: Native to E. & Central U.S. Leaves heart-shaped & notched. Flowers saucer- to bell-shaped, white, with tiny petals deeply cleft, in very slender 6 in. racemes on erect stems. Lacy looking. Flowers of the second yellowish green with 10 stamens. Delicate.

M. caulescens & *M. stauropetala:* W. Am. natives, woodlands, wet meadows & swamps. To 1–1½ ft. Leaves of the second often purplish tinged. Flowers greenish.

M. pentandra: N. Am.; Alaska, Alberta, Colo., Calif. Tiny flowers with greenish petals.

M. breweri: N. Am.; high mtns. Alberta, British Columbia, Mont., Idaho, Calif. Leaves kidney- to heart-shaped to 4 in. in diameter. Flowers greenish yellow.

M. trifida: Only available from a specialty nursery. Periodic watering in dry weather. Top dress.

Omphalodes: BORAGINACEAE. Navelwort, Creeping Forget-Me-Not, Blue-Eyed Mary.
Eur., Asia, Mex.
Herb. or evgrn. Spreading neatly to a loose mat 30 in. in width. Low, clumping, good foliage, healthy & fresh looking. Leaves a pointed oval, ridged by deep veinage.
Shade. Soil moist & fert. Division.
Restrained g.c. The name, Blue-Eyed Mary, also applied to *Collinsea verna.* Bloom spring. Plant with *Brunnera, Viola, Primula.*

O. verna: Spreads by underground stolons. To 8 in. tall. Leaves evgrn. in a warm climate; basal leaves often heart-shaped, rough textured, pointed; stem leaves smaller. Bloom in spring, in deep shade. Flowers in short few-flowered clusters, bright blue with white throats. Look like miniature Forget-Me-Nots. Also *O. v.* var. *alba,* rare.

O. cappadocica: Creeping rhizomes; erect stems; densely hairy, prominently veined, heart-shaped leaves to 4 in. Foliage of softer texture & less neat than that of *O. verna.* Flowers bright blue, white-eyed, ½ in. across, in long racemes. Blooms for 6 weeks, spring.

Ophiopogon: LILIACEAE. Lilyturf or Mondo-Grass.
E. Asia.
Evgrn. Looks like *Liriope.* Clump-forming. 6 in.–1 ft.
Shade & ½ sun. Semi-hdy. Ordinary cult. Groom. Division.
G.c. or r.g. Containers. The dark cv. needs its own space. Bloom summer & fall.

O. jaburon: Japan. Nonspreading. To 2 ft. Leaves arching, dark green. Flowers white; fruits blue-violet, just above foliage. Variegated varieties.

O. clarkei: Sikkim. Rhizomes. Forms tufts. Leaves to 1 ft.

O. japonicus: Stolons spreading rapidly to form a dense, coarse, wavy turf.

O. planiscapus: Japan. Thickened roots & slender stolons. Leaves to 1 ft. flaring from the crown. (Spelling varies, sometimes *planiscarpus.*)

O. p. var. *arabicus (O. arabicus):* Leaves & stalks nearly black. 4 × 4 in. Flowers pinkish. Fruits blue-green. Restrained & slow. Hdy. to New York City, in U.S.

O. p. var. *nigrescens:* May be available. (Or may be a synonym). Display these oddities in a pot.

Osmunda: OSMUNDACEAE. Royal Fern or Flowering Fern.
Widespread.
Herb. or evgrn. Unusual fern. Distinctive personality. 1 ft. w.
Shade. Soil moist, fert. Cut back spent fronds. Division.
Use as accent. Place in center of a ground covering fern or in front of a per. with unusual form as *Macleaya.*

O. regalis: To 4 ft., often less. Blades broadly ovate, twice pinnate. Leaflets oblong, to 3 in.; finely toothed. Upper parts of the fert. fronds in erect panicles with numerous globose clusters of spore cases, first green later brown; look like tiny flowers.

O. cinnamomea: The fertile fronds in groups of 4 show earlier in spring than the sterile fronds. To 5 ft., with branching upper parts, warm-brown. Then the sterile fronds surround these spires—in a vase-shape, as a wide collar.

Oxalis: OXALIDACEAE. Wood-Sorrel.
S. Afr., N. & S. Am.
Herb. & evgrn. So many kinds, some pests, some restrained houseplants, some suitable for ground covers. Sev. fold their leaves downward at night, or when a shaft of sun hits the area. (An ingenious way to protect themselves from a sunburn.) Differ in hardiness according to habitat.
Shade & part shade. Ordinary cult. Control. Division.
Foliage varies widely in shape & size & color. Some leaves are clover-form; some are small & round, some oval, some plain, some with shadings. The more handsome the foliage, the more invasive the plant, it would seem. 6 plus in. Flowers invite some investigation from the side as well as from the front. Often the petals flare from a short, narrow tube. There are sev. white forms of various spp. for those with a predilection for white. Some of the spp. are a little fussy whereas we know that others are overly vigorous. Bloom, mostly spring.
O. adenophylla: Chile & Argentina. To 6 in. Grey-green clover-like leaves which disappear by late summer. With 12 to 20 leaflets forming a whorl. Flowers pink or white with deeper color in throat. Bell-shaped. May through June.
O. acetosella: Usually white flowers, veined with purple-pink but there is a pink form. To 6 in. Moist woods.
O. oregano: leaflets to 1 in. long. Flowering stem to 10 in., rosy-pink sometimes white. Difficult to eradicate if the carpet overgrows its space. Typical redwood g.c.
O. deppei: Mex. Leaves long-stalked with 4 nearly round leaflets, ½ in. long & wide. Minute teeth. Glabrous. Petals spatulate. Tubers edible. Flowers red in clusters of 5–12 at top of long stalks. A white flowered form, 'Alba'.
O. alstonii (not a var. of *O. hedysaroides*): Fire Fern. River banks, Brazil. To 8 in. Leaves exquisite, clear red, esp. with light behind them. Texture thin. Leaves with 3 leaflets, the broad end of the heart attached to stalks. Delicate, graceful branchlets. Flowers small, yellow; bloom off & on, but not conspicuous. *O. a.* 'Rubra'. Charming shrublet for a pot.
O. regnellii: S. Afr. 3 leaflets appear sheared & the resulting wide apex then notched.

Pachysandra: BUXACEAE. Japanese Spurge.
Asia, Am.
Evgrn. Slender underground rhizomes. To 6+ ft. In some sections of the U.S., it grows too readily, esp. in cemeteries. A leafy carpet. Attractive foliage design. Flower inconspicuous.
Sun or shade. Soil moist, fert. Division.
Plant under trees, on banks, in strips, in courtyards, in woods. Must be lush to be effective.
P. terminalis: Leaves thick, shiny, coarsely toothed through center, leathery. Flowers few, in spikes, fragrant, white, not noticeable.
P. t. 'Variegata': Nice pattern of silver & green. Also *P. t.* 'Silver Edge'. Much more restrained than the sp.

Paris: LILIACEAE. Herb Paris.
Eur., Japan, Temp. Asia.
Herb. Creeping rhizomes. Like *Trillium* but parts in fours. Arrangement in fours unusual in LILY family. Sculptural. Amazing miniature flower at top of foliage umbrellas. No. of parts may be more than 4.
Shade & ½ shade. Soil friable & moist. Roots increase each year producing more shoots. Spreads to 2 ft.
Once used as medicine & aphrodisiac but overdoses result in death. No one is apt to investigate as to whether the pharmaceutical property is in root, leaf or flower. Unique appearance deserves an open special setting. Bloom spring, summer & fall.
P. quadrifolia: Moist woodlands, Eur. & Asia, N. to Arctic Circle. To 1 ft. Stem very erect. Leaves 4–6 in., in 2 layers, one towards the top of the stem, the other beneath the bloom; this one is made up of seals but looks like the first (only a little smaller). It forms a collar or ruff (whorl). 4 outer thread-like yellowish green perianth segments, 4 inner—the outer greener, broader & longer, within yellow stamens & a violet colored knob-like stigma. Styles 4; stamens 8; conspicuous. Fruit black, if present.
P. polyphylla: Himalayas. To 3 ft. May have more than 4 leaves, up to 9, linear, 6 in. long, 4 in. across. Flowers with 4 to 6 outer segments, green & the same number of inner segments, yellow. Fruits contain red seeds. Though muted in color, a plant stands out in an opening of the woods as a masterpiece of design. Treat like *Trillium.*

Pasithea: LILIACEAE.
Chile & Peru.
Herb. Hardy where there is only a little frost.
Sun or part shade; openings in woods. Soil rich. Good drainage. Division.
Resembles *Anthericum* in habit. When cutting, condition well. Only 1 sp.
P. caerulea: Rhizomous roots travel underground in the dormant period. Roots may be divided if a leaf clump is attached. A colony, in 3 years may produce 20 stems. Leaf narrow, strap-shaped, rather limp after flowering stem develops. Flowering stem firm, smooth, green; at the top, there is a branching cluster of starry blossoms, each 1 in. wide. Purplish bright blue; spring & early summer. Graceful sprays.

Patrinia: VALERIANACEAE.
Cent. to E. Asia.
Herb. Leaves broad, basal. Foliage light textured, incised pattern. Bloom summer.
Part shade. Soil well-laced with compost. Division.
Each plant 1 ft. w.; grow in a group.

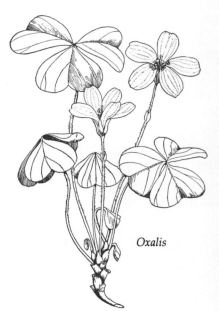

Oxalis

Paris

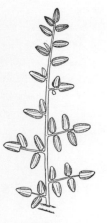

Pellaea

Phlox

Phyllodoce

P. gibbosa: Japan. Leaves broad, basal. Stems to 18 in. Curious small flowers pale yellow with one long petal of greenish yellow. Late summer. (Peculiar odor.)

P. triloba (P. palmata): To 2 ft., mostly shorter. Leaves basal, palmately lobed, coarsely toothed. Flowers in loose, 3-branched cluster well above foliage. Bright yellow. Dainty. Woodsy. Goes well with *Tiarella, Sanguinaria, Alchemilla,* dwarf *Pieris.*

Pellaea: PTERIDACEAE. Cliff-brake.
S. Am., S. Afr., & Calif. in U.S.
A fern growing mostly among or on rocks. Clusters of spore capsules close together along the margins of the frond segments & covered by the turned under edges. Spp. many, of various size & form. Only 2 described.

P. atropurpurea: Purple Cliff-brake. N. Am.: Vt. to Brit. Col., Ariz.; & Guatemala. Pale green, then blue-green, with dark purple to black hairy stalk. Blades to 10 in., 1 to 3 times pinnate.

P. andromedaefolia: Coffee-Fern. S. Calif. in U.S. & Baja in Mexico. Dry rocky ravines & moist shady banks of streams. Leaves thin, rounded, grey-green, spaced along a wiry stem. Delicate with subtle charm.

Phlox: POLEMONIACEAE. Moss-pink or Wild Sweet William.
N. Am. (except *P. sibira*).
Herb. Two distinct kinds, the tall herb. per. & alpines. Bloom spring & summer. Flowers of soft texture in usually rounded heads.
Sun & partial shade. Soil moist & fert. Division.
Low growing spp. & hybs. for r.g., for slopes or open woods (tall growing: described in General Plant Description).

P. divaricata (P. canadensis): Sweet William Phlox. N. Am., Quebec to Ala.; soils rich, slightly acid, loose. Partly evgrn. Part shade. To 1 ft. from creeping underground stems. Leaves oval, to ½ in. Flowers blue or white, in open clusters. Spring, somewhat fragrant. Look for *P. d.* var. *alba* & *P. d.* 'Fuller's White'.

P. d. var. *laphamii:* (May be a hyb.) N. Am., Wis. to Tex. with petals NOT notched at apex. Lavender-blue to pale violet & white with masses of flowers in loose branched clusters. Spring. The var. does best with some sun. Seek.

P. arendsii (or × *arendsii*): *P. divaricata* × *P. paniculata.* Dwarf race. Showy. 1 ft. × 1 ft. Lavender leaves. Flowers mauve or white, long flowering season. One of the best is 'Lisbeth' with clear lavender-blue color.

P. subulata: Moss Pink. Mat forming. Creeping stems to 6 in. Leaves evgrn., stiff, needle-like to ½ in. Flowers in heads, pink, rose, lavender, white; late spring, producing sheets of color. Part shade or sun. Cut back half way after flowering. Cvs. e.g.: 'Betty', salmon-pink (Hillier's catalogue); 'Sensation', deep pink (Blue Hills catalogue). A cv. 'Blue Hills'. May & June.

P. frondosa: Probably hyb. *P. subulata* × *P. nivalis.* Good forms. *P.* 'Vivid', bright pink & compact from the same parents. The strain,

"Alexander's Subulata hybrids" reportedly excel.

P. nivalis: Trailing Phlox. Loose mats to 6 in. Leaves evgrn., narrow. Flowers pink or white, in clusters, late spring. Best in r.g.; part shade or sun. Cvs. e.g., 'Camla', 'Avalon White', 'Gladwyne'.

P. amoena: To 4 in. A carpet. Leaves small, dark green. Flowers in heads, rich pink or white. R.g.

P. stolonifera: Appalachians in U.S. Creeping stems grow from the tops of those of the previous year. Rosette-like clusters along the length of spatula-shaped leaves to 2½ in. long. At ends, flowering stems to 6 in. or 1 ft.; flowers 1 in. wide, pink to reddish purple with yellow anthers.

P. procumbens: *P. stolonifera* × *P. subulata.* Flowers mostly bright purple.

P. p. 'Millstream': Flowers pink with white ring & star of deep red.

P. adsurgens: N. Am., acid woodlands, Ore. to Calif. Leaves nearly round. Flowers in few-flowered clusters, tones of clear pink with a dark stripe up each petal. Variants & hybs.
A number of other spp. & cvs. should be sought by the r.g. enthusiast & tested in the alpine house. E.g.: *P. gracilis, P. douglasii, P. missoulensis, P. diffusa, P. hoodii.*

Phyllodoce: Called Yellow Heather. Dwarf spp. with closed bell. See Subshrubs.

Pleione: ORCHIDACEAE. Ground Orchid.
China, Taiwan, India.
Bulb. Sev. spp. Some spp. bloom when in leaf. Clump to 1 ft. w. Foliage attractive during period of no bloom. Flowers sev. to a stalk. Two-toned, somewhat orchid-like.
½ shade. Cool r.g. as well as containers for greenhouse or lath-house. Division.
Leaves deeply pleated. A variegated form. Growth 3–4 in. taller when planted in the ground instead of in a container.

P. bulbicoidinoides: Leaves 2, thin to 1 ft. long. Flower stems just a little taller. Flowers with young leaves. Flowers deep mauve to paler mauve-pink, rarely white. Lips paler & marked with red & magenta. Winter & spring. Sometimes blooms better when grown in containers.

Podophyllum: BERBERIDACEAE (or separate May Apple family). Mandrake or May Apple. Woods of N. Am., India, China.
Herb. Rhizome. Leaves large. A carpet of *Podophyllum* is astonishingly decorative. May colonize but not easy to establish.
Shade & ½ shade. Soil moist, loose, fert. Protect site. Plants hdy. Young leaves frost-tender. Division.
More than one attempt may be necessary but worthwhile. Bloom spring. Flowers nodding, cupped white, pink or purple according to sp.

P. peltatum: The leaf comes through the ground folded like an umbrella; opens to 1 ft. across. 2 half-round leaves at top of flowering stem; 7–9 wedged-shaped, toothed lobes. From the crotch formed by the leaf stems, a flower, 2 in. across, cup-shaped, nodding, 6 to 9 petals, white, traced with transparent veins. Fragrant. Fruits

Euphorbias can be coarse or weedy in the height of bloom. One of the more interesting species makes a show of its rounded heads of chartreuse green, *E. characias*. D.D.

The Newberry Garden near Portland contains the species collection of the Rhododendron Society. Here companion plants for Rhododendrons flourish in suitable terrain and climate. This stand of *Cornus canadenis* is hard to believe. D.D.

Euphorbia is well known for its spreading proclivities. E.B.

Sisyrinchium striatum shows its rounded form especially well at the height of bloom. At the base of steps, this plant has served an architectural purpose. D.D.

PERENNIALS WITH MUTED COLORS

Athyrium nipponicum var. *pictum:* Shown is a portion of this multi-colored fern so that you may see more clearly the markings on its fronds. The various tones are highlighted by a grey central stripe and purple petioles. For 9 or 10 months a space in the woods is occupied by this graceful fountain. E.B.

Helleborus lividus var. *corsicus* is the tallest of the four best known Hellebores. Here you see only the top of the plants since you are looking down on the fine trusses of bloom. E.B.

The foliage of *Helleborus* spp. have various shades of green. Several species grow in this glade associating well with each other. *H. niger* is shown here. E.B.

A *Digitalis* stem repeats the straight, strong line of the Redwood trunk. Plant in deep shade, either the hybrid *D.* × *mertonensis* or the species *D. ferruginea,* the second more slender. E.B.

WOODS—UNUSUAL

One sees a pleasing combination of two diverse forms in two perennials of similar color. The second brighter tone in the *Penstemon* heightens the relationship. The edging plant whether it is grey or white, as it is here, should be low and dense to finish but not detract from the central attraction. (Rockefeller Garden.) K.B.

In open woodland, a perennial with a wide spread is often effective. In this garden, *Anemone nemerosa* has conditions to its liking. Plant woodlanders with it such as *Vancouveria* and *Tiarella.* D.D.

Erinus alpinus is a restrained ground cover to be planted on the edge of shade so that ample light can bring out its clear pink. *Androsace* is at once similar and different and makes a good companion. E.B.

Shades of pink are interwoven with grey in this planting of mostly succulents. Some *Crassula, Mesembryanthemum* and *Kleinia,* with a dwarf Jade tree in the center for accent. E.B.

COMBINATIONS

This garden has a seemingly casual mixture of several long blooming perennials. In this center circle, you will find *Salvias, Astilbes, Verbascums* and all manner of low ground covers . . . Roses are here and there. In the right hand corner of the photo is part of a bush of the McCarthy Rose, *R. bracteata,* sometimes called Fried-egg Rose, but it is altogether more refined. B.W.

Angelica pachycarpa creates the focal point with its sculptured glossy foliage. *Alstroemeria* sets the key for the color harmony with the *Iris* accentuating the softer end of the scale. *Campanula persicifolia* is a blending agent. B.W.

Hidcote. In this woodland setting, a sculptured effect is produced by very broad, thick leaves with wavy edges. Ornamental rhubarb and *Gunnera* are good in this role. In this swale, since the soil is extra damp, candelabra Primroses flourish. J.Z.

A number of perennials are woven together in a harmony of form and color. Yellow is provided by *Hypericum* 'Moonlight' and *Aurinia.* The *Euphorbia* is taller and wider and yellowish green; the bright magenta-pink is *Geranium incanum.* Bulbous plants are introduced not only for flowers in their season but also for the dissimilarity of their blade-shaped foliage. B.W.

COMBINATIONS

lemon-yellow to rose to 2 in. long, edible, plum-like.

P. p. 'Splendens': Leaves to 1 ft. Substance & texture usually improved.

Polemonium: POLEMONIACEAE. Jacob's Ladder, Greek Valerian, Charity.
N. hemis., esp. Brit.
Herb. 2 × 2 ft. & some very dwarf alpines. Best known, *P. caeruleum,* often 18 × 24 in. Basal clumps of finely divided foliage. Bloom summer.
½ shade. Sun in cool climates. Soil fert. Keep moist in summer. Division.
Explanation of common names not commonly known. Grown since time of Roman Empire.
P. caeruleum: Old-fashioned garden plant. To 3 ft., usually less. Leaves pinnate, with delicate texture. Flowers many, silky, light lavender cup-shaped with orange stamens. Early summer.
P. c. var. *van-brutiae:* Esp. long stamens. Seek.
P. foliosissimum: W. N. Am. Little taller than most. Deeper lavender. Flowers many, cup-shaped, silky, sev. weeks in summer.
P. carneum: W. N. Am. Pink flowers. 'Rose Queen' is deeper. Seek *P. c.* 'Album'.
P. flavum: S. N. Am. Flowers yellow. Not common.

Polygonatum: LILIACEAE. Solomon's Seal or David's Harp.
N. hemis.
Herb. Thick, knotty, horizontal, creeping rhizome with erect arching, graceful stems. Rhizomes spread underground. To 4 ft. w. Sev. spp. other than those described.
Shade or partial shade. Soil moist, loose. Division.
Foliage clear green or in one sp. there is a white edge. Leaves to 4 ft., abundant on curving stem from the underside of which hang the bell-shaped flowers. When fully open the bells sometime show multiple curly petals. Bloom summer.
P. latifolium: Eur. Not endemic on the E. Coast of U.S. as sometimes reported. Splendid texture. Flowers off-white.
P. multiflorum: Cylindrical stems to 4 ft. Leaves stem-clasping, pointed to 5 in. with up to 9 veins. Flowers white, constricted at middles; pendulous, in clusters of 3–5.
P. hybridum: P. multiflorum × *P. odoratum*; characteristics of both.
P. odoratum (P. officinale): Eur. To 2 ft. Stems angular, not cylindrical.
P. o. var. *thunbergii (P. japonicum):* To 3½ ft. with leaves to 6 in. & flowers to 1 in.
P. o. var. *variegatum:* Leaves with longitudinal white stripes.
P. o. 'Flore Pleno': Flowers "full".
P. hookeri: Less common sp.; not in *Hortus.*
P. commutatum: Great Solomon's Seal. N.H., U.S. to Mex. To 7 ft. Lower portion of stems naked, upper leafy, with leaves 6½ in. by 4 in. 7–19 veins along length. Flowers on stems to 1 ft. long, yellowish green to greenish white, 1, or in groups to 15.
P. biflorum (S. caniculatum): Small Solomon's Seal or Eastern Solomon's Seal. Width 3 ft. plus, up to 6 ft., usually 2 ft. Only center vein

conspicuous. Flowers sometimes 1–3 as well as 2. Colonies formed in fert., moist woodland. Dormant until late spring. Not attractive to snails.
P. alpinum: 3 ft. × 3 ft. Somewhat invasive. Bushy plant; narrow leaves. Num. branching spikes. Cream white flowers; 2 mos. flowers for 2 mos.

Polystichum: 3 w. U.S. spp.

Primula: PRIMULACEAE. Primose, Cowslip, Oxlip, Auricula.
N. hemis., mostly higher altitudes, except common Primrose found at sea level.
Herb. The genus is classified in 30 botanical sections. (Sometimes classified as to countries of origin.) In this account, sections will be mentioned only to show a relationship. The spp., hybs. & cvs. will be grouped according to shared characteristics or to behavior in the garden. Dwarfs are esp. good for a woodland.
Part shade. Soil porous, fert. Moisture. Seed or division.
Mostly restrained growth. 1–2 ft. w. Foliage usually crinkled in basal rosettes. Flower stems straight scapes of various heights. Bloom winter, spring & summer.

The garden primroses of early spring:
P. vulgaris (P. acaulis): English or Common Primrose. Leaves wrinkled, toothed to 3 in. Flowers solitary 1½ in. across, on stems to 6 in. Garden selections with purple as well as yellow bloom; color, in the wild, soft "primrose-yellow". Dbles. also. Fairly true from seed.
P. veris, Cowslip & *P. elatior,* Oxlip: Eur. Leaves in rosettes, soft-hairy, round-toothed to 3 in. Flowers in many flowered umbels, fragrant on erect stems to 8 in. Yellow, rarely purple. In many Primroses, each bloom is constricted at the center, forming a sort of saucer. Oxlip does not have this contraction & therefore is without folds & with a flatter face.
P. polyantha: A hyb. with *P. vulgaris, P. veris & P. elatior* as parents. "Munstead Strain", England; "Pacific Giants", W. Amer. (the latter slightly less hdy.). Leaves in strong rosettes, round-toothed, wrinkled. Flowers single & dble., to 2 in., in umbel; excel. colors.

Primroses for r.g. & moist shady garden: Most not easy. Most require space.
P. floribunda: Himalayas. Glandular-pubescent (not mealy). Leaves in loose rosettes to 5 in., irregularly toothed. Flowers on stalks to 8 in., *whorls* with leafy bracts; well spaced. Petals rounded or slightly notched. Yellow, fragrant. Winter & spring.
P. f. var. *isabellina:* Sulphur-yellow.
(*P. florindae* is described with spp. of the Sikkemensis section.)
P. verticillata: Bigger than the above. Coating of white meal on leaves, bracts & calyces (not glandular-hairy). Leaves in loose rosettes, long-oval, irregularly toothed to 8 in. long. Flowering stalks to 2 ft. Flowers 1 in. wide, less golden-yellow than that of *P. floribunda,* petals slightly notched. Leafy bracts to 3 in.
P. kewensis: Kew Primrose. Intermediate

Polemonium

Polygonatum

Primula

Primula

between *P. floribunda* & *P. verticillata*—chance seedling at Royal Botanic Gardens. Sterile. A tetraploid has been raised, from which seed may be produced. The fert. kind has more vigorous growth & greater size of leaf & flower. Plants vary as to the amount of white, mealy coating.

P. auricula: European Alps. Farinose. Fleshy. Leaves long oval to 4 in. Flowers (of sp.) yellow to 1 in. wide in many flowered umbels (3 to 20). Petals notched at apexes. Horticultural variants with various patterns of various colors.

P. pubescens: Hybs. of *P. auricula, P. rubra* & *P. viscosa.* Variable.

The candelabra primroses flower in whorls. Fert., very moist soils in partial shade. Sev. spp. e.g.:

P. japonica: Japan. Probably the best known & perhaps the easiest. Leaves to 1 ft., crenate, dentate. Scape to 18 in. with 2 to 6 whorls, many flowered. Many forms yellow, red, purple or white. May & June.

P. 'Potsford White': Rich looking. Easy. The white shaded pink. Seems to come true from seed.

P. anisodora: China & Burma. Scent of anise in all parts. Leaves to 10 in., hairless, meal-less. Flowers tubular, funnel-shaped; brownish purple with greenish centers. 5 to 10, in whorls.

P. aurantiaca: Yunnan Province, China. Leaves dentate to 8 in. Flowers 6–12 in 2–6 whorls. Reddish orange to dark red. Scape to 1 ft. July.

P. beesiana: Yunnan Province, China. Leaves dentate to 8 in. long, narrow at base. Flowers 8 to 16 in 2 to 8 whorls. Rosy carmine with yellow eye. Scape to 2½ ft. June.

P. bulleyana: China. Leaves irregularly toothed, almost hairless. To 2½ ft. Whorls, sev., many flowered. Stalks with white meal below each whorl. Petals notched; blooms 1 in. wide; calyces cleft to middle. Deep orange to apricot-orange to deep apricot. June.

P. pulverulenta: W. Szechwan Province, China. Farinose. Leaves to 1 ft. Scape to 3 ft. Deep red. June.

P. cockburniana: China. (Short-lived.) Leaves minutely toothed to 5 in. To 1½ ft. Flowers 1 in. wide with white mealy tiny bracts, brilliant orange. (A cv. 'Red Hugh', of superb color, perhaps derived from above.)

Species of the *Sikkimensis* section like the same kind of situation. But they usually have only a single umbel of blooms. Flowers bell-shaped.

P. sikkimensis: Himalayas. Leaves crinkled to 6 in. To 1½ ft. Flowers bell-shape in an umbel, drooping. Clear yellow.

P. florindae: Looks like a giant *P. sikkimensis.* To 4 ft. Umbels of up to 60 flowers, fragrant, pendulous, bell-shaped, sulphur-yellow. Wet, fert. soil & partial shade. Needs space; difficult. See "Bog".

P. alpicola (P. microdonta var. alpicola): Like the above but smaller. To 1½ ft. Bells less drooping & flatter. Umbels more mealy,

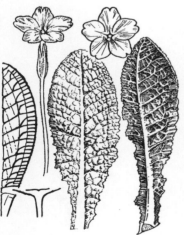

Primulas

fragrant, yellow, sometimes creamy white. Difficult but worth effort.

Spp. with flowers in heads

P. capitata & *P. c.* var *mooreana:* Himalayas. (The variety more robust.) Dense, globular heads. Leaves to 5 in., white mealy underneath; in the sp., on both sides, above & below. Flowers ½ in. wide, bell-shaped, fragrant on 9 in. stems, stems & calyces white mealy. Purplish blue. June to Aug. "Chinese Star Sorts" on scapes to 1 ft.

P. denticulata: Denticulata section wherein the blooms face upward instead of being pendulous. Flowers soft lavender with small yellow eye.

P. d. var. *cachemiriana:* Differing from the sp. in that leaves nearly mature at time of flowering. Coated with yellowish meal. Also *P. d. c.* var. *alba.*

P. farinosa: Flowers pale purple with a yellow eye.

Dwarfs

P. juliae: Transcaucasia. Close relative of *P. vulgaris.* Mats made up of tufts rather than of rosettes. Leaves red-stalked, hairless, coarsely toothed with blades to 1 in. long. Flowers many, solitary, magenta with yellow throats, petals deeply notched.

P. pruhoniciana (P. juliae): Group name for hybs. with *P. juliae* as main parent. Juliana hybs.: good dwarf plants, various colors. Spread to 1 ft.

P. parryi, P. rusbyi, P. chionantha: Alpines very hard to domesticate.

Oddities: for specialists.

P. vialii (P. littoniana): China. Only member of Muscarioides section commonly grown. Easy from seed. Difficult to find. Flowers in slender stalked spikes, narrow, erect to 5 in. topping stalks to 1½ in. tall. Amazing color. Upper part made up of calyces, bright orange-red narrowing to a point; lower part crowded with open flowers, striking violet-blue.

P. halleri: High mtns. Eur. Leaves to 5 in., undersides dusted with yellow meal. Stalks to 7 in. Flowers up to 12, in umbels, deeply notched petals; violet.

P. mollis: Himalayas. Unlike a primrose. Leaves heart-shaped, softly hairy, slightly lobed. Flowers in loose tiers on very slender stalks, pink to crimson, dark centered. (Last two from Cortusoides section comprised of woodland spp.)

Pulmonaria: BORAGINACEAE. Lungwort, Blue Cowslip, Jerusalem-Sage, Bethlehem-Sage, Spotted Dog.

Eur., Middle East & N. Asia.

More or less evgrn. except *P. angustifolia.* Most spp. form a low, almost flat mound. Usually less than 1 ft. high. Leaves rugose. Bloom early spring & some spp. late spring. In certain spp. combination of blue petals with pink in buds a decorative feature. After flowering foliage enlarges & spreads to form a pleasing mat. Improves each year but slow-growing.

½ shade. Soil moist, fert. Groom. Division. More or less open woodland. For spotted leaves: Spotted Dog. Not a sage, even though this name is found in 2 common names.

P. officinalis: Jerusalem-Sage, Blue Lungwort. To 1 ft. Once considered a specific for lung diseases. Creeping roots spread slowly to 2 ft. Leaves to 4 in., oval, pointed & heart-shaped at base. White spotted, the spots somewhat irregular. Flowers in forked clusters with curved branches. Bugle-shaped tube with 5 blunt lobes forming corolla. In bud, purplish red opening to violet.

P. o. var. *immaculata:* Unspotted leaves.

P. saccharata: Bethlehem Sage. To 1½ ft. Leaves with very pointed tips; blotched white or almost grey; a large proportion is light. Flowers white to reddish violet; calyces purplish, velvety. Cvs. e.g.:

'Mrs. Moon': A fine cv. with flowers first bright pink then blue.

'Margery Fish': Believed to be still better & perhaps the best of the lungworts. Jan. through April.

P. angustifolia: To 1 ft. often only 9 in. A mound of coarse, all green leaves, crinkled & prickly, on stems growing more or less horizontally. Flowering stems parallel projecting beyond foliage. Flowers bell-shaped, in sprays.

P. a. var. *azurea* & *P. a.* 'Johnson's Blue', the bluest.

P. a. 'Salmon Glory': Coral-pink & uncommon.

P. rubra: Leaves light green, velvety. Flowers coral-red in nodding heads as early as Feb. A white form & a red form.

P. lutea: A more or less dense, spreading carpet. Leaves small, overlapping. Even more crinkled than those of *P. angustifolia.* Flowers pendant, soft yellow, numerous, often early, continue sparsely to prolong season.

P. mollis: Largest sp., 18 in. × 2 ft. Velvety. Flowers rich color. Prolific. Uncommon.

Pulsatilla: RANUNCULACEAE. Wind Flower. Eur. & Brit.

Herb. Ferny, downy, foliage often decorated with silky hairs. Deeply divided on short stems to form a clump. Lovely in seed head as well as in blossom. Bloom fall.

Sun or partial shade. Soil fert. Drainage perfect. Seed or division.

Formerly included in *Anemone.* Personality esp. delicate.

P. vulgaris (Anemone pulsatilla): Pasque Flower. 1 ft. × 1 ft. Leaves "filigree" fern-like. Flowers delicate, poppy-shaped, with hairy calyx as a collar. Mauve, pink, purple.

P. v. var. *grandis:* Purple-violet.

P. halleri var. *slavica (Anemone halleri):* Switzerland, Austria. To 2 ft. Basal leaves to 12 in. pinnate, very hairy with narrow linear segments. Flowers purplish inside, rarely white, hairy outside, campanulate at first, later spreading, erect. This sp. has esp. fine leaf division. 'Budapest': Color of flowers forget-me-not blue.

P. hybs.: P. montana × *P. halleri.* Some of those with darkest flowers.

P. alpina var. *apiifolia:* Flowers sulphur-yellow, seed-heads silvery. Rare.

Ramonda: GESNERIACEAE.

Mtns. of S. Eur., generally in limestone.

Evgrn. R.g. or pot. Choice. For alpine specialists. Decorative small rosette of crinkled leaves, lying flat upon the soil. Very slow growing.

Shade. Soil open, moist. Drainage Will go dormant in drought. Propagate by leaf cuttings or division. Offsets may develop around main rosette.

Stemless. Best in a rock crevice. Bloom a rare event; flowers look precious.

R. myconi: Rosette Mullein. Pyrenees. Rosette very flat on the earth, to 8 in. wide. Leaves deeply toothed, fleshy as well as rugose; very wrinkled, few pale hairs above, many reddish hairs beneath. Flowering stalk to 4 in., 1–5 flowers, 1 in. plus across, lavender-blue or purple. Sharp-pointed yellow anthers. Bloom May or June. *R. m.* var. *alba, R. m.* var. *rosea* & *R. m.* 'Wisley Pink'.

Raoulia: COMPOSITAE.

Mostly N. Zealand.

Evgrn. Mats. Creeping. For foliage.

A warm place; does not need full sun. Soil lean. Perfect drainage. Division.

Ground covers of various habit; restrained.

R. australis (R. lutescens): Creeping mats, to 3 ft. wide, of minute, silver, rosettes forming a close, solid carpet. Leaves less than ¼ in. wide with silvery hairs. Imbricate, spatulate. Flowers hardly apparent, in yellow heads.

R. glabra: Very compact mound. Leaves tiny, green. Flowers minute, white. The mounds seen from a distance grown on hillsides in N. Zealand look like sheep asleep.

R. tenuicaulis: Said to be easiest. Leaves ½ in.; grey-green & silver. May be used as a cover for small bulbs.

Reineckea: LILIACEAE.

Japan, China (Woodlands at low altitudes).

Evgrn. or herb. G.c. Close relative of *Convallaria.* Small, non-rampant spreader. Leaves large to 18 in.

Part shade. Soil loose. Moisture med. Division.

Flowers starry with protruding stamens. Not prolific. Fruit a globular red berry.

R. carnea: Something like *Ophiopogon.* Leaves narrower than those of *Convallaria.* Clump spreads to 1 ft. Leaves to 1 ft. Flowers, starry in dense spikes, fleshy, pale pink, fragrant, with protruding stamens. Bloom April. Fruits small, round, few-seeded.

Rhodohypoxis: AMARYLLIDACEAE.

S. Afr.

Herb. Tuber. Small & low plants appearing late in spring. Leaves strap-shaped to 4 in. long in dense clumps. To 1 ft. w. Remarkable show of upfacing flowers.

Partial shade. Soil limefree. Excel. drainage. Tender in the north. Needs mild winters. Division.

Excel. in containers. In woods, provide a special pocket. Appears fragile. On the contrary, a vigorous grower when in propitious situations. Bloom summer.

Pulmonaria

Pulsatilla

Rodgersia

Sanguisorba

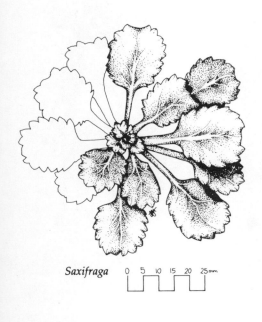

Saxifraga 0 5 10 15 20 25mm

R. baurii: Grows from small ovoid tubers. Leaves strap-shaped to 4 in.; 2 chief veins; sparse stellate hairs. Flowers solitary with 6 spreading petals. Deep pink or rose. A little over 1 in. in diameter. Should be masses. June through Aug. *R.* 'Apple Blossom' with light shade of pink.

R. b. var. *platypetala* is white.

R. rubella: Should be sought.

Rodgersia: SAXIFRAGACEAE.
E. Asia.

Herb. Rhizome. 5 spp. Related botanically to *Astilbe* which it does not resemble. Leaves are compound & often large, 1 ft. or more across. Handsome. Look like a broad hand. Seed heads with reddish tints in fall. Available in NW. U.S. & England.

Part shade. Soil friable, holding moisture. Some kinds grow well in the Berkshires of the U.S. with snow-cover of 16 in., Jan. to Mar. Cuttings. Division. Seed if available.

Watch it unfold soon after it emerges, a work of art. Plants develop annually becoming wider & reaching heights of 3–6 ft. according to sp. Slow to attain full growth. A stylish look. Excel. in a container; leaves then remain much smaller. In woods, allow space for mature width, to 3 ft.

R. pinnata var. *alba* & *R. p.* 'Superba': Leaves exceedingly coppery. Flowers fluffy, cream or pink in clusters.

R. sambucifolia: To 3 ft. Leaves pinnate. Flowers small, yellowish white in flat-topped panicles to 1 ft. across.

R. tabularis: Leaf stalk supports middle of peltate, circular leaf 3 ft. wide.

R. podophylla: China, Japan. Leaves palmately compound with jagged lobes, bronze when young, turning to green, then coppery when fully mature. 3 ft. by 3 ft. Slow to emerge. Sparse bloom.

R. aesculifolia: Leaves crinkled & bronze tinted. Flowers in a pyramid.

Rupicapnos: FUMARIACEAE.
N. Afr. & Spain.

Evgrn. 32 spp. Nearly stemless. Leaves pinnate. Flower subcorymbose raceme.

½ shade. Drainage. Semi-limey. Semi-hdy. Seed.

Greek rupi = rock; knapnos = smoke.

R. africana: From calcareous, rocky & partly shady cliffs. Variable. Leaves glaucescent, segments ovate or linear. Flowers ½ in. long; spurs on uppermost petal tips (turned downward often); rose-purple with dark purple—smokey.

Sanguinaria: PAPAVERACEAE. Bloodroot, Red Puccoon.
N. Am.; Nova Scotia to Ontario, Manitoba, Fla., Ala., Okla.

Herb. Fleshy underground rhizome; usually only 1 leaf from each bud of the rhizome. Low plant with unusual foliage. See sp. description. Bloom, spring. Spreads to 1 ft.

Shade. Soil moist, loose, fert. Division.

From rich woods. Try to duplicate. Somewhat temperamental.

S. canadensis: Leaves on 8 in. stalks, rounded with 3–9 palmately arranged toothed or wavy edged lobes. Not fully mature at time of bloom. Blue-grey. Flowers on 8 in. stems. 4 or 8 or 16 petalled, in 2–4 rows, 1½ in. across, white or tinged pink. Numerous stamens.

S. c. var. *multiplex:* Extra petals instead of stamens. The flowers of this form last longer. Spring.

Sanguisorba (Poterium): ROSACEAE. Burnet. Temp. parts of N. hemis.

Herb. Decorative spp. as well as the culinary herb. To 6 ft. × 2 ft. Most spp. robust. Pinnate foliage. Flowers bottle-brush like. Late summer.

½ shade. Soil moist, fert. or lean. Division.

No sp. common in the marketplace. The Japanese sp. hard to find.

S. canadensis: American Burnet. Damp & wet soils in the mtns. from Labrador to N.C. in U.S. From 4 ft. to 6 ft. Leaves 1½ ft. long; leaflets 7 to 17, more or less ovate. Flowers in cylindrical spikes to 5 in., white with protruding stamens. Bottle-brush like. Fall. Looks something like *Cimicifuga:* looks well with Japanese Anemone.

S. obtusa: Japanese alpine meadows. Rare. 2 ft. to 4 ft. Leaves greyish overtopped by flowers, summer. Flowers pale, rose-pink.

S. o. var. *albiflora:* White.

S. minor: Salad Burnet. Culinary herb but ornamental. Flavor like cucumber. Sun, drainage, moisture, rather poor soil. To 1 ft. Leaves deeply-toothed, in a rosette. Flowers, thimble-shaped, pinkish white. Cut before buds open; cut whole plant back half-way, often.

Saxifraga: SAXIFRAGACEAE. Saxifrage, Rockfoil, Strawberry Geranium, London Pride, Prince's Feather.

Worldwide, mostly temp., subarctic & alpine regions.

Herb. & evgrn. Mostly low to 1½ ft. although one sp. 3 ft. Plants spread to about 1 ft. 370 spp., sev. sections. Some difficult. One or two easy. Various foliage, all decorative. Flower color white—or white with spots or pink. Spring & summer.

Sun & ½ shade. Soil moist, open, fert. Some will divide.

G.c., r.g. & edges. Place the low growing spp. where personality is well displayed. Spread 1–3 ft.

S. stolonifera (S. sarmentosa): Easy. Leaves rounded, marbled on thin stems, arching over the plant seeking a spot to lay down a root. Flowers pinkish, in small sprays, spring.

S. 'Apple Blossom': An easy one. Short lived.

S. s. var. *tricolor:* Semi-tender. Leaves conspicuously marbled.

S. cortusifolia var. *fortunei:* Japan. (*S. fortunei* given sp. stature by some authorities.) Another of the Diptera group (as is *S. stolonifera*). Herb. & somewhat tender. Grows in wet rocky places & on banks of streams. Leaves lobed & toothed with reddish undersides; flowers white, shaggy, spotless. Fall. Cv. e.g. 'Wada's Form' (or 'Wada's Variety') has leaves & stalks wine-purple, or mahogany. Rather short flowering shoots.

S. c. var. *compacta:* More dwarf; leaf shape round, scalloped.

S. umbrosa (Robertsonia section): London Pride or Mother-of-Thousands. Eur. & British Isles. Flourishes in native areas but only occasionally lush in N. Am. Leaves round to spatula-shaped, slightly round-toothed, often with a narrow margin of white; leathery. Forms a neat patterned carpet. Flowers small on stalks to 2½ ft., in panicles, white to pink, red-dotted & each petal with a yellow spot.

S. u. var. *primuloides:* Smaller & neater. Leaves look like those of a primose. Flowers pale pink in panicles to 2 ft.

S. u. p. 'Elliot's Variety': With deeper pink color; seek. Source in the Pacific Northwest.

S. michauxii: From SE. U.S. Available in at least one U.S. nursery. 1½ in. × 7 in. Leaves coarsely toothed. Flowers ¼ in. long, white.

S. × arendsii: Hyb. of mixed parentage. Leaves in dense tufts, dissected. Flowers larger, redder.

The mossy *Saxifrages,* the encrusted, the kabschias as well as some representatives from other groups are for the connoisseur. Excel. for pots or troughs. (Rosettes of sev. *Saxifrages* die after blooming. Young rosettes require a number of years to mature enough to bloom.) Here are included only a few examples:

S. longifolia: Pyrenees. *S. longifolia* × *S. callosa* = *S.* 'Tumbling Waters'. Cv. hard to find. Develops offsets.

S. crustata: Alps. Densely tufted with leaves silvered.

S. aizoon 'Baldensis': Light silvery mats. Flowers white.

S. a. var. *rosea:* Encrusted, good to grow between & over rocks. Flowers pink. A "mountain saxifrage".

S. petiophylla: One of the best for a trough.

S. fernandi-coburgii: Balkans. A kabschia. Parent of many hybs. Compact cushions of silvery grey, spiny leaves. Flowers bright yellow, to 2 in. A variegated cv.—very flat & decorative.

Try *S. apiculata, S. andrewsii, S. geum* 'Gentata'.

Schizostylis: IRIDACEAE. Kaffir Lily or Crimson Flag.

S. Afr.

The flower does not suggest a lily or an iris; it resembles more nearly a dwarf gladiolus. Its appearance leads one to expect a bulbous root; but the underground stems are tough, thick & spreading. It appears here & there but not too extensively.

Part shade. Ample water during summer to insure good quality. Divide every 3 years.

Flowers good for cutting; stems to 2 ft. in habitat; in Calif., U.S. closer to 1 ft. Foreground or mid-ground of a mixed planting. Color of type sp. bright crimson; selected clones with various soft colors. Period of bloom differs; growth starts in late spring; height of bloom Aug., Sept. or Oct.

S. coccinea: Grassy leaves. 2 ft. × 9 in. Flowers silky, cup-shaped in slender spikes, Sept. & Oct. 'Mrs. Hegarty', pale pink (1921); 'Tambara', warm, rose-pink (1970). Two of many cvs.

S. biformis: Phillipine Islands. Crowded clumps of soft arching fern-like fronds to 8 in. & finely divided.

S. erythropus: Very lacy.

Selaginella: SELAGINACEAE. Resurrection Plant, Rose-of-Jericho, Clubmoss.

All continents except Antartica.

Evgrn. More or less moss-like plants. Called a "fern ally" because this term is used for non-flowering plants. (Some look something like a fern.) Lacy pattern close to the earth. Spreads to 6 ft. or more.

Shade. Humidity. Soil moist, open. Warmth. Division.

Greatly valued in Japan. Harold Epstein introduced sev. to U.S. Leaves often in 4 rows, those of the lower plane bigger than those of the upper plane. Appearance lacy. Light green or variegated. Seek dwarf var. & cvs. from Japan or from collectors.

S. kraussiana: Afr. & Azores. Creeping, trailing, moss-like, bright green. Stems slender, jointed. Grows rapidly, makes good g.c. Often found under benches in humid greenhouses; likes warmth & moisture. Easy to control. Also *S. k.* 'Variegata'.

S. k. var. *brownii:* More compact & moss-like, from Azores.

Shortia: DIAPENSIACEAE. Oconee Bells or Nippon Bells.

Mtns. of Japan, Taiwan, China & one in E. US.

Evgrn. Stemless, herb., creeping rootstock. 6 in. mat, 1 ft. wide. Excel. foliage. Bloom spring.

High shade. Soil moist, fert. Mulch. Division.

Abundant along Oconee River in N.C. U.S. Fruits a capsule. Distinctive. Sheen of the leaves of the following sp. give certain visibility.

S. galacifolia: To 8 in. Sim. to *Galax* except that leaves are smaller & flowers have longer stems. Leaves roundish, glossy with shallow rounded tips. Soft green, then bronze, then wine-red. Stems to 6 in., March & April. Flowers single, nodding, white or slightly pinkish to 1 in. wide, a bell with toothed edges. Can be difficult. Grow in moist, acid, duff-filled soil in high shade (where *Rhododendron* grows esp. well). Less difficult than *Galax.* Worth a lot of preparation & effort.

S. soldanellöides: Fringe Bells. Petals deeply fringed, pink to rose. Seek *S. s.* var. *ilicifolia.*

S. uniflora: Nippon Bells. Japan. Leaves thin, heart-shaped to 3 in. long with wavy margins. Flowers on slender scapes white to soft pale rose-pink.

S. u. var. *grandiflora:* Flowers bigger.

Stylophorum: PAPAVERACEAE. Celandire-Poppy.

E. N. Am.

Herb. Seldom seen in gardens. Over 1 ft. tall & 1 ft. wide.

Part shade. Cool. Soil moist, rich, leafy, humusy. Seed or division.

Rich, moist woods of E. N. Am. Those from E. Asia not in cultivation. Somewhat resembles the Greater Celandine.

S. diphyllum: A downy, hairy plant for cool woods. To 18 in. Leaves light green with a

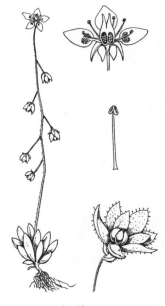

Saxifraga

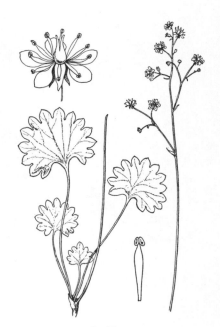

Saxifraga

Synthyris

Tanakaea

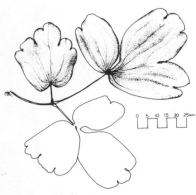

Thalictrum

shape like an oak leaf, but lobes cut to the base. Flowers numerous for many weeks. Yellow poppies, spring & summer. Silvery pods in the fall. Transplants without difficulty.

Synthyris: SCROPHULARIACEAE.
Mtns. of W. N. Am.
Herb. Low. Leaves all basal, broad blades toothed or lobed. Flowers blue-purple (rarely pink or white). 2 stamens, which protrude. Winter & spring.
Light shade. Soil moist & leafy. Division.
Scarce. Observe in the wild.
S. reniformis: Collected in Ore., U.S. by W. Roderick. Flowers Feb.
S. stellulata 'Alba': Plant 12 in. by 8 in. Leaves notched. Flowers almost ½ in. bells. Type color—violet. Order from an alpine specialist.

Tanakaea: SAXIFRAGACEAE.
Japan & China.
Evgrn. & herb. 1 sp. Rare. Low, matting. Leaves excel., glossy, leathery, acute. Choice small plant with decorative form & habit.
Shade. Soil moist, open. Division.
Found among wet rocks in the shade. Try to duplicate habitat. Restrained; yearly enlargement of small clump. To 1 ft. Habit graceful.
T. radicans: Only sp. Creeping rhizomes, slender & rooting as nodes reach porous soil. Leaves not over 3¼ in. long or over 2 in. wide; leathery, irregularly toothed, green above, paler on undersides. Flowers in panicles, on stems 4–12 in., feathery, astilbe-like, tiny, whitish. 10 stamens. Bloom Apr.–June.

Tellima: SAXIFRAGACEAE. Fringecups.
N. Am., Alaska to Calif.
Evgrn. Anagram of "mitella" which does not have the 2 beaks on its seed capsule typical of *Tellima*. One sp. only.
Shade & ½ shade. Soil loose. Water in dry weather. Division.
Small rosettes, restrained growth. Looks well among rocks or on a streamside in association with relatives & ferns.
T. grandiflora & *T. g.* 'Rubra': Flowers on stems to 10 in., sprays of creamy bells in late spring. Greenish look. Good evgrn. g.c. plants.
T. g. 'Purpurea': Leaves purplish in winter.

Thalictrum: RANUNCULACEAE. Meadow Rue.
Eur., N. Afr., N. Asia, Himalaya, Tibet.
Herb. All except *T. minus* & a few others grow to 3 ft. or often 5 ft. Stems are slender & upright; often side branches interweave. The effect of the plant is delicate. Leaves are mostly columbine-like. Flowers have a fluffy look, showy, stunning. Summer & spring.
All spp. will grow in shade although sun is recommended for some. Soil moist. Staking is needed except in the quietest spot or where shrubs will support. Division. Seed.
Plant sev. spp. in a woodland, singly or in groups. Each plant 1–2 ft. w.

T. aquilegifolium: 2–5 ft. tall. Leaves with 3 or 6-lobed leaflets (the sp. with leaves most columbine-like). More or less glaucous. Flowers in umbels in large much-branched panicles. Tiny greenish to white sepals which soon fall. Stamens to ½ in. Handsome.
T. a. var. *album, T. a.* var. *atropurpureum, T. a.* var. *roseum,* the third is pinkish-lilac.
T. delavayi: (commonly sold as *T. dipterocarpum,* which is a distinct sp. though sim.; one distinction—achenes with narrow wings) To 5 ft. Foliage very dainty. Loose panicles of many flowers (not fluffy heads); pyramidal in shape, may be 2 ft. tall by 1 ft. wide. Cup of 4–5 rich lilac petals from which protrude a tuft of cream colored stamens. The white form 'Album' is available.
T. d. 'Hewitt's Double': Seemingly brighter lilac because of the extra petals. Flowering sprays invaluable for upper tracery in a flower arrangement. (No seed)
T. speciossisum (T. glaucum): This is the proper name for plants called *T. flavum* var. *glaucum* & *T. rugosum.* (*T. flavum* & *T. lucidum* have green leaves.) Blue-green foliage remains handsome after flowers have dropped. Flowers in fluffy heads, lemon-yellow.
T. dioicum: N. Am., moist woodlands, Quebec to Mo. To 2½ ft. Leaves 3-lobed. Flowers yellow to greenish yellow. Early spring.
T. polygamum: N. Am., wet meadows & stream banks, Canada to Colo. To 6 ft. 3-lobed leaflets. Flowers whitish in panicles, to 1 ft.; tiny, broadly spaced. The stem will reach up through the branches of a tree, using them for support.
T. minus: Varies greatly in growth habit. Choose a plant to 1 ft. tall with fern-like leaves. Dense clumps. (May be labelled *T. adiantum.*) Yellowish stamens prominent.
T. kuisianum: Japan. Spreads slowly by underground rhizomes. To 5 in. Leaves purplish with 3–9 toothed leaflets. Flowers tiny, lavender-pink to purple sepals. Dilated stamens. A dwarf for r.g. or woods.
T. alpinum: Eur., Asia, N. Am. Usually no taller than 5 in. Leaves few, under 2 in. long. Leaflets toothed at apex. Greenish sepals.

Tiarella: SAXIFRAGACEAE. False Miterwort or Foam Flower.
SE. U.S. & NW. N. Am.
Almost evgrn. Herb. Both creeping & clumping. Leaves almost triangular, thin texture in basal clusters.
Shade. Moisture. Abundant organic matter in soil. Mostly hdy. Division.
Flowers in delicate panicles or racemes with protruding stamens. A dainty erect spike. Wild garden, r.g., or small scale planting. Single plant to 8 in. w. Good with ferns, with Columbine, with *Astilbe.* Bloom, spring into summer.
T. cordifolia: Allegany Foamflower. N. Am., Nova Scotia to Ala. Stolons (above ground runners). Compact mats. Leaves broad to 3 in. across sometimes marbled with bronzy red. Flowers ¼ in., star-shaped, white, in slender spikes, May & June.
T. c. var. *purpurea* & var. *marmorata:* Leaves

marbled with bronzy red. Flowers maroon.

T. wherryi: S. Appalachians, U.S. No stolons. More compact. Leaves nearly heart-shaped, 3-lobed, blotched near bases, turning red in fall. The clump about 8 in. × 8 in. Many stems to a clump. Flowers in small narrow graduating pyramid, slender racemes, narrower than those of *T. cordifolia.* Flowers tiny, narrow-petalled, creamy white tinged pink in early spring. A few through summer. Delicate appearance.

T. polyphylla: China, Japan, Himalayas. Leaves ovate, toothed, 3-lobed, hairy-stalked, to almost 3 in. wide. Stems to 2 ft. Branchless racemes with minute blooms, white to reddish. Petals so threadlike, they are hardly noticeable. (Sometimes there are none.) Grow from seed if plants unavailable.

Tradescantia: COMMELINACEAE. Spider-wort.

Americas, warmer parts.

Herb. & evgrn. A few hardy spp. Mostly dense clumps. Some trailers, some erect.

Shade & ½ shade. Soil moist & fert. for best growth. Ordinary cult. Division.

Foliage not tidy in habit, but shiny & deep green.

T. andersoniana: Group name for hybs. of 3 spp. including *T. virginiana* (of gardens). Both fancy & Latinized names for varieties. Flowers 3-petalled, in clusters on 2 ft. stems.

Cvs. e.g.: 'Osprey', white; 'Innocence', white; 'Purple Dome', brilliant; 'Rubra', deep rose-red. All summer into fall.

Trillium: LILIACEAE. Wake Robin, Wood Lily, Toadshade, Stinking Benjamin.

Americas & E. Asia.

Herb. Sev. spp. tame fairly easily. None are easy or tough. Give a special place. All *Trilliums* have a long life when their garden situation is correct.

Soil moist & fert. in "cool woodland". Plants increase but very slowly. The westerners do not resent year around water. The easterners adapt to western climates except that they do better in the NW. than in Calif.

Characteristics: 3 leaves, 3 calyces, 3 petals. Bloom, spring & summer.

T. grandiflorum: Wake Robin. The easiest & best known E. native. From thick rhizomous roots. To 18 in. × 1 ft. Leaves ovate to nearly round, almost stalkless, to 4½ in. long. The flower is stalked. Flowers at first erect & white, 2 in. across on 2 ft. stems. As they age, the petals fade to pink & nod. (Varies to parts in 4s)

T. g. subsp.: A form with green & white flowers may be a result of a virus; found in a particular rock formation. Whatever— beautiful, the green a pointed sliver in the center of each petal.

T. g. var. *plenum:* Dble. Flowers 2 in. across on 2 ft. stems.

T. g. 'Roseum': Variation with pink petals.

T. ovatum: N. Am.; Brit. Col., Mont. & Calif. Closely related to *T. grandiflorum.* Smaller. 1 ft. × 9 in. Petals narrower & flowers only 2 in. wide. More upright than nodding.

T. o. 'Kenmore': Fully dble. & pale pink; rare.

No petals, no pistils or stamens.

T. o. 'Tillicum': Semi-dble.; no stamens, 9 petals, normal pistil.

T. chloropetalum (T. sessile var. *californicum):* Best known sp. in the U.S. West. Leaves to 6 in. with red mottling. Whorl handsome. Stems reddish green. To 2 ft. Flowers sit on the leaves. Usual color, crimson-maroon (also white or pink). The maroon form sometimes listed as *T. c.* var. *giganteum.* Reproductive parts outstanding.

T. sessile: Toadshade. Eastern counterpart but smaller. To 1 ft. Leaves to 4 in. Leaves not mottled (or mottled occasionally). Petals erect, narrowing to their bases. Normally brown-purple, sometimes yellow or green. Stamens ½ as long as petals.

T. viride: Wood Trillium. Cent. U.S., S. Appalachians & S.C. to Fla. Sim. but stamens with straight anthers ⅓ as long as petals. Sev. forms; leaves mottled or plain green. To 1½ ft. × 1 ft.

T. v. var. *luteum (T. luteum):* Plant smaller than sp. 1 ft. × 9 in. Leaves mottled. Flowers soft-yellow. Lovely!

T. cernuum: N. Am., Newfoundland to Del. & *T. c.* var. *macranthum:* N. Am., mtns. to Ga. & Ala. To 2½ ft. Flowers stalked but stalks nearly concealed. Flowers nod; segments small & recurving. Fragrant. Creamy white, or rarely pink with maroon center, anthers, & green sepals.

T. undulatum: Painted Trillium. N. Am.; S. Canada, Mich., Wis., & Pa. & mtns. to Ga. & Tenn. Prefers acid, wet soil, even a bog. Not easy. To 2 ft. Leaves stalked, blue-green. Flowers stalked. Petals pointed, wavy-edged, to 1½ ft. long. White with pinkish center, stenciled with radiating rosy purple or magenta lines. Sometimes with flowering parts & leaves in 4s or 8s. Only *Trillium* with scarlet fruits.

T. erectum: Birthroot or Lamb's Quarters. N. Am., Nova Scotia to Tenn. Unpleasant odor when crushed. To 1 ft. Leaves large, rich green. Flowers with segments recurving. Nearly erect, long-stalked to 3½ in. across. May have clusters of flowering stems from the one tuber. Flowers mostly maroon with indigo center & paler anthers.

T. e. var. *albiflorum:* Not ill-scented. Segments greenish-white.

T. e. 'Ochroleucum': Whitish green. Charac-teristics of the sp.

T. nivale: Dwarf White or Snow Trillium. N. Am., rich woodlands, Pa. to Mo. Like a miniature *T. grandiflora.* Leaves stalked to 2 ft. Spread 9 in. Flowers short-stalked; white sometimes pink-striped at bottom of petals. Blooms earliest. Only kind which tolerates lack of acidity.

T. rivale: N. Am., Siskyou Mtns. of Calif. & Ore. (Sim. to *T. nivale.*) To 10 in. Flowers long-stalked, small. Petals ascending. White streaked with rose-carmine.

Trollius: RANUNCULACEAE. Globe Flower.

N. hemis.

Herb. Many spp., some flowers globular, others flat to cupped. Leaves shiny green, much cut, plentiful. Petals shiny, also.

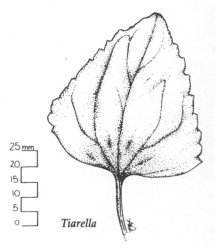

25 mm
20
15
10
5
0

Tiarella

Trillium

Trollius

Vancouveria

0 5 10 15 20 25mm

Viola

Viola

Heights from less than 1 to almost 3 ft. Bloom spring & summer.

Part shade as well as sun. The soil does not have to be waterlogged but it must not dry out. Frequent watering in dry weather. Yearly fertilization. Division.

From damp to wet places. The lower growing kinds are more adaptable to woodland plantings.

T. × cultorum or *T. hybridus:* Popular race of garden plants to which sev. spp. have contributed. Cvs. e.g., 'Goldquell', 'Golden Queen', 'Orange Globe', 'Earliest of All', & 'Canary Bird'. Sometimes 3 ft. tall × 18 in. w. Leaves deeply divided & lush.

T. ledebourii: NE. Asia. 2–3 ft. × 18 in. w. Mostly orange with petaloid centers. Blooms later than most. A cv. 'Golden Queen'.

T. pumilus: To 1 ft. Leaves glossy, cut into 5-toothed segments. Flowers solitary, yellow, sometimes green-tinged. 8 spreading sepals, petals hardly longer than the stamens.

T. laxus, to 1½ ft., cream-colored.

T. acaulis, to 1 ft. Flowers deep yellow with 5–9 sepals & 12–16 petals shorter than the stamens.

Uvularia: LILIACEAE. Bellwort or Merrybells. E. N. Am.

Herb. Related to *Polygonatum.* Combine with this and *Dicentra* and *Eucomis.*

Succeeds in shade but when wet enough tolerates sun. Mulch & ann. fertilizer helpful. Seed. Root cuttings.

Increases in a woodland site. Green or cream on curving stem.

U. grandiflora: Stems arch to 2 ft. Leaves fresh green, perfoliate. Flowers creamy yellow, hang below the stems.

U. g. 'Variegata': Good pattern.

U. perfoliata: A smaller plant. Leaves ovate to 3½ in. Flowers pale yellow, bells more conspicuous since they are carried above the leaves. Inner surfaces of perianth segments clothed with short glandular hairs.

U. sessilifolia: Ground cover.

U. carolinianum: 10 in. with flowers to 1 in.

U. pudica: Not perfoliate. To 1 ft.

Vancouveria: BERBERIDACEAE. Inside-Out-Flower or Redwood Ivy.

N. Am., Pacific Northwest.

Evgrn. & herb. (*V. hexandra,* herb.) Related to *Epimedium.* 3 spp. Spread by slender, underground rhizomes. Clump 8 in. × 3 ft. wide. Leaves mostly glossy. Leaflets mostly hastate. Flowers with petals mostly recurved. Bloom, summer.

Shade & ½ shade. Soil moist, porous. Division.

Plant on a slope or on flat, level ground; superior g.c. for woods or shady site.

V. hexandra: To 1½ ft. Thinnish leaflets. Flowers in loose drooping panicles, up to 30; white.

V. planipetala (V. parviflora): To 1 ft. Leaves 2, but sometimes 3 times divided, ovate leaflets with slightly wavy margins; dark green, glossy on upper sides. Flowers white, tiny in loose panicles, 25–50, unequal sized parts. Probably, the most common & the fastest spreader.

V. chrysantha: Leaves evgrn.; quite leathery; 2–5 times divided; leaflets to 1¼ in., crisped at the margins. Dark green above. Flowers up to 15 in very open panicles. Golden yellow. Not over ½ in. long.

Viola: Some species prefer shade. See general plant descriptions.

9. Planting on a Sloping Site

Treatment varies according to the size of a sloping site and more especially its steepness. When does a slope become a bank? No way to state categorically, let us just say that a long and steep slope is a bank. The smallest slope is just a strip of uneven ground for which you will find some suggestions in the chapter on strips together with the idea that a short slope may be made level by terracing with a wood, rock, brick, etc. retaining wall. Suppose, however, that this rather narrow slope remains sloping. Does it have a boundary? What does it abut upon? If its lower edge meets a path, or a terrace we must limit ourself to plants with stems somewhat restrained lest we be clipping continually along the path edge.

It might be best to look for sprawlers instead of trailers. One of the dwarf *Potentillas* will keep to its place while one of the trailing species will be a nuisance. If the sloping bed is bounded, especially on the lower side, you have less worry about the trailing habit. Stems which travel, rooting as they go, may be confined by this barricade. You can use one of the ground covers like *Duchesnea* or *Ajuga* or *Rubus*. *R. calycinoides* has very decorative foliage; it really does better if it has room to roam. Now go to the chapter on strips for examples of plants which mix well in a narrow space.

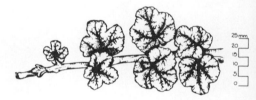

Rubus

With the short slope out of the way we proceed to consider a bigger slope— approaching the "bank" status. There will no doubt be a mixture of perennials put together with imagination and every hope of success.

With only a little more space on our slope, it is best not to choose all trailers, or creepers. A design is called for which rises as well as falls; the ups will be produced by erect stems while the downs will derive from horizontal stems. Some mounds should be introduced since we could not get enough variation in shapes without some circles.

Small, low-growing, fragrant herbs are most suitable for a slope. Planted in the foreground, they are available for touching and cutting and also enjoying the little flowers in their season. In such a situation, plant savory and thyme. Summer Savory, *Satureja hortensis* (Satureya), is desirable for the delicacy of the flavor of its leaves, but it is an annual and therefore its cousin, Winter Savory, *Satureja montana,* is preferred since the plant is not only useful, but is also attractive and it continues to produce its crop in health and vigor year after year. It is never higher than 15 inches, but this tight subshrub is at least that wide when in full leaf and hardly smaller after it has been sheared. Clip at the beginning of the flowering season for drying and clip again in the fall for the renewal of the health of the clump. The stiff, narrow to roundish leaves, on manylittle stems, are never more than an inch long and produce an orderly dark green

Satureja

Origanum

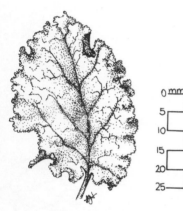

0 mm
5
10
15
20
25

Teucrium

Penstemon

look. When the mound is in full bloom with its many short stems bearing whitish flowers in whorls, the plants are nearly covered with contented bees. Winter Savory looks well along the edge of a raised bed. It can be planted in a row, or scattered here and there and in places where half the shrublet lies along the top of a wall.

Both of these savorys are from the Mediterranean, but a third is native to California and gave its name to the area that is now San Francisco. Yerba Buena, *Satureja douglasii*, is a creeping, spreading perennial and should only be planted where it can spread without usurping the space of a more valuable plant; although the foliage is sparse, it is attractive. There are flowers in both spring and fall. Its dried leaves make a tea which many people find refreshing.

The savorys like a sandy soil and the good drainage which a slope provides.

Thymes like the same conditions; let them sit upon a wall or trail down the bulge of a slope where you can brush the foliage and breathe the delightful aroma. *Thymus vulgaris* is the culinary thyme and it forms a dense hummock less than a foot high. Harvesting by shearing keeps the plant tidy, but to use the harvest one must separate the leaves from the stems and this can be tedious: they are both so small. No matter, the thymes are all attractive whether used in the kitchen or not. This sp. has a good dark green foliage, but is yellowish in 'Aureus' or green and white in 'Variegatus'. The latter, unlike many variegated sports, is very floriferous.

It is not always easy to identify thymes. Some of the species are quite variable and *Hortus III* says simply that most of them grown in American gardens "appear to be of confused identity and often erroneously named."

The distinctive odors of certain thymes are of some help in identification. *T. × citriodorus* is lemon scented, as is *T. serpyllum,* sometimes called Lemon Thyme. But there are cultivars with differing leaf colors, 'Silver Queen' being silver and 'Aureus' gold. A thyme with a dependably unusual scent is *T. herba-barona,* which has the fragrance of caraway. One Thyme has seed clusters which look like conifer cones.

One of my favorite thymes is commonly known as Wooly Thyme. It is a very flat creeper with only an occasional flower, but it makes a soft grey-green mat that will spread out over slopes and walls and interweave with the other mats and the rocks.

One of the flattest thymes is *T. caespititius.* It grows not more than three inches tall, but is usually shorter. *T. praecox* is another low-growing one. Its common name is Mother-of-Thyme and it has cultivars with differently colored flowers. *T. p.* 'Coccineus' is desirable for its crimson flowers and 'Splendens' for its red ones. (For a hangover, add one tsp. thyme, one tsp. honey and a pinch of salt to one cup of boiling water.)

With the thymes and savorys, combine another small herb good for a slope. One is Sweet Marjoram, *Origanum majorana (Majorana hortensis).* It will grow in dry rocky places; it is too tender to be perennial in some climates. Its somewhat trailing stems bear greyish leaves and short spikes of white flowers. The leaves dry for flavoring soups and stews.

O. vulgare is the stronger flavored oregano, but this is a variable species and if you want the very pungent flavor, it is well to test a leaf of any specimen before buying it. Some of the scents seem quite dull.

One of my favorite herbs is *Origanum dictamnus,* Crete Dittany, but not for its flavor. It is never cut to eat, only to renew the vigor of the little plant. It is aromatic, but really grown for its cosmetic value. Round, greyish, fuzzy leaves decorate arching and trailing stems usually less than one foot long. Small purplish pink flowers bloom summer to fall. The rose-purple cone-like fruits are reminiscent of the imbricated sections of the rattle of a rattlesnake. This charming Mediterranean herb may also be used in a container, a rock garden or a hanging basket; to rub the foliage is pleasing for the texture as well as the scent.

If blooming time of the bank covers coincides, do the flower colors blend and augment each other? Plant a drift of Dittany and *Origanum pulchella* and any other herb with pale lavender flowers. *Teucrium scorodonia* combines artistically with the *Origanums.* At the bottom plant *Aster alpinus* with a deeper bluer, lavender color, or one of the dwarf hybrids, e.g. 'Dark Beauty', deep violet. One takes the eye to the other. (The mat of the *Aster* has thick roots which hold the soil in place.) *Androsace* is a good holder and its color is another shade which combines well—a pinkish lavender. Go all the way to magenta if you want to make your scheme brighter. Put blues with your crimson, cerise and lavenders. *Penstemon heterophyllus* is blue, *Penstemon barbatus* is lavender, *Penstemon b.* 'Coccineus' is crimson.

We could stay here all day planning combinations but let us face the big slope, the real banks. One slopes away from us, another rises above us; both are large enough for a few shrubs. The shrubs, especially on the bank going downhill, will be at the bottom serving the dual purposes of holding the soil (preventing erosion) and acting as a backdrop for smaller plants. There is no time to talk about the many shrubs and small trees which would be appropriate. To name a few: *Hypericum androsaemum* (Tutsan), *Grevillea tripetela, Rhamnus* 'Eve Case', *Rosmarinus officinalis, Myrceugenella, Ugni molinae, Correa* 'Ivory Bells', *Olearea stellulata*. These shrubs will hold the earth and also contribute to the personality of the planting.

Salvia

The *Hypericum* is rounded; it has yellowish green leaves (bronze when young), yellow flowers and fruits, first peach colored, then red, then black. Perennials which would go well with this well-behaved *Hypericum* are *Linum flavum, Solidago* or *Solidaster* and *Papaver californica* for the yellow spectrum, *Zauschneria* for its complimentary orange-red to reflect the color of autumn leaves. And then another color for contrast; the lavender of *Lavandula* and of some Sages, perhaps *Salvia pratensis*, Meadow Clary, and a tall, slender, dark, bright one, *Salvia nemerosa* 'East Friesland'.

So many spp. of *Salvia*, and what better site for all of them than a slope or bank. This is a fine stage on which to compare their fascinating characteristics. It is good culturally because of the excellent drainage provided and the open exposure. What a mixture of fragrance on a warm evening. And in midday their area makes a hummingbird heaven; we hear that hummingbirds have territories but it is possible that when there is a superior feasting place they share the riches. *Salvia* is one of the genera which is enjoyable for the collector. To add to the numerous forms available there are always new discoveries; they all mix and match so well together, from 6 ft. shrubs to 6 in. ground covers. It does not spoil the satisfaction of the collector to allow a few outsiders in a planting. The *Correas* and the *Oleareas* mentioned above blend very well with the bush Salvias; the *Artemisias* and the *Origanums* dwarf or trailing add finishing touches to the herbaceous Salvias. There are other genera with various spp. for which a slope is a superior site, to mention only two, *Geranium* and *Eriogonum* and they promise fulfillment for the urge of a collector. *Salvia* however is the most versatile; the shapes of the various flowers are pictorial. Eg. *S. autumnalis, S. clevelandii, S. leucophylla, S. sonomiensis, S. elegans, S. leucantha, S. patens, S. quaranitica, S. uliginosa, S. cacaliaefolia, S. garandiflora* var. *pitcheri, S. coccinea* 'Crimson King.'

Salvia

Have you noticed most of the spp. considered so far are upright, one or two quite stiffly erect? We must intersperse some low mounds and some tailers. The Lavender from Spain, *Lavandula stoechas* mounds as does that wonderful grey-white plant *Calocephalus brownii*. We can allow some Thymes to fill in the spaces and plant some Yerba Buena to trail down from the upper edges. As you have already guessed this is a drought tolerant bank but not one to be neglected. It has only a few natives in the combination planting, although there could easily be several others. *A native plant is no panacea for neglect.* Some are useful and beautiful. Never select them because you want plants to go it alone. Many spp. of the genus *Gaultheria* are excellent for slopes in the shade, but some are tricky. One of the easiest is *G. procumbens*, a wide spreading ground over.

Let's try the other bank. We look up instead of down and the shrubs act as backdrop first and then accents to break the sharp descent of the slope. The shrubs could be *Vaccinium ovatum* or *Hydrangea quercifolia*. These two are densely branched and green and make a curtain at the top against which to plan a complimentary mixture. *Vaccinium ovatum* is included since the bank may be in partial shade at the top. (*V. oxycoccus* will be described in the paragraphs on trailers.) Smaller shrubs might be the prostrate *Cotoneaster dammeri* with good autumn color and *Erica carnea* 'Springwood White' for a dense mound of light green when its white flowers have been sheared away. The perennials should all have interesting foliage. Examples: violets can be spotted here and there; small sprawling *Penstemon* in strategic spots and *Mimulus* in the wetter places. If the bottom of the bank is retained by a board or a wall, some perennials with trailing stems can be placed here and there to spill over. I think again of good old *Geranium incanum*; to be innovative let's plant *Helianthemum* cultivars. A plant with long trailing stems like *Helianthemum* must be placed quite a ways up the bank to give the stems room to begin their fall. This is a biggish bank which you are planting and the possibilities have only been touched upon. For a smaller bank you would select smaller subjects both above and below.

Hypericum, St. John's Wort is known for its shrubby spp.; there are some delicate low spp. which spread on a slope. They are studded in summer with yellow

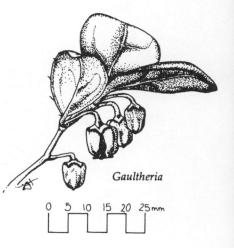

Gaultheria

0 5 10 15 20 25mm

Hypericum

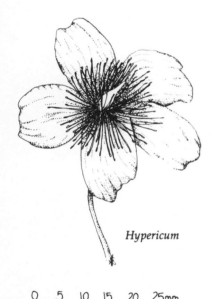

Hypericum

0   5   10   15   20   25mm

Alchemilla

flowers bristling with stamens. See suggestions on the best of trailers.

You have a bank in the shade. At the top you have room for a few shrubs, perhaps *Vaccinium* again, *Viburnum* spp., and *Osmanthus* spp. and some ferns—tree-ferns if you have a really big bank. Towards the bottom put plants which like it cool—*Francoa* spp., *Heuchera* spp., *Saxifraga* spp. and which look well together with their spikes of different height and density. As trailers, you could use *Alchemilla*, although it likes the sun as well. In particular, the cousins *Vancouveria* spp. and *Epimedium* spp. really grace a slope. As a focal point, plant a dwarf cascading shrub with a rock to tumble over. It might be a dwarf cranberry which seems to cling to a rock. Add ferns of the matting kind like *Azederach,* on the lower part of the bank, to repeat the ferns above. The base is held by logs. No splash of color on this shady bank, only a little cream in the foreground and the sparkle of berries in the fall.

The base of a bank, the one which slopes toward you, is a special situation which I call the "chin" of the bank. The contour descends from the "shoulder" near the top, not too evenly, to reach a final last rounded dip. This chin should be planted thickly with perennials possessing sturdy roots. These when mature will hold the soil without the assistance of logs, boards, railroad ties, rocks or bricks—meanwhile, use temporary supports which can later be removed. On the other hand, you may find that one of these material soil holders—"retaining walls"—suits your landscaping very well. Whatever you choose you may still want to plant the chin of the bank with perennials or shrubs which will spill over the top of your short wall.

Suggestions for a "chin": *Sedum* spp., Thymes, *Ceratostigma,* Strawberries, Violets, even Ivy if you can find a dwarf with interesting foliage. Ivy Geranium if you are willing to keep it groomed. *Vinca* spp., if you can find the very small cultivar 'Atropurpurea'. *Myoporum debile* has trailing branches to four feet; therefore you must plant it high on the bank. You must be aware of future length when you place—especially true of trailing shrubs and subshrubs.

Some shrubs which trail: *Hermannia, Pimelia, Cistus, Jasminum* (especially *Jasminum parkeri*), (See chapter "Subshrubs") *Rosmarinus, Euonymus, Lorepetalum, Coprosma kirkii* (or *C. repens*). Perhaps the most attractive shrub for a bank is *Arctostaphylos uva-ursi.* Another western native is *Ribes viburnifolia* but it needs full shade. There is *Baccharis;* obtain the cultivar which better withstands a very wet winter, 'Pidgeon Point'. *Juniper,* if you must, but only Shore Juniper or a very low cultivar like 'Bar Harbor'. If you admire conifers, look for several which cascade, e.g. *Taxus baccata* 'Repandens';* there is even a prostrate Redwood. *Grevillea:* there are many decorative species. Several *Gaultherias* are subshrubs for shade.

You will not buy a piece of property just for sloping ground, I guess, but be glad if you have a bank, it makes a good showcase. All manner of trailers increase the length of their stems immeasurably when grown on a bank. Many become wider and more luxuriant also. A slope can easily be curtained with foliage drapery while flowers are added in their season. And there are several other suitable sites for trailers.

Top of a stump, top of a rock, top of a wall: fringers, spillers, spreaders, sprawlers, trailers.

Here we have three sites where perennials which have a habit of growth suitable to the situation are needed. Several kinds send out stems more or less horizontally from the crown, sometimes increasing gradually in length, and may be called spreaders. Spreaders may sprawl, and often when the stems reach an edge they spill. Other kinds have stems which elongate considerably more, trailing from the central crown and descending when there is an opportunity. These might be called "hangers". There are kinds with stems of in-between length used on the "fringes" of a garden bed where the edge needs the softening of spreading stems.

The softeners include *Alchemilla, Arabis, Arenaria, Aubrieta, Campanula, Cerastium, Dianthus, Geranium, Heliotropium, Iberis, Saponaria, Sedum, Silene* and *Nepeta. Nepeta* has many stems which first arch then droop; the fall is greater if their position is raised.

Suppose the bed needs a small retaining wall (board or rocks or brick); the ample growth of *Nepeta* will drape over the edge and nearly hide the wall. *Nepeta* can also be placed in a drift within the bed; then the stems lie upon each other; a mass of grey plus lavender results.

Other exemplary candidates are *Geranium incanum* already mentioned and *Silene maritima.* The first has quantities of stems branched and tangled, enlarging the mound with the new growth meanwhile spilling over a barricade. The *Silene* also makes a mound and its stems descend abruptly when they reach an edge. In the chapter on containers *Silene* is mentioned as a plant to hang from a pot. And two more: a dwarf *Hypericum, H. cerastoides* makes a waterfall of tiny stems; *Alchemilla alpina* or *A. guatemalensis* spreads and runs ad infinitum. There are several other excellent spp. of *Alchemilla*. The stems of *A. mollis* are shorter than most; but it is a fine spreader and its beautiful leaves make a pattern close to the earth. The stems of *A. guatemalense* are probably the longest of any. They trail 6 ft. or more down a slope tumbling over each other but in very orderly fashion. The leaves are scalloped and crimped and incised and have a sheen which gleams as the light catches the surface.

It is interesting that stems which have a chance to hang will become considerably longer than those which lie on the ground. It is also true of "climbers"—when stems have some object to which to attach or to twine around much greater length occurs. An Ivy Geranium has been known to climb up through a hedge, or even a tree, and spread its blossoms as a bonnet at the top. These habits are useful when we want to cover something.

Let us consider the stump. Stumps look part of the scene in a forest but often untidy in a garden. Sometimes a stump can be used as a stand, just the right height above ground. On the other hand, you might want to cover the stump or at least to camouflage it with stems long and numerous. You have seen Honeysuckle, Roses (old-fashioned) or Jasmine used in this manner. Vines are often too rampant, with stems seeking to cover neighboring plants in addition to the elected stump. You must not be enticed by a plant too luxuriant, like Ivy or *Polygonum* for you will be unsuccessful in keeping it within bounds.

A species *Clematis* could be chosen; *C. tangutica* is easy to prune and has delightful seed heads. *C. lanuginosa* grows to only six feet, has creamy white flowers and a myriad of silky seed heads. But *Clematis* is mostly deciduous; do you want a year around leafy cover?

I have a couple of candidates from the subshrub category. *Whipplea modesta* both sprawls and hangs, with semi-woody stems, for some distance and in a graceful cascade. A big shrub, *Jovellana*, will cover a stump in a different manner; the many branches, densely clothed with foliage tumble over the top.

Some creeping perennials like stumps so much they root in the crevices of the bark. *Jasminum parkeri* is a good example. Its luxuriant growth can make a thing of beauty of the ugliest stump.

Here is a little soft-stemmed vine which climbs trees attaching with tiny tendrils to flakes of bark. The white form of *Cymbalaria*, Kenilworth Ivy, is less rampant than the lavender and looks temporarily like a lacy tracery. One advantage is that it is easy to pull; it seeds itself very readily. There is a delightful *Tropaeolum, T. tricolor*, with small and bright flowers which is a tree climber with just a little assistance.

Convolvulus mauritanicus is a rampant trailer and its stems would drape themselves over any obstacle in its path.

Let us leave stumps and think of rocks. Again we must not choose a spreader with stems so questing that they will cover completely. If you have a nice rock, you will find that you want to thin any vigorous covering from time to time to let the best part of the rock show. Prostrate dwarf subshrubs are the best accompaniment for rocks. Their stems seem to embrace the contours. *Putoria*, somewhat woody, also prefers a rock over which to drape its stems. I will give three other examples:

Genista kewensis, Grevillea humisifusa, Vaccinium oxycoccus: the stems have amazing length; they are numerous, slender and trail down the hill after having clambered over a rock.

Perhaps my favorite draping perennial is the *Gentian* called Willow Gentian. It likes a pile of rocks, for the stems arch rather than curve. It may need one or two *Helleborus foetidus* behind it to hold it up enough for us to enjoy. I am partial to *Gentian* in general; this one is not temperamental and improves every year—perhaps in the fourth year a dozen stems ending in a series of deep blue-purple narrow trumpets. There is a white form. Please find in the Woodland chapter some other candidates to accompany rocks.

But there are rocks in the sun also. Some of the thymes, such as *T. praecox*, will develop long descending stems when they have a place to hang but others will climb a rock and seem to become a part of it—Interesting flowers and seed pods add to the decoration.

Helianthemum performs well when it has a place to hang; the stems elongate on

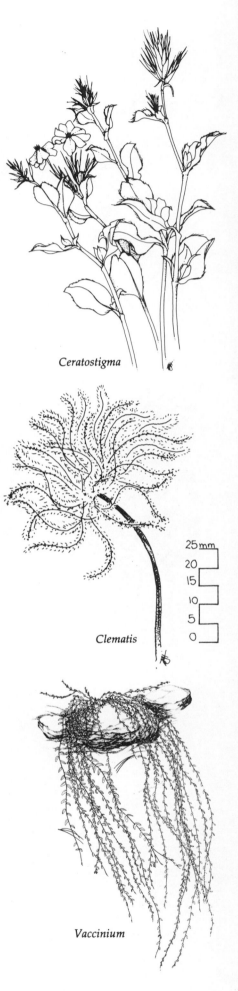

Ceratostigma

Clematis

25 mm
20
15
10
5
0

Vaccinium

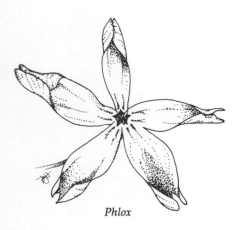

Phlox

Anagallis

Anagallis

a slope (as noted in the previous chapter). A rock placed in its path will be trimmed, or perhaps covered. There are many beautiful colors; a pale yellow cultivar associates well with granite.

Phlox is a spreader not a hanger. It likes the drainage provided by a slope. A rock in proximity makes a partnership with the mound of *Phlox,* the *P. subulata* with leaves bright green and prickly looking. Excellent cvs. e.g.: 'Intensity', 'Cerise', 'Scarlet Flame', 'Scarlet Ruby', 'Schneewitchen', a tiny white.

True hangers can, of course, be grown over stumps and over rocks but find their best role decorating a wall. From the top of a wall they may hang inches or feet. I will talk about some hangers such as *Sedum sieboldii* and *Campanula isophylla* as candidates for containers and "hanging baskets". They are especially appropriate at the top of a wall. How high is the wall? The short wall was considered when we talked about fringers.

Now let's look at some walls which are waist to head height. To the long hangers we must add *Asparagus, Pelargonium peltatum,* Ivy Geranium and a *Lotus.* The best *Lotus* is *L. bertholettii,* well behaved and less apt to seed all over. The flowers cover the many trailing stems for weeks. Always our thoughts move to vines for wall treatment but these can be combined with trailing perennials. Semi-trailing vines are good choices such as the shrubby jasmines. You may like the look of the wall and do not want to *cloak* it with plant material.

Whatever, some pruning is involved. Thinning is a better word. For the best stems are chosen to stay while others are cut back to the crown.

Now there is one particular case of pruning which is noted in "Containers". The cascade *Chrysanthemum* entails more pinching (and tieing) than trimming and thinning. A plant, even less than perfectly trained, is fantastic at the top of a wall.

Perhaps if you do not already have a wall you will now build one somewhere—leaving room for planting at its top.

PERENNIALS FOR SLOPES

Alchemilla	Goniolimon	Scaevola
Anagallis	Helianthemum	Sedum
Antirrhinum	Helichrysum	Sempervivium
Artemisia	Heliotropium	Silene
Arabis	Heuchera	Sisyrinchium
Arctostaphylos	Hieracium	Sphaeralcea
Asarina	Hippocrepis	Stachys
Asparagus	Hypericum	Statice
Asphodeline	Iberis	Teucrium
Asphodelus	Jasminum	Thymus
Aurinia	Keckiella	Tropaeolum
Campanula	Lantana	Vaccinium
Canarina	Limonium	Veronica
Cerastium	Lotus	Vinca
Ceratostigma	Lysimachia	Whipplea
Cheiranthus	Malvastrum	Zauschneria
Chrysanthemum	Monardella	
Clematis	Nepeta	
Convolvulus	Onosma	
Crucianella	Origanum	
Cymbalaria	Pelargonium	
Dianthus	Penstemon	
Duchesnea	Phlox	
Erica	Potentilla	
Eriogonum	Prunella	
Eriophyllum	Pterocephalus	
Euphorbia	Putoria	
Gaultheria	Rubus	
Genista	Salvia	
Gentiana	Saponaria	
Geranium	Satureya	

Alchemilla: See General Plant Descriptions.
Three spp. esp. good for slopes: *A. conjuncta,* Lady's Mantle; *A. pectinatus* & *A. guatemalense:* Leaves crinkled, palmate, shiny, yellow-green. Flowers tiny sprays, chartreuse.

Anagallis: PRIMULACEAE. Pimpernel.
All continents, esp. trop. Afr.
Herb. Ann., bien., per. Habit various. Small. Sprawls to 1 ft.
Sun & shade. Soil med. Semi-hdy. Seed.
(Not to be confused with *Anaphalis* which is erect, with small flower-heads, COMPOSITAE.)
Blue color of flowers striking in the blue spp. of *Anagallis.* Sev. buds will open as current flowers fade.
A. linifolia: A per. in nature. Its spp. & vars. sometimes available.
A. fruticosa var. *breweri:* Not listed in ordinary encyclopedias. Worth seeking. R.H.S. states *A. fruticosa* is a synonym of *A. linifolia,* "annual somewhat woody . . ."
A. monelli 'Phillipsii': Bien. but often seeds itself. Leaves usually in threes. Flowers longer than the type. Spain. Strong blue. Sometimes listed as a form of *A. linifolia.*
A. arvensis: Scarlet Pimpernel, Poor-Man's Weatherglass or Shepherd's Clock, so-called because the flowers close as sun retires. An ann. weed but not a pest. A rare blue form as well as common orange-red.

Artemisia: COMPOSITAE. Wormwood.
Eur., N. Am., Asia.
Herb. & evgrn. Foliage often intricately dissected, mostly grey. Tall & wide, to 4 ft. high & low spreaders, also to 4 ft. wide. Sev. dwarves. See For a Large Site.
Sun. Summer & fall. Med. water. Soil more lean than rich. Groom. Some spp. semi-

tender. Cuttings. Division.
Some are called Dusty Miller. Some aromatic. Some medicinal.
A. dracunculus: Tarragon. Vaunted for vinegar.
The following spp. are low herb. foliage plants for edges, for foregrounds, for banks or for r.g. Flowers may be pruned before buds open. Less than 1 ft. tall, often well over 1 ft. wide. Plant all 4 if you can but have at least one.
A. pycnocephala: Sandhill Sage. N. Am.: Ontario, Can.; Ark., N. Mex., Calif., U.S. Sprawling subshrub, growing from a rhizome. Compact when young; unkempt looking with age. Keep cut back. Leaves white, hairy beneath. Velvet look.
A. schmidtiana or *A. schmidtii:* A. s. 'Nana', 'Silver Mound', 'Angels's Hair', 'Silver Frost'. The cvs. available. Soft & feathery. Bright silvery filigree mats. Flowers grey, twice cleft.
A. frigida: Fringed Wormwood. N. Am.: Alaska to Tex., U.S. Subshrub with tufted base of prostrate stems to 20 inches h. To 1½ ft. wide. Silvery-silky-hairy, 4 times pinnately cleft, making linear segments. Silvery down. Winter dormant period.
A. canescens, of gardens: Chain Link. The most intriguing & the most reliably spreading carpet to 1½ ft. wide. Detailed pattern of silver leaves, their coils entwining. Once named *A. versicolor,* a listed name only. *A. splendens* is sim. Both have been confused with *A. armeniaca.*

Asarina: See Containers Plant Descriptions.
Stems to 1 ft. long will drape over a low wall. Or climb. Allow to trail or provide a framework around which tendrils can twist.

Asphodeline: LILIACEAE. Jacob's Rod. Yellow Asphodel.

Artemisia

Artemisia

Hardiness: When hardy, I have said nothing about hardiness. I have used semi-hardy to indicate that a plant is less than perfectly hardy. This plant needs protection against frosts to survive. I have used tender to indicate that the plant will not tolerate *any* frost. I have used semi-tender to mean that a plant may survive a short period of frost but not prolonged frost or often repeated frost. This plant may lose its above ground portions but its roots may survive if mulch is used to protect the root area.

Explanation of the order: When there are varying heights in a genus, the spp. are often described in groups, Tall, Medium and Low. When the spp. are divided according to use, sometimes a group will appear under one heading and sometimes another group under a different heading. When there are two or more entries under different headings of various spp. a general plant description will occur under only one of the headings but reference to the list which includes the plant is included.

The spp. are not listed alphabetically. One sp. follows another because it is related or similar in appearance. One sp. may follow another because it has a similar habit. Occasionally the better known spp. are described first and spp. hard to find are given at the end of the spp. descriptions of the genus. Very often a dwarf sp. will come at the end both because it is smaller and because it is more uncommon. Occasionally the spp. will be arranged one below the other because I like the second better. You will have to judge from the text whether I like it equally well. I put them this way so that you might better see relationships horticulturally. When you wish to find a certain sp. in the descriptions, you may find its position in the text by means of the alphabetical index. Please do not read the descriptions of the spp. as if the whole were a jumble.

Hybrids: When a cv. name follows directly after the genus name, no name has been given to the hybrid and the parentage of the cross has not been recorded.

Asphodeline

Mediterranean region & W. Asia.

Herb. Narrowly linear leaves in tufts. Clump forming. Erect stems clothed in grassy foliage.

Sun. Water in periods of drought. Division.

Known in antiquity. Homer writes of asphodel meadows of the dead. Equally appropriate for a flat site. Bloom spring or summer.

A. lutea: To 4 ft. Pale grey-green, slim leaves. Flowers top of stiff stems, in spikes; fragrant. Buff bracts nearly as long as flower. *A. l.* var. *flore-pleno:* Double.

A. liburnica: 2 ft., with green midrib on yellow flowers. Upper part of stem naked of foliage.

A. taurica: Unbranched, erect to 2 ft. Densely leafy at base of raceme. White striped with green in dense raceme to 12 in.

Asphodelus: LILIACEAE. Asphodel.
Mediterranean region, S. Eur.

Long grassy leaves in dense basal clumps. Almost leafless flower stems to 3 ft. Closely related to *Asphodeline.*

Sun. Soil deep. Sandy loam. Division.

Sev. spp., e.g. *A. aestivus, A. albus.* Flowers white, yellow, or pink, funneled-shaped on tall erect stems, some branching, some not. Brownish reverses or brownish tint of the calyx and veins makes the color muted. Uncommon.

Aurinia: CRUCIFERAE. Basket of Gold, Golden Tuft.
Eur.

Partially evgrn. 7 spp. which were formerly a section of the genus *Alyssum.* Tufted rosettes.

Sun. Soil med. Cut back after flowering. Division.

In early spring, flowers can almost cover leaves. Spreads at moderate rate to form mat less than 1 ft. high. For bedding, r.g., foregrounds of borders; dry walls, top of a wall. G.c.

A. saxitile var. *compacta:* A form less lax than the sp.

A. s. var. *citrina* (*A. s.* var. *lutea* & *A. s.* var. *sulphurea*): Flowers soft yellow.

A. s. var. *plenum:* Dble.

A. s. 'Luteum': Evgrn., an improved form of the well-known Basket of Gold.

A. petraea: 6–24 in. high. Leaves toothed & wavy-edged. Flowers in racemes, yellow.

Calocephalus: COMPOSITAE.
Coastal areas of Aust.

Wide, nearly all-white rigid subshrub; slender branches entangling. An uneven, dense mound, to 2 ft., the spread wider. Brittle look.

Sun. Sandy porous soil. Dislikes wet soil but unharmed by water on foliage. Tolerant of salt spray. Semi-tender; only warm climates. Flower spray may be sheared or left on plant when dry. Cuttings, best taken in autumn and rooted in sand.

Greek kalos = beautiful & kephale = head, referring to the clusters. Clusters made of tiny flower heads; bloom in summer. Twigs good for small bouquets. Collections featuring grey. The wooly hairs are so short

as to be invisible.

C. brownii (*Leucophyte brownii*): Stiff, brittle, compact subshrub to 2 ft. Tangled branchlets will cascade over a bank or wall. Stems & leaves, whitest-grey. Flower sprays stand erect above foliage mass a few in., white to palest yellow as the flowers age. Not obnoxious when spent. Can be sheared, early fall.

Campanula: CAMPANULACEAE. Bellflower.
N. hemis., esp. Mediterranean.

Herb. & evgrn. Many spp.; many with evgrn. handsome basal leaves. Many forms, low mats to towering spikes. Many with bell-shaped flowers, others star-shaped.

Part sun but some shade in the hottest part of the day. Drainage. Soil reasonably fert. Water in dry weather. Feed in early spring. Repot those in containers annually to refresh. Certain alpine kinds need special r.g. conditions & attention. Combat slugs. Keep crowns clear of clutter (some danger from water molds). Division.

Many, many kinds; look for those not covered here. See page 38 & 39 in Alan Bloom's *Perennials for your Garden* for color pictures of *Campanulas.* See Perennials for Containers for trailers. Spp. following, divided according to habit—short to tall.

Following are examples of short kinds:

C. poscharskyana: Dalmatia. Wide spreader. Trailing stems: elongated when they hang or lean. Flowers stars, sev. mos. of summer; lavender, white or uncommonly pink. White one is best.

C. portenschlagiana (*C. muralis*): *C. p.* 'Bavarica', superior form. Contained spreader. Stems to 5 in., leaves small, dark green.

C. cochlearifolia (*C. pusilla*): Mtns. in Eur. Confined spreader. Stems to 6 in. Leaves tiny, numerous, shiny. Flowers tiny, perfect, partly nodding. Cvs., e.g., 'Oakington Blue', 'Cambridge Blue', 'Blue Tit'.

C. c. 'Hallii' & *C. c.* 'Alba': Diminutive, white, numerous dangling bells.

C. c. 'Miranda': Flowers tiny, light "China" blue. Only for specialists' gardens. Unsurpassed for r.g. Container. Trough.

C. carpatica: Tussock Harebell. Carpathian Mtns. Looks like a pincushion. Basal leaves small & dense. Stems 6–15 in. Flowers wide bells, upturned. Many garden variants & cvs.—purple to white. Parent of sev. hybs.

Cvs., e.g.: 'Dark Star'; 'White Star'; 'Moonlight', very light blue; 'Blue Gem', tiny.

C. c. var. *turbinata:* A geographical form with stems somewhat procumbent; bells somewhat smaller & longer than those of the type.

C. c. var. *turbinata albescens:* Very pale blue.

C. × haylodgensis: C. carpatica × C. cochlearifolia. Wide spreader. Sprawls. Flowers broadly campanulate. A good cv., i.e., 'Warley', & a good cross.

C. raineri: N. Italy—in limestone. Enough like *C. carpatica* to be sometimes mistaken for it. Grows from a tuft. Has a good white form. Broad bells, face-up. Solitary.

C. cephallenica: Islands of N. Greece. Like *C. elantines.*

Campanula

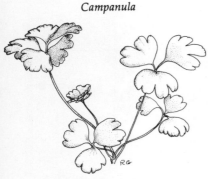

Campanula

0 5 10 15 20 25mm

Gardens in the even, cool climate of the Monterey Peninsula often contain perennials with especially vigorous growth. This occurrence adds to the leeway in choice of bedfellows. Here a wallflower of the West Coast, U.S., which is seen often only one foot tall has almost reached the height of the "old" rose. Duchesse de Brabont also obviously likes the sea breezes. B.W.

Rockefeller Garden. The long border disappears in the distance. This section, in this season, is dominated with orange and yellow with grey as the cooler. The perennials are closely related to trees and shrubs. K.B.

This bed has tall shrubs as its bone structure. The *Viburnum* is a cv. of *Viburnum tomentosum* var. *plicatum;* the one called 'Lanarth' very similar to the popular 'Mariesii'. The undercover is hardly taller than 10 in.; *Helleborus, Epimedium, Alchemilla* and a *Potentilla* compliment the strong horizontals of the *Viburnum.* E.B.

In a garden in Palo Alto, Calif., U.S., roses are used as the basic plants. Here we see 'Marquis Boscella'. *Yarrow, Verbena, Oenothera* and the like grow well as accompaniment. B.W.

PERENNIALS TO COMBINE WITH SHRUBS

This border is against shrubbery; the paths make a peninsula. The deep purple of bedding *Salvia* separates the large drift of white from the scattered white in the center of the bed. The rounded forms of full grown perennials are woven together. (Rockefeller Garden). K.B.

A long border (Rockefeller Garden) is densely packed with interweaving foliage forms. But the plants do not seem to crowd one another; they touch but do not push. The picture was taken in late Summer when many perennials were in bloom. K.B.

Amy du Pont gardens near Santa Barbara. Specimen trees and shrubs provide the setting. Perennials edge the lawn. K.M.

Instead of coping with the planting of a steep bank, this slope became two levels by terracing. On the upper level, the central feature is a wavy perennial border. Over the top of the plants one sees just the roof of the house below. *Penstemon* and *Physostegia* provide deep pink accents. E.B.

COMBINATIONS

Polygonatum is a woodlander which should be planted on a rise, if possible, in order to give more visibility to its bells which hang below the foliage. *P. odoratum* clumps increase in size each year, spreading by underground roots in woodsy soil. E.B.

Cyclamen for every season; those which bloom in September when summer turns into fall seem very welcome. This sp., *C. coum* var. *atkinsii*, waits for Spring and blooms together with its leaves. There are several white *Cyclamen*, all delightful. The leathery leaf contrasts with the delicate texture of *Kirengeshoma*, nearby. E.B.

A Primrose species grows in a damp clearing. *Primula alpicola* is not like the stunning bold spp.; it is delicate and shy. The stem stands very straight. E.B.

All spp. of *Vancouveria* make such a beautiful mass of compound foliage that they would be grown even if they did not flower. When the blooming stem rises above the leafy cover, it is an exquisite extra benefit; note the recurve of the petals, hence the common name Inside-out-Flower. E.B.

A shaft of light has caught the brilliant color of this unusual *Epimedium*. The foliage makes a dense mat below the blossom; this is a species in which the leaves are decidedly heart-shaped. The leaf color is the new light green of early Spring. E.B.

Tiarella wherryi has a light green leaf with a slightly darker mottling. Do you see that the shape is almost triangular? The flower spikes are nearly erect, at the tips pinkish where the buds have not yet opened. E.B.

Trillium. The big, gorgeous *Trilliums* are masterpieces of floral art. Some spp. are smaller and add a subtle charm on the floor of the woodland. *Trillium ovatum* is a clear white, noticeable against the adjacent greenery. E.B.

The foliage of *Trilliums* has three divisions. Parts in threes give this extraordinary genus its botanical name. In the photograph, the leaves have their young freshness and are a fitting background for the deep color of the flower. L.H.

C. elantines: Italian Alps. Several forms as *C. e.* var. *elatinoides.*

C. e. var. *glabra, C. e.* var. *fenestrellata:* Leaves tiny; flowers 4–5 on lateral stems, delicate, open, flat, lighter ring in center, prominent pistil.

C. e. var. *garganica* (known as *C. garganica*): Compact tufts. Flowers numerous in lateral sprays, open-petalled, "blue". Good wall plant.

C. raddeana: Caucasus. R.g. Tufted. Stems slender to 9 in. long. Basal leaves roundish heart-shaped, toothed, pointed, glossy green. Flowers wide funnel-bell-shaped with spreading lobes; violet-blue, nodding, large. Bloom July. Dark. Campanulate. Rapid growth in open soil. Uncommon.

C. orphanidea: Biennial. Macedonia. Deep roots. Rosettes. Hairy. R.g. or container. May live several years.

C. aucheri: Mtns. Armenia to Iran. Tufts. Pubescent. Trailing 4 in. stems. Flowers large bells, deep violet or pale blue. Mostly solitary.

C. arvatica: N. Spain. Leaves tiny, rounded heart-shaped at base, merge into small, sharply-toothed leaves on 3 in. stems. Flowers many upright, solitary, purple 1 in. bells. July. Specialists.

C. pulla & C. pulloides: Creeping growth. Dangling, fat, purple bells. The second twice the size of the first.

C. pilosa: Siberia; Alaska. To 3 inches. Leaves crowded at base. Stems hairy. Upper leaves linear, with roundish teeth. Flowers funnel-shape; hairy in mouth. June. R.g.

C. dasyanthus (C. pilosa): 3 in.

C. incurva, pale violet, Greece, *C, bakeri, C. spruneriana, C. hondoensis* & many others excel. for r.g.

C. glomerata var. *acaulis:* 3–6 in.

Canarina: CAMPANULACEAE. Canary Bellflower.
Mex., Canary Islands, trop. Afr. & Moluccas.
Characteristics of *Campanula.* Parts, however, usually in 6. Fruit an edible berry.

C. canariensis: Semi-tender. Fleshy root. Clambering. Flowers soft orange. Specialists only.

C. campanula: Needs greenhouse. Herb. to 4 ft. high. Ample water while in growth.

Cheiranthus: CRUCIFERAE. Wallflower or Gilliflower (also used for other genera).
Evgrn. & herb. Long ranging roots. Flowers with unique fragrance.
Sun. Tolerates poor soil. Preferably limey. Control pests & diseases. Groom. Semi-hdy. Division. Cuttings. Seed.
Undemanding. Borders, cutting beds. Greek: cheir = hand, anthos = a flower. Related to *Erysimum.* Sev. diseases typical of CRUCIFERAE. Keep plants vigorous.

C. allionii = Erysimum hieracifolium. Siberian Wallflower.

C. mutabilis: A synonym of *C. semperflorens* according to some authorities. Canary Islands, Madeira. Habit open. Flowers pale yellow, age to lilac-purple.

C. cheiri: English Wallflower. To 2½ ft. Originally yellow to yellow-brown; cvs.

various. Old garden favorite.

C. suffruticosum: Blister Cress, Treacle, Mustard. To 20 in.

C. semperflorens: Morocco. Shrubby to 3 ft. Flowers at first cream becoming purple or striped. *C. s.* 'Wenlock Beauty': 6–9 in. Smoky purple.

C. 'Constant Cheer': Hyb. parents? Morocco. Compact mounds of dark foliage. Flowers dusky red.

C. capitatum: N. Am.: Brit. Col., Can. to Idaho, U.S. Properly a bien. Flowers to 1 ft., soft cream color or orange-yellow. Grow from seed. Also *E. concinnum.*

C. linifolius: Synonym of *Erysimum linifolium.* *C. l.* 'E. H. Bowles': Compact, but branches few, grey-leaved. Flowers single, lilac. Short-lived.

C. l. 'Variegata': Compact, dwarf bush. Flowers mauve with amber. Delicately attractive. Short-lived.

Crucianella: RUBIACEAE. Crosswort.
Mediterranean to Iran & Cent. Asia.
Evgrn. Flat g.c. Semi-tender.
Sun or partial shade. Ordinary cult. Drainage. Division. Seed.
Crux = cross, the leaves being placed crosswise.

C. stylosa: Reported as ann. but may live a 2nd year. As yet untested for longevity & spread. Synonym of *Phuopsis stylosa.*

Cymbalaria (Linaria): May be included in *Linaria.* SCROPHULACEAE. Kenilworth Ivy.
Temp. parts of Eur.
Evgrn. Mostly ann. but seed themselves. Trailers or creepers. G.c.
Sun, partial shade. Gritty, porous soil (not rich) with moisture. Seed.
The common trailers may become invasive; easily pulled. A white form is somewhat less rampant. The many flowers with snapdragon-like shape. Greek kymbalon = cymbal; refers to roundness of leaves of some kinds.

Duchesnea: ROSACEAE. Indian Strawberry or Mock Strawberry. Asia.
Foliage shiny & fresh-looking; typical strawberry shape. G.c.
Sun or partial shade. Does not mind heat. Or cold.
Drainage. Moisture. Division.

D. indica: Naturalized on the E. & the W. Coast of N. Am. Long slender runners, rooting at the nodes forming a fairly dense carpet. Fairly clean looking but removal of old leaves improves health & looks. Flowers bright yellow, fruits bright red but flavorless.

Eriogonum: See Subshrubs Plant Descriptions.
Spp. good for slopes include: *E. crocatum, E. fasciculatum, E. latifolium, E. umbellatum, E. subalpinum, E. ovalifolium.*

Eriophyllum: COMPOSITAE. N. Am.
Herb. Rarely subshrubs. Mostly woolly.
Sun. Will rot if water stands around its crown. Good drainage. Seed. Division.

E. lanatum: Good for a dryish bank not in the

Cheiranthus

Crucianella

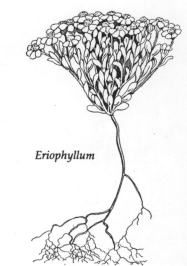

Eriophyllum

Geranium

Geranium

Helianthemum

path of drainage from above, or r.g. Tufted to 12 in. high. White woolly. Many short-stemmed yellow daisies all summer produced in great numbers. Limp stems, clothed with silvery, crinkled leaves, reach out to form a 1-ft. circle.

E. l. var. *arachnoideum* & *E. l.* var. *achillacoides:* Are interesting varieties. There is a cv. 'Oregon Sunshine'.

Euphorbia: See General Plant Descriptions.
E. myrsinites: Trailer. Good draped on a wall. Leaves white-grey.

Geranium: GERANIACEAE. Cranesbill. Widespread.

Evgrn. & herb. Many kinds, trailing, mounding, or upright. Leaves lobed, usually thin-textured. Fine or broad segments. Look totally unlike the Pelargonium called Geranium.

Sun. Soil med. Ordinary cult. Trim & groom. Seed, division & cuttings.

Seek modern cvs. as 'Birch Double', 'Bressingham Flair'. (Avoid G. 'Robertianum'.) Greek: geranos = a crane; alludes to beaklike fruits. Combine with any & all border pers. The trailing spp. best for a slope.

G. armenum: Tallest, to 3 ft. Color brilliant.
G. incanum: Trailing as well as mounding. Covers a space 2 ft. wide & 1 ft. high. Dense but delicate looking. Leaves feathery. Flowers bright magenta. Mos. of bloom.
G. renardii: Caucasus. Clumps to 1 ft. across. Leaves puckered, olive-green, veined. Flowers in pairs, violet, purple centered.
G. sanguineum var. *prostratum* (*G. s.* var. *lancastrensis*): Mounds less than 1 ft. Leaves smallish & deeply lobed. Flowers usually solitary, magenta-pink.
G. s. var. *splendens:* A pleasing pink.
G. s. var. *lancastrense:* Prostrate. Flowers pale pink, red-veined.
G. sanguineum 'Alpenglow': introduced by the Canadian Nursery "Alpenglow". 6 in × 18 in. Leaves evgrn., dark. Flowers vivid rose-red. Summer
G. ibericum: Caucasus, SE. Eur., SW. Asia. Sev. varieties & cvs., including *G. i.* var. *album, G. i.* var. *flore-pleno, G. i.* 'Johnson's Blue', bright blue
G. wlassovianum: To 1 foot. Upper part of stems hairy. Leaves roundish-kidney. 3 to 5 lobed. Flowers 1½ inches across, purple-violet.
G. stepfiana: Grows from a corm. Creeps slowly. 6 in × 10 in. Foliage mottled.
G. tuberosum: Short life. 10 in. × 12 in. Leaves shaped like snowflakes; last only until June. Flowers purple, May..
G. pratense: Eur. & temp. Asia. To 3 ft. Flowers cup-shaped, in pairs, lavender to purple. *G. p.* var. *album, G. p.* var. *albo-plenum, G. p.* var. *atro-purpureum.* Look for 'Kashmir White.'
G. wallichianum: Himalaya. To 1 ft. tall; trailing stems to 2 ft. Leaves lobed & jaggedly toothed. Flowers in pairs, 2 in. across, pet. emarginate, lavender-pink, white centered, veined with purple. Aug. & Sept. Sheltered site.
G. w. 'Buxton's Variety': Flowers violet-blue; clear white eyes, 1¼ in. across, May thru

Aug. More erect than the type sp.
G. himalayense (*G. grandiflorum*): To 1½ ft. Leaves lobed & toothed. A good white form.
G. phaeum: Mourning Widow. Color so dark, appears to be black. July.
G. sessiliflorum 'Nigrum': Leaves dark, interesting.
G. endressii: Wet places SW. France. Creeping rhizomes; rampant.
G. dalmaticum: Yugoslavia & Albania. Leaves quite small, clump quite tight. White form.
G. macrorrhizum: S. Eur. To 2 ft. tall, dense clump; leaves larger than most. Some leaves have autumn colors. Can groom. 'Wargraves Pink', very good cv.
G. m. 'Variegatum': Leaves splashed creamy white.
G. maculatum: N. Am. Erect stems, 2–3 ft. tall, 2–3 from leaf axils, with 2–3 1½ in. flowers, rose-purple.

Goniolimon: PLUMBAGINACEAE. N. Afr. to Mongolia.
Herb. Closely related to *Limonium.* Looks like a *Limonium* dwarf.
Sun. Soil fair. Ordinary cult. Drainage. Semi-tender. Seed. Cuttings.
Flower heads in fans of delicate design. Nearly horizontal branching.
G. tataricum: To 1½ ft. tall. Leaves lanceolate, pale green. In basal rosettes. Stalks more than twice branched & angled, broadly winged. Flowers whitish. Beautiful dried.

Gunnera: See Site for a Large Perennial Plant Descriptions & Containers P.D.
G. magellanica: Carpet forming about 3 in. high. Stems slowly spreading, flat & tight on the ground. Leaves small, kidney-shaped, creased & toothed. Flowers small, green, inconspicuous; summer. Part shade, moisture. Most hdy of New Zealand spp.

Helianthemum: CISTACEAE. Sun Rose. Eur. to Cent. Asia, N. Am. & S. Am.
Evgrn. Subshrub, low & trailing. Leaves small, narrow, numerous. Flowers solitary or in clusters. From single to near double. For r.g. & banks.
Sun. Needs drainage & good soil. Semi-hdy. Cuttings.
Some are hybrids with *H. glaucum.*
H. nummularium: To 1 ft. and 2 ft. wide. Green above; grey down beneath. Leaves to 1 in., flat. Flowers yellow or white.
H. n. var. *grandiflorum:* Leaves green, thinly hairy beneath. *H. n.* var. *tomentosum* with larger flowers.
H. apenninum & *H. a.* var. *roseum* (*H. rhodanthum*): Leaves green above. Flowers pink. *H. croceum,* leaves nearly white. These 3 have contributed to variants & hybs.; vigor is inherited perhaps from *H. apenninum* var. *roseum;* cvs. e.g., single: *H.* 'Butterpat', yellow; *H.* 'Dazzler', bright crimson; *H.* 'Flame', bright pink; *H.* 'Goldilocks', soft yellow (grey foliage); *H.* 'Peach' & 'Apricot', color nearly apricot, & *H.* 'St. Mary's' white, dble.: *H.* 'Boule de Feu', crimson; *H.* 'Snowball', white; *H.* 'Sun Fleck', golden yellow; & *H.* 'Ball of Gold', burnt-orange (semi-double).

H. canum var. *scardicum:* Subshrub. Compact to 6 in. Foliage downy.

Helichrysum: For genus description & for the most dwarf spp., see Outdoor Room Plant Descriptions.

H. psilolepis 'Meg's Gold': From Drakesburg Mtns., S. Afr. Prostrate. To 1 ft. Leaves shiny, silver colored. Flowers ball-shaped, yellow "straw" flowers in fall. Sun. Drainage.

H. 'Sulphur Light': Probably a hyb. Leaves narrow, white-woolly. Flowers sulphur-yellow like "everlasting" flowers.

H. petiolatum: Licorice Plant, S. Afr. Tender. To 4 ft. tall, most of length trailing. Trails 3 to 6 ft. on a bank. Quite erect on the flat. Cut back to 1 ft. Leaves small, white-grey, velvety. Flowers small, cream, with white bracts.

H. petiolatum 'Nanum': Dwarf version. More branching. Softer texture. Compact. Velvety.

Hieracium: COMPOSITAE. Hawkweed.
Eur.
Some Hawkweeds complete pests. Orange color of *H. aurantiacum* is tempting. Avoid this & other invasive spp. Sun or ½ shade. Soil poorish, well-drained. Division.
The best spp. good as g.c.

H. lanatum: 1 ft. by 1 ft. Leaves ovate, mostly lobeless & toothless, grey. Flowers yellow 1 in. across in clusters. Remove flower stems while still in bud for control.

H. maculatum: Leaves mottled.

H. waldsteinii: Leaves light grey with brownish mauve markings.

Hippocrepis: LEGUMINOSAE. Horseshoe Vetch.
Mediterranean & Canary Islands.
Herb.; prostrate. G.c. Widespread from center. Looks somewhat like *Lotus.*
Sun. Soil med. Ordinary cult. Semi-tender except *H. comosa*—hdy. Seed. Division. Cuttings.
Flowers papilionaceous, yellow on axillary peduncles.

H. comosa: Leaves with about 15 linear leaflets. Flowers 5–12 in tight clusters; calyx 5 lobed; wing petals flat; keel beaked; 10 stamens. Bloom spring & summer. Seed pods curved.

Hypericum: HYPERICACEAE (GUTTIFERAE). St. John's Wort, Aaron's Beard, St. Andrew's Cross, St. Peter's Wort, Tutsan. Widespread, temp. regions.
Herb. & evgrn. Shrubs, spreaders & trailers. About 300 spp. Some weedy. Many types of foliage. Leaves of the dwarf cvs. short & narrow, closely arranged on procumbent stems. Flowers plentiful with usually num. stamens. Bloom spring—fall.
Sun & part shade. Soil med. Ordinary cult. Semi-hdy. Division.
Seek the choice spp., esp. the small & restrained.

H. cerastoides (H. rhodopeum): Delicate, refined look. Tufted; procumbent or ascending branched stems 6 in. long. May be erect or may make a cascading drift. Leaves glaucous, grey-green. Flowers yellow from leaf axils. Prominent stamens. Early spring

& summer. Hdy. only in mild climates.

H. aegypticum: Mediterranean region; not Egypt. Foliage has a look of *H. cerastoides.* Also for mild climates. A much-branched small shrublet to 1 ft. with crowded, grey-green, mostly oval leaves. Bloom Aug.

H. ericoides: Spain, possibly Portugal. Evgrn. subshrub 3–6 in. high. Very like a low Heath. Leaves whorled, imbricate, much recurved, linear-oval, mucronate, grey patterned, ⅛ in. long. Flowers in terminal, few flowered cymes. June to Aug. Semi-hdy.

H. empetriformis or (*H. empetrifolium*): Evgrn. subshrub to 1 ft. Stems prostrate to erect. Leaves grey-green in whorls (circles) of 3, rolled under edges. Flowers golden yellow 6 + in., in terminal loose panicles. Sun or part shade. Semi-hdy.

H. kelleri: Very Small.

H. yakusimanum: Difficult to find. One of smallest.

Keckiella: SCROPHULARIACEAE.
San Luis Obispo County & nearby, in Calif., U.S. Chaparral.
A close relative of *Penstemon,* not over 1 ft. tall. Sun. Heat. Good drainage. Heavy pruning. Semi-hdy. Seed.

K. cordifolia (Penstemon cordifolius): To 10 in. Prefers site sim. to habitat—situated on dry slopes and in canyons below 4000 ft. Flowers red & yellow.

Lantana: VERBENACEAE. Shrub Verbena.
Tropics & sub-tropics of Americas & warm parts of Old World. Best so they hang. Also g.c. Leaves toothed.
Sun & part shade. Med. soil. Somewhat drought tolerant. Semi-tender. Seed. Division.
Will completely shroud the wall of a raised bed. In Hawaii, some become troublesome weeds. Will cascade from a pot.

L. hybrida: Group of hybs. Spreading hairy stems. Leaves small. Flowers colorful. One a good pink with dark green leaves, another 2-tone orange.

L. montevidensis: Trailing or Weeping Lantana. Used on steep slopes, esp. in S. Calif. Leaves coarsely toothed. Flowers in clusters, rosy lilac 1 in. across. Combination: *Plumbago,* purple *Clematis* with this sp. of *Lantana.*

Leucopogon: EPACRIDACEAE.
L. fraseri (Cyathodes fraseri) Otago Heath Trailer. 6 in. × 9 in. Leaves glossy on low spreading stems Flowers in axils, pink, fragrant. Cultivate as for *Erica.*

Limonium (Statice): PLUMBAGINACEAE. Marsh Rosemary or Sea Lavender.
Bulgaria, S. Russia, Algeria, Canaries.
Evgrn. & herb. 200 plus spp. For dryish sites & seasides.
Sun. Ordinary cult. Groom. Semi-hdy. Division.
Noted for angled spreading branches of inflorescence.

L. latifolium: Dry grasslands. Leaves spatulate, narrowing to stalks 10 in. long. Flowers on stems to 2½ ft. with branching panicles of dryish-looking small flowers in 1-sided spikes. White calyces with mauve, pink-

Hieracium

Hypericum

Limonium

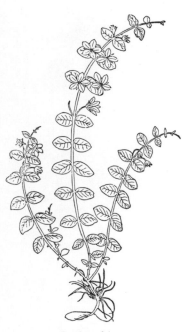

Lysimachia

Monardella

Origanum

purplish corolla. Stems wirey. Cvs., e.g., 'Violetta', 'Collier's Pink'.

L. *vulgare*: European Sea Lavender. Salt marshes. Tough. To 1 ft. Basal leaves to 5 in. Flowers in flat-topped panicles, reddish violet, 2 rows along upper sides of branches.

L. *gougetianum*: Salt marshes, esp. Algeria & Balearic Islands & Italy. 7–12 in. tall. Leaves leathery, 1–2 in. long, margins revolute, tapering to the stalk, obovate-spatulate in dense rosettes. Flowers pale violet with reddish calyces. In panicles to 10 in. high, branched low. Bloom July & Aug.

L. *psilocladon*: Evgrn. compact mat. To 10 in. tall in flower. Many stems with light sprays of lavender flowers. Good for r.g. All summer into fall.

The following more dwarf:

L. *bellidifolium*: Saline soils, Eur. & Baltic. Hairless to 9 in. Leaves obovate to lanceolate to 1½ in. Flowers in 1-sided spikes.

L. *minutum*: Limestone cliffs, Mediterranean coast. To 6 in. Hoary grey, spatula-shaped to ½ in. Cushion-like. Flowers tiny, lavender, in sprays.

L. *cosyrensis* or L. *cosyrense*: S. Eur. Hard to find. Tight, tiny clumps, closely packed. Scape to 6 in. high branched. Bloom June. Leaves linear spatulate, margins recurved.

L. *puberulum*: To 9 in. Leaves white-hairy lozenge-shaped. Flowers with violet calyces, yellowish corollas.

Lysimachia: PRIMULACEAE. Loose-strife or Creeping Charlie.

N. Am., E. Asia & elsewhere.

Herb. Creepers, some invasive. Some dwarfs.

Sun or part shade. Soil med., moist. Division.

Summer bloom. Sev. look like *Veronicas*. Sev. spp. do well in waterside plantings.

L. *nummularia*: Creeping Charlie, Creeping Jennie, Moneywort. Rampant trailer. Leaves to 1 in., almost round. Flowers golden yellow, spotted red in axils.

L. *japonica* var. *minuta*: Tiny flowers yellow, in axils. Miniature for a pot.

L. *'Minutissimum'*: Perhaps still more dwarf.

L. *punctata*: To 3 ft. Far too invasive.

L. *ephemerum*: Non-invasive. Clump forming. Leaves grey. Flowers in slender spires, grey-white, late summer.

L. *clethroides*: Flowers in tapering spikes (recalls *Buddleia* or *Clethra*); white.

Malvastrum (Modiolastrum): MALVACEAE. Trop., subtrop. & temp. S. Am.

Herb. & subshrubs. Related to *Malva*, Mallow. 80 spp.

Sun or ½ shade. Semi-tender. Seed.

Two or three spp. spread to create g.c.

M. *lateritium*: Argentina & Uraguay. Herb. Quite prostrate. Hairy. To 6 in. high. Lobes 3–5, wedge-shaped. Flowers 5 petaled, brick-red, solitary, fall. Hdy.

Monardella: LABIATAE. Mountain-Mint or Coyote-Mint.

W. N. Am.

Herb. Aromatic. Leaves entire or nearly so, small. Flowers in term. heads each

somewhat 2-lipped, tubular with a 5-toothed calyx, the lower lip 3-lobed, the upper lip erect 2-lobed.

Sun. Ordinary cult. Not easy to establish. Semi-hdy. Division.

Stamens exerted. Flowers in close terminal heads.

M. *macrantha*: Native in dry soils, Calif., U.S. To 1 ft. Leaves ovate to 1 in., shiny upper surface, hairy-margined. Flowers in loose heads of 10–20. Scarlet to yellowish with collars of purplish bracts. Bloom fall.

Onosma: BORAGINACEAE. Golden Drops.

Eur. to the Himalayas.

Herb., mostly. Low mats formed by rosettes. Slow spreader. Leaves hairy, may rot if care not used in watering.

Sun. Soil sandy, deep, rather rich. Drainage. Semi-tender. Division.

Flower shape like a fat drop. R.g.

O. *stellulatum*: White bristly hairs. To 1 ft. Leaves often linear. Flowers short-stalked, pale yellow, stalkless.

O. *tauricum (O. stellulatum* var. *tauricum)*: Fewer hairs. Flowers in curved racemes, pale yellow.

O. *alboroseum*: To 6 in. Constant wetness at roots destructive. Leaves grey-hairy, oblong to spatula-shape, in tight rosettes forming an attractive mat. Flowers velvety-hairy on outsides, 1 in. long; soft pink (or white), becoming deep pink & then purplish, in tight racemes. Mat may be divided & groomed to remove damaged rosettes; new growth will follow.

Origanum: LABIATAE or LAMIACEAE. Marjorum, Oregano, Dittany-of-Crete.

Eur. to Cent. Asia, esp. Mediterranean.

Herb. or evgrn. Some culinary herbs to dry; also ornamentals. To 18 in. Bracts important. Many excel. on a slope. Plants leafy & stems tipped with soft clusters of cream or lavender flowers.

Sun. Soil med. Semi-hdy. Seed or division.

Name from "origanon", which was used by Greeks for sev. plants meaning "joy of the mountain". Bees like *Origanum*.

O. *majorana*: Sweet Marjorum, Garden Marjorum. To 2 ft. Usually grown as an ann.

O. *vulgare*: Wild Marjorum. Flowers lavender, thyme-like. For a good crop keep plant trimmed.

O. *v.* 'Aureus': Young leaves golden yellow.

O. *laevigatum*: Easy. Wiry stems. Leaves tiny, blue-grey.

O. *dictamnus (Amaracus dictamnus)*: Dittany-of-Crete, Hop Marjorum. Mt. Dicty, Crete. Hardy to Washington, D.C. A non woody shrublet to 1 ft. Branches ascend then decumbent. Keep moist in a pot. Sun. Excel. drainage. Leaves white, wooly, marjorum-like fragrance, very round to 1 in. across, neatly arranged on the stems which are spreading & trailing. Flowers in compact, hop-like spikelets arranged in loose panicles. Summer & fall. Corolla tubular, pink to purplish. Pale purple bracts, ovate & overlapping, change to rich rose purple as seeds form. Looks like a tassel. Plant with *Androsace lanuginosa*.

O. pulchellum: To 18 in. Like *O. dictamnus* but smaller throughout. Leaves toothed. Calyx with sepals overlapping. Flowers pinkish.

O. sipyleum: SW. Turkey. To 2 ft. Airy. Bushlet, dense. Stems wiry, wand-like, flexuous. Leaves blue-grey, tiny. Flowers pinkish purple, many small inflorescences.

O. × hybridum (O. dictamnus × O. sipyleum): Clones vary. Long, pink bracted, almost shrimp-like inflorescences in summer. Cut spent stems after frost. Not as fussy as *O. dictamnus.*

O. rotundifolium: Plant is smooth. Leaves smaller than those of *O. dictamnus.* Hop-like inflorescence with round chartreuse bracts. Cuts well.

O. tournefortii (O. acutidens): Dittany of Amorgos. Subshrub to 12 in. Leaves somewhat heart-shaped. Flowers pink in denser spikes than in *O. dictamnus.* Looks like *O. dictamnus.*

Paronychia: CARYOPHYLLACEAE. Whitlow-wort, Nailwort, Chickweed.

Widespread, Eur., S. Am. & U.S.

Evgrn. & herb. Mostly small often tufted, even caespitose. Bulbous plants may grow through this loose g.c.

Sun & part shade. Med. light, sandy soil. Drainage. Division. Seed.

Used in r.g. To be recommended for slopes with exclusive spots for unusual subjects. The sp. selected to describe looks delicate & worthy of cherishing.

P. kapela subsp. *serpyllifolia:* Spain, Pyrennes, Alps, Apennines. 3 in. Slender stems procumbent, crowded with very small narrow leaves, ciliate. Spreads slowly to form restrained mat. Somewhat drought tolerant. Flowers May, June, July, tiny round clusters silvery looking as a result of prominent bracts.

Phlox: See Woodland Plant Descriptions.

Two spp. for slopes are *P. divaricata* & *P. subulata.*

Polygonum: POLYGONACEAE. Knotweed. Widespread.

Gonu = knee joint, from often swollen nodes Per. or ann. Avoid spp. which might become invasive.

P. capitatum: A rampageous trailer. Leaves evgrn. in tones of pink. Flowers small balls, pinkish.

P. cuspidatum var. *compactum (P. reynoutria):* To 2 ft. h. and spreading to 3 ft. Leaves to 2 in. darker green than those of sp.; crimped. Flowers erect panicles, white.

P. c. var. *spectabile:* Less vigorous with leaves mottled white, green & red. *P. c.* var. *variegatum:* creamy white variegation.

P. affine & *P. vaccinifolium:* Himalayas. Herb., the first with deep rose spikes, the second, pink to red spikes, both 3–9 in., both erect. Mat forming. Leaves bronze in winter. Foliage undistinguished.

Potentilla: ROSACEAE. Cinquefoil.

Temp. & subarctic regions of the N. hemis.

Herb., subshrubs or spreaders. About 350 spp. Many weedy & many choice for the r.g.

The flowers look like the flowers of strawberries.

Sun. Soil fair to good. Not particular. Drainage. Seed. Cuttings. Division.

Bloom mostly spring; long season. See General & Subshrub Plant Descriptions for other spp.

Spp. & cvs. good for slope, edging or r.g. Mostly semi-hdy.

P. recta 'Warrenii' & *P. r.* 'Alba' & *P. r.* 'Nana'.

P. r. var. *pygmaea:* To 4 in. Neat mat. velvety, hairy stems. Flowers to ½ in. June & July.

P. alba: Cent. & E. Eur. Mounding to 4 in. Deeply divided. Leaflets 5, spread widely, toothed at apex, green on the upper side, white silky hairy beneath. Flowers white, less than 1 in. Sometimes hidden by leaves, 2 to sev. on slender stalks. Bloom Apr.–Aug.

P. nepalensis: W. Himalayas. To 18 in. Width 2 ft. Stems many, branching. Leaves with 5 leaflets, coarsely toothed, green on both sides, to 3 in. Cvs. e.g.: 'Rosana' (Roxana), rosy orange; 'Willmottiae' ('Miss Willmott'), (or var. Miss Willmott), warm cherry pink; 'Master Floris', primrose & coral-red. July & Aug.

P. nevadensis: Dry rocks & screes, Spanish Sierra Nevada. Flat pancake. Leaves much divided, downy. Flower stem splaying with 3 or 4 blooms, yellow. July, Aug.

P. cinerea: Alps. To 4 in. Tufted. Leaves grey, hairy, woolly beneath. Does not like overhead water. Flowers pale yellow. Bloom May–June.

P. argyrophylla: Himalayas. Leafy stems. Leaves grey, silky, deeply divided to 2½ in. long, coarsely toothed, silky hairy above, white hairy beneath. Flowers to 1 in., yellow in loose clusters, on branching spray. Bloom May–September.

P. fragiformis: Siberia. Grows from a thick rhizome. To 10 in. Leaves thick with thick whitish hairs (adverse to water standing on foliage). Rounded in outline with 3 deeply-toothed leaflets to 2 in. Flowers golden yellow with orange blotch.

P. megalantha: Another with soft, fuzzy leaves. Edges scalloped. Slow, difficult & uncommon.

P. gracilis & *P. gracilis* 'Nutallii' & *P. villosa:* W. U.S. to Alaska. Erect to 2 ft. Stems slender, downy. Basal leaves palmate; 5–7 leaflets. Flowers yellow in panicles, June to Sept. Not readily available.

P. hybs.: With *P. argyrophylla, P. atrosanguinea* & others. (*P. atrosanguinea* looks more like a strawberry than any other.) Various colors, yellow, scarlet, maroon.

Spreading, creeping or cascading: Need enriched soil & good drainage.

P. oweriana: Mystery sp. highly praised.

P. tonguei (P. tormentilla var. *formosa): P. anglica × P. nepalensis.* To 1 ft. with adcending and sprawling or trailing stems. Basal leaves palmate. Leaflets to 5, coarsely-toothed. Flowers to ½ in., buff-yellow to apricot-yellow (burnt orange) with small red-brown blotch (dusky brick-red) at base of each petal.

P. alchemilloides: Pyrenees. 4 to 12 inch. h. Basal

Polygonum

Potentilla

Potentilla

Saponaria

Scaevola

Sedum

leaves palmate. Leaves silky & like the leaf of a very dwarf *Alchemilla*. Flowers to 1½ in., white. Restrained, pleasing.

P. tridentata: Greenland & the midwest U.S. To 1 ft., woody at the base. Somewhat downy. Stems spread, ascend & fork. Leaves palmate ("tridentata" means 3-toothed); leathery, toothed at the tip, all green, & evgrn. Flowers white.

Prunella: LABIATAE. Self-Heal.
Eur., Asia, NW. Afr., N. Am.
Herb. Decumbent or sub-erect. To 6" h, wide mats.
Sun or shade. Ordinary cult. Vigorous in any damp soil. Invasive. Division.
Flowers in whorls. Overlapping bracts. Dense spike.

P. vulgaris: Self-Heal or Heal-All. Most familiar sp. Weedy. Best in poor, dry soils where flowers, magenta pink, violet-purple or white, grow only to 6 in. For collectors of medicinal herbs.

P. grandiflora & varieties: Leaves usually toothed. Erect to 2 ft. Flowers pink, red or white. Remove seedlings when young.

P. lacianata: (*P. vulgaris* var. *lacianata*) Uncommon. Slightly more interesting. Leaves indented deeply cut. Flowers whitish. Good as edging.

P. × webbiana 'Loneliness Pink'.

Pterocephalus: DIPSACEAE. Mediterranean region. Mtns. of Greece.
Herb. & evgrn. Stems in tufts forming a broad cushion, leaves entire to pinnatifid. Ovate, crenate often pubescent. Plant with *Origanum, Androsace, Hypericum* dwarves, esp. those somewhat pubescent.
Sun & ½ shade. Soil open. Drainage. Dislikes heat & humidity. Hdy. to N.Y. Division.
Well-drained slope or pan pots or sunny r.g. (pteron = wing, cephala = head; the fruiting head appears to be covered with feathers.)

P. parnassi (Scabiosa pterocephala): Carpeting to 4 in. & to 1 ft. wide. Leaves fiddle-shaped, pinnately toothed & silvery-grey pubescent. Crinkled & crowded. Flowers in concave flower heads like a flattened scabiosa head. Pale lilac. Summer. Conspicuous stamens. After flowers fade, the head has a feathery appearance.

Saponaria: CARYOPHYLLACEAE. Soapwort or Bouncing Bet.
Eur., Asia & N. Afr.
Lather from the leaves used to clean old tapestries. Good annual for arrangers.
S. officinalis: Colonizes on roadsides. Untidy & invasive. To 1 ft. Flowers single or dble.; white with purplish veins or pink.
S. ocymoides: Trailing stems form 3 in. mounds; useful for slopes or top of walls. Flowers on slender, spreading stems, bright pink. Looks like *Phlox* or *Campion*. Spring or summer.

Scaevola: GOODENIACEAE.
Tropics & subtropics esp. Aust. & Pacific Isles.
One sp. grown in Hawaii called *Naupakas*.
To 100 spp. Shrubs & spreaders.
Spp. for g.c. not well-known in U.S.
S. plumieri: Shrub to 6 ft. grown in Florida & W.

Indies, spreads by underground stems. Flowers are fragrant.
S. hyb.: Sold under cv. names. Stems spread wide & close to ground, num. & well-clothed with foliage. Leaves alternate. Flowers small, num., pale lavender marked with stripes. Flowers assymetrical; 5 petals with slit down one side. 5 stamens; 1 bent style. Spring & summer. Fruits berry-like.

Sedum: See Containers & General Plant Descriptions.
Some spp. for slopes are: *S. stahlii, S. spurium, S. spathulifolium, S. anglicum, S. album, S. australe, S. dasyphyllum.*
S. acre: Gold Moss. Foliage evgrn., almost mosslike. Shoots to 2 in., thickly clothed with blunt, conical leaves. Flowers starry, ½ in. wide, yellow in clusters on stems to 3 in. Invasive but useful on a bank.
S. dasyphyllum: Leaves soft blue-grey, ovoid. Flowers ¼ in. across, white with pinkish undersides.
S. spurium: Wide mats; stems creeping & branching. Leaves more or less evgrn. to 1 in. long. Flower stems reddish. Flowers in flattish clusters, white, pink, red.
S. stoloniferum: Sim. but stems bright red. Flowers pink.
S. rupestris: A persistent weed.

Sempervivum: CRASSULACEAE. Houseleek.
Eur. Eur., N. Afr. & W. Asia.
Evgrn. Usually spreading to form a dense mat with small rosettes. Sun. Drainage. Some spp. semi-hdy. Division.
Many good for a rock crevice, or slope with rock accompaniment. All good in containers. "A large proportion found in gardens are ... unnameable." Dr. R. Lloyd Praeger, monographer of the groups. Each sp. very variable & all hybridize easily.
S. tectorum: The common Houseleek. Often grows in old walls & roofs. Rosettes of various sizes (& ages) for mats.
S. t. var. *calcareum:* Dark purple tips on its leaves, in rosettes to 2½ in. across.
S. arachnoideum: Cobweb Houseleek. Pyrenees to Carpathians. Dense rosettes to 2 in. wide of incurved green or reddish leaves, connected with a cobweb of fine hairs. Flowers bright rose-red in smallish clusters.
S. a. var. *glabrescens:* Leaves hair-fringed, tips not united with a cobweb. Flowers in branching clusters & ½ in. wide with 10 or so petals.

Silene: CARYOPHYLLACEAE. Catchfly, Campion, Cushion-Pink, Wild-Pink, Fire-Pink, Indian-Pink.
Widely distributed in temp. & cold regions.
Herb. & semi-evgrn. Many spp. Tufts, mats, upright, or trailing. Baggy calyces. Leaves small oval, mostly silky texture, plentiful. Stems numerous to form a mound.
Sun or shade. Soil med. Ordinary cult. Seed or cuttings.
Some are good as g.c. Others for pots. Floriferous. Summer
S. acaulis: Cushion Pink. Name describes habit.
S. schafta: Caucasus. Tuft of wiry stems to 1 ft. Studded with "rose-purple" flowers in late

summer. Might refuse to flourish for a few years; seems to require time.

S. vulgaris (S. latifolia, S. cucubalis), sea coasts & cliffs of Eur., & *S. v.* var. *maritima (S. maritima),* similar, variable & with subspp.: Bladder Campion & Sea Campion. Evgrn. mats. Calyces, greenish, puffed-up, inflated like miniature balloons. Many stems cascade to 1 ft. Top of wall, raised bed or container. Shear off stems occasionally for renewal of growth. Flowers whitish, numerous in summer.

S. v. var. *maritima* 'Plena': Looks like a dwarf carnation. Flowers sterile. R.g. or pot as well as slope.

S. fimbriata: To 2 ft. Leaves hairy, dark green. Flowers white with fringed petals.

S. virginica: Fire Pink. Eastern U.S. 2–3 ft. Leaves basal, spatulate to oval-lanceolate, to 4 in. long. Stem leaves nearly sessile. Inflorescence 7–11 flowered, petals 2-lobed, scarlet.

Sisyrinchium: IRIDACEAE. Blue-Eyed Grass, Golden-Eyed Grass, Satin Flower.
S. Am. & N. Am.
Somewhat naturalized spp. of W. U.S. Seed themselves readily, but pull easily. Every flower stem causes the death of the leaf stem from which it grows: in years when flowering is abundant, plants "bloom themselves to death" & must be discarded. Seedlings will carry on. Leaves of seedlings, very narrow always, look tiny in youth & might be mistaken for grass. Some spp. more than others have a substantial and stylish personality.
Sun. Ordinary cult. Some semi-tender. Seedlings. Division late summer.
Plant in a drift or in a strip or mix with low slope genera. Seed themselves.

S. bellum: Most common, from coastal Calif., U.S.

S. bellum 'Variegatum': Rare; should be sought.

S. × *macounii* 'Alba' = *S. bellum* × *S. macounii:* Brit. Col., Can. Tiny rhizomes. To 10 in. Leaves quite wide & firm-textured. Trim tufts make stylish edger, small-scale g.c.; a slow multiplier.

S. douglasii: Grass Widow or Purple-Eyed Grass. Leaves rigidly erect, bract-like. Flowers nod. Reddish purple. 1 ft. stems.

S. californicum: N. Am.: Moist soils from Ore. to Calif., U.S. Leaves ¼ in. wide; to 1 ft. tall; greyish with black vein. Flowers yellow on broadly-winged, branchless flower stalks, to 1½ in. across.

S. boreala & *S. brachypus:* Close to *S. californicum.* 2 spp. of the W. Coast of N. Am. (as far N. as Vancouver) with yellow flowers & markings on petals. Good habit. Leaves of firmer texture than those of most spp. & more blue-green.

S. striatum: S. Chile & Argentina. Sword-shaped basal leaves ½ in. wide, grey-green in erect clumps. Flowers bell-shaped, petals wide spreading. Outside of petals streaked brown or purple. Good in flower garden. Looks like grass when not in bloom.

S. s. 'Variegatum' ('Aunt May'): Leaves quite grey, cream striped.

S. bermudiana: 4 in.–2 ft. Flower stalks flattened & winged to 2 ft. Flowers violet-blue, yellow throat; or yellow with darker veins.

S. angustifolia: N. Am.: damp meadows & open woods, Newfoundland, Can. to mtns. of N.C., U.S. Leaves ¼ in. wide, wider than those of *S. bellum.* Flowers bright violet-blue.

Sphaeralcea: MALVACEAE. Globe-Mallow, Desert-Mallow, Desert Hollyhock, Prairie Mallow.
Americas.
Herb. Subshrub. 18 × 18 in. Dies down in winter. G.c. or with sim. herb. subshrubs. Not elegant; color of flowers unusual.
Sun. Not tolerant of very wet weather or of cold; some more hdy. than others. Good drainage. Division. Seed.
Long period of bloom. Not long-lived.

S. ambigua: Apricot Mallow. To 3 ft. with many stems; hybridizes.

S. fendleri: Subshrub, erect to spreading to 2½ ft. Leaves usually velvety or downy. Flowers round, silky, mallow-like in spikes, orange-red to pink or mauve. In axils of leaves, continuous through summer & until stopped by winter weather.

S. coccinea (Malvastrum coccineum): Prairie Mallow. White-hairy herb.; sprawling stems to 9 in. Flowers 1 in. wide, brick red in short terminal racemes. The most hdy. species.

S. munroana: Woody but dies to the ground. Leaves greyish, shallowly 3–5 lobed. Flowers coral with minute starry hairs. Color sometimes described as "grenadine-red to apricot pink".

Stachys: LABIATAE. Woundwort, Betony, Lamb's Ears, Chinese Artichoke, Crosnes, Knotroot.
Temp. & warm temp. regions.
Herb. Many coarse or weedy.
Sun & part shade, esp. *S. macrantha.* Soil poorish. Control. Semi-hdy. Division.
Mostly solid mats. Dense growth produced by leaves of various size.

S. byzantina (S. lanata, S. olympia): Strong & sturdy plant not higher than 18 in. Wide spreading mass of grey. Leaves tongue-shaped, soft, thick & white-woolly. Frost damages the leaves & heavy rains make the hairy surface mushy. New leaves grow quickly. Don't allow to bloom; cut off flower stems while in bud; flowers would be purplish in summer on spikes to 1 ft. tall.

S. b. 'Silver Carpet': A form which does not flower. Foliage with good quality.

S. macrantha: From the Caucasus. Green, downy leaves in a mat to 2 ft. wide. Flowers hooded, mauve in whorls on erect stems.

S. saxicola: Morocco. Subshrubby, to 1 ft. Soft white hairy. Flowers white. A delightful dwarf.

S. coccinea: Stems slender. Leaves green, soft, floriferous. Flowers light scarlet. Hummingbird favorite. Grow from seed.

Statice = Limonium.

Teucrium: Several spp. are excellent for sloping sites. See General Plant Descriptions. See Outdoor Room Plant Descriptions for spp. good for containers.

Sempervivum

Silene

Sisyrinchium

Stachys

Vinca

Geranium

T. scorodonia: Wood Germander. G.c. Spreads underground to form a drift & above ground to make a tracery with its sprawling stems. Basal rosettes tight to ground. Leafy flowering stems with frilly foliage, very crinkled, scalloped, thick textured & velvety. The basal leaves make a mat & the flowering stems arch away from its center. Flowers in very narrow spikes, cream-colored; delicate, along leafy tips. Seek 'Crispum'.

T. aroanium: Compact tufts. 2 in. × 6 in. Leaves small, round, silver. Flowers purple-veined. July.

Vinca: APOCYNACEAE. Periwinkle, Running Myrtle, Creeping Myrtle.

Eur. & Russia.

Evgrn. More or less vining. Leaves shiny green when healthy. G.c.

Shade & ½ shade. Ordinary cult. Trim. Do not allow to dry out. Division.

Some invasive. These 2 spp. hdy.:

V. major: Mediterranean region. Rampageous, tenacious.

Eradicate it by burying it below 8 or more in. of leaf mulch & using a herbicide on any *Vinca* leaf which shows through the mulch.

V. minor 'Bowles Variety': Hdy. & valued as a g.c. *V. m.* var. *multiplex*, with dble. plum-purple flowers might be found in catalogues. Still harder to find is a variant with smaller leaves, more slender stems & with small, single flowers deep, dark plum-purple. It would be listed as 'Purpurascens' or as 'Atropurpurea'. This form lies very flat on a slope; its stems elongate rooting often at the nodes. The drift increases but in a much less rampant manner than the type sp.

Zauschneria: ONAGRACEAE. California Fuschia or Hummingbird Flower or Hummingbird's Trumpet.

Herb. Related to *Fuchsia.*

S. & W. U.S.

Related to *Fuchsia.* May be transferred to *Epilobium.*

Herb. Often evgrn. in mild climates. Semi-tender. Survives all but worst winters. Can be cut to the ground. Twiggy subshrubs & herb. trailers. Leaves small, tightly packed, various shades of grey. Flowers trumpet-shaped, orange to scarlet, late summer. Also a white form.

Sun & part shade. Soil dryish. Division. Cuttings.

Much visited by hummingbirds; trumpet sometimes thrusts out-ward to present an open door for visitors. G.c. Edges. Plants easily cross-pollenize.

Z. californica: Dry, gravelly & stony soils. To 2 ft., upright. Leaves green to greyish; more or less pubescent, to 1½ in. long. Flowers to 2 in.; 4 sepals, 4 petals & 8 protruding stamens.

Z. c. var. *alba:* A choice restrained plant.

Z. c. var. *angustifolia:* Stems slender; leaves grey-hairy.

Z. c. subsp. *latifolia* (*Z. arizonica*): Oreg. and Calif. U.S. Stems short not woody at bases. Leaves broader. Mostly ovate, often glandular. A form with distinctive foliage.

Z. arizonica: A distinct sp. of merit.

Z. cana (*Z. microphylla*): Calif., U.S. Stems woody at bases & sprawling. Leaves grey-hairy, narrow, fascicled, crowded. Flowers narrow, plentiful; seem brighter scarlet in contrast to silvery grey of foliage. *Z. cana* appears to be low because of its habit.

Z. septentrionales (*Z. latifolia* 'Etteri'): Herb. Makes a mat which dies to the ground in winter. Roots live. Stems closely set; to 6 in.; leaves grey-green. Flowers numerous; scarlet trumpet on almost every tip. Scarce.

10. The Bog

A real bog is a place where water naturally collects and stays, so saturating the ground that the soil is never completely dry. The consistency of the soil becomes different: sticky and soggy. A few plants like it that way; among them are *Anemopsis*, *Gunnera*, *Maianthemum*, *Malanthium* and *Darlingtonia*. Some of the *Primulas* want wet feet, especially *Primula floridae*. *Iris ensata* wants to be soggy during its growing season but must dry out while dormant.

Kirengeshoma palmata comes from a wet habitat and does not thrive in the ordinary garden situation, preferring the border of a stream where the winter overflow has thoroughly wet the soil. *K. palmata* is herbaceous but becomes, in early spring, a lovely shrublet with attractive branching habit and leaves of unique shape and color. The indentation is distinct and the lobes sharply pointed. The time for the odd shuttlecock bloom is summer but it is fleeting. You must remember to watch for the soft yellow flower half hidden by the beautiful foliage.

Kirengeshoma

Some of the *Heucheras* seem to prefer a site near a water course. One smallish sp., *H. pilosissima*, has delicate pale sprays of flowers which are discernible against the grey faces of rocks.

The flowers of *Petasites* come up early and then disappear beyond any trace, letting the big, tough foliage take over and cover a large area quickly. Stolons travel over the top of the ground hardly stopping to root. All spring and summer the large leaves overlap and completely shade the earth. Is *Petasites* an enemy even in a good sized bog? I find its questing stems can be grubbed easily enough to control the spread.

Two plants which flourish in boggy ground can be considered enemies. The first is beautiful.

Equisetum hyemale, Horsetail: great sweeps of the ferny fluffy stems shimmer in shafts of light. Their roots travel under ground, quite deeply, and may send up tree-like—somewhat prehistoric—stems far from their boggy home. They look right in a group in a natural setting but quite messy when they invade a planting of *Hellebores* and *Astilbes*.

The worst enemy is Baby's Tears, *Helxine Soleirolii*. Its roots are not only on the surface but also far deeper than you think. When you try to eradicate it you will lose quite a bit of soil in the area. Better keep after it. In weeks it seems, you find that the bright green carpet is back and bigger.

Let us consider some plants which are less rampant. Two spp. provide splashes of yellow, noticeable against the overall green in a place of almost deep shade: one is *Ranunculus cortusifolius* (Creek Buttercup) with stems three feet tall and petals of such a glossy surface that they shine even from a distance. The other is the bright-yellow, creeping *Mimulus guttatus* which will wander anywhere, in sun and in dryer situations,

Ranunculus

Monarda

Inula

Maianthemum

as well as this damp place; little monkey faces decorate many stems. It seems to look best on a shady streamside. This is the site to find it in the wild. On roadsides it may grow taller, with twigs to lean against, and is noticeable to the dilatory motorist. It is the yellow one you want for wet shade, but look for other spp. with muted colors for your edgings.

Another wanderer is *Maianthemum* but both pace and distance is less than that of *Mimulus*.

While *Hosta* is not a true bog plant, it flourishes in full shade in a place where it receives ample moisture through its growing season. If you have a place for *Hosta*, there are many sizes, shapes and flowers from which to choose. I like the white ones better than the lavender. One with white flowers is *Hosta minor* var. *alba* with a dozen or more one foot spikes above a clump of narrow, pointed leaves. You might like to choose a bigger one. One example is Fragrant Hosta, Royal Standard, a hybrid, *Hosta subcordata* var. *grandiflora*. It has two foot spikes of white lily-like flowers for many months. This is one which tolerates more sun and less moisture. *Hosta* is good to cut, both flowers and foliage.

Select *Hostas*, however, primarily for their foliage; the leaves vary in shape and color and include variegated forms. Of all the patterns of variegation, I like 'Thomas Hogg' the best since its white marking is in a quite neat stripe around the leaf-edge. *Hosta sieboldii* is the most handsome because of its leathery texture, its decided heart shape and its blue-green color (it retains the bluish caste better if not fertilized well).

Hosta is herbaceous; snails and slugs will find the tips of leaves even as they break through the surface of the earth; put out bait and a ring of ashes well before there is any sign of growth. *Hosta* likes good soil but moisture is essential.

Flowering perennials for bogs? *Hosta* blooms but is mostly grown for its foliage. *Filipendula* blooms better in wet soil than in ordinary soil. *Monarda* will bloom in ordinary soil but is taller and more colorful in a semi-bog site.

Not many people have a bog, i.e. a true bog. However, if you plant a subject noted as good for bogs in the garden proper, you will surely give it ample water.

PERENNIALS FOR BOGS

Aciphylla	I. pseudoacoris
Acorus	I. chrysographes
Amsonia	Juncus
Andromeda	Kirengeshoma
Anemopsis	Lilium
Arisaema	Lobelia
Asarina	Lysichitum
Asclepias	Lythrum
Calla	Maianthemum
Caltha	Malanthium
Carex	Monarda
Chelone	Osmunda
Claytonia	Peltiphyllum
Coptis	Pennisetum
Darlingtonia	Petasites
Equisetum	Primula florindae
Eupatorium	Rheum
Filipendula	Rodgersia
Gunnera	Rubus
Habenaria	Ranunculus
Heuchera	Sarracenia
Hibiscus	Saxifraga
Hydrocotyle	Smilacina
Inula	Trillium undulatum
Iris ensata	Trollius
	Viola lanceolata

Aciphylla: UMBELLIFERAE. Speargrass. Wild Spaniard. N. Zealand.

Herb. Slow growing, compact clumps. Leaves basal, compound, pinnate. To 2 ft. long. Grey-green. Narrow leaflets spine tipped. Inflorescence often spikelet, many small umbels, yellow or white. Grown mainly for foliage.

Semi-shade. Soil moist, peaty, gritty. Well-drained. Seeds when ripe.

A few spp. available. Large leaved ones picturesque. Spp. to seek: *A. aurea, A. glaucescens, A. horrida, A. scott-thomsonii.*

Caltha: RANUNCULACEAE. Marsh Marigold. N. Am.: Can. to Alaska, S. to Nebr. & S.C.

Herb. Low & fleshy. From cold marshes of N. & temp. zones. Leaves alternate, petioled, entire or serrate. No petals. Stamens many.

Sun & semi-shade. Soil moist, acid. Best where conditions stay wet. Division of roots when dormant; seed.

Seen in marshy meadows. Edge of ponds. Bloom, spring.

C. palustris: Clumps. 2–3 ft. Tall robust stems to 12 in. Leaves glossy, kidney-shaped. Flowers on stalks which rise above leaves; satiny, rich yellow.

C. leptosepala: Alaska to N. Mex., U.S. To 8 in. tall. Leaves longer than broad, dentate. Flowers white, unimpressive; April. Likes moisture.

Darlingtonia: SARRACENIACEAE. N. Calif. to SW. Oreg., U.S. Wet swampy sites.

Evgrn. Leaves form basal rosettes, to 30 in. Hooded, cobra-like; attracts & digests insects. Flowers inflated, tubular, translucent, novel. Obtain from specialist.

D. californica: Pitcher Plant. Occasionally available. Needs bed of moss & peat, always moist. Flowers yellowish green, summer. Not easy to tame.

Equisetum: EQUISETACEAE. Horsetail, Scouring Reed.

Widespread. Mostly wet places.

Herb. Spreads extensively in a damp site. Fluffy masses. Some leaves with central cavity; leathery looking.

Shade. Control, if possible. Root division.

Looks exceedingly "wild". Beware of over production even without help from you.

E. variegatum: Evgrn. Stems to 2 ft. Slender.

E. telemateia var. *braunii:* Giant Horsetail. Best in a natural setting, perhaps in a public garden for education. to 7 ft. How eradicate?

Eupatorium: Some spp. like wet soil esp. *E. perfoliatum.*

Filipendula: Will grow quite well without a bog, but likes the soil quite wet. See Woodland.

Heuchera: See Woodland Plant Descriptions. A suitable sp. for the bog is *H. tiarelloides.*

Hydrocotyle: UMBELLIFERAE. Pennyworth, Water Pennyworth or Navelworth.

Trop. Asia, Afr., N. Zealand, Eur.

Semi-evgrn. Low tight g.c. Leaves nearly orbicular or peltate, palmately lobed or veined. Leaf shape interesting. Flowers inconspicuous.

Semi-shade. Moisture. May be invasive but most spp. spread slowly. Semi-hdy. Seed. Cuttings. Layers.

At least one sp. a pest.

H. vulgaris: Marsh Pennyworth. Leaves round, peltate, lying flat. Will float.

H. sibthorpioides (H. rotundifolia): Leaves nearly round, scalloped. Flowers tiny, greenish, inconspicuous. Impossible to control in a lawn.

H. moschata & H. dissecta: Both from N. Zealand, 1–2 in., the first with leaves notched & the second deeply cleft. Carpeting for damp soil.

Inula: COMPOSITAE. Elecampane.

Eur., Asia & Afr.

Clumps of narrow leaves sometimes hairy. To 3 ft. Leaves basal. Flowers yellow composites, summer. Rays narrow & separate.

Sun & semi-shade. Soil moist, or bog. Semi-hdy. Division. Seed.

Ray flowers very slender. Arrangement creates a frilly look.

I. ensifolia: Makes a full mound, 1 ft. × 1 ft. esp. between rocks. To 2 ft. overall i.e. including flower stems. Flowers num., on wiry stalks, yellow to 2 in. wide. July.

I. magnifica: As name implies. Needs at least 3 ft. for width. Grows to 6 ft. Broad, rough foliage.

Iris: For genus description, see General Plant Descriptions.

Waterside spp.:

I. pseudoacoris: Yellow Flag of Europe, N. Afr. & Asia Minor. Fleur de Lys of heraldry. Naturalized in N. Am. Waterside. Colonizes luxuriately. Leaves broadly sword-shaped to 3 ft. long but often only 1 ft. Flowers bright yellow. Early summer. Erect falls 2 in. long & shorter, narrow standards. Will grow in shallow water. *I. p.* var. *variegatus:* Leaves striped yellow. Division.

I. delavayi: Marshes, Yunnan Province, W. China. (Related to *I. sibirica*). May be a hyb. of *I. chrysographes.* To 4 ft. Leaves linear to 2½ ft., conspicuously veined. Flowers purplish, much of falls area yellow.

I. chrysographes: Stream-side. To 1½ ft. Leaves linear to 1½ ft. Narrow, grassy, lax. Flowers deep velvety violet, gold veining. Hybs. & cvs. with dark (almost black) indigo-violet, e.g. 'Black Knight'. Short period of bloom, early spring.

I. ensata: Beardless, rhizomeless. Clumps of growth buds & sheaves of erect leaves. 2 ft. × 2 ft. Hybrids of *I. kaempferi,* Manchuria & *I. laevigata,* Japan. Developed in Japan, Eur. & Am. Moist soil & water plants. Can be grown in containers for the express

Caltha

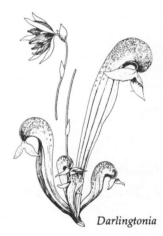

Darlingtonia

Equisetum

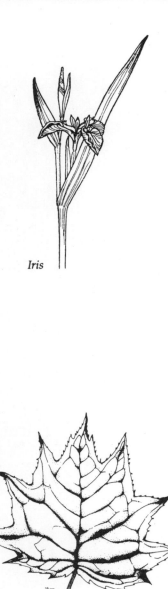

Iris

Kirengeshoma

Maianthemum

purpose of standing them in water, during summer blooming season. Boxes are stored out of water but continue to be watered & fed. Only iris to prefer lime-free soil. Likes humus. Flower unique in shape: 3 short standards & 3 large drooping falls. (Some hybs. have multiple petals which detract from basic form.) Texture important: noted for the "velvet" surface. Colors white, pale lavender, dark blue, purple, red-purple, pale pink, two-tones, flushed & streaked with veins of a different shade.

(One authority lists *I. ensata* as a sp. from Japan with red-purple blooms 4 in. wide with elliptic falls yellow at their bases. Perhaps many spp. have assisted the breeding of "Japanese irises".)

Kirengeshoma: SAXIFRAGACEAE. Yatabe. Moist mtn. woods, Japan & Korea.

Fairly open bushlet. Clear pale green, indented leaves. Handsome, unusual, sev. weeks before flowers open, early fall.

Shade. At least part-time light. Soil good, deep, woodsy, acid. Moisture. Semi-hdy. Division. Seed.

Improves each year. Eventually 3 ft. × 2 ft. Unusual form in leaf & flower.

K. palmata: Reported to 4 ft.; only 2 ft. in gardens in Calif., U.S. Leaves indented, green, opposite, broad like a plane's on branching black stems. Flowers bright yellow, shaped like shuttlecocks with translucent texture—airy lanterns on tips of stems.

Lysichitum: ARACEAE. Bog Arum. N. Am. & Asia.

Herb. Aroid. Related to *Symplocarpus, Zantedeschia* (the Calla Lily), *Anthurium,* & *Philodendron.* For a large site.

Shade. Bog best. Division or seed.

Edge of pond or stream.

L. americanum: Yellow Skunk-Cabbage. Alaska to Calif., U.S. Wet soils in woodland & the open. Large clumps to 4 ft. wide. Leaves 4–6 ft., paddle-shaped. Follow flowers, which arise from soil early spring. Spathe, yellow or greenish yellow to 8 in. Flowers tiny, crowded to form the spadix, to 5 in. All parts with disagreeable odor.

L. camtschatcense: Kamtchatka. Spathes pure white or palest green. Spadix white & with smaller flowers than the U.S. sp. Scent pleasant. Somewhat smaller sp. 3 ft. × 3 ft.

Maianthemum: LILIACEAE. False Lily-of-the-Valley.

Eur., Asia, N. Am. (N.Y. to Tex., U.S. in damp soils.)

Herb. (not long without leaves). Only 3 spp. Thick rhizomes. Underground stems. Leaves 2–3, simple, glossy, irregular in shape; many of various sizes according to age.

Shade. Soil rich, moist. Division.

Suitable for a wide, damp, gentle slope. Easy; colonizes, but slowly. Shiny green g.c. to 4 in.

M. bifolium (Smilacina bifolia): To 9 in. Leaves triangular-ovate.

M. canadense: Canada Mayflower or Two-leaved Solomon's Seal. Wide range in U.S.

& NW. territories. Carpeting to 8 in. Leaves almost sessile. Narrow V-shaped sinus. Leaf blades with narrow opening between. Flowers in thin, white clusters in the center of greenish bracts, 2 in. long at tips of slender stem. Fragrant. Fruit brilliant red. Hybs.

M. kamtschaticum: Alaska to Idaho & Cent. Calif., U.S.; E. Asia. To 14 in. Leaves cordate to 8 in. long. Flowers in racemes to 2 in. Fruit a pale red.

Monarda: LABIATAE. Horse-Mint, Oswego Tea, Bee-Balm, Fragrant Balm, Wild Bergamot.

Am.

Herb. Mostly tall, erect & aromatic. Plant in groups. Hybs. Leaves entire or toothed. Basal leaves make dense spreading clump. Spread to 6 ft.

Shade or ½ shade. Grow in borders if soil moist enough. Spring division.

Attractive to hummingbirds. Hybs. Shaggy look. Bloom summer.

M. didyma: From moist thickets & woodlands, Maine to Mich. & N.C., U.S. To 4 ft. when planted in rich, moist soil. Erect, square stems. Leaves ovate-acuminate to 4 in. Flowers bright crimson with bracts tinged red. Cvs., 'Croftway Pink', 'Cambridge Scarlet', 'Prairie Glow' (salmon-red), 'Prairie Night' (violet-purple), & 'Adam' (good habit).

Peltiphyllum: SAXIFRAGACEAE. Umbrella Plant.

Banks of streams, Calif. & Ore., U.S.

Herb. Fleshy horizontal rhizome. Slow to reach maximum growth. 3 ft. or more. Leaves large, lobed.

Shade. Not easy to tame. Division.

Leaves on single stems arise after flowers are over.

P. peltatum: Peltate = shield-shaped. Leaves to 2 ft. across on long hairy stalks 3 ft. tall, growing from end of rhizome; nearly round, depressed in the center, 5–15 lobes. Flowers starry, before leaves, on pinkish brown hairy stalks, many in a terminal rounded panicle. Spring. *P. p.* 'Nana': Only 1½ ft. tall with blades 9 in. in diameter. Wavy, large leaves of a size more adaptable to the average garden.

Pennisetum: GRAMINEAE. Fountain Grass.

Widespread. Warm areas, including Asia, Afr. & Arabia.

Evgrn. Tall grass. Some variegated. See Grasses.

Sun or shade. Ordinary cult. Semi-hdy. Division.

Sev. spp. good for ornament. Colors affected by back lighting. Clumps to 3 ft.

P. setaceum (P. atrosanguineum): Naturalized in Calif., U.S. To 3 ft. Ornamental. Arching stems, narrow leaf blades. Flower spikes slightly curving, 1 ft. by 1 in. Flowers copper, rose-pink or purplish.

P. s. var. *purpureum:* Leaves dark reddish purple. Flowers deep purple-crimson. Spring to fall.

P. s. var. *cupreum:* Foliage reddish.

Petasites: COMPOSITAE. Butterbur, Winter Heliotrope, Sweet Coltsfoot, Bog-Rhubarb, Butterfly Dock.

Eur., Asia & N. Am.

Herb. Increases widely by rooting stems & underground roots. Some invasive. Large, indented leaves follow flowers.

Shade. Cut back. Control. Division.

Sweet scented flowers in winter. Need *very* large space.

P. hybridus (P. vulgaris): Eur. & Asia but naturalized in N. Am. Toothed blades 6 in. to 3 ft. across, kidney-shaped, shiny on the upper side, underside—cobwebby, hairy on stalks to 2 ft. Flowers rayless, reddish purple, in tight ovoid panicles, on stems to 1½ ft., in winter. Flowers before leaves. Situation must allow strong roots to roam; best site a shady stream-side.

P. japonicus var. *giganteum:* Wavy margined blades to 4½ ft. across on 6 ft. stalks. Stalks eaten as vegetable in Orient.

P. frigidus (P. nivalis): Widely distributed in N. parts of 2 hemis.; appears in Calif. Leaves almost triangular, lobed & toothed to 10 in. wide. Flower stalks with foliage. Flower heads whitish in panicles.

P. fragrans: (Considered by some only a listed name.) Called Winter Heliotrope because of vanilla fragrance. From Mediterranean region.

Primula: See Woodland Plant Descriptions.

Some spp. which like it wet are: *P. anisodora, P. japonica, P. aurantiaca, P. beesiana, P. bulleyana, P. pulverulenta, P. cockburniana, P. sikkimensis, P. alpicola, P. florindae, P. capitata.*

Ranunculus: RANUNCULACEAE. Buttercup, Crowfoot, Fair Maids of France, Lesser Celandine.

Widespread, 3 are from cold & temp. regions.

Herb. Many spp. Various. Leaves small, indented, glossy. Shade. Moisture. Control invasive kinds. Division. Seed. The shiny & rounded look of a buttercup.

R. repens: A weed. Eliminate the single-flowered spp. To 10 ft. w.

R. r. 'Flora Pleno': Vigorous carpeter. Rooting at any node of runners. Flowers small, bright yellow buttons. Better than sp.

R. 'Molten Fire': Glistening flowers. Fine color. Parentage unknown.

R. aconitifolius 'Flore-pleno': Fair Maids of France or Fair Maids of Kent. Grown since 16th century. To 2 ft. Leaves deeply cleft into usually 5 segments deeply toothed. Pure white buttons rosette-like on many branching stems. (Sometimes yellow.) Apr. & May.

R. cortusifolius: Azores. Semi-tender. Needs sharp drainage but moisture. Completely disappears for sev. mos. New foliage looks exceedingly fresh. Clump 1 ft. Stems to 3 ft. Shiny, yellow buttercups very bright when seen in deep shade. Early summer.

Rodgersia: See Woodland Plant Descriptions.

Good for marshy soil, by pond or stream.

Sarracenia: SARRACENIACEAE. Pitcher Plant or Side Saddle Flower.

From acid sphagnum bogs in E. N. Am.

Herb. Oddity. Carnivorous.

Trillium: See Woodland Plant Descriptions.

A good sp. for the bog is *T. undulatum.*

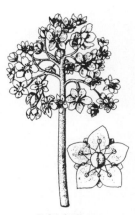

Peltiphyllum

Petasites

Hardiness: When hardy, I have said nothing about hardiness. I have used semi-hardy to indicate that a plant is less than perfectly hardy. This plant needs protection against frosts to survive. I have used tender to indicate that the plant will not tolerate *any* frost. I have used semi-tender to mean that a plant may survive a short period of frost but not prolonged frost or often repeated frost. This plant may lose its above ground portions but its roots may survive if mulch is used to protect the root area.

Explanation of the order: When there are varying heights in a genus, the spp. are often described in groups, Tall, Medium and Low. When the spp. are divided according to use, sometimes a group will appear under one heading and sometimes another group under a different heading. When there are two or more entries under different headings of various spp. a general plant description will occur under only one of the headings but reference to the list which includes the plant is included.

The spp. are not listed alphabetically. One sp. follows another because it is related or similar in appearance. One sp. may follow another because it has a similar habit. Occasionally the better known spp. are described first and spp. hard to find are given at the end of the spp. descriptions of the genus. Very often a dwarf sp. will come at the end both because it is smaller and because it is more uncommon. Occasionally the spp. will be arranged one below the other because I like the second better. You will have to judge from the text whether I like it equally well. I put them this way so that you might better see relationships horticulturally. When you wish to find a certain sp. in the descriptions, you may find its position in the text by means of the alphabetical index. Please do not read the descriptions of the spp. as if the whole were a jumble.

Hybrids: When a cv. name follows directly after the genus name, no name has been given to the hybrid and the parentage of the cross has not been recorded.

Ranunculus

11. *The Site for a Large Perennial*

Yucca

There are practical advantages in using one very large plant instead of several of ordinary size. There it is, growing by itself, growing apace, filling its space in a few years; when it overfills its space it can perhaps be cut back. All these big plants are exceedingly permament——unless tender ones are killed in a winter of more than average frost. They all have big strong roots to suit their size and some would require a mammoth operation to move. It is wise to make sure that the mature plant will be to your liking and place it where it will stay forever.

Where is there a proper site for it? It should have space from an esthetic stand point as well as a practical one. Many huge plants have a distinctive personality which needs to be set off as an individual to be appreciated. Many are of such a decided character that only plants of a similar character look well in combination. On the other hand, sometimes the use of something very different will be effective—creating a contrast which is arresting. Some careful study is important when combining strangers. Who would have thought *Yucca* would go with the traditional plants in a perennial border? Gertrude Jekyl did and now some of us copy her experiment. *Yucca* is one of those subjects—one plant of which is often enough. If your space is large enough, three plants make a wonderful show. The towering spires with quantities of cream flowers bear repeating expecially if you have sky for their backdrop.

Those plants which are bigger than just large are sometimes overpowering and inappropriate in combination with the usual herbaceous perennials. In the dooryard garden, however, there are some very possible sites. Earlier, I reminded you that planting along the base of the house used to be called "foundation planting". The shrubs selected for this trimming of a building often become so tall that the roof becomes a hat pulled down over the ears of the windows. Windows are put there to let light come inside; shrubs often cut the window in two or block it altogether. Rather than these woody plants try some of the big perennials. A row of three or more will fill the space and still have room enough to display their personalities. No need to clutter the planting area with accompanying perennials, although a ground cover might be suitable.

Strelitzia is one of several candidates for this bed against the house. It can also be used standing free—one plant at a path crossing or corner of the terrace paving or two or three in their own island bed.

Strelitzia needs a prominent position; it is a spactacular plant, either *S. reginae*, Bird of Paradise or *S. nicolai*, Giant Bird of Paradise. The latter is huge, a tree of 30 feet in tropical countries; in temperate zones, it needs a setting like a courtyard of a public building, where it can be protected by an overhang. It is supposed to stand the cold down to 28 degrees. The dramatic foliage is described as banana-like; the evergreen leaves are more leathery than that and arranged fan-like to display their shape and texture. I like the muted coloration—the floral envelope is purplish grey, the flower is bluish white with a dark blue tongue. The smaller one is easier to grow and easier to place. Containers are good because the very tough roots like to be crowded; but heavy, regular feeding is required for fine flowers so confined. The orange, blue and white is an arresting combination and the form looks like something from outer space.

The foliage shape is narrow-oval and the texture very leathery. The flowers are decorative for a long season and at a time when the average beholder wants color above all else. Many flowers make a startling effect. I passed a little garden where a row of *S. reginae* filled a strip against the house wall; the roof had a wide overhang—no plant need suffer from winter storms, or a moment of heavy hail. When several plants are used the effect is a crowded mass; the character of the leaf and its fan-like positioning is then almost lost; when *Strelitzia* grows too vigorously it must be thinned. It does not combine well with shrubs, first because one will surely lean against the other but principally because it is hard to find a shrub of a compatible character. When a plant stands alone with space around it the imagery of "Bird of Paradise" becomes evident; the term "boat" is applied to the tongue; its point is like a prow and its margins are turned inward, and the purple-edged bracts repeat the boat motif. Perhaps the prime reason for selecting Bird of Paradise is that it is spectacular when cut. An arrangement of two or three leaves and a flowering stem or two is appropriate for a desk or table in a hospital or library.

Aristea is not useful for cutting. The flowers are sapphire blue and spaced on a long stalk but they open one at a time and each lasts only about one day. The sword-shaped leaves grow in a wide clump.

Agapanthus may be used for a large strip or for foundation planting. It looks well in a row when it is young but becomes congested after the third year; it is then difficult to groom. When the foliage is used as salad by deer, the clump has a sawed-off look; the flower stalks are munched in the process. The flowers are otherwise excellent for cutting. An alternative scheme is to plant in groups of three with enough space between groups for a low compatible perennial, for example *Liriope*. The old-fashioned expression, "too much of a muchness" can soon apply to *Agapanthus*. When you must divide, resist the temptation to enlarge the group. Give half or more of the plants away.

Clivia is not all that large. It is a good selection for a strip next to the house on the shady side. It does, however, need ample space for display since its weight and strength should be in scale with its surroundings; it has a personality which deserves a fitting show-case. It is an all season plant in temperate climates with handsome, waxy, leathery, evergreen foliage arching away from the crown and during its blooming time, with full heads of red to orange trumpet-shaped flowers. (Perhaps all of you know that *Clivia* makes an excellent container plant and houseplant.) Beware slugs and snails.

Agapanthus and *Clivia* are quite small compared to the succulent plants which are sometimes used in the front yard. Really huge plants are often much better well away from the house. Some genera need placement out of competition with other plants. I have seen one big sp. of a succulent genus make a handsome display of great orange-crimson spikes, street-side, outside the hedge of the doorway garden. It is sheltered by branches of tall trees since it is not hardy. This is *Doryanthes,* Spear Lily, one of those enormous succulents; it really belongs in a park or an arboretum. But if you are looking for a strong plant with sword-shaped leaves, here it is; there can be up to one hundred in a clump, about six feet long by four inches wide. Look in Botanical Gardens for exotics of this type for suggestions to fill that large space.

Phormium tenax, New Zealand Flax, has sword-shaped leaves which can become almost as big as the house. I think it is overpowering—to both house and other plants if placed near them. But a clump by itself, allowed to do its thing, say in front by the street-side or in the back in a lower corner, makes a bold effect (the dwarf forms are six feet). If you have occasion to do huge arrangements anywhere, the foliage is just what you need for the vertical line; you may prefer a bronze kind (there are cultivars); you may even use the flower stalk which is especially dramatic when dry and dark brown.

Puya alpestris is just possible in a garden used as a feature plant in an otherwise empty corner. If you think it needs companions, you could try *Amarcrinum* or some of

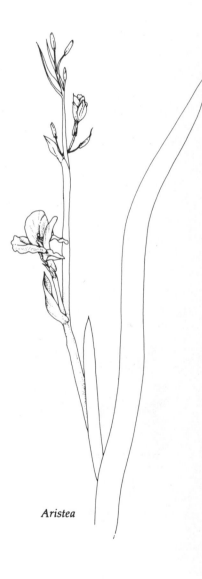

Aristea

Hedychium

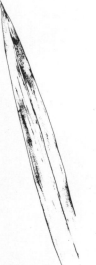

Watsonia

Lilium

the medium sized *Aloes*. (There are many *Aloes* from which to choose; the big ones are trees.)

Puya won't develop its curious flowers unless it has water and food; it does not bloom often even in the best of places—perhaps every seventh year. It comes from Chile. The sword-like leaves are in a crowded clump two feet tall. They have a very strong personality and are a stunning centerpiece during the six years between blooming. When it blooms (on stalks of about four feet), it is a miracle of form and color. Imagine "metallic blue-green and steely turquoise" and "orange" together in a flower! I see it recommended for "pots" but a container to suit would have to be both big and handsome.

Anigozanthos is an amaryllid from West Australia. It is tall but not overly wide. It has short sword-like leaves of interesting shape and texture. The roots are tuberous or "swollen". It needs a protected position and one with excellent drainage. Tall stems carry branching heads of curious flowers suitable for a striking flower arrangement in which the oddity of the flower rather than beauty is the keynote—perhaps standing alone uncluttered by competition. The common name is Kangaroo Paw; the stems and flowers are downy and the tubular blooms have starry mouths. One species is *A. flavidus,* to five feet, yellowish-green tinged with red-brown; another is *A. manglesii,* flowers deep green, red at the base; others are available, all with odd tones—some lighter, some darker. This plant needs to be put in an appropriate situation in the garden as well as in the vase; it does not "go with" such plants as Larkspur and Columbine. It needs sun, sand in the soil mix and good drainage as well as shelter.

Hedychiums are large dominant plants which look better planted alone—anyway, not next to Tulips or *Dianthus.*

The foliage of Gingers (Hawaian gingers), Zingiber family, looks to some visitors like crowded corn stalks. I am willing to have a clump in a conspicuous place especially when a cluster of uniquely scented flowers develops at the top of some of the leafy stems. In some years on the San Francisco Peninsula it is warm enough for satisfactory bloom, especially if plants have been mulched and well fed. Try a Ginger as a doorway plant, to enjoy the wonderful odor as you enter the house and to admire the massive colorful spike. In the winter, the stems must be cut back; the space is empty for only a few months. The space can be kept narrow by periodic division of the thick clump of rhizomes.

Less tropical looking and much more hardy are most lilies. Because these are herbaceous, they must be sited amongst evergreen plants (See Woodland). Some of the spp. are very grand looking, especially those which bloom in a tiered spire. The sp. in our drawing is not the largest but it is certainly regal, *Lilium martagon.* What is more regal looking than *Fritillaria imperialis?* This hardy, bulbous genus is described in Woodland but this sp. needs a large site with special conditions and only succeeds in special climates.

Alpinia speciosa may bloom in a wide, warm, wet, protected spot; although a tender plant, it acclimatizes more readily than some other exotics on the borderline of hardiness. Its bright dangling beads are unusual looking.

Watsonia marginata is an irid from South Ameica which is quite hardy in my garden. In colder climates, it would have to be lifted and stored for the winter; its corm is big and strong; it is clothed in a heavy overcoat of coarse fibre and needs strong hands when it is time to divide. The foliage is at full height all winter, often five feet and is in no way damaged by storm or cold. Cut it to the ground after the flowering period. The leaves have extremely solid substance, a nice color—slightly blue-green: the midvein is prominent, the margins of leaves are darker and thickened, modifying the flat surface and giving the foliage character. The leaf has a dramatic shape—really sword-like, coming to a sharp point. This sp. grows in a tight, stiff erect fan. When I cut leaves, as I do for big flower arrangements, I cut all the way to the ground so that the sheaf stays together. A flower bud may be destroyed in the process but the colony is large enough so that there will be plenty of "orchid" pink bloom to cut in early summer. The spikes reach to six feet, showing above the foliage and sometimes against the sky which makes a nice combination.

There is another tall species, *W. pyramidata (W. rosea)* which grows to five feet with small plentiful, clear-pink flowers in a one-sided spike. There is a white hybrid, *W.* 'Ardernei', which is highly praised by G. S. Thomas but I have not seen it. Nor have I seen *W. beatricis,* described as apricot, blooming in late summer and only three feet tall. Another with apricot colored flowers is *W. meriana;* blooms in Spring and reaches only

The light has caught the sheen on the leaves of *Kirengeshoma*. It reveals the grace of the stems, spreading to allow full view of the leaf form. The flowers will be later, a delicate spray of shuttle-cocks. E.B.

Eucomis is too distant in this picture to see with clarity all the intricate details of its flower column. The shape of its top-knot stands out, however, against the dark background of woods. E.B.

Fairybell is an apt name for this charming woodsy plant. *Uvularia hookeri* needs a close look to view its short-stemmed bells. In pairs they dance under a canopy of foliage. L.H.

Narrow strap-shaped leaves form a basal clump when this So. Afr. plant emerges in earliest Spring. *Bulbinella robusta* blooms in mid-summer in its natural habitat. Here we see the flowering spikes bending at their tips as the buds prepare for a full opening. This bending in the early stage is typical of a few perennials. E.B.

The white form of *Lapeirousia laxa*. The variety spreads less rapidly than the species. Here its low blade-shaped leaves are in a dark space; the sun has picked up a leaf of a Wood Strawberry. E.B.

Anthericum liliago opens its delicate flowers in Spring, sometimes only one at a time. In this picture a number of buds are still tightly closed above the flaring open blossom. E.B.

Fritillaria needs an opening in a woodland in order to display its exquisite form. This sp. may have a third bell-shaped flower on its graceful stem. L.A.

So many exquisite *Erythroniums*. This one, *E. purpurescens*, is called Plainleaf Fawn Lily because its leaves are not mottled. The recurve of the petals is seen clearly in a shaft of light. E.B.

DEEP SHADE TO FILTERED SHADE

Here is John Brook's design for a patio. A clay jar is the focal point with a cluster of small pots at its base. The bright colors contrast with the pale yellow and whites of the perennial backdrop. J.Z.

Fern pots for a terrace are better than upright pots. They must be as wide as 14 in. to accommodate any of the daisy bearing sub-shrubs. This one is the best, *Chrysanthemum anethifolium,* since it shears well and blooms heavily. C.A.

Leadbetter Gardens, Santa Barbara. A terrace is designed to compliment an imposing house. Its furnishings of pedestals and pots not only soften the formal lines but give the house a friendly intimacy. K.M.

At the corner of a path, a composition is made with two complimentary perennials. *Geranium incanum* provides the bright magenta pink as contrast to the bright blue of *Lithodora* 'Grace Ward'. *Lithodora* must have a site to its liking to become this full and floriferous. D.D.

TERRACES AND PATIOS

Sedum in an urn. At the height of full growth in the Fall, *Sedum sieboldii* spills over the rim of its container. E.B.

On a wall, low pots are more complimentary than those of regular height. Terracotta bowls have a good shape for herbs, for annuals, for bulbous plants and for succulents. This succulent is a *Haworthia;* it has not filled the bowl as yet but it is well enough established to bloom. E.B.

Geum georgenberg has a more shy and at the same time more elegant personality than its robust cousins. Only a few flowers at a time but new ones keep opening for weeks. E.B.

An association of foliage plants in a shady corner. The sun, for a few hours at midday, spotlights first one and then another. The light is now focused upon a fancy-leaved *Ligularia.* The background plant, *Loropetalum chinensis,* is raised on a stand. E.B.

CONTAINERS

2 feet.

There are a number of *Watsonia* hybrids which we grow for cut flowers in late summer, about three feet or a little taller which come in good pastels including white. When the main spike is finished, short side branches can be cut for low arrangements.

I usually lift them mainly because the corms multiply so fast. While pulling them apart, the thick thatch peels off so single bulbs are later planted, clean and shiny. Since the plant is narrow and the corms can be planted close together, a stand of hybrid *Watsonias* takes little room. However, find a big space for *W. marginata* both because it wants to spread and because its majestic foliage needs a proper setting.

Crinum has been noted as a garden plant but should be brought to your attention again as a candidate for such containers as boxes and barrels. Look for a hybrid, *Crinum × powelli* with silvery-mottled foliage which gives it distinction when not in flower; the lily-like flowers are of good quality. Find also the bigeneric cross, *Amarcrinum*.

This amaryllid has a bulb the size of a football which must have its long neck above ground. The limp leaves make messy clumps too big to hide but we can put up with the foliage in order to have only one or two stems topped with clusters of fragrant, lily-shaped blooms in summer. *Crinums* need rich, deep soil, continual feeding and plenty of moisture. In cooler climates, a place against a sunny wall might be chosen; you might want to grow them in an unconspicuous place, in some shade, in a corner behind trees because the foliage, even without damage by snails, is not an asset to the permanent picture. Not much bloom can be expected without ample light.

Alocasia is a tropical looking plant from Asia. It needs room as it becomes a dome-shaped plant four feet across and five feet high. It is sometimes referred to as "elephant's ear"; its leaves are arrow-shaped and big—two feet long. The flowers have been likened to calla flowers.

Colocasia esculenta (*Caladium esculenta*) truly deserves the common name, Elephant's Ear. The shape of the leaf has been described as heart-shaped but it is a very elongated heart; the leaves grow almost directly from the ground and may reach six feet. It is very lush looking. Some people in warm climates grow it as an herbaceous perennial! In cooler climates, it can be lifted and the tubers stored over the winter. It comes from tropical Asia and Polynesia. It reaches only three feet in the first three years but in the fourth it may reach almost full stature and become exceedingly vigorous and handsome. The soil should be rich and moist; if there are tree roots nearby, the area should be given extra water in a dry season. Put it in filtered shade and out of the wind.

There are several large plants which are usually grown in containers instead of in the ground, because they are tender and may need to be moved to shelter. Another reason may be that they are particularly suitable to create a bold display for exterior decoration.

You will note that there are a large number of members in the group of plants called "big" which have sword-shaped or blade-shaped leaves. Those genera described in this chapter have been those with many leaves which form wide clumps. Most of them are evergreen and often supply a sturdiness and stability if used in a bed or border. This narrow, linear form is useful for developing variation and interest in the basic parts of the design. If the line of the leaves is erect, they make a sharp vertical; if it is curved, they make a wavy line. A waving mass of foliage produces a sense of motion which makes the design seem alive.

How much of this linear form should be incorporated in your plant combination? Not half and half; not one or two spots in a 30-foot space. Let us say an eighth of the vertical pattern in a mixed border should be made with sword-shapes. Various types can be used together separated perhaps by other forms but repeating the linear type in variation, here a wide clump of foliage stiff and erect, there a smaller statement with the leaves noticeably arranged in a fan, and further, a drift of that foliage with softer substance which results in the more curved line. You have seen perhaps very lush and, what might be called, billowing borders in which not eight but 80 percent of the blade-shaped has been used. These gardens are very permanent looking; their very fullness is an element in their design. And they are effective. Although this type of perennial takes up room, it is suitable in a small garden. The neighbors must be also big; a Violet would no doubt be overshadowed.

Do you have that place which is a strip along the neighbor's fence in which you

Zantedeschia

Phyllostachys

Romneya

Rodgersia

Polypodium

want to plant large perennials in a row? How would you like a sp. with tall stems carrying bright flowers all summer? You might try *Cannas*. They are strong looking, almost coarse but if planted alone, there are no delicate perennials with which to be compared and they are sturdy enough in their growing period to be looked upon as an extension of the fence. If you plant a line of one of the yellow cultivars, and also plant marigolds in the beds by the front door, you have to like yellow a lot! You may like *Canna* a lot but in other colors.

This dividing place is also a site for Callas, *Zantedeschia*, Calla Lily. Not so big and strong but big enough. This side should be in the shade. There is a place on your property which may need a very large plant. Suppose your lot is fenced from the adjacent lot. But you can see over or through the fence and would like a better barrier. If there is a narrow strip in which to plant you might like to try Bamboo.

It will flourish in little sun or shade once established. Bamboo is admired for stem and leaf rather than flower, in fact, most species die if by chance they flower. Bamboo is admired for its history and its traditions as well as its looks. It is ancient and it is practical; it has been used in a number of ways and it is edible. It makes a fair wood substitute for decorative purposes; a number of kinds have been planted, especially in Japan, to replace wood and in that country it has also been made into paper.

It is grown for the straight, erect lines of its strong stems. This habit makes it suitable for the fence line or in a corner of the boundary line. One has variegated leaves. The most interesting feature, however, is the smooth stalk trimmed by the rings which indicate its sections. I have seen Bamboo indoors in large containers producing a very stately effect; the boxes must be movable so that plants can vacation out of doors.

Phyllostachys nigra is one of the most difficult Bamboos to grow in a container. This is disappointing since the black sheen on the stems is outstanding. It thrives in good soil and with adequate water. I have seen a grove a block long, with many stems young and old, some two inches through; the black gleams as shafts of light penetrate the thick growth. It has become a forest. It makes a beautiful screen. This species does not grow as fast as a number of other species.

There are many kinds of Bamboo and dwarfs as well. Ask before you buy to ascertain what kind of roots the plant has since some can become invasive very quickly and are besides terrifically tenacious.

Romneya, Matilija Poppy needs space since when it thrives it makes a stand 8 ft. wide or more. It is over six feet tall. The strong stems are densely clothed with handsome foliage. Its best position is against a green background or in an opening with sky or sea as its backdrop. The big white poppies are attractive against blue. Few herbaceous perennials combine well with *Romneya;* it fills its role best standing by itself—against a fence perhaps or a green hedge or just against an Oak or a Redwood Tree. It will associate with a few shrubs or large evergreen perennials. As we have seen, not all big plants prefer sun. Some prefer ample moisture and these are best in shade.

Gunnera, the spp. with the huge leaves, really need a large site perhaps only to be found in a park. They require not only a wide space but soil almost bog like.

The large ferns should have a site under trees. Tree ferns are beautiful in a grove but should not be crowded. Several fern genera have species which need room. *Woodwardia radicans* will grow to 6 feet tall (although usually only 4) with proportionate width. Large ferns can play the basic role in a shady garden with all manner of smaller ferns and woodland perennials to accompany them. The fronds of the tender Hare's Foot Fern, *Polypodium aureum* are deeply cut. A secondary design is created by spore patterns.

Perennials with large foliage have an important role in a garden under trees. The strong leaves relate to the sturdiness of the trunks. A massive leaf produces a sense of drama; perennials with large leaves act as transitions between the tree canopy and the floor of a woodland.

Petasites and Ornamental Rhubarb are examples. The foliage of *Rodgersia* has stunning texture as well as size. When there is space enough several plants should be positioned to make a wide drift in order that the pattern of the leaves may have the emphasis brought about by repetition.

Have you other candidates for the large site? Those here described were selected to give examples of diverse personalities. Some of them are evergreen, some of them are hardy etc. You must choose a genus which will grow well in your site but also which has a character which appeals to you.

PERENNIALS FOR A LARGE SITE

(f = foliage)

Acanthus	Crinum	Houttuynia
Aeonium	Cynara f	Indigofera
Agapanthus	Dianella	Liatris
Agave f	Dierama	Libertia
Alocasia f	Dietes	Lupinus
Aloe f	Dimorphotheca	Lysichiton
Alpinia	Diplarrhena	Lythrum
Amarcrinum	Doryanthes	Moraea
Amaryllis	Echeum	Oxypetalum
Anigozanthos	Echinops	Pachyphragma
Aralia f	Eupatorium	Panax
Aristea	Euphorbia	Peltiphyllum
Arundinaria	Euryops	Phormium
Arundo f	Gaura	Polystachys
Asclepias	Gonospermum	Puya
Beschorneria	Goodyera	Rheum
Beta	Gunnera	Rodgersia
Celsia	Haplopappus	Romneya
Centranthus	Hedychium	Strelitzia
Chloragalum	Heliconia	Valeriana
Colocasia f	Heliopsis	Verbascum
Crambe f	Hemerocallis	Wachendorfia
		Yucca

THE SITE FOR A LARGE PERENNIAL PLANT DESCRIPTIONS

Acanthus: ACANTHACEAE. Bear's Breeches. S. Eur.

Herb. Many large leaves, dark green, shiny. Large clumps. 5 × 3 ft.

Sun ½ shade. Soil fert., well drained. Cut foliage back to the ground. Division.

Design of the leaves, inspiration for Corinthian column. Flowers summer in tall spikes. Good to pick fresh or dry. Beware of thorns on the hooded calyx lobes.

A. mollis var. *latifolia:* Commonly grown in the U.S. Broad full clumps. Leaves long, cut deeply, almost pinnate lobes. Shiny, arching.

A. spinosus: Bold, strong clumps for large gardens. 5 × 3 ft. Leaves deeply divided with spiny points. Flower stems to at least 3 ft., summer, mauve with white; the hooded calyx lobes end in sharp prickles. Spikes foxglove-like, handsome.

Aeonium: Seek hybs. Warm climates only.

Agapanthus: LILIACEAE. Blue African Lily, Lily of the Nile.

Natal, Cape Province, Transvaal, etc.

Evgrn. & herb. Wide clumps. 3 × 3 ft. Leaves broad strap-shaped. Mostly waxy.

Sun or ½ shade. Soil ordinary. Water well and feed weekly in growing season & when in containers. Likes crowding. Needs grooming. Snails. The evgrn. spp. are semi-tender. Division.

Flowers in rounded heads, good to cut, with long or short stems. Early & late summer.

Evergreen spp.:

A. africanus: Was the first sp. introduced; *A. umbellatus* (of gardens) sim. is usually seen instead. Abundant sword-shaped leaves in a clump about 3 × 3 ft. Large heads 10 in. or more across of lavender-blue or white, made up of num. funnel-shaped flowers.

A. umbellatus var. *mooreanus:* A dwarf form only 1½ ft., replaced by modern cvs., e.g., *A.* 'Lilliput', a dark blue, 'Peter Pan', both lavender and white.

Deciduous spp.:

A. inapertus: Deciduous. To 2½ × 2 ft. Reported to reach 5 ft. Foliage blue-green. New leaves fresh. Up to 100 tubular flowers, it is reported; "spode" blue, hang as they open.

A. campanulatus: 3 ft. × 18 in. Stems strong. Leaves narrow, greyish green. Flowers white or various shades of soft blue. Rather flat (not spherical) heads. Late summer.

A. × Headbourne Hybrids: *A. inapertus* × *A. campanulatus.* Many cvs. Sev. cvs. of sev. hybs. are not readily available in the U.S. trade. Mixed seed strains are available.

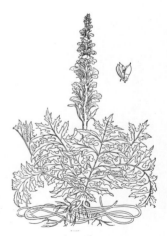

Acanthus

Agave: AGAVACEAE (AMARYLLIDACEAE). Century Plant. or Am. Aloe.

N. Am., Mex. & N. S. Am.

Evgrn. Mostly large, shrub-like to 20 × 8 ft. Some 12 ft.; a few 4 ft. Rosette of some spp. may reach 6 × 6 ft. Leaves grey-green, sharply pointed. In age, 30 to 40 years will have immense flower spike. Summer.

Sun. Perfect drainage. Protection from winter rains. Division.

Good in containers. Look for spp. of smallest stature.

A. shawii: Leaves densely prickly-margined. Flower panicle to 10 ft.

A. victoriae-reginae: Unusual rosette, leaves dark green with white line. Handsome habit. Seek other sim. spp.

A. striata 'Nana': Mex. Foliage plant for a container. Stylish.

Alocasia: ARACEAE.

Trop. Am. & Indonesia.

Evgrn. Some giants. Leaves arrow-shaped. A few oval. Markings & veinage in strong patterns.

Sun. Soil moist and fert. Groom. Semi-tender. Division.

Flowers with spadix and spathe (like a Calla Lily).

A. odora: Leaves 3 ft. long on 3 ft. stalks. Trunk to 6 ft.

A. amazonica: Clear white veins & midrib on dark green narrowly heart-shaped scalloped leaves.

Aloe: See Containers Plant Descriptions.

Some large, shrub-like with thick trunks. Others about 2 ft.

A. ferox: National floral emblem of Republic of S. Afr.

Alpinia: ZINGIBERACEAE. Ginger Lily, Shell Ginger.

S. & E. Asia.

Evgrn. Large clumps. 6 × 5 ft. Tall stems. More slender than *Hedychium*.

Aloe

Sun. Warmth. Feed. Division.

Cut flower clusters most unusual. Blooms assymetrical. Racemes. About 4 ft. Arching & drooping at the lip with pointed buds of polished texture.

A. sanderae: Greenhouse except in the tropics. Prized for variegation.

A. speciosa: Blooms in a sunny, protected, warm position as far north as San Francisco, Calif., U.S. Late summer. Typical ginger stalks; leaves browning a little on the edges in cold mos. Aromatic when rubbed. The flower a work of art & ingenuity. The corollas shiny, shell-like.

Amarcrinum:

A productive intergeneric cross between *Amaryllis* & *Crinum*; *Brunsvegia* & *Nerine* now being used also in the crosses. Several cvs. grouped under *A. memoria.*

Warmth. Soil moist & fert. Most are semi-tender. Division.

In an established clump, many strong spathes, many flowers to an umbel opening over a long period. Several soft pinks; excel. white form.

Amaryllis: AMARYLLIDACEAE.

S. Afr.

Bulb. Herb. Leaves strap-shaped. Flowers wide, colorful trumpets.

Sun & shade. Soil fair. Feed hybs. Semi-tender. Division.

Audacious mixture to plant together: *Agapanthus* with *A. belladonna.*

A. belladonna: Leaves appear after flowers, called "Naked Ladies", good heads of trumpet-shaped flowers. Pink or yellow (pink the most common).

A. hybrids: Especially good for pots. Sold by mail order catalogues almost ready to bloom.

Anemone: Some spp. are so invasive that they require a large space.

Hardiness: When hardy, I have said nothing about hardiness. I have used semi-hardy to indicate that a plant is less than perfectly hardy. This plant needs protection against frosts to survive. I have used tender to indicate that the plant will not tolerate *any* frost. I have used semi-tender to mean that a plant may survive a short period of frost but not prolonged frost or often repeated frost. This plant may lose its above ground portions but its roots may survive if mulch is used to protect the root area.

Explanation of the order: When there are varying heights in a genus, the spp. are often described in groups, Tall, Medium and Low. When the spp. are divided according to use, sometimes a group will appear under one heading and sometimes another group under a different heading. When there are two or more entries under different headings of various spp. a general plant description will occur under only one of the headings but reference to the list which includes the plant is included.

The spp. are not listed alphabetically. One sp. follows another because it is related or similar in appearance. One sp. may follow another because it has a similar habit. Occasionally the better known spp. are described first and spp. hard to find are given at the end of the spp. descriptions of the genus. Very often a dwarf sp. will come at the end both because it is smaller and because it is more uncommon. Occasionally the spp. will be arranged one below the other because I like the second better. You will have to judge from the text whether I like it equally well. I put them this way so that you might better see relationships horticulturally. When you wish to find a certain sp. in the descriptions, you may find its position in the text by means of the alphabetical index. Please do not read the descriptions of the spp. as if the whole were a jumble.

Hybrids: When a cv. name follows directly after the genus name, no name has been given to the hybrid and the parentage of the cross has not been recorded.

Anigozanthos: AMARYLLIDACEAE. Kangaroo Paws.

W. Aust.

Evgrn. Leaves sword-shaped. Tall stems with woolly coating.

Sun. Warmth. Sharpest drainage. Division.

Bizarre look. See drawing, p. 122, showing the paws which give this common name. Bloom late summer.

A. flavidus: To 4 ft. Basal clump of sword-like leaves to 2 ft. wide. Flowers tubular with "open mouths" on branching stems at the top of a 4 ft. stalk. Downy. Yellowish tinged red-brown.

A. flavidus 'Bicolor': Less red than *A. coccineus.*

A. coccineus: Rusty red.

A. manglessii & *A. viridis:* Less tall; to 3 × 2 ft. Yellowish green without appendages on anthers. Flowers of all spp. bloom in summer & look well in "contemporary" compositions; keep well cut.

Aralia: ARALIACEAE.

N. Am., Asia & Aust.

Mostly large shrubs or trees. 6 × 6 ft. Some herb. Deeply cut foliage on arching stems. Often spiny. Flowers greenish cream in open panicle. Maroon-black berries.

Shade. Soil moist & fert. Semi-hdy. Seeds, spring.

Rich woodlands. Grow for handsome foliage. Massive plant to grow as a specimen.

A. racemosa: American Spikenard. 5 × 4 ft. Brownish stems. Leaves to 2½ ft., deeply-cut, hand-like. Greenish white flowers in umbels on a large spike. Summer. Berries, dark purple.

Aristea: IRIDACEAE.

S. Am. & Trop. Am.

Evgrn. Large clumps. Leaves linear, clean, strap-shaped, somewhat flaring. Flowers deep blue. Early summer.

Sun or shade. Soil, any. Drainage. Semi-tender; need warmer parts of temperate zone; not hdy. north of Calif., U.S. Seeds itself readily. Hard to transplant the mature clumps but will divide.

Not a huge plant but takes considerably more space in the small garden than is warranted by its qualities. Leaf clumps are fresh green & attractive. Arista, Latin = a point.

A. ecklonii (or *eckloni*): Clumps, from woody rootstocks with fibrous roots spread to 2 ft. in a year or two. Leaves many, linear, "sinuous" & pointed; flower stalks to 2½ ft., rise above foliage; flowers small, deep blue; many buds which open every day as the previous day's die.

A. thyrsiflora: Leaves rigid, ribbed, linear; flowers clear blue, fragrant, close at midday. Bloom for many weeks in early summer.

Artemisia: See Slope.

Some species are woody, and wide. One is herb. The following need space.

A. ludoviciana var. *albula* 'Silver King': Colo., Tex., U.S.; Mex. 1½–4 ft. high. Thicket of stems; silvery white stems & leaves (like willow leaves). Flowers whitish in loose panicles. Feathery look.

A. pontica: Roman Wormwood. 1 to 4 ft. tall. Leaves broad-triangular, cut in slender segments; flowers whitish yellow in long, loose, slender panicles.

A. absinthium 'Lambrook Silver': Seek. Grey color as name implies.

A. (sp.?) 'Silver Queen': A curving rather than erect cv., many silver leaves much divided.

A. arborescens: Maritime cliffs, Mediterranean. Silkiest & laciest. Semi-tender. Needs protection & dry soil.

A. nutans: Silver-leaved. Most reliable according to Bloom.

A. stellereana: Old Woman or Beach Wormwood. From sandy beaches in Japan. Naturalized in parts of E. N. Am. Leaves felted, with few lobes. Flowers yellow. Also Old Man, *A. abrotanum,* seldom grown. Leaves greenish with thread-like segments.

A. lactiflora: China & India. Herb. 4–6 ft. May become top-heavy or invasive. Erect stems form thick clumps. Leaves green, numerous. Flowers, plumes of creamy white. Good to cut for mixed bouquets. Layout 3 & 13. Clearly for the highest rank in a border.

Arundinaria: GRAMINEAE. Reed

Evgrn. Most running bamboos should be avoided because invasive. Perhaps 150 spp. usable, sev. graceful.

Sun & shade. Ordinary cult. Control. Division.

Bamboo valuable as background or screen.

A. pumila: To 2½ ft. Probably smallest & hardiest. Canes, dull purple; leaves 7 in. pubescent & tessellated.

Arundo: GRAMINEAE.

Evgrn. Some from banks of Nile & Bible lands.

Sun or shade. Soil moist. Control. Division.

The personality of a reed is definite & strong.

A. donax: Giant Reed. Used for screens, lattices, mats, fishpoles, bagpipes, clarinets, organs through the centuries.

A. versicolor (*A. variegata*): Stripes yellowish. Less vigor, less hdy.

Asclepias: ASCLEPIADACEAE. Milkweed, Butterfly Silk-Weed, Pleurisy Root.

N. Am. Cent. Am. & S. Am. or E. N. Am.

Herb. Sap generally milky. Stout 3 × 2 ft.

Milkweeds popular for dried seed receptacles. Silky seeds.

Sun. Soil light, sandy, deep, no lime. Some spp. tender. Seed. Fleshy, spreading roots; plant 4 in. deep.

Dedicated to Asclepios, the Greek god of medicine.

A. tuberosa: Stems 1–3 ft. Leaves rather coarse; flowers numerous of a striking bright orange-red with small reflexed petals in rounded heads. Bloom fall. No milky sap. 'Vermilion' of esp. rich color.

A. speciosa: Leaves greyish. Flowers star-shaped in branching heads.

Beschorneria: AGAVACEAE.

Mex.

Evgrn. herb. 10 spp. The best known is 8 × 3 ft.

Sun. Warmth. Division.

Handsome large rosette of sword-shaped leaves, grey-green with thick texture.

B. yuccoides: Basal leaves to 2 ft. Inflorescence to 4 ft; a much-branched candalabra with

Aralia

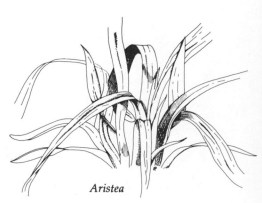

Aristea

Asclepias

Centranthus

Crambe

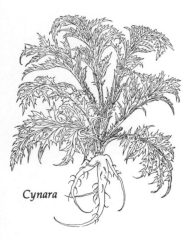

Cynara

red arching stems. Bracts coral-red & pink, flowers green. Blooms only in occasional years, in summer.

Beta vulgaris: Chard. Stems of red chard brilliant. See Rheum.

Celsia: SCROPHULARIACEA. Cretan Bear's Tail, Cretan Mullein.
Mediterranean.
Herb. Biennial. Closely related to *Verbascum*.
Sun. Soil med. Not hdy. north. Seed, sown in June.
Also grown in greenhouses. A hyb. between *Celsia* & *Verbascum* is *Celsioverbascum*, with fine qualities.
C. *cretica:* 4–6 ft. tall. Stiffly erect. Spire of closely arranged outfacing flowers on upper third of stem. 2 lobed upper lips somewhat deeper yellow than 3 lobed lower lips. Chocolate-brown marks at the base of upper lips. Bearded stamens.

Centranthus: VALERIANACEAE. Red Valerian, Jupiter's Beard.
Eur. & the Mediterranean.
Herb. Bushy. Tall clumps. Leaves fleshy, glaucus. Flowers in large long heads.
Sun. Ordinary cult. Division.
Naturalizes readily, esp. on stony banks.
C. *ruber* (*Valeriana rubra, Valeriana coccinea*): To 3 ft. Leaves oval to 4 in. long & stalkless, high on stem. Flowers minute red, fragrant. Summer & fall.

Chlorogalum: LILIACEAE. Soapplant, Amole.
W. N. Am.
Bulb, large, clothed with coarse fiber. Invasive. Plentious in the wild.
Sun. Soil unimproved. Division.
Greek chloros = green; gala = milk; refers to color of sap. Unusual contrast between tough bulb & delicate flower spray.
C. *pomeridianum:* N. Am. Indians relished the bulbs; used them to stupify fish; rubbed the young bulbs in water to make a lather (hence common name). Above a clump of limp, sword-shaped leaves, a spray of delicate flowers on a stalk to 8 ft. Flowers white with green midribs; open at night. Summer. (Some other spp. have flowers open in the day.)

Crambe: CRUCIFERAE. Seakale.
Canary Islands to W. Asia.
Herb. Sometimes woody at base. Deep rooted. Used as a vegetable in Europe; some spp. ornamental.
Sun & part shade. Soil rough, well drained. Tender at 20° F. Give space. Root cuttings. Seed.
Handsome, bold plant with unique foliage.
C. *maritima:* Sea Kale. Seacoasts of Eur. A wide plant, over 3 ft. across with strong, deep roots. Leaves rather cabbage-like, thick & fleshy, notched, curved & lobed, to 2 ft. long & 2 ft. wide. Flowers small, numerous, in dense clusters on 3 ft. stalks, pure white. Pea-like seed-pods. Allow a space 3 ft. wide. It dislikes transplanting. Deep, well-drained soil on the alkaline side. Hdy. to N.Y. City, U.S. To eat: cut & blanch the succulent spring shoots.
C. *cordifolia:* Colewort. Caucasus. To 7 ft., stout.

Grown as ornamental because of striking appearance. Leaves cordate sometimes over 2 ft. across, coarsely toothed, more or less hairy. Flowers in large panicles. Obviously needs space.

Crinum: AMARYLLIDACEAE. Crinum-Lily, Milk-&-Wine Lily, Poison Bulb.
Mostly trop. S. Am. & Afr.
Bulbs, large to 10 in. Clumps. 4 × 3 ft. Some spp. deciduous.
Sun or shade. Soil, deep fert., moist. Fertilize twice yearly or dilute fertilize weekly. Groom. Some from wet places; plant these by water-sides. Some prosper only in deep S. U.S. Some semi-hdy. If leaves persist, cut back to neck of bulb, Oct. Cover when frost expected.
Greenhouse plants for large containers. Or plant in warm site, e.g. against a wall. In pots, leave long necks of bulbs above soil level (in garden, tips just below). Extra water in blooming period.
C. *bulbispermum* (*C. longifolium*): S. Afr. Common in S. U.S. gardens. Semi-hdy. Bulbs, flask-shaped. Leaves many, deciduous, to 3 ft. long, pointed. Flowers trumpet-bell-shaped, the tips of the petals flaring, to 15 in., an umbel; flowers somewhat drooping, white to pink with streak down the inside & outsides reddish purple. June.
C. *moorei:* Woodlands of S. Afr. Differs in that edges of the broad leaves are smooth; they are however wavy. Umbels on 4 ft. stalks. White to pale pink or deep pink. Fragrant.
C. × *powellii:* Hyb. between the above 2 spp. 4 × 3 ft. Pink. Summer. Inherits hardiness from C. *bulbispermum*.
C. *powellii* 'Album', the white form, or 'Ellen Bosanquet', deep-rose. Leaves to 3 ft., flower stalks to 4 ft. Leaves of these *Crinums* grow in something of a jumble; become shabby in the fall; position the bulbs mid-rank in a mixed planting to somewhat conceal the foliage.
C. *amabile:* Trop. Asia & Indonesia. Leaves tapering, to 4 ft. Flowers narrow tubes with spreading petals, deep crimson outside, white, flushed red inside.
C. *augustum:* Seychelles Islands. Larger. Less fragrant.

Cynara: COMPOSITAE. Cardoon.
Eur.
Herb. Plants too big for most gardens. Leaves divided, recurving, silvery, spiny, to 4 ft. long.
Sun. Ordinary cult. Division. Suckers. Seed.
Resembles artichoke. Larger & magnificent. Flower known best in dried state.
C. *cardunculus:* 6 × 3 ft. Leaves to 4 ft. long, silvery grey, pointed, deeply divided. Flowers on stout grey stems. Summer. Big, purple thistle heads seen in the dried flower market. Cut back leaves and stems to ground.

Dianella: LILIACEAE. Flax-Lily.
N. Am. & W. S. Am., E. trop. Afr., Madagascar to China, Aust., N. Zealand, Pacific Islands including Hawaii, U.S.
Evgrn. Leaves numerous, strap-shaped.

Clump increases. Invasive? 2–4 ft. Flowers early spring & summer. Nodding tiny, lily-like, white or light blue.

Sun & part shade. Soil, med. moist, more water while actively growing. Feed regularly with liquid fertilizer. Hardiness marginal in Seattle, Wash., U.S. Division.

From Diana, goddess of the hunt. Branched slender rhizomes not visible amongst thick entangled roots. Grown in containers, must be replanted every 3 years.

D. tasmanica: Aust. To 4 ft. Basal leaves to 4 ft. & 1 in. wide, keeled & channeled below, edges with small spines, rigid, purplish green or greyish green. Flowers small, starry, in many branched panicles, on stems longer than leaves, light blue, beginning to open in Feb. & continuing many weeks. Bright dark blue berries ¾ of an in. across, long lasting.

D. revoluta: Aust. Leaves to 3 ft., with rolled-under margins. Flower stalks to 4 ft., flowers deep purple-blue (richer blue than other spp.) to 1 in. across in loose panicles. Berries, small, richer blue than other spp.

D. intermedia: Blueberry. N. Zealand. Woods & open areas. Leaves in 4s. Flowers white or delicate blue. Berries ½ in., blue.

D. caerulea: Aust., New S. Wales. To 2 × 1 ft. Leaves more grassy than tough. Flowers summer, tiny, light blue. Berries shiny, royal blue.

Dierama: IRIDACEAE. Wand Flower, Angel's Fishing Rod, Venus's Fishing Rod.

S. Afr.

Evgrn. & herb. To 5 ft. (1 sp. only 2 ft.). Leaves in clumps, narrow blades. Wide, arching growth or upright.

Sun. Soil moist, fert. Dislikes lime. Drainage. Division. Seed.

Corms liked by mice & gophers; plant in wire baskets. Corms multiply if unmolested. Tender, if temperature goes to 10°F for more than three days.

Some arrangers like the tall delicate line. Bloom late summer.

D. pulcherrimum: Classed formerly as *D. pendulum.* Either sp. name fits its character. The Slieve Donad Nursery in N. Ireland has selected forms, named after birds. Another breeder's cv. names are for fairies, others for characters in legend, e.g. 'Ceres', cobalt-violet; 'Oberon', carmine-purple; 'Puck', soft rose; 'Titania', light pink. To 5 × 1 ft. The tall, arching stems sway in the breeze as if on springs. Leaves long, grassy. Blossoms, many, bell-shaped, arranged so they look like the showering sparks of a rocket. Bells beautifully shaped, opening from end of stems first. Deep lilac-rose color, violet-mauve, mallow-pink. Silvery calyces. Summer.

D. pumilum: Sim. but growing only to 2 ft. A cv. 'Hermia'. Spreads vigorously to 1 ft. more upright than arching. "Grassy" foliage. Flowers satiny rose-pink, plentiful but for short season. Used in the hybs.

D. hybridum: A name to cover spontaneous crosses; cv. names for bred crosses. Mostly upright in growth. Midway in height between tallest & shortest.

Dietes: IRIDACEAE.

S. Afr., Aust.

Evgrn. Close to *Moraea.* Sword-shaped in broad clumps. 3 ft. or more.

Sun or part shade. Soil sandy & peaty; not wet or stagnant. Feed annually. Water in long dry periods. Choose permanent site. In mild climates, easy. Division.

Leave stems which have borne flowers; more buds are hidden within the sheathing bracts. If cut to use for an arrangement, leave lower part of stem with at least two nodes. Flowers are "fugaceous", i.e., each lasts but a short time; buds preparing to open meanwhile. Long flowering period, summer & fall.

D. vegeta: To 2 ft. Leaves stiff, narrowly sword-shaped, numerous, 2-ranked forming a crowded fan. Flowers 2½ in., white. Outer perianth segments with yellow or brown spots. Crests of style marked with blue.

D. v. var. *johnsonii:* African Iris. The var. taller, with leaves over 2 ft. Flowers 4 in. across.

D. bicolor: S. Afr. Flowers bright yellow, with maroon to purplish brown blotches at base of outer petals & spots of same on inner; 2 in. across, on branching stalks.

D. "Oakhurst hybrids", *D. bicolor* × *D. vegeta:* Flowers larger, of firmer texture & with repeated bloom. Sev. cvs. developed in W. U.S. as 'Lemon Drops', 'Orange Drops', & 'Contrast'.

D. robinsoniana: When not in bloom said to look like New Zealand Flax. Leaves to 6 ft. long & 2 in. wide. Flowers to 4 in. across, fragrant, creamy white with reddish yellow basal blotches. Sev. years before blooms. More tender than others. Flower stems not per. Needs large setting.

Dimorphotheca: COMPOSITAE. Cape-Marigold.

S. Afr.

Ann., per. & subshrubs with daisy-like flowers.

Sun. Soil med. Dislike humidity. Not hdy. to frost. Best in Mediterranean type climates. Dead-head. Cuttings.

Not good for arrangements since flowers close at night & in cloudy weather.

D. cuneata: Shrubby. Flowers 2 in. wide, ray florets white with colored undersides—blue-violet shaded with copper.

Diplarrhena: IRIDACEAE. Peacock Iris.

S. Aust., Tasmania.

Evgrn. Growth habit like that of *Libertia, Moraea* & *Dietes.* Leaves sword-shaped in 4 ft. clumps. Leaves narrower than those of *Moraea.* Looks smaller.

Sun or part shade. Soil well-drained with sand & compost, somewhat moist. Not hdy north. Division.

Do not cut flower stems all the way, since flower buds are present within the green sheath. Fragrant. Greek: diploos = double, arrhen = male; alludes to just 2 stamens.

D. moraea: Short creeping rhizomes invisible in root mass; leaves pointed, stiff, linear to 18 in. Flowers sev. at the top of a strong stem to 2½ ft. Curious in shape: 3 broad white segments in center, 3 small erect

Cynara

Dianella

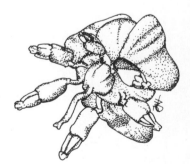

Gaura

Gonospermum

Hedychium

segments, 1 yellow & 2 purple. Each flower lives a short time but others open each day.
D. latifolia: Grow from seed. This sp. is available although uncommon.

Doryanthes: AMARYLLIDACEAE. Spear-Lily. E. Aust.
Evgrn. Huge. Goes with large succulent plants. Sun. Soil deep, fert., well drained. Tolerant of drought, not frost. Division. A number of years before first bloom.
D. palmeri: A sp. grown in S. Calif., U.S. Leaves up to 100, each leaf 6 ft. by 6 in. Flowers funnel-shaped, red with pale centers, interspersed with leafy bracts.

Echinops: See general Plant Descriptions.
Two spp. which can grow large are:*E. tournefortii* (to 5 ft.) & *E. spaerocephalus* (to 7 ft.).

Eupatorium: See Woodland Plant Descriptions.
About 300 spp., some large. Examples of large spp. are: *E. maculatum, E. dubium,* & *E. purpureum.*

Euphorbia: See General Plant Descriptions.
E. characias & some other spp. grow to form a clump 4 × 3 ft. and more.

Euryops: COMPOSITAE.
S. Afr. to Arabia & Socotra.
Evgrn. Many green leaves fancifully cut. Yellow daisies on dense subshrub.
Sun. Soil med. Drainage. Groom. Shear to induce second bloom. Plant new every 3 years. Semi-tender. Cuttings.
Good in tubs. Useful as punctuation for bed or border. Look for *E. acraeus* more dwarf.
E. pectinata: A subshrub, 3 × 3 ft., evgrn., stems and leaves densely coated with grey or white hairs. Flowers numerous, a soft yellow daisy on 6 in. stem, with 20 ray florets. Spring & summer.

Gaura: ONAGRACEAE.
SE. U.S. & Argentina.
Herb. Basal tufts evgrn. Wide & tall. Flowers dainty on willowy stems. Very long blooming period, summer & fall.
Sun. Soil ordinary. Somewhat tolerant of drought. Cut back to within 6 in. of ground. Hdy. as far north as N.Y. City in U.S. Cuttings. Seed.
Racemes sim. to those of Gasplant but larger & with less conspicuous stamens. Plant with shrubs & subshrubs, *Digitalis, Penstemon* & other sturdy perennials.
G. lindheimeri: Clump 4 × 4 ft.; airy. Slender, waving stems. A willowy plant. Leaves thin textured, small, narrow, oval, numerous, spotted with rose in the fall. Flowers pale pink with white.

Gonospermum: COMPOSITAE.
Canary Islands.
Herb. & semi-evgrn. Subshrub. Foliage grey with intricate pattern, very finely divided.
Sun. Drainage. Ordinary cult. Prune. Cuttings.
Sometimes becomes overly woody. Start new plant periodically. Sometimes confused with *Chrysanthemum ptarmieiflorum.* See Bramwell's *Wild Flowers of the Canary Islands.*
G. canariensis: Evgrn. Subshrub to 5 ft. Leaves

look like grey lace. Tolerant of winter rain; no insects or disease. Not long-lived. Semi-tender. In cold weather climates, the lower leaves shrivel. Flowers small white daisies often appearing rayless; in wide clusters early summer. Foliage has unique pattern.

Goodyera: ORCHIDACEAE. Rattlesnake Plantain or Latticeleaf. N. Am., Japan.
Herb. Rhizome. Terrestrial. Stems leafy. Cool greenhouse or warm climates.
½ shade. Drainage. Compost of peat, leaf-mould & sand or pieces of soft sandstone.
Sepals & petals meet at tips forming a helmet. Bloom spring & summer.
G. oblongifolia (G. menziesii): Synonyms *G. decipiens, Spiranthes decipiens* or *Epipactis decipiens.* Giant Rattlesnake Plantain. Woodlands. Leaves elliptic in basal rosettes to 4 ft., dark green, with whitish central stripe & veined with white. Flowers in dense racemes to 6 ft., small, white tinged green. Summer.

Gunnera: HALORAGIDACEAE. Water Milfoil family.
S. Am., Chile, Ecuador, Columbia, S. Brazil.
Herb. Very large & very small.
Part shade & shade. Soil moist. Division.
See also Bog Plant Descriptions. Some spp. are long stemmed trailers.
G. manicata & *G. chilensis:* Huge plants with leaves 6 ft. across, lobed & sharply toothed, to 8 ft. long, prickly, on stout stalks. Rhubarb-like, suitable for damp places in large settings, as arboretums.
G. manicata, the largest sp., crown as large as a man's body (R.H.S.). *G. chilensis:* crown almost as large as that of *G. manicata.* See text.

Hedychium: ZINGERBARACEAE. Ginger-Lily.
Warm parts of Asia & 1 sp. in Madagascar.
Herb. Mostly naturalized in Hawaii, U.S. More or less tuberous & rhizomous. Tender below freezing. Battered by heavy, fall rain.
Sun. Warmth. Soil moist & fert. Ample water in growth period. Cut back to rhizome not injuring next year's buds. Division.
Fragrant. Bloom Oct. Spread doubles each year.
H. coronarium: White Ginger-Lily or Garland Flower. Flowers used for leis in Hawaii. Roots hdy. in Ca., U.S.
H. flavescens: Yellow Ginger-Lily. Uncommon except in warm climates.
H. gardneranum: Kahili Ginger-Lily. To 6 ft. Leaves to 1 ft. long; turn blue-green in maturity. Flowers in spikes or clusters terminate leafy stems; 4 in. across, yellow with projecting red stamens.

Heliconia: HELICONIACEAE. Lobster Claw, False Bird of Paradise. W. Indies, Cent. Am. & S. Am.
Evgrn. 2–6 ft. Large clumps. Stems & leaves very dramatic. Brilliant bracts.
Sun. Warmth. Soil, rich loam. Ample water. Tender. Drainage. Division.
Sometimes cut flowers shipped from Hawaii to mainland U.S.

Heliopsis: COMPOSITAE. False Sun Flower. N. & S. Am.

Herb. Related to *Helianthus*. Background per. 5 × 2 ft. Spreads annually.

Sun. Ordinary cult. Cut to ground. Division. Seed.

Spp. seldom seen; replaced in gardens by cvs.

H. helianthoides var. *scabra*: (The variety sometimes given genus status.) To 4 ft. With sev. variants. Cvs.: e.g., 'Light of Loddon', deep lemon-chrome-yellow; 'Gold Greenheart', dble., yellow with green centers. Cvs. less tall, more compact.

Hemerocallis: LILIACEAE. Daylily.
Japan, China, Cent. Eur.

Herb. & evgrn. Cvs. numerous. Seek a cv. which is compact. Leaves strap-shaped, soft. Ideally, foliage creates a dense mound of curving leaves, the clump becoming over 3 ft. wide. Flowers & buds, fresh or withered, are considered a delicacy as a food.

Sun & part shade. Soil, tolerant of any sort. Ordinary cult. Groom. Division.

Breeding extensive. Diploids & tetraploids. Spp. used: *H. minor*, toward more dwarf size, *H. flava*, the Lemon Daylily to contribute fragrance, *H. fulva*, for colors & shapes: throat long, segments narrow, margins recurved. Many cvs.

Examples are 'Apollo, 'Black Magic', 'Hyperion', 'Pink Charm', 'Pink Damask', 'Gusto'.

Liatris: COMPOSITAE. Kansas Gay Feather or Blazing Star. U.S.

Herb. Colorful in mixed planting. Leafy stems from tufts of grassy leaves.

Sun or ½ shade. Soil med. Plant every 2 years. Seed.

Flowers at the top of spike open first (unusual). Summer.

L. pycnostachys (or *L. pycnostachya*): Kansas Gay Feather, tallest. To 4 ft. Stems topped by a spike, to 1 ft., of small, fluffy, mauve-pink flowers, resembling bottle brushes.

L. spicata (*L. callilepis* of gardens): To 3 ft. Brilliant mauve-pink, esp. 'Kobold', occasionally white (var. alba).

L. 'White Spire' is listed.

Libertia: IRIDACEAE.
Chile, N. Zealand.

Evgrn. Clumping. 3 × 2 ft. or 1 sp. 2 × 2 ft. Leaves sword-shaped, narrow, flaring.

Sun or part shade. Drainage. Moisture, esp. in the air.

Division.

Begins to bloom in Mar.; long period follows. Will cut. Pick when buds partly open.

L. formosa: Chile. Thick clumps of narrowly sword-shaped leaves. When leaves brown at the tips, remove. Flowers on stiff stems to 3 ft. Flowers white, in bud rounded, close to stalk on the top one-third. Open to saucer-shape. Brown calyces between the flowers, do not detract. Orange seed pods are described; none developed in my garden.

L. ixioides: N. Zealand. Sim. but much shorter & opener than *L. formosa*. Leaves narrower, more flaring. Flowers with greenish outer petals, inner ones white. Very attractive oval seed vesicles, first soft green then turning yellow from the base upward. Altogether very refined.

Lilium: See Woodland & Outdoor Room. Some of the spp., especially those native to West Coast U.S. woodland are tall and stout and increase to form wide colonies. One example illustrates the text, p. 106.

Lupinus: Several spp. are quite shrubby and may become over 3 feet wide. See General for herb. spp.

L. albifrons: Calif. Really a shrub, 4 × 3 ft. Leaves silky, silver colored. Flowers cream, yellow, lavender in short spikes.

L. arboreus: Bush or Tree Lupine. Bushy, woody shrub; to 8 ft. in the wild. Can become a weed. Suitable on a sunny bank with pers. of like personality. An older shrub may not last through a wet winter & younger plants more suitable. Sow seed (preferably in plant bands) every other year. Flowers soft yellow & fragrant.

Lythrum: LYTHRACEAE. Purple-Loosestrife.
N. Am., Asia, Afr., & Aust.

Herb. Some spp. naturalized along lakes & rivers. Seed themselves freely. Prefer boggy soil but will grow in a well watered site.

Part shade. Soil moist. Ordinary cult. Seed.

Bloom in summer. Slender spikes.

L. salicaria: Erect to 5 ft. Flowers purple-red or strong magenta-pink in racemes to 1 ft., with leafy bracts. Sway in the wind on wiry stems.

L. 'Dropmore Purple': A deep, strong shade.

L. 'Morden's Pink': Most popular cv. Good pink. Goes with *Monarda*. 'Firecandle', intense rosy red. Best with grey foliaged perennials.

Moraea: IRIDACEAE. Fortnight Lily, African Iris, Butterfly Iris, Peacock Iris, Peacock Flower.
Afr.

Evgrn. Roots complex with corms attached. Erect clump of narrow blade-shaped leaves parallel-veined. 3 × 3 ft. *Dietes* is separate botanically but is sim.

Sun & ½ shade. Warmth. Soil loose. Good drainage. Division.

Roots become a tough, tangled mass in which corms are invisible. Clumps of some spp. may become as wide as 4 ft. with a strong permanent appearance. Alternate for a shrub.

M. polystachya: (This sp. poisonous to livestock.) Leaves 2 ft., 3–4 to a clump. Stems to 3½ ft. with 5–20 clusters of flowers each with 3–6 flowers. Lilac with bright yellow blotch at bottom of 3 spoon-shaped outer petals. Each flower short-lived. The flower stem is wrapped in a sheath & side clusters continue to emerge from productive nodes.

M. spathulata (*M. spathaceae*) (*Dietes huttonii*): Considered best sp. for gardens. Variable. Leaves to 4 ft. bend over to sweep the ground. On erect (or bending) stems to 1½ ft., flowers to 3 in. across, bright yellow with darker markings at base of outer petals; inner petals narrower & suberect. Flower after flower is produced, late spring.

M. villosa: Peacock Iris. Single slender basal leaf. Flowers on stems to 2 ft. Beige, yellow, orange, light lavender with colorful

Hemerocallis

Lupinus

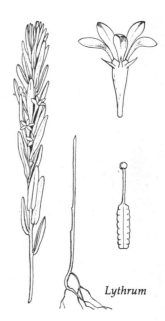

Lythrum

Romneya

Valeriana

Woodwardia

blotches at base of outer petals, peacock-blue or green, margined with orange, yellow, deep purple or almost black. Each lasts 4 days. Flowers do not close at night.

M. tripetala: Flowers remain open for 3–4 days. One leaf. Slender stem to 2 ft. Flowers in clusters of up to 3. Dark lilac to turquoise-blue with triangular patch of yellow at base of outer petals (or plain purple). Outer ones droop, inner, small & narrow, angle outward.

M. tricuspidata: S. Afr. Single leaf. Blooms "propeller"-shaped, white with light blue veins and metallic, blue-black blotch; small inner petals with creamy white crests.

M. johnsonii: Robust: Must have summer water.

M. irioides (or *M. iridoides*): To 2 ft. Grows from a rhizome. Semi-hdy. Flower white, waxy with orange, brown, purple stippling & lilac-blue crests. Stem branches into more flowers after terminal flower fades.

M. dwarfs: To 6 in. 2 in. leaves thread-like. Seldom seen in cultivation. Open after 2 p.m. when sun is out. 3 petals flat, pale. Flower lavender, pencilled purple with 3 petals upright with soft yellow marking.

Panax: ARALIACEAE. Ginseng.
N. Am., Asia.
Herb. Tuberous. Used medicinally in the Orient. Some spp. being used throughout the world. Roots aromatic.
Sun or shade. Ordinary cult. Seed, but stratify.
Leaves palmately arrayed; leaflets spreading from top of stalk.

P. quiquefolius: American Ginseng. To 2 ft. Leaves usually 5-pointed, coarsely toothed, leaflets to 6 in. Center leaflet larger than 2 basal ones. Flowers greenish white, in July & Aug. Berries bright red.

Petasites: Compositae, Senecio tribe. Butter-bur. Sweet Coltsfoot
Eur. N. Asia and N. Am
Herb. 3 spp. Spreads widely with strong under and overground stems. Large and bold appearance.
Shade. Soil somewhat damp. Division. Seed.
Suits a natural garden with a sloping site under trees.

P. albus: Leaf blades to 16 inches. Two seasons, one for flowers early Spring. Flowers on 12 inch scapes followed by foliage. Lobed and denticulate, glabrous above.

Phormium: LILIACEAE. New-Zealand-Flax
N. Zealand.
Evgrn. Tall. Can grow to 10 ft. Wide spreading. Strong stiff sword-shaped. Flower stems top leaves by 4 ft. Upper 3 ft. a stiff branching spray of dull red flowers. Flower stems and seed pods, almost black when dry.
Sun or shade. Soil med. Needs space. Semi-hdy. Groom. Division.
Cvs. either smaller and/or more colorful.

P. tenax: Needs space; at least 3 ft. wide to 7 ft. tall. Leaves evgrn., sword-shaped; good for arrangements of the largest kind. Seek cvs., e.g., 'Bronze Baby', 'Smiling Thorn': Variegated pink & green stripe.

P. cookiana: Hardier sp. 4 × 1 ft. At least 2 good cvs., 'Tricolor' & 'Dazzler'. Leaves striped pink, green & purple. Flowers green plus brown.

Puya: BROMELIACEAE.
S. Am., Andean region.
Evgrn. Flower stalks sometimes to 15 ft. Taller in native habitat. Leaves in rosettes. A handsome plant without bloom.
Sun & part shade. Warmth. Maritime area advantageous. Semi-hdy. Drainage. Plants die after blooming; new rosettes have formed around outside. One of these will bloom in 7 years? The bloom defies description.

P. alpestris (*P. whytei*): Chile. Hardiest. Main axis & flower branches extend beyond blooming part (thought to be perches for birds). Leaves thorny, prickly, recurved, to 3 ft. long, 1 in. wide at base in a great rosette, bright green above & thickly coated with white scales underneath. Flowers in erect yucca-like spikes on stalks to 4½ ft. To 20 spikelets, lax panicles, metallic blue-green with reddish stem & reddish bracts. Survived 3 freezes in San Francisco, Calif., U.S.

P. berteroniana: Chile. Leaves to 4 ft., 2 in. wide at base, with long spines on margins. Vivid chartreuse.

Rheum: POLYGONACEAE. Rhubarb.
Temp. & subtrop. Asia.
Herb. Ornamental as well as edible. Usually 6 × 6 ft.
Sun. Soil fert. Ample water. Seed.
Translucent stems. Excel. crimson. Bloom early summer. Seeds attractive.

R. rhaponticum: Common edible rhubarb. *R. officinale:* Medicinal rhubarb.

R. palmatum 'Atrosanguineum': To 6 ft. Leaves large, deeply cut, vivid red when young & red on undersides until blooming time. Flowers "cerise-crimson" in big fluffy panicles; early summer. May take seeking.
R. palmatum 'Bowles Crimson': For a damp place, esp. waterside. Flowers in big panicles. Deep red. June & July.

Romneya: PAPAVERACEAE. Matilija-Poppy.
N. Am., S. & Baja Calif.
Evgrn., partially. Tall, branching, spreading. Leaves indented. Poppies huge.
Sun & part shade. Soil med., fert. Water in growth period. Division.
Will grow under poor conditions. More lush with good conditions.

R. coulteri: To 8 ft., bushy. Leaves glaucous blue-grey, to 4 in.: margins sparsely fringed with hairs. Flowers with crinkly, crepey petals, to 6 in., white with a large, fluffy, yellow central section.

R. c. var *trichocalyx:* Leaves with narrower lobes.

Hybrid: *R. coulteri* × *R. c. trichocalyx.* Difficult to discern a difference or improvement but probable nevertheless.

Strelitzia: STRELITZIACEAE (or MUSACEAE). Bird of Paradise.
Mostly S. Afr.
Herb. or woody-trunked. Fans of 2-ranked blades, paddle-shaped, thick, leathery,

bluish green. Flowers unique. For large containers & ample space in the garden.

Sun. Soil, deep fert. Drainage. Semi-tender. Division.

Flowers in succession from large, stiff pointed spathe; 3 sepals, 3 petals, 2 of which make arrow-shaped tongue. Stamens & style lie in the groove. Bold. Curious.

S. reginae (S. parvifolia): Bird of Paradise. To 4 ft. Leaves paddle-shaped, the blades 6 in. wide, leathery. Flowers with orange-red sepals & purple-blue petals; beak & head formed by greenish spathe. Bloom spring & summer. Outdoors in warm climates.

S. r. var. *humilis* is more dwarf; look for *S. r.* var. *juncea,* odd.

S. nicolai: Giant Bird of Paradise. Huge leaves from a trunk to 25 ft. Leaves strong, deeply veined. Flowers blue & white. Nestled in axils of upper leaves; arising from reddish chestnut spathes.

S. alba: To 18 ft.; all white.

Valeriana (Centranthus): VALERIANACEAE. Valerian, Garden Heliotrope.

Widespread except Aust.

Shrubs, anns., pers. Invasive. Appearance inelegant.

Sun. Soil poor. Tough. Division.

Large in the sense that spread is unrestrained.

V. offinalis: Common Valerian. From Eur. & Asia naturalized in N. Am. Robust. To 5 ft. "Cats Valerian" since cats love it. Stems may rise out of anywhere from a hedge or thick shrub.

V. rubra: A rough, tough plant sometimes used in a poor quality situation such as an unimproved slope. Flowers white, crimson, pale red in late spring, in sun or shade; compound heads of tiny flowers.

Wachendorfia: HAEMODORACEAE.
S. Afr.

Herb. Bulbous & tuberous roots. Often 6 ft. ×

18 in. Leaves large & plicate.

Sun. Ordinary cult. Semi-hdy. Division.

Flowers in panicles, color bright & rich orange or yellow, funnel-form. Bloom early summer.

W. thyrsiflora: To 6 ft. Leaves 3 ft. long & 3 in. wide. Looks like a tall coarse *Aspidistra.* Flowers in dense cylindrical panicles 1 ft. long. Each side shoot with sev. starry blooms, yellow-orange.

W. paniculata: Sim. but flowers yellow.

Woodwardia: POLYPODIACEAE. Chain Fern. Eur., Asia, No. Am.

Large strong-growing. Prefer moisture

W. fimbriata: British Columbia to Mexico. In wet coastal forests to 9'.

Yucca: AGAVACEAE or LILIACEAE. Adam's Needle, Joshua Tree, Our Lord's Candle, Spanish Bayonet, Spanish Dagger.

Not exclusively desert.

Evgrn. Some to 40 ft. Large strong clumps. Leaves stiff, sharply pointed. Flower stalk often to 10 ft. Pyramidal head magnificent for huge arrangement.

Sun. Excel. drainage. Cut back flower stem. Groom. Division.

Lower growing spp. better for the garden. See text.

Y. recurvifolia: One of smaller kinds. To 6 ft. Trunk branches.; sev. leaf clusters, a stalk of flowers possibly for each. Cut off these great stems with a saw & from a ladder. Flowers creamy white, saucer-shaped, crowded. Grow sev. plants in a large setting or grow one plant with carefully chosen companions. Good in a large container.

Y. smalliana: Adam's Needle, Bear Grass. Leaves to 2 ft. No teeth on margins; instead curly threads (see *Hesperaloe*). Panicles to 15 ft., with white flowers to 2 in. across.

Sev. spp. of *Yucca* have variegated forms.

Gunnera

12. For Cutting

PLANT DESCRIPTIONS TO BE FOUND IN ONE OR ANOTHER CATEGORY

When you say "There is nothing to cut in the garden", you have not been out that day to look around. You may not have gorgeous stock, snapdragons, lilies, etc.; but something can always be made interesting with bits and twigs from different plants as they were gathered in your hand—to fit in a mustard jar or wine bottle.

I think one should reserve a little space which is named the "cutting garden". It may be a corner where a few plants of some new color or some new cultivar are being introduced, primarily to use for picking. There is no reason why this corner cannot be at the same time as decorative as any other corner, but it will have no unspoken sign, "touch me not". Picking frequently will reduce the mass of color somewhat, but on the other hand, picking stimulates more and longer blooming. No more labor is required to keep up a cutting garden than any other garden space, since dead-heading will be cut at least in two.

Pickables, however, can be thoroughly scattered in the garden to serve the primary purpose of landscaping but when chosen, their use as cut flowers is taken into account. I will describe an assortment of plants which I would like to have to pick. You will like others better since personal taste is such a strange factor in flower arranging. You will find some suggestions perhaps among my favorites which you can work into your garden. Or plant in containers, for example *Eucharis*.

I would always want at least one peony plant; I would like two or three but all of different kinds of the hybrid herbaceous Peonies and at least one Tree Peony. I prefer the single flower to the double. The doubles look gorgeous but they have lost some of their special form. In a single flower the spacing of the petals contributes to the design and the center is another "work of art". If I could have but two, one would be *Paeonia* 'Scarlet O'Hara' for brilliance and then a white one, there are several named cultivars: perhaps *P.* 'Krinkled White', single, pure white with a yellow center; or *P.* 'Minnie Shaylor', semi-double; or *P.* 'Bowl of Cream', fully double. I would search for the species with a waxy, small, single yellow flower on a bushy plant—the texture extraordinarily shiny. This is the species you pronounce like Molly-the-witch. This peony deserves a place of honor in your garden; the leaves, beautifully cut, are somewhat bronze when young, changing to deep green—very glossy. It is herbaceous and every year makes a full mass of foliage mounded to two and a half feet almost hiding the flowers. The flowers are attractive balls in bud and open to a bright yellow cup. Many buds continue to open all summer. All peonies need sharp drainage, sun and nourishment. Peonies fit easily into any and all gardens.

Eucharis

Alstroemeria is more difficult to incorporate in a small garden. The colorful hybrids like a place to themselves and if one wants straight stems of the big flowered *Ligtus* for picking, special support systems must be devised. I would certainly go to a lot of trouble to fix a site if I could get hold of roots of some of the new hybrids—the flowers are fantastic. There is at this point a corner on the market and some of the newest cvs. have not yet been released.

A species from Brazil, *A. pulchella,* is much less imposing and will grow anywhere in the garden with no attention. It is an example of the curious combination of red and green in a flower color. *A. pulchella* is probably identical with *A. psittacina;* the odd coloring makes the common name, "Parrot Lily" seem appropriate. At the top of a firm, erect two to three-foot stem is a cluster of upright flaring trumpets, each close to two inches long, though varying in length, dark-red, tipped with green and brown spotted. Odd looking in a mixed bouquet, this is quite certain to be a conversation piece. A few stems are in full flower most of the year. It is not greedy for space or nutrition but those growing in a good spot will be more handsome than those from a poor one. The handful of pulpy fingers, the roots, are easily moved with a spadeful of soil. This *Alstroemeria* will travel all over the garden but is not hard to control; just pull off the out-of-bounds stems. When it is time to divide it, the roots will be several inches deeper than they were when planted; those queer soft fingers descend even in firm soil. If this species were planted adjacent to other species of *Alstroemeria,* when the bed is to be remade, this one can be identified; the fingers are shorter, firmer and browner. There will be enough to give away; the roots of this particular species can stand exposure for a few days.

On the contrary, roots of the *A. chilensis,* and relatives, Chilean Lily, resent any air which may dry the pulpy fingers. When the roots are to be moved from one place to another, the place should be so ready that the roots may be popped into the hole—or rather laid on their side spread apart on the loose earth. Even so they may sulk. If you have enough to give away, your friend must be instructed. Wrap the roots in damp sphagnum moss when they make that immediate trip to another garden. After they have been placed in the hollow already prepared, the hole should be filled only part way. When the delicate shoots show on the surface, soil should be added preferably little by little.

In their own island-bed or in a deep box, platforms of wire mesh can be made at different heights. The mesh will help hold the flower stems erect. If this is too much trouble, several slender stakes placed to encircle a whole clump will do the job. There are so many good colors—pink, salmon, coral-orange, even light crimson, often with beautiful markings. Bloom continues for several weeks. They are exceedingly long-keeping if only one cleans off the foliage well on the part of the stems which will be under water in the vase. *Alstroemeria* flowers keep many days.

A. peruviana, Peruvian Lily, actually from Chile, is a good cut flower too. But roots grow large and thick and wander in an uncontrollable manner.

A. pelegrina (A. violaceae) is a very choice *Alstroemeria* which should be grown in boxes rather than in the ground since the containers can be moved under cover in a cold spell. Probably, this is the real Lily of the Incas.

"Alstroemerias . . . may be planted out in Spring, lifted after blooming, and stored over winter," says Hortus III, and further "pot plants in the greenhouse . . . shaken out annually." There is no further advice as to how to store. I am glad I do not have to store. A thick mulch over the ground level keeps the roots safe in cool climates when *Alstroemerias* are grown in the garden. Only *A. pulchella* will tolerate full shade.

Let us think about *Gerbera.* It is without rival in the world of daisies. What an addition to a vase of mixed flowers! It is hard to place in the garden since it will not flower without adequate nourishment and perfect drainage. Is there room in a small garden for a raised bed just for *Gerbera*? A possible solution is containers; but will we wish to pick the flowers which look so rich and colorful in the pot?

Now I think of another perennial which cannot be added to the garden casually no matter how good it is for picking. This is *Hosta* which is especially valuable for its foliage. To have enough to pick you must grow quite a few plants. *Hostas,* nearly all, need shade; they must have slug control; the roots must be unmolested for a long season of dormancy. I suggest you select the cultivar that you like the best and somehow create a site just to its liking.

Bergenia is another perennial which is picked mostly for foliage. It has many uses. If I were to have just one small patch, I would get the white flowering cultivar

Alstroemeria

Alstroemeria

Bergenia

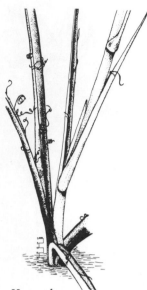

Hesperaloe

Angelica

named "Silberlicht". The greatest problem is snails and slugs.

I will append a list of perennials to grow especially for foliage useful in arrangements. However, I would like to star the four which follow.

Hesperaloe sends up a tall stalk bearing flowers of a lovely color. But you could grow it just for the foliage—leathery leaves trimmed with curly hairs.

Rohdea is sometimes grown as a container plant. It is a highly prized genus in Japan where breeding has resulted in many leaf variations. Even a plain leaf is valuable to anyone who likes to use sword-shaped leaves or narrow-oval leaves with flowers in a bouquet. Look in Japanese nurseries for forms of *Rohdea japonica*.

Aspidistra is easy to find in a house plant store. This is a broader leaf with more curve and especially attractive when variegated. Slugs and snails are particularly fond of it.

Angelica pachycarpa might be hard to find but it will grow from seed. This leaf is a work of art—intricately cut and glossy dark-green. Plants will grow in the shade but need moisture to produce good foliage. One or two can be squeezed into a corner since they are tolerant of lean soil and will beautify their site by their sculpture and sheen. Flower is a composite—a flattened head.

Chrysanthemum, so many kinds and many pickable. In other chapters you will find described certain species for various purposes. Several have a second use as cut material. Notes on a few follow:

C. coccineum (Pyrethrum roseum): Painted Daisy. 30 or more varietal names, white, pink, crimson, single, double; 'Evenglow' by Alan Bloom is considered one of the best.

C. parthenium (Pyrethrum or *Parthenium):* Feverfue. Improved forms including doubles; these look like buttons on stems to one foot. Good as a filler in a vase.

C. 'Aureum': Lots of flowers on bushy plants. Useful to clip for a knot garden. Foliage aromatic. May be sloppy or invasive. Flowers small, white, good for fillers in mixed bouquets.

C. yezoensis (C. arcticum of gardens): Pink form and yellow form. Stems to one foot. Recommended by Thomas as a ground cover.

C. rubellum of gardens: May be a hybrid of unknown origin. Clones include 'Clara Curtis', clear pink and 'Duchess of Edinburg', coppery red. Fertile soil; drainage; division every three years.

C. nipponicum: Nippon Daisy. Like Shasta Daisy but three feet; tender.

C. × *superbum nipponicum:* To three feet; especially good for cutting.

C. Korean hybrids: Treat as annuals. These are single or double, daisy type or ball type, small and somewhat large. Traces of their early form may be seen in the more simple moderns.

A further look at the common *Chrysanthemum* is in order.

Hybrid Garden *Chrysanthemums:* Old-fashioned kinds valuable for picking especially in October and November.

Hybrid moderns: Many shapes, forms, size and colors—the petals incurved, reflexed, quilled, pompon, spider, etc. Examples of cultivars for picking:

C. 'Red Rover': big, daisy-type, rich color

C. 'Emperor of China': white spider

C. 'Silver Lace': chartreuse spider

C. 'Waikiki': orange spider

Please see the index for outline of Culture.

Chrysanthemum is a mainstay in any garden in any quantity from one or two plants to dozens. It is generous with bloom and when cut will last weeks not days. It takes little care and goes on indefinitely provided it is cut back and divided when needed. Tiresome? Not really if you have the more interesting kinds and colors. Even satisfactory in pots if you cannot give it room in the garden. Let us turn to some other genera.

Have you a penchant for white? You might choose the *Phlox* which picks the best *P. caroliniana* 'Miss Lingard' and look for white kinds of a number of ordinarily colored perennials of several species, those named 'White Lustre', 'White Swirl', 'White Cloud', 'Icicle'. Renew, in any case.

The white clones of *Scabiosa* can be purchased if you prefer white instead of mixed. *Scabiosa* takes little room—unless you want lots to pick. There is no other perennial which responds better to being picked; the more often you pick it the more it blooms. If you don't pick it, it stops blooming.

One is always having to make room it seems. It is often good to find a plant which takes up little space—that is for what it gives in foliage or flower. What then would I advise you to tuck in somewhere if only to cut?

It would be very useful to have enough true lilies to cut. Once in awhile, you might want to demolish a display in a container, in order to use the unique form in your arrangement.

There is a lovely herbaceous perennial not that generous and not that easy to find. It is so slender it will push its delicate stem up through clumps and mounds of neighboring plants to arch perhaps two feet above them. This is *Anthericum liliago*. See p. 122. Not a showy flower to pick, but excellent for a "bud vase", now back in style. Not to pick in quantity: it produces only a few stems. Tempting to leave in the garden where it curves with such lasting beauty opening new tiny "lilies" one by one. It grows from neither bulb or corm although it has strap-shaped leaves and belongs to the Lily family.

Chrysanthemum

I have pointed out to you the benefits of narrowness in some of the candidates for picking. These look well coming into bloom and are not missed after they have been picked. Sometimes the picking will cause them to bloom again. One is *Anigozanthos*: tall, slender stalks with a moist curious flower on top. I will mention three other narrow plants. One is *Pasithea caerulea*: it has a slender, unbranching stem reaching usually over the top of its neighbors; the form of its intense blue-lavender flower is beautiful; it can be cut for a "bud vase" although it has little lasting quality. 'Kalistrum' is tall and delicate looking. Another is that easy *Alstroemeria, A. pulchella*, I have previously extolled, and described which lasts over a week. It can be allowed to travel in the garden and come up singly (or perhaps in groups) amongst annuals, perennials or shrubs. It takes up little room even when over productive. It provides an unusual note in a mixed bouquet.

I have sworn off including bulbs in these pages. But how can I skip over several of my favorite bulbous perennials for picking. Some take up little room and do not need to be lifted. I will mention a few. Two *Ornithogolums, O. arabicum*, with its black, shiny, shoe-button centers and *O. thyrsoides* with cream-colored pointed pyramids. This one lasts weeks when cut.

Chrysanthemum

There are two *Gladioli*, not quite white but very useful for mixed arrangements or for a stem or two in a slender vase. *Gladiolus tristus* var. *concolor* is softest yellow, blooms in earliest spring, multiplies its small corms and seeds all over the garden. Subtle fragrance adds to its value. Its cousin, *Gladiolus callianthis (Acidanthera)*, has fragrance also, quite unique. The small trumpet is decidedly pointed and its white is traced with purple. It may bloom in summer or not until fall. The slender stems of both *Gladioli* take up little room in a flower bed but are tall and distinguished enough to make a statement. These suggestions may suffice to interest you in searching out bulbs and corms to incorporate in your plantings simply for flowers to cut, white or bright colored.

Think now of a few perennials you might like to have because their colors are unusual. "Burnt" orange is often a sparkling introduction to an otherwise unexciting combination. There is a *Geum* with many small flowers in bloom a long time. Buy when in bloom in order to get the best muted orange.

A small poppy has an orange color which exemplifies the term "burnt" orange. This is *Papaver atlantica*. Not room-consuming like Oriental poppy—although it seeds itself readily—and more or less evergreen. Quantity of flowers is greatly increased by constant picking.

Plant *Clivia* if you have room and choose one of the hybrids for the best orange. Look for a species of *Helenium* with a shade you may call tangerine. *Telephium* 'Autumn Joy' becomes more and more russet as it ages.

Odd shades have been brought to your attention in the chapter on color. You will recall that often a cultivar will be selected which has a muted mixture in its color. The species which comes to mind is an out of the ordinary kind of Columbine, *Aquilegia escalcarata*, a small flower—fat and double and with no prominent spurs; the shade might be called "dusky" rose instead of "dusty" rose.

Many genera with grey foliage will be valuable for cutting. Grow *Ballota* for its all grey look and unusual form.

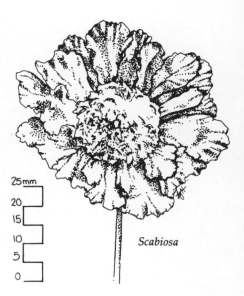

25 mm
20
15
10
5
0

Scabiosa

Intense colors are also valuable, as we have seen. Perhaps one of the brightest is *Hesperaloe* called Red Yucca, a strong stem, good for a modern arrangement. The color? "Shaded coral" is a fairly close description. Wonderful bronze in the leaves although only a few to cut. The plant takes up little room in the shrubbery border.

Anthericum

Alpinia speciosa is big for most gardens; it has a similar color. Of course there are true lilies with wonderful brilliant shades from yellow through red and exquisite for picking.

You will be guided in selecting spp. to provide cut flowers by two factors: one, the colors you have in your house; two, the colors you like the best. Perhaps these two will coincide? Find the descriptions of spp. in the various P.Ds.

PERENNIALS FOR CUTTING

(f. = foliage; b = bulb-corm; a = annual)

Anigozanthos

Ornithogolum

Acanthus	Clivia	Jasione
Achillea	Dahlia b	Kniphofia
Acidanthera	Daucus a	Lapeirousia
Aconitum	Delphinium	Lavandula
Adenothera	Dianthus	Leonotis
Aeonium	Dicentra	Lespedeza
Agapanthus	Digitalis	Leucocoryne b
Ajuga	Echinacea	Leucojum b
Alchemilla	Endymion b	Libertia
Allium b	Eremurus b	Ligularia f
Alpinia	Erigeron	Lilium b
Alstroemeria	Eriogonum	Limonium
Anaphalis	Eryngium	Linaria
Anemone	Erythronium b	Lindelofia
Angelica f	Eucharis b	Liriope
Anigozanthos	Eucomis b	Lunaria a
Anthemis	Euphorbia	Lupinus
Anthericum	Euryops	Lychnis
Anthurium b	Felicia	Lycoris b
Antirrhinum a	Fibigia	Lythrum
Aquilegia	Filipendula	Macleaya
Arabis	Foeniculum	Matthiola a
Artemisia	Francoa	Mertensia
Arum f	Freesia b	Monarda
Asarina	Fritillaria b	Muscari b
Asclepias	Gaillardia	Narcissus b
Asphodeline	Galax	Nicotiana a
Asphodelus	Genista	Nigella a
Aspidistra f	Gerbera	Ophiopogon
Astartea	Geum	Origanum
Aster	Gladiolus b	Ornithogalum b
Astilbe	Gloriosa	Paeonia
Astrantia	Gypsophila	Papaver
Babiana b	Haemanthus b	Paridisea
Ballota	Hedychium	Pasithea
Baptisia	Helenium	Pelargonium
Belamcanda b	Helichrysum f	Penstemon
Bellis	Heliopsis	Petasites
Bergenia	Helleborus	Phlomis
Brachycome a	Hemerocallis	Phlox
Brodiaea b	Hesperaloe	Physostegia
Bulbinella	Heuchera	Platycodon
Calocephalus f	Homeria b	Pleione
Camassia b	Hosta f	Polemonium
Campanula	Hunnemannia a	Polianthes b
Catananche	Hyacinthus b	Polygonatum
Cephalaria	Hymenocallis b	Primula
Chrysanthemum	Iberis	Ranunculus
Cimicifuga	Iris	Rehmannia
Clematis	Ixia b	Rohdea f

Clivia will flourish in a tub or large pot if given ample water and food. The most common sp., *Clivia miniata,* has cvs. with extra quality. E.B.

Lavandula stoechas looks attractive in a wood box. In a container it grows less wide and less dense than in the ground; the curious flowers with flaring top-knots can be better viewed when the plant is small and open. E.B.

A trough made of wood; not traditional to be sure, but a nice shape and texture for dwarf plants. This is not a scene in miniature but a collection of small perennials of varying form arranged with harmony as the goal. E.B.

On a wood deck or on wood steps or with wood as a background, wooden containers are suitable. All spp. of Lavender grow and bloom well in wood; several may be placed in a line or in a group. Here see a cv. of *Lavandula officinalis.* E.B.

Brick. These steps are left unadorned first because their full width is needed to express a welcome to the house and second because stark steps are more formal. The clipped hedges and closely trimmed *Ficus* carry out the severity. The grey rosette of the *Dudleya* is both contrast and compliment. M.M.

Steps must rise several feet in this garden, but the ascent can be broken by a platform part way up. Stone is elegant looking but the irregularity of its pattern makes the stairway more informal than formal. Perennials are planted near the front of the beds so that their stems may drape the edges of the steps. K.M.

Rustic steps mount a steep bank to the north terrrace of a house. *Rubus* is the main ground cover; it will flower little in so much shade but the leaves are rich in texture and shiny green. *Vancouveria* grows in a crevice between two branches of cascading Manzanita. E.B.

Aggregate pavement used for a series of steps. They are wide enough to border with pots either side. The larger containers contain sub-shrubs, e.g. dwarves of *Pieris, Arbutus, Ilex* and *Carissa, Pernettya, Loropetalum*. Smaller pots of perennials are added in their season. E.B.

Much attention has been given in recent years to the decorative qualities of vegetables. Some common edibles are allowed to go to seed for the beauty of the flower heads. Others are valuable for foliage form. Here is a true edible garden with decorative parallel lines. K.M.

Why not combine vegetables with non-use plants? Many have handsome foliage and none can surpass that of Artichokes. Cuts if you condition it well. B.W.

On this slope, a raised bed has been built up with logs to house some herbs. The leaves of the Comfrey stand out fresh looking and flaring from their 2 ft. stems. A sturdy plant of *Aloe vera* is accent for the softer leaves. In the foreground, *Santolina* has been allowed to tumble down the bank, giving a quite different effect from the stiff hedge it makes when clipped. E.B.

Mostly shade in a shrubbery border except on the forward edge. Grey foliaged perennials are used in combination to create contrast against the dark green of the background. Here an *Achillea* cv. is half as tall as the *Ballota nigra* and more blue-grey. Dittany, Marjorum and Thyme grow for looks as well as use. E.B.

FEATURING VEGETABLES AND HERBS

Portland. A broad brick path leads to the terraces. Two
risers are necessary to lift us to the slightly higher level.
Strips and beds are filled with perennials and pots stand
in strategic places. In this narrow space, the character of
the vines, shrubs and trees must be in harmony with the
perennials. J.Z.

Where does the path go? The more intriguing since it
changes character in mid-distance. It is lined in a natural
manner with casual perennials. J.Z.

Planting on two levels increases the impact of the design.
Here the basic lines are provided by foliage. Splashes of
lavender color below are repeated above for emphasis.
Colors must "go with" the color of the pavement. E.B.

This garden is planted on three levels. Its perennials
bloom in Spring as well as Summer. At the time of this
picture the lavender colors in the beds reflected the color
of the *Wisteria* on the house. L.H.

MORE THAN ONE LEVEL

Romneya
Rosmarinus
Rudbeckia
Ruta f
Salvia
Satureja
Scabiosa
Scilla b
Sedum
Senecio f
Solidago
Solidaster
Spathiphyllum b
Sprekelia b
Stachys

Sternbergia b
Stokesia
Strelitzia
Tanacetum
Telephium
Thalictrum
Thermopsis
Tiarella
Tigridia b
Trachelium
Trachymene a
Trillium
Trollius
Tropaeolum a
Tulbaghia b

Tulipa b
Uniola
Urospermum
Valeriana
Verbascum
Verbena
Veronica
Viola
Watsonia b
Yucca
Zantedeschia
Zephyranthes b
Zingiber f

Ballota

Papaver

Section III: Concentration

Lingularia

13. The Outdoor Room

The day of the container plant has certainly arrived, with all manner of places to display it.

There are a number of names for outdoor rooms; loggia, lanai, atrium, gazebo. These are modern, mostly sophisticated living spaces, or at least visiting places, a setting for container plants, one, two or many. These spaces have to some extent replaced the enclosed porches, conservatories, orangeries, sunrooms, vestibules, and verandas of our forbears. Today the outdoor room is usually more outdoors, especially in the climates where outdoor rooms can be lived in many months of the year. In such areas, there are terraces everywhere; one may be just an enlarged entry way—another may be almost as big as the house, with several rooms created by dividers for sitting, sunning, or eating, as well as looking.

Annexed to the terrace may be one or more features, places for container plants. The most likely is a set of steps to another level and the doorway to the terrace. If this is the front door there may be an entryway or a covered terrace along the house wall. The terrace may have its own wall for a practical purpose such as retaining the earth of a higher grade or for the purposes of enclosure or as an element of architecture. If the wall is designed to provide privacy or for architectural reasons, it may go all around the terrace and then we have a patio.

Decks have become popular. A deck is usually a continuation of the house and frequently made of wood planking. A house in the city often has a deck; the deck may be at the top of a flight of steps or down at the bottom or halfway as the steps angle, but it is always a place for plant containers. Since there is often protection and shade from trees or overhang in this situation, it is an excellent place for tender plants. Certain genera can be included in the design of a covered deck which you will see classed as "indoor-outdoor plants"; they would be different according to climate but you would find the fancy-leaved Begonias and a number of other mainly foliage plants as well as dozens of flowering plants. One example is *Pleione*, Chinese Ground Orchid.

Other protected sites for containers are a balcony, a loggia, and the part of the patio over which the house roof projects.

A house in the city might be only one room wide. The back door from the kitchen may open onto a small courtyard, with a circle of paving in the middle surrounded by plants or a square of paving edged with containers probably Pelargoniums. What if you live instead in a condominium, flat or apartment? I recently saw a new building with glass greenhouses projecting out from the south wall. Several units were already taken, the shelves in the greenhouses half full. The more likely place for a garden upstairs is the balcony.

There is another place which has become part of life in the modern age, a "retirement home". This can be quite different from the idea the phrase connotes. You

Pleione

Bolax

Anemone

live in a cottage with your own front door which you reach through a minuscule patio. Another retirement complex is more congested; the wall of both your house and tiny patio is the neighbors' as well as yours. It will hold, however, a dozen or so plants. The upper floor dwellers must settle for balconies.

A houseboat would be my favorite retirement place, but not without a porch for plants. See the Sept., '83 issue of *Gardens for All*. The cover pictures an ingenious deck—a barge anchored and cabled to the house. It is mostly garden space, with perhaps a little sitting space. There are plants in barrels and boxes of several shapes and sizes.

It is now my intent to decorate all of these settings. Selection of perennials for use in the various outdoor rooms is guided by the type of building, the landscape, the setting itself, and, of course, the person. Let us look at the stage. You do not need a fancy setting as the stage. But you do need props: steps and shelves and also movable staging such as blocks, pedestals, stools, benches and tables, all of which you may move around from time to time as your plant material changes. Arrange your container plants even more carefully than you do the chairs and tables and lamps in your house. The same principles apply to decoration with container plants as in the garden proper but they are more important since the container plant is a showpiece. The container itself may be a showpiece—for instance, a trough. Not all plants are suitable for troughs. One must be dwarf, but also have an element of distinction in its character. There must be artistic lines in your design; you will need vertical and horizontal lines. The final design objectives will be with the achieved shapes and characteristics of the plants you select, but good lines can be enhanced by extensions made by your props, which elevate or display the plants to set off their form.

About containers: Plain clay is the first choice. It breathes and absorbs the salts in earth and water. Usually it is best to use a pot which is as low as possible, taking into account the needs of the roots of the plant. Several shapes can be assembled in an outdoor room but not without planning for harmony or contrast. There is also fancy clay in the market which can be selected for special plants which need a special setting.

Wood is the second choice. It is first choice for a large plant, such as Bird of Paradise, and also for a small plant when the small plant is worthy of something different. Wood is obvious for a composition of several plants in the same container. Boxes used to be attached to the house and were called "window-boxes"; they are coming back into style but are being used in or on a wider variety of places, not just under the windows. The narrow, rectangle shape is still good for displaying perennials. The box may be placed on the top or at the foot of a wall or against the house or on the ledge of a balcony. A box can be allowed to just float on a terrace or be permanently placed to make a "room" divider. Wood can be used for a trough instead of concrete.

Old concrete sinks, basins and tubs were often left lying around after they had been replaced by more modish fixtures. Gardeners discovered them and decided they were a fine depth and shape for plants. They became containers for treasures. Costly copies are now being made to sell to gardeners. They are indestructible and are quite handsome, properly placed and planted. The same plants, however, look well in a box of approximately the same shape, made of wood rustic enough to look a little antique.

Cement forms can be urns as well as baskets; often, however, there remains too much evidence of the method of manufacture. Sometimes one can find a decorated cement box which looks quite antique. Usually it is wretchedly shallow but it suits the terminal part of a rock wall.

Glazed pottery: Use only with the understanding that earth soon becomes stale for want of air. Semi-glaze is somewhat safer. The color and texture of a glazed pot may be just right to set off a rare perennial in a special way, for example a cv. of *Rohdea japonica*. If you use glazed ware, you will have to change the soil every six months.

The "lavabo": Almost always glazed. Special drainage must be provided. Perhaps best for *cut* leaves or flowers.

"Japanese pots" or "Raki pots": These breathe. They are good for plants we associate with Japanese landscapes. Good for bonsai. Good for specialties, e.g. *Anemone blanda*: Cut foliage; dainty daisies not much taller than leaves. They do not combine easily with plain clay. So use them in a particular place, probably several of them together of different shapes and sizes.

Strawberry jars: These are sometimes glazed but clay is to be preferred. They are inviting as containers for perennials other than strawberries. Herbs are very suitable; plant all of one kind or a mixture—as many as there are pockets. Watch the soil in the pockets to make certain that your water floods each one. Strawberry jars are good for small succulents; those with russet or dusty-rose hues in their rosettes compliment the terra-cotta of the container.

There are jars with no pockets; these look best when a perennial spills over the rim. Sometimes they are made of concrete instead of red clay and may be plain or decorated. If genuine antiques, don't plant in them.

An urn is another form, often concrete and usually figured. Either an upright or trailing dwarf plant will work equally well. Example, *Sedum.*

Barrel-shaped containers: Made of red clay, the curve of the sides is pronounced and the shape looks quite modern. They are available in sizes large enough to accommodate a very large plant. There is a barrel-shaped container available in oriental stores; eggs are packed within them in China and shipped to "Chinatowns". The semiglaze is in two complimentary colors; the inside is that turquoise-blue so typically Chinese; I like it so much that I do not plant in them. Hibachis I also leave empty.

The body of a pot can be shaped in a variety of ways—the sides may be straight, they may curve inward or outward; they may be jug-shaped, bowl-shaped, barrel-shaped or ball-shaped. Some have ridges or other markings. A tall one with outward bending walls may have a naturalistic design.

Top edges are greatly varied. Some flair out a bit from a somewhat narrowed neck. Such pots suit certain shapes of plants, for instance, plants with horizontal branches. A very low bowl is appropriate for a short, almost stubby plant. If the plant grows upright to reveal the edge of the pot, a rolled edge is attractive. Some pots are designed to imitate a basket. Low and distinctly flaring terra-cotta used to come from Italy with a rolled edge and a fine basket weave. You have perhaps seen custom-made pots of cement with a heavy basket weave. The weave is heavy, the pot itself is heavy and only a very sturdy looking plant looks well in it.

More about wood: It looks well in many situations. Boxes should be plain, no bands in sight, either bright copper or rusty. But not just planks knocked together; better to miter the corners. Sides flaring a little often set off the plant better than do straight sides. Decorated wood is very nice when it is well done; carvings of quail, squirrels or cones often have charm without taking anything from the plant. Wooden boxes can be perfectly plain or they can look like a window box—with a lip around the top, or they can be carved with either animals or a geometric design. Pots or cans can be set into the long boxes, the cans hidden and the plants growing well; they will look as if they were planted.

There is a fad for baskets. The word basket is used commonly for a container which is designed to hang—the "hanging basket". This is not a woven basket; it can be made of any material from pottery to moss; it usually has a rounded bottom and comes with wires attached to the rim with a hook on top. It may hang from a rafter or an overhang or a ceiling of an Outdoor Room. It may be planted with a trailing plant or with a mixture of perennials and annuals. This combination is used mainly for the basket made of a wire frame and stuffed with sphagnum moss; the effect is very colorful; the culture is difficult.

The other type of basket is used as a jacket for another container—or occasionally on a temporary basis for the ball of the plant. You can plant directly in the basket if you line the basket with plastic; but drainage would not be possible over a period of any length. It works better to leave the plant in its growing container; if the rim is well hidden with moss, the container is not noticeable. For holiday or special occasion gifts, baskets are "made-up" with a mixture of several plants. First the basket is lined with plastic, which is concealed because the containers are jammed close together and the moss fills any spaces. Some of the plant material is for foliage, usually a houseplant type; often perennials are added with colorful flowers to brighten the scene. Can you recall being tempted by a combination of variegated foliage and Poinsettias just before Christmas?

Sometimes you wish to display a large plant, usually a shrubby houseplant, presently in a five gallon container; a Chinese type basket, wicker or reed, with handles is deep enough to accommodate the depth of the plant's container. Many styles of baskets are manufactured to hold a gallon container; the perennial only spends the weeks of blooming in its basket cover, being returned to a holding area until the next

Sedum urn

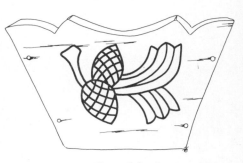

Carved box

Sedum

Pelargonium

show date. For terrace decoration the basket jacket is only used in an emergency. All perennials, even those destined for a minor role show to better advantage in an appropriate container into which they have been moved from their can or carton. I have seen some beautiful plants displayed in the plastic container in which they were bought; no one should be that lazy or unobservant.

The outdoor room is a stage. Hopefully it will be lived-in but at the very least it is a showcase. The most important role of a plant in a container is as a showpiece. Some plants will be permanent furnishings, others may be put on display only when at their best. Design with containers offers more latitude of placement than the garden proper because the outdoor room offers a variety of vertical dimensions or aspects not available in the garden. Where and how the containers are placed will determine whether the plants in the containers decorate the setting successfully. Remember you are dealing with a three dimensional space—a volume—which demands the perceptions of an architect or sculptor.

The container selected must not overpower the plant itself. As I have noted above, in most instances the pot should be low, taking into consideration the needs of the roots, and the material should usually be plain. Highly figured or strikingly colored pots detract from any plant with a definite personality. You cannot go wrong with plain clay.

Containers often need to be raised off the ground both for drainage and to accentuate the vertical line. Instead of another container upside down; give it a proper stand, table, box or pedestal. Make several levels in your design. A ladder design is often effective.

Vertical gardening is in vogue, necessitated by the limited space available in some outdoor rooms. Tiered containers are available which allow you to plant at every level. (I once did one with members of the ROSE family, as many as I could find. This flowershow project received applause at the moment, but was soon abandoned because of the upkeep required.) Another kind of tiered effect is easily produced with a do-it-yourself table; a set of shelves rise from the table set back halfway on each level. Shelves can be as long as you want, perhaps taking up one whole side of the patio fence. You have seen bonsai displayed on such a bookcase. Your choice of perennials to fill the containers is only restricted by the size of your space. If you are considering tender subjects, you should build a pitched roof over the top; then you can grow a collection of dwarf orchids.

How about herbs; these would be of use to you as well as decorative. Add to the herbs some fragrant-foliaged Geraniums with leaves to smell or cut for bouquets. Perhaps you had a liking for some particular genus when you had a larger garden. For example, *Campanula* with its bells and stars; choose some of the miniature spp. to bloom in pots on a tiered table. The dwarfs of many spp. have intricate patterns in their foliage, evident when the flowers have been cut. There is a cv. of *C. nitida* with a tiny architectural tuft, a top-knot. Another has a name almost bigger than the plant: *Campanula elatines* var. *fenesterella*.

Corner shelves are another possibility, like those cabinets in which our ancestors displayed china. You will probably become a "collector" if you get started with dwarf plants. You will collect oddities because the marvels of nature as it designs its curious members are marvelously intriguing. You can collect until there is no more room on your cabinet shelves to display your trophies.

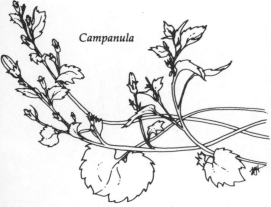

Campanula

There are other props to assist you with vertical gardening. Frames and trellises may be purchased or made. You may buy the kind used for training tomatoes, with expandable legs, on which the tiered hoops can be raised. When fully extended you can create a pillar with a vine such as *Clematis* or *Tropaeolum* or Jasmine. For small pots, you can make small trellises. Natural bamboo is best but any flexible bare branch will serve. You can build a horizontal trellis for an espalier. The plant's branching and foliage personality shows off well on a flattened plane. Or you can construct a tepee (best to use copper wire to hold your bamboo together). On it train perennials with trailing stems, inducing them to go up instead of down. An example is *Asarina*. Usually your plant will do better on a support of three or more stakes rather than one. You will not want to reform the habits of all the trailers; some will go on the top shelf of a tiered table or the cabinet to hang. Train the stems of delicate vining plants on one-strand fishing line.

A flight of steps coming to or leading away from the terrace is an excellent showcase for containers. There may be a ledge either side of the steps or there may be a wall or just a balustrade. First, however, let us think of steps wide enough that an arrangement of pots may be made on the steps themselves. Here is a setting which has leeway in its treatment. Containers can be placed in rows or can be staggered. A pleasing effect is brought about by plants all of the same sp. in pots all of the same kind. On the other hand, with ingenuity you can make an attractive design with a mixture. What a wonderful showcase for a wedding reception, or a "coming-out" party! You can use *Delphinium, Lilium* and *Petunias* in late spring or in summer, you can bank together a number of pots of *Astilbe* to make a solid mass. In the fall, you would no doubt start with the obvious *Chrysanthemum* but you would use interesting flower forms like the squill or the spider. At the base of the *Chrysanthemum* pots you would use some smaller pots, for once for color only, and probably an annual. Small pots in quantity each containing the same sp. are excellent for a seasonal show. *Cyclamen persica* is without equal in displaying value for a shady site. Now the day-by-day ordinary show on the steps will be more modest and more permanent. For suggestions please see the descriptions of *Primula* and *Pelargonium* (fragrant-foliaged Geraniums). Explore succulents and in particular the suggestions for the spp. which look well in little pots to accompany the larger containers (described later in this chapter). Sometimes a trailing perennial looks well on a step but the best place for a trailer is a shelf or the top of a wall. A trailing *Kalanchoe* may sit on a table or a stand. See p. 146.

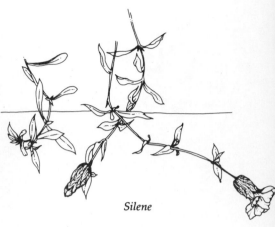

Silene

The wall may have upright plants as well as trailers but it is a natural setting for hanging plants. It is a conspicuous place. Stems which trail serve the function of tying and relating the container to the wall and they are very visible. The wall may be waist or eye level; if it is higher the selection of plants must be confined to spp. which need little care. It will not be easy to water, weed and groom or rearrange them; when you use a high wall as a showcase you must like the plants you place there. A wall at waist level is ideal for displaying novelties, rarities or oddities. The visitor sees the choicest plants almost as if in a museum. Your plant may be rare, just unusual or a curiosity such as *Kalanchoe daigremontiana.* A very simple genus may give equal satisfaction because of its ardent growth and innate charm. (Please see the paragraphs on "Vertical Gardening" and the tiered showcases.) The owner has these specialties under close observation to assist in their care; the small pots need almost daily surveillance and attention. On shoulder height walls, plants are just as visible and at this height the cascaders are especially appropriate.

Plants placed atop a wall can be either a number of the same spp. in a row or several spp. interspersed in containers of various sizes. Two or three spp. are easier to assemble in a pleasing geometric display. Smaller pots often flank larger pots but may be interspersed between them. The most decorative arrangement is achieved by combining perennials which look well together.

This is a place to give some examples, especially of trailers. (Please see the chapter on trailing perennials for further suggestions.)

Silene vulgaris subsp. *maritima*, what a distance its slender stems trail! It has curious pale flowers with a puffed-up "bladder" behind the flare of the petals. Trim it now and again to induce it to bloom for a longer season. In the winter the tuft of leaves remains healthy and holds the promise for the trailing stems of next year.

Pelargonium peltatum is Ivy Geranium. Pots may be used effectively on the top of a wall or on a step. These trailing forms are especially good in a hanging basket.

Growing a "cascade" *Chrysanthemum* to near perfection takes much trouble and time but the result is magnificent. As I have already pointed out, the best site is the top of a wall or a pedestal.

A shelf is a fine site for a hanging plant. Several of the *Campanulas* with trailing stems may be grown in pots as small as six inches across. If you have a place for a hook in a ceiling or on a wall, grow *Campanula isophylla* in a hanging pot—the stems will hang further and the trailing mass can be seen from all sides. The container should be of the "fern" type; or a bowl-shape seems to be complementary. It does a fair enough job in a standing container placed against a background or on a wall, but the side toward the light will be fuller and longer so the plant expresses itself better when hanging. Flowering stems, sometimes two feet long, look as if they were studded with many, many stars—the white form 'Alba' more so perhaps than the blue. A cv. of the blue, 'Mayi', has large, star-shaped, lavender-blue flowers on soft, hairy, grey leaves. When at its best it makes a really striking cascade. The common name for *Campanula* is Bellflower and as it implies many of the spp. have flowers of a bell-shape. But others, in addition to *C. isophylla*, have stars instead of bells; *C. fragilis* is one. Its stars are blue with

Campanula

Rohdea

Ligularia

Isoplexus

white centers; its stems are slenderer and shorter than *C. isophylla*. Both bloom in late summer and fall; both are cut back to the ground and the leaves start their growth in spring. (The common name, Star of Bethlehem, is sometimes given to *C. isophylla* but should be reserved for *Ornithogalum umbellatum*, or vice versa.)

Arrangement of your container plants is of paramount importance. Whether the pots are on pedestals or other props or on the ground placement must be according to a plan. It is good to have a collection of containers look plenteous but the result must not look cluttered. If you have an exacting site like an atrium, "just a few" is a good rule of thumb. There should be more than one size of pot unless the design calls for pots in a row. The placement of the plants should be "random" and natural in feeling. Several compositions can be made, with more or less related plants. Place them in groups with space between groups. Sometimes a group will cluster nicely at the base of a potted shrub or a pillar. Even though perennials are permanent plants, you will want to rearrange them from time to time both to alter the sense of the display and for cultural advantage; the backside of a plant with reduced light and air becomes sparse and unsightly.

You may have just a simple terrace. It is approached by steps, has a wall on one side and you go to the front door through a covered portico (we will decorate those adjuncts afterward). What is the easiest way to use container plants on the terrace? The form of the plants must relate to the door, the windows, the roof, the pillars and to the type and materials of each. You may want to stress vertical plants to harmonize with the vertical architectural elements. Alternatively use widely spreading horizontal plant elements to contrast with the verticals. The color of the plants determines where they are placed and with which architectural element. The scheme is apt to be successful if the color is mostly green throughout—different shades of course—perhaps a little white added. This scheme will produce a restful, cool and dignified effect.

Exposure is of course a factor. Let us take as our exercise in decorating with containers a terrace in part shade.

Pieris, Ardisia, and ferns will work in the shadiest corners. The tallest plant is a *Sciadopitys* and the widest is a *Viburnum davidiana* cv. What smaller plants shall we add to these basics? Try some permanent spp. for their decorative form, such as *Rohdea*, *Aspidistra* and fancy-foliaged *Begonias*. Then add some temporary pots of spp. chosen for color according to season. In the early spring, Primroses with *Freesia, Scillas* and Daffodils; in later spring, *Violas* with Tulips; in early summer, *Pelargoniums*, in late summer, *Geraniums* and shade loving succulents; in autumn, *Chrysanthemums* or *Cinerarias* with *Impatiens* in whatever shades go with the other plants.

The foundation of this scheme is made up of foliage of various heights and shapes. The ferns chosen are the more leathery spp. with fronds of distinctive pattern, rather than the dainty ones like Maidenhair. If you use the variegated form of *Aspidistra*, cut away the plain green (perhaps you can use it in a flower arrangement). The leaves of the *Begonias* may be either the pointed shape or the rounded shape; most of them will have pleasing crimson-red on their backsides and in their stems. The *Rohdea*, which the Japanese horticulturist likes to collect in all its various forms, may only be available in its plainest form. You will like it when the plant fills out; the angle of the leaf is graceful and the green is lush and shiny. You may need a taller and wider foliage plant, one that makes a mound instead of a spike. Select one of the *Ligularias* which you like. I would skip the one called Spotted Dog and look for those with unusual indentations or leaves curled or crinkled. The leaves of one cv. have a curly ruffle. *L. dentata* 'Desdemona' as you might guess has dark stems. My favorite sp. is *L. tussilaginea*. The cv. 'Argentea' has bold rounded leaves edged with creamy white. In the shade, planted in rich, moist soil, a plant in an eight-inch fern pot will have a dozen handsome leaves.

I hear you saying, "I want more color, color." *Isoplexis canariensis* is colorful. It is seasonal but it can be kept going a long time. While from the Canary Islands it is somewhat cold tolerant. You should place it in as good light as possible; perhaps you can get it to bloom two or three times a year. *I. canariensis* grows to about two and a half feet in a container. There will be several flower stems to a plant; the upper foot of the stem is a dense spike made up of many hooded flowers overlapping. The flowers are tubular with pronounced lips, the leaf color is two-toned, a fine bronze predominating. *Isoplexis* is distinctive.

If you live in a warm climate, you can use all manner of tender plants such as *Anthurium* and *Eucharis*. For a frost free terrace, there is a charming twining shrub,

Clerodendron thompsonii, with pointed green leaves for many months and flowers all summer into fall. Clusters of short stems with imbricated calyces have several phases. First the calyx is white, then it turns pale green, then it turns a dusty magenta-rose. Meanwhile, the flowers are inconspicuous but they become fascinating seed vesicles. The pod is orange-red velvet which the seed splits open as it becomes big, black and shiny. This contained vine can be easily trained on a frame to whatever height you need to produce your vertical line. Add seven or eight pots of white *Primula* at the base of the big pot containing the *Clerodendron.* Try other twiners on frames such as *Asparagus* or any of the *Ampelopsis. Lygodium japonicum,* Climbing Fern, is grown for its foliage and will climb to amazing heights. It shows off the unique pattern of the leaves as the slender wiry stems wind tightly around the standards of its frame. *Gloriosa* is a climbing Lily. It winds by tendrils on a frame and produces gorgeous "Lilies". Two or more species have floriferous seasons and are fragrant.

Lygodium

How about a deck? The treatment differs only a little from that of the terrace. A deck may stretch all the way across the house, in lieu of a terrace. Another deck abuts onto a room with easy access to the outdoors and there is enough space for at least an "ice cream table" and two chairs. Here is another natural stage for container plants. The principles are the same for choosing and arranging as for a terrace or porch, except that the whole is on close view from the inner room. The deck may really be lived in, also. There must be a plan to make changes and replacements; he who has a deck should surely have a storage place for alternates. But there is always the nursery up the street for replacements.

As we leave the terrace or deck we approach the door to the house. There is a place for potted plants at the entrance to a doorway. It was once called a stoop. Do you remember that in earlier days the members of a household used to have their photographs taken on the "stoop"? Often steps go to the door, sometimes wide enough to put a row of pots either side or on one side. On either side there is sometimes a ledge, ostensibly holding up the staircase but it is a perfect place for container plants. Sometimes just one on either side will look well, perhaps a perennial with a tree-form. One of the succulents, especially Jade Tree, can be ornamental. Sometimes several pots, or a single box, can be placed to cover the whole length; usually all the same kind of perennial should be used. On the other hand, some person who lives here may be adventuresome and will try a combination of several kinds.

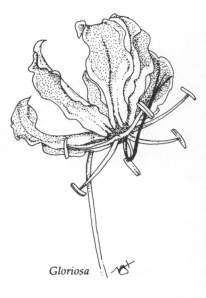

Gloriosa

The facade of the house has a part in the staging, both from an artistic and a practical standpoint. "Doorway" plants have a special character; sometimes the twin shrubs selected to introduce the entrance need no smaller plants with them; at another house, a grouping of pots might be developed in the entrance way, near the door although not at the door.

Sometimes you see the words "portico" and "foyer"; usually these are indoors. These places must be decorated in such a way that the plants enhance the architecture. If a portion of the architecture is a special feature with artistic proportions, its form should not be obliterated or even shadowed by plants.

Here is a case in point. The entrance porch is covered and the roof is held up by pillars. The area can be crowded with plants on the wall, on shelves, on pedestals; the effect will only be good if selection and placement are carried out with ideal staging. The many perennials suitable for containers do often combine well—*Aquilegia, Campanula,* and *Viola* are a few examples.

Dwarf shrubs, such as *Pieris, Camellia sasanqua, Ilex* and many others both coniferous and broad-leaved are an ideal basis in an arrangement. Their containers remain in place when perennials both evergreen and deciduous must be taken away. Bulbous plants are mostly only visitors; they conclude their stay when they start to go dormant. A few with evergreen foliage may have permanent residence. Several spp. may be attractively arranged with other perennials; choose especially the smaller spp. e.g. *Scilla, Freesia, Zephyranthes, Muscari, Crocus,* and the dwarves of *Narcissus.*

Quite another type of design is made with *Pelargoniums,* Geraniums. Think of the number of choices in *Pelargoniums.* Several spp. can be combined or several cvs. of one sp.

Doorway

Pelargoniums can be used on that balcony off the main room of an apartment or flat. When it is small, there is hardly enough room for one chair but there is enough room for a few plants. Crowd the plants but skillfully. There is a ledge along the top of the balcony wall. One small box or several pots may be fixed to this railing; since it will hold more soil, the box will be better than pots for growing plants. (Even

Narcissus

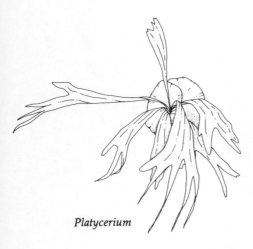

Platycerium

Begonia

undemanding genera like *Pelargonium* grow better with ample soil.) If the space on the top of the wall is too narrow make a shelf just below the top—attach it with brackets. Is the owner putting these plants on the balcony for his own enjoyment or to please the passerby? In any case, geraniums are the best bet; they are number one for window boxes also. In the Netherlands, every window of every building is full and bright with geraniums. These are usually *Pelargonium hortorum* but *Pelargonium peltatum*, Ivy Geranium, runs a close second. The blooming time of *P. peltatum* is long, the stems trail down and the plants don't look messy quickly—anyway from the street.

On this tiny balcony, there must be room for a watering can and a basket with tools, shears, a miniature rake and plant food. Sometimes apartment dwellers become African Violet devotees; if they live on the north side of the building, they can air these and their other indoor plants part-time on the balcony. The primary plant will no doubt be one you had and very much liked when you had a garden.

Sometimes the balcony is much larger. Suppose you select a number of different plants. They will need varied, and constant care. You will need to screen off a little section at one end with a small table in the corner with a bin underneath for soil or shelves to store pots and hooks for a couple of implements to hang on the wall. You must be able to repot when necessary. Each plant should be in optimum condition. Many small pots can be crammed together in a design of compatible foliage—shrubs, perennials and annuals to bloom in all seasons even in this small space.

If the balcony is really large, you can make a real garden. You may live in the windy part of a windy city. At the end, against the prevailing wind, build a windbreak of strong plastic; angle it around the corner. Now build a deep box in front of it all the way across the end. In this raised bed you can plant conifers or other strong evergreens. They hide the plastic and give the impression of deflecting the breezes even though the wall might do it without them. Even so, some of the plants you try to grow will suffer in the gusty winds. Many perennials will adjust to it: The sturdier ferns will take it. Several genera include tough spp. as *Asplenium, Blechnum, Ceterach, Ctenitis, Cyrtomium, Davallia, Doodia, Humata, Nephrolepis, Pellaea, Phyllitis, Polystichum.* Strangely enough, among the annuals Petunias are the most wind tolerant; their seemingly fragile petals just bend but return again. You will not leave room enough to sit in this outdoor room, but you might put out a stool, perhaps on which to place another plant which requires some height. You might put out a bench but this will be soon covered with the little pots and perhaps a wooden trough. Your guests can stand quite awhile to look, sniff the good odors and praise you for your efforts.

Let us return to the ground floor. What specific principles are required for decorating with container plants in places other than a terrace where you have more leeway than anywhere else? A porch is one place and takes some study. It has the house wall as a backdrop and doors and windows to decorate around; pots will most definitely have to be placed in groups. The choice of spp. and the design of the pots should go with your architecture. Taller genera will be chosen to flank the doors. Or perhaps a genus thick and wide: *Clivia* is incomparable for a shady doorway. There will be mostly shade but in certain seasons for a limited time there will be sun on the forward edge.

The very narrow porch which is like an extended entry way was surely invented more for decoration than for use. There is only a little traffic and no place to sit. Containers can be massed, taking up more than half the floor space. Banks of pots can be arranged in a bleacher fashion. Baskets can be hung from wall and from ceiling. Urns can be attached to the wall. There may be a showcase for small pots. Even on a narrow porch boxes may be added containing seasonal bright flowers; but usually the general scheme will be mostly green.

At another house, the entrance way is again narrow; the door is at the end. A group of containers is concentrated on the side wall of this passageway. It may be enclosed with glass on one side.

A most attractive architectural feature is a covered porch which passes along a house wall. The door is again on the end wall instead of on the side. The wall has no windows; the other side is open. The porch is wide enough so that a planting bed can be installed along the wall. It is planted with exotic subjects; it is even wide enough for Tree Ferns. Staghorn Fern, *Platycerium* hang on the wall behind the bed. Container plants can be set temporarily in the bed for additional form or color. Plants with variegated leaves are appropriate. This is a place where a red color on the backs of leaves or in stems looks well; some Philodendrons have crimson stems as well as backs. Use the various fancy-leaved *Begonias*, Beefsteak or Angel.

    Begonias are very good on shelves since many of them grow branches of considerable length. *Begonia foliosa* has numerous hanging stems with crowded round scalloped leaves and small pink flowers for a long period. Use them extensively, and alone or perhaps combined with ferns, in a north side entry way. On the blank walls either side of a door, attach tiers of shelves at levels of five, seven and nine feet on which smaller containers with interesting leaf shape and color are placed.

Tropaeolum

    The furnishing of a patio may be somewhat different from that of a terrace. Do you have a feature in the center? Perhaps a fountain with a base to decorate with plants. Or a fountain which spills into a moat edged with a geometric wall. The wall of the hexagon (or sexagon) can be crowded with pots all the way around or the number can be reduced by confining the pots to spaces at the angles or between. Absent water, there may be a sundial or statue in the center; tiered steps can be built to rise all the way around from ground level to the raised centerpiece. Quantities of potted plants can be sited here. Examples are *Calceolaria, Heuchera, Pelargonium, Tropaeolium.*

    When the center of the patio is clear, the main plantings will be placed around the inside of the walls. Plants may be grown in beds here or alternatively, containers, boxes, barrels, bowls of every shape and size can be used. Either way, a wide variety of spp. can be combed for possibilities.

    But let us turn back to the minuscule patio. A tiny patio can be a plant connoisseur's paradise. There is only room for one small tree, two small shrubs, a corner hidden by a piece of bamboo screening (for mechanics) and somewhere between ten and twenty potted plants. You will buy nothing at a cut-rate counter (though I admit you can occasionally find a treasure) but almost everything at an Arboretum Plant Sale. You will have mostly foliage plants because you will look at your patio more than once a day and at very close range. You will collect the unusual; you will not have enough room for a large collection but the ones you acquire must give you much pleasure. Put *Ophiopogon*, the black one, in a small pot to enjoy its personality at close range.

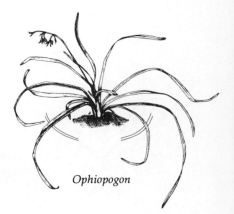

Ophiopogon

    Many of the container plants of a completely furnished outdoor room will be permanent inhabitants and their appeal will be derived mostly from some attribute of shape, texture, personality of foliage or fragrance of leaf or flower. Some plants when leafless offer an extra value in the wood and its branching. In the very small patio, there will not be room for the deciduous or herbaceous plant which should be on view only at its best. There are a number of plants elegant at all times to be the permanent residents here. Some dwarf spp. will look like miniature trees as *Teucrium* or *Erica*. After pruning they may look like bonsai. The number of foliage and habit types does not increase with the expanding size of your space; it may enlarge, however, the variety of spp. open to selection.

    Let us think about possible genera for containers. I would like to tell you about several perennials which I find very decorative. You will have heard of many of them as candidates for one or another of the outdoor rooms. Let us look first at Primroses.

    Primula malacoides, the flowerful and dainty annual, may be brought into bloom very early just by setting the seedlings in pots in late fall. Or, allow the growers to bring it to full stature and bloom; then select the colors you like for that year and stuff the root balls as tightly as possible into their containers. This alternative to raising plants yourself applies to all spp. and cvs. of Primrose.

    The most colorful perennial Primrose is *Primula polyantha,* the hybrids of which are grown in several excellent strains—Pacific, or Clarke's or Barnhaven. The particular strain need only concern us if we wish to grow them ourselves from seed; otherwise we just buy the best looking plants at the nursery. Some others may catch our eye. Be on the lookout for *Primula obconica* which tends to be a nearly ever-blooming Primrose with flowers in white, pink and many shades of lavender. This sp. is a fine subject for pots but the plants may wear out after awhile—they bloom so constantly—so plan to renew. Put them in several low, five-inch pots and make a cluster of the containers on a flight of steps in the shade. I have suggested using them clustered at the base of a large container. Or line them up in a box. Both the width and the depth of this container should accommodate a plant which has come out of a gallon plastic container with a little soil beside and below the roots to continue growing. All one color and all one kind in a box might be best. However, I must admit that a mixture of the several colors of *P. obconica* looks very fresh and gay. The white looks well alone. Some container plants need a mass of white for balance or blend. White looks well in

Primula

Primula

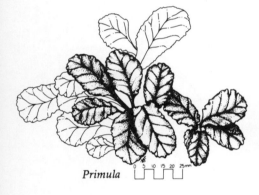

Primula

0 5 10 15 20 25mm

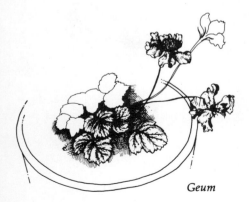

Geum

front of ferns or other foliage plants, and also in all white groupings containing white *Astilbe,* white *Narcissus,* etc.

Primula auricula, although it may be grown in boxes, is more suitable for low, wide, round pots. The mealy coating on the leaves and the combination of colors in the flowers need individual settings; the flowers are of many muted shades decorated with eyes of white or yellow. It is wise to start them under glass; they suffer in stormy weather. They are tortured by snail and slug attack; check the hole in the bottom of the pot constantly for this is one of the slug's hideouts.

The hybrids of *Primula juliae,* Juliana Primrose, look best planted in bowls. They improve in growth every year making a fine show of bright, dwarf flowers beginning in February. The magenta shades of several cvs. are especially cheering on a cloudy day.

A number of other spp. of Primrose do well massed in containers but are better as specimens in single pots. Those described thus far can all be grown to make a mass display.

Some genera commonly grown in the garden bloom very well in pots, especially the spp. which are more dwarf; examples are *Campanula,* and *Geum* (use a choice small sp. of *Geum*). *Teucrium,* known best for its large spp., is especially good for slopes. *Teucrium polium* var. *aureum,* a dwarf, thrives in a pot. See general Plant Descriptions for *Teucrium.*

Now herbs in containers are probably not colorful, certainly not spectacular and have no qualities which accentuate a display. From a practical standpoint, however, they are excellent in boxes as they can be sited nearer the kitchen than can an entire herb garden. Many have delightful if unobtrusive flowers, in case you are willing to let them come into bloom. Take chives; I grow them in pots mainly for their small lavender heads which add a needed form to a small bouquet. The flowerhead of Dill is far from unobtrusive; a broad platter of greenish-yellow. Dill would seldom develop bloom when grown in a pot, especially when it is kept pruned by harvesting.

I grow Thymes which are out-of-the-ordinary in containers. Sometimes I put one in a pot for its trailing stems with generous bright flowers. Marjoram and Savory I grow in boxes because they have flowers I like and leaves I eat.

So-called succulents, from many genera and several families, make fine subjects for container planting. Their contribution is primarily their foliage; some have amazingly colorful flowers which are a bonus. Most of them are somewhat tender; therefore it is best to use them in situations with some protection, for instance under the overhang of a roof, on a porch or in an atrium. Plant various sizes and heights together; perhaps a four-foot *Kalanchoe beharensis,* Felt Plant, down to tiny *Sempervivum arachnoideum,* Cobweb Houseleek. Habits may vary; include trailers. Use occasional oddities. An exotic looking *Aloe* can be used as an accent.

Those with similar form or color or texture of leaf should be grouped together. A number have a rosette-type of growth, e.g., *Echeveria* spp., *Cotyledon* spp., *Dudleya* spp., *Crassula* spp.; these are for the sunniest steps. The *Crassula* called Jade Tree, has a branching form and is woody enough to suggest the name "tree". It is very floriferous in its season. For a shadier spot try several pots of Haworthia spp. with their neat, stacked towers of speckled or striped leaves.

Some of the succulents have a glossy coating on their foliage; while others are tomentose (covered with "hair"). Nature has invented a variety of methods to protect plants from the elements which are intriguing to look at while being efficient—such as the minute hairs of some of the rosettes. Succulents display a wide and interesting range of protective coatings which can be used to good design ends and to satisfy severe site conditions. Mix or match them in keeping with the quality of their leaf effects for some very satisfying container displays.

None of the succulent plants require much care, except grooming, of course. They are willing to do without water for a time, though not forever. Feeding is beneficial at least once a year. The soil may become packed or poor so the top inch or so can be renewed if you are short of the time necessary to repot completely. Occasionally though a complete replanting is in order.

Should more than one sp. go in the same container? When a dish garden of succulents begins as a mixture of varieties, perhaps because of a compulsion to fill it full right away, it is usually best to remove a few you like the least quite soon. My rule is— not more than two different spp. to a container. Two compatible kinds can be used in a bowl or other wide pot, usually a ground cover type below the main feature, with a rock or two and a finish of pebbles. If you are a collector of succulents, then you will want to pot your prizes one to a container with no distracting companion.

There is good reason that succulents differ so greatly. They are members of various families and come from a wide range of environments. One genus which varies tremendously within itself, *Sedum*, Stonecrop, has spp. native in Europe, Asia Minor, North Africa and the west coast of North America from British Columbia to Mexico. The character of the numerous spp. is so different that only a few can be recognized as cousins. At least three make excellent container plants: *S. morganianum* is the one we know as Donkey Tail or Burro Tail which drapes in curious fashion from a hanging basket.

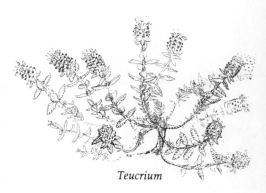
Teucrium

Another which trails is *S. sieboldii*, usually to nine inches, and looks best in an urn-shaped container so that the stems drape over the edge. The small, almost-round, fleshy leaves are blue-grey, attached to the stem without stalks, and are notched on the edges creating an embroidered look; the stem ends in a small curly blossom rosette. These leaves turn reddish in the fall; stems are only cut back when the leaves drop. Soon little leaf rosettes are seen at ground level and these remain as a miniature ground cover until March. This *Sedum* flowers in fall with flat clusters of dusty-pink flowers—an added attribute, but I value it most for its foliage.

Sedum spectabile (from China and Japan) is upright and bigger, to 18 inches tall, but one can note some resemblance—its stems die down in winter, the flower cluster is of similar shape and the leaves are blue-green, roundish and fleshy. This one is grown in pots for its fall flowers which make a colorful display at the tops of many tall stems. There are cvs.—'Carmen,' 'Brilliant' and 'Meteor'.

Telephium (Sedum telephium) is similar in size and shape; some authorities consider it a subgenus of *Sedum*. The color of the cv. 'Autumn Joy' is at maturity tawny-copper. You must read a book on succulents to discover the many possibilities among them. There is even one *Sedum* with fragrance.

Dill

One is always tempted to put a plant with extraordinary fragrance in a container so that the visitor is welcomed by the scent. *Convallaria*, Lily-of-the-Valley, is an example. Again the foliage suggests a bulb or corm; its curious root is called a "pip". It is far from easy to get luxurious bloom from *Convallaria* in the gardens of temperate climates. The growers will force them for us to buy when in flower.

Chlidanthus has wonderful fragrance. It is an *Amaryllid* from the Andes called Perfumed Fairy Lily. The flowers are soft yellow on ten-inch stems. There are two spp. from tropical South America; I have grown the one called *C. fragrans*. This sp. has strap-shaped, ten-inch basal leaves. The flowers form a few-flowered umbel blooming with the leaves. The tube is long and slender, the lobes lanceolate, there are six stamens. It blooms in summer—and what a lovely thing it is.

Eucharis, Eucharist Lily, has a subtle fragrance. This tender *Amaryllid* for tropical terraces is from the Andes of Columbia and Peru but must be grown indoors except in tropical regions.

Polianthes tuberosa has a bulb-like tuber, and it is more apt to bloom in a container than in the ground in a cool garden because the Tuberose likes it really hot; heat brings out the fragrance. Grow them in a greenhouse or you can buy a pot in full bloom.

Freesia is famous for its fragrance. I like *Freesia* in bowls.

Hymenocallis narcissifolia, Spider Lily (or Basket Flower or Peruvian Daffodil), is another fragrant bulb which is easy in a warm climate. It should bloom in June.

You have observed that most of the plants chosen for fragrance are bulbous or cormous. A number of bulbous plants even without fragrance look especially well in containers. *Cyrtanthus* is well behaved in a pot and is available in apricot as well as yellow.

Dwarf forms from a number of bulbous genera offer many candidates; for instance, try to find an Iris from north Afghanistan, *I. baldschianica*, if you are as intrigued as I was by its photograph.

Sometimes you may be tempted to underplant regular sized bulbs with annuals or trailers to cascade from the pot edge. A ground cover in a pot makes watering and slug control more difficult. *Lobelia* is a prolific self seeder and may often smother a container. Colorful and lush in full growth.

Sprekelia is an *Amaryllid* from Mexico and in cool climates must be stored over winter (not removing the dry tops). In areas where it may safely be left in the ground, several blooming periods may be induced by drying out and then increasing moisture.

Convallaria

Polianthes

0 5 10 15 20 25mm Cyrtanthus

Lobelia

The dark crimson bloom, on 12-inch stems, is very rich looking because of its waxy texture as well as the brilliance of its color. The flower shape is unusual: the three upper segments curl only a little and are erect while the three lower segments cascade from a tube which is formed at their base by their being rolled together—this seems to me an ingenious mechanism. The flowers stand well above the daffodil-like leaves. There are three common names—Jacobean Lily, Aztec Lily, and St. James Lily. *Sprekelia* can be used in pots, as one grows *Amaryllis*.

Zephyranthes, Zephyr Flower, Fairy Lily, a bulb from warm regions of the western hemisphere, generally blooms in August and September, although it may be induced to bloom at odd times by giving it a period of drying out and then some good soakings. In the wild, flowers appear a few days after a rain and as a result are often called "Rain Lilies".

Lapeirousia is a small South African. A white form as well as a pink form can be found.

Schizostylis, Crimson Flag, is easy to grow in pots. It is an *Irid* from South Africa.

Vallota is a true fall bulb, not just a carry-over from summer. What a lovely flower it is! A good color of clear coral-crimson is combined with an exquisite texture, firm but translucent. Two or three rounded trumpets (in shape between a cup and a trumpet), remain fresh after opening for several weeks, retaining their sheen until the petals shrivel.

Tritonia is related to *Freesia*. The common name Flame Freesia is given to *Tritonia crocata* which is the best known sp. and which has several color forms. A bright red one, *T. c.* 'Miniata', is the cv. most often seen in the western United States. It is easy to grow in pots and it is a bright addition for late spring.

Nerine belongs to the Amaryllis family and comes from South Africa. It has pink, lily-like flowers on stout stems. *N. bowdenii* is the best known sp. and has several forms. *N. humilis* grows to less than 18 inches and is a dainty miniature.

Foliage fanciers have been investigating some of the spp. of *Haemanthus*. There are some 60 spp. The leaves of some spp. are good looking in a strong, weird way—they have a thick, fleshy, leathery texture. I have not been able to find a word which describes their shape—it is not a blade or a spoon or a pad—it is a curved oval and massive in some spp.

Haemanthus is only one of many bulbous plants which is called "Lily". The term is used sometimes because the flower is more or less lily-shaped and also because the plant does belong to the Lily family.

Plants of the genus *Lilium* are the "true" lilies—there are almost a hundred. Most of them look well in containers and are notable for their fragrance. Many of them do better in containers for several reasons: the two most important reasons are watering can be better controlled and enemies foiled. Lilies are subject to a mosaic virus for which there is no cure, so plants must be discarded which are stunted or have mottled leaves. The plants are attractive to aphids, which spread the virus; early control of aphids is best handled if the plant is in a pot. In the open garden, gophers will delight in the succulent bulb above all else; they will be frustrated by the pot—one place where they are unable to furrow. Light and heat can be best adjusted with a pot plant.

There are 80 or 90 spp. of lilies and approximately one-fifth of these are commonly planted in U.S. Zones 6–9. Some of them grow to five or six feet in the garden but will not reach such heights in a container. Choose from a number of hybrids in several categories. From among the Olympic Hybrids, select one of the "dragons", either "Green" or "Black". Their heavily textured trumpets open in July and August on tall stems. The Mid-Century Hybrids overlap but start to bloom a month earlier. Their flowers are upward facing and wide open; their colors are yellow through orange to red. Two of the most adaptable for pots are 'Enchantment', a nasturtium-red, and 'Cinnabar', an orange-red. But every year new cvs. are named with colors equally vibrant; the photographs in the catalogs and lily books give quite exact shades. Some Golden Chalice Hybrids which bloom in May would be better for the family who goes to the mountains or the seashore in the summer. One selects according to time of bloom and for color but also for other purposes—the situation where the pots will be staged may need special emphasis on fragrance—the situation may be at a doorway or on a sitting terrace—or the pots may be destined for a wedding or anniversary when the lily color must follow the dominant color scheme (or determine it) or the lilies may be grown primarily for cutting. Those best for cutting

Here growth of foliage has mostly shrouded the framework. Pink, white and cerise are woven into the pattern. Round or oval forms predominate in the foliage. L. & L.H.

Tiers of raised beds are an effective showcase for mixed perennials. The relationships of foliage forms can be seen very well when similar groups are placed on different levels. Seasoned redwood is used here to make the framework. Tubs on the deck reflect the wood structure and the plant materials are related. L. & L.H.

Beds in tiers in another garden are deeper and higher. The material used for the walls is adobe brick. The rough texture and brown tone make a good background for green foliage. This garden contains cooking herbs combined with *Pelargoniums* and *Salvias*. A few clumps of sword-shaped leaves break the monotony of the leaves of the other perennials. G.S.

A bed on a deck follows the wall along one side and around the corner. The deck is so built that the shadow of the boards produce a second shade of brown. The bed contains mostly cooking herbs showing flowers in muted colors with the soft greens of the foliage. E.B.

Bodnant, Wales. Circular concrete steps trimmed with a
ruffle of *Campanula*. They rise gently to a panel of lawn
ending in an inviting bench. A rock wall separates the
two levels with perennials gracing the corners. J.Z.

For an island bed, a circle is a variation in form. Here one
is set on a chipped stone base of warm grey-brown. Only
three spp. are used; all have excellent foliage, decorative
in full growth as well as after having been trimmed back.
Along the edge is *Helianthemum* which sprawls over the
low wall and later when clipped creates a neat compact
finish to the picture. E.B.

A garden in Oregon. A circular brick wall and clipped
Teucrium making a second circle above it. If this design is
formal, the patio is made informal with a variety of container plants. Perennials border the patio on the house
side. J.Z.

Two levels in this garden, separated by a wall which is draped by rolling waves of cascaders. The varied color of flowering trailers and sub-shrubs provides a fitting contrast to the cool green of grass and specimen trees. J.Z.

Western Hills Nursery, Occidental, Calif., U.S.A., is the work of two eminent horticulturists. Their rural property has been molded into a garden of hills and dales where perennials which have been propagated are planted in quantity. Our picture was chosen, instead of others showing the contours, in order to provide a glimpse of one of the intriguing masses of vibrant flowering perennials. Here in this garden, most of the mounds are too big to be called berms. J.Z.

Roadway, lawn, border, hedge at Gravetye. The unique shape of the bench suggests the importance of displaying shapes, as carried out in the related forms of the planting. Most of the lines are curvaceous even when the flower is a spike, e.g. Lupine and *Penstemon*. J.Z.

Strip planting has a tendency to be unexciting. Consider choosing a perennial with variegated leaves, to provide liveliness and color while the plants are out of bloom. For a strip of accommodating width, *Iris pallida* is a good selection. Here it is grown in a full and flourishing row. J.Z.

UNUSUAL SITES

Old stone is a perfect setting for both foliage and flowering plants at the top of the wall. The shades of pink to rose to apricot all interweave with the grey and green as blenders. K.B.

A curving edge to a bed adds more visibility to the perennials, especially along the edge of the planting. Here we see enlarged drifts of *Aurinia, Arabis, Mimulus* and *Dianthus* as they finish the deeply indented bays. Rocks are planted in strategic places amongst the plants in the border. E.B.

A rock of substantial size lends itself to a number of treatments. Grasses make good accompaniments because of their shape and because of their earthy look. This grass is a dwarf, *Milium effusum* 'Nanum'. A soft, full ground cover seems to belong at its base, here *Pulmomaria lutea.* D.D.

A perennial bed with low stone wall as background, in the John Lovelace Garden near Santa Barbara, Calif. Note the array of pinks and reds to reflect the *Bougainvillea* on the roof: *Dianthus, Penstemon,* Lupinus are three which carry out the scheme. Over the wall drapes *Lantana,* a lavender with pink in its color. White does the melding, *Phlox* at the top and *Iberis* along the front. Boulders tie the border to wall and chimney. W.G.W.

WITH ROCKS

have foliage all the way down the stems, some of which will be left to nourish the bulb. Those which are best for fragrance depend on how much scent can be tolerated in a constricted space; the lily catalogs do not often include information about fragrance. Two that are definitely fragrant are *Lilium regale,* Regal Lily and *L. longiflorum,* Easter Lily. The latter only blooms at Easter because the growers have manipulated its growth to bring it to the right stage for its seasonal sale. 'Croft' is a good cv. for pot culture and midsummer bloom; it's fragrant and only about a foot tall.

Zephyranthes

Easter lilies are usually sold one plant to a pot—the reason no doubt economic—but lilies look best several plants to a pot. Most lily bulbs are large but five may be put together in a deep 16-inch wide pot or box. Include much organic material in the mix to provide not only good nutrition but good drainage. When planting, spread out the roots and place the bulbs two-thirds of the distance down from the top upon a layer of this prepared mix. An extra special practice is to cover the bulb at planting with only an inch of the mix and then fill the pot gradually as the stems reach upward. The mix must be moist from the start since lilies never go completely dormant. When purchased, the bulbs should have some live roots—still moist though not soggy. If you receive a shipment of lilies take care of them immediately; if perchance the bulbs have become dry, hold them in wet sand until the scales become plump. Water and feed all during the growing period; when the foliage turns yellow, reduce water.

Sometimes, as with daffodils, it is advantageous to plant lilies from pots out into the garden the second or third year because there is a spot in a mixed planting which they would enhance tremendously. Dollars spent on a large quantity of lilies for a special occasion can be spread over many years ahead. It is a pleasing venture to grow a number of bulbous potted plants for a party; in early spring there are daffodils. *Narcissus* has so many spp. that it is hard to choose. The dwarves are especially delightful in containers. Then comes the time for tulips and last the season for lilies (which is three or more months long). In any case, there could be no further and better suggestion than a lily as a bulb for a container.

Whether the root of a plant is a bulb, a corm, a tuber or just an ordinary root, many in each category are possibilities for containers.

Remember to search for plants out-of-the-ordinary such as grasses many of which have subtle charm. Do you know *Imperata,* Japanese Blood Grass? And another, *Carex morrowii* var. *variegata*? Grasses show off their special grace when displayed in a container.

So now I will leave you to search.

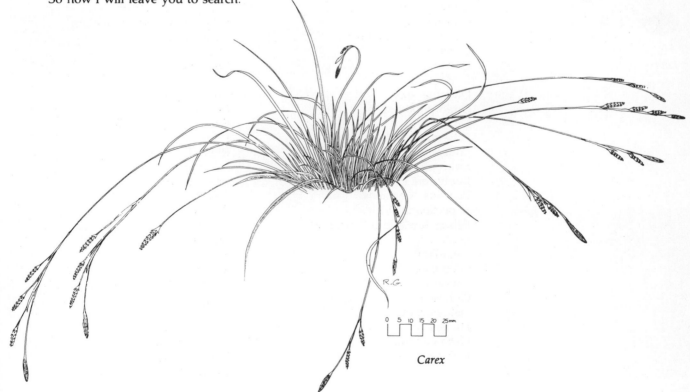

Carex

Some Examples

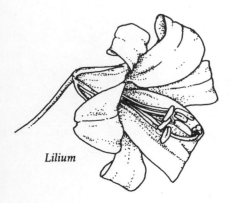

Lilium

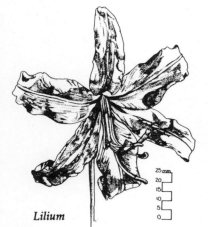

Lilium

Agapanthus 'Peter Pan'
Agapanthus 'Queen Anne'
Agapanthus 'Rancho Dwarf'
Agave
Allium
Alocasia
Aloe
Alstroemeria
Amarcrinum
Amaryllis
Anthemis
Anthurium
Aralia
Ardisia
Armeria
Asarina
Asperula
Aspidistra
Astilbe
Begonia
Bletilla
Calceolaria
Campanula
Catananche
Centaurea cineraria
Chrysanthemum anethifolium
Chrysanthemum frutescens 'Kayo
  Watanabe', 'Maxine', 'Snow
  Cap', 'Pink Lady'
Chrysanthemum, Garden & Florist, e.g.
  "Large flowered", "Cushion"
Clivia miniata
Convallaria
Convolvulus cneorum
Cotyledon
Crassula
Cyrtanthus
Dianthus spp.
Dimorphotheca
Dudleya
Echeveria
Edraianthus
Eriocephalus
Euphorbia biglandulosa
Euryops × acraeus
E. pectinatus 'Viridis',
Felicia amelloides 'Variegata'
Francoa
Geranium
Globularia
Gloriosa
Gunnera
Hakonechloa
Hedera
Helianthemum
Helichrysum

Heliotropum
Hesperis
Houstonia
Hutchinsia
Imperata
Iresine
Iris
Isoplexus canariensis
Kalanchoe
Lantana
Lavandula
Leptospermum humisifusa
Leptospermum scoparium, 'Nicholsii
  Nanum'
Lewisia
Ligularia
Lilium
Linum
Lithodora
Lithospermum
Lobelia
Morisia
Mutisia
Nelumbo
Ophiopogon
Orchids
Origanum
Oxalis
Pelargonium crispum
Pelargonium domesticum
Pelargonium fragrans
Pelargonium hortorum
Pelargonium odoratissimum
Pelargonium peltatum
Phormium
Phyteuma
Polianthes
Primula auricula
Primula kewensis
Primula obconica 'Gigantea'
Primula sinensis
Rhodohypoxis
Saxifraga
Scleranthus
Sedum
Sempervivum
Spiraea
Stokesia
Strelitzia
Thymus
Trachelium
Tropaeolium
Viola
Wahlenbergia
Zantedeschia
Zephyranthes
Zingiber

Bulbs and Corms for Containers,

Babiana
Brusvigia
Eucharis
Haemanthus
Hesperantha
Hippeastrum
Homeria
Hymenocallis
Lachenalia
Nerine
Pleione
Streptanthera

Perennials for Alpine House

Allardia
Androsace
Andryala
Dionysia
Erinacea
Erictrichum
Gypsophila aretioides
Helseya
Lewisia
Saxifraga
Weldenia

Perennials for Troughs

Acer orientale
Aethionema
Alyssum serpyllifolium
Androsace
Anemone
Anemonella
Antennaria suffruticosa
Aquilegia saximontana
Arenaria
Armeria caespitosa 'Bevan's Variety'
Armeria
Aruncus aethusifolius
Asperula gussonii
Astilbe chinensis var. pumila
Aurinia saxatile 'Tom Thumb'
Bellium
Bolax
Calluna
Campanula
Dianthus
Douglasia
Draba
Draba hispanica
Elmera
Erinus
Franklinia thymifolia
Gentiana verna

Geranium subcaulescens
Globularia
Gypsophila artioides
Helichrysum selago
Helichrysum milfordiae, H. hookeri
Houstonia cabralia 'Fred Miller'
Hutchinsia
Hypericum yakusimanum
Limonium
Mentha requienii
Morisia monanthos
Penstemon caespitosa
Phlox
Potentilla nitida
Pratia angulata
Raoulia australis
Rhodohypoxis
Saxifraga petiophylla & other dwarfs
Scleranthus biflorus
Sedum anglicum & other cushiony kinds
Selaginella
Teucrium
Thalictrum
Vaccinium
Vancouveria
Viola adunca 'Silver Hart'
Viola verecunda var. yakusimana

Imperata

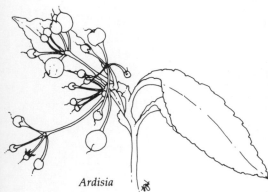

Ardisia

Asarina

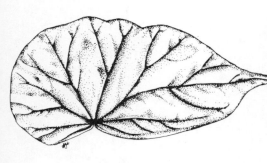

Begonia

Aloe: LILIACEAE.

Mostly S. Afr., trop. Afr., Madagascar, Arabia.

Evgrn. 6 in. to l8 ft. 325 spp. Succulent for burns, even X-ray burns. In South, bloom every mo. of year from a collection of spp. Leaves pointed, fleshy in rosettes. Flowers lily-like, erect, raceme or candelabra. Summer.

Sun. Ordinary cult. Groom. Drainage. Dislikes a wet winter. Division.

Containers may be moved to shelter in winter.

A. variegata: Partridge Breast Aloe. Leaves 4–6 in. long, over 2 in. wide. Handsome cross bands. Stylish looking in pots. Likes roots crowded. Soil sandy, loamy & clayey. Semi-hdy. Offsets. Cuttings.

A. haworthioides: One of sev. with interesting foliage. Good for pots. Rosettes of about 30 leaves, 2 in. across.

A. aristata: Dense rosettes of pointed, fleshy leaves. Dark green, white marked. Lily-like flowers in slender spires. Usually forms clusters of up to 12 rosettes.

Anemone blanda: Cut foliage. Dainty daisies not much taller than leaves. Small pots; shade. See woodland.

Anthemis: COMPOSITAE. Golden Marguerite. Mostly Eur.

Evgrn. Shrublet. Leaves quite finely cut, num. Daisies num. on stems to 5 in.

Sun. Ordinary cult. Tolerant of heavy rains. Trim. Cuttings. Replace.

Needs a container at least 7 in. across & 1 ft. deep.

A. tinctoria: Bush-like plant (3 × 3 ft.). Foliage carroty or parsley-like. Yellow daisies summer. Best if dead-heading constant, or shear on a regular schedule.

Anthurium: ARACEAE. Flamingo Flower. Trop. Am.

Evgrn. Mostly for greenhouse with moisture in the air.

Sun & part shade. Soil moist & fert. Division.

Leaves graceful, strap-shaped. Will grow in a container from 6–10 in.

A. andraeanum: Columbia. Also some 50 other spp. & hybs. & cvs. Amazing & various leaves. Flowers of the spathe & spadix type.

Ardisia: MYRSINACEAE. Coralberry.

Japan.

Evgrn. Mostly known as houseplants. Used outdoors in S. U.S. climate or as a container plant with protection. Tender in Seattle, Wash.

Shade or ½ shade. Soil moist. Cut back. Cuttings. Division.

Leaves glossy. Habit neat. Size of container for mature plant to 14 in.

A. wallichi: Differs to a marked degree from the well known spp.

A. crenata. Without hairs except on youngest parts; leaves obovate, oval 3–5 in. long; flowers white, num., axillary. Red fruits. May become dense shrubby plant 2 ft. tall & almost as wide. May be pruned.

Armeria: PLUMBAGINACEAE. Thrift or Sea Pink.

N. Am., Asia & Eur.

Evgrn. Herb. Flat. Some quite dwarf.

Sun. In cold climates cover with branches. Tolerant of sea air. Soil lean, sandy. Drainage. Fertilize in early spring. Division.

Dwarfs good for troughs. The spreaders can be used when young as cover for potted shrubs.

Hardiness: When hardy, I have said nothing about hardiness. I have used semi-hardy to indicate that a plant is less than perfectly hardy. This plant needs protection against frosts to survive. I have used tender to indicate that the plant will not tolerate *any* frost. I have used semi-tender to mean that a plant may survive a short period of frost but not prolonged frost or often repeated frost. This plant may lose its above ground portions but its roots may survive if mulch is used to protect the root area.

Explanation of the order: When there are varying heights in a genus, the spp. are often described in groups, Tall, Medium and Low. When the spp. are divided according to use, sometimes a group will appear under one heading and sometimes another group under a different heading. When there are two or more entries under different headings of various spp. a general plant description will occur under only one of the headings but reference to the list which includes the plant is included.

The spp. are not listed alphabetically. One sp. follows another because it is related or similar in appearance. One sp. may follow another because it has a similar habit. Occasionally the better known spp. are described first and spp. hard to find are given at the end of the spp. descriptions of the genus. Very often a dwarf sp. will come at the end both because it is smaller and because it is more uncommon. Occasionally the spp. will be arranged one below the other because I like the second better. You will have to judge from the text whether I like it equally well. I put them this way so that you might better see relationships horticulturally. When you wish to find a certain sp. in the descriptions, you may find its position in the text by means of the alphabetical index. Please do not read the descriptions of the spp. as if the whole were a jumble.

Hybrids: When a cv. name follows directly after the genus name, no name has been given to the hybrid and the parentage of the cross has not been recorded.

A. caespitosa 'Bevan's Variety': Quite dwarf, very good for a trough. Collar of papery bracts add to personality. Easy. R.g. or in groups in foreground of border as well as in containers.

A. maritima: Carpet of threadlike leaves, balls of pink or white. 'Laucheana' more dwarf and of a deeper color.

A. plantaginea 'Bees Ruby': Clumps of broad, long leaves. Flowers deep, brilliant "shocking"-pink. "Formosa Hybrids", a strain with tints deep carmine to terra-cotta. Early summer.

Asarina: SCROPHULARIACEAE. Creeping Snapdragon.
N. Am. & Eur.
Evgrn. Short stems, trailing or climbing. Leaves nearly triangular. New leaves continually opening.
Sun or ½ shade. Soil med. Cut back. Seed.
Flowers look like snapdragons or "butter and egg" flower. Summer. Will grow in a 5 in. pot.

A. procumbens (Antirrhinum asarina): Soft stems climb by coiling petioles. Leaves sticky, light green with round-toothed margins; flowers solitary in the axils, cream or pinkish. 1½ in., 2-lipped.

A. erubescens: Leaves triangular, toothed, hairy. Flowers with red stripes.

A. scandens: Leaves arrow-shaped; not hairy. Flowers 1 in., purple.

Asperula = Galium: A few spp. remain in this genus and these should not be overlooked.

Aspidistra: LILIACEAE. Cast Iron Plant.
Japan, Taiwan, China, Vietnam, Himalayas.
Evgrn. Valuable foliage. Oval, with pointed tip & broadened base. New leaves constantly push up from soil level.
Shade. Moisture. Snail & slug control & grooming. Division.
Old-fashioned pot plant, good to cut. Manicure for best performance. Best in fern pots, to 14 in. Spreads vigorously so divide often.

A. elatior var. *variegata:* Leaves striped with creamy white. Flowers stubby, colorless, curious, at soil level, only in old, lush specimens. Sp. quite hdy. (outdoors, under shelter, N.Y. City). Excel. in containers.

Azorella: UMBELLIFERAE
Herb. Differs little from *Bolax*
Cushions. Leaves entire or dissected.
Soil well-drained. Full light Alpine house or trough.

Begonia: BEGONIACEAE.
Malaysia, China, Japan.
Evgrn. Many spp. & cvs. Some grown solely for foliage. For flowers *Rieger* hybs., bred in Germany, most useful for containers.
Shade and ½ shade. Soil moist, fert. Cuttings. Seed.
Very various. Only 2 of many kinds listed here. Containers may be 5 in.; continued growth will require 6 in. container.

B. foliosa: A floriferous evergreen Begonia with many hanging stems. Small, rounded to oval overlapping leaves. Numerous pink flowers. Houseplant except in warm climates. Good for a shelf.

B. semperflorens-cultorum: Horticultural derivatives of *B. cucullata* var. *Hookeri* (Brazil). Wax Begonia. Easy to grow; free flowering. Wide variety of foliage color & flower color. Regrow annually.

Blechnum penna-marina: A tight ground cover. See Woodland. Angles of the fronds are displayed to advantage when the dwarf fern is grown in a pot.

Bletilla: ORCHIDACEAE.
Herb. with pseudo-bulbs. A clump-forming terrestrial orchid. Tough.
Sun or ½ shade. Soil humusy & rich. Plant 2 in. deep. Division.
Flowers in wavy, dainty sprays.

B. striata (B. hyacinthina): Leaves narrow, sword-shaped pleated to 1 ft. long. Flowering stems erect & wiry to 2 ft. with sev. rose-purple flowers. E. summer.

Bolax: UMBELLIFERAE.
Herb. 2 or 3 spp. Differs little from *Azorella*.

B. glebaria: Magellan. Chile. Tufted cushion leaves cut thrice, glabrous, leathery lobes ovate, obtuse. Flowers almost sessile; four flowered umbels.

Calceolaria: SCOPHULARIACEAE. Slipperwort, Slipper Flower, Pocketbook Flower, Pouch Flower.
Mex. s. to Chile and Argentina.
Herb. & subshr. Variable in habit.
Part shade. N., greenhouse; warm areas in the open.
Typical flower with a decided pouch. Division.
Several pots in blooming time make a show of yellow. See General P.D.

C. biflora: Herb. Basal rosette. Flower yel., less than 1 inch across.

C. polyrrhiza: Chile. One of hardiest. Corolla yellow, spotted purple.

C. tenella: Chile. Hardy on Pacific Coast. Creeping subshrub. Leaves almost sessile. Flowers on stems to 6 inches. Corolla yellow, spotted orange-red inside.

Campanula: For genus description, see Slope Plant Descriptions. For other spp. see General Plant Descriptions.
Some Campanulas are especially fine for containers. A few to be described here are trailers and most suitable for hanging baskets. The size of baskets or pots should be 5 in. or more for best growth.

C. fragilis: S. Italy; non-hdy. Very like *C. isophylla.*

C. hondoensis: 3 × 12 in. Close to *C. isophylla.* Flowers dble., fluffy, pure white.

C. isophylla: Italy; not hdy. in the north. Excel. in a greenhouse. Leaves heart-shaped, oval, becoming narrower as they approach the flowers. Flowers in profusion, saucer-shaped to flat, style conspicuously protruding.

C. i. var. *alba:* Almost hairless, many white flowers.

C. i. var. *mayi:* Foliage clothed with soft grey down.

C. i. var. *variegata:* White striped leaves appear more pointed.

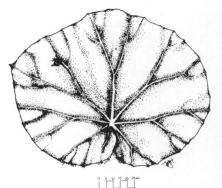

Begonia

Blechnum

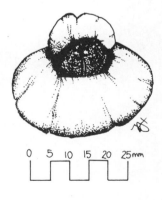

0 5 10 15 20 25mm

Calceolaria

Clivia

Convallaria

Crassula

C. pilosa: Compact clump. Leaves in tufts, oval. green. Flowers one to a stem; deep trumpets outfacing, two-toned.

C. pilosa var. *dasyantha:* Japan. 4 × 12 in. Blue bells one for each stem; lined with white; deep trumpets outfacing.

One large sp. handsome in a large container:

C. pyramidalis: Chimney Bellflower or Steeple Bells. Grow as a bien. Seed. Herb. Partial shade. 5 to 7 ft. in pots. Full, handsome, towering columns.

Carex: See Grasses

Clivia: AMARYLLIDACEAE. Kaffir Lily.
S. Afr.

Evgrn. Tuberous roots. Handsome foliage. In colder climates, grow indoors.

Shade; light but not sun. Moisture: sprinkle foliage. Drainage. Fertilize twice a year or biweekly with dilute fertilizer when grown in a container. Plant with roots just level with surface of soil. When dividing, "tease out" carefully old soil from root-mass, prying apart roots which are entangled. Partial dormancy Nov. & Dec.; start giving water & food in Jan.

Site pots in groups rather than in a row. Or use as single specimen, either in the house or in the ground. Needs 17 in. container. Best in fern pot. Bloom winter.

C. miniata: Belgian hybs., Zimmerman hybs.: selections for leaf quality & variety of flower color. Leaves thick, glossy, 1½ ft. long & 2 in. wide, curving away from center of clump. Flowers on strong erect stems to 18 in., funnel-shaped in clusters. Orange to orange-red or rarely soft shades to white.

C. caulescens: To 18 in. Flowers green, tipped orange.

C. gardenii: Funnels droop, making the cluster appear to tumble from stem top.

Convallaria: LILIACEAE. Lily of the Valley.
N. hemis.

Noted for fragrance. In pots, may be part of a display of bloom for the outdoor room.

Open shade. Rich soil with ample humus. Top-dress yearly. Water thoroughly all summer. When grown in pots, remove in fall, wash soil off roots, store in vegetable drawer of refrigerator & plant out, in pots or ground, in Nov. To start a new patch from an established patch cut a cube of roots about 6 in. by 6 in., plant in prepared bed— part leaf or bark & large enough to accommodate *Convallaria* by itself (it likes to keep its own company). Another method: lay a piece of thong-like root horizontally about 1 ft. deep & cover with soil. Some pieces may "take". Pips are available or plants in pots already blooming. Patience: the most important ingredient for success. In the ground, keep old patch growing well: shear before winter, feed periodically, pick constantly. Leave a few stems in order to see the scarlet berries. (Some plants are barren.)

Containers from 4–12 in. Boxes appropriate.

C. majalis: A cv., 'Fortin's Giant', highly praised & 10 days later than sp. *Convallaria* thrives in northern states of E. Coast of U.S. & inland;

only weedy looking if neglected. Slow to become established on the W. Coast of the U.S. & flowers never as luxuriant as in moister, colder climates. Leaves broad, basal to 6 in.; flowers small, drooping, waxy, white bells on 9 in. stems—fragrant. Pull to pick.

Cotyledon: CRASSULACEAE.
S. Afr.

Evgrn. Sev. succulent spp. well displayed in containers. Size of container varies with sp.

Crassula: CRASSULACEAE. Jade Plant.
Mostly S. Afr.

Evgrn. Many succulent spp. Tree-form & rosettes.

Sun. Drought resistant. Soil with sand.

Latin "crassus" = thick; succulent leaves & stems. For flowers as well as foliage, e.g., *C. argentea, C. falcata.* Fern pots best for most spp. To 14 in. for multiple rosettes.

C. hybrids: many oddities.

Cyclamen: See woodland.

The florist type are very colorful over a long season. Choice spp. are valuable.

Use in quantity especially on steps or surrounding an architectural feature.

Cynoglossum: Fill a large bowl with 5 to 7 seedlings. Fine show of blue. See woodland P.D.

Cyrtanthus: AMARYLLIDACEAE. Fire-Lily or Ifafa-Lily.
S. Afr.

Some spp. evgrn. "Fire-Lily" because some kinds bloom well after a veld fire. These spp. & others still more uncommon are tender.

Light shade both in pots & in the garden. Soil porous, sandy, fert. Drainage. Ample water when in active growth. Water spp. with evgrn. leaves throughout year but less in winter. In cool climates, dig up & store & replant in spring. Division. Or grow in containers; plant bulbs close together, tops just below surface.

In the garden best site is r.g. & edging for mixed plantings. In pots position sev. together in order to increase the less than potent fragrance. Size of container 5–7 in.

C. mackenii: Up to 6 leaves, to 1 in. long & ¼ in. wide; flowers ivory-white, up to 10, in umbels on stalks to 1 ft. Also pink & apricot pink. Fragrant. Waxy. In warm climates, may remain in the ground.

C. m. var. *cooperi:* Leaves narrow, arching with the flowers. Flowers cream to yellow.

C. o'brienii: Leaves glossy green, develop with or after flowers. Flowers scentless, bright red.

C. ochroleuca: Leaves narrow after the flowers. Flowers 2–4 in. an umbel, pale yellow.

Dudleya: CRASSULACEA.
N. Am., Ariz., Baja Calif.

Evgrn. Succulent. Very like *Echeveria.* Mostly rosettes. Best in a wood container. Needs at least 12 in. in width. Low best.

Sun. Soil with sand. No overhead sprinklers. Division.

Named for W. R. Dudley, first Prof. of Botany

at Stanford Univ.

D. brittonii: Leaves white-mealy, pointed, oblong; may reach 10 in. in length. Flowers on stems to 1 ft. tall, in clusters.

D. candida: Still whiter than *D. brittonii*. Leaves broader & shorter.

Echeveria: CRASSULACEAE.
Warm parts of the Americas. esp. Mex.
Evgrn. Succulent. Container 5 in. for specimen, to 10 in. for clumps.
Sun. Soil with sand. Drainage. Tender. Water roots, not leaves. Control slugs & snails. Groom. Division.
Many sizes, shapes & textures, some hairy, some smooth. Some with odd encrustations. Some with flowers of bright colors. Sev. varieties & cvs. for the collector, e.g.:

E. 'Set Oliver': This cv. has a wooly texture.

E. setosa: Small, neat, geometric mound. Curiosity.

Galium: A tight mat of pleasing foliage will fill a low pot. A few small dainty white flowers will bloom Spring and Summer. See woodland.

Geum: The smaller spp. bloom well in pots.
G. georgenberg has very crinkled leaves in tight rosettes and flowers of a pleasing orange color.

Globularia: See Woodland Plant Descriptions.
Dwarfs esp. good for containers: *G. repens, G. cerastioides, G. trichosantha, G. incanescens, G. aphyllanthus.* All worth seeking for use in small pots in which individuality of dwarf character may be portrayed.

Gloriosa: LILIACEA. Climbing-Lily or Glory-Lily.
Afr. & Asia.
Herb. Grows from pronged tubers. A curling tendril at end of each leaf.
Sun, warmth. Soil porous, fert. Perfect drainage. Appropriate trellis. Division.
Flower shape very intricate. Good in a bud vase or in suitable container. Pot 6–7 in., regular depth.
Latin: gloriosus = splendid.

G. rothschildiana: Trop. E. Afr. To 6 in. Leaves narrow to 7 in. long, ending in tendrils. Flowers downfacing; petals to 3 in. strongly reflexed, first bright red & yellow changing to red. Summer & Fall. Also *G. r.. var. citrina.*

G. suberba: With crisped petals & *G. simplex* with undulating margins, less common but available.

Gunnera: See Site for a Large Perennial Plant Descriptions.
G. hamiltonii & G. dentata: Attractive in a container. N. Zealand. Leaves grey-green. In the second the leaves evenly toothed & in rosettes, crowded to form mounds.

Hakonechloa: GRAMINACEAE.
Wet rocky cliffs, Cent. Japan.
Evgrn. Grassy cascading tufts. G.c. & r.g., besides pots.
Half shade. Soil moist. Drainage. Division.
Uncommon. In the wild, rather rare. Only 1 sp. Name from Japanese place, Hakone, & Greek kloa = a grass.

H. macra & variegated forms including *H. m.. var. albo-variegata:* Curving, pointed blades to 1 ft. long, to ½ in. wide. Flowers in spikelets to 6 in., 3–5 flowers yellowish green. Handsome.

H. m. var. *aureola:* Yellow leaves with green lines.

Helichrysum: COMPOSITAE. Everlasting, Immortelle, Strawflower, or Curry Plant.
S. Afr. & Aust.
Anns., pers. & subshrubs. Ev. Both common & choice.
Sun. Soil loose. Cuttings.
Bank. Pan or trough for dwarves.

H. angustifolium: Curry Plant. Mediterranean. Tender, woody-based-subshrub. Many-branched to 1 ft. tall; leaves slender, grey-hairy, crowded, with an odor of curry when brushed against. Flowers yellow to ¼ in. wide in clusters at top of erect stems. Can be trained as a standard.

The following for troughs or small pots:

H. psilolepis 'Nanum': White-grey. Silky texture. Spreads to form round, low mat. (See Slope Plant Descriptions).

H. selago: N. Zealand. Evgrn., many-branched, small shrub to 1 ft. The branches angle; clothed with imbricated, scaley leaves, green with white edges. Flowers minute, sessile, solitary. Pan or trough.

H. hookeri: Sim. Choice.

H. milfordiae: S. Afr. Low, compact cushion. Leaves small, oval, clothed with silvery hairs. Crimson or brown on the undersides of the bracts. R.g. in mild climates or alpine house.

H. frigidum: High warm places, Corsica & Sardinia. Only for a specialist.

Heliotropium: BORAGINACEAE.
Warm parts of Eur. & Am.
Herb. Subshrub. Size determined by pruning. Stems somewhat limp. Foliage of shades of green; dense in flourishing plant. Crinkled.
Sun & part shade. Soil moist, fert. Tender. Cuttings.
Unique fragrance. Bloom Summer, Fall. Can be trained as a standard or trained against a trellis. Container should be deep & at least 8 in. across.

H. arborescens: Cvs. selected for compactness & size & color of flower.

Hesperis: CRUCIFERAE. Sweet Rocket, Dame's Rocket, Dame's violet.
S. Eur., Siberia.
Herb. Fragrance strongest in the evening. Sprawling habit.
Sun or part shade. Easy. Soil limey, water retentive. Drainage. Might be invasive. Seed. Division. Cuttings.
Good as g.c. in low pots alone or with bulbs. Best grown as ann. Increases expansively by underground runners.

H. matronalis: Naturalized near old N. Am. gardens. Invasive but easy to pull. Flowers in terminal racemes, purple or white. Flowers look like *Phlox* flowers.

H. m. var. *flore-plena:* Dble. Temperamental.

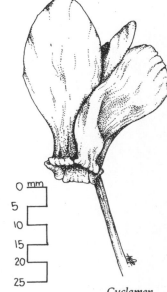

Cyclamen

Globularia

Heliotropium

Homeria

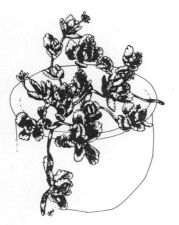

Houstonia

Homeria: See text

One of the South African bulbous plants which will bloom in a container. Tall stems and splendid show of apricot orange.

Houstonia: (*Hedyotis*) RUBIACEAE. Many stems. Delicate blue flowers, many weeks. Low pots. Three pots better than one.

Hutchinsia: CRUCIFERAE.

Eur.

Evgrn. Draba-like.

½ shade. Soil loose. Division. Seed.

Good for trough as well as r.g. When grown in its own container, needs soil area at least 5 in. deep × 5 in. wide.

H. alpina var. *brevicaulis:* To 4 in. Small, compact. Leaves mostly basal, 1–4 lobed, pinnate. Flowers small, white 4 petaled, narrow.

Isoplexus: SCROPHULARIACEAE.

Canary Islands & Madiera.

Herb. Related to *Digitalis.*

Sun. Soil fert. & moist. Cut back. Seed.

Erect, full, colorful spikes; plant sev. to a pot. Container 7 in. or more. See text.

I. canariensis: To 6 ft. in native habitat, 4 ft. in W. U.S., 2½ ft. in a container. Survived sev. frosts & bloomed 2 or 3 times a year, W. Coast of U.S. Erect, leafy stems. Flowers tubular with pronounced lips, 1 in. across at the opening. Flowers overlapping forming a dense spike over 1 ft. tall. Rich bronze.

Kalanchoe: CRASSULACEAE.

Afr., Madagascar.

Evgrn. Succulent. Many spp. with varied & extraordinary leaf forms. Shrubs to 12 ft. when planted in the ground. Some spp. 6 in.

Sun. Soil as for most succulents. Feed twice yearly. Cuttings.

Many spp. good for containers of various sizes according to spp. Plant should fill surface of pot. Group with other succulents or to accent plants with grey foliage.

K. blossefeldiana: Known in horticultural varieties for quantities of colorful flowers.

K. diagremontiana: Leathery leaves unusual, with trimming of plantlets on their edges.

K. beharensis: Felt Plant, Velvet Elephant Ear. Shrubby. Leaves large, 15 in. long & almost as wide, peltate or nearly hastate, felted, rusty brown on upper surface, silvery grey beneath. Triangular, indented.

K. tomentosa: Panda Plant. Madagascar. Stems densely leafy to 10 in. Leaves thick, silvery white, velvety hairy, coarsely toothed above middle & each tooth with dark brown blotch at tip; about 3 in. long.

K. pumila: With stems trailing from pot edge. Combines the colors grey, violet, lavender, pink. Sev. other smaller sp. excel. for pots.

Ligularia: COMPOSITAE. Leopard Plant.

Eur. & Asia.

Evgrn. & herb. Mostly grown for foliage interest. One can easily become a collector. Branching stem of yellow composite flowers may be removed in bud. Bloom summer & fall.

Part shade. Soil rich, moist. Groom. Protect from snails & slugs. Some need space. All need pots with at least 1 sq. ft. of soil. Divi-

sion. Seed.

Group containers on stands or on a wall for best display. Five or more leaves in a 6 in. pot. Aborting bloom increases health. Damage by slugs & snails defeats purpose of growing for handsome foliage. *Senecio* differs botanically only in the bracts of the involucre.

L. kaempferi var. *aureo-maculata* & var. *argentea:* "Leopard Plant" applied esp. to this sp. Japan. Extraordinary markings on 10 in. leaves: blotches yellow, white or sometimes light rose. Flowers light yellow on branching stems, often removed to increase value of foliage.

L. wilsoniana: To 6 ft. Flower heads in cylindrical racemes. Clumps 2 ft. wide of num. large basal leaves.

L. veitchiana: To 7 ft. Sim. to *L. wilsoniana.* Leaves triangular or almost circular toothed to 1 ft. across. Flowers look like *Eremurus* spires, slender, stiff.

L. macrophylla: To 6 ft. Large leaves glaucus-blue-grey. Flowers crowded in conical panicles. Uncommon.

L. stenocephala: China, Japan & Taiwan. To 4½ × 2 ft. Thick clumps of reniform-shaped leaves coarsely (jagged) toothed, 1 ft. across. Flowers light yellow in slender racemes, the stems often purplish.

L. przewalskii: Resembles *L. stenocephala* except in having leaves deeply palmately lobed, dark green extending up nearly black stems. Flowers in narrow spire. 'The Rocket', a fine cv.

L. dentata: Hybs. & cvs. E.g., 'Othello', with leaves purplish on undersides; 'Desdemona', leaves rich, dark brownish green above & with stems, stalks, veins & undersides dark purple or mahogany red. The cvs. more compact & refined than the type sp.

L. hodgsonii: To 3 ft. The large kidney-shaped leaves sharply toothed or smooth. Flowers often orange, with purplish brown calyces. When flowers are yellow, foliage is all green. Flowers more densely clustered than those of *L. dentata.*

L. tussilaginea: (*L. kaemferi*), (*Farfugium japonicum*). Evgrn. Sp. green-leaved. Varieties & cvs. with different patterns, spotted, blotched or segmented with white.

Many hybrids and cultivars.

Lilium: See Woodland Plant Descriptions.

Many spp., hybs. & cvs. may be grown in containers. Examples of those most often used follow. Use tubs, boxes or pots 12 in. or over. Hybs. are listed in the catalogues in strains (with " "). For colors, refer to your catalogues & the publications of the Lily Society. Heights given should be reduced for expectancy in containers.

Species:

L. candidum: Madonna Lily. To 4 ft. June. Fragrant. White. Dies down after bloom. Plant top of bulb only 2 in. deep. Sun.

L. longiflorum: Easter Lily. Forced for Easter. Spring or early summer normal. Trumpet. Very fragrant. Cvs., e.g. 'Croft'.

L. regale: Regal Lily. White, fragrant. July.

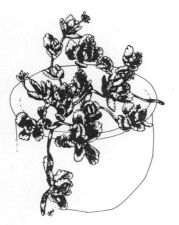

Kalanchoe

L. canadense: A native of E. coast of U.S. to 6 ft. Plant in tubs for first year. Cv. Coccinea brick-red with spotted yellow throat. Campanulate.

Hybrids: Parentage mixed. Examples: *L. auratum, L. japonicum, L. rubellum, L. speciosum.*
"Golden Chalice": To 3 ft. May.
"Coronado or Rainbow": To 3 ft. June. Tulip-shaped, upfacing.
"Bellingham": To 6 ft. June, July. Flowers recurved, 20 or more.
"Fiesta": To July. Flowers nodding & recurved. "Citronella" or "Golden Wedding".
"Harlequin": To 5 ft. June, July. Flowers recurved.
"Mid Century": To 4 ft. July. Flowers upfacing, wide open. E.g., 'Enchantment', nasturtium-red.
"Aurelian": 3–6 ft. Includes 4 sections: 1) Trumpet, e.g., 'Golden Clarion' & 'Golden Splendor'; 2) Bowl-shaped; includes special strain called "Heart's Desire"; 3) Pendant, drooping flowers; 4) Flowers flared with narrow segments, e.g. "Sunburst".
"Olympic": To 6 ft. July–Aug. Trumpet-shaped. E.g. 'Green Dragon', 'White Sentinel'.
"Oriental Hybrids": To 1 ft. July & Aug. Trumpet-shaped. Powerful fragrance. E.g. "Imperial" or "Jamboree".

Mitella: See woodland. See text.
A ground cover for shade. In a container, the foliage becomes an overlaid mass of triangular leaves—rich texture.

Morisia: CRUCIFERAE.
Sardinia & Corsica, sandy places at low altitudes.
Herb. 1 sp.
Best in Pacific NW., U.S.
Sun. Soil sandy. No severe heat or severe cold. Division.
Good for troughs or pans as well as r.g. or alpine garden. Shallow containers best. Bloom spring or early summer.
M. monathos (M. hypogea): No above ground main stem. Leaves lanceolate, dark, glossy, pinnate in rosettes flat to the ground. Flowers solitary on slender stems, golden yellow 4 petaled. Look like individual flowers of Wallflower. The flower stem bends down to the earth & buries the seed in order to continue its ripening.

Mutisia: COMPOSITAE.
S. Am.
Evgrn. Climber, slender stemmed. Leaves steel-grey.
Sun. Not hdy. in the north. Hard to establish. Seed.
Container large enough to hold a trellis.
M. decurrens: Chile & Argentina. Flowers to 5 in. with about 15 rays, brilliant orange with a yellow disk.

Narcissus: See Woodland.

Ophiopogon: See Woodland Plant Description.

ORCHIDS
Evgrn. Many spp. of various hardiness, size, shape & color. Orchid fanciers know which ones they wish to grow. Listed are two common, easy ones.

Epidendrum: ORCHIDACEAE.
Warm parts of the Americas.
Estimated number of spp. 400–800. A few more or less easy.
Light. Soil very loose, fert. Division.
Greek: epi = upon & dendron = a tree.
E. o'brienianum: E. evectum of Columbia × *E. ibaguense:* Mex. to S. Am. Stems, slender, reed-like. Flowers small, in rounded clusters, spring & summer, carmine with yellow on fringed lips. Also pinkish white. 12 in. pots & supports.

Cymbidium: ORCHIDACEAE.
Evgrn. About 40 spp. Thousands of cvs. Many, esp. dwarf forms, excel. for containers.
Sun & shade. Warmth. Soil loose. Seed.
Greek kimbe = a boat; refers to hollow in lip of flower.

Oxalis: See Woodland for genus description. *O. alstonii,* Fire Fern is excellent in a pot showing off its deep wine red foliage. *O. regnellii* is one of the spp. in which the tips of the leaflets appear decidedly sheared. The drawing on p. 148 shows the cv. with numerous white flowers sold in the market in early Spring.

Pelargonium: See General P.D.: 1000 spp. which grow well in a container—some for flowers; some for interesting foliage.

Phyteuma: CAMPANULACEAE. Horned Rampion.
Eur. & Temp. Asia.
Evgrn. & herb. Spp. from high altitudes difficult; others easier. Basal rosettes. Dense.
Sun. Soil with lime. Drainage. Rocks or large pebbles over surface of soil. Seed. Division.
Trough as well as r.g. Individual containers should be shallow & 6 in. wide.
P. comosum: Limestone mtn. cliffs, Alps. To 6 in. Leaves glossy, coarsely toothed. Flowers "flask-shaped" tubular with lower part bulbous, in dense heads of 15 to 20. Blue or purple with paler lavender or pink at base.
P. scheuchzeri: Hard to find?

Platycerium: Attach this fern to a wall. Its moisture preference can be met by immersing the plant in a tub twice a month. See text. Called Staghorn Fern. Exotic.

Pleione: ORCHIDACEAE. See text.
A genus to be used in the garden in temperate climates or in containers for a partly shaded site.

Polianthes: AGAVACEAE. Tuberose.
Mex.
Semi evgrn. From bulb-like tubers. Scape to 4 ft., usually less. Leaves in clumps, wide soft blades. Flowers in spikelike clusters, white or pinkish, tubular, waxy. Summer bloom can be expected in the garden only in southern climates.
In containers, plant root 2 in. deep. Use fern pots at least 10 in. wide. Water in growing

Ligularia

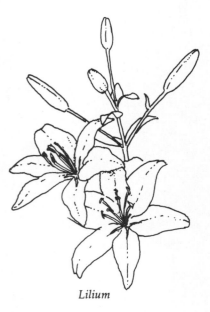

Lilium

Mitella

Epidendrum

Oxalis

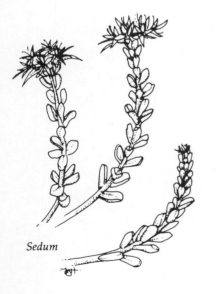

Sedum

season; dry off in winter. Feed on regular schedule while growing. Division.
Good to cut. Fragrant.
P. 'The Pearl': Dble., more often grown than the single.

Primula: See Woodland Plant Descriptions.
Primroses esp. for pots & boxes & bowls.
P. *malacoides:* Plant the annual in a grouping of pots for a show of white, pink or lavender for many weeks.
P. *seiboldii:* Japan. Leaves to 3 in. Whole plant downy. Flowers 6–10 in. an umbel, white, rose, purple. May. Plant is out of sight by summer. For moist beds as well as containers. Many cvs., e.g., 'Alba'.
P. *obconica:* Called German Primrose. Low elevations China to Himalayas, Sikkim. Glandular hairs on underside of leaf. (Sometimes cause a skin rash.) Long season. Flowers sturdy-stalked, 6–10 in. an umbel. Pink, lavender, purple-red & white. Calyces form a fleshy cone. P. o. var. *gigantea:* Sometimes available.
P. *sinensis:* Natural habitat unknown. The Sinensis section is segregated for bladdery calyces with broad, flat bases. Leaves to 5 in. across, cleft into sev. irregular lobes. Flowers notched to fringed, to 1-½ in. wide, pink, red, lavender, purple & white. Some flowers in this section have flowers in whorls. Winter, spring. Grow cvs. in greenhouse for a colorful display.
P. *polyneura:* Yunnan. Suggests P. *sinensis.* Plant downy. Scape to 1 ft. Flowers 9–12 in an umbel, pale rose to crimson with yellow eye.

Rohdea japonica: A choice foliage plant with many cvs. See text.

Scleranthus: CARYOPHYLLACEAE. Knawe.
Aust. & N. Zealand.
Evgrn. One a low weed of roadsides; another a good member in a trough.
Sun. Ordinary cult. Division.
S. *biflorus:* Loose mat, 2 × 8 in. wide. Yellowish green. Flowers in pairs, tiny, yellow.

Sedum: CRASSULACEAE. Stonecrop, Orpine.
Far East, Eur., N. hemis., China, Mtns. of Tropics.
About 600 spp. Succulent. Mostly perennial herbs & subshrubs. Heights from 2 in.–2 ft. Leaves often small & overlapping, inflorescense mostly a cyme. Genus divided into 8 groups.
Sun. Some spp. tolerant of poor soil. Semi-hdy. Seeds. Offsets. Cuttings.
Wide hardiness range. Some grown under glass. Many hdy. kinds. Some spp. esp. for containers alone or as companion plants. Spp. with small foliage will cover surface of soil in a pot. See General & Slope Plant Descriptions

Descriptions for spp. to be used in pots:
S. *anglicum:* Tiny plant. Leaves pinkish grey, only a little larger than a pin head arranged in short clusters which look like tassels.
S. *a.* 'Minus': Even smaller.
S. *sericea:* Very low but foliage increases to make a carpet. Leaves reddish, circumference about 1/16 in.

S. *spathulifolium:* Gormania group. Spreading & rooting slender stems. Will fill & spill over a pot; will fill cracks between paving stones, esp. good with slate or rock. Leaves in tiny flattish rosettes, grey-green & purple-grey. Flowers yellow, ½ in. wide in a flat-topped cluster. Faint fragrance.
S. 'Capo Blanca', S. 'Casa Blanca': 2 forms (may be only difference in spelling) with improved habit of growth, the rosettes tight & fat.
S. *suaveolens:* Leaves in rosettes. Only really fragrant *Sedum.*
S. *kamtschaticum:* E. Asia, esp. Japan. Tebar Daki. Stout rhizomes. Stems to 1 ft. Leaves dark green spatula-shaped, bronze in Fall. Flowers yellow in flattish clusters with yellow anthers. Makes a mound.
S. *morganianum:* Donkey's Tail. Leaves white-grey overlapping on long thin trailing stems. Best in "hanging basket".
S. *spectabile:* Upright sp. with cvs. 'Meteor', 'Brilliant' 'Carmen.'
S. *sieboldii:* China & Korea. Trailing, grey succulent foliage. Basal leaves no bigger than 1/16 of an in. in tiny rosettes, increasing to form a bumpy cover. Then, stems 8–10 in. grow to cascade over the edge of pot; leaves scalloped in a neat arrangement. Then tipped with pinkish flowering heads. In the fall, after flowers dry, leaves turn a rosy bronze. When leaves wilt, cut stems all the way to ground level where new rosettes are forming. Place on top of a wall to allow stems to hang.

Teucrium: RUBIACEAE. See General. One sp. excel. in a container.

Teucrium:
T. *polium* var. *aureum:* Velvety foliage with teeth on leaf edges, producing frilly look. Uncommon habit: stems grow at angles from main stem.

Tropaeolum: TROPAEOLACEAE. Nasturtium. Mex. to Chile.
Mostly anns. or vines. Leaves distinctly round.
Sun. Good drainage. Not hdy. Only mild & dryish climates. Seed.
Let sprawl from container or build a trellis. Excel. in hanging baskets. At least 6 planted in a container; low type.
T. *polyphyllum* & T. *speciosum:* Chile & Argentina. Fleshy-rooted pers., prostrate or climbing. Leaves roundish, deeply divided into 5 to 7 ovate lobes. Flowers yellow or orange-red with notched upper petals.

Viola: See General Plant Descriptions.
Miniatures for the greenhouse designed for alpines. Leaves very small, heart- or kidney-shaped. Mostly herb. Good planted in wood containers. Seek other small spp.
V. *verecunda* var. *yakusimana:* White. Tiny. Petals about 1 in. long.
V. *dissecta* var. *chaerophylloides:* Japan. To 4 in. Leaves divided. Flowers to 1 in., rose-pink. Fragrant.

Wahlenbergia: CAMPANULACEAE.
Wide distribution.
Herb. Close to *Edraianthus.* Bloom late Spring, early Summer.

½ shade & sun. Soil moist. Drainage. Grit or scree for the dwarf spp. Division.

Trough as well as r.g. Or a container to be placed where trailing stems can be seen.

W. hederacea: Moist soils, Eur. Ann. or per., 9 in. to 2 ft. Flowers narrow, bell-shaped, pale blue. Spills over edge of a pot. Place container on shelf or wall.

W. trichogyna: Aust. & N. Zealand. To 2 ft. Bristly hairy. Leaves lanceolate to 2 in. long. Flowers funnel-shaped; petals blue-violet, corolla tubes white, yellowish based.

W. saxicola: Evgrn., tight. Tufts resemble foliage of smallest *Campanulas*. Leaves narrow, spoon-shaped in tiny rosettes. Stems 3 in. Flowers tiny, blue. Late spring, early summer. Sun or light shade. Should be allowed to fill the surface area of a fern pot.

W. graminifolia & *W. serpyllifolia:* Might be found in a list of plants for a r.g. A trough would be a suitable situation.

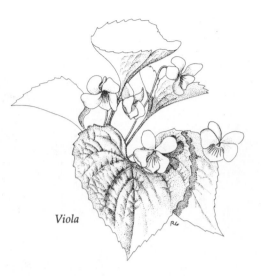

Viola

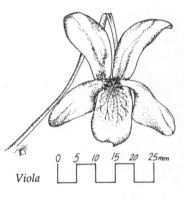

Viola

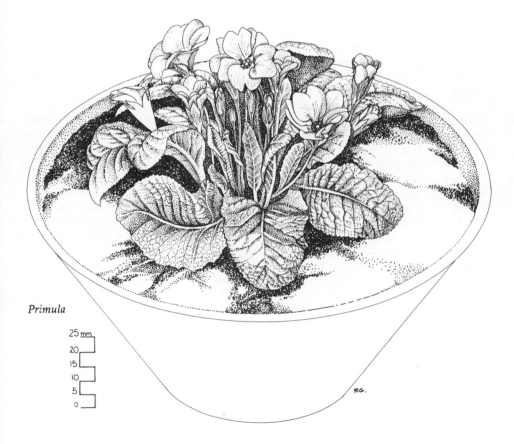

Primula

Lavandula

Pelargonium

Astilbe

14. The Strip

In almost every garden there is a bed which edges a path, a walk, stairs or driveway. This kind of s bed is called a strip; it is longer than wide, indeed, it may be no wider than a foot or two. Because it is used to decorate a permanent architectural feature, often dividing the architecture from the garden grounds, it must be planned and executed with care. The paths and walks etc, are usually level so no great amount of site preparation is called for. But in the case of steps or stairs or a sloping driveway, the strip must be terraced with retaining boards, rocks, bricks, or some other material fitting to the garden. Preparing terraced beds will require planning of the site as well as the planting design. The ground may slope away from the path; whether the the strip is level or terraced, its far side when lower than the path should not fall off from the near side. It must be built up and retained on the low side.

A strip need not be a straight line. It can be serpentine, with a continually curving edge. It can be straight but with additions to break the line. "Scallops" at regular intervals are decorative and appear somewhat formal. The scallops may contain a special plant, a perennial or subshrub of appropriate shape.

The narrow even strip, a foot or so wide is best planted with the same species throughout, in a row. Strips are often planted with a dwarf shrub, which is easily pruned, frequently Boxwood. If you like a neat, formal style there are a few perennials which can be trimmed in the manner of Boxwood, making a hedge but departing from a treatment so traditional that it is almost trite. My favorite candidate is *Iberis* which is dense and leafy enough for the hedge shears. If you would like a double hedge, plant *Buxus* and *Iberis* together, in two lines side by side. This will make a stepped hedge, the *Buxus* twice as high as the *Iberis*. A hedge type planting is appropriate either side of the approach to the front door. *Teucrium, Lavandula, Santolina* are three perennials which clip well. A number of subshrubs look well in a row and may be trimmed a bit to produce a neater more formal feeling. Heaths and Heathers respond to this treatment and *Convolvulus cneorum* is a perennial which grows in a soft mound needing little if any clipping. There are many choices if you want a more casual look. *Pelargonium hortorum*, the garden geranium, is neat and leafy especially when young. There are several more or less dwarf spp. or cvs. of *Pelargonium* which trimming makes compact, e.g. *P. odoratissimum*. If you are a rose fan, miniature roses look well in a strip.

Alternately, consider a sprawling or trailing or carpeting perennial. A mixture could be used but mixtures are more easily carried out in a space wider than most strips; herbs might be a possible exception.

All edgers need to have their straggly shoots trimmed regularly, for the sake of health as well as tidyness. Neatness does not necessarily produce a formal effect. Perhaps there are some people who have a basic aversion to the artificiality of trimmed plants; they can't admire or abide a perennial clipped to make a hedge. Clipping and trimming have admittedly been greatly overdone. For the non-clippers, there are a few perennials with a naturally geometric habit. This is more likely in dwarf species; look for them in genera such as *Teucrium, Limonium, Campanula, Aquilegia*. Some alpines grow in an even mound—almost a ball. Most of the smallest plants are choice and rare and not affordable for strip planting unless the site is equally miniature. But dwarf species can be found in several genera. A dwarf conifer is a very elegant plant to use in a strip; some grow in a tight, tidy round ball. *Chamaecyparis obtusa* 'Juniperoides' is neatly rounded, *Picea abies* 'Little Gem' is a dense small mound.

Fragaria

There are flowering plants which can be used in imitation of a hedge, e.g. certain spp. of *Begonia, Chrysanthemum, Dianthus. Penstemon*. Just a little trimming of those with fairly regular growth habit will keep the line neat. *Astilbe* is a very stylish strip plant—herbaceous but in leaf almost all through the year. Space the young plants of these perennials four to ten inches apart according to kind so that at maturity the outer edges of the foliage will just touch or overlap a little. Meanwhile, as they grow (hopefully at equal rates), the small plants will be attractive standing free; the soil between them and beside them should be kept neater and nicer because a strip is usually in a conspicuous part of the garden. There will be more months without than with flowers. After the flowers have made their show, any out-of-season buds may be removed; the foliage strip will do its own job of decoration when made neat by the removal of odd shoots and unwanted leaves. You will have a second show when plants have berries; *Fragaria vesca* is attractive planted in a row in a narrow strip. This is a species strawberry which is clumping instead of carpeting and its foliage, flowers and fruit are smaller than those of other spp. and cvs.

Aquilegia is a clumping perennial; its basal foliage is usually full, rising from crowded rosettes. The mound made by the foliage of the dwarf species is more dense, neat, low and round than the mound made by the many species grown for tall stems and large flowers. Each leaf flares out from the center, overlapping when in maximum size, but still face-up showing the pattern. Columbine leaves make a beautifully patterned mass when the foliage of the plants overlap; when planted far enough apart so that the leaves do not touch, the shape of each rosette is more visible. When it is time to remove last year's leaves, you will find the new ones just beneath.

Cyclamen: Several species increase readily, in time producing a tight mass. The foliage has fascinating form and design! When in bloom, there may be myriads of small crowding flowers.

We should talk about other bulbous plants which are out of sight part of the year. Some have attractive, lasting foliage which is neat for several months, often both before and after flowering. Bulbous plants can be grown in a strip with a perennial or annual ground cover. Some candidates are *Allium, Iris, Muscari, Zephyranthes, Scilla* and the dwarf spp. of *Narcissus*. The slender, numerous leaves of *N. bulbicodium* have a grassy look during the months before flowering. The leaves of bulbous or rhizomous plants usually have a distinctive character.; they are sword-shaped or blade-shaped, varying in form, texture and habit. We should select bulbs for a path edging with consideration of the foliage personality. They may flare from a central crown; they may grow in uneven clusters or in fans. Their habit may be neat and attractive.

Aquilegea

I will only give you examples of two genera which have forms with variegated foliage. These may be planted in a mass to fill the whole bed; or, in a narrow strip, they may be planted in a row. Perennials of this sort need some watching and clipping to keep the straight line straight. One is *Liriope*. The spp. increase by underground stems which must be cut away or dug when out-of-bounds. The variegated *Liriope, L. muscari* 'Variegata', is less rampant than a green-leaved one like *L. m.* 'Lilac Beauty'. *Liriopes* grow better in the shade. A variegated leaf with plenty of white or cream in the pattern shows up well in a shady place, lightening the various shades of green. Another sp., which looks quite like *Liriope* from a distance, is a grass, *Acorus gramineus* 'Variegatus'; it is striped with ivory the whole length of its slender blade. Do not overlook a number of other grasses.

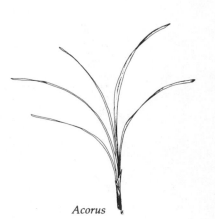

I would like to define again what I mean by "edger". The word describes a habit of growth which has a neat, attractive and more or less regular form. This type of plant is particularly suitable for the edge of a bed, to bind or trim a bed containing a different type of plant behind the edge. This type is equally useful for the edge of planting or the edge of a lawn or a path. But I have enlarged its scope to include plants of the same character for a special purpose, namely the strip.

Plants of two families, the succulents and the ferns quite different from each

Acorus

Adiantum

Heuchera

Diascia

other, look natural planted in a row, or rows. Some of the succulents, especially the succulents which form rosettes, e.g. *Crassula, Echeveria, Haworthia,* are very decorative planted close together to form a solid band. I have seen a mixture of succulent perennnials planted together to make a succulent "garden". This requires a space wider than a strip; a successful design can only be achieved if species which associate well are chosen and if they are arranged in a pattern which hits it off. I have described elsewhere some of the spp. of the succulent type which have greyish foliage; try combining two or three of different size and shape. A scheme can be developed with some spp. which are basically green but are trimmed with bronze. Spp. of both *Sedum* and *Sempervivum* produce handsome carpets which look well in strips. The majority of succulents prefer sun.

Ferns for the most part like shade. A fern with a small neat fountain of fronds makes a successful edging in a single row, e.g. *Pellaea rotundifolia.* Western Sword Fern, *Polystichum munitum,* is an orderly fern but needs a strip at least as wide as two feet. In a narrow strip *Adiantum,* Maidenhair makes a forest of delicate lacy fronds. Or a mixture of ferns can be tastefully assembled. *Phyllitis, Cyrtomium* and *Pteris* make a pleasing combination.

The strip bed can be treated in a different manner. A ground covering plant can be used provided it has enough form and personality to make a decided statement. If the habit of growth is very flat, the bed should be raised; a one-foot header board will give the bed enough height to create a demarcation and will give the flattish plants some stature relative to the path. For an informal style, the bed can be raised with rocks rather than a board. If the plant used is a trailer, it may be allowed to break the edge, but in this case, you will be hard pressed to keep that neat effect. Again, let's remember that flowers are incidental and should be sheared at the slightest provocation.

One of the following might be selected: *Prunella, Rubus, Aethionema, Aubrieta, Ajuga, Arabis, Aster, Viola. Nepeta* is good in hot sunny locations but hard to keep neat; *Heuchera,* Coral-bells, is a natural candidate for a shady bed but choose a sp. with small leaves. *Tiarella* grows in a neat clump, the little leaves radiating face-up from a center, too small for any purpose other than a narrow, shady strip. It suits best a woodsy setting.

Ajuga and Violets offer a wide choice of varieties. I like the giant *Ajuga* for its healthy-looking, low-lying mat of green; it sometimes appears overly healthy perhaps because we guess its intent to travel. I like a Violet with small close rosettes easy to groom after blooming; those which are rampant often look messy. Half the leaf stems must be cut back on *Aubrieta;* half the year there will be spaces between plants; part of the time it will look ratty. *Prunella* will look ratty if its flower stems are left on after they have gone to seed. Some people think of *Prunella* as a weed but one sp. has close growing foliage with a marvelous design. *Rubus* may take off over the edge of the strip and into the path but it makes a tight, crinkly carpet. The stems are easy to cut.

Sometimes three different genera can be combined in a strip. *Heuchera, Francoa* and *Brunnera* have some common traits and their habits of growth suit a strip situation. Sometimes two species of one genus will make an interesting combination. E.g. *Diascia rigescens* can be used for the dominant mass and *Diascia cordata* can be placed at intervals for interest.

The design of this one to two-foot bed is a little demanding if you use more than one species. Its restricted form requires a simple treament—probably with a selection of not more than three different spp. with one of the three taking a major role. Its relationship to the site and its well-being are important; you may have a sad little strip of tawdry appearance. If the layout of your garden permits you no greater width, your narrow strip can be made a success if you will but use your seeing eye.

Let us turn to a situation with more leeway. Your strip can be three or four feet wide. The wider strip is still in a prominent postion, bordering an architectural feature or defining the garden spaces. The setting may call for larger plants. Perhaps *Agapanthus* is used too much in southerly gardens and the chore of keeping it clean is a nuisance but it has some fine attributes. Choose one of the smaller cvs. like 'Peter Pan', if the large spp. seem gross or out of scale. When the handsome flowers are finished, the clumps of blade-shaped curving leaves can become a foliage feature if one is willing and able to groom.

Clivia has a similar form but it seems more elite: mainly due to the excellent texture of its foliage. It grows in a fine architectural way and has rich, choice flowers. The glossy foliage of the hybrids is outstanding; some may come under a group name

"Belgian hybrids", some under "Zimmerman hybrids". Without doubt breeding is continuing at the present time.

Moraea grows in a flaring clump of sword-shaped leaves. The foliage is dull rather than glossy but is not without interest; the leaves are narrow and numerous and form a plant over three feet wide. When planted along a path, its odd flowers can be seen at close view. Some other similar genera e.g. *Dietes* are equally appropriate; one which is hard to obtain is *Diplarrhena*. Some of the clumping perennials with sword-shaped leaves are too invasive or overpowering for the strip of a small garden.

If you like a genus but the most common species is too big, hunt for a cousin of smaller stature. Search for *Libertia ixioides*, smaller in every way than its better known relative.

Libertia

A more open growth is associated with certain genera which grow from a rhizome. Several kinds of *Iris* look very well planted en masse along a path. Choose from the Oncocyclus and Spuria groups. *I. japonica* and *I. foetidissima*, with a different look, have bright green clean foliage. *I. sibirica* cvs. must be cut back in fall but have pleasing upright foliage for many months. *I. unguicularis* has a tendency to over-spread but can be divided. *I. pallida* has wide leaves with handsome variegation. The big hybrids of Bearded *Iris* are stunning in parallel rows during their season of bloom but their foliage is very difficult to keep healthy and tidy during the off season. Many of the dwarf *Iris* have flowers the shape of the big bearded; they are decorative in leaf and furnish an added design element in their small above ground roots. The foliage of Pacific Coast *Iris* has a pleasing form but again the clean-up job of removing old leaves is a chore. I like *Iris innominata* so much that I would go to a great deal of trouble to keep plants neat in order to grow it along a woodsy path.

One of my favorite genera (as you have discovered) is *Bergenia;* the big, round leathery foliage is exceedingly glossy. When *Bergenia* is planted in the shade, the surface of the leaf catches any glimmer of light coming through the canopy of tree tops. When it is planted in the sun, it shines as well; the color in the green of the leaf is then often tinged with red. Of course, I like best one of those with white flowers; *B. cordifolia* 'Alba' is an example. The character of *Bergenia* is bold rather than dainty, not too bold for the small garden like *Acanthus* or *Yucca* but strong enough so that some care in the selection of its associates is called for. *Asarum.* and *Francoa* go well with *Bergenia*. *Bergenia* does spread but the retaining wall of the strip would contain it.

Asarum

Let us find some practical applications of these suggestions, which have been classed as strip plants and sometimes called "edgers".

We will walk along a sidewalk in a residential district. Next to the curb is a strip of soil in which there may or may not be planting. This was in the old days called a "parking" because it lay next to the curb along which cars parked. If this strip is planted, it requires a great deal of care with little reward. Neither animal nor man has any regard for anything alive there. Imagine three boys rushing along bouncing a ball carrying on a heated conversation about the kind of thing which fully occupies boys' attention. They cannot be expected to distinguish sidewalk from strip so another effort to beautify has failed. It is safer to divide the site along the curb into two or more squares instead of the strip and plant them with a small tree or shrub. The boys will have to go around the planting not through it. The tree well requires only occasional raking.

There is an alternate way to treat this area outside the hedge along the front of the house. Let the path be next to the curb and the planting strip against the hedge. There will be space for two or three small bushes and for perennial cover. This strip will get overflow from water and food given the hedge. The plants are close to a traffic lane and beyond the boundaries of day to day care; it is best to select something with excellent behavior.

A few plants are very very tough indeed, such as Ice Plant, *Delosperma* 'Alba', *Drosanthemum floribundum*, and "Highway Daisies", *Osteospermum fruticosum*, etc., but neatness is not the dominant characteristic of either. Their untidiness is not improved by their unfortunate use as a receptacle for gum wrappers, cigarette stubs and bits and scraps. Ice Plant can be considered a downright menace, a close tie with ivy. As for Highway Daisies, they behave much better along the roadside than they do any place even faintly similar to a garden.

Some of the spp. of *Oxalis* are uninvited guests in our gardens and most become real pests. But the one with many stems of yellow flowers in early spring is fresh and colorful in its short season of bloom; it will do well in a strip. There are a few perennials we can invite, and hope they stay, which are strong enough to take some

Thymus

neglect and to stifle the worst weeds. If some care can be programmed, *Lantana* is a possibility; it is bright and floriferous; when it has a place to trail it will go a long way. There is a tough *Verbena, V. rigida* with good strong color. *Pelargonium peltatum,* Ivy Geranium, looks well for a while; sometimes it will climb up the hedge and bloom on top. Should *Vinca* be the chosen plant, it might as well be tramped upon since it looks so mangled at the end of its season anyway. There is a well-behaved *Vinca,* however, a cv. of *Vinca minor,* probably found under the name of *V. m.* 'Purpurascens'; its stems lie close to the ground and neatly. But even then it trails and spreads vigorously.

Among the other perennials suggested for strip planting, there are a number which might be useful here outside the hedge. But this is a difficult space because it gets too little attention despite good intentions. If these which are the toughest for me don't appeal to you, choose one of the perennials recommended for strips which might be tough for you. E.g. Certain spp. of *Artemisia* close ranks to make a most pleasing strip planting.

Now we will enter up the driveway or the path, toward the house; here there is less hazard and more control of our plants. There could be a strip either side or perhaps only on one side of the path. We may turn a corner to arrive at the door. In the angle of the building wall, there will no doubt be a bed, for which you must make a new plan. Perhaps the plan has a small tree in the middle or a bush in the corner or in the center. There will be a perennial ground cover at its base. Something in proportion and green and hopefully flourishing is allowed along the facade and under the windows, something low with a compact habit. Container plants at the entrance and sometimes in a vestibule or covered walkway may take the place of planting next to the building. A low, trim strip of planting along the edge of the path is an alternative decoration for the approach. The plants could be flowering to obviate the need for flowering shrubs against the house wall.

Landscape architects often make the strips along paths too narrow allowing so little room for soil that there is little scope for choices. Perhaps there is only room for one row of a small perennial which may well look skimpy. Recall some of the suggestions for perennials adaptable to row planting in the discussion of narrow strip beds. The upright *Thymes* especially the spp. with natural rounded forms may be improved with a little clipping. But do not take the design of a landscape architect lying down, widen the strip a bit. If you build a house yourself and have an architect, keep him out of the garden except in rare cases. He does have to fit the building comfortably onto the lot but have your plan for paths and plantings ready for him to take into account as part of the site with which his plan must harmonize.

In a country garden, there may still be strips along the paths but they are usually wider, and when wide enough they become beds or borders. The composition of edgers in a strip in the country might be influenced by the open and natural setting—the wide view, the hills and the sky, but the principles guiding the selection of plants apply everywhere whether a path leads to a shop or a condominium, a cottage or a mansion.

Strip planting does not command your interest and attention? You just believe that plants-in-a-row is not aesthetic garden design? You think of a neat plant as not a "natural" plant? But a strip is a very common occurrence. It will not be tiresome or dull if a better than commonplace plant is selected for it. If it gives you pleasure to contemplate it, the extra effort you expend upon it turns out to have been worthwhile. It is possible to produce a pleasing effect in more than one fashion; if I have made some suggestions, they are not given to be followed automatically. This is a place, like all other places in the garden, where imagination should play a significant role.

If you live in a warm climate, you might grow a stylish strip of *Spathiphyllum.* If you do not mind a dormant period, you might plant in your seasonal strip a row of *Hosta.* Altogether different would be a solid mass created by a row of *Phlomis.* Or, small and low again—*Dianthus.* Foliage, grey or green, flowers, spring or summer, sun or shade there are too many possibilities to even mention any more.

Artemesia

Grey is featured on this bank with several perennials of varied form and texture. *Fibigia* is in the foreground, white-grey but showing its brown seeds. The rounded shape is silvery *Convolvulus cneorum*. The fluffy mats are three low species of Artemisia, *A. frigida, A. schmidtiana, A. canescens.* Rocks have two functions: to stabilize and to decorate. E.B.

Boulders are features in a rock garden taking up the whole steeply sloping lot (house on the upper fringe). Plants of like shape and of quite different shape are needed to accompany the large rocks. This is a colorful slope at every season; yellow, orange and red predominate in this view at this time of year. H.H.

Rocks delineate the beds which rise in irregular tiers on this nearly perpendicular bank. Rocks are functional, as well as decorative, and no space between them is without a perennial. Note the unusual hairy mop in the foreground, a *Carex* sp. H.H.

A path dissects a bank, making two, the upper long and steep, the lower shorter but also fairly steep. On the left some grey mounds, notably *Calocephalus brownii;* on the right side, in half shade, *Astilbe, Helleborus* and *Epimedium.* The vista ends in tall *Viburnums, Exochorda* and *Corylopsis.* E.B.

SLOPES WITH ROCKS

Raoulia glabra: This species comes from the hill country in New Zealand. It is a curious plant—a tight mossy mound ... The tiny white flowers tucked into the foliage only disturb the smooth surface a very little. E.B.

Androsace is a sprawler rather than a mat former. Numerous limp stems overlay each other, densely trimmed with soft, grey foliage. Many tips are trimmed with colorful rosettes. A. lanuginosa spreads neatly. E.B.

Here is a spreader with rough hirsute green foliage close to the ground. New tufts arise from underground stems to widen the mat. The flowers, palest yellow, have exaggerated protuberances from wide open mouths. This is an unusual sp. of Pulmonaria, P. lutea. E.B.

Clumps of low grasses may be planted close together to form a crowded cover. A variegated cultivar is more refined and slower growing. Variegated Liriope is similar but more open in habit. E.B.

A border at Filoli Center is longer and broader than any which you could put in a small yard. The size offers great opportunity to associate shrubs and sub-shrubs with wide expanses of mature perennials. The garden has passed through its developing years; some of the genera have been divided and replanted several times. Do not overlook such a border as a model. True, you cannot copy it, but you can make use of all its combinations. Think of it as a blown-up picture enlarged for ease in understanding the principles involved.

Here is a portion of a garden concentrating on yellow and white. Low and procumbent shrubs are used with sub-shrubs which repeat the scheme on a smaller scale. K.B.

A border rises abruptly from the edge of a path, producing the effect of a rounded tapestry hedge. The circular heads of one of the tallest perennials are projected above the solid mass for accent. (Rockefeller Garden). K.B.

White flowering shrubs make the background for several shades of rose and pink. The form of the plants is naturally rounded, so moderate pruning accentuates this natural shape. K.B.

This is an example of the famous English border. The background is formally vertical—the hedge clipped to allow no stray leaf. The perennials appear clipped as well; they are round forms in contrast to the rectangular sheet of the hedge. Perennials have been chosen which grow in a compact manner; their colorful flowers indicate that the hedge shears have not been in use recently. (*Dianthus, Teucrium, Iberis, Senecio, Erica, Calluna*—some of the spps.) K.B.

Strybing Arboretum border photography courtesy of the Helen Crocker Russell Library of Horticulture. Design by R. G. Turner. A traditional perennial border in an Arboretum along a main path and bisected by a side path leading to another section. Outstanding genera which contribute long seasons of bloom are *Heuchera, Coreopsis,* and *Delphinium.* A variety of forms is the means of creating the design, the tall spires, the round mounds and the low mats. A diversity of foliage lends interest; note the sword-shaped leaf of *Hemerocallis* and *Liriope* and the finely cut lacy leaf of a grey *Artemisia.* The planting can be replenished from the growing grounds of the arboretum. No gaps can be allowed in a teaching border, and the visitors' expectations of color for most days of the year must be satisfied. R.T.

The Strybing border seen from another angle. As one walks down the path, a design is seen in the forms of the plants and their overlapping drifts. Clumps and mounds and tufts and spikes are melded into a pleasing pattern. R.T.

The colors blend with each other on a muted canvas with highlights of vivid shades. In this view, orange and yellow are combined. R.T.

Approaching the border from the West, the cerise is seen in the distance which gives brilliance to the foreground in view #1. The visitors are comparing impressions. R.T.

STRYBING ABORETUM, SAN FRANCISCO

PERENNIALS FOR STRIPS

See other Plant Description list for descriptions of Strip Plants.

Achillea
Adiantum
Aethionema
Aquilegia
Arabis
Arrhenantherum
Artemisia 'Silver Mound'
Asarum
Aster
Aubrieta
Aurinia
Begonia
Beta
Calluna
Campanula
Canna
Carex
Chrysanthemum
Cyclamen
Dianthus
Diascia
Erica
Fragaria
Francoa
Geranium

Gypsophila
Hemerocallis
Heuchera
Hosta
Iberis
Iris
Kniphofia
Lavandula
Limonium
Liriope
Neomarica
Ophiopogon
Pelargonium
Penstemon
Phlomis
Platycodon
Potentilla
Sedum
Sempervivum
Spathiphyllum
Thalictrum
Thymus
Vancouveria
Veronica
Viola
Watsonia
Zephyranthes

Spathiphyllum

Hosta

15. Plans for Beds and Borders

Now that you have listened to my precepts and accumulated a lot of information about plants, it is time to put into practice some combinations. We will take a closer look at some sites where perennials may be concentrated. We will not place them completely by themselves; a few shrubs and trees are or must be put in and then the surroundings will always be present. You may think perchance of a walled garden which shuts off the planting to some extent but the wall does not obliterate the building nor the landscape nor the geographical setting, and besides, it is a feature which influences the design of the perennials in the strips or beds or borders within it.

Here is quite a different approach. You are building a house so start your garden on the vacant lot. This is immensely satisfying—the plantings will get a start so that when the house is finished the garden will be well on its way. However, this cart which comes before the horse must be made to fit its horse and to suit it.

Whatever you want to produce and wherever it goes, you will want to review some principles of design to guide you. Let me restate a few which are indispensable.

Let us think first of the relationship in a design of herbaceous and evergreen perennials. In warm climates you will have many semievergreen spp. Their locations will not be bare during the dormant period but mantled and decorated with rosettes of some spp., tufts of others and mats with only the briefest period before the new leaves take the place of the old. These spaces in the perennial garden look quite different during that time when the plants' upper growth has been cut back. The foliage patches look neat and flourishing and have individuality of form while the plant is in its semi-resting state. But the garden in these spaces has no vertical lines and obviously the spaces occupied by the herbaceous perennials will not be visible at all. So how does our design look while nature takes a seeming leave of absence?

The best solution is a selection with all three kinds, evergreen, semievergreen and herbaceous. Then, intersperse them with one another. It will normally turn out that while arranging various forms you will conscientiously place the evergreen plants in strategic positions. Many are subshrubs and their solidity is a factor that is connected with the habit of keeping the leaves. Go ahead with your plot plan placing your spp. according to form. When your drawing is complete, check over the positioning of the plants. If you have inadvertently put too great a concentration of evergreen perennials in one section, it will be an easy matter to exchange a piece or two without disturbing either contours or the combination of color.

In any case, most of your evergreen material will be improved by strategic

Arenaria

shearing. Thus its foliage will be reduced in overall size and will be then in better relation to the rosettes and tufts left in your pattern after cutting back the flowering stems of your semi-herbaceous to the ground.

As for the positioning of the spp. which disappear altogether, they can be intentionally staggered on your plan so that the areas of bare ground are not all at one end or the other. Again, this placing is incidental to the contribution each sp. will make when mature. You will find yourself, however, selecting certain bays in the plot plan for some of those perennials which take up a large space when in growth but stay out of sight for an extended period. You will see examples in other chapters. For instance, in "Woodland and Shady Places" you have seen the use of herbaceous *Athyrium,* which I have warned will completely die back in November. Also I have alerted you about the disappointment you will feel when a large space has been allotted to Oriental Poppy, *Papaver orientalis.* Perhaps even just three plants will leave a spot of bare ground too big for too long.

This is not to say, avoid the truly herbaceous. Such a principle would cut you off from too many excellent choices. Besides earth well cultivated and mulched is beautiful and full of promise.

I think a few more guide lines should be reiterated here. Even if you have finished your main paper plan you may need to give it a further look and some last minute adjustments and finishing touches. Have you enough variety in your forms especially shapes resulting from plant habit?

You may want to make a substitution with either a plant which branches at angles or a plant with branches stiffly erect. You may want to move your one drift of grey edging down away so that grey is not concentrated in one place. You may want to change the contour of a drift so that some of the rather tall spikes of a sp. come forward into the rank of medium height.

Finally, of course, you must check your own plant index for breadth of growth and exposure preference. To the facts in the plant descriptions in these chapters, you will add notes from your own experience and observation. A card catalogue is bound to have become part of your equipment. First, a review of the principles which apply to all mixed plantings.

Size of drifts: Not too small so that the personality of the plant is lost; not too big because a personality should not become overpowering.

Shape of drifts: Not just oval. There are a number of similes all of which are useful as guides: fish, clouds, deflated balloons, etc. One expert designer calls them "bubbles". A kite is good but the corners must be softened.

Position of drifts: Interweave. Drifts should be pulled forward occasionally and then pushed backward.

Arrangement of heights: Bring some heights to the front; run some low drifts back into the middle range.

Association. Not dainty next to coarse except for shock in the design.

Accents: Make some focal points with material which is heavy, definitely outsize or merely different.

Repeats: A species should appear at least twice in a bed of any reasonable size. Or it might be complemented by a close relative. Or again it could occur just once as an accent or as a connector for a change of type. A repeat of color is essential, except again when there is need for an accent.

Selection of color: Some color you especially like should be predominant. Various shades of this color can be incorporated. A general scheme may focus on one color. In a design with muted colors something bright can be introduced but it must blend and emphasize a tone in one of the predominant muted colors. Something white or cream is important as a blender and a cooler.

Edges: The drift of some small, low plant may be thin and long. Do not use too much of any kind of ground covering plant which finishes its flowering quickly or has poor foliage for more than a very short time.

Variation of shapes: The shape of the drift is of paramount importance. But both the shape of leaf and of flower should be taken into account when placing any two plants in juxtaposition. Contrast is important but similarity is indispensable for carrying out a scheme. Repetition is a tool of emphasis.

You may not place your plants perfectly on paper. It is all very well to say, "Here there should be a kite-shaped space to be occupied by a round-shaped, medium-height perennial." How many plants of this perennial do you need? One school of

Eriogonum

Godetia

Phacelia

Ramona

Zygadenus

thought errs on the too-many side and often with a poor result because the weaker plants of the sp. just grow less well and look stunted or puny in the foliage mass. I am of another school. I like the plants to just touch and may have to wait two years for that to happen; also I am niggardly about the riches in my soil, therefore, I like each member of the colony to get its maximum share. Take, for example, *Coreopsis verticillata*, the foliage of which forms a rounded mass. Plants may be placed close enough together so that they will overlap in full growth; still, however, you may want to see the form—the roundness of the individual plant. How do you place the plants to carry out the outline of the drift you want to make?

When you position three of a more than medium-sized perennial, make a triangle with equal spaces between each plant but set your triangle so that no two plants appear to be in a row. When you position seven of a less-than-medium-sized perennial, begin with one at one end, increase to two, then to three, then decrease to two, each row with its parts between the parts of the other.

If you wish to make a circular or an oval-shaped drift with quite small plants, mark the outline and place plants on its circumference four to eight inches apart depending on growth habit of your sp. Then fill in the middle, putting inner plants in spaces between plants of the outer circle.

Suppose you wish to trim the forward edge; the drift behind the straight front may be made irregular, the oval line bending inward to one side of center.

Experiment with many shapes. Try cumulus clouds. Think of a ribbon or rope, start it at one spot, loop it back of a drift of another sp. and bring it forward again to the edge. Or make a crescent. This will be narrow, one plant wide at the tips and fuller with two to three plants in its fattest portion. A triangle often fits well between several more or less oval drifts. The meeting of the hypotenuse and one of the sides comes nearly to the edge, seeming to bring the form down to the viewer. The plants in the triangle are placed as in an oval, the outside plants spaced after the first plant begins the outline at the forward point.

Suppose you wish to make just an exclamation point or a period. Often this is easy with just one plant, with a sp. of considerable width and density or height and slenderness.

Have you been practicing? You might want to make a rough plan or two before embarking on the final draft.

Yucca

16. The Beds

Take a garden where a plot can be established which will be the home specifically of perennials. This area may be created on the plans of a new garden; in an old garden, it may be a space freed of discarded plantings such as annuals or shrubbery or it may be carved out of a plot of grass. The plot may be a geometric shape, round, oval, square, rectangle, triangle. A shape between rectangle and oval may evolve in which the sides are straight but the corners are curved; the planting for this flattened oval would be hardly different from that for a rectangle unless you believe that any curve makes a shape more informal than straight lines. "Island bed"—an oval with curves on sides as well as corners—like an island. Technically this bed is surrounded by grass. "Serpentine" is a good description for a bed with a curving edge. "Flower garden" is a good name for any bed or border with some plants incorporated.

Suppose we considered first a measured shape which has a rather strong tendency to be formal. It is not very common in the modern garden so we can dispatch with its treatment fairly quickly. This is the shape resulting from a square which is dissected from all sides with paths. Four beds have been formed, each a square except that usually the inner corner of each has been bitten off. There may be a circle in the middle, large enough to hold some planting or small enough to merely make a place for a seat, a birdbath or a weather vane. As you can readily see, the corners of the beds were removed to facilitate traffic flow around the center and to the adjacent right angled paths. If the circle is reserved for a specimen tree, a trimming with perennials is usually redundant. The tree could be a flowering fruit; in a smaller situation the centerpiece could be a standard shrub like a Wisteria or a "P.G." Hydrangea. In either case, the circle of soil in which the plant is growing is best covered with bark, gravel or rock. (More later about planting under trees.) The center might be just planted like the four squares and without a special feature but it is really too tempting to use it as a focal point. If roses were used in the square beds, the center could have a standard rose. How have you decided to pave the paths? You have to choose between grass, cement, aggregate, gravel, bark; this cover will be one element which helps to set the stage for the type of planting.

But the character of the whole composition is affected most strongly by the choice of edging for the four beds. As mentioned, the form lends itself to a formal treatment; the plant selected for the boundaries of the beds should conform to the following requirements. It must be naturally neat or easy to keep neat; it must be naturally small; it must grow at a predictable rate so that its height and width will be more or less even; it must have an inherant vigour. It should probably be evergreen— surely not herbaceous, at least in a temperate climate.

Besides Boxwood, which is the most common formal edging, there are a few dwarf shrubs which have a fair chance of success—Red Barberry, a species which loses

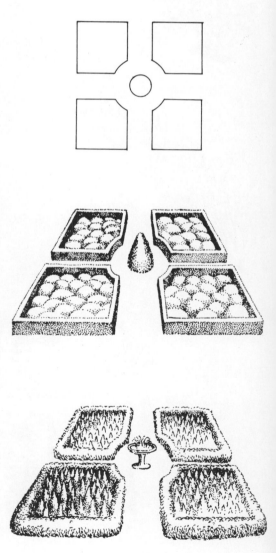

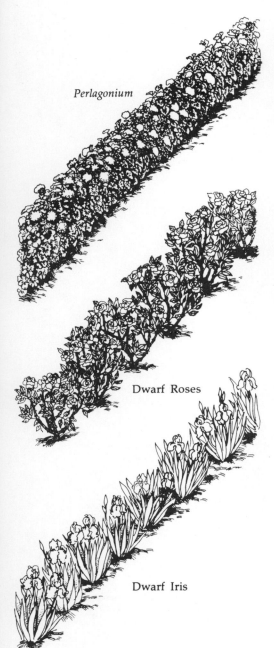

Perlagonium

Dwarf Roses

Dwarf Iris

its leaves for a while, *Euonymus,* a dwarf; a privet, the small, rare sp.; a heather; or "Baby" roses. If you are crazy about Ivy, you can make a rounded frame and train a dwarf kind over every wire and keep it trimmed. You could do the same with dwarf *Ficus.* Another possibility is a subshrub which takes to clipping. And you will think of Lavender, which gets too big for most sites with this divided pattern; if you have a strong liking for Lavender, you will find one of the most dwarf cultivars. This search will be relevant also in selecting a *Pelargonium*—the different kinds are so various in size and habit that both research and trial elsewhere in the garden may be in order. The look of a plant in youth is often so very misleading; normal growth, perhaps increased by sun, soil and water may develop a plant so out-of-scale that it will not fit its space no matter if clipped weekly.

What about Lavender-cotton—the number of clippings needed depends upon such things as weather and nourishment. The most commonly seen *Santolina* is grey, *Santolina chameacyparissus,* but here is *Santolina virens* if you prefer a green edging.

Remember if you wish to make a hedge type edging, you must find a kind of plant which responds to clipping. The best place to see possibilities is in a well conceived "knot garden": usually a number of varieties are worked together to form the design and all must be clipped. A subshrub which is fundamentally neat-growing may be clipped for greater neatness and greater formality. To make and keep a Knot Garden is a chore beyond the scope of most gardeners. A very ambitious individual can not only find books which prescribe the various designs and suggest the plants to carry them out, but will visit gardens with fine models.

For our all-of-one-kind hedge for a courtyard we do not need quite as much perfection as that which is expected in a Knot Garden, although the more the better. A few perennials will serve and still not be too demanding; how about *Iberis* of which we do not tire even when it is put to every use in the garden? Another look can be brought about with an upright blade shape; three examples are dwarf *Iris, Liriope* and a grass like *Festuca glauca.* No one of the three is perfectly orderly but all are plants which look well in a row. In the bed proper there are a number of possibilities which I will tell you about in a later chapter.

Now let us look at another situation which requires very similar plant material. To go back to our squares, a less patterned square might develop between natural boundaries such as buildings or hedges. Sometimes a path bisects this plot usually at an angle. The result will be two, more or less, equal triangles the hypotenuse being the front edge of the beds. If the path is straight, or with geometric angles, the edge of the beds will perhaps have a semi-formal treatment less stiff perhaps than the pattern of the four-square bed just described. If the path curves, the edge will be wavy in which case the edging plant may be less erect and less neat. When this square is small, it is often fully paved; the manner of paving may leave spaces between stones, slate, brick, and wood blocks. The kind of ground cover to plant between paving of any kind is a special category for which I should make yet another list. (See Index)

A small square whether or not bisected may be planted fully with a low perennial; probably a more satisfying effect can be achieved with just one species; its height can be considerably greater than that of a species to be used just between stones.

Westringia, Teucrium, clipped *Santolina.*

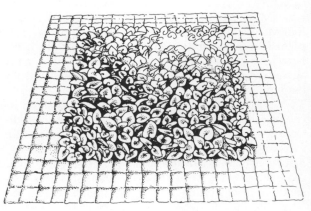

Asarum in small square.

Above all, the species chosen must possess good foliage, that is with leaves of attractive texture and color and with a habit of growth on the stems which is regular and dense. In all probability you are aiming to create a restful carpet. I think of two examples: for a shady space, *Asarum*, Ginger, and for a sunny site *Rubus calycinoides,* or the best kind of Strawberry. (See Plant Description) It is sometimes reasonable to fill the space with an herbaceous perennial such as *Convallaria.*

If the square is large or larger, the planting may be more mixed, since in a free standing rectangle, perennials with at least medium height can be incorporated. When the square is raised, the proportions don't change but less height is needed. For example, a solid mass of *Veronica* can be edged with *Lantana.* Combining two perennials works in raised oblongs, also.

If the square has a more or less formal feeling, accent perennials may be placed in the corners or in the centers—all the same kind in a regular fashion; this perennial could be a subshrub or it could be an evergreen mound; in any case, it should be a neat grower. Choose one which does not have to be replaced every year because it grows too fast and soon becomes out-of-scale. Members of the daisy group have this tendency. The so-called Paris Daisy is quick to become woody and together with all daisies has to be constantly dead-headed. The best daisy, if you want yellow, is probably *Euryops pectinata.* The plant becomes three feet by three feet. The second best is *Chrysanthemum anethifolium* if you want white. The foliage is small as are the daisies. Both of these last longer in good condition if constantly clipped and groomed. Certain *Pelargonium* are manageable—some restrained growers of the fragrant foliage group. There are handsome variegated ones if you like variegation.

The circle has entered our survey in connection with a type of square. But there is more to say about circle planting. A circle is very seldom put into a landscape plan as an artistic design for its own sake. I saw a circle in the middle of a lawn the other day, with flowers filling it; it was made level with a brick wall; it was in place of a border. A circle may develop around a tree as previously described or at the convergence of paths; a round bed may be situated on an artificial platform for the purpose perhaps of breaking a seemingly boring line, or of providing a special spot for "flowers", in an otherwise severe or starkly green part of a picture. A secondary reason for such a raised bed could be the need of a screen; it might be a decorative addition to partially block off the garage entrance from the house entrance court. The fewer the kinds of perennials in this bed the better. Concentric circles of plant material certainly look contrived. This circle has a tendency to resemble a cake; when the circle is solid white in the center, it may look like a meringue pie. It takes a lot of effort and care to get two or more perennials to come to bloom solidly and in unison.

Is there another treatment for a free standing circle? Certainly not a casual mixture; inevitable bare places would mar any sense of an integrated whole displayed within a frame. Probably the most successful treatment is a planting of just one kind— maybe a trailer when the circle is raised; I have seen Rosemary or *Trachelospermum* used to good effect in a large circle and *Helianthemum* in a small circle. Maybe an upright perennial, say to 18 inches, can be planted as a solid bed. I have three or four suggestions quite various: good old *Agapanthus* but no doubt one of its dwarf cultivars;

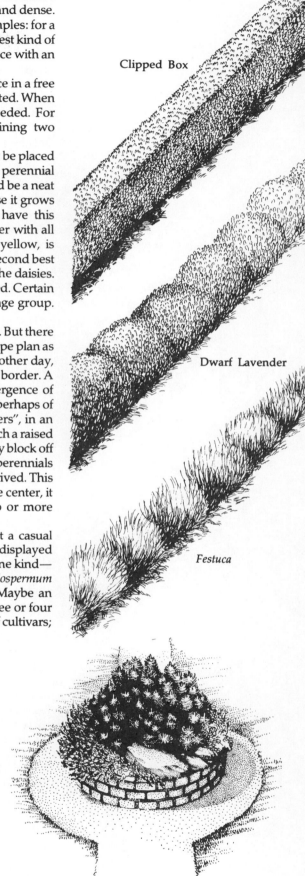

Clipped Box

Dwarf Lavender

Festuca

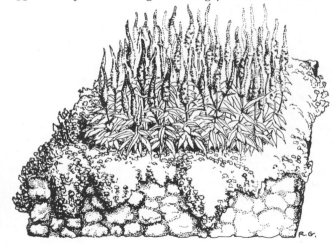

Raised bed: *Lantana* trailing, *Veronica* in middle.

Mugho Pine, *Helianthemum.*

Pelargonium (Geraniums), either the flowering or the foliage type; daisies or Daylilies; or something more stylish, for instance, *Gerbera*. A special bed is advantageous for *Gerbera*, first because the site may be made just right as to drainage and richness, and second because this colorful flower needs its own stage for display. Or *Begonias*—any kind of *Begonia* may be featured in a circular bed in a solid mass—or in any bed of any shape—squares, or rectangles or strips. The modern bedding *Begonias* have been improved in breeding.

Now if there is a tree in the middle of the circle, that is another matter. See page 163. The tree should dominate the scene and any other planting should be subservient. to it. If by chance the species is one which dislikes wet feet, like an evergreen oak, it can only be accompanied by some plant which does not need constant water. If the tree is deciduous, there will be two seasons, one of sun and one of shade, so you must choose a companion tolerant of various exposures. With a tree tolerant of regular watering, there are a few ground covers which are appropriate. How about *Ajuga?*—quite pleasing foliage together with a season of strong blue in its flower spikes. (It may send stems wandering over the edge of the bed—ones not difficult to cut.) Hybrid Primrose—or species Primroses—may be tried especially if their colors go with the color of the spring flowers of the tree. Probably all one color will be more pleasing than several. Now, if the circle is in a shady area, *Epimedium* or *Helleborus foetidus* are very decorative in a mass planting—with or without a feature of tree or shrub. *Pachysandra* has the requisite qualities; when healthy it is dense and lush.

An annual instead? Excellent for a special season—*Primula malacoides* or *Nemesia* for spring and *Impatiens* or *Cinerarias* for the fall. (*Cinerarias* are classed as perennial but are best planted fresh every year.) *Alyssum* (the annual) is stylish only when fresh; Larkspur may fall over. A mixture of low growers? If one tries to plant a carpet—to neglect—it will look moth-eaten very soon.

Of course you have realized that no particular shape of bed demands specific plants exclusively; many of the suggestions made for one shape will equally well suit another. But let us touch upon some variations.

The strip, the long and narrow bed, is given special treatment elsewhere in these pages. "Serpentine" is a good name for a strip with a curving edge. A bed which curves along its edge making an uneven outline can be called "free-form". The modified geometric shape is presently more in vogue than the strictly plain shape whether circle, panel or rectangle. Beds must fit into their surroundings and into the landscape; they may be carved out of an expanse of grass, or the pavement or the floor of a patio.

The panel: Does it stand free? What are its measurements? It is longer than a strip; it is shorter than a border; it is wider than a strip; more or less the same width as the averge border. Its lines are geometric although they can be modified with curves along the sides or by bites taken out of the corners. It can have similar plant material to that in any other bed except probably fewer kinds. There are "rococo" panels and there are "baroque" panels. In a formal garden, the treatment of a panel would probably be traditional with a clipped edging and regularly spaced accents. It might be a solid bed of one perennial but it would more likely be filled with an annual or a perennial grown as an annual; the planting would be changed two or three times a year. It could be more informal with a soft edging and with rising height from edge to middle not unlike seats in an amphitheatre but with more undulating levels.

The oval: What kind of a setting would ask specifically for this shape? It might be used instead of a circle because it fits better into the surroundings. There may have been a cut in the grade which developed a space just about oval. Its lines, softened into curves instead of squared off will result in a more natural shape. Sometimes we soften the straight lines of a rectangle by the planting. Often we bring a plant, used in a drift for the edge of the end, around the corner creating the look of a curve instead of an angle. The choices for an oval are about the same as those for a rectangle. Sometimes the oval backs up against some boundary, straightening its back line. This situation allows taller perennials on that line; then the arrangement of the several kinds selected will be very similar to that used in a "border". Is there any type bed in which the arranged pattern typified by border designing would not give the most attractive results? Very seldom does ribbon planting—rows one behind the other—have a pleasing effect; an exception might be a formal bed in which a progression of colors might be the paramount object. But it would be hard to imagine ribbon planting in an oval bed or in its relative, the island bed.

The "island bed": Start with an elongated oval; make indentations at will; the contours should be more uneven than even. You are trying to make an imitation of a natural island. This is the popular form made famous by Bloom. It is a modification of designs in existence for centuries. There is a great deal of scope in the pattern of the planting and ample opportunity for the exercise of a sense of imagery. The shapes within should enhance the outline.

The island may have a path all the way around it but as noted earlier the path is not authentic. The British version has no need of a path; the island sits in the navigable sea of the English lawn. The small, low plants go all the way around; the heights mount from the edge to the higher central plants. Of course the gradation is not exact; the heights mingle on the way to the summit. To see the other side, you must go around the corner when you may find a different scheme not visible from your first view. But even as the scene changes the planting forms are related. The form from a distance is a pyramid of pleasing, melding shapes and colors. Each composition can be unique.

The planning of a border is not exactly stereotyped either—what a lack of interest if it were cut and dried! I will put several types of beds and borders on paper for you, expecting you to make drastic changes. No one, I trust would follow any paper plan exactly. My selections will be of a certain size, shape and color and you will make substitutions with plants you like of similar character.

Be always searching for new cultivars and for unfamiliar species for either beds or borders. The most common perennials may be easy, tough, available and beautiful but they lose all sense of excitement and adventure when seen along highways and in every dooryard. But don't forget the old standbys; sometimes plants go out of favor and then sink into oblivion; upon rediscovery, they prove to be plants of merit. And if you find a very odd species, place it well.

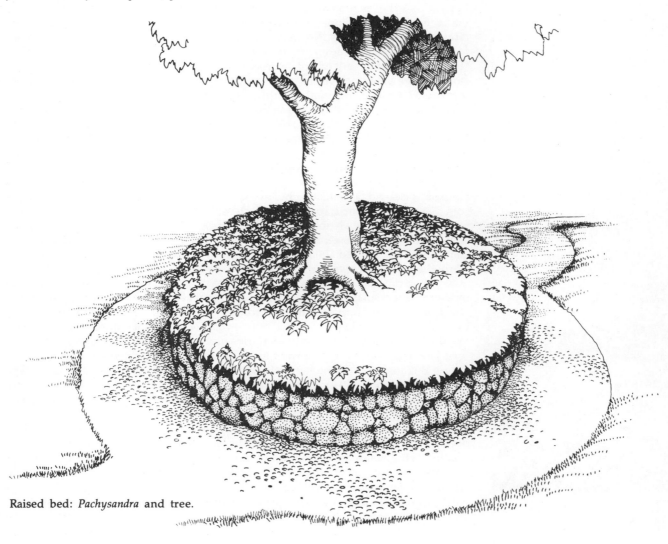

Raised bed: *Pachysandra* and tree.

17. The Borders

Of course, the situation suitable for a combination of the greatest number of perennials is the "perennial border". It is no longer designed just in the old-fashioned manner. It is not a feature with fixed rules as to contents and sizes and shapes. Nowadays anything goes. Probably it would be a good idea to enlarge our conception of the "border" to include all the areas which have heretofore gone under the name of "beds". The definition need not be precise; the one basic ingredient must be an inclusion of more than one species of perennial. How many? Shall I say three would be minimum? Another component of the definition is the shape of the site; the area should be longer in one dimension than in the other. As to the outline, no rules are necessary. Have I broadened the meaning too much? Do you see that my enlargement brings the "island beds" within the class called border? Why was it called a bed in the first place? First because it is surrounded by lawn, supposedly giving it a special status. Second, because the British think of a border as a traditional border.

A modern border can be a limitless mixture of trees, shrubs, subshrubs, annuals, rocks and perennials either evergreen or herbaceous. Of all sorts of character some yes, old-fashioned, some comebacks, some known previously in the wild and now tamed, some newly introduced, some lowly, some fancy, some easy from seed, some hard to grow, some found at the bargain counter, some sought in remote corners, some you have learned about in books, seen in the borders of Botanical Gardens or learned of on the screen during a talk by a specialist.

You can not have them all. Only a few will last you for a lifetime; most have an indeterminate span of life, some need replacement periodically. Perhaps, although the word perennial is supposed to mean forever, you should plan to redo your border every three years. Whether in three or five years, you will then divide the plants you like the best and perhaps make wider drifts of them. You will have enough to give at least half away since you will want to make room for newcomers.

But how to make the start? What perennials do you use for your design? There are restrictions imposed by the place you live. First climate. How many days of warmth and how many hours of sun? In a cool or cold climate you will plan for a short season garden; your time of active growth is so short that the maturity of perennials more closely coincides. Climates having many growing days in the year, have their disadvantages. The roots of some perennials like a rest period and some like the shock of cold as a trigger for the beginning of a new growth period. In a climate where growth is almost constant, you will find that some familiar perennials are hard to control. If you are new to this warm area, you perhaps do not know the meaning of "invasive"; you will learn soon enough. You will see in the literature expressions like "questing roots" and "rampant growth". In a mixed border, perennials of this sort may encroach upon other perennials less aggressive. Now you must put these plants only where you are

Maples, ferns, *Gaultheria*

pleased to have them travel. These fastest growers are the ones called invasive; another type is slower but persistant, wandering too far beyond the space allotted in your plan. If you are willing to watch these energetic types, you can control their growth by clipping and pulling on their periphery. Corydalis is one example.

Some other restrictions brought about by climate are given special treatment in another chapter where some methods of protection are suggested. Wind seems to me the hardest element to contend with but I have pointed out to you the remarkable resilience of some perennials to the battering of gusts and gales. A very hot area as well as a desert requires special selection and attention and extra water and shade. As for damage and death caused by low temperatures, in many cases you must learn how well your choices can withstand cold by trial and error. You can not go by the USDA Hardiness zones; within the zones there are many mini-climates. How to select for hardiness can follow a course of caution or of daring. There are quantities of perennials which are borderline cases. I will outline for you the conditions which sometimes allow the tender species to get by. Meanwhile you will lose out on many kinds you would like to have if you are not adventurous. So many gardeners in temperate zones have holding areas and those especially who specialize in container plants enlarge their scope to include "indoor-outdoor plants". So I will include in the Plant Descriptions a number of names which will cause alarm. Don't say, "We can't grow that" until you have tried out some of the semi-hardy and the semi-tender, helping them to become acclimatized and providing as much warmth as can be devised in your garden.

Corydalis

There are other general guiding principles for selecting the perennials for your border. Do you still have in mind an old-fashioned perennial border? Your choices may be influenced by your past; you may have been born in Boston, Bogota, Naples, London, New Orleans. You will think first of some old-fashioned perennials; *Delphinium*, Foxglove, Hollyhock. Sunflower, Black-eyed Susan, Peonies, *Phlox* and towards the front, *Aurinia*, English Daisies, *Violas*, Primroses, *Ajuga*, *Aster*, *Chrysanthemum*. You will certainly include *Nigella*, Love-in-a-Mist. When you become acquainted with the value of the many perennials which contribute to the design by leaf structure, you will replace on your plan some of the familiar perennials best known for their flowers.

What is more beautiful and stately in the highest rank than the tall hybrids of *Delpinium*. If you hanker after *Delphinium*, grow a less demanding species and perhaps a leafier one. *D. bellamosa* is less regal but it is tougher. For the back of the border, mostly look for substitutes for *Delphinium*. You will see some in the layouts. *Fritillaria imperialis* and *Eremurus* are very regal indeed, with substantial foliage, but will they survive? When only one of three to six roots sends up a tall spire, you have failed in your purpose of a strong period, a single column looks very lonely. In any case few gardens require either the size or the grandeur.

Digitalis, the tall biennial, used to be in the back row of every perennial border. Now look for more perennial species, or hybrids, which carry out the spire form but are less tall. *D. ferruginea* is almost as tall as the tallest but it is more slender and leafy and looks less heavy than the common species.

Nigella

Besides Foxglove the old-fashioned perennial border contained *Aster*, *Coreopsis*, *Helianthus*, *Valeriana*, etc. Look now for genera with especially decorative foliage as in some *Veronicas*, some *Salvias*, *Macleaya*, *Cimicifuga*. Sometimes the decorative value of the foliage of a number of species carries over a long period—many months before bloom and usually some weeks after.

Let us come down one range in height. *Phlox* was always present in an early century border. It should not be absent in a late century border unless you find an alternative with similar habit of growth and similar shape of flower head. *Paeonia* anyone would want in the today's border when there is room enough. Cultivars may be selected for the leaf growth as well as for the bloom.

Daylilies: Always a mainstay because of that rounded clump which gives solidity to a border. The foliage of today's selections is lusher. How to choose from among the many cultivars? You might select for instance, 'Heavenly Harp', both for its fragrance and its lovely shade of yellow; the flower is not normal, the petals have ruffled picotee edges. With *Hemerocallis*, or instead of, you can use other genera with sword-shaped leaves. Some genera differ from *Hemerocallis* in foliage and habit of growth, broader or higher or stiffer; hardly thicker, since a well-grown Daylily has about as dense a habit of growth as you can find. Or combine with *Hemerocallis* a genus

Dictamnus

Anagallis

Houstonia

with a quite different habit and leaf as *Baptisia* or *Pelargonium* or *Dictamnus*.

We have skimmed over the back and middle of a border and will give the low front even less attention. After all you have a lot to read about possibilities in other chapters. This edge is the ideal situation for plants of interest: some quality of foliage or the value of being out-of-the-ordinary will recommend them. Low plants are described not only in the layouts but in the special treatment of small plants for strips, beds and carpets.

You will find as you search, several improvements to take the place of your preconceived notions. Perhaps you will just discover a different species of a well-known genus, or a cultivar or a hybrid. Cultivars have often been bred for better behavior. Even if you are a devotee of true species preservation there are some cultivars you will not be able to resist. You will not break away from the natural entirely but your choices will reflect your discoveries of values in both behavior and appearance.

Where will you make a border? Someone said, "I would like a border but I just have not any room"; there is an old adage which applies here but need not be repeated. Another said, "A border is too much work". True, if you cross out the "too". Most of the work comes in preparation, in the improvement of the soil and the making of the plan.

At the moment, let us just list some possibilities: Have you a lawn? Down one side of the lawn, down both sides of the lawn, around three sides of the lawn, right in the middle of the lawn. Carve off the lawn whatever space you would rather have in perennials. Have you a paved area? A border may be alongside or within. Have you a house wall or a fence or hedge? Put a border against. If this gives you a very narrow border, select slender plants e.g. *Linaria*. Have you a part of the garden you do not like? Put in a border instead. When? At least start your plan today.

Would model paper plans be a guide or a hindrance? The layouts which follow are merely suggestive and, of course, come nowhere to a point of coverage of the field. A large number of species will be found in the Plant Descriptions which have not been assigned to any layout. If a plant sounds good to you, you will look for it and put it in your own plan.

I strongly recommend a paper plan even if you do not expect to follow it. It will be helpful in a number of ways. You will be able to observe whether you have chosen the right proportions of varying heights and widths and the best proportion of broad leaves and narrow leaves. As you have heard me say before, one good principle to guide you in making your plan is repetition. If you believe you have found a pleasing association between two or three kinds of plants, do the same combination further along, either copying the relation of the drifts or changing it a little. You can take a piece of one of the layouts, if you wish, in case a special combination fits both your site and your preferences. None of the sample layouts are meant to be exact as to size and shape: some had to be curtailed in length in order to fit the page. Some may contain too many different species of plants; do you think perhaps a few were tucked in in order to have a reason to describe them? Perhaps your space allows you only a single border; the double border is just a further challenge if your yard is wide enough. And the two can be only five or six feet apart if you put between them a grass (or other) path instead of a lawn. How much space do you need? Very little.

Measurements: almost limitless latitude. A border can be anywhere from 10 to 100 feet long and its depth can be 2 to 20 feet. If you have a short border, you will have fewer different kinds of plants, especially few because you will still practice repetition. If you have a narrow border, you may want to confine your selections to allow only two heights, low and medium or medium and high.

Additions? If your border will be over five feet in depth you may want to incorporate shrubs, or subshrubs. If you will need extra color for a season, you will want to incorporate annuals and bulbous plants.

Adjustment to the site: If your border will be near Eucalyptus, its inhabitants must be not only drought resistant but tough. If it will be near any kind of tree, its nature will be dictated by how much water and food the trees demand, how much shade they cast and when and what effect the tree's type of root growth will have on the health of the roots of the perennials in its vicinity. But trees and shrubs can provide some wind protection; what will you choose to plant which does not suffer from being battered about?

Drainage: The ground need not be level. If the garden slopes, the border may be "stepped up"—terraced to allow for a succession of flat raised beds, or left sloping if the slope is gentle. A gentle slope will perhaps have natural dips and rises. These can be accentuated. If your sloping border goes downhill evenly, it is best for both cultural and aesthetic purposes, to create some mounds. On these mounds (an elongated mound may be called a "berm", originally the name for the long mound following a ditch) you will plant some of your tricky species and also some of your rarer species for which you wish a sort of pedestal. What happens to the water which descends from your mounds? It will make a natural track for itself but you can assist in planning its direction; it should not end in a hollow from which another track does not exist to carry the water on a gradual descent through the length of the border. This type of border— with hills and dales—is particularly suited to the inclusion of rocks; it is often inhabited by a tree or trees and therefore partly shady. This meandering border will have more foliage than flowers.

"Flower garden" is, however a good name for any bed or border. Now, you wish to make a flower garden on a site with a little depth and more than a little length and at least enough light for your flowering species to come into bloom.

Let us suppose that you contemplate mixed perennials in quantity and you have drawn an outline more or less to scale. How do you proceed? Perhaps a plant list first and then the drifts to fit the plants or the other way around. How big the drifts and how many plants to each drift depends of course on the eventual size of the plants selected. Vary the size and the shape of the drifts (see chapter on preparation.) Do not make a checker board.

You will acquire your perennials in a number of ways; if purchased they will be in four-inch plastic or clay pots or more likely in a one gallon container. Do you know how much and how fast they will multiply in size? Plant dictionaries and catalogues seldom provide the eventual width of a plant. Some books say how far apart to place them. This seldom indicates width at maturity. Many plants reach their best size in three years; some which increase by underground roots grow as wide as you allow. Take the average perennial, however; about how wide will it eventually become? Many will spread horizontally until they touch their neighbors; stems will overlap and finally climb into each others' laps. How wide will an individual become which has no obstruction in its way? You can only go by a rule of thumb and foresee that each healthy specimen will triple in size in the foreseeable future.

Do you see that I am giving you a principle? If you are putting dots within your drifts to signify the placing of plants, do not put too many. Sometimes you may be tempted to plant closely so that the border will look full right away. You will have to remove some plants the second year; you can avoid some replacing if you will only give the plant space in which to grow. If given room when being planted, some species may remain in place for 8–10 years (a few forever). The following genera are samples: *Baptisia, Bergenia, Dianthus, Kniphofia, Helleborus, Ophiopogon, Liriope, Polygonatum, Paeonia, Trollius, Yucca.* Meanwhile, some will have been divided. The clumps of some perennials continue to spread sideways; at some point, the plant with which you started will do poorly and be quite worn out in its oldest parts. You will dig it up, cut it up, throw away the aged center and plant a group of pieces at least a foot apart.

But this is down the line a bit. The paper plan is for now. Many species which have a medium rate of growth may be spaced a foot apart, e.g. the roots of *Aquilegia* and the rhizomes of *Iris*. Plants which make a large clump will need between two and three feet. In one of your drifts on the paper plan, you can place one *Hemerocallis* or in a larger border a group of three. There are many large clumpers which need strategic positions for them and will be the bones of the border ten years or more hence. How about the hundreds of species of smaller perennials? On the average, leave six inches for those you believe to be upright growers without much root spread and modify the measurement of the spacing according to your observance of that kind of plant in a mature garden.

Should the drifts touch, on paper? Not quite since the plants on the periphery need room for spread. But don't leave any biggish holes unless you are saving that space for a specific addition. The drifts should interweave but not interlace. You should leave more spaces between drifts than between plants. Somebody said, "a community of plants comfortably adjusted to one another, cooperating instead of co-elbowing".

I have not put dots on the sample layouts. They would make the plan look as if it had the measles. Dots could be a help when planting, however. The clouds and fishes and worms of your drifts can not be adhered to exactly; you will make adjustments

Linaria

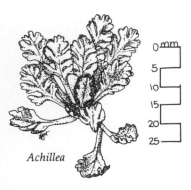

Achillea

when you are on your hands and knees where you can better visualize the outcome of your handywork.

The General Plant Descriptions follow wherein you will find a number of suggestions for a sunny site. Please refer to Woodland and Shady Places Plant Descriptions for suggestions for a shady site. When you are making your plans, check one of these to find out as much about the spp. as possible.

General Plant Descriptions

Achillea

Achillea: COMPOSITAE. Yarrow.
Eur., Brit., Asia Minor.
Evgrn. Basal leaves; finely cut. Some spp. leather-like, some velvety. Flowers in flat heads, spring & summer. Yellow, white & 1 sp. crimson. Spread 1–3 ft. Good to cut. Sun. Soil med. Cuttings. Division.
Low spp. 4 in. for r.g. & borders. Medium & tall 2–4 ft. for beds, strips & borders. Bloom spring & summer.

Low spp.:
A. ageratifolia, A. argentea, A. clavennae var. *argentea:* Greyish foliage. Low, thick carpeting. Small, white daisies in clusters.
A. umbellata: Greece. To 6 in. Spreads slowly, to 1 ft. Leaves tufted, pinnately toothed, white-wooly. Flowers white in small dense heads, spring.
A. tomentosa: Dark green, feathery, more vigorous than grey spp. Flat heads of strong yellow top 7 in. stems, summer. Cv. 'King George': Soft yellow variation.
Cv. 'Maynard's Gold': Foliage very tomentose. Flowers on 5 in. stems.
A. ptarmica: Sneezewort. Narrow, green, often messy foliage, not leathery. Invasive; to 6 ft. or more. Small, button-like flowers on 18 in. stems. Summer, sun, poor soil.
Cvs. 'The Pearl' ('Boule de Neige'), dble.; 'Perry's White', more lax. Good to cut for small bouquets.

Med. spp.:
A. × *taygetea* (of gardens): Possible cross—*A. millefolium* × *A. clypeolata* (of gardens). Foliage copious grey-green, feathery. Dense 4 in. mat. Width at maturity, 2 ft. Flat heads, summer, on 2 ft. multiple stems, sulphur-yellow. Plant with *Ballota, Eryngium* & *Origanum.*
A. 'Moonshine': Hyb. by Alan Bloom. *A. taygetea* × *A. clypeolata* (both of gardens). Bright to light sulphur-yellow. Very prolific.
A. millefolium: Common Yarrow, Milfoil. Many erect flower stems to 30 inches. Leaves crowded, full rosettes, feathery, green. Flowers muted-white, flat-topped. Best in a "wild" garden. Spread difficult to control; somewhat weedy. Invasive.
A. m. 'Cerise Queen': Bright cerise-crimson for mixed bouquets. Flat heads on 2 ft. stems, 2½ in. across, in clusters.

Tall spp.:
A. filipendulina: Robust. To 4 ft. Back of border. Between shrubs. For cutting. Best known as dried flower with brownish yellow 5 in. plates on tall stems which are self supporting in the garden. Tolerant of dryish conditions. Found in nursery catalogs under names such as 'Golden Plate' 'Golden Pride', 'Coronation Gold', from a cross with *A. clypeolata* (of gardens).

Adonis

Hardiness: When hardy, I have said nothing about hardiness. I have used semi-hardy to indicate that a plant is less than perfectly hardy. This plant needs protection against frosts to survive. I have used tender to indicate that the plant will not tolerate *any* frost. I have used semi-tender to mean that a plant may survive a short period of frost but not prolonged frost or often repeated frost. This plant may lose its above ground portions but its roots may survive if mulch is used to protect the root area.

Explanation of the order: When there are varying heights in a genus, the spp. are often described in groups, Tall, Medium and Low. When the spp. are divided according to use, sometimes a group will appear under one heading and sometimes another group under a different heading. When there are two or more entries under different headings of various spp. a general plant description will occur under only one of the headings but reference to the list which includes the plant is included.

The spp. are not listed alphabetically. One sp. follows another because it is related or similar in appearance. One sp. may follow another because it has a similar habit. Occasionally the better known spp. are described first and spp. hard to find are given at the end of the spp. descriptions of the genus. Very often a dwarf sp. will come at the end both because it is smaller and because it is more uncommon. Occasionally the spp. will be arranged one below the other because I like the second better. You will have to judge from the text whether I like it equally well. I put them this way so that you might better see relationships horticulturally. When you wish to find a certain sp. in the descriptions, you may find its position in the text by means of the alphabetical index. Please do not read the descriptions of the spp. as if the whole were a jumble.

Hybrids: When a cv. name follows directly after the genus name, no name has been given to the hybrid and the parentage of the cross has not been recorded.

Adenophora: CAMPANULACEAE. Ladybell. China.

Herb. Tufted. Often taken for a *Campanula.* Long period of summer bloom. Leaves oblong, ovate. Flowers in branched racemes. Summer.

Sun or part shade. Ordinary cult. Cut spent stems to the ground. Division.

Somewhat invasive. Fleshy roots go deep.

A. tashiroi: Japan, Korea. A less common sp. worth seeking.

A. confusa: Most common sp. Lavender bells on erect 2 ft. spikes.

A. megalantha: Supposed to be superior.

A. bulleyana: China. Reputedly to 4 ft.

Adonis: RANUNCULACEAE. Pheasant's Eye Eur. Far East.

Growth in winter—to 18 in. Stems leafy.

Leaves deeply divided into narrow lobes. Flowers buttercup-like.

A. vernalis: Best known & easiest. Fol. feathery; lasts until Summer. Flowers yellow.

Aethionema: CRUCIFERAE. Stonecress.

Herb. Low mound with small leaves & flowers.

Sun. Soil loose, light, sandy. Drainage. Ordinary cult. Seed.

See this in Victor Reiter's garden, San Francisco.

A. × warleyense: A decorative form. R.g. or front of border. 3 to 5 in. Dense terminal heads. Fragrant.

A. cordifolium: Horticultural hybrid. Dense heads on stiff, upright stems. Leaves ½ in. blue-green.

Ajuga: LABIATAE. Bugleweed.

Temp. Old World.

Evgrn. Foliage mats by rooting stolons.

Shade or ½ sun. Need water & food to thrive. Cut flower stems to ground.

G.c. Weedy-looking if neglected.

A. reptans: Carpet Bugle. Solid carpet increased by runners. Leaves may be green, bronze, metallic purplish or mottled. Flowers strong, erect, intense color, some 10 in. tall. Good to pick. Cvs. include "Giant" strain & "Jungle" strain.

Alcea: MALVACEAE.

Probably Asia Minor. Now widespread.

Herb. Tall, stately. Flowers in pastel colors.

Sun. Soil med. Water med. Seed.

A. rosea: Hollyhock. (*Althea officinalis* = Marshmallow) 7 to 9 ft. Sturdy usually without staking. Only garden strains today grown as ann.

Alchemilla: ROSACEAE. Lady's Mantle.

Asia Minor.

Evgrn. Spreaders & creepers. Round foliage ruffled or notched or toothed. Scalloped effect outstanding. Invasive?

Sun or shade. Soil med. Trim back in fall for fresh growth early spring. Division.

G.c. & r.g. Short stems, both leaves & flowers to cut.

A. vulgaris: Probably the one to which the common name was applied—the pleating & scalloping of the leaves suggested the headdress of the Virgin Mary. Native to mtns. of E. Eur. & Asia Minor. Leaves with

shallowly-toothed lobes. Flowers yellowish green over sev. mos. To 1½ ft.

A. mollis: Carpathians to Turkey. Both flowers & leaves useful to flower arrangers. Leaves kidney-shaped, softly hairy, soft green, fringed. Flowers tiny, a delicate cloud of soft greenish yellow. Tough. Control by division & preventing seed from developing. Cut back.

A. alpina: Alpine Lady's Mantle. Mtns. Eur. More compact, less rampant. Leaves silky-hairy beneath. Flowers insignificant. Self-sows.

A. conjuncta: Alps Eur. Like *A. alpina* but leaf segments joined for a little distance. Silvery beneath. To 1½ ft.

Alstroemeria: AMARYLLIDACEAE. Peruvian Lily, Chilean Lily.

Chile & Brazil.

Herb. Many spp. & cvs. Numerous slender stems, 10–36 in., soft or firm according to sp.; often forming a wide clump, to 2 ft. wide. Produces drifts to 10 plus ft. Divided foliage, in masses before flowers. Fine flowers to cut, mostly summer.

Sun. Soil good. Water while growing. Provide special framework for hybs. Initial support results in extra substance & sturdiness. Division.

Seek superior cvs. not on the market at this writing.

A. pulchella: Increases. Blooms many mos. Odd green & red. Easiest.

A. aurantiaca: Peruvian Lily. Spreads vigorously underground, becoming invasive. 6–10 ft. A "stand" produces many cut flowers, orange-yellow. A number of cvs. of varying shades & size.

A. ligtu var. *angustifolia:* Now a rare plant, was used with *A. haemantha* to produce a strain called Ligtu hybrids—in salmon, coral, pink, crimson, some streaked & spotted. Flowers many with more firm stems if supported, 1–2 ft. tall. Long-keeping if lower leaves removed so none below water line. Chilean *A. ligtu,* St. Martin's Flower, is robust.

A. "Parogo hybrids" recently developed in Holland. Only available cut. Various muted to deep shades; small, flaring trumpets. Flowers scattered instead of in rounded heads. Admired by arrangers. Varied muted colors.

A. "Dr. Salter's hybrids": Superior.

A. hybrids (of the late 20th century): As yet unnamed. All gorgeous.

Anacyclus: COMPOSITAE.

Morocco.

Evgrn. Spreading to 18 in. Stems slightly woody, prostrate.

Sun or ½ shade. Ordinary soil. Summer. Cuttings.

Rosy, glossy seed pods. Leaves small, oval, many, pinnately cleft, sticky.

A. depressus: Contained, flat little plant. Leaves num. & lacey. Flowers 2-toned, small "daisies", ray florets white with pinkish purple on the backsides, visible, since flower is open only part-time.

Anchusa: BORAGINACEAE.

Caucasus, Eur., W. Asia, N. & S. Afr.

Ajuga

Alcea

Alstroemeria

Anemone

Antirrhinum

Aquilegia

Herb. Stalwart almost heavy. Foliage rough, almost coarse.

Sun. Soil med. Some spp. dislike humidity. Division or seed.

Hearty. Strong growth, strong color of flowers.

A. azurea (A. italica): Italian Bugloss or Alkanet. Mediterranean region. 3 to 5 ft. tall. Bristly hairy. Flowers forget-me-not like in large panicles of purple-blue. Wide clumps with a dozen or more stems make strong display.

'Little John': A cv. with lesser measurements.

'Loddon Royalist': Cv. with rich shade of blue. Tall.

A. barrelieri: Early Bugloss. To 2 ft. Leaves rough, wide. Flowers dark blue. Soil porous, will drained. Light shade.

A. caespitosa & *A. angustissima:* Per. about 1 ft., not tolerant of hot, humid summers. Good in Pacific Northwest, N. Am.

A. myosotidiflora: See *Brunnera*

Anemone: See Woodland & Shady Places Plant Descriptions.

"Poppy Anemone" or "Florist's Anemones" provide many cut flowers. Strains for garden use, e.g. "de Caen", "St. Bridget", "Au Creagh Castle".

A. coronaria, A. hortensis & *A. pavoninina:* The descendents of these anemones grow from a curious irregular, knobby, tuberous root, planted 2 in. deep, in the fall. Parsley-like leaves show in warm climates as early as January. In warm climates, roots may be left in the ground. Leaves may then appear as early as November. Cover with hardware cloth since birds & rabbits appreciate the delicious salad provided by every young leaf. Clump to 10 in. wide. Flowers pink, purple, scarlet, "blue", with dark centers. Spring.

Some cvs.: e.g., 'His Excellency', single crimson; 'Mr. Fokker', single blue; 'The Admiral', deep pink, semi-dble.; 'The Bride', single white; 'Sylphide', single mauve. Sun. Dead-head to keep flowers coming. Division.

The tall kinds are cvs. of *A. hybrida (A. elegans)* resulting from crosses of *A. hupehensis* & *A. h.* var. *japonica* (to 2 ft.) with *A. vitifolia.*

A. vitifolia: Grape-Leaved Anemone. Upper Nepal. (The group is called "Japanese Anemones".) Leaves lobed "grape-like". Stems of type sp. are shorter by 2 ft. than most other Japanese Anemones, some to 4 × 1 ft. wide. Flowers white, with yellow stamens. Early fall. *A. vitifolia* 'Robustissima' (of gardens): Soft pink.

A. tomentosa: From Tibet. Vigorous to 4 × 2 ft. The pink sim. to the pink hybs. but blooms earlier beginning in late summer. Many cvs. e.g.: 'Margarette', dble. pink; 'Profusion', deep rose-pink; 'September Charm', delicate pink shaded with rose-pink; 'Bressingham Glow' by Alan Bloom, compact, almost dble., rose red; 'Queen Charlotte', semi-dble., rose-pink, darker in bud. White is represented by *A. hupehensis* var. *alba* & an exquisite white sport, 'Honorine Jobert'; 'Whirlwind', semi-dble., pure white, is a cv. often listed in the U.S.

Anethum: UMBELLIFERAE. Dill.

A. graveolens: Useful. Very delicate. Worth sowing often.

Anthericum: LILIACEAE. St. Bernard's Lily. S. Eur.; also Am. & Afr.

Herb. Clump forming. 300 spp., only 1 or 2 hdy. or available. Slow to become established. Graceful. Leaves strap-shaped, delicate. Flowers delicate. Bloom spring & early summer.

Sun or part shade. Soil med., fert. Water in dry weather. Fertilize annually. Easy. Stolon division. Some spp. produce seed.

Clumps increase to produce more flower stalks each year. Good in borders, with shrubbery & to eventually colonize. Cuts. Plant with relatives & *Pasithea* & *Astilbe.*

A. algeriensis: May be a form. of *A. liliago.* Similar.

A. liliago: To 3 ft., (often lower) × 1 ft. wide. Only a few flower stems.

A. l. var. *major:* Branchless, erect. Leaves num., slender grey-green to 1 ft. long. Stalks so wiry they sway in a breeze. Flowering spathes with delicate starry small, white, open trumpets. Clumps increase to produce more flowering stalks each year. Flowers somewhat resemble those of *Camassia* & are unlike its cousin *Asphodelus.* Quite like another relative, *Paradisea liliastrum,* sometimes given as a synonym.

A. ramosum: Branching, to 3 ft. Grassy leaves. Smaller flowers producing airy, cloud-like spikes.

Antirrhinum: SCROPHLARACEAE. Snapdragon.

Eur.

Well known as the colorful border annual & cut flower. See Annuals Plant Description.

Sev. unusual spp. Related to *Asarina.*

A. glubinosum: Spain. Tender. 8–12 in. Prostrate. Flowers yellowish white, tip striped red.

Aphyllanthes: LILIACEAE.

Mediterranean.

Herb. Only 1 sp. Fibrous roots. Leaves rush-like. Chaffy bracts.

Shade & part sun. Soil, moisture retentive. Division.

A dwarf member of the Lily family; might be difficult to find.

A. monspeliensis: Basal leaves minute. Scapes to 10 in., rush-like. Flowers blue or white; to 1 in. across.

Aquilegia: RANUNCULACEAE. Columbine.

Eur., N. Am., Japan, Mex.

Herb. & evgrn. 3 in.–3 ft. Leaves indented. Foliage with excel. patterns. Flowers with or without spurs; spring & summer.

Sun to ½ shade. Soil with organic matter. Ample water spring & early summer. Needs drainage. Basal leaves of some persist through winter. May need replacement at end of 3rd or 4th year. Grooming increases health. Seed or division.

"Aquila" means "eagle" & refers to the claw-like curve at the end of the spur. Hummingbirds like to visit. Dwarf spp. for

The end of the border is seen some 40 ft. to the south. This is summertime when the mats on the forward edge are allowed to spill over the path. Across from the border you can see the first row of the Rose Garden. The two garden features are traditionally associated. T.C.

A center section has been chosen as a demonstration. Here we see the green hedge as backdrop and the interesting colors of shrubbery foliage. The reddish copper is the bronze form of *Cotinus coggygria* and one of the greys is *Teucrium fruticans*, trimmed to make a dense dome. The grey is repeated in *Stachys* on the forward edge. *Penstemon* and *Diascia* provide rose tones, pale to deep; *D. rigescens* stays in fresh full bloom for 3 mos. C.A.

Cotinus used at intervals as dusky focal points. Common Lavender is the big grey ball beside the copper. In the center is *Coreopsis verticillata*. C.A.

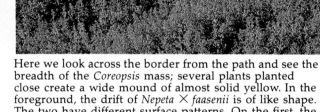

Here we look across the border from the path and see the breadth of the *Coreopsis* mass; several plants planted close create a wide mound of almost solid yellow. In the foreground, the drift of *Nepeta × faasenii* is of like shape. The two have different surface patterns. On the first, the daisies make many circles and on the second, the racemes make curving lines. L.E.

BORDERS AT FILOLI

This view shows billowing forms in the rear and a progression of heights to the forward edge. *Penstemon* with its bending spike is prominent in the center range. *Agapanthus* 'Peter Pan' with a stiffer vertical form, finishes the edge at this point. Sword-shaped leaves are good contrast. C.A.

A foliage with distinct character can be seen close-up in a portion of the drift of *Stachys olympica*. The photograph does not fully portray its velvety look. The white-grey is excellent as a foil for nearby bright colors. C.A.

Here we see again the *Stachys* in its role of background for the delightful coral-pink of *Diascia rigescens* seen in number 2. There are pink overtones in the copper of the *Cotinus*. C.A.

In the central portion of this long border we have seen the use of shrubbery plants and sensed their connecting and stabilizing function. Here is another shrubby perennial, *Perovskia atriplicifolia*, outstanding for appropriate habit of growth and special features varying from season to season. At this summer season, its foliage is lacy, its branching graceful, its color excellent, both the grey of its leaves and the bright lavender of its flowers. C.A.

BORDER AT FILIOLI

Rectangles have been cut into a deep lawn. *Thuya* and other fine conifers make a background of deep green. The beds stand free and out in open sun, where perennials are planted with bright colored flowers. In early Spring, the palette will contain much yellow since bulbous plants are combined with perennials. K.B.

An example of a traditional border with lawn as its setting. It is not difficult to grow excellent grass in Vancouver. The border contains masses of mostly old-fashioned perennials such as *Achillea, Phlox, Lythrum.* D.D.

Victorian. Two features adorn this parterre. The gazebo at the far end is fanciful in design, belonging in a romantic story. The border planting is quite low, acting as a fringe to the woodland beyond. The bowl shape in the foreground is accompanied by a clump of perennials to give a complementary rise in the planting level. J.Z.

A scene in a Northwest garden, U.S.A.—a long border with curving edge. Perennials with stems of medium height were brought forward toward the edge, accentuating a raised effect for the whole design. In the season of the picture, the prevailing color was pink, expressed by *Geranium, Linaria, Phlox,* etc. and carried through to the far end. Pink roses as background set the color scheme. J.Z.

WITH LAWNS

Perennial beds border a lawn with a sweeping expanse of perfect grass. Color and sunshine contrast with the large, dense, dark trees behind them. K.B.

The mountains make a stunning backdrop for many properties in the Santa Barbara area. In such a setting and in a semi-tropical climate, palms are picturesque and proper. Beds of perennials divide lawn from house and terrace.

This is the famous white garden at Sissinhurst, especially beautiful in summer moonlight. Any number of perennials can be added to increase the intensity of white contributed to the bloom of the deciduous and ever-green shrubs. K.M.

The Chatto garden is famous for its pond and pond-side plantings. In this picture you can glimpse the still water in the mid-distance. The site invites the use of perennials with bold foliage both of the sword-shape form and the palmate form. K.M.

SCENES WITH SPECIAL THEMES

r.g. Usually with well-designed clumps of basal leaves. 6–18 in. wide.

A. hybs.: Derived from many spp. A. "Longissima hybrids": strain of mixed colors; mostly pastel but sometimes rich purple or with red spurs. Breeding has enlarged spurs as a primary aim.

Cvs. & strains: 'Snow Queen' (white), 'Mrs. Scott Elliott' (an oldtimer), "Spring Song" (of good repute), "Biedermeier" (a dwarf strain). Modern strain, "Langdon's Rainbow". Flowers look delicate but are quite sturdy for picking; buds continue to open. Plant in wide drifts. Sun or part shade. Look for seedlings in order to increase collection. Somewhat true from seed.

'Black Star': One example from many cvs. To 3 ft., long-spurred, semi-nodding, almost black.

A. longissima: S. N. Am., the sp. with probably the longest spurs, yellow, to 2 ft.

A. vulgaris: To 3 ft., with short spurs, may be the one seen in old flower paintings. Crossed with A. alpina, Switzerland, hyb. in old gardens. Almost a weed. Flowers rather squat, very plentiful.

A. canadensis: American Columbine. N. Am. To 2 ft., red & yellow. Delicate texture. Bright colored.

A. caerulea: N. Am., Colo.; purple & lavender, to 18 in.

A. chrysantha: S. & N. Am., to 3 ft., 2-toned yellow. Important parent of hybs.

A. formosa: W. N. Am., to 3 ft., yellow & coral-red.

A. pubescens × A. truncata: N. Am. A natural hyb., Mono Pass, Calif., 8,500–10,000 ft. (perhaps only to be seen in its habitat).

A. 'Nora Barlow': To 3 ft., fully dble. Airy, graceful foliage. Flowers blend of red, pink & green.

A. pyrenaica: S. Eur. 1 ft. Often 2 shades of blue, with spurs nearly straight.

A. discolor: Spain. 1 ft. Blue & white with spurs noticeably incurved.

A. snockleyi: Seek.

A. ecalcarata: China. Wine to rich purple, spurs nearly lacking. The genus Semiaquilegia, where this sp. was formerly placed has been discontinued.

A. flabellata 'Nana Alba': Clump of basal leaves, full & fat, grey-green, substantial texture. Flowers short spurred on short stems. Spring. Sp. lavender. Sev. forms of A. flabellata, e.g. alba, nana as well as 'Nana Alba'. The leaf of A. flabellata is quite distinctive; it is often twice divided, thickish, scalloped on the edges & a bluish green. Structure of spurs varies considerably.

A. sibirica: Sim. to A. flabellata. Less leafy. Color of flowers shade to claret.

A. saximontana: N. Am., Colo. An alpine gem. One of many alpines difficult except for the specialists.

A. akitensis: Leaves green, flowers lavender on 8 in. stems. Some authorities consider A. akitensis a synonym of A. flabellata var. pumila. The structure of leaf is a distinguishing feature. See A. flabellata.

A. glandulosa, A. jucunda & A. siberica: Siberia.

1–2 ft. The first bright blue with short incurved spurs; the second white, smaller & with broader petals; the third close to A. flabellata, lilac-blue sepals & petals (or white), spurs curved & coiled inward; twice divided basal leaves.

Arabis: CRUCIFERAE. Rock Cress & Wall Cress.

Temp. N. Am. & Eurasia.

Semi-evgrn. Low mats, 4–9 in., of irregular shape. Leaves in rosettes. Bloom spring & occasionally fall. The West Coast native blooms in Feb.

Sun or ½ shade. Soil med. Ordinary cult. Division. Seed.

Slopes, strips, borders. The most dwarf, excel. in pots & r.g. A. f.-c. 'Variegata', a gem for a special site.

A. koehleri: Shrubby Rock Cress. Small & tight. 6 × 8 in. Flowers pink.

A. procurrens: Rampant.

A. caucasica (syn. A. albida) & A. c. var. flore-pleno & A. c. var. variegata: Loose mats of grey-green leaves (or splotched with pale yellow). Flower stalks 6–9 in.; white flowers look like Phlox. The dble. flower lasts longer when cut than the single. Makes a broad spread in the foreground; needs severe shearing after spring blooming. May repeat bloom in fall. Cvs. are available.

A. alpina: True sp. rare in gardens; more compact, smaller rosettes, greener leaves than common Arabis. Less than 6 in. tall.

A. ferdinandi-coburgii: Tiny. Flowers 6–10 in., in loose racemes.

A. f.-c. 'Variegata': A fine dwarf form with attractive variegation. Lies flat on the earth as if etched.

A. sturii (of gardens): Tight green cushions.

A. androsaemum: Silky-silvery in dense tufts to 2 in.

A. blepharophylla: N. Am., Calif. Small, low, dense mats; in tufts, to 4 in. tall. Flowers purple-pink, 1 in. in diameter & fragrant. Bloom begins Feb. Less hdy. than other spp. described above. Best to grow annually.

Argemone: PAPAVERACEAE. Prickly Poppy.
N. & S. Am. and Hawaii

Leaves & calyces spiny. Yellow or orange sap.

Sun. Good soil. Grown as an annual.

Leaves lobed, clasping. Flowers to 6 in. across.

A. mexicana: Mexican Poppy. One of several spp. To 3 ft. Decidedly prickly. Flowers white.

Artemisia: See Large Site & Slope

Aster: COMPOSITAE.
U.S., Eur., Asia.

Evgrn. Basal leaves in tufted mats or clumps. Num. "daisies".

Sun but with some shade. Soil fert. but not too rich. Ordinary cult. Don't water the foliage (some kinds susceptible to mildew). Drainage. Dead-head. Division.

Low Asters esp. those with solitary flowering heads are very good for the fronts of per. borders, for edgings & for ordinary r.g. Tall Asters good for back of borders with shrubs & on banks. Combine with Solidago, Veronica, Salvia.

Argemone

Arabis

Artemisia

Aster

Babiana

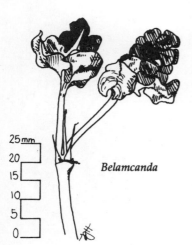

Belamcanda

A. nova-belgii & *A. novae-angliae:* Michaelmas Daisy. U.S. As much a natural of the fields of New England as the rocks & grasses. Many cvs., 2–5 ft., white, pink, lavender, purple. E.g.:

'Harrington's Pink', 3 ft., Sept.; 'Climax', strong to 6 ft. with color called "spode" blue (Thomas); 'White Lady', quite white; 'Crimson Brocade', well named.

A. cordifolius: Native from Nova Scotia to Minn., Ga. & Mo. in U.S., to 5 ft. Also sev. spp. from midwestern to S. states from 1–4 ft. Arrangements of the inflorescense vary.

A. amellus: Italy. Not over 2 ft., often 1 ft. Shades of violet & shades of pink. See catalogues for named forms.

A. thomsonii: A. t. 'Nana', most popular. A cv. listed, 'Little Red'.

A. × *frikartii* 'Monch': Considered the best of 3 seedlings raised from a cross between the above 2 by Frikart of Switzerland.

A. × *frikartii* 'Wunder von Stafa' (in U.S. 'Wonder of Stafa'): A later seedling, admired but perhaps less erect & less blue than 'Monch'. Attractively branching subshrub; bloom from late July to late fall. Clear lavender-blue with ray petals well-placed. Hyb. not reliably hardy; however, when the skeletons of last year's branches look very dead, new shoots will appear at base in spring. Useful as cut flower.

A. tongolensis (*A. subcaeruleus*) & *A. farreri:* Both spp. from China. Mats of hairy, dark green leaves. Flowers large, lavender with vivid orange centers; daisies carried singly instead of on branching stems. Width to 1 ft. Height 1½ ft.

A. t. 'Napsbury' (*A. yunnanensis* 'Napsbury', of gardens) & *A. t.* 'Berggarten'. Stout stalks. Better in fert. soil.

A. alpinus var. *albus:* Rock Aster. Eur. & Rocky Mtns. Only 9 in. Flowering heads solitary, to 2 in. across, late spring, with clear, white rays.

A. hybridus: Oregon Aster, 9–15 in. Flowers semi-dble. & dble. Cvs. e.g.: 'Nanus', 'Niobe', 'Mt. Everest', 'Gay Border Blue', 'Blue Radiance'.

A. "dwarf": Sev. cvs., e.g. 'Winston Churchill', 'Twinkle', 'Marjorie', 'Nancy', 'Ronald'.

A. Oregon: Semi-dwarf 'Adorable.'

A. 'Finalist': Cv. of uncertain parentage.

Astrantia: UMBELLIFERAE. Masterwort.
Eur. & W. Asia.
2 ft. × 18 in. Good basal divided foliage. Flower unique.
Sun or ½ sh. Soil good; drainage. Spreads by runners.
Branching wiry stems. Collar of bracts important feature.
A. major: Foliage divided. Flowers tiny forming a dome. White. *A. m.* var. *involucrata*, with extra large collar.
A. maxima: Foliage tripartite. Flowers pinkish. Collar prominent, rose-pink.

Aubreita: CRUCIFERAE.
S. Eur. to Iran. Usually alpine.
Herb. Small mats. Foliage past its prime looks straggly.
Sun. Soil, sandy with compost & other

organics. Drainage. First bloom early spring. Shear to ground & top-dress; often second season. Division.
Close to *Arabis* & *Aurinia.* Bright g.c.
A. deltoidea: A horticultural group; hybs. not true from seed. For separate colors propagate by division. Cvs. e.g.: 'Pink Parachute', 'Vindictive'.

Babiana and Belamcanda: One a bulb, one a rhizome; to mix with herbacious perennials and subshrubs.

Ballota: LABIATAE. Black Hourhound.
Mostly Mediterranean.
Evgrn. Related to *Stachys*. Upright stems well clothed with velvety leaves from soil to tip.
Sun. Soil lean & dryish. Easy. Semi-hdy. Seed. Division.
Some writers say "of no account". Subtle appeal. Addition for the collector of grey foliage. Herb garden or mixed border. Combine with *Origanum dictamnus*, *Artemisias*, *Lavandula* & *Thymus*.
B. nigra: Two varieties of this sp. naturalized in waste places of N. Am. Leaves, stems & calyces almost white—pubescent. Square foliage stems make a 1 ft. clump of softest grey; upper part of flowering stem crowded with smaller leaves. Arranged in whorls. Flowers very small 2-lipped, purplish pink close within the axils, replaced with scalloped tiny saucers.
B. pseudodictamnus: Crete. 2 ft. tall. Leaves white-wooly; flowers white, purple-spotted. Probably less hardy than *B. nigra.*

Baptisia: LEGUMINOSAE. False-Indigo or Wild Indigo.
N. Am., E. U.S.
Herb. Shrubby to 4 ft. Leaves blue-green clothe grey-green stems. Spp. with flowers white or flowers yellow & a cross, *B. bicolor*, blue standards & cream colored wings & keels. Frosts turn leaves black. Deep roots unaffected.
Sun & ¼ shade. Soil fair. Somewhat drought resistant but thrives better with moisture. Summer bloom. Semi-tender. Division.
From Greek "to dye". Cut flowers will keep if picked when young but buds will not open in water. Use dried, both pods & leaves, the latter turning a nice grey with glycerine treatment.
B. australis, *B. a.* 'Exaltata', *B. a.* 'Madam Mason': Best known, most commonly planted & considered most ornamental. Herb., multiple-stemmed. To 4 ft., 2–4 ft. wide, increasing in width annually. Stems grey-green, branching, covered by blue-green leaves by June, forming soft foliage mass. Numerous lupine-like spikes in violet-blue. Spikes are narrow, erect but not stiff. Seed pods, like pea-pods but big & leathery, dark grey—elephant grey. Leaves turn coal-black after first frost or first spell of heavy rain; at this time cut back to the ground, marking the space.

Boltonia: COMPOSITAE.
N. Am.
Herb. Feathery mass of flowers on tall stems. Sun or shade. Easy. Tender. Seed.

Background filler. Also dwarf pink kind.

B. latisquama: To 6 ft. Heavy: requires support. Leaves insignificant. Flowers small lilac daisies in clusters.

B. asteroides 'Snow Bank': To 4 ft.

Bulbinella: LILIACEAE.
S. Afr. & N. Zealand.

Herb. Leaves, shiny green, narrow, strap-shaped in a clump. Flowers in a spire-shaped spike at top of 2 ft. stem. Tip of spike bends until all flowers are mature. Winter & summer.

Sun or ½ shade. Soil rich, moist, cool, peaty. Don't allow to dry out. Stake stems or allow to flop a bit. Division. (Use a saw or sharp spade.)

For arrangements, straighten curved stems by bundling & supporting them in the soaking pail. Odor when crushed, none in bouquet. S. Afr. sp. with excel. winter flower, bright yellow, full spike-like inflorescence on 2 ft. stems. 1 sp. less robust.

B. floribunda (*B. robusta* or *B. robusta* var. *latifolia*): Roots fleshy, growing from a woody erect rhizome, forming clumps 1 ft. or more wide, clothed in thick brown fiber. Leaves basal, narrow, tapering strap-shaped, deeply grooved, rather lax, with an unpleasant odor when crushed. Leaves sheath each other at bases. Favors swampy soils.

B. hookeri: N. Zealand. Grassy tufts. Leaves narrowly sword-shaped. Hardier than S. African spp. Blooms in summer. Flowers starry, deep yellow.

B. alloides: S. Afr. & N. Zealand. Many slender stems wrapped with linear light green leaves to 10 in. Flowers in narrow racemes, yellow. Spreads easily to make a wide clump, to 3 ft. Pull apart to divide.

Caltha: RANUNCULACEAE. Marsh Marigold. N. & S. temp. zone.

Herb. Low, fleshy. From cold marshes. Needs moist soil which does not dry out in Summer. Division.

C. palustris: E. US. Best known.

Campanula: See genus description in Slope Plant Description.

Described herewith some of the medium tall kinds, excellent for borders & cutting gardens. Bloom summer & fall.

C. vidalii: Canary Islands. Short-lived. Sensitive to wet weather. Suffruticose; upright but branching semi-woody stems. Almost evgrn. Almost succulent. Temperamental. Leaves obovate, toothed, leathery, glossy in clusters. Flowers somewhat like Canterbury Bells but more slender, more sculptured. Exceedingly waxy. Pink. Possibly other colors besides pink. Bloom all open at once on a pyramid, 1 ft. × 1 ft., which looks like a nursery rhyme. Possible from seed.

C. × *burghaltii* 'Burchaltii': *C. latifolia* × *C punctata.* A hyb. of distinction. To 2 ft. x 1 ft. Flowers large with most attractive points on the pale grey-lilac petals. *C.* 'Van Houttei' is sim. but the flower color is darker.

C. alliariifolia: Caucasus, Turkey. To 20 in. Leaves heart-shaped, basal. Flowers in a 1-sided spike; nodding bells. 'Ivory Bells': A graceful wand to 2 ft.

C. rotundifolia: Caucasus. To 18 in. Leaves quite unlike the idea of round suggested by the sp. name. Flower deep lavender.

C. primulifolia: Spain, Portugal. Herb. Grows from a clump, 3 ft. × 1½ ft. Sev. erect stems. Leaves rough. Flowers 2 in. across, broadly campanulate, soft lavender, in spikes, narrow-paniculate. Late summer bloom. New leaves look like *Primrose* leaves. Clumps increase. Volunteers from seed.

C. persicifolia: Peach-Leaved Campanula. Eur., N. Afr. & Asia. To 3 ft. tall, but usually less. Flower stems grow erect from basal rosettes of narrow leaves, almost evgrn. forming a spreading mat, 1 ft. plus wide, less rampant than *C. glomerata.* Flowers cup-shaped, nodding on short stalks. Division easy; also from seed.

C. p. 'Alba': Size & form like the lavender sp. Good cvs. include dbles. & semi-dbles. Seek *C. p.* 'Fleur de Neige' & *C. p.* 'Moorheimii' for tall slender stems excel. for cutting. In bloom sev. weeks.

C. latiloba (*C. grandis*): Close to *C. persicifolia.* To 3 ft. Flowers stalkless facing rigidly outward. (*C. l.* var. *alba,* Siberia) 'Percy Piper': *C. persicifolia* × *C. latiloba,* wide mound of light green leaves to 9 in. More vigorous than sp. Flower color a darker bluish lavender.

C. barbata: Full mound of pointed, arrow-shaped leaves, to 1 ft. wide. Stems leafy to 18 in. Flowers purple bells decorated with tiny hairs—ciliate.

C. glomerata: Eur. & Asia. Many flower stems from a spreading mat, to 4 ft. Wild form is rampant. Leaves rough. Basal leaves, to 5 in., narrow heart-shaped, differ from stem leaves. Flowers funnel-shaped to 1 in. long, petals flaring. In dense bunches to form crowded, globular heads at tips & in upper leaf axils.

C. g. 'Joan Elliot': Selected for improved habit & finer flowers. Smaller green leaves on looser stems, than those of sp. Prolific flowering. Scarcely rests. Flower heads less conglomerate; flowers more noticeably bell-shaped. Behaves well in a container.

C. g. var. *dahurica:* Stems usually 2 ft. but attain 3 ft. Vibrant purple, more deep lavender or more "rosey" than sp. 'Superba' even more vigorous & darker colored.

C. g. 'Schneekrone': Strongly recommended white cv. Longest vase life of any *Campanula.* Needs dividing & feeding for num. fine flower stems. Less rampant.

C. latifolia: A tall sp., to 4 ft. Distinctive foliage.

C. l. macrantha is noteworthy.

C. lactiflora: Caucasus. To 6 ft. & 2 ft. wide. Branching stems. Leaves toothed, stalkless 2–3 in. long. In windy areas, staking required. Flowers in groups of 3 in angled panicles; broadly bell-shaped. Pale blue. June, July. Excel. with shrub roses.

C. l. var. *caerulea* & *C. l.* var. *alba:* 2 good forms. Seek 'Pouffe' (Bloom).

C. rapunculoides: Even a bulldozer could not eradicate; a ground cover which spreads by fleshy roots & seed. Avoid.

Ballota

Baptisia

Bulbinella

Campanula

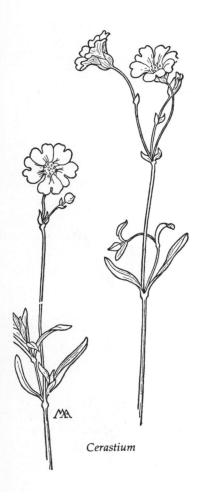

Cerastium

Canna: CANNACEAE.
Cent. & S. Am.
Herb. Leaves of firm texture from green to reddish bronze. Young foliage is rolled up. Flowers top of tall stems, various shades yellow to red.
Sun. Soil med. Ordinary cult. Circle complete plant' with slug & snail bait. Semi-tender. Only hdy. to Oreg. Division.
To use for arrangements, submerge overnight in cool water.
Canna hybs.: To 4 ft. Large clumps from tuberous roots. Cvs. e.g.: 'Wyoming', apricot-orange flowers & purplish leaves.
C. cretica: 4–6 ft. tall. Stiffly erect biennial. Spire of closely arranged outfacing flowers on upper third of stem. 2 lobed upper lips somewhat deeper yellow than 3 lobed lower lips. Chocolate-brown marks at the base of upper lips. Bearded stamens.

Catananche: COMPOSITAE. Blue Cupidone, Love Plant, Cupid's Dart.
Mediterranean.
Herb. 2½ × 1 ft. Somewhat short-lived. Heads of calyces admired for dried arrangements. Calyx papery enclosing a dark-eyed daisy. Summer.
Sun. Soil dryish. Drainage. Root cuttings. Seed.
Greek women used in love philters.
C. caerulea: To 2½ ft. Looks like chickory. Distinctive for its papery calyx. Leaves basal; clump; greyish, shaggy; hidden by sev. flowering stems. Flowers lavender-blue, dark eyed; sev. weeks in summer. Dry by cutting before flowers fully open & hanging bunches upside down. Cvs. e.g.: 'Major', 'Perry's White', 'Bicolor'.

Centaurea: COMPOSITAE. Knapweed, Basket Flower, Cornflower, Dusty Miller, Mountain Bluet, Sweet Sultan.
Eur. & N. Am. & S. Am., Armenia, Caucasus, 1 in Aust.
Herb. & evgrn. 600 spp. Leaves often grey, others dark, ferny. Bracts in sev. overlapping rows, often fringed sometimes prickly. No true ray florets but marginal florets often enlarged & frilled. Ann. & per. Hdy. & non-hdy.
Sun. Soil less than rich. Water 4 times during long dry spell. Grey group prefers water at roots & porous soil. Division. Seed.
C. ragusina, C. cineraria (C. candidissima) & *C. gymnocarpa:* Dusty Miller: this vernacular name also applied to some *Artemisia, Senecio* & *Lychnis,* etc. Leaves deeply pinnately cleft. Grow new annually.
C. hypoleuca: To 2½ ft. Leaves dull green, white-hairy beneath, num., subject to insect damage. Buds produced all summer. Heads to 3½ in. across, frilly, lavender-pink to rosy purple. Looks like a thistle. Shaggy.
C. h. 'John Coutts' is in favor, 18 in. stems & brighter color.
C. macrocephala: Globe Centaurea. To 3 ft. Leaves large at bottom, small top of stem. The bracts shiny, rusty-colored & fringed; enclose the bud. Head thistle-like, to 4 in. across & yellow.
C. dealbata 'Sternbergii': A per. cornflower.

Flowers lilac-pink.
C. ruthenica: To 3 ft. Leaves dark, ferny. Flowers fluffy, pale citron-yellow.
C. simplicicaulis: Clump. Leaves to 3 in., dainty, toothed. Flowers pink 8 in., balls.
C. moschata, Sweet Sultan, *C., cyanus,* Bachelor's Button. Annuals excel. to mix with per.
C. montana: Mountain Bluet or Perennial Cornflower. To 1½ ft. Leaves oval, pointed, plentiful. Florets petal-like, fringed; bright blue, white or rosy red. All summer. Wide drifts. Prefers light shade. Feed early spring. Remove worst portion of mat formed by spread of underground roots.
C. m. 'Parkman': Flowers lavender-purple.

Cephalaria: DIPSACEAE.
Mediterranean, W. Asia to S. Afr.
Herb. 6 ft. Clump. Restrained spreader. Open tuft of divided leaves.
Sun. Soil fert. & not too dry. Staking in windy areas. Flowers on slender, bending stalks. Summer.
A position at the back of a border or amongst shrubbery is ideal with the reservation that in full shade, plants will not flourish. Readily from seed. Sources few.
C. gigantea: Siberia. Often misidentified as *C. tatarica* of gardens or *C. alpina.* 6 ft. tall. Num. side-branches on a well-developed plant. Leaves large, pinnately lobed. Flowers cream to yellow, primrose yellow, in flattish heads 2 in. across, outer florets larger than the others. It looks like a *Scabiosa* & should, as it is a relative.
C. flava: Smaller with buff-yellow flowers; may be the sp. listed as *C. leucantha.* In any case, not generally available.

Cerastium: CARYOPHYLLACEAE. Snow in Summer, Silver Carpet, Mouse Ear, Chickweed.
Eur., temp. Asia & N. Am.
Herb. Mat mostly less than 1 ft. Leaves insignificant. Flowers make sheet of white. Foliage in a mound of small leaves.
Sun. Soil almost any. Drainage. Average moisture. Groom. Mostly hdy. Division. Sheer after blooming.
C. tomentosum & *C. biebersteinii:* The latter superior in that it has more compact growth, whiter stems & leaves—perhaps larger flowers. Sheets of the small white flowers in summer make a fine display as edging to a border & esp. in an informal r.g. Perhaps 1½ ft. tall in the higher parts of the billowing mound.

Chelidonium: Papaveraceae. Greater Celandine, Wallow Wort.
Eur. Asia.
Colonizes in open shade. Orange-red sap.
C. majus: 2 ft. × 18 in. Leaves divided. Flowers many, small, yellow. E. U.S. Summer.

Chrysanthemum: COMPOSITAE.
Caucasus, Brit., Japan, Middle East.
Annuals, perennials. Various in size & habit.
Sun or part shade. Water. Feed. Watch for pests. Stake. Deadhead. Seed. Division. Cuttings.
Bloom summer & fall.

C. mawii: N. Afr. Atlas Mtns. Low, small, clumping, to 1 ft. Leaves triangular to oblong to 1 in., usually pinnatifid, soft, loose, woolly hairs. Semi-hdy. The flower small, with pink reverse on petals.

C. anethifolium: Bushy. May be clipped. To 2 × 2 ft. Good behavior in a container. Leaves delicate in texture, num. Small white daisies.

C. frutescens: Paris Daisy. Suffruticose; good for containers. Severe shearing beneficial. Seek cvs. for improved habit, foliage & flowers, e.g. 'Kayo Watanabe', 'Maxine', 'Snow Cap'.

C. coccineum (Pyrethrum roseum): Painted Daisy. 2 × 1½ ft. 30 or more varietal names—white, pink, crimson, single, dble. 'Evenglow', rich salmon-scarlet by Alan Bloom is considered one of the best. A strain "Robinson's Hybrids"; by James Kelway. 'Kelway's Glorious' is a single crimson.

C. maximum: Shasta Daisy, Pyrenees. Considerable variety of size & shape. Mostly hybs. Many have fringed petals. Watch out for nematodes. Can be invasive. Cvs. e.g.: 'Mark Riegal': N. Am. cv., has been praised. 'Esther Read': Fairly short stemmed, fully dble., an oldtimer. 'September Snow': Seen in some catalogues; reported to have second crop of its dble. white flowers. 'Powis Castle': A dwarf, may be hard to find.

C. nipponicum: Nippon Daisy. Like Shasta Daisy but 3 ft. Tender.

C. × superbum var. *nipponicum:* To 3 ft.; good for cutting.

C. leucanthemum: To 2 ft. Easy bedding plant with many small, yellow centered white daisies on upright stems. A mat of many tufts easily divided. Spreads to 18 in.

C. haradjanii: A dense grey g.c. often classed as a sp. of *Tanacetum.* To 3 ft. wide.

C. rubellum (of gardens): May be a hyb., origin unknown. Should probably be assigned to *C. zawadskii* var. *latilobum.* The sp. is 18 × 18 in., much divided foliage & flowers for many weeks. Clones include 'Clara Curtis', clear pink & 'Duchess of Edinburgh', coppery red. 'Royal Command' is popular. Fert. soil; drainage; division every 3 yrs.

C. rubellum × C. vestitum helped to produce Korean hybs.

C. coreanum & 'Ruth Hatton' a pompom, were also used & the results merged with other strains.

C. Korean hybs.: Valuable for cutting. Treat as annuals. Bushy plants. 3 × 1½ ft. with varicolored daisies in profusion. Some progeny were named after planets. Bloom fall.

C. yezoensis (C. arcticum of gardens): A pink form & a yellow form as well as white. Stems to 1 ft. Branching sprays to 1 ft. Fall.

C. parthenium (Pyrethrum or *Parthenium):* Feverfue. Leaves finely cut dark green. Forms a low tangled mat 2 ft. plus wide. Improved forms including dbles.; these flowers look like buttons on stems to 1 ft. 'White Bonnet' fully dble., neat, rounded flowers. See Layout 3.

C. p. 'Aureum': Lots of single flowers on bushy plants with yellowish leaves. Clip for a knot garden. Foliage aromatic. If not controlled, will be sloppy & invasive. Flowers small, white, good for fillers in mixed bouquets.

Hybrid Garden Chrysanthemums: Crossed & recrossed since 1800 when they arrived from China but raised since before 500 B.C. Old-fashioned & un-named spp. & cvs. valuable for Oct. & Nov. Often less sophisticated looking than modern cvs. & excel. to combine with late fall perennials, e.g. *Aconitum, Salvia, Gaura, Eupatorium.*

Hybrid moderns: Apt. to bloom earlier than autumn. May also be held back. Choose for size & character as well as color. Many shapes, forms, sizes & colors—incurved, reflexed, quilled, pompon, spider, etc. 'Red Rover': Big, daisy-type, rich color as coppery red with streaks of yellow. 'Emperor of China': Old-rose. The foliage in Nov. is shaded crimson, suffused as well as veined. Nov. is bloom time. 'Royal Command' & 'Clara Curtis': Look for these. 'Silver Lace', white spider; 'Emerald Isle', chartreuse spider; 'Waikiki', orange spider. 'Shodoshina': White turns pink; good to train as cascade. (A nameless yellow with naturally limber arching branches also esp. good for cascade training.)

Chrysanthemums for containers: Raised from cuttings—choose a bud with a short stem; raised from "Irish cuttings"—a leafy shoot with a piece of root; choose one which is straight & vigorous. Or divide clumps in the normal fashion keeping best parts.

Chrysanthemums in the cutting garden: Plant in rows—those with sim. heights in same row. Stake whole row with horizontal support at one or more levels. See index.

Chrysanthemums in the border: Pinch for branching or allow to develop naturally.

Cimicifuga: See Woodland Plant Descriptions.

In cool climates, *Cimicifuga* grows well in sun. *C. racemosa* is the sp. with the erect plumes.

Clematis: RANUNCULACEAE. Virgin's Bower. China, Eur.

3 or more shrubby spp. to be treated as herb. pers. except for the most woody spp. which should be left to 10 in. tall for next year's stems.

Sun for the top, shade for the roots. Control slugs & snails. Soil fert. & porous; maintain alkalinity. Prune to ground except a few, e.g. *C. heracleifolia.*

Stems of all *Clematis* very brittle; best to rig separate cages, for certain kinds in particular, either inconspicuous metal hoops or twigs of bamboo (or other plants with slender stems) with parallel horizontal circles of tie material as dull in color as possible. Cages may be left in place during dormancy, helping to prevent injury to the delicate crowns. (Small pinkish buds appear in Feb. on plants growing on the W. Coast of U.S.) Sim. support needed for shrubby types.

C. heracleifolia: China. Thick, firm, woody base with several leafy stems. Leaves with 3 leaflets, irregularly toothed, with roundish

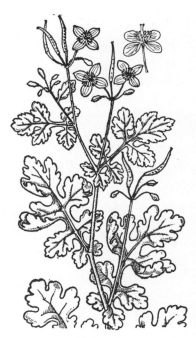

Chelidonium

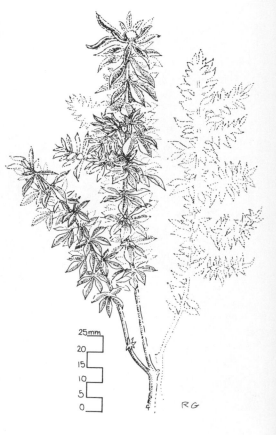

25mm
20
15
10
5
0

RG

Coreopsis

Cynoglossum

Dahlia

bases. Flowers num. in clusters, light lavender-blue, more or less tubular but with reflexed sepals, on the ends & in some axils. Shape that of Hyacinth flowers. Soft fragrance. Very fluffy seed heads.

C. h. var. *davidiana (C. davidiana):* Differs from the sp. type by having leaves with wedged-shaped bases, brighter blue flowers, up to 15 in some clusters, & male & female flowers on separate plants (the type usually has both sexes on same plant). Slight support.

C. integrifolia: S. Eur. Sprawling if not supported. To 2½ ft. Leaves undivided, oblong, toothless. Flowers to 2 in. solitary terminal, violet-blue, rarely white with conspicuous yellowish stamens. The flaring bell (the petals separated) often hangs but sometimes turns to face one. The stamens form a whitish cone which looks something like an oversized clapper.

C. × *eriostemon* 'Hendersonii' *(C. integrifolia* × *C. viticella):* Like a superior *C. integrifolia.* Plumed achenes.

C. × *jouiana (C. heracleifolia* var. *davidiana* × *C. vitalba):* Good forefront of shrubs in mixed border.

C. recta: S. Eur. A shrubby sp., looking like a vine although it does not twist or twine; it likes to lean or be enclosed in a cage which will hold the 4 ft. stems straight during the summer blooming time. Stems, strong but not brittle. Cut to the ground in fall; new shoots begin to show in March. Leaves more or less oval & pointed. Flowers small creamy white in full clusters, resembling from a distance the clusters of *Clematis montana.* Clouds of silvery seed heads (plumed achenes). Unique fragrance: good planted near the turn of a path or by a flight of steps—esp. with a wall as background. Cvs. e.g.: 'Grandiflora' & 'Plena', flowers 2 in. plus.

Convolvulus: CONVOLVULACEAE. Bindweed or Dwarf-Morning-glory.
S. Eur.
Herb. & evgrn. Some with superior horticultural value. One sp. with silky grey leaves in a round mound.
Sun. Soil med. Good drainage. Semi-tender. Occasional haircut improves shape & encourages new growth. Cuttings.
Bank, a good position; also containers. Morning-glory flowers keep opening from April to July. Cut short stems of silky silvery foliage for additions to pastel bouquets.
C. cneorum: Limestone cliffs, S. Eur.; semi-hdy. in vicinity of N.Y. A subshrub 1 ft. tall by almost 2 ft. wide, with firm, twiggy branches forming a more or less regular full mound. Leaves silvery silky, stand up well during cold winter weather with deluging rain. Flowers soft texture, white with yellow throat in crowded clusters at stem tips; hairy calyces. Height of bloom mid-summer; scattered bloom other mos.
C. althaeoides: Herb. or subshrubby, pubescent, trails to 3 ft. From dry areas.
C. cantabrica: Dry open areas in Spain, Portugal, Italy. Erect, herb., pubescent with somewhat woody base.

C. mauritanicus: Trails. Semi-tender. Less hdy. than *C. cneorum.* Flowers blue-mauve with paler throats, to 1 ft., solitary or in groups. Lacks distinction.

Coreopsis: COMPOSITAE. Tickseed.
E. U.S., Hawaii, trop. Afr.
Herb. Fruit looks like a bug. Yellow daisy flowers.
Sun. Ordinary cult. All those described are hardy except the 2 from Calif.
Greek koris = a bug; opsis = resemblance. Old-fashioned kinds are useful for mixed borders, cutting-beds, etc. Sev. ann. Tickseeds worth growing to incorporate with pers.
C. maritima: Sea Dahlia, to 3 ft. & *C. gigantea,* both of Calif.
C. 'Goldfink': A dwarf to 1 ft., worth growing from seed.
C. tinctoria: Most interesting for flower arrangers. To 3 ft.; flowers to 3 in. on slender branches, with purplish bracts, discs 7, at petal bases.
C. verticillata (C. tenuifolia): E. U.S. Cvs. usually grown: 'Grandiflora' or 'Golden Showers'. Forms a broad mound of fine, densely packed dark green leaves—neat, bright & shiny; the foliage an asset before & after blooming period (height of summer). Flowers light textured, only 2 in. across, extremely numerous. Good soil. Shear after first full bloom for second lesser show. No support required. Plants increase at the root & can be divided.

Cortusa: PRIMULACEAE.
Closely related to *Primula.*
Eur., No. Am.
C. mathioli var. *pekinensis:*
Herb. Hairy leaves geranium-like. Scapes 8 in. Flowers intense crimson.

Cosmos: COMPOSITAE
Warmer parts of the Americas.
Herb. or ann. Leaves delicate. Need several plants for a drift.
Tender.
Greek: komos = ornament.
C. diversifolia: Usually grown as an ann. To 1½ ft. Flower heads to 3 in. across, yellow disks & lilac-pink rays. Or white.
C. bipinnatus: Horticultural varieties to be found in seed catalogues; early, late, anemone flowered & dble. flowered.
C. atrosanguineus: Black Cosmos. Mex. Growth starts in May from tubers planted 3 in. deep. To 2 ft. Bloom late summer. Protect with deep winter mulch in cooler climates. Flowers with red disks & rays of dark velvety red.
C. ssp. *seamannii:* Only to be seen in a specialist's garden. (Sp. unknown.)

Cynoglossum: Grow from seed each year for masses of large, blue forget-me-nots.

Dahlia: COMPOSITAE.
Ancestors mostly Mex. & Cent. Am.
Herb. Tuber; curious tubers look like sweet potatoes. Leave in the ground only in warm climates. Foliage bright green in clumps. Flowers various. Hybs. with sev. parents esp. *D. pinnata* & *D. coccinea.* Many sizes &

colors & types as single, dble., "anemone", "collarette", "peony-flowered", "formal", "ball", "cactus", "orchid-flowered". When cutting apart to divide, each section must have a portion of old stem. Or divide after new stems have started.

Sun, full. Good air circulation. Soil fertile with a well-balanced content. To at least 1 ft., add liberal quantities of potash & phosphorus as well as nitrogen & trace elements. Drainage. First, after digging up clumps, cut stems to 6 in., turn clumps upside down for 3 hours outdoors & 1 week indoors so the cut stems can drain. Dust with sulphur, ferbam, etc. any injured portion. Store in a cool dark place over winter; in order to prevent drying of the tubers, cover with slightly damp material as vermiculite or sand, or wrap in thick layers of newspaper & box, or pack with damp vermiculite in plastic bags left open, for 1 month. Or prepare a bed in the soil with material above & below the tubers to maintain conditions advantageous to their life & health. In any method, check at regular intervals in order to discard any sick parts. Tubers multiply.

Dahlias make great cut flowers, if carefully conditioned; probably the smaller the kind the better it keeps. Dis-branching & careful supporting will improve flowers. Perhaps the very smallest cvs. make the most attractive garden plants. All add fine color in summer and fall to a mixed border or bouquet.

Delphinium: RANUNCULACEAE. Larkspur. N. hemis.

Herb. Anns., biens. & pers. Pers. short-lived. Leaves lobed, cut or divided. 1 ft. to 6 ft. Tall spp. spire-like.

Sun or part shade. Soil, deep, well-drained, thoroughly tilled. Stake tall kinds. Shelter from wind. Water at roots instead of overhead. Give plenty of fertilizer, but not fresh manure. In dry weather, weekly deep soaking. Obtain superior seed. Mulch young plants. Protect from birds. Control snails & slugs. Circle clumps with solid barricade of something sharp esp. wood ashes since crawlers might find this barrier irritating to their soft bodies. Baits also. Don't bury the crown. Mildew is an enemy where the nights are cold; best defense—select seed of finest strains. It is said that continued breeding makes a plant more susceptible to disease; but breeders strive for resistant clones.

Greek "delphinion" from delphis = a dolphin; alludes to the shape of a single flower. Difficult to plan a substitute for *Delphinium* in a border for July. Tall, columnar, stately, massive display of color. (There are even yellow & pink ones being developed. At Longwood, even red strains are being worked upon.) *Delphinium* will always be thought of as "blue". Handsome as a cut flower but not long keeping—shatters. When picking, cut leaving some foliage since the leaves continue to nourish the roots; when foliage has wilted, cut stub of flowering stem all the way to the ground to make way for new shoots. White is best

color to pick since blue becomes more lavender within doors. Or pink.

D. *elatum:* Introduced to England 17th century from Siberia.

D. *grandiflorum* & D. *cheilanthum:* Probably first parents of a hyb. Chinese or Bouquet hyb. Treated as bien. or ann.

"Connecticut Yankee" strain, D. *elatum* × D. *cheilanthum:* Spire-like hybs.

D. modern hybs.: e.g. "Blue Fountain series". Excel. cvs. Shorter stems.

D. *belladonna* & D. *bellamosum:* Early named seedlings, from work by breeders Lemoine, Kelway, Langdon, Samuel, Bishop in England, Vanderbilt, Spingarn, Leonian, Barber & Vetterle & Reinelt in the U.S. Med. height. No staking required. Flowers various shades of blue to white.

D. English hybs.: Best for cool summers & not too cold winters.

D. *belladonna* hybs.: To 4 ft. Cvs. 'Bellamosa', 'Casa Blanca', & 'Cliveden Beauty' (turquoise blue).

D. Pacific hybs.: To 8 ft. Flowers big, many colors with colored eyes. Best grown as ann. or bien. Easy & quite true from seed. Look for 'Blue Spire'.

D. *chinensis:* Various forms of D. *grandiflorum*, often called Chinese Delphinium. To 2 ft. Live to 3 years. Flowers in loose sprays. Wide-spreading sepals, various blues, purples & white. D. *grandiflorum* comes from dry meadows & stony slopes. To 2 ft. Leaves with 5 lobes. Flowers few, bright blue in loose racemes.

D. *cardinale:* Scarlet Larkspur. Dry chaparral & woodlands, Calif., U.S. To 6 ft. Deep, woody roots. Leaves lobed & cleft. (Basal leaves wither before buds fully open.) Flowers on slender stems in loose panicles, brilliant scarlet (rarely yellow). Cornucopia-shaped with prominent spurs. Not easy. Needs dedicated effort.

D. *nudicaule:* To 1 ft. Reddish; together with sev. other spp. only for the collector.

D. *ajacis:* Larkspur. Ann.

D. *bicolor* & D. *hanseni*, & D. *consolida:* Oldtimers.

Dianthus: CARYOPHYLLACEAE. Pinks, Carnation. N. hemis.

Semi-evgrn. Greatest claim to fame is fragrance, often potent. Single & dble. Many different sizes & shapes.

Sun & part shade. Soil porous, not acid, with drainage. Never soggy or even very wet. Bonemeal mixed with a spring top-dressing. Stone-chips around the foliage clump—of benefit & look well. Rot, wilt & rust may attack but not usually healthy plants. Long periods of drying winds are harmful. Slugs, cutworms, aphids, caterpillars, thrips & red-spider mites enemies which can be controlled. Birds & rabbits are to be discouraged by wire covers. Plants in bloom must be groomed. Bloom mostly summer. On the whole fairly easy. Seed or division.

Greek: dios = divine, anthos = flower.

Carnations, sometimes grown for picking under special conditions, (even in special

Delphinium

Delphinium

Dianthus

Dictamnus

25 mm
20
15
10
5
0

Dictamnus

greenhouses) are derived from the following sp.

D. caryophyllus. Carnation. Two sizes.

D. barbatus: Sweet William, a bien. which sometimes lives more than 2 years. Blooms well in part shade. Comes in excel. colors & adds appreciably to borders. Selected forms. 1–2 ft. × 1 ft. wide. Flower heads rather flattened & composed of 5 to 10 individual *Dianthus* flowers.

Garden pinks, variable. They may have grey foliage or green. Mostly low growing, to 1 ft. wide. Flowers single or dble., simple or fancy. There are many named forms, most of uncertain parentage. It is best to look in old gardens as well as in the market place. "Clove Carnations" are in bloom July & Aug. & seldom available in the trade.

D. 'Little Joe' must be loved for its name as well as for its crimson-red flowers above a blue-grey clump only 6 in. across.

D. plumarius: Cottage Pink. Old-fashioned. Mat of very narrow leaves, bluish; flowers on 12 in. stems, pink, red, rarely white—with an eye. Petals with fringe to ⅓ of depth. Very fragrant.

D. gratianopolitanus (D. caesius): Cheddar Pink. Leaves soft, narrow, blue-green in a loose mat. Flowers 1 or 2, rarely 3, rose-pink, 1 in. across, bearded in throat, petals toothed. Parent of many good cvs.

D. chinensis: Chinese Pink, Rainbow Pink. Many cvs. Short-lived.

D. c. 'Hedewigii': A fringed clone.

D. "Highland Hybrids": A group with single flowers on 1 ft. stems, white & pink with maroon centers. 'Highland Fraser' less tall, markings attractive. Fine for picking. Bloom June. Grow from seed. Plant at the base of shrub roses.

D. superbus: Leaves mostly green. Stems mostly branched, 2–12 on a stem. Pale lilac, deeper lilac, rose-pink or rarely white; frilly & curly, the petals slashed into narrow segments. To 2 in. across. Special fragrance. May be short-lived. Not difficult to increase. Cvs. 'Loveliness' & 'Lavender Lace', perhaps derived from this sp.

D. monspessulanus: Spain & the Caucasus, relative of *D. superbus.* Lower, with longer branches, to 1 ft., pink, carmine or white, deeply lobed with frilled edges.

D. knappii: Hungary & Yugoslavia. Leaves green. Stem to 1½ ft., slender, branched at top with flowers in clusters, lemon yellow, scentless. Open growth.

D. deltoides: Maiden Pink. Gr. Brit. to Japan, naturalized in some parts of N. Am. Wide spreading, flat mats of green foliage. Flowers less than 1 in. across, on stems mostly less than 1 ft. tall, light to dark rose or magenta-pink more or less spotted or speckled. Toothed petals. Numerous. June–August.

Many cvs. of unknown parentage, e.g. 'Helen', 'Doris', 'Parfait', 'Zing Rose', 'Beatrix'.

D. latifolius 'Silver Mine': A recommended cv.

Many dwarfs. Many spp. & cvs. worth seeking for r.g.

"Alpine Hybrids": A group name for several 6 in. high × 8 in wide.

D. alpinus: Alps to Greece & Arctic Russia. Low green cushions. Flowers on 4 in. stems,

solitary, to 1½ in. across, pink to crimson with an eye. Throats bearded. Fragrant.

D. a. var. *albus:* Scentless.

D. glacialis: Quite like *D. alpinus* but petals are not as flat. Tight green mound. Flowers solitary, short-stemmed, pale & deep pink with whitish centers. Fragrant.

D. petraeus var. *noeanus:* Green cushion. Leaves rigid, sharp-pointed, prickly to touch. Arching flowering stems to 1 ft. with fringed white flowers of flimsy texture less than 1 in. in diameter. Blooms late. Fragrant.

D. 'La Bourbrille': With a really tiny mound, 4 in. × 4 in. Excel. for trough.

Diascia: SCROPHULARIACEAE.

S. Afr.

Ann. & per. Colorful & floriferous.

Sun. Soil fert. Water moderate. Division.

Greek "di" = two; askos = a pouch. Corolla has twin spurs on lower lip. Many stems from spreading clump. Leaves mostly opposite. Calix 5 lobed. Lower lip 3 lobed, upper 2 lobed. 4 stamens; slender style. The perennials make a colorful display over a very long period. Names found in the market place may be faulty.

D. barberae: The ann. called Twinspur.

D. rigescens: Spreading with flowering stems more or less erect in full clumps. Flowers in racemes interspersed with small leaves. Num. & very long lasting. Two toned pink to coral or salmon.

D. cordifolia (D. cordata): Clump less wide & less dense. Branches & leaves smaller. Flowers dainty, small, brighter than *D. rigescens.*

Dictamnus: RUTACEAE.Burning Bush, Gas Plant, Dittany.

Eur., Asia.

Herb. To 3 ft. × 2–4 ft. wide. Aromatic: lemony. June & July. Foliage attractive when blooming season finished.

Partial shade or sun. Soil well-drained, fert. Bonemeal in base of prepared area. Patience; long-lived but development may take 4 years. Combine with *Aquilegia, Lupinus & Geranium.*

Can withstand some dry periods. Difficult to establish. Gas content unusual; a lighted match held to the base of a spike when seed pods are ripening will ignite the volatile oil. Seed pods brought indoors for drying, will explode & shoot out seeds; the lining will crackle.

D. fraxinella var. *albus (D. albus):* Fraxinella or Dittany. To 3 ft., often less. Leaves dark green, pinnate, leaflets 9–11, toothed, 3 in. long. Flowers erect racemes at the top of 3 ft. stems. Petals gracefully bent with 10 long, conspicuous stamens. The most common form is white; others are mauve-purple, dark red. *D. f.* var. *ruber* = *D. albus* var. *purpureus.*

D. caucasicus: Larger & less common than *D. fraxinella.*

Doronicum: COMPOSITAE. Leopard's Bane.

Eur., Brit., N. Afr., Temp. Asia. Mostly mtns.

Herb. Stems stiff, erect & sturdy, withstanding heavy rain. Leafy. Leaves of some spp. more hairy than those of others. Sometimes heart-shaped, sometimes with scalloped edges or coarsely toothed. Mostly such early bloom, as to be called winter.

Part sun & part shade. Soil fert., well-drained, preferably slightly acid. Division. Seed.

Excel. for cutting. Tuberous roots somewhat invasive. Since foliage disappears in summer, place clumps in small groups. Pots.

D. pardalianches: Great Leopard's Bane. Spreads by underground tuberous stolons. Invasive. Leaves lush during flowering time. 'Bunch of Gold', a cv. with canary-yellow flowering heads. Name often used for other finer spp.

D. cordatum (D. caucasicum): Spreads by underground stolons; plants colonize but without encroachment on companion plants. To 2 ft. tall. Somewhat hairy. Leaves basal, coarsely toothed, with heart-shaped bases. Flowers 2 in. wide, solitary. *D. c.* var. *magnificum:* Has larger flowering heads.

D. 'Miss Mason': Later bloom, perhaps April.

Dorycnium: LEGUMINOSAE.
Mediterranean, Canary Islands.

Evgrn. or deciduous. Shrublet. Soft grey foliage. Many small leaves crowded on branchlets. Seed pods excel. brown. Hardy in S. New England, U.S.

Sun. Soil porous, not too rich. Drainage. More dryish than wet. Propagate from seed & less easily from cuttings.

Uncommon.

D. hirsutum: (Has been grown in gardens as *Cytisus lotus*). Woody at the base with white hairy foliage. From base new soft leafy stems annually. To 2 ft.; longer stems tend to sprawl. To 2 ft. wide. Trimming at intervals will keep this shrublet less tall, less wide & also more neat & compact. Flowers in small heads, white with rose lines & purple keel, papilionaceous in shape, not conspicuous. Clusters of cylindrical legumes are more noticeable; dark brown in contrast with soft grey. Pods oblong-ovoid, nearly ½ in. long.

Echinacea: COMPOSITAE. Coneflower.
E. N. Am.

Herb. Helianthus Tribe. 3 spp. Coarse, rough, hairy. 4 ft. × 18 in. Leaves simple, large. Purple cones (purplish brown) except for a few cvs. with greenish cones. Sim. to *Helenium* & *Helianthus* with the difference that the discs of these two are not cone-like.

Sun. Soil rich, moisture retentive. Easy from seed. Cut off flowers before any seed has dropped. Cuttings. Division.

Greek: echinos = a hedgehog; alluding to the prickly bracts protruding from the flower head. Seeds of the cvs. will produce variable tints, mostly better than the color of the sp. For mixed plantings. Combine with *Rudbeckia, Aster, Cosmos, Gaura.* A late summer daisy good to pick.

E. purpurea (Rudbeckia purpurea): Purple Coneflower. Best known. To 6 ft., usually 4 ft. Leaves oval to lanceolate, rough textured. Flower heads to 6 in. across. See Layout 1.

E. p. 'Robert Bloom': Spreading ray florets, intense, rich, cerise-mauve-crimson. Prominent central boss.

E. p. 'The King': Drooping rays, crimson-pink. Popular for many years.

E. p. 'White Lustre': Off-white but useful in mixed planting & as a cut flower. Orange-brown central cone.

E. tennesseensis: A rare & endangered sp. The petals of this rose colored (purple) coneflower are notched. The flowers of the cone are openly spaced. Blooms first year. Color: "Ashes of roses". Obtain seed.

Echinops: COMPOSITAE. Globe-Thistle.
E. Eur., Cent. Asia & Afr.

Herb. Full, leafy clumps. Excel. pattern of indentations.

Sun. Soil dryish. Drainage. Seed.

Deep borders, with shrubs or as accent. Good to pick, good to dry. Head made up of tiny florets & bracts. Greek: echinos = a hedgehog; in this genus, the whole head is prickly.

E. exaltatus: Siberia. (Sometimes mistakenly called *E. ritro* or *E. sphaerocephalus*). Shrubby, with num. stems 3 to 10 ft., all prickly. Leaves grey on their backsides. Flower heads bluish, to 2 in. across. 'Taplow Blue': A cv. of long standing. 'Veitch's Blue': Is newer.

E. ritro: Grows to about 2 ft. & the leaves felted with white hairs beneath.

E. r. var. *tenuifolium:* (May be listed as *E. ruthenicus* of gardens). Stems coated with white. Leaves spiny-toothed, over 1 ft. long. Flowers bright blue. Easy.

E. emiliae: Introduced from Turkey by John Watson. Flowers jade-green.

E. tournefortii: Large plant to 5 ft. tall. White stems, white thorns, grey leaves. Flowers white in late summer. Extremely prickly.

Eomecon: PAPAVERACEAE. Snow Poppy, Dawn Poppy, Poppy of the Dawn.
E. China.

One sp. in this genus. Slender rhizome. Colonizes. Average size 18 × 18 in. Large, rounded leaves.

Partial shade. Soil cool & moist. Needs drainage. Annual application of fertilizer. Permanent. Invasive? In humusy rich soil it may want to wander. Plant under greedy shrubs, (3 in. deep).

Greek: heos = eastern, mekon = poppy. A rare relative of *Sanguinaria.*

E. chionantha: Deciduous, herb. per. with wide-spreading underground rhizomes. Leaves many, heart-shaped to kidney-shaped with undulated margins, 4 in. across, fleshy, palmately veined, bluish green. Flowers late spring & summer, on 1 ft. stalks, sev. in loose panicles, nodding, petals roundish, pure white with sev. yellow stamens, each flower short-lived.

Eremurus: LILIACEAE. Foxtail Lily or Desert Candle.
Himalaya, SW. Asia Minor, Turkestan.

Herb. broad roots form crown. Leaves, some narrow, some broad. *E. robusta* has the most broad and the bluest green. Majestic spikes magnificent for picking as well as for features in a border or mixed planting.

Sun. Perfect drainage. Full protection from any wind. Bloom about the time of Bearded

Dorycnium

Echinacea

Erigeron

Erigeron

Erodium

Iris. (It is said that the two like similar conditions.) Choose the right place since the roots are very difficult to move. Two people should undertake the lifting, each with a fork endeavoring not to break or injure any root. The rootstocks consist of a central crown from which spread horizontally, in starfish manner many thong-like roots, the health of which determines whether or not the plant will manufacture its great spire. When the roots arrive from the grower, all roots will not be intact & it will take a year for all the spokes of the wheel to mend & grow back. The crown should be placed just below the surface & be enveloped in a bed of coarse sand. If staking is planned it should be done during planting in order to place the tip of the stake between roots rather than pierce one which has been covered. It is said that the root system will finally take up more than a square yard of ground. Water should be withheld for a rest period. Therefore, the plants are not apt to flourish when planted in an area with plants which must be given constant water through summer. They are certainly worth an attempt to find a site to their liking. In cold climates, & as far north as S. New England, the roots are frost hardy but gardeners there mound over the root area with sand, peat or sawdust being careful to detect the early spring growth pushing up through the mound. At this time, in the expectation of further frost, boughs or improvised nightly shelters are placed. Young leaves are frost tender. Site where early A.M. sun does not reach. Once established, *Eremurus* is a long lasting per. When applying the annual spring fertilizer, do remember those roots which do not withstand damage.

A place should be found, suitable aesthetically as well as horticulturally. Against a dark background has been suggested; but the site must be far enough away from questing roots of big shrubs or trees so that these do not entangle the *Eremurus* roots. Success would be worth not only time & trouble but a lot of space.

E. robustus: Probably the tallest; one form has been reported, to 10 ft. Rigid cylindrical spikes, made up of num. flowers pink with brown keel.

E. himalaicus: Spikes only 3 ft. tall. White flowers. Easiest.

E. stenophyllus: Spikes to 4 ft.; flowers yellow. This sp. & *E. algae* both from Iran.

E. hybs.: Many—some less high that the tallest. Every pastel shade & white. "Shelford hybrids" are praised. *E. algae* × *E. stenophyllus* = × Shelford.

Erigeron: COMPOSITAE. Fleabane, Orange-Daisy.

N. Am. Widespread.

Herb. Some evgrn. Leaves mostly in short tufts to form mats. 1 × 1½ ft. Flowers resemble Michaelmas Daisy. Low clumping evgrn. spp., useful for edging, g.c. Summer bloom.

Sun. Soil med. Needs drainage. Semi-hdy. Division.

Flowers keep well cut; good for small bouquets. Plant with *Aster* & *Achillea*.

E. hybs.: Mostly short, narrow rays & yellow center. Cvs. many, of various colors, e.g. 'Charity', soft pink; 'Felicity', clear pink; 'Festivity', lilac-mauve; 'Sincerity', mauve-blue; even 'Prosperity' & Alan Bloom's 'Darkest of All', purple. Bloom's 'Dimity' is dwarf, pink with orange buds.

E. speciosus, E. speciosus var. *macranthus* & *E. glaucus:* Spp. from W. N. Am. On cliffs near the ocean, the first particularly tolerant of sea spray. Mats spread to 2 ft. Leaves clammy texture, greyish green, flowers on many stems not over 2 ft. The rays bluish purple.

Erodium: GERANIACEAE. Heron's Bill.

Cent. Spain & the Pyrenees.

Herb. Wide distribution. Closely related to *Geranium;* flowers without spurs. Tufts. Foliage varies, some only lobed, some finely divided almost carrot-like.

Sun. Soil dryish, very well-drained, non-acid. Cover with branches in cold climates. Semi-hdy. Seed.

Greek: erodius = a heron; refers to beaked fruits. Those growing in dense mounds good for damp r.g. Taller kinds for foregrounds of beds & borders. Smaller kinds for r.g. Dwarfs for pots or pans in alpine greenhouse. Flowers in summer.

E. chamaedryoides & *E. corsicum:* Native on rocks, islands of Mediterranean. Leaves round, toothed. Flowers pink or white or with darker veinings.

E. petraeum: From mtns. Ferny foliage. Close mat. Flowers bright pink.

E. moschatum: To 6 in. Flowers pink, June and July.

E. pelargoniflorum: Asia Minor. To 1 ft. Leaves ovate, heart-shaped. Flowers up to 10, in clusters, pinkish white with streaks & blotches.

E. hybridum: Covers sev. successful crosses. Some with greyish foliage.

E. cheilanthefolium 'David Crocker': To 4 in. Mtns. of Spain or Morrocco. Leaves all basal with erect white hairs. Twice pinnate. Segments of leaf are short, finely cut. Flowers, petals white, veined with rose. 2 upper petals larger & red splotched at the base.

Eryngium: UMBELLIFERA. Sea Holly.

Eur. & S. Am.

Herb. Habit & foliage vary. 1–8 ft. Leaves with firm texture, deeply toothed. Noted for cone-shape of flower & ruffled collar, called a "piccadil" by Thomas.

Sun. Ordinary cult. Needs drainage. Some spp. need room, to 3 ft. wide; others 1–2 ft. wide. Sometimes dies after flowering bountifully. Hdy. to Wash., U.S. Seed. Or from root cuttings.

Summer bloom. Pick before heads fully expanded & hang for drying. Wonderful color sometimes called "steel blue"; or nearly white in a few spp.

E. alpinum: Meadows in mtns. of Eur. To 2½ ft. Basal leaves heart-shaped to triangular to 6 in. long. Stems, upper leaves & flowers bluish or whitish. Cylindrical flower heads to 3 in., 25 dissected bracts, prickly-looking & frilly. The largest flower of all the spp. Pineapple-like cones, blue with blue calyx-frills.

E. amethystinum: Italy, dry places. Herb. To 1½ ft. Leaves—the basal ones leathery & pinnately divided, to 6 in., segments spiny-toothed. Upper stems, leaves & flower heads—amethyst-blue. Bracts 5–9, spines in pairs.

E. × zabelii: A name which covers a group of hybs. In breeding prominent bracts have been selected.

E. paniculatum: Handsome.

E. protaefolium: High altitudes, Mex. To 3 ft. Leaves 2 ft. long, pointed linear, both margins with long, white spines forward pointing, silvery green, forming broad rosettes. Flowers light blue in a collar of many leafy silvery white bracts, 8 in. across. All greyish white.

E. proteiflorum: Evgrn. Mex. May be the same as *E. protaefolium.* Astounding if not beautiful. Leaves long, narrow, pointed with long prickles, forward pointing. Flower a big head with leafy bracts—all greyish white.

E. involucratum: Like *E. proteiflorum* but smaller.

E. giganteum: Caucasus. To 6 ft. Leaves to 6 in. Heads to 4 in. Bracts to 4 in. Bold. Bluish to sea-green. *E.* 'Miss Willmott's Ghost': Quite white. Quite large.

E. yuccifolium: N. Am. To 4 ft.; usually less. Beautiful rosettes of curved flaring leaves, blue-green, shiny, with curving spines on the margins. Bloom late summer.

E. tripartitum (of gardens): 2½ × 2 ft. Long spreading bracts. Flowers steel blue. Bracts dark blue, spiky.

E. planum: Sim. to *E. tripartitum.* 'Blue Dwarf': a shorter form.

E. bourgatii: Dry stony places, Spain & the Pyrenees. To 1½ ft. tall. Rounded bush, more sparse-looking than others. Leaves deeply-cleft. Upper parts usually bluish.

E. decaisneana: Uraguay & Argentina. To 8 × 4 ft. Very odd indeed. Narrow pointed graceful leaves with spiny edges to 6 ft. high. Stout stem with greyish sheathing leaf carries a huge head. Num., tiny brown-purple heads, size of peas.

Erysimum: CRUCIFERAE. Blister Cress or Siberian Wallflower.

Mostly temp. regions.

Herb. or evgrn. Differs from *Cheiranthus* in type of nectary glands. Leaves narrow, to 4 in. Flowers in rounded heads.

Sun. Soil average (not rich), porous, well drained; annual top dressing of fresh soil. Easy from seed or grow where seedlings are welcome.

Many valuable spp.

E. allioni: The Siberian-wallflower is probably a horticultural form of *E. hieraciifolium* (*Cheiranthus allionii*). Usually a bien. To 1 ft. Bushy; freely branched. Leaves narrow, to 4 in. Flowers in rounded racemes which lengthen as lower flowers fade & upper buds gradually open. Orange or yellow.

E. capitatum: Coast-wall flower. Bien. To 1½ ft. Leaves to 3 in. long, linear, toothed or toothless. Flowers white or yellowish, small round heads, lovely. Native N. Am., Calif. to Brit. Col. & Idaho.

E. concinnum: Sold by specialists. (*Hortus* says it is *E. suffrutescens.*) Many cream colored flowers. 'Ballerina', a fine cv.; hard to find.

E. linifolium: Alpine-wallflower. Spain. Per. To 1 ft., quite broad mound. Leaves narrow, usually toothed & greyish. Flowers on 1 ft. stalks, muted lavender or lilac. A variegated form: restrained & attractive. Short-lived.

E. pumilum: To 6 in., sulfur-yellow, slightly fragrant & *E. alpinum,* to 1 ft., lemon-yellow, sweetly fragrant—mtns. of Eur.

E. kotschyanum: Cespitose per., stems to 6 in. Leaves narrow-linear to awl-like; petals bright yellow to ½ in. long. High mtns., Asia Minor.

Euphorbia: EUPHORBIACEAE. Spurge, Milk-weed.

Brit., Eur., SW. Asia.

Herb. & evgrn. 1–6 ft. high; 1–3 ft. wide. Foliage plentiful, yellowish green. About 2000 spp. Poinsettia & Crown-of-Thorns belong to this genus.

Sun or part shade. Soil poorish. Needs drainage. Tall spp. may need 1 or 2 stakes. Seed. Pull up seedlings when invasive. Division.

Liked by arrangers for odd color. Look for *E. g.* 'Fireglow', with bright rose tints in the green color. When picking, burn the ends, at the site; the milk within the stem helps keep the stem. Use gloves; the milk stains black with allergic reaction in a large percentage of people. Plant with shrubs or subshrubs. Bloom in spring, summer & fall.

E. characias: To 3 ft. Leaves bluish green, linear to 5 in. long, clothing dull purple stems. Greenish bracts forming a cup around the flower; flowers in a small cluster greenish also.

E. wulfenii: (According to one authority is a subsp. of *E. characias;* is very similar.)

E. venata: Synonym of *E. wulfenii* or mistaken for *E. characias.* Sp. is variable. Leaves plentiful, muted green, attractive in winter, covering the stem from the base to the top where the flowering head is developed in early spring; first bright green, then chartreuse.

E. griffithii: Himalayas. To 2 ft. Stems more slender. Leaves with pink midribs. Heads more broad & loose with brick-red tint to bracts. Cvs. 'Fireglow' & 'Fire-fly', bright orange-scarlet.

E. wallichi: To 18 in. Leaves dark green with purplish edges & white central vein. Bracts large & greenish yellow.

E. epithymoides (E. polychroma): Cushion Spurge—from the shape of the rounded dome. To 18 in., clump-forming, 3 ft. across. Bracts to 1 in. long & bright sulphur-yellow. Full flowering heads cover the top of the plant in spring.

E. cyparissias: Cypress Spurge. 1 ft. Leaf so narrow that it looks almost cypress-like. Blooms late spring & early summer.

E. sikkimensis: Purplish red shoots.

E. myrsinites: S. Eur. Looks like a succulent. Trailing: long stems from a tub or from the

Erysimum

R. G.

0 mm
5
10
15
20
25

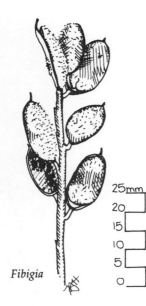

Fibigia

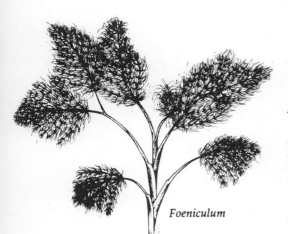

Foeniculum

Fragaria

edge of a raised bed, to 1 ft. from a common center. Leaves light blue-green. Bracts yellow.

E. biglandulosa (E. rigida): Like *E. myrsinites* except stems erect. Leaves fleshy, grey-green distinctly lanceolate. Flowers chartreuse-yellow in domed heads.

E. robbiae: Asia Minor. Subshrub to 2 ft. × 2 ft. Leaves dark green, leathery. Attractive foliage plant. Flowers of no account. Useful foliage g.c. from spreading roots. Rosettes of dark green, flowers at top of stems in green spires.

E. mellifera: Canary Islands. Low & neat. Flowers green. Foliage pleasing. Spreads by underground stems. *On the endangered list.*

Fibigia: CRUCIFERAE.
Mediterranean to Afghanistan.
Herb. (Sometimes included in Farsetia.) From Johann Fibig, a German physician & prof. Leaves small & narrow, alternate on lower stems. Flowers yellow, early summer, on 1 ft. stems, sev. to a clump.
Sun. Dry walls or dry banks where soil drains quickly. Not hdy. in cold climates; grow then as an ann. Seed.
Fruits flattened with beak-like tips—velvety pods. Cut stems for dried arrangements. Grow in a collection of grey mats.

F. eriocarpa: Greece. Erect. Leaves velvety, white. Flowers bright yellow, ½ in. across. Seed pods to 1 in. long with long hairs.

Filipendula: ROSACEAE. Dropwort, Meadow-sweet, Queen-of-the-Meadow, Queen-of-the-Prairie.
Eur., Brit., N. Am.
Herb. To 4 × 2 ft. Leaves feathery or ferny, full basal clumps.
Sun or ½ shade. Some spp. prefer very moist soil, grow taller & wider where soil continually wet.
Good to cut. When fully open petals tend to shatter. Bloom summer.

F. vulgaris (F. hexapetala, Spiraea filipendula): Dropwort. Rootstock tuberous. Old plants can be divided with a saw. Tufts of carrot-like foliage. Occasionally taken for a fern when without flowers. Hdy. in warmer climates. Needs less moisture than other spp. described below. Flowers on 2 ft. stems in summer, fluffy, white in clusters.

F. v. var. flore-pleno: The dble., larger, flowers look more white & last longer.

F. 'Grandiflora': A selected form. Flowers creamy yellow. Slightly fragrant.

F. palmata (Spiraea camtschatica, Spiraea gigantea of gardens): To 3 ft. Leaves palmate. Flowers pinkish esp. in bud, pale pink fading to white in age. Sim. to *F. rubra*.

F. p. 'Digitata Nana': Reported worth seeking for compact habit & finely cut foliage. Height reported as 18 in.

F. rubra: Queen-of-the-Prairie or Martha Washington Plume. To 7 ft. Best for a "wild garden".

F. r. 'Venusta': Flowers deep rose. Stamens longer than the petals.

F. purpurea: From Japan, perhaps a hyb. 1–4 ft. × 2 ft. wide in big clumps, handsome leaves, 5–7 lobed; flowers carmine in rather loose large clusters. Perhaps not in the U.S.

market. A white form 'Alba'.

F. ulmaria: Queen-of-the-Meadow or Meadowsweet. Wet places in Eur. & Asia, naturalized in parts of N. Am. Best for boggy woodland. To 8 ft. but often 3 ft. × 1 ft. wide.

F. u. var. aureo-variegata: Planted for golden foliage.

Foeniculum: UMBELLIFERAE.
Herb. Seeds prolifically. Look for the dark one, the bronzy leaved form of *F. vulgare*. Foliage very feathery, almost like hair & very plentiful.
Sun. Soil poorish. Ordinary cult. Seed. Cuttings. Division.
Interesting to cut. Adds interest to a bed or border.

F. vulgare: To 6 ft. × 2 ft. Leaves green, very finely divided. Fragrant.

F. v. var. purpureum: Deep purplish mahogony; as foliage ages becomes bronze. Somewhat smaller than sp.

Fragaria: ROSACEAE. Strawberry.
Temp. Eur., Asia, N. Am., S. Am., Hawaii.
Creeping or tufted. 3 in.–12 in. Leaves indented forming a triangle. The less rampant spp. good for r.g.
Sun or part shade. Soil good, fert. Ample water. Division. Seed.
The edible strawberries also ornamental; the divided leaves are handsome with rich texture & sculptured division. A successful cv. is "# 25".

F. chiloensis: A parent of modern strawberries.

F. vesca: Eur. & N. Am. The Wood Strawberry known as "Fraise de bois", has sev. improved forms: e.g. 'Baron Solemacker', old-fashioned, and modern 'Rugen's Improved'.

F.v. var. alba: White berries.

F. v. var. variegata: Also white berries. Green leaved crowns should be removed; being stronger growers, they would take over.

Gerbera: COMPOSITAE. Transvaal Daisy, Barberton Daisy.
Afr. to Madagascar to Asia & Bali.
Semi-evgrn. To 1½ × 1½ ft. A raised bed the best site or pots or boxes. A large, elegant daisy.
No water over crown. Crown ¼ in. above surface. Soil rich. Feed often. Sharp drainage. Division.
Good cut; slit stem 1 in. Grow under glass for cut flowers. Plants for outdoors plentiful in temp. climate markets. Considerable hybridization to obtain whites & pinks. May–Dec. Stylish.

G. × cantabrigiensis: *G. viridifolia* × *G. jamesonii* & cvs. of the hybs. Semi-dbles. & dbles. & duplex with 2 rows of rays. Can be grown in containers if given ample water & nutrition. Does not mix well with most old-fashioned perennials in the garden.

Geum: ROSACEAE. Avens.
Widespread.
Herb. & semi-evgrn. Foliage basal, reliably clean-looking, often in tight crinkled rosettes. Flowers over a long period, on branching stalks, to 2 ft. above leaves.

Part shade. Soil med. Ordinary cult. Mostly hdy. Division. Best when divided every third year.

Good to pick for the bright colors & prominent stamens of its flowers. Goes well with *Potentilla, Oenothera, Achillea*.

G. triflora var. *campanulatum*: Scarce.

G. quellyon (*G. chiloense*): Chile. Often misidentified as *G. coccineum*. Cvs. e.g.: 'Mrs. Bradshaw', scarlet; 'Lady Stratheden', yellow, to 2 × 1½ ft. wide. Newer cvs. e.g.: 'Rubin' & 'Red Wings', semi-dble. & red; 'Fire Opal', flame, single; 'Dolly North', orange-yellow. 'Princess Juliana' is choice.

G. coccineum (of gardens): Is *G. chiloense* which in turn is *G. quellyon*.

G. reptans & *G. bulgaricum* & perhaps also *G. coccineum*: Parents of a hyb. named for King Boris of Bulgaria, given the name *G. borisii*, a dense mound of light crinkled leaves of pleasing texture; flowers deep orange in May & June on 1 ft. stems, up-facing with prominent stamens. The name *G. borisii* may be applied to another hyb. with orange-scarlet flowers. Of sev. hybs., one has excel. attributes: namely *G.* 'Georgenberg'. (Often given sp. status) Very compact. Foliage curly, overlapping in decorative fashion. Flowers over a long period, a more muted scarlet than other cvs. of this hyb.

G. rivale: Water Avens. Wet meadows & swamps in Eur., temp. Asia & N. Am. 1 × 1 ft. Flowers bell-shaped, nodding. 'Leonard's variety' is recommended. Flowers also bell-shaped, soft, coppery, creamy pink blushed with orange.

G. rossii: Carrot-like foliage in a neat tuft; color butter-yellow.

Glaucium: Red Horned Poppy.

G. phoeniceum to 2 feet. Flowers poppies, "scarlet" with a black spot.

Gypsophila: CARYOPHYLLACEAE. Baby's Breath, Chalk Plant.

Eur., Asia, N. Afr.

Herb. Tall & wide to 4 × 4 ft., or small, low mounds & dwarfs, 6 × 6 in.

Sun. Soil alkaline, friable, deep & rich. Excel. drainage. Seed. Some from cuttings. Tap-rooted: difficult to transplant.

Dwarf spp. for r.g. or troughs. Wide spp. have many stems for cutting, fresh or dry. Bloom summer.

G. acutifolia: Caucasus. Sim. to *G. paniculata*.

G. paniculata: The most common & the largest sp.

G. p. 'Perfecta': Leaves 3 in., grey-green. Flowers tiny but larger than sp.

G. p. var. *flore-pleno*: To 3 ft. Flowers in billowy clouds. Other dbles.: *G. p.* var. *ehrlei, G. p.* 'Bristol Fairy', with dense clouds of small, white flowers.

G. p. 'Rosy Veil': Quite prostrate cv. Dwarf to 1½ ft., rose-pink dble. flowers. Grows well from cuttings.

A number of other spp. & cvs. are dwarves.

G. repens var. *rosea*: Only 6 in. tall. Flowers pink.

G. bodgeri: A hyb. between *G. r.* var. *rosea* & *G. paniculata* var. *flore-pleno*, to 1 ft. Lower stems

prostrate; upper making loose panicles of dble. pink, or white, flowers.

G. cerastioides: Mouse-Ear Gypsophila. Himalaya. Cushions to 4 in. Flowers white, pink-veined, with notched petals, in loose clusters. Or lilac. May die out.

G. aretioides: Iran. Dense firm, grey-green mats. Flowers white.

G. petraea: (and the other very dwarf spp., Good for troughs. Obtain from a specialist.

Helenium: COMPOSITAE. Sneezeweed.

N. Am. & S. Am.

Herb. Daisy with a cone. To 5 ft. Sev. stems from a clump, to 18 in. w.

Sun. Ordinary cult. Easy. Division in autumn or spring.

Legend: sprang from ground, watered by tears of Helen of Troy. Seek 'Copper Spray'.

H. autumnale: 3–5 ft. Cvs. selected for variations of color. Hybs. with *H. bigelovii*. Cvs. e.g.: 'Gold Fox', a rather new gold; 'Bruno', mahogony-red. 'Coppelia', bronzy red with flattened disc, blooms earlier than other cvs. June through Aug. Cvs. with shorter stems to 2½ ft. include—a yellow (with brown cone) 'Pumilum Magnificum'; 'Riverton Beauty', yellow & maroon 'Peregrinum', sometimes listed as a sp. but merely a cv.

H. bigelovii, 4 ft. & *H. hoopesii* to 3 ft.: W. N. Am., natives from moist meadows. Heads to 3 in. in diameter with yellow rays & with cones reddish purple. Bloom in July & Aug. The shorter cvs. derive their height from selections of these 2 spp.

Helianthus: COMPOSITAE. Sunflower.

Mostly N. Am.

Some kinds invasive weeds. To 15 ft., the tallest.

Sun or part shade. Mostly seed, esp. annuals.

H. tuberosus: Jerusalem Artichoke. Used by American Indians. Presently seldom grown; roots may be cooked & frozen for soups or eaten raw. Division.

H. multiflorus = *H. annuus*, an annual × *H. decapitatus*, a perennial. To 6 ft. Leaves pointed & toothed to 10 in. long. Flowers golden yellow; single, semi-dble. or dble.

H. cvs.: e.g. 'Loddon Gold', vivid oldtimer. To 5 ft. dble. 'Capenoch Star': With lighter color than many others.

Hesperaloe: LILIACEAE. Red Yucca.

N. Am., S. U.S. & Mex.

Evgrn. Stylish. Open clump of sword-shaped leaves. Flowers num. in tall spikes. Only a few leaves & flower spikes from each crown.

Sun. Soil good. Needs drainage. Feed Division.

Handsome to pick, esp. leaves, narrow, curving, thick, leathery, brownish green. Noted for curling threads along margins.

H. parviflora (*H. yuccaefolia*): Smaller by far than any *Yucca*. To 4 ft. usually less, 1½ ft. wide. Leaves narrow, leathery; attractive, curled, thread-like frayings on the margins. Arching from the crown. Flowering stalks rise above clump of leaves, the top portion crowded with small trumpets of a two-toned apricot color. A few stalks to each crown with blooms many weeks, summer.

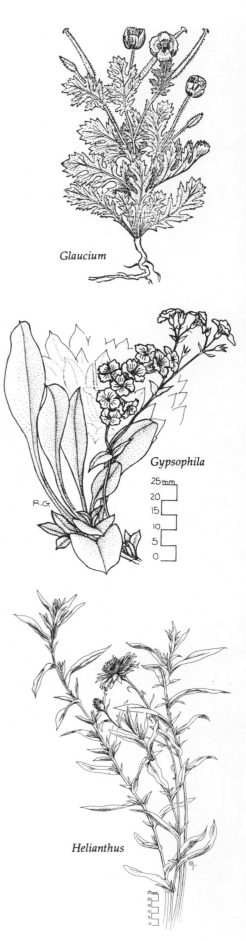

Glaucium

Gypsophila

25 mm
20
15
10
5
0

Helianthus

Hesperis

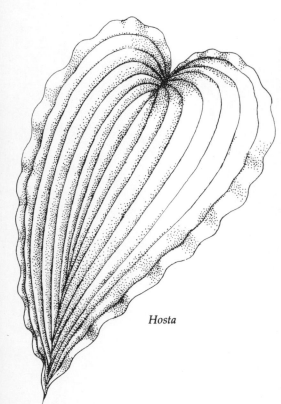

Hosta

Hesperis: See annuals. Useful to underplant bulbs.

Hosta: LILIACEAE. Plantain Lily, Gibosh, or Daylily. (Funkia)

Japan, China, Korea.

Herb. 1–3 ft. Spread 1–3 ft. Included under General instead of shade since the genus needs the space, moisture & nutrition, not sufficiently available under most trees. Grown primarily for varying & interesting foliage. May be puckered, ridged, wavy, tips pointed or blunt—rolled in a scroll, but mostly more broad than linear & more thick than thin. Green of different textures & colors & many patterns of variegation. Flowers more decorative in some spp. than others. *Hosta* even though requiring space combines well with *Helleborus, Filipendula, Astilbe.*

Shade. Dense or partial. Soil fert. & moist. In sun, more humus in the soil & more water will be needed. During dormancy mark position of the roots to prevent trespass. At very first sign of a leaf, circle with snail & slug bait & renew. Very deep roots, to 5 ft. it is reported. Best on a slope in wide drifts under undemanding trees. Division.

Excel. for arrangers. Veins, sometimes called nerves in the literature, either side of midrib give character to leaves. In some spp., veins more pronounced. Sev. yrs. for all spp. to reach maximum growth.

The order in which spp. are described show similarities & relationships.

H. subcordata var. *grandiflora:* One to seek.

H. fortunei (H. f. var. *gigantea = H. elata):* *H. fortunei* is "of gardens" & probably a hyb. with *H. sieboldiana* as a parent. Glaucus. Some cream with green edges, some green with yellow margins. (The one edged with white is probably *H. crispula.*) Flowers pale lilac late spring.

H. 'Thomas Hogg': Probably a cv. of a hyb. Impervious to "tree drip". Shiny surface. White or silver edges.

H. elata (once named *H. fortunei* var. *gigantea):* Large. 2½ ft. Leaves glossy, narrowly ovate to heart-shaped, undulate deep green with paler undersides. Flowers white to pale purple, loose racemes, about 40 blooms. June & July.

H. plantaginea (Funkia subcordata): Fragrant Plantain. Stout rhizomes. Leaves yellowish green (olive), glossy, heart-shaped, 1 ft. long. Making broad mounds, 2 × 2 ft. 8 or 9 pairs of lateral veins. Flowers waxy white, 3 × 6 in., trumpets, flaring horizontally. Open in evening, close as sun goes down, next day. Very fragrant.

H. p. var. *grandiflora:* Longer leaves, longer, narrower flowers.

H. sieboldii (H. albomarginata, H. lancifolia var. *albomarginata):* Seersucker Plantain Lily. Japan. To 3 ft. Leaves mostly elliptic to 6 in., 4–6 veins. Narrow, marginal band of white or yellowish white. Flowers 30 in erect raceme, funnel-shaped, violet with darker streaks.

H. s. var. *alba:* Plain green. Flowers white.

H. 'Honeybells' *(H. plantaginea × H. sieboldii):* Leaves green 12–6 in., 10 pairs of veins.

Flowers white, fragrant, marked with violet lines; 60, in racemes on stems to 4 ft. Flowers open in the morning. Aug.

H. 'Royal Standard': Parents unnamed, distributed from Wayside Gardens, U.S. Flowers near white, scented, Aug. Highly praised in the catalogues.

H. lancifolia (H. japonica): Narrow-leaved Plantain Lily. To 2 ft. Leaves dark, glossy, to 7 in. long, making a mass of foliage, 1½ ft. tall. Flower stalks to 2½ ft., 15 to 30 bell-shaped blooms whitish, streaked violet.

H. l. var. *variegata:* Leaves variegated with white. Look for 'Louisa'.

H. l. var. *albomarginata (H. sieboldii):* A special variegation, neat white stripe around edges.

H. sieboldiana (H. glauca): Not the same as *H. sieboldii.* Leaves grey or bluish green in gardens. In the wild, green, as well as glaucus: result of a light coating of wax. Almost as broad as long, over 1 ft. Spreading. 12–14 veins. Flowers 2 in. long, white. Late June, early July. Sev. cvs. E.g.: 'Frances Williams', leaves with white edges.

H. tokudama (Funkia sieboldiana var. *condensata):* Very sim. to *H. sieboldiana* in color of foliage—blue glaucus. Leaves with erect stalks but spreading blades, broadly heart-shaped & wrinkled (puckered like seersucker). Flowers in crowded, short, one-sided racemes, deep mauve, white & pale purple. In Japan, forms with leaves variegated with pale green are considered choice. June, July.

H. undulata: Midsummer Plantain Lily or Wavy Leaved Plantain Lily. Probably a hyb. 18 × 12 in. Prominently wavy-edged, elliptic, blades 6 × 2½ in., veins 10 pairs; noted for broad white centers with 2 shades of green on either side. On stalks to 2 ft., about 10 blooms, light purple; July. Leaves look curled in their tight mass. May be spirally twisted.

H. 'Univittata': Has one broad stripe down the center of the leaf. Sim. to *H. undulata.*

H. u. var. *erromena:* More robust with stems to 3 ft. & pure green, less wavy leaves than the sp.; rich green, broad, shiny. (No longer found in the wild) One of the tallest.

H. decorata: Leaves long-stalked, blunt elliptic, to 6 in., dark green with clear irregular white margins. Flowers dark violet; Aug.

H. d. var. *normalis:* Plain green. To 2 ft.

H. crispula (see *H. fortunei):* Leaves with white edges. Leaves large, to 8 in., pointed, undulate. Dull above, lustrous below. Veins 7–9 each side of midrib. Irregular pure white margins broader than those of *H. decorata.* Flowers funnel-shaped in a loose, many-flowered raceme. Up to 40 on stalks 3 ft. tall; white flushed purple. June, July. Esp. vigorous.

H. ventricosa: Blue Plantain Lily. China. (*H. coerulea, H. ovata*) Full, broad clumps. Leaves with channeled stalks; blades spreading, nearly heart-shaped to 8 in. across, wavy-edged, slightly shiny above, glossy beneath, as if shellaced, rich green. Inflated. Flowers violet-blue with darker veins; Aug., Sept. Flower suddenly opens, widens, in upper one-half.

H. v. 'Variegata': Green edges around light center; or green center with cream edge.

H. rectifolia: U.S. hyb., 'Tall Boy'. Probably the tallest. To 3 ft. Leaves to 12 in. Lance-shaped, pointed. Flowers to 2 in. across in many flowered racemes "cobalt violet".

H. 'Blue Skies': Leaves heart-shaped, steel blue in a neat rosette.

The following 5 spp. are esp. good for rock gardens:

H. minor 'Alba': Leaves short, broad-orbicular-ovate. Flowers low, white.

H. tardiflora (H. lancifolia var. *tardiflora):* Compact to 12 in. Leaves dark green, shiny, leathery, 6 × 12 in., 5–7 veins. Stalks to 1½ ft. with crowded racemes of 24 flowers; pale violet to whitish or dark violet to purple. Sept., Oct. No longer found in the wild.

H. tardiana: H. tardiflora × H. sieboldiana. Scarce. Look for cv. 'Dorset Blue'.

H. nakaiana: To 1½ ft. Leaves small, 3 in., thin, long, pointed. Flowers 2 in. across, campanulate, lilac to purple.

H. venusta: Thumbnail Plantain Lily. Suziki, Cheju Islands. Miniature, grown in the NW. U.S. Leaves to 2 in.; 3–4 veins. Blades under 2 in. long & less than 1 in. wide. Flowers funnel-form, pale purple, summer. (Shallow clumping rhizomes)

Houstonia: See Outdoor Room.

Hylomecon: PAPAVERACEAE.
Temp. Asia.
Herb. Slowly spreading clumps, fresh green foliage.
Sun. Soil cool, moisture retentive. Seed.
Interesting Poppy relative. Bloom April. Dainty.

H. japonicum: To 1 ft. high, 9 in. wide. Leaves with irregularly toothed leaflets. Flowers up-facing, golden-yellow, 2 in. across; spring & summer.

H. heterophylla: Orange Wind Poppy. Uncommon.

Hypoxis: AMARYLLIDACEAE. Star Grass.
Trop. Asia, Aust., Madagascar, Trop. & S. Afr., Trop. & N. Am.
1 sp. in Cent. U.S. (which follows).
Herb. Rhizomes. Grass-like leaves.
Semi-shade. Soil sandy, peaty, leafy. Division.
Not a grass; has a sim. look.

H. hirsuta: From open sandy pinewoods. To 2 ft. Leaves to 6 in., linear, hairy. Flowers 1 in. across, star-shaped, bright yellow, with green outside, in racemes, 2 to 6 from common stalk, to 8 in. May–July.

Iberis: CRUCIFERAE. Candytuft.
Eur. & Mediterranean, esp. limey soils.
Evgrn. Low compact, somewhat woody at base. Num. branches. Makes a mound; more dense if pruned. Leaves narrow, entire or dentate. Flowers in heads, usually white, sometimes lavender.
Sun & ½ shade. Soil alkaline but tolerant. Semi-hdy. Seed. Cuttings. Division.
Excel. for edging; clip like a hedge or leave loose. Or use for bedding. Bloom spring & for a long season, again after shearing.

I. gibraltarica: Gibralter Candytuft. Gibralter & Morocco. Cespitose. Flowers light purple,

young clusters somewhat flattened.

I. sempervirens: Edging Candytuft. S. Eur. Evgrn. subshrub to 2 × 1 ft., usually less because of the practice of clipping. Much branched. Leaves linear, entire, blunt. Flowers white. Cvs. e.g. 'Compacta', 'Nana', 'Superba': bred for more dwarf habit & finer flowers. 8 × 8 in.

I. s. var. *correifolia:* This form was used for cvs. e.g. 'Little Gem', 'Snowflake'.

Iris: IRIDACEAE.
Widespread.
Variable. Divided into sections, groups & classes. See *Perennial Garden Plants* by Thomas, *Dwarf Bulbs* by Mathew & *Iris for Everyone.* Sev. spp. are mentioned in discussions of mixed planting & in layouts. Find descriptions in books, accounts & catalogs of many spp. not covered here.
Sun & shade. Culture according to spp. Division.
Rhizomes spread to form clumps 1–5 ft. wide. Most spp. good to cut.

Iris, bearded: Best known class. Many cvs. Rhizomous. A "German" *Iris* was one forebear. The classic form is that of the "fleur de lis". Now modified. Colors originally white, yellow & lavender. Now spectacular; see catalogues & many accounts.

Iris, bearded dwarf: Cvs. with *I. chaeiris* & *I. pumila* as parents. Beard plush-like on narrow part.

I. pumila & *I. pumila* 'Alba': Leaves to 5 in. in tufts. Flowers nearly stemless. Various colors; early spring. Cvs. e.g. 'Lemon Flare'.

Iris, bearded, spp. & hybs.:
I. pallida: Leaves variegated. Flowers small, soft lavender.

I. p. var. *dalmatica:* Flowers white.

Iris, Spuria group: Beardless; sev. blooms to a stalk. Recently bred for new cvs. *I. spuria × I. monnieri,* a productive cross. Bronze, blue, purple, violet & blends. For mild climates.

I. spuria: Herb. To 4 ft. Flowers white, yellow, few weeks in spring.

I. monnieri: Herb. Sim. Leaves blue-green & narrow-sword-shaped.

I. kernerana: Uncommon. To 18 in. Many stems to a clump. Flowers soft yellow, unique shape. Strongly recurved falls. June.

Iris, Louisiana: A hyb. complex. Natural & artificial crosses. Main contributors: *I. fulva, I. brevicaulis, I. giganticaerulea:* Offspring: 1 to 5 ft., with firm substance, white, creamy white, yellow, bronze, copper, purples. "Flight of Butterflies" a strain with good colors. 'Cajun', 'Jeunne Fille', 'Joyeuse', examples of cvs.

I. chrysphoenicia & *I. versicolor:* Rich red-purple. (*I. virginica* belongs to another series.)

Iris, Aril: E. Mediterranean, Himalayas & China. Regelias, Pseudoregelias & Onocycluses & hybs. between. Also hybs. between these & bearded iris—Oncobreds & Regelia-breds. All these best in the U.S. Pacific States since they are accustomed to dry summers. Examples:

I. hoogiana: Turkestan. Leaves 1½ in.; stalks 2½ ft. Flowers grey-blue to purple with falls to 3 in. Beards, golden to orange.

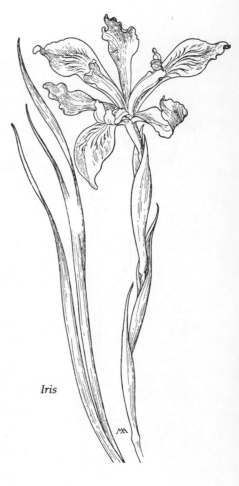

Iris

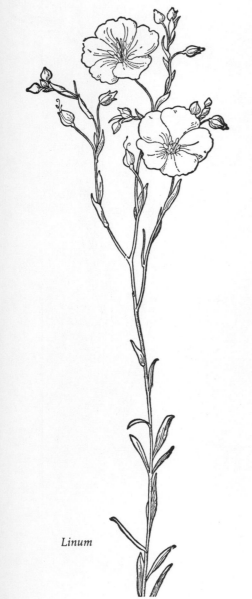

Linum

I. susiana: Mourning Iris. Flowers pale grey, heavily pencilled & dotted with blackish purple; brownish purple beard; nearly black velvety patch. Flowers unusual looking.

I. sibirica: Eur. & N. Asia. A clump of many stems; crowded growth buds make dense sheaves of foliage. (No rhizomes or bulbs.) Leave 6 in. of leaf above ground when cutting back. 'Swank' is one of many cvs.

I. sibirica with *I. sanguinea* produced many hybs. & cvs. To 3 ft., lower also. Wide color range, purple, blue or white, & wide range of form of flower & length of season. (See catalogues of *Iris* specialists.)

Iris, beardless, rhizomeless:

I. ensata: Clumps of growth buds & sheaves of erect leaves. Hybs. of *I. kaempferi*, Manchuria & *I. laevigata*, Japan. Developed in Japan, Eur. & N. Am. Moist soil & some water-plants. Can be grown in containers. Only *Iris* to prefer lime-free soil. Likes humus. (Further coverage in "Bog".)

I. pseudoacoris: Yellow Flag of Europe, N. Afr. & Asia Minor. Naturalized in E. N. Am. Waterside. Leaves broadly sword-shaped to 3 ft. long. Flowers bright yellow. Erect falls 2 in. long & shorter, narrow standards.

I. chrysographes: Another for the stream-side.

I. delavayi: Needs moist soil. (Related to *I. sibirica*.)

I. foetidissima: Gladwin or Gladdon Stinking Iris. Evgrn. Foliage has unpleasant odor when crushed. Grown for seed pods which open to show 3 rows bright orange seeds. Easy. Somewhat unrefined. Flowers dull purple or yellow. (Poisonous to livestock.) Not particular about conditions. 2 cvs. to seek if you like colored foliage: 'Citrina', the foliage with yellow shadings, & 'Variegata', the foliage streaked with cream.

I. unguicularis (I. stylosa): Algerian Iris or "Winter Iris". To 2 ft. in thick tufts, spreading to form a colony, 2 ft. wide. Flowers barely taller, often many; Sept. to April on the W. Coast of N. Am. Flowers with delicate texture & unique fragrance. Pale lavender & the white form somewhat difficult to find. Poor, dry soil, sun & part shade.

Iris, botanical subsection Evansia: Crested Irises. Not hdy.

I. wattii: Assam & W. China. To 3 ft. Leaves thin, ribbed to 2½ in. wide. 40–50 flowers to a clump, April. Color soft lavender spotted with darker lavender. Margins of standards wavy. Crests large, fringed yellow or orange.

I. w. 'Nana': Smaller version of the sp.

I. japonica: Japan. Sim. Leaves to 2 ft. Flowers lilac, crisped falls.

I. tectorum: China. Roofs of Japan. May be grown in a border. To 1½ ft.

I. gracilipes: Japan. Leaves (after bloom) to 1 ft. Flowers only 2 or 3 to stem, pale purple to pinkish lilac. Ruffled texture. Poise on stems-mothlike. Also *I. g.* var. *alba.*

I. cristata: N. Am., acid woodlands & cliffs from Md. to Okla. & Ga. Dwarf. Leaves first 8 in., then 10 in. Flowers just above foliage. Light purple, lilac or pale violet, the crests whitish to yellow with white band edged with line of violet or purple. Also, *I. c.* var. *alba.*

Iris, N. Am. Pac. Coast: Rhizomes. Graceful form. Exquisite etching. Collect.

I. bracteata: Oreg. To 10 in. Leaves few to a tuft, rigid to ¼ in. wide. Look braided at the base. Spathes 2 flowered. Flowers bright yellow with 4 bright purple veins. May.

I. purdyi: Near *I. bracteata.* Sometimes confused with *I. douglasiana* cvs. Flowers of pale straw color with long narrow tube. May & June.

I. tenax: 10 in. leaves, slender, linear with tough fibers. Indians used fibers. Flowers often grey to reddish claret. Falls clawed & reflexed; middle ridge of falls yellow.

I. hartwegii: Related closely to *I. tenax.* But flowers yellow & num.

I. longipetala: To 2 ft. Leaves narrow, firm to 1½ ft. Flowers white, veined violet, falls obovate, clawed. Spreading, drooping, 3½ in. deep by 1½ in. wide. Standards erect to 3 in. Short clawed yellow keel.

I. macrosiphon: Leaves linear to 1 ft. long, finely ribbed. Spathes to 6 in., 1–3 flowers. Flowers lilac or cream. Falls wedged, 2 in. deep, ¼ in. wide.

I. douglasiana: Widespread, Pac. Coast. Hybs., both natural & man-made. Leaves wide-spreading, growing from rose colored rhizomes which branch upon the top of the ground. Flowers on 1 ft. stems. 6 crinkled segments, lilac, & sometimes white or yellow with white, yellow & violet markings. Examples of cvs. with interesting color blends: 'Agnes Irmes', 'Pegasus'.

I. innominata: Mtns. in Calif. & Oreg. Sometimes exhausts itself. Renew. Distinctive habit of growth. Leaves narrow, many, splay out in a circular fan-shape to 1 ft., the mound bright green & shiny. Flower stems angle somewhat but rise above foliage. Bright yellow is the original color. A strain has developed with white, lilac, amethyst, violet. The clear yellow is often marked with tracery & flecks. No other *Iris* can surpass the grace of the poise of the segments.

Iris, bulbous (subgenus *Xiphium*): Spanish, English & Dutch. Many forms & colors. Some bulbous spp. are *I. reticulata, I. histrioides, I. danfordiae, I. plicadee* var. *violacea, I. baldschiana.*

I. sintenisii: S.E. Eur., Asia Minor. Tuffet of narrow leaves 1 × 1 ft. Stem round, 12 in. long, 2 flowered. Flowers violet-purple; tracery on the falls. Falls are veined & dotted on a white ground. Early summer.

Jasione: CAMPANULACEAE. Sheep's-Bit-Scabious or Shepherd's Scabious.

Mediterranean region & Asia Minor.

Herb. Looks like *Globularia.* Leaves simple on lower ½ of stems. Flowers quite num. height of season. Summer.

Sun. Soil sandy. Drainage. Deadhead. Division.

Fronts of borders. Combine with spp. which look alike or with Lavender, Thyme, *Nepeta.*

J. perennis (J. laevis): To 1½ ft. Clump. Somewhat hairy leaves to 4 in. Mounds of

The training of Chrysanthemums as cascades is an art to be practiced by the dedicated. In this photograph they have a proper stage to show both the length to which they hang and the masses of bloom which have been developed. D.D.

Here is an unending wave of Gloriosa Daisy in a space which allows it to grow unheeded and unaccompanied. The heads of this *Rudbeckia* are mostly unequal height making a thick carpet of brilliance. D.D.

A collection of perennials in Vancouver, B.C. Several species, all with yellow flowers, were planted together to produce a sheet of yellow: *Achillea, Coreopsis, Ligularia,* etc. D.D.

Clary Sage. The larger *Salvias* need a wide bed to accommodate the full growth of their flourishing clumps. The soft lavender cloud made by this Sage, *S. sclarea,* is an excellent transition between other shades and colors. T.C.

SOME PERENNIALS IN WIDE SWEEPS

Artemisia pycnocephala is a Sage of the sand dunes of the West Coast. The tips of the branches, with young leaves, are very silky, velvety. E.B.

A western U.S. *Arabis, A. blepharophylla,* blooms in March. The foliage is a maze of tiny tufts. E.B.

The lower growing *Zauschnerias* are more useful in most gardens than those spp. with taller stems. This one has a mass of blooms in September. *Z. arizonica* is a sp. with especially brilliant color. Of course, the Hummingbirds are attracted. E.B.

Eriogonum spreads on a slope to form a low mat. This one should be in front of its taller relatives. The excellent yellow begins to cover the mat in May and continues for several weeks. E.B.

FOR GARDENERS WITH AN INTEREST IN NATIVES

Convolvulus: Is known best for its trailers, one a pernicious weed. This mounding sp. is quite different. The foliage is silky, shiny grey.

Campanula: Many spp. are prostrate and some are spillers. This one is colorful against the grey of the pavement.

Lilium: Several spp. are native to Pacific Coast woodlands. *L. pardalinum* blooms well in captivity.

Mimulus: The genus is variable. Considerable breeding has brought about some fine colors, some muted, some bright as this one.

SOME PARTICULARLY ATTRACTIVE PERENNIALS

Clivia: Here is an unusual species, the flowers more hanging than erect. The light on the edge of the woodland brings out the strong color.

Calochortus: Photographers have been fascinated with the design of the Globe Tulips. Here we look in the throat of one of the Sierra spp.

Erythronium: Blooms well in a light patch in a woodland. The Trout Lilies are hard to tame. Some nurseries stock the bulbs of the more common spp.

Tiarella: This perky small plant is a natural for a glade. Its spikes taper to a pinkish point. It is *T. wherryi.*

Eriogonum: Buckwheats have a wide distribution in the Pacific states. Some of the compact forms are decorative in a sloping garden.

SOME PARTICULARLY ATTRACTIVE PERENNIALS

tiny rosettes. Flowers in rounded heads, 2 in. in diameter on erect stalks; lavender, summer. A fuzzy look.

J. montana: Ann. or bien.

Knautia: DYPSACACEAE.
N. Afr. & Eur., Caucasus, W. Siberia.
Herb. Looks like *Scabiosa.*
Sun. Soil loose, fert. Cut back. Cuttings.

K. macedonica (Scabiosa rumelica): To 2½ ft. Stems slender, branching, curving. Corolla 4–5 lobed; bristles. "Dark purple" but more accurately deep wine red.

Kniphofia (Tritoma): LILIACEAE. Poker Plant, Red Hot Poker, Torch Lily.
Mostly E. & S. Afr.
Herb. Leaves narrow, blade-shaped. Clumps to 2 ft. wide, wider if not divided every 3 years. Division needed for health. Many hybs., the tall cvs. 4 ft., the dwarves 3 ft. or less.
Sun. Somewhat tender but tough. Ordinary cult. Division.
Useful for erect spikes, sev. to a plant. Good poker-shape, less than 3 in. across at the bottom & tapering to a point. Summer & fall.

K. uvaria, K. u. var. *maxima, K. u.* var. *nobilis,* & *K. praecox:* 4–6 ft. Leaves tough. Flowers in cylindrical spikes. Flower color changes from scarlet to greenish suffused with red to orange-yellow & greenish yellow.

K. triangularis: Usually less than 2½ ft. Leaves more grass-like. Flowers flame color Sept. & Oct. One parent of dwarf hybs. At least 3 clones: *K. galpinii,* bright reddish orange well into autumn; *K. macowanii* & *K. nelsonii,* all sim. Flower lobes are splayed except in *K. galpinii.*

K. hybs.: 2–3 ft. Breeding produced pastels. Pure white to delicate shades of yellow & pink as well as rosy reds. Cv. e.g. 'Vanilla', one of pale pastels. Useful cut flowers if stems selected when young.

Lavandula: See Subshrubs Plant Descriptions.
Many uses: Strips, beds, borders, containers.

Linaria: SCROPHULARIACEA. Toadflax or Butter & Eggs.
N. hemis., mostly Mediterranean.
Herb. Per., ann. & subshrub. Leaves narrow, small, mostly on thin stems. Flower with a lip. Some invasive.
Sun. Soil lean. Ordinary cult. Seed.
Find, in fields, the true Butter and Eggs.

L. dalmatica & *L. genistifolia:* To 3 ft. Leaves small, blue-grey. Flowers yellow. June onward. Snapdragon-shaped. Poor, gravelly soil.

L. purpurea 'Canon Went': Pink variant of lavender sp. Leaves bluish green. To 3 ft., it is reported, but less in gardens since it is pruned & picked. Dainty spikes, light pink. Seedlings.

L. triornothophyros: Three-Birds-Flying. Portugal. Erect to 4 ft. Herb. Leaves glaucus, glabrous small on thin branching stems. Flowers pale lavender, striped with dark lavender or lavender-purple with crimson dot. Different.

L. supina: Toadflax. Eur. Sparingly naturalized in E. U.S. A clumping herb. Num. stems nearly erect or decumbent. To 9 in. Small flowers along 6 in. of the top of the stems. Flowers in May & June. Muted colors— pale yellow with cream & lavender with cream.

L. spuria: Round-leafed Toadflax To 4 in. Oldtimer.

Lindelofia: BORAGINACEA.
Temp. Asia, Himalayas.
Herb. Uncommon. Less coarse than *Anchusa.* 18 × 18 in.
Sun. Ordinary cult. Seed.
Bloom late summer & early fall.

L. longiflora (L. spectabilis): To 2 ft. Leaves long, narrow, hairy throughout. Flower stems leafy with side shoots. Flowers from gentian-blue to lavender to purple; racemes curve like those of *Anchusa,* Hound's Tongue. Stamens which protrude from throat. May.

Linum: LINACEAE. Flax.
Widespread, mostly temp.
Herb. & semi-evgrn. One sp. a weed, others choice. Leaves needle-like in common spp.
Sun. Soil med. Ordinary cult. Division.
Only a few hardy: examples follow.

L. perenne: To 2 ft., whispy-looking. Leaves bluish green. Flowers light lavender or white in *L. p.* var. *album.* Seeds so readily, may become a nuisance.

L. narbonense & *L. n.* var. *album:* To 2 ft. but stouter, stronger. Flowers bluer, white-eyed. Superior.

L. flavum: To 2 ft. Stems somewhat woody at base. Leaves green, broader than those of *L. perenne.* Basal leaves in small rosettes, spoon-shaped. Flowers golden yellow, to 1 ft., num. Seek *L. f.* var. *compactum.*

L. aretioides: Mtns. of Eur. To 2 in. Leaves tiny, forming a tight cushion of branched woody stems. Flowers golden.

Lobelia: CAMPANULACEAE. Cardinal Flower, Indian Pink or Indian Tobacco.
N. Am., Eur., E. Afr.
Herb. Ann. & per.
Sun & shade. Ordinary cult. Semi-hdy. Seed or division. Used by Indians medicinally.

L. cardinalis, from N. Am.; *L. fulgens,* from Mex.; *L. tupa,* from Chile: 3 ft. to 5 ft. & decreasing in hardiness. Red, summer blooming, 2-lipped flowers in a tall spike. Need deep, rich, moist soils. Stake only when young.

L. × milleri (× vedrariensis): Hybs. with *L. splendens, L. cardinalis, L. siphilitica:* Some very good reds.

L. siphilitica: E. U.S. To 3 ft., reputedly. In dry West Coast gardens only 2 ft. Seek 'Blue Peter', a cv. from Alan Bloom. A clumping herb. per., several one-sided spikes to a plant, flowers bluish lavender. Interspersed with narrow bracts. Set closely against a leafy stem, slender & erect. Although from wet soils, this sp. is tolerant of the average soil of the average garden. Divide every 3 yrs. Good for cutting. Good with all border perennials esp. *Campanula, Salvia.*

L. erinus: S. Afr. Ann. or herb. The small mounding border plant which comes in

Lobelia

Lupinus

Lychnis

Mentha

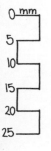

sev. shades of blue. Reseeds. Sev. fine cvs.

Lopezia: ONAGRACEAE. Mosquito Plant or Mosquito Flower.

Mex. & Cent. Am.

Herb. Dainty. G.c. Bloom spring & summer.

Sun or shade. Ordinary cult. Tender. Seed.

Leave damaged tops on for protection until danger of frost is over.

L. hirsuta: Somewhat sprawling subshrub to 3 ft. Flowers deep pink, coral or salmon with purplish red sepals. Odd shape. Bloom summer.

Lupinus: LEGUMINOSAE. Lupine.

N. Am., S. Am., Eur. & Afr.

Subshrubs. Anns. Mostly with a taproot. Inchworms may infest.

Sun. Soil with no lime, compost or manure. Need nitrogen; buy organic nitrogen or grow with legumes. Drainage. Seed.

Bloom summer. Spire-shaped; good design value. Grow woody spp. in a large space. See The Site for a Large Perennial Plant Descriptions for other spp.

L. polyphyllus: N. Am.: moist soils, Calif., U.S. to Brit. Col., Can. Leaves 9–16 pointed leaflets to 6 in. long. Flowers in crowded erect racemes to 2 ft. Purple standard petal, blue wing petals & a dark-tipped spur.

Hybrids: *L. arboreus, L. polyphyllus* with some anns. to produce cvs. The cvs. are often compact, more dwarf, leafy & good for pots. Examples: 'Little Lulu', 'Minarette'.

L. regalis: Hybs. with *L. polyphyllus* & other spp. Includes "Russell Lupines". Colors—pure white, pinks, rich reds, lavender, purple, creamy white & yellow. Many are 2-toned with peach, apricot, bronze; all blend. Hybs. less long-lived than the spp. If grown from seed, select strongest plants & grow from basal cuttings of spring growth.

L. excubitus var. *hallii* forma *alba:* To 5 in. Uncommon. White flowers. No summer water.

Lychnis: CARYOPHYLLACEAE. Rose-of-Heaven, Mullein-Pink, Flower-of-Jove, Cuckoo Flower, Maltese Cross, German Catchfly, Campion.

Temp. parts of N. hemis.

Herb. Closely related to *Agrostemma* & *Silene*. Clumps to 1½ ft. or more wide. Stems often weak. Unsophisticated. Use with old-fashioned perennials.

Sun. Warm, sheltered position. Ordinary cult. Drainage. Seed.

One sp., *L. coronaria,* with grey foliage to cut. Flowers of some value. Summer. Plant *Lychnis* with perennials having lavender or blue flowers, as *Aster, Anchusa.*

L. chalcedonica: Maltese Cross or Scarlet Lightning. E. Russia. Naturalized in E. N. Am. Good as a bog plant. To 3 ft. Leaves somewhat hairy. Flowers in terminal heads of 10–50 with notched petals; brilliant scarlet (also pink, white & dble.). Shape of individual flowers cross-like.

L. haageana = *L. fulgens* × *L. coronaria. L. haageana* crossed with *L. chalcedonica* resulted in hybs. called *L. × arkwrightii,* having flowers with an orange tone. Summer. *L.* 'Vesuvius' has the best reputa-

tion. The hybs. have some individuality & qualities such as longer life & sturdiness. To 12 in.

L. viscaria 'Splendens Plena'; To 10 in. Flowers dble. cerise-pink, carnation-like.

L. coronaria (Agrostemma): One of many plants called Dusty Miller. Spreads widely & vigorously. Leaves grey. Mat to 8 in. high. Flowers many, small on twiggy growth, cerise-red. Not an elegant plant. Tolerates dry & poor soil. Looks well only the first year.

L. flos-jovis: To 18 in. Leaves grey, woolly in dense tufts. Flowers reddish purple.

Macleaya: (*Bocconia*) PAPAVERACEAE. Plume Poppy or Tree-Celandine.

Japan & China.

Herb. Tall almost shrublike growth. Erect to 7 ft. × 2 ft. wide. Leaf structure excel. & with 2 colors; most decorative with rounded, large lobes. Back lighting for best display. Excel. for tall, upright form with *Spiraea, Anemone, Abutilon,* shrubs & ferns. Bloom summer.

Part shade or sun in cool climates. Soil loose, friable. No staking required. Cut back. Division.

Contains yellow sap. Picks well. Foliage unique—angled outline. From crown up the stem, becoming smaller. New stems emerge some distance from center root. Whole plant should be in view.

M. cordata: To 7 ft. Stems strong, from root, rather compact. Leaves heart-shaped in outline with edges indented; the undersides bronzy green & covered with short white hairs; leaves to 1 ft. long but decreasing in size from bottom to top. Flowers small in erect sprays, a delicate yellow or cream color. Stamens conspicuous 24 to 30.

M. microcarpa: Coral Plume. Sim. to *M. cordata.* Not over 12 stamens. Fleshy roots which travel underground in light soil making a colony. Num. leafy stems. Flowers in branching plumes, summer. Buff or flesh tinted, soft in texture as well as color. 'Coral Plume', raised in England by Kelways, early in the century. Colors deep coppery buff.

Melissa: LABIATAE. Balm, Lemon Balm, Common Balm, Bee Balm.

Eur., Brit.

Herb. Less rampant than the mints.

Sun. Soil poor, dryish. Division.

Cut back to the ground.

M. officinalis: To 2 ft. Seeds itself freely but easier to control than the mints. Lemon-scented, grown as a sweet herb for the kitchen garden. Used for medicine as well as seasoning.

Mentha: LABIATAE. Water Mint, Field Mint, Scotch Mint, Peppermint, Spearmint, Apple Mint, Orange Mint.

Some spp., sweet herbs of value. All with vigorous underground runners, never to be eradicated. One a dwarf for carpets.

Sun or shade. Soil fair, more moist than dry.

M. pulegium: Pennyroyal. (pulegium = fleabane) Leaves small, tight on creeping stems spreading widely & seeding. Flowers lavender on erect 1 ft. stems in summer. Cut with hedge shears & hang to dry. Flat carpet appearance reestablished. Invasive g.c. Fragrant to walk upon. (*Hedeoma pulegioides:* American Pennyroyal)

M. requienii: Corsican Mint. A miniature creeper forming a flat mat to ½ in. Flowers lavender, in summer but microscopic. Good along the top of a wall, in order to rub foliage & receive fragrance from fingers. Also stepping stones. Sometimes mistaken for the pest "Baby Tears"; it is tinier. Moisture, good soil, shade.

Mimulus: SCROPHULARIACEAE. Musk or Monkey Flower.

N. Am., Rocky Mtns. to Pacific Coast & from Newfoundland to Va.

Semi-evgrn. Shrub & g.c. Leaves various, some very green, shiny, some rough or downy.

Mostly sun or shade. Soil mostly moist. Control. Division. Pleasant musklike odor has disappeared in latter years of 20th century. Some unusual hybs.

M. moschatus: Musk. Creeping slimy rooting stems to 1 ft. Leaves to 1½ in. Flowers funnel-shaped, yellow dotted brown.

M. luteus: Chile, moist soils. Stems rooting, creeping to 1 ft. Leaves to 2 in., sharply toothed. Flowers long stalked, few in loose racemes, yellow, spotted red & purplish, with gaping throats. Sev. variations with distinctive colorations.

M. guttatus: Wet soils Alaska, U.S. to Mex. Hardier than some. Herb. Sim. to *M. luteus* but throats almost closed by 2 hairy ridges. Flowers num., yellow with red-brown or purplish spots. These 2 spp. have been crossed.

M. aurantiacus: Pale orange to bright orange-red. Woody with downy & sticky leaves.

M. hybridus: Showy, large flowered vari-colored garden hybs. Sev. spp. have contributed to these fine hybs.

M. bartonianus = *M. cardinalis* (scarlet) × *M. lewisii* (rose-red, pink or white): Needs dry situation & sun. Excel. cross with range of tones.

Narcissus: AMARYLLIDACEAE.

W. & E. Mediterranean, China, Japan, N. Eur.

Bulb. See *A Handbook of Narcissus*, E. A. Bowles, & *Key to the Identification of Native and Naturalized Taxa of the Genus Narcissus*, A. Fernandez. Many spp. & thousands of cvs. Fragrance potent.

Little water in the vase. Use strap-shaped foliage from another per. in arrangements leaving *Narcissus* leaves to feed bulbs. New introductions every year to suit changing popularity.

Use the dwarf & small spp. to naturalize or to combine with herb. per. in mixed plantings. 8 × 8 in. clumps.

Neomarica (Marica): IRIDACEAE. Apostles Plant, Twelve Apostles, Fan-Iris, House-Iris, Walking-Iris, Toad-Cup Lily, False Flag.

Trop. & subtrop. S. Am., West Indies & W. trop. Afr.

Herb. *Iris*-like with short rhizomes. Long season. Begins May & June. Handsome intricate structure & color.

Sun. Well-drained rich soil. From Nov. to Feb. it is advantageous to reduce water but not so much that rhizomes might shrivel. When planted in a garden with winter rainfall, best to lift during season of rain. Grow in a greenhouse in cool climates. Division of rhizomes, sand with bottom heat.

Structure unusual & decorative. Use in a container for cultural reasons & for display.

N. caerulea: Guinea & Brazil. To 5 ft. Leaves sword-shaped, 1½ ft. wide to 6 ft. long, slender, pointed. Flower stalk also wide & with bract-like leaves. Flowers bright blue; claws yellowish marked at bases with brown & orange crossbars.

N. gracilis: Mex. to Brazil. Leaves to 2½ ft. × 3 in. with distinct midrib. Flowers white or blue, 2 in. across. The flower stalk is conspicuously winged in its upper part (hence the common name). Flowers short-lived but succeed each other. Not hdy.; may be grown on windowsills in cold climates.

N. northiana & *N. longifolia:* Both with flowers reminiscent of *Tigridia*. The 1st: to 3 ft. with leaves to 2 ft. Flowers fragrant, 4 in. across; white outer petals mottled with yellow & purple at bases & sky blue inner petals, marked low down. The 2nd: from Brazil, to 2 ft. Flowers yellow crossbarred with brown.

Nepeta: LABIATAE. Catmint.

Eur., Asia, N. Afr. & mtns. of trop. Afr.

Herb. Aromatic. Attractive to bees. Sprawling.

Sun. Soil not too rich, not too moist. Ordinary cult. Cut back at least twice a year. Not fully hardy. Hdy. N.Y. Cuttings or division.

Edging or g.c. Sheets of lavender, 2 seasons.

N. faassenii (Sometimes shown with an "x" since it is a hyb. Confused with *Nepeta mussinii;* true *N. mussinii* more lax.): Feathery, fringing, the stems leaning rather than prostrate. Leaves small, bluish grey-green. Haircut after first full outburst induces second crop. Second pruning in fall. Flowers soft lavender, June–Sept. Stems overlap to form a fluffy mat to 1 ft. Good top of a wall.

N. 'Six Hills': To 2 ft. Also 'Blue Beauty', 'Souvenir d'Andre Chaudron', cvs. with large flowers. (*N. nepetalla* 'Blue Dwarf' may be a parent.)

N. cataria: Catnip. Less ornamental. More aromatic. Grown for cats.

Nicotiana: SOLANACEAE. Flowering Tobacco.

N. Am. & S. Am., Aust. & Polynesia.

Herb. Small leaves, often clammy or sticky. Fragrant.

Sun & part shade. Soil med. Seed.

N. alata: Tender per., cultivated as an ann. Cvs. with various colors: white, chartreuse, wine red, etc.

Oenothera: ONAGRACEAE. Evening-Prim-rose, Sundrop, Golden Eggs.

N. & S. Am.

Herb. & evgrn. Some weedy as *O. ovata*. Some spp. wait until evening to open their flowers & close next a.m. Some spp. with colorful foliage; leaves shiny, num.

Sun. Soil med. Good drainage. Division. Most

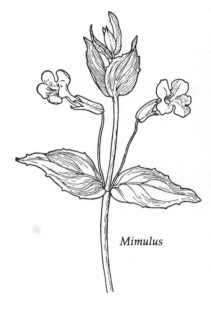

Mimulus

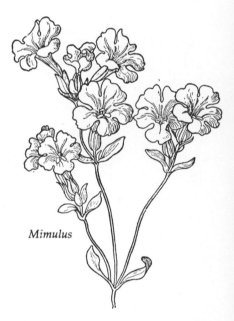

Mimulus

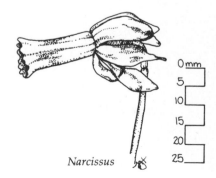

Narcissus

Neomarica

Paeonia

Paeonia

spp. hdy. A few will not survive in too much cold, e.g. *O. aucalis*, *O. caespitosa*. Treat these as annuals.

O. californica: Desert places, U.S. Calif. & Baja. Running underground rhizomes. Leaves mostly spatula-shaped & coarsely-toothed. Flowers over 2 in. across, white turning pink as they age. Like *O. caespitosa*.

O. tetragona (*O. fruticosa* of gardens) *O. youngii* & *O. t.* var. *fraseri* & *O. t.* 'Highlight': To 3 ft., usually shorter. Flowers to 2½ in. wide, the cv. free flowering. Bright yellow, reddish buds & tinted spring foliage. Many garden seedlings named. Look for 'Yellow River' & 'Lady Brookborough'. *O. glaber* (of gardens) related. Foliage with mahogony tints.

O. speciosa: Usually per. To 2 ft. Flowers white fading pinkish, to 3 in. across, blooming in upper axils. Spreads on underground runners: invasive.

O. cheiranthifolia, *O. deltoides* var. *howellii*, *O. hookeri*, *O. pallida*, *O. decorticans*—Oenotheras with merit.

Paeonia: PAEONIACEAE. Peony.
Asia, Eur., N. Am.
Two groups: herb., 2 ft. wide, & shrubby, 2 ft. wide. Many excel. hybs. & cvs. Foliage lobed—lovely tints in new, mature & old. Bloom spring. Noted for full, round flower heads.
Sun. Soil moist & fert. Keep crowns clear. Propagate with pieces of root with "eyes".
Patience required for full maturity. Join American Peony Society. Only a few of many spp. to be described.

P. daurica: To 1½ ft. Leaves lobed. Leaflets broadly ovate with undulate margins. Flowers yellow; April, May.

P. mlokosewitschii: Mollie-the-Witch, easy way to say sp. name. (May be a variant of *P. daurica*.) Caucasus. To 2 ft. Leaves dark bluish green with paler, shorthairy undersides. 3 divisions each of 3 leaflets. Flowers yellow to 5 in. across, 8 petals, numerous stamens, a purple stigma & 3 hairy carpels. Flowers April.

P. × *smouthii*: *P. lactiflora* × *P. tenuifolia*. Hyb. has best qualities of 2 parents. Leaves finely dissected. Stems 2 to 4 flowered. Single crimson. Fragrant.

P. obovata: Japan, China, Manchuria. To 2 ft. Rare. Pink & rose. A form has pale flowers really yellow although described as white.

P. wittmanniana: Caucasus. To 3 ft. Leaflets pointed. Pale yellow flowers. April.

P. w. var. *nudicarpa*: More usually seen than sp. Both this & the sp. hard to find.

P. californica: N. Am.; dry slopes, Calif. to Wyo., Nev. & Brit. Col. To 2 ft. Leaves medium green; 3 primary divisions. Petals blackish red, pink margined.

P. brownii: Somewhat fleshy leaves with 3 divisions of each of 3 leaflets. To 1½ ft. Petals brownish red with yellowish or greenish margins.

Herbaceous hybrids: Many variations in foliage & flower from extensive breeding over the years. In the catalogues, sev. divisions are given names as "Chinese Type", "Japanese Type", "Estate Peonies". These are groupings made according to dominant characteristics. (The photographs in the catalogues are excel.) A few examples are here briefly described.

Chinese: Mostly from *P. lactiflora*: Huge white single silky flowers. Reddish brown foliage & stems. Num. yellow stamens. Early summer. Often called "Garden hybrids".

Japanese: Singles. E.g. 'Krinkled White' with very wavy edges; 'Karen Grey', Camellia-like in form, 'Pink Dawn', irregular form, coral pink, lightly speckled.

Estate: Multipled petals. Petaloids emphasized in hybridization. E.g. 'Bowl of Cream', pale & soft colored; 'Top Brass', yellow with shading, mostly petaloids. The petals look like a narrow collar. Innumerable variations. Hard to surpass as cut flowers. Some of them with stems 3 ft. tall for early, med. & late seasons. New introductions every year. Meanwhile, the bushy mound of foliage is handsome in the garden for many mos.—a landscape plant without comparison.

Edwardian: The "Saunders hybrids": a strain of many crosses producing many cvs. The collection now carried on by Dr. David Reath of Vulcan, Michigan.

Tree Peonies: A completely different plant horticulturally—a shrubby base, the trunk & main branches woody. It is pruned like a shrub. The leaves are divided & handsome & clothe the annual stems in a graceful manner. Whenever the top becomes heavy with foliage & flowers the "tree" may need support. Foliage varies in shape & texture, flower form & color is almost as important; choose your horticultural variety when fully mature whenever possible. Bloom mainly early summer. 4–6 ft. × 2–3 ft. Sev. spp. contributed to the hybrid lines. The 2 main spp. are *P. suffruticosa* & *P. lutea*. *P. lemoinei* is the name for hybs. between the 2.

P. suffruticosa: To 6 ft. Leaves twice-pinnate with lobed leaflets, hairy on undersides. Flowers to 6 in. wide, with 8 or more concave petals, rose-pink to white.

P. lutea: To 4½ ft. Hairless. Flowers yellow, sometimes with purple at the base.

Brief descriptions of a few cvs.:

'Black Pirate': Decorative leaf. Flowers of a color called "crimson-mahogany". The flare is nearly black & the center is velvety black. The full cluster of staminodes is golden.

'Tria': Lacy foliage. Sometimes 3 flowers to a stem yellow, open faced. Petals crinkled & curly. Staminodes crisp & twisted. Probably first of the Tree Peonies to start blooming & continues for a long period.

'Harvest': A fluffy dble. with amber tints in the yellow. The petals have a picotee edge.

'High Noon': Semi-dble. Four rows of petals, the inner row curled like a cup around the gorgeous staminodes. The lemon yellow color is highlighted by a flare of crimson. Lemon fragrance. 4–5 ft. in 6–8 years. May rebloom in Sept. or Oct. (Called a *P. lutea* hyb.)

Papaver: PAPAVERACEAE. Poppy.
N. Am., S. Afr. & Aust.
Herb. Leaves pinnately lobed or divided or

toothed. Flowers nodding in bud, upfacing when open, usually 6 petals & num. slender stamens. Bloom mainly early summer.

Sun or ½ shade. Ordinary cult. Deadhead. Semi-tender according to area of origin. The spp. to be described are hdy. to Seattle, Wash., U.S. Seed. Division.

The poppy form & the poppy papery petal texture should be sought in other genera besides *Papaver*.

P. somniferum: Opium Poppy. An ann. Illegal in U.S.

P. rhoeas: Field Poppy or Corn Poppy. Ann. The poppy of Flanders fields. Small & delicate crimson flowers on 8–12 in. Broadcast & hope for at least a few.

P. nudicaule: Iceland Poppy. From Asia Minor. To 2 ft. tall. Per. but often grown as ann. Sev. related spp. Horticultural variations such as 'Amurense', 'Delicatum', 'Croceum', 'Rubro-aurantiacum' with many shades of white, yellow, orange, pink & dble. Flowers to 2 in. wide, texture crinkled. Fragrant. "Champagne Bubbles" is a popular strain.

P. alpinum: Collective name for a group from sev. spp. Looks like a miniature Iceland Poppy. To 1 ft. Flowers to 1½ in. across.

P. rhaeticum: One of the sp. contributing to *P. alpinum*. Less tough.

P. orientale: Armenia. To 4 × 3 ft. Hairy, lobed leaves in full basal clumps; in some cvs. on the stems as well. Foliage dies away in July. If plants are cut back directly after flowering, a good crop of new leaves may develop. It is best, however, to plan for annuals to fill the gap (or *Gypsophila paniculata*). Roots impossible to remove totally if you want the space for another per.; plants will grow from any small piece, even with only one eye left in the ground. Increase with sections of healthy roots, best with 3 eyes.

Many clones of many colors. Breeding over the centuries has created a "race", a group with at least somewhat divergent characteristics between its members & many given cv. names. All have a feature of the type sp.—a maroon blotch at the base in the center of which the maroon stamens & velvety knob of the seed capsule is prominent. *A. bracteatum* has been used in the hybridizing & some offspring have a characteristic of leafy flower stems derived from this parent. An example of this type is 'Goliath' which has a striking red flower.

It is only possible to name a few of the many cvs. Other reds are 'Marcus Perry', a tall red & 'Indian Chief', a maroon-red. There is a brilliant red cv. esp. desirable because it is more dwarf than the general run of cvs.— 'Peter Pan'.

White is represented by a well-known cv. 'Perry's White' but its white is not bright white. 'Barr's White' is whiter. 'White Queen' has pink spots, stems to 2 ft. The texture is satiny.

The original color was vermillion. There are still orange cvs. of value. One, fully dble., is called 'May Queen'. 'May Sadler' has a profusion of flowers & bold foliage.

Pink has probably been given the most atten-

tion by the breeders. 'Mrs. Perry' (1906) was an early success, a clear pink. Now there are cherry-pinks & salmon-pinks, the second the most popular. One named 'Salmon Pink' is dble. & would probably be chosen unless you prefer the singles in order to keep the typical fantastic center. 'Pale Face' to 3 ft., opens out flat. 'Helen Elizabeth' has an excel. shade of pink, with dark spots. There are also semi-dbles. with petaloids around the center sometimes partially hiding it.

Selection will be mostly by form & color of flower since all will have sim. habit of growth (except for the few somewhat dwarf). Here is just one more name in case your appetite has not been sufficiently whetted—the name indicates the character—'Crimson Pompom'. Oriental Poppies are handsome in flower arrangements. Pick in bud; dip stem ends in hot water; soak in cold water for 12 hours.

Sev. spp. from the Mediterranean region are closely related. 18 × 18 in. Leafy bases & rising, branching stems. The top flowers open first. Early summer.

Other species

P. atlanticum: Morocco. Basal leaves densely hairy. Leaves coarsely round-toothed, oblong, the largest to 10 in. To 2 ft. Stems branch from the crown. Flowering stalks to 1½ ft. carry flowers 1½ in. Soft orange to brick red. Some call it tangerine. Silky texture. Seed capsules wrinkled. Plants make a colony. Sow seed in peat-pots. Keep some stock in reserve for loss or damage. Will take part shade.

P. pilosum: From one mtn. in Turkey, UluDag. More leafy than most of the Mediterranean spp. Flowers in racemes. Orange with white stamens. About 3 in. across.

P. rupifragum: Spain. Very sim. to *P. atlanticum* but less hairy esp. in the case of the flower buds which have no hairs.

P. lateritium: Turkey & Caucasus. Very like *P. rupifragum*. Seed capsules bluish black. Hairy. Excel. basal leaves. Nearly leafless stems. Flower large tangerine-orange.

Paradisea: LILIACEAE. St. Bruno's Lily. S. Eur.

Herb. Closely allied to *Anthericum*. Larger & more lily-like than *Anthericum*. Slender, delicate plant, however. Short underground rhizome & fleshy, clustered roots. Flowers funnel-shaped like small white lilies in loose spikes; up to 20 flowers in a spike. Flowers 2 in., white with delicate green spot at tip of each segment. Early summer.

Part shade. Soil moist & fertile. Cut to ground.

Seed difficult to find. Use 'Magnificum' in a bed or border with plants of open growth in order not to smother the fragile form, as *Patrinia* or *Pasithea*.

P. liliastrum: Closely allied to *Anthericum liliago*, St. Bernard's Lily. 2 × 1 ft. Leaves linear, channeled. Leafless, green almost erect flowering stalk to 2 ft. Few to sev. flowered racemes. Flowers fragrant, funnel-shaped to 2 in. long. Corolla of 6 petals with 6

Papaver

Papaver

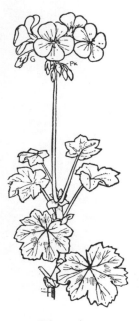

Pelargonium

stamens. *P. l.* var. *major:* Taller & bigger. Easy from seed. Needs light but can be planted near shrubs or trees if no greedy roots.

Pelargonium: GERANIACEAE. Geranium. S. Afr. mostly.

There are three large groups, the main spp.: *P. hortorum*, Zonals, *P. peltatum*, Ivies, & *P. domesticum*, Pelargoniums. *P.* hybs.: Many. Low shrubs. Spp. valuable as foliage plants. There is a 5 volume work called *Geraniaceae* (an exhaustive study of *Pelargonium*). In most treatises the information about cvs. is often of only local importance & soon outdated.

Zonals: *P. hortorum:* Zonal, Bedding, Fish or Horseshoe geraniums, best known simply as Geraniums. Complex hybs., main parents *P. zonale* & *P. inquinans*, undertaken in late 18th century & since augmented with other spp. From giant subshrubs, to miniatures. Semi-tender. Normal size to 3 ft., or 1 ft. in a pot & pruned. Leaves circular to kidney-shaped, slightly scalloped & round toothed. Usually a darker zone inside the margin (hence "zonal"). Flowers mostly in rounded umbels. Many colors & shades. Hundreds of cvs.

Zonals are divided into groups of individuals having common characteristics. This division will be followed here & only one or two examples will be given in each group. The gardener will choose, in any case, by the plant seen & liked rather than by cultivar name, & one which has single, semi-dble. or dble. flowers according to preference. The main criterion will be vigor & health of plant. This outline may act as a guide.

1. With plain green leaves: 'Fiat', salmon, semi-dble.; 'Olympic Red', clear red.
2. Variegated zonals:
a. Tricolor. 'Happy Thought', 'Skies of Italy'.
b. White or cream margined. 'Mme Salleron', no bloom. Good delineation. 'Wm. Langsluth', low habit. Flowers dble. vermillion. 'Hills of Snow', a very white look to foliage.
c. Yellowish. 'Cloth of Gold'.
d. Bronze. 'Distinction', a narrow ring of brownish black around each leaf.
e. Miniature. 'Sprite', margined with white.
f. Carnation flowered. Petals toothed. 'Fiat', salmon, semi-dble. with plain green leaves (see above).
g. Rosebud geranium. 'Apple Blossom' 'Rosebud', name implies color.

In developing new cvs. breeders give attention to compactness & texture. Cvs. are often put on the market as a series. Here is an example: 'Hollywood Series', 'Hollywood Star', 'Hollywood Red', 'Hollywood Salmon'. These are compact, early flowering dbles. Scatter proof. Leaves well zoned or heavily zoned.

Zonals may be grown as temporary indoor plants. They require light to bloom. They may be trained as espaliers or standards. None of the three spp. like humid or stagnant air. Zonals are more susceptible to attack by worms than others. Worms eat holes in leaves & also devour flower buds.

Ivy-leaved Geraniums: P. peltatum: Ivy-leaved Pelargonium or Geranium. Stems weak, trailing, to 2 ft. Leaves with 5 angles (look like ivy leaves), attached to their stalks well in from the margin. The blade toothless, hair-fringed. Flowers asymmetrical, the 2 upper petals with blotches & stripes darker than base color; white, pink, wine-red, purple-violet, crimson. Dble. as well as single. Variegated cvs. with white or cream markings. Many modern cvs. very vigorous. E.g.: *P. p.* 'L'Elegante': Useful for hanging "baskets", top of walls, bloom most of the year. *P. p.* 'Apricot Queen', dble., 'Sybil Holmes', dble. silvery pink. There are hybs. with Zonals. There are cvs. with elongated stems & candy-striped flowers. All very useful in situations where they may hang or climb.

Regal or Show Geraniums: P. domesticum: Lady Washington or Martha Washington Pelargonium or Geranium. This sp. often is called by its genus name, *Pelargonium.* A hyb. complex with a number of S. African spp. involved. Woody stem & stiffly branched to 3 ft. Prune as a shrub. Blooming season only a few weeks in spring but extra crops obtainable. Leaves with kidney-shaped bases, crinkled, & edged with pointed teeth. Green, without the darker zone of the zonals. Flowers to 2½ in. in full clusters, various pinks to wine-red, salmon & peach, often 2-toned & crimson & pure white; the 2 broader upper petals usually blotched toward their bases. Best in pots. Many cvs. One example, 'Mary Bard'. Flowers assembled in clusters. Have been compared to *Azalea, Petunia* & Pansies. Petals are somewhat crimped & usually have a blotch of another color. American breeders have produced many named varieties. The names are somewhat fleeting as popularity comes & goes. E.g.: 'Cover Girl', 2 shades of pink, deeper shade in upper petals & white throat. 'Senorita', salmon-red with paler ruffled margins. 'Black Knight', very dark wine-red.

P. domesticum must be pruned like a shrub & fertilized in early March. Soil should be not rich in nitrogen but rich in potash & superphosphate. Wood ashes & bonemeal are sources. Cut back. Keep old plant but make cuttings of green healthy tips. Transplant into porous soil but not sandy to renew. Pick away old soil from roots. Plant into a container which is no larger than necessary to hold roots comfortably. Pack soil firmly. For full & compact growth, 2 pinchings are better than one. Pinch out a terminal bud just beyond a leaf in front of developing flower bud.

Scented-leaved Pelargoniums (Scented Geraniums): More highly scented if grown in poor soil. Trim to make compact, bushy form. 1 × 1 ft. to 3 × 9 ft.

P. odoratissimum: Apple Scented Geranium (or Cinnamon Scented). Short main stem to 1½ ft. Bushlet 10 × 10 in. if kept trimmed.

Leaves small, rounded, light green & numerous; hairy, kidney-shaped, toothed, frilly looking. Flowers small, whitish, few in umbels.

P. *fragrans:* Apple Geranium. Shrubby, much-branched. Leaves to 1 in. Heart-shaped, blunt toothed. Flowers white, upper petals red-veined.

P. 'Ninon': Apricot Scented (or Nutmeg). Leaves triangular, with 3 lobes, rough-hairy. Flowers small, num., white to pink (& red). Purple veins & carmine spot on upper petals.

P. *crispum:* Lemon Geranium or Finger-bowl Geranium. (P. *limoneum,* a hyb., & P. *citrosum,* a hyb., also lemon-scented) Stiff upright growth to 3 ft. Leaves usually in 2 ranks, rounded to 1 in.; bluntly toothed, crisped, or crest-like. Flowers to 1 in., pink with darker markings. Flowers often absent. P. *c.* var. *minor:* With smaller leaves.

P. *crispum & variegated varieties & cvs.:* P. *c.* var. *variegatum:* Leaves blotched with yellow, rounded bush if trimmed. Or 'Variegatum'. P. *c.* 'Prince of Orange' or 'Orange': Leaves to 2 in., less crisped than the sp. P. *c.* 'Lady Mary': Flowers deep pink. P. *c.* 'Prince Rupert': Variegated. Stiff, erect stems. Leaves larger, shorter stalked than sp. Crinkled. Light green edged with yellowish ivory border. Good.

P. *nervosum,* a hyb., & cv. 'Village Hill Oak': Perhaps a derivative of P. *crispum.* Leaves toothed, ovate, softly-hairy. Lime-scented. Small, rounded, slightly 3-lobed, sharply toothed, slightly ruffled edges. Flowers in umbels, lavender-pink, 2 broader upper petals marked with dark veinings at bases. Quite showy.

P. *graveolens:* True Rose, Rose Geranium. Varieties & hybs. Leaves greyish, cleft ½ way, the 3 lobes again lobed, toothed. Variegated cvs.: 'Lady Plymouth', lobes blotched with cream; 'Grey Lady Plymouth', leaves edged with white (popular). Variegated forms smaller & slower.

P. *capitatum:* Pine Scented (or Minty-Rose Scented). Leaves many, toothed & lobed with straggling white hairs.

P. *denticulatum:* Compact plant. Thick bushlet, tree-like to 3 ft. with slender branches. Leaves rounded, wavy, lobed, toothed; triangular; with a sticky upper surface. Lacy-looking. Flowers lilac-purple to 2 in. 'Clorinda', bright pink, translucent.

P. *blandfordianum:* P. *graveolens* × P. *echinatum:* To 1 ft. Delicate plant with slender stems. Pungent, musky scented, silvery. Leaves white hairy, bluish grey, deeply cleft. Flowers white with lilac & violet spots & veined purple (but no red spot as in the second parent).

P. *echinatum:* Sweetheart Geranium or Cactus Geranium. Long blooming season. Stout, succulent-looking stems with curious spines (hence "Cactus"). Leaves broad, medium-sized, wavy, toothed & lobed, green. Bluntly heart-shaped to ovate, with hairs on undersides. After leaves turn yellow, reduce water for 3 mos. Branched stalks. Flowers white with red, heart-shaped spot in upper petals. Flowers sometimes rich purple. Petals notched at apexes. Flower buds very hairy.

P. *glaucifolium:* P. *gibbosum* × P. *lobatum.* Night Scented Geranium. Compact, woody dwarf shrublet. Leaves large, smooth, pinnately lobed, ruffled. Flowers small in sprays, or umbels, maroon-black, yellow-margined. Hard to propagate.

P. *acetosum:* Related to P. *peltatum.* To 1 ft. Leaves small, slightly grey-green, fleshy. Taste like sorrel. On thin stems. Stalks join at bottom of wedge-shaped bases. Flowers narrow-petalled, spreading, pale shrimp with darker veining or salmon-pink. Look like butterflies or spiders.

P. *ardens:* P. *fulgidum* × P. *lobatum.* Dormant in summer, loses foliage. Knobby stem, short branches. Leaves to 8 in. across, lobed, hairy. Petals garnet-red, paling towards edges, upper ones with darker spots.

P. *quercifolium:* Oak-leaved Geranium. Pungent scented. Thick, wide spreader. Leaves large, elongated, numerous, black-green. Lobed to beyond middle. Flowers pink with darker veins on narrow petals. Cvs. e.g. 'Fair Ellen', 'Giant Oak'.

P. *tomentosum:* Peppermint Geranium. Spreads widely or climbs to sev. ft. or hangs. Tender. Leaves large with blades to 5 in. across with 5 to 7 shallow lobes. Velvety, hairy, thick & spongy. Rich green. Truly peppermint-scented. Becomes poor in old age. Grow replacements.

P. *Madame Salleron:* Variegated. Tender. 4 forms of different height & size of leaf. Leaves rounded, apple-green with a white edge. Will grow in half shade.

Some cvs. of pelargoniums with uncertain parentage are: 'Happy Star': Leaves rounded, with a gold center. 'Mrs. Taylor', 'Pretty Polly', 'Joy Lucille', 'Mme. Margot': Unattached ladies of value. Many fascinating other kinds.

Penstemon: SCROPHULARIACEAE. Beard Tongue.

N. Am.

Herb. or evgrn. Divided into sections or subdivisions. Habitats range from moist mtns. to dry, hot plains. Spp. from high altitudes are difficult.

Sun or part shade. Soil med. Ordinary cult. Groom. Deadhead. Some only semi-hdy. Bloom summer & fall. Seed. Cuttings. Division.

Grow dwarf spp. in sunny r.g. Only fairly long-keeping cut. Join American Penstemon Society.

P. hybs. & cvs. Garden penstemons. Sev. spp. esp. 2 from Mexico: P. *campanulatus* & P. *hartwegii,* leaves mostly green, shiny & full; flowers tubular in spikes.

P. *hartwegii:* Mex., a parent of the hyb. P. *gloxinoides.*

P. *gloxinoides:* A hyb. name with many cvs; e.q. 'Firebird', older cv.; 'Huntington Pink', 2-toned with good growth habit; 'Apple Blossom', very floriferous. Two fine dark ones, 'Midnight', very tall, & 'Prairie Dusk'.

P. *barbatus* (*Chelone barbata*): Beard-lip Penstemon. Colo., Utah., U.S.; Mex. One of

Penstemon

Penstemon

sev. red-flowered spp. To 3 ft. Flowers tubular, strongly 2-lipped. 'Rose Elf', smallest, 2 × 2 ft., light pink, grows well, picks well. Other cvs. e.g.: 'Praecox', 'Coccineus', 'Roseus'.

P. digitalis: To 5 ft., but usually much less. Basal rosette. Leaves glossy, dark green. Flowers pink or white, the white almost pure white. Good growth habit.

P. hirsutus & *P. h.* var. *pygmaeus:* E. U.S. Decumbent at base 1–3 ft. Flowers purplish.

P. antirrhinoides: Evgrn. shrub. 6–8 ft. Branches woody; leaves small. Will bloom in shade. Flowers yellow. Protruding staminodes with yellow hairs.

P. spectabilis: Calif., U.S. To 4 ft. Greyish leaves hairless & glaucus, to 4 in. long. Flowers blue-lavender. Tall, loose, narrow pyramidal panicles.

P. ovatus: Cent. U.S. To 2 ft. Slender, erect, downy. Flowers bluish.

P. confertus: N. Am.; Alberta, Wash, & Rocky Mtns. 9 in.–2 ft. Variable. Leaves hairless, linear up to 2 in. Flowers cream to yellow in spires, erect. Dense tuft of brown hairs on lower lip.

P. strictus: Wyo. to Colo. & Utah, U.S. Variable. 9 in.–2 ft. Leaves linear to spatula-shaped. Flowers deep blue to violet-blue, 1 in. long in 1-sided spikes. Staminodes naked of hairs but stamens with long hairs at tips.

P. newberryi (Syn. *P. menziesii* var. *newberryi*): Mountain Pride. Calif., U.S. Grows in crevices of rocky cliffs. To 1 ft. Woody stemmed. Leaves pointed. Flowers carmine to scarlet. Difficult to tame on the flat.

P. davidsonii (Syn. *P. menziesii* var. *davidsonii*): Related to *P. scouleri* & *P. newberryi:* High altitudes N. Calif. to Wash., U.S. Mats 4 in. high. Small hairless, toothless leaves. Flowers blue-lavender to purple-violet, 1 in. long, in racemes of 1 to 5. Staminodes hairy. *P. d.* var. *alba*, *P. d.* var. *menziesii* & *P. d.* var. *thompsonii:* High mtns. of Sierra Nevada, often in gravel.

P. gardneri: Idaho to Oreg., U.S. 4 in.–1 ft. Grey-hairy. Leaves spatula-shaped, 1 in., margins rolled. Flowers lavender-purple to ½ in. long with petals widespreading. *P. g.* var. *oreganus:* Almost white.

P. rupicola: Wash. to N. Calif., U.S. Woody based mat. Pubescent, freely branched shrublet with prostrate stems & erect branches to 4 in. Leaves ovate, thick, round-toothed, bluish glaucus. Flowers 1 in., numerous, look like Snapdragons, rose-carmine, to rose-crimson to rose-purple. *P. r.* var. *alba:* Few in sprays. Anthers woolly. Long stamens. Difficult.

P. pinifolius: SW. N. Mex., SE. Ariz. in U.S.; & Mex. Shrubby to 2 ft. Leaves often 4 in., crowded, filiform. Flowers scarlet to 1½ in. Tubular. Staminodes yellow, bearded. Difficult.

P. procerus: N. Am.; Saskatchewan, Brit. Col., Colo., Calif. 8 in.–1¼ ft. Leaves ovate, toothless to 4 in. Flowers ½ in. long, deep blue-purple, down-pointed & in ball-like clusters. Insides & end of staminodes bearded. *P. p.* var. *tolmiei:* Dwarf. Leaves shorter, broader in basal rosettes. Flowers sometimes yellowish. 'Crystal Freeze', a cv.

Penstemon

to seek.

P. caesius: Mtns. Cent. & S. Calif., U.S. Leaves entire, leathery. Flowers 1 in.

P. fruticosa: N. Am.; Alberta to Wash., Wyo. & Oreg. Shrubby. Dense clumps 4 in.–1½ ft. Leaves lanceolate, toothless, to 1 in. Flowers lavender-blue to purple. Staminodes bearded.

P. heterophyllus 'Purdyi': Calif., U.S. Common. Easy. To 1 ft. 2-toned "blue", July. When grown as an ann. & used as a g.c., called "Blue Bedder".

P. rattanii: Oreg. to N. Calif., U.S. To 4 ft. Leaves 2 in. long, lanceolate to elliptic, undulate, serrate. Flowers lavender to purple. Beard 2½ in. long. Staminode exerted.

P. cordifolius=Keckiella.

Phlomis: See Subshrubs Plant Descriptions.
P. rotata: W. China. Rosettes of small round leaves hug the ground. Flowers purple-blue to 2 in. Available? G.c.

Phlox: See genus description in Woodland Plant Description.

P. paniculata: Border or Summer Phlox. Native of moist fert. soils N.Y. to Kans. to Ark. in U.S. Hybs. & selected forms are chosen for color & form. White, pink, rose-crimson, lavender, sometimes with eyes of contrasting color in dome-shaped or pyramidal clusters on stems 3 ft. or more. Aug. Plants grow in clumps increasing every year. Basal mat can be 6 × 6 ft. square if not divided. Divide at least every three years. Flowers fragrant; when cut, must be conditioned well. Control mildew, spider-mites & eel-worm. Discard any plants attacked by the latter; keep healthy. Sun but cool around roots. Deep rich bed with bark, sand & compost. Feed. Mulch in winter. Water deeply in growing season; in the morning & the soil only. Grow in a bed with *Platycodon, Penstemon, Paeonia & Delphinium.*
P. p. 'Sandra': Good flower color. *P. p.* 'Nora Leigh': Interesting for white variegated mottled foliage. Plant somewhat stunted in growth. To some gardeners, looks diseased. *P. p.* 'Bright Eyes': One of the popular cvs.

P. carolina: Thick-leaved Phlox. Light woodlands Md. to Miss., U.S. The shiny surface of the leaf is some protection against pests & disease. Bloom is earlier & longer. Flowers a little smaller in more tall, columnar, cylindrical clusters. Fewer colors & less brilliant. 'Miss Lingard' can not be surpassed as a white. (It may be a hyb. between *P. carolina* & *P. maculata*.) Root cuttings from healthiest plants best for future stock. *P. c.* 'Miss Willmott': Seek, for superior flowers.

Physostegia: LABIATAE. False-Dragonhead or Obedient Plant.

N. Am.

Herb. Tufted mats which spread to 6 ft. if not divided. Spike form, num. stems, to 3 ft. tall.

Sun. Soil moist & fert. Cut back. Division.

Flowers have hinged stalks & will remain in any position they are placed. Good for per. borders & cutting. Bloom early summer & for many weeks.

P. virginiana: Dense clumps by second year.

Very straight firm stems. Tubular flowers lie close to stem. Cvs. e.g.: 'Alba' & 'Summer Snow', white; 'Vivid', 2 ft., rose-pink. 'Vivid' spreads faster than other cvs.: invasive.

Platycodon: CAMPANULACEAE. Balloon Flower.
Far East, NE. Asia.
Herb. Stems narrow, erect. Clump forming. Slow spreader. Plant 7 plants to make a drift 3 × 5 ft. Leaves lance-shaped, glaucus beneath, closely arranged up the stem. Shape of puffed bud important. Bloom summer into Sept.
Sun. Soil fert. Ordinary cult. Deadhead. Cut back. Seed. Division.
Leaves of *Platycodon* show the end of March with sunny days. Stay quite small as stem proceeds to elongate. The miniature cv. has a spike of pleasing proportions.
P. grandiflorus: Erect stems to 2½ ft. tall. Stems are firm but gentle support of a group of stems advantageous. Leaves soft, blue-green, neat, short-stalked, sharply toothed, to 3 in. Flower buds look like puffs, or balloons. Flowers when open, like cups; sev. on branches of upper stem. Deep lavender, whites, occasionally pinks. Aug. bloom & continues if deadheaded. *P. g.* 'Mariesii': In demand. Stems to 1 ft.; flowers same size as sp. Buds of cv. open July. Usually deeper colored than the sp.

Potentilla: For genus description, see Slope Plant Descriptions. Also see Subshrub Plant Descriptions for woody spp. Two spp. described here grow in clumps.
P. rupestris: Prairie Tea. Eur. & Asia. To 2 ft. Lower leaves pinnate to 7 leaflets, upper leaves with 3 leaflets. Flowers over 1 in. wide, white with prominent yellow stamens.
P. recta: Eur. & E. Asia (naturalized in N. Am.). To 2 ft. Stems ascending in a thick clump. Leaves palmate, green, quite hairy. Flowers yellow, June. Coarse & inferior.
P. r. var. *warrenii* (of gardens) (*P. r.* var. *macrantha*): Much superior. Bright yellow. *P. r.* var. *sulphurea*: Pale yellow on ascending stems to 2 ft.

Ranunculus: See genus description in Bog Plant Description.
Persian, Turban, French, Peony-flowered Ranunculuses: Developed from *P. asiaticus.* Leaves 2–3 times palmately divided, the segments cleft or toothed. In most areas tubers are stored until early spring. Headstart in flats & under cover. Moist, sandy, good medium. Become leafy plants, 1 ft. × 8 in. Complete protection from birds, esp. youngest sprouts. In Cent. Calif., U.S. tubers may be left in the ground in a place with very good drainage. Tubers must not rot in the ground before they acquire roots. Young shoots can withstand winter rains. To plant or replant, place 2 in. deep, with prongs downward. (No need to soak before planting—as was at one time the custom). Flowers Feb., Mar., April. Sev. strains, e.g. "Tecolote". Each tuber may manufacture 50–75 blooms over 2-mo. period. Single, dble., semi-dble.: yellow, orange, cream, red, pink, white.

Plants may sometimes be obtained in separate colors. Petals may be frilly; edges may be shaded with darker tone; centers, often black.
R. gramineus, R. parnassifolius, R. montanus: 9 & 6 in., suitable for r.g.
R. lyallii, R. insignis: N. Zealand, to 5 ft. × 3 ft., white to creamy white & yellow respectively. Rare large alpines.

Rubus: ROSACEAE. Bramble, Blackberry, Baked Apple Berry.
N. hemis.
Evgrn. & herb. Large shrubs or vines or creepers. Typical Rose Family flower.
Sun or part shade. Soil med. Control. Division.
G.c. R.g. Woods. Edge. Bank.
R. calycinoides: Stems woody but tight to the ground & to each other. Stems dotted with white, hidden by thick covering of foliage. Leaves leathery, curly-edged, roundish, dark green. Makes a carpet either on the level or on a slope. Flowers look like strawberry blossoms. Invasive? Travels far when rooting-stems find humusy earth. Not difficult to control. Good to fill step risers.

Rudbeckia: COMPOSITAE. Coneflower, Black-Eyed Susan, Gloriosa Daisy, Golden Glow.
N. Am.
Herb. Mostly grown as ann. 2–6 ft. tall. Spreads in a basal mat to 3 ft. wide if left in the ground. Cones prominent. Many variants. Bloom summer & fall.
Sun. Ordinary cult. Soil moist rather than dry. Seed. Cuttings. Division.
"Gloriosa Daisy", popular for cutting. "Black-Eyed Susan" because of black central cone.
R. fulgida: Natural variants & improved horticultural cvs. e.g.: 'The King' to 3 ft., deep old rose with a copper tone; 'White King', prominent cone; 'Goldsturm', ray flowers flat & neatly arranged; 'Oriole', seen in the catalogs.
R. hirta: Black-Eyed Susan. Many variants, some with fancy names.

Rumex: POLYGONACEAE. Dock or Sorrel.
Temp. regions.
Evgrn. Some are coarse weeds. Wide distribution.
Sun. Soil rich, moist. Snails. Division.
R. scutatus: French Sorrel. Herb garden or vegetable garden. Useful.

Ruta: RUTACEAE. Rue or Herb of Grace.
Mediterranean & W. Asia.
Herb. & evgrn. Forms a mound 2 × 2 ft., if pruned. Grown for flowers & decorative foliage. Strongly pungent. Flowers small, chartreuse-yellow, may be removed in bud which practice improves foliage.
Sun. Soil somewhat dry & lean. Cut back. Cuttings.
Dislikes excessive moisture.
R. graveolens: Scent very pungent when leaves crushed. Remove chartreuse bloom to improve vigor of foliage. Leaves with special color green. Cvs. with foliage color esp. bluish—e.g. 'Blue Beauty', 'Jackman's Blue'.

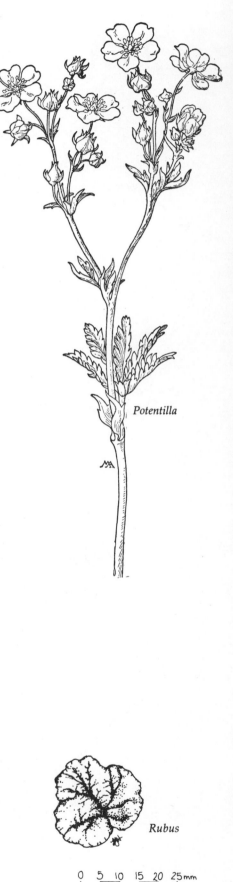

Potentilla

Rubus

0 5 10 15 20 25mm

Salvia

Salvia

Salvia

Salvia: LABIATAE. Sage or Clary.
Wide distribution.

Herb. & evgrn. Annuals, perennials, shrubs. Variable. Leaves differ considerably but some can be recognized as Sage leaves. Typical flower with upper petals forming a hood. Most of the spp. aromatic. Many spp., only a few to be described.

Sun & ½ shade. Soil med. Needs drainage. Cut back. Cult. various. Semi-hdy. Seed. Cuttings. Division.

Combine well with grey-foliaged genera, *Artemisia, Helichrysum, Hyplopappus, Calocephalus.*

Annuals

S. farinacea: Mealy-Cup Sage. Grown as an ann. where winters are cold, & often in warm climates also. After second year base becomes woody & foliage less lush. To 4 ft. Pubescent. Flowers in slender racemes on whitish stems to 9 in. & freely branching. Corollas blue-violet ½ in. long with white woolly calyces. Cvs. more compact, e.g. 'Blue Bedder'; 'Royal Blue', developed in S. N. Am. Very long flowering period, summer into fall. *S. f.* var. *alba:* With white corollas. (or 'Alba')

S. columbariae: China. N. Am.; Calif., Baja, Utah to Ariz. Ann., to 20 in. Leaves mostly basal. Flowers bluish. May.

S. carduacea: Thistle Sage. Cent. Valley & inner coast range of Calif. & south to Baja, N. Am. Ann. To 2 ft. Stems stout. Leaves to 6 in., spiny. Tomentose. Flowers lavender. The middle lobe of the lower lip, fringed. In whorls with large woolly-haired spiny bracts. Calyces woolly.

S. spathacea: Pitcher Sage. Calif., U.S. Coarse, herb. per. or ann. Creeping rhizomes. Leaves mostly basal, rough-surfaced to 8 in. long. Stalk to 2½ ft., erect. Flowers in dense narrow spike, purplish bracts & purplish red flowers.

S. viridis: S. Eur. Ann. Often grown for colorful bracts. Good for strip planting or beds. *S. v.* var. *alba, S. v.* 'Bluebeard', *S. v.* 'Oxford Blue', *S. v.* var. *purpurea.*

S. patens: Gentian Sage. Often grown as ann. Stems num. Well-covered with hairy, arrow-shaped, green leaves. Flowers intense blue, noticeably lipped. *S. p.* 'Cambridge Blue': Light blue.

S. argentea: Bien. Erect, shaggy to 3 × 2 ft. Basal leaves wedge-shaped, intricately lobed, white-woolly, wrinkled margin, irregularly toothed. Flowers in large panicle on branching stems. Grey-white calyces. Corolla pinkish white, hooded.

Perennials

S. guaranitica (S. ambigens): S. Brazil, Paraguay & Argentina. Semi-hdy. Grown often as ann., but in warm climates as herb. To 2½ ft., sometimes 5 ft. Stiff erect stems; few to a clump. Spreads to 3 ft. Leaves wrinkled to 5 in. long. Flowers in spike-like racemes spread at right-angles to the stems. Unique 2-lipped form, rich bluish purple. Often calyces almost black. Scent, oily lemony.

S. officinalis: Common Sage. To 2 ft., bushy, with white hairy shoots. Also called Garden Sage & used for seasoning, fresh or dried. Remove flowering lavender spike in early summer. When foliage is cut often for use, fertilize. *S. o.* var. *aurea, S. o.* var. *purpurascens, S. o.* var. *tricolor, S. o.* var. *crispa:* Less vigor. Grown for foliage.

S. sclarea: Clary or Clary Sage. Bien., sometimes per. Flavoring herb. To 4 ft. tall & almost as wide. Many stems densely clothed with flowers. Leaves oval, round-toothed & hairy to 9 in. long. Flowers in whorls of about 6, pinkish purplish. Bracts broad, white toward bases, pink or lilac at tips. Often seeds itself. *S. sclarea* var. *turkestaniana:* Bracts very conspicuous. Flowers whitish.

S. pratensis (S. haematodes): Meadow Clary. Eur. & Brit. *S. p.* var. *haematodes:* Greece. To 3 ft. Branching stems many from large basal rosette; leaves dark green. Flowers in sprays, bluish lavender with paler throat. Compact forms with rich color. Cvs. e.g., 'Indigo', 'Mittsommer'.

S. jurisicii: Balkans. Tufted. Odd habit—flowers grow upside down. To 18 in., often as wide. Leaves (upper) finely once or twice pinnately divided; lower leaves not cleft. Flowers with widely divergent lips, hairy, ¼ in. long. Deep bluish purple. Sometimes pink or white.

S. nemerosa 'East Friesland': Many slender erect spires; to 2½ ft., pinkish purple. *S. n.* 'Superba': SE. Eur. Bushy flowers in erect spikes, blue-violet with bracts of crimson-purple. After flowers drop, bracts hold color. *S. superba*, a sterile hyb., unknown parentage (mistaken for *S. nemerosa* which is probably no longer in cultivation). Flowers in slender spikes, sev. to a stem, violet-purple.

S. uliginosa: From S. Am. To 6 ft. Flowers bluish with white interspersed. Stems slender, curving.

S. cacaliaefolia: This sp. cannot be found in the usual encyclopedias. When it is, you may find the spelling *cacaliifolia*. It is enough like *S. patens* in flower to sometimes be mistaken for it. It is smaller, however, in all parts except for the width of a plant; it forms a bushy, woody clump to 6 ft. across. The stems are hairy & the leaves thick & hairy. Roots of this sp. run underground, sending up fresh shoots. In native habitat, it grows to 3–4 ft.; in the garden it should be kept lower and fresher by pruning. It may be pruned to the ground for the winter. The shape of the leaves is equally hastate as that of *S. patens* and the blue color of flower equally intense. In branched racemes.

S. azurea: SE. U.S. To 6 ft., usually lower. Stems slender, ascending, clothed with narrow, greyish green leaves, making quite a dense mass to 3 ft. wide. Flowers in slender spikes at top of stems; clear, light blue.

S. azurea var. *grandiflora (S. azurea* var. *pitcheri)* & *S. azurea* var. *pitcheri (S. pitcheri):* To 5 ft. or less. Grey-green leaves hairy. Calyces hairy. Flowers large, velvety & deep blue with branching habit. Seen more often than sp. but less tall, less wide & less vigorous.

S coccinea: Texas Sage. So Afr. A good crimson and a pink form raised at Brenthurst.

Dwarf:

S. caespitosa: To 1 ft. wide but often only 6 in. tall. Leaves grey. Flowers lavender.

Subshrubs:

S. leucantha: Mexican Bush Sage. Less shrublike than many others. Tender. Woolly-stemmed. To 4 ft., nearly as wide. Leaves wrinkled, pointed, white woolly on undersides. Flowers white in branching slender sprays to 1 ft. Stems & calyces thickly clothed with violet woolly hairs, causing an appearance more purple than white. Fall bloom.

S. leucophylla: Purple Sage or Grey Sage. Mtns. of S. Calif. Quite a bit more woody than *S. leucantha* with brittle, branching stems. Makes a leafy dense mound 2–6 ft. & as wide. Characterized by whitish stems; leaves small, grey, crinkled, an overall white look. Leaves drop in long dry spells. Flowers light, pinkish purple in whorled clusters. May & June.

S. clevelandii: Another native of S. Calif., part of the chaparral. Much larger & more shrublike (4 × 4 ft) than *S. leucophylla.* Rounded bush which in the garden, must be pruned annually, else top-heavy. Leaves grey-green, potent when crushed. Flowers bluish in whorls. May through Aug.; greyish brown when dry. Scent pungent & very pleasant, in foliage & flowers, both fresh & dried. Cvs. worthwhile as 'Allen Chickering', a cv. of a hyb.

S. sonomensis: A compact, green, leafy subshrub. To 2 × 2 ft. 'Dara's Choice', a selection, sometimes available. Ample flower stems, with flowers in whorls, lavender, smaller than those of *S. clevelandii.* Prune only to groom. Not long-lived; grow replacements from cuttings.

S. apiana: Definitely shrubby. Over 2½ × 1½ ft. wide. Compact & neat at least in youth. Could be grown solely for its white-grey foliage. Leaves of firm texture, oval & pointed, shaded lavender in summer. Flowers pinkish lavender or whitish in tall slender racemes, on long curving flower stems. Remove complete stem.

Santolina: COMPOSITAE. Lavender Cotton.
Mostly Mediterranean. Escaped to U.S.
Evgrn. Aromatic. Often geometrically clipped.
Sun. Soil poor, dryish. Groom. Dead-head. Shear. Tender. Division.
Prevent flowering for best foliage.

S. chamaecyparissus (S. incana): Compact, bushy, evgrn. Can be clipped. Stems stiff & quite woody but fully clothed with foliage. To 2 ft. usually kept to 1 ft. Leaves tiny, rough. Flowers small, round, yellow, button-like (all disk florets); may be removed by shearing. *S. incana* 'Nana': More dwarf & compact. Leaves "frosted".

S. neapolitana (S. rosmarinifolia): S. Italy. Evgrn. To 2½ ft. Leaves to 3 in. long, dissected into thread-like segments, white-felted.

S. virens (S. viridis): To 2 ft. & as wide. May clip. Leaves green, pinnately cut into num. sharp teeth. Flowers solitary, yellow.

Satureja: LABIATAE. Yerba Buena, Calamint, Savory.

Calif. to Brit. Col.
Herb. & ann. Clumping or trailing.
Sun or shade. Ordinary cult. Cut back. Division.
Two savories decorative as well as useful. Plant top of a wall or along a path. One Savory trailing with long, delicate stems.

S. hortensis: Summer Savory. Ann. but may extend life. "Use plant" but decorative. Flowers small, pale pink to rose, in whorls. Allow to bloom after "harvest" has been taken.

S. montana: Winter Savory. Evgrn. subshrub. Mound to 15 in. Leaves to ½ in., stiff, close together, on many stems. Best leaves for drying at very start of spring flower season. After clipping, flowers develop soon on new blooming stems, white to lilac. Boxes as well as herb beds or edges. Less flavor than *S. hortensis.*

S. douglasii (Micromeria chamissonis): Yerba Buena. Found widely distributed on the hills of San Francisco under the native oaks & amongst chaparral. Gave the first name to this California city. Creeping, evgrn. Likes rich, moist soil. Best in sun esp. along foggy coast line. Stems to 3 ft. long, clamber around vigorously in between & over plants more especially if the situation is sloping. Not overly aggressive. Leaves scalloped, to 1 in., with a minty scent. When dried, a pleasant flavor for tea. Flowers small, lavender-white, inconspicuous, summer.

Scabiosa: DIPSACACEAE. Scabious, Mourning Bride, Pincushion Flower.
Eur., Asia, Afr., most from Mediterranean.
Herb. Ann., bien. & per. Foliage plentiful, shiny, clear green, much cut. Branching open growth to 3 ft. Quadruples in size the second year.
Sun. Soil fert., alkaline rather than acid. Drainage. Dead head. Protective covering in winter in cooler climates. Seed. Cuttings.
Mixed borders. The dwarf spp. for edging & r.g. Cutting; long season. Flowers look like pincushions, some flat, some full.

S. columbaria: Many stems. 3 ft. × 3 ft. Small flowers, lilac-blue.

S. ochroleuca: To 3 ft. Branches carry many smallish, yellow cushions. A wide bushy plant 3 × 3 ft. in form very like *S. columbaria.*

S. caucasica: Well-known garden sp. with improved forms. 2 × 2 ft. Cvs. e.g.: 'Blue Perfection', bluish lavender; 'Miss Willmott', white; 'Clive Greaves', mauve. Stems 18 in., branching. Flowers slightly flattened pincushions with prominent stamens. To 3 in. across. If flowers are picked every week beginning June, bloom will last into fall. If flowers are not dead headed & picked, plants deteriorate. Leave 6–8 in. when cutting back.

S. scabra var. *pterocephala:* Mat, 1 ft. wide formed by grey-green, leathery leaves. Stems to 6 in. Flowers pale bluish lavender. R.g.

S. variifolia: Subshrub. 2 × 2 ft. Num. flattened cushions, lavender.

S. graminifolia: Hummock. To 6 in. Leaves grey, grassy. Flowers pale mauve.

25 mm
20
15
10
5
0

Salvia

Senecio

Senecio

Silene

Knautia macedonica (S. rumelicus): (*Knautia* repeated here because it cannot be distinguished from *Scabiosa* by the layman.) To 2 ft. with soft, curving, branching stems. Flowers smaller, more rounded & dense than *Scabiosa*; deep dull red or dark crimson. Many to a clump. Picks well.

Sedum: See genus description in Container Plant Descriptions & Slopes Plant Descriptions for other spp.

Here are some members of the genus which fit into neither category; although they may be used in pots or on sloping ground, they may also be incorporated in beds & borders. They are hdy. but defoliation may occur after the first frost. The flower stems are herb. but a mat of foliage rosettes persist or is renewed. The spp. prefer sun & soil light enough to drain well. Bloom is mainly late summer. Increase by division.

S. maximum: Eur. A giant. Cv. 'Atropupureum', uncommon.

S. alboroseum: The lowest since it has lanky stems which sprawl. Pale green leaves with wide central splashes of cream. Flowers in flat heads, white petals, pink centers; often omits a blooming period.

S. spectabile: China, Korea. Herb. Robust. Foliage feature through summer with stems upright to 2 ft. A medium sized sp. with clumps 2 ft. wide as well as tall. Leaves flat, elliptic, fleshy to 4 in., blue-grey. In Sept., flat heads of small, starry flowers on num. stems, mauve-pink in the type. Sev. cvs. e.g. 'Carmen', 'Meteor', 'Brilliant', the latter said to be both rosier & more vivid. 'September Glow' has excel. color. *S. s.* var. *album:* Not often seen.

S. telephium: Some authorities give *Telephium* genus status, (treated thus in this text). Other authorities consider it as here a sp. of *Sedum* or a subsp. of *S. spectabile,* the type sp. of a group. In any case it hybridizes with *S. maximum.* It has deeply serrated leaves. *S. t.* var. *purpurascens* has excel. color. Those authorities who give it less than genus status often call it a "subgenus". All agree that it has upright stems which die down in winter & that it has leaves thin, flat, fleshy & blue-grey. Leaves obovate to 3 in. Flowers in large clusters with stamens about as long as petals. Cvs. with deep colors. 'Autumn Joy' has been considered a cv. of *Telephium* by those who give this cousin genus status. Another opinion follows. By any classification, this is a fine plant.

S. 'Autumn Joy': A chance hyb. between *S. spectabile* & another member of the *Telephium* group. (Muriel Hodgman, Journal of the R.H.S., Vol. 105) Perhaps nectaries defective in the individual flowers of the cross since they do not attract butterflies. Handsome colors which change with the seasons. Three stages: soft green, dusky orange-rose & copper. Sometimes all present in midseason.

S. cauticolum: Crossed with *S. maximum* produced cvs. e.g. × 'Vera Jameson'. Crossed with *S. spectabile,* 'Ruby Glow'.

S. roseum: Preferred name *Rhodiola rosea:* Na-

tive of circumpolar region. Rootstock globular buds with overlapping purple scales, silvery brown to blue-green. Perfume of dried root like that of Damask roses. Leafy shoots to 6 in. Flowers in tight clusters, gold-green, in May.

Semiaquilegia: RANUNCULACEAE. Japan, Korea, E. China.

Herb. Properly *Aquilegia.* Foliage *Aquilegia*-like. *S. escalcarata:* Flowers short-spurred, cream & chocolate.

Senecio: COMPOSITAE. Groundsel, Cineraria, Dusty Miller, Leopard's Bane, Ragwort, German Ivy, California-Geranium, Candle Plant, String of Beads, Vertical Leaf.

Ann., per. & shrubby. Perhaps 3000 spp., one of the largest genera of flowering plants.

Sun. Soil med. Ordinary cult. Seed. Cuttings.

Our prime interest is in those with grey foliage, useful in mixed plantings & for cutting, but other spp. described below.

S. hybridus: Correct group name for florist's Cineraria. Pots. Bedding in mild climates. 2 types: 1) grandiflora group, flowers large, full, circular, in large, round, compact trusses. Sev. colors, bicolors & tricolors with hues in concentric zones; 2) stellata group, starry flowers in looser trusses. Colors white, pink, lilac, purple without marked zoning. Bloom fall.

S. petasitis: Velvet Groundsel, Velvet Geranium, California Geranium. Mex. To 8 × 4 ft. Almost circular leaves. Shallowly lobed & wavy. Velvety-hairy. Flowers in large, showy clusters, small, with up to 6 ray florets, yellow. Long season. Cut to ground. Large shrub in one season.

S. cineraria (Cineraria maritima or *Centaurea maritima):* Dusty Miller. S. Eur. One of the best plants called by this popular name. Only semi-hdy. Sometimes grown as an ann.; gently trimmed to shape for a season; used as edger or for bedding. When allowed to grow, foliage forms a mound, 3 × 3 ft. Leaves deeply divided, pleasing pattern, velvety texture. Should not be allowed to flower. Find forms with foliage esp. silver-white. Good drainage.

S. leucostachys: White-grey foliage. Leaves finely divided.

S. vira-vira: Ovate leaves even more finely divided, deeply pinnately clefted into 2 to 4 pairs of narrow, linear, toothless, pointed lobes. Flowers with florets only disk type, whitish to cream-colored.

Silene: See slope.

Solidago: COMPOSITAE. Goldenrod. N. Am., esp. E. N. Am.

Herb. Sev. improved forms. Breeding has attempted to reduce pollen which causes hay-fever. Foliage is good esp. in compact forms. Tall spp. with graceful spires Sept. & Oct. Feathery. Plant with *Phlomis, Aster, Achillea.*

Sun. Soil med. All are greedy. Spread & seed vigorously. In 3 years a stand may have 15 stems grown from a thick mass of tufts 6 or more ft. wide. Division.

Cvs. developed for compact habit usually to 2

ft.; e.g. 'Cloth of Gold', 'Peter Pan', 'Golden Baby'.
A few suitable for r.g.: *S. multiradiata* var. *scopulorum, S. virgaurea* var. *alpestris*.

Solidaster: *Solidago × Aster ptarmicoides.* Herb. Bigeneric cross.
S. hybridus: To 2 ft. Flowers daisies, canary-yellow. The *Aster* look predominant. Likes fert. soil.
S. luteus (Aster hybridus var. *luteus*): To 2½ ft. Stems which branch near the top. Pubescent. Flowers in flattish clusters to 4 in. wide. Numerous. When first open, disk & rays both golden yellow; rays soon fade to cream-yellow. Good in a mixed border.

Stachys: See Slope Plant Descriptions. Very good g.c. for the edge of the border.

Stokesia: COMPOSITAE. Stokes Aster or Cornflower.
N. Am., S.C. to La.
Herb. or evgrn. Strong clumps. 1½ × 1½ ft. Flowers have shaggy appearance. Improved forms available.
Sun. Ordinary cult. Cut back. Winter protection in coldest climates; hdy. in S. New England, U.S. Division.
Foliage in quite flat, basal mound more vigorous when plant out of bloom. Flowers good to cut. Dead heading improves quality. Bloom summer.
S. laevis (*S. cyanea*): Evgrn. To 2 ft. Leaves basal to 8 in., lanceolate. Flowers shaggy looking, with about 15 wide outer florets resembling petals. Horticultural varieties with latinized names & cv. names indicating colors. Cvs. e.g.:
S. l. 'Silver Moon': The white more pure than that of *S. l.* var. *alba*.
S. l. 'Blue Star' with very large flowers & 'Spode Blue', less lavender & with a creamy center.

Symphytum: BORAGINACEAE. Comfrey.
Eur., temp. Asia. Somewhat naturalized in N. Am.
Herb. Ancient lore being revived.
Some shade preferred. Slug & snail control important. Division. Inv.
Controversy over contribution to health.
S. officinale: Leaves to 8 in., big, rough, hairy, clustered in big clumps; smaller leaves equally rough follow up stem. Stems to 3 ft. Flowers lavender tubes in clusters hanging from branches. Also, dull yellow or whitish.
S. asperum: Prickly Comfrey. Stems covered with stout, flattened, recurved prickles. Flowers often bigger & bluer.
S. uplandicum: S. officinale × S. asperum. Russian Comfrey. To 6 ft. Coarse growth. Flowers pink in bud, purple when open. *S. u.* var. *variegatum:* Leaves with broad margin of creamy white.
S. grandiflorum & *S. rubrum* (of gardens): To 4 ft. Probably hybs.

Tanacetum: COMPOSITAE. Tansy.
N. hemis. including N. Am.
Evgrn. Related to *Chrysanthemum.* Strongly scented. Common Tansy naturalized in N. Am.
Sun. Soil lean, dryish. Groom. Division.

Foliage to cut with short stems.
T. camphoratum: San Francisco Bay area, Calif., web of fine whitish hairs.
T. haradjanii: 8 × 12 in. Wider unless divided. Pure silver, feathered. Often named *Chrysanthemum haradjanii.*
T. nuttallii: A silver cushion. Uncommon; difficult to obtain.

Teucrium: LABIATAE. Germander.
Wide distribution; esp. Mediterranean.
Herb. or evgrn. Per. & shrub. Aromatic. Leaves various.
Flowers in whorls, few to many in spikes.
Sun. Soil med. Ordinary cult. Easy to grow. Trim. Semi-hdy. Light winter protection. Seed. Cuttings.
Habits mostly unusual. Sev. dwarves.
T. fruticans: A true shrub. Leaves & stems grey. Flowers light lavender. Stems slender & easily pruned for shape of plant. To 8 ft. × 8 ft. if not trimmed. Gets woodier & poorer if neglected in a year of drought. Good for back accent in a large border. *T. f.* 'Nanum'.
T. chamaedrys: Only slightly shrubby; evgrn. mound to 2 ft. wide. Leaves toothed, shiny, dark & set closely on stems. Shear at least twice a year to make neater, fresher, fuller. Or clip way back for a dwarf hedge. Flowers mauve-pink, on sev. inches of the tips of 1 ft. stems. Spring. Good for the chin of a bank.
T. lucidum: Erect & shiny. Also good to shear.
T. c. var. *prostratum:* Only 6 in.; may spread to 3 ft. Hard to find.
T. subspinosum: A grey shrublet.
T. hyrcanicum: Persia. To 2 ft. Leaves grey, buds grey. Flowers in late summer, in slender spikes, tiny, dark lilac. Uncommon.
T. scorodonia: See Slope Plant Descriptions.
T. polium var. *aureum:* See Outdoor Room Plant Descriptions.

Thermopsis: LEGUMINOSAE. Carolina Lupine.
N. Am. & temp. Asia.
Herb. Bushy clump to 4 ft. Leaves light green, numerous. Flowers erect spikes to 10 in., resemble those of Lupine. Early summer.
Sun. Soil well-drained. Fertilize annually. Cut back. Seed or division.
Use 3 to 5 plants for a wide drift.
T. caroliniana: Leafy clump to 4 × 2 ft. Flowers erect, canary yellow, in spikes to 10 in.
T. montana: N. Am., Rocky Mtns. to Wash. Spread too rapid for most gardens. Flowers straw-yellow; looks more like *Baptisia* than Lupine.
T. lanceolata: Does not have a questing root. Sim. otherwise to *T. montana* 3 × 2 ft.
T. fabacea: Look for this sp. from Kurile Isles.

Thymus: LABIATAE. Thyme.
Temp. parts of Old World, esp. Mediterranean.
Evgrn. Subshrubs as well as carpeting spp. Often minute foliage. Aromatic. Some spp. not reliably hdy.
Sun. Soil lean. Drainage. Some moisture. Division.
Grow on the flat or better on a slope. Raised bed suitable. Between stepping stones or in open areas in a r.g. Try a tapestry, sev. kinds in a pattern. Flowers in midsummer

Solidago

Thermopsis

Thymus

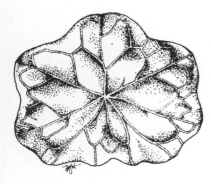

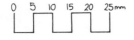

Tropaeolum

Uniola

25 mm
20
15
10
5
0

Valeriana

add to design; white, pink or lavender. Spread to 1 ft., often to 2 ft., sometimes to 3 ft.

T. vulgaris: Culinary Thyme. Dense hummock to 10 in. Leaves dark green. *T. v.* 'Aureus': Foliage yellowish green. *T. v.* 'Variegatus': Green & white.

T. × *citriodorus: T. vulgaris* × *T. pulegioides.* Lemon Thyme. Tender. Low shrublike. Flowers tiny, pale lilac, cylindrical clusters. 'Silver Queen' with variegation creamy white, very pleasing.

T. serpyllum: Sp. rarely cultivated.

T. praecox-arcticus (T. britannicus) (T. druce) (T. serpyllum of gardens): Mother-of-Thyme. Leaves minute, hairy. Flowers tiny, lilac-pink in small heads. Cvs. & vars. e.g.: *T. p.-a. coccineus,* crimson; *T. p.-a. splendens,* red; *T. p.-a.* 'Albus', numerous white flowers.

T. hirsutus var. *doerfleri:* Balkans. Matting to 3 in. Leaves linear, hairy, ½ in. long, with rolled-under hairy margins. Flowers in clusters ½ in. across, tiny, lilac.

T. caespititius: Iberian Peninsula, Azores & Madeira. Matting. Stems slender, prostrate; branches hairy to 2½ ft. Leaves with hairy margins. Flowers in loose clusters, pale lilac.

T. camphorifolius: An uncommon sp. with interesting scent.

T. pseudolanuginosus: (Origin unknown) More common in gardens than *T. lanuginosa* which has stems hairy all the way around. Mat, very tight to the ground. Leaves of both densely hairy. Flowers light pink, not in head-like clusters, grow in the leaf axils.

T. quinquecostus 'Albus': Uncommon evgrn. sp. Worth seeking.

T. herba-barona: Corsica & Sicily. Not completely hdy. To 6 in. Caraway-scented. Flowers in loose clusters ½ in. long, deep pink.

T. broussonetii: Morocco. Erect, bushy to 1 ft. Stems hairy; leaves almost smooth. Flowers in rounded clusters, reddish with conspicuous bracts: prominently veined, purplish red, ½ in. long, fringed with hairs.

Trachelium: CAMPANULACEAE. Throatwort. Mediterranean region.

Herb. 6 in.–3 ft. Leaves pointed ovate, dark green, plentiful. Num. small flowers in terminal clusters. Sev. stems from a wide clump to 4 ft. w.

Sun & shade. Soil moist & fert. Semi-hdy. Division.

Plant with leafy perennials in pale colors, for accent.

T. caeruleum: Leaves to 3 in. Flowers in rounded heads—flattish clusters—starry, bluish or lavenderish mauve. Slightly fragrant. Produce a noticeable splash of color towards back of a border. Less hdy. than the dwarf sp.

T. rumelianum: Limestone soils in Greece & Balkan Peninsula. Not over 6 in. tall. Leaves sharp-toothed, ovate. Will sprawl over rocks. Flowers fluffy.

Tradescantia: COMMELINACEAE. Spider-wort.

Americas.

Evgrn. & herb. Some trailers, some erect.

Foliage lush but not very tidy. Dense clumps to 2½ × 2½ ft.

Shade or ½ shade. Soil moist. Ordinary cult. Division.

Good filler for mixed planting. Flowers good to cut. Summer & fall.

T. × *andersoniana:* Group name for hybs. of 3 sp. including *T. virginiana.* Flowers 3-petalled, in clusters on 2 ft. stems. Cvs. e.g.: 'Osprey', white with blue eye; 'Purple Dome', brilliant; 'J. C. Wequelin', pale blue; 'Purewell Giant', red-purple. All summer into fall.

Tropaeolum: Nasturtium. See Outdoor Room.

Tricyrtis: LILIACEAE. Toad Lily.

Japan.

Herb. Colonies. Gradual spread. Short rhizome usually branchless, arching stems. Foliage sword-shaped to oval, to 6 in. Leaves semi-clasping. Buds unique. Flowers in open erect sprays each flower a flared trumpet. 6 petals & prominent stamens & style. Use in pots or r.g. as well as in beds & borders. Bloom fall.

Half shade. More sun in cool areas. Soil moist, fert., humusy. Division.

Flowers with curious speckled markings. Some with rich reddish purple tints. Clumps of ascending & arching stems. Slow development.

T. hirta: Japanese Toad-lily. Clumps; to 2½ ft. tall. Leaves hairy, oval. Flowers erect, white with spots. *T. h.* 'Alba': Off-white. *T. hirta* 'Variegata': Foliage, white hairy. Bloom with the leaves. Flowers with slender spurs. An orchid look.

T. formosana: Taiwan. Clumps to 3 × 1½ ft. Leaves glossy, deep green. Flowers in panicle-like clusters, erect, white, slightly cupped with flaring segments. So spotted they appear from a distance to be red-purple.

T. macrantha: Brown, hairy stems to 2 ft. Leaves oval to lance-shaped. Flowers pendulous, yellow with purple-brown spots.

Tulbaghia: LILIACEAE. Sweet Garlic.

S. Afr.

Rhizome or corm-like. Related to *Agapanthus* but unlike. Small clumps. To 2 ft. tall. Leaves narrow, blade-shaped.

Sun or shade. Soil warm & well-drained. May damage at 25 degrees but recover. Protect in cold climates. Division.

Good in pots. Peak of bloom spring & summer except one sp. in winter. A variegated cv. has slender, thin-textured leaves with vertical stripes. Plant with *Aquilegia* & *Platycodon.*

T. violacea: Society Garlic. To 2 ft. × 9 in. Leaves rather fleshy with an onion odor when cut or crushed; once in a vase no odor is evident. Flowers in umbels, narrowly bell-shaped, rosy lavender; 6 spreading lobes & 6 stamens.

T. v. 'Silver Lace': Leaves longitudinally striped esp. along margins.

T. fragrans: Blooms in winter. In an area where winter rains could beat down the stems, grow under cover. Flowers lavender-pink, truly fragrant.

T. natalensis: Uncommon. Flowers white; green central cups turn yellow.

Uniola: GRAMINEAE. Sea Oats.
N. Am. to S. Am.
U. paniculata: To 8 ft. Much smaller in the garden since old stems are cut to ground. Graceful, wavy stems. Will tolerate shade. Interesting flowers.

Urospermum: COMPOSITAE. S. Eur., Mediterranean.
Herb. Per. or bien. in cultivation. Bloom summer.
Sun. Continuous grooming. Seed.
A curiosity. Somewhat coarse looking but unusual. Grow in a forward bay for best viewing.
U. dalechampii: Spreading clump of toothed green leaves. To 1½ × 2 ft. wide. Flowers look like fancy dandelions. Good lemon-yellow.

Valeriana: Seen often on the waysides.

Verbascum: SCROPHULARIACEAE. Mullein.
Eur., temp. Asia & naturalized in N. Am.
Herb. & semi-evgrn. Some very large, some coarse. Basal rosettes large & often with an intricate pattern. Leaves various, green, smooth, glossy, to thick grey velvety. Tall narrow spikes. 1–4 ft. Bloom summer.
Sun. Soil common. Ordinary cult. Most spp. invasive. No staking. Seed or division.
Intergeneric cross, *Celsioverbascum,* is excel. hyb. of dwarf stature. Spike form useful in mixed plantings or in groups in the landscape. Grow with *Digitalis, Penstemon, Scabiosa.*
V. thapsus, Common Mullein, *V. thapsiforme, V. phlomoides, V. olympicum, V. longifolium, V. vernale* (of gardens) & sev. undetermined spp. are too gross for the home garden.
V. bombyciferum: Also big but has esp. noteworthy foliage; a dense covering of silvery white hairs over all parts. Bien. Leaves to 1 ft. Sometimes called "Arctic Summer".
V. blattaria: Moth Mullein. To 6 ft. Flowers yellow with a lilac throat. Also *V. blattaria* var. *albiflorum:* Flowers white.
V. chaixii: To 3 ft. Leaves glossy green, grow in a basal rosette. The parent of sev. horticultural hybs. Flowers on straight firm stems, the upper 1 ft. crowded. Flowering branches off the main stem bloom after those of the central stem finish. Flowers corolla yellow, filaments purple woolly.
V. chaixii 'Album': To 3 ft. Hard to find. Flower white with mauve center.
V. phoeniceum: Purple Mullein. S. Eur. & N. Asia. Short-lived but seeds readily. Early summer. Parent of a fine strain of hybs., "Cotswold hybrids". Basal rosette of dark green leaves. Stems from 3–4 ft. White, pink, yellow, purple.
V. 'Cotswold Queen': With a color called "bronzy salmon".
V. 'Letitia': Dwarf & 1 ft. wide. Very attractive shape.
V. 'Golden Bush': Hyb. by Hillier. Excel. To 2 ft. Flowers clear yellow. (Available in the U.S.)

Verbena: VERBENACEAE. Vervain.
Eur., naturalized in N. Am.
Evgrn. & herb. Small, irregular, dark, toothed leaves. Best grown as ann. since subject to pests & diseases. Bloom summer & fall.
Sun. Soil med. Needs drainage. Semi-tender. Seed.
Low growing spp. more useful in gardens. Best where winters are fairly mild.
V. bonariensis: S. Am. To 5 × 2 ft. Dense tuft of lavender flowers, fragrant.
V. rigida (Verbena venosa): Brazil, Argentina. To 18 in. with many stiff branches. Spread 1 ft. or more. Leaves rough, hairy, sharp-toothed. Flowers small, of a rather strong violet color. Useful as g.c. on a bank in warm climates.
V. r. var. *alba* & *V. r.* var. *lilacina:* Often cultivated as anns.
V. canadensis: N. Am. Perhaps only available in seed. To 1½ ft.; wider than tall; dense mounds, to 3 ft. wide. Leaves rough, small, dark green, indented on the edges. Flowers clear reddish purple, many, in many mos. Dead-head.
V. tenera var. *maonettii:* Called "Italian verbena" but comes from S. Am. Trailing stems thickly branched. Leaves rough-hairy, 3 parted, pinnately cut. Flowers of the sp., violet-rose-pink. The var. is candy-striped, the petals a carmine-pink edged with white.

Veronica: SCROPHULARIACEAE. Speedwell.
Widely distributed, chiefly temp. regions.
Herb. & evgrn. Some spp. subshrubby. Many kinds from 1 in.–4 ft. Foliage various.
Sun. Soil moist & fert. Respond to good cult. Cut back. Summer. Easy. Seed or division.
Many uses. Listed according to height. Combine with *Physostegia, Platycodon, Asphodiline, Penstemon.*

Tall ones:
V. exaltata: Siberia. Jagged, large leaves continue up the single stems. Plumes of light blue, tiny flowers. 4 × 4 ft.
V. longifolia: From Eur. & Asia. 4 × 1 ft., lavender. *V. l.* var. *subsessilis:* Japan. 2 × 1 ft. Far superior. Spikes large & with deep color.
Hybs. between *V. longifolia* & *V. spicata* & *V. virginica:* E. N. Am. Flowers in spikes lilac, purple, white. Look for 'Red Fox', upright spikes to 14 in. tall, reddish pink.
V. spicata 'Nana': Useful for the small garden.

Medium in height:
V. perfoliata: To 2 ft. Subshrub. Seldom seen. Leaves leathery, glaucus & clasp the stem. Flowers blue-lavender in sprays.
V. latifolia (V. teucrium): May grow to 3 ft. but its best known form, 'Crater Lake Blue', is more like 2 ft. & compact.
V. spuria: Look for the cv. 'Royal Blue'. There are sev. other cvs. with the word "blue" in the name, some of them from the crosses, *V. spicata* × *V. longifolia.* E.g.: 'Blue Charm', 'Blue Spires', 'Blue Champion', 'Blue Fountain', 'Sunny Border Blue'—this last esp. good for a mass of color toward the front of a mixed planting. Long blooming. 'Icicle' an excellent white with flowers of rich texture. 'Minuet' is low, with silvery grey

Verbena

Veronica

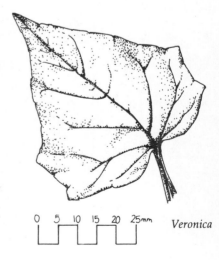

0 5 10 15 20 25mm

Veronica

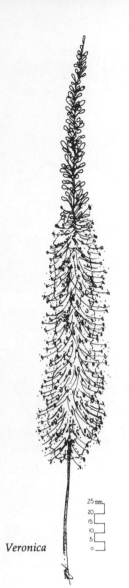

Veronica

Viola

foliage & soft pink flowers. All have spikes, dense with many tiny flowers. Look for *V.* 'Saraband' with grey foliage to 20 in. Some of the cvs. have shorter stems than the type sp.

V. spicata 'Nana': Useful for the small garden.

V. grandis var. *holophylla*: Himalayas. Different. Leaves dark green, glossy with good texture, almost triangular, toothed along margins, to 2 in. long. Foliage an asset, dense & leathery. Stems to 1 ft. with terminal spikes, looser than those of others described. Color, deep blue-lavender, July to Sept. Clumps to 10 in. Less vigorous than most spp. Liked by rabbits.

Low kinds: (Some of the lowest are weeds.)

V. incana: Wooly Speedwell. Although the flower stems rise to 2 ft. occasionally, the foliage classes it as low. Clumps of low shoots many of which do not flower. The silvery look is as much silky as wooly. Leaves to 3 in. form a tight g.c. to 1 ft. wide. Flowers in narrow spikes, bright blue-lavender, terminal arching stems. Cvs. One is 'Candida'.

V. gentianoides: Caucasus. Mat forming; makes a bright-green carpet. Restrained to 18 in. Stems to 18 in., erect. Flowers ½ in. wide in spikes, palest blue with darker margins; gracefully arranged on branchless slender stems. Does not flourish as well in W. U.S. as in England. Some other spp. also are more vigorous in beneficial climates.

V. armena: To 4 in. with long trailing stems & tiny leaves & with vivid blue flowers.

V. pectinata: To 6 in. with rooting stems densely white hairy, & with white-eyed flowers. These last 2 spp. are examples of prostrate *Veronicas*.

Viola: VIOLACEAE. Violet, Heartease, Johnny-Jump-Up.

Temp. & cold parts of N. & S. hemis.

Herb. & evgrn. Includes "pansies", derivatives of *V. cornuta* & "violas", derivatives of *V. tricolor*. Leaves solitary or in clumps, various light to heavy-textured, kidney- to heart-shape.

Sun or shade. Soil moist, lean or fertile. Spp. with runners invasive. Some will not domesticate; some from shady bogs & some from dry sunny slopes. Seed or division.

Only a few are fragrant. Large bed required in order to provide enough violets for a bunch to pick. Bloom mostly spring.

V. rugulosa: Travels. Leaves 4 in. Rich green, pointed, copious. Flowers white, bluish tinted.

V. canadensis: Sim. But does not wander. Neat clump to 1 ft.

V. odorata: Sweet Violet. Cvs. vary in fragrance. Single or semi-dble. Flowers of 5 petals. The lower one larger & with a spur. 4 in 2 pairs dissimilar. Cvs. e.g.:

'Mary Louise': Dble., 2-toned, white & bluish lavender. 'Royal Elk': Leaves to 7 in. across & flowers 1½ in. across. Spreads.

'Swanley': Dble. white. Trailing stems make it suitable for hanging baskets.

'Lady Lloyd George': Flowers dble. Lavender-mauve.

'Rosina': Small, dainty & contained. Not easy to establish.

V. alba: Parma Violet. Cent. & E. Eur. Close to *V. odorata* in that it has stolons & fragrance. The fragrance of *V. alba* is special; used for perfume. Not overly invasive. Foliage undistinguished, shabby if attacked by insects. Flowers many. Often 2-toned. Flowers ½ in. across, mostly white or violet (sometimes pink or reddish).

V. hispida: France. Another which contributes to the production of scents.

V. hederaceae: Australian Violet, Ivy-leaved Violet or Trailing Violet. Stemless, tufted, stoloniferous. Leaves reniform, entire or toothed. Petals blue varying to white. Scarcely spurred.

V. jooi: SE. Eur. Rhizomes. Small. Flowers ½ in. across; mauve streaked with purple. Fragrant.

V. tricolor: Johnny-Jump-Up, Love-in-idleness, Heartease, Pink of My John. Eur., naturalized in N. Am. Not always per. Varies greatly in habit, size & flower color. *V. t.* var. *subalpina* (*V. saxatile*): Usually per. To 1 ft.; often with violet upper petals & others yellow, veined with violet. "Faces" quaint.

V. lutea: Mountain Pansy. W. & Cent. Eur. Creeping rhizomes. Leafy branchless stems. 3–6 in. high. Flowers yellow or violet or a combination, over 1 in. across; petals twice as long as the spur. Flowers sparse but most attractive.

Spp. of N. Am., E., Midwestern & W., sometimes divided into 2 groups, one with leafy stems & one without. Or they could be listed according to geography or to color, or to size or to behavior or to habitat. The system in these paragraphs is subjective. No fragrance except when noted.

V. sororia (*V. papilionacea*): Sunny but damp meadows & open woodlands from Quebec, Can. to Okla., U.S. The wooly blue violet. Dark violet to lavender to white with densely bearded side petals.

V. s. var. *priceana*: Confederate Violet. Flowers greyish white, heavily veined with lavender. Strong spreader. Invasive to 6 ft. or more.

V. lanceolata: Lance-leaved Violet. Nova Scotia to Tex., U.S. Stolons; leafless stems. Leaves tapering. Flowers white with brown-purple lines on lower petals. Delicate.

V. adunca: N. Am.; Quebec, Can. to S.D., U.S. Stolons. Leafy stems. Stems in tufts; become prostrate. Leaves to 1 in., nearly round, with short hairs. Flowers violet to lilac, white at the center, lower petals veined. Bloom spring. Gravelly, sandy, infertile soils.

V. a. var. *puberula*. Might be hard to find.

V. labradorica: Very like *V. adunca*. These 2 may be invasive.

V. striata: N.Y. to Ariz., U.S. Clumps; stems to 1 ft. Flowers ivory with purple veins. Scent of "newly mown grass".

V. pubescens: Downy Yellow Violet. N. Am.; from Nova Scotia to Okla., U.S.: rich woods.

V. p. var. *eriocarpa*: Smooth Yellow Violet. Clear yellow, brown-veined near bases of petals. Slow. Choice.

Digitalis: The spikes of no other genus can excel the straight spires of the various Foxgloves. Here are a few stems of the the commonest kind blooming in part shade.

Delphinium: A stately column which is very hard to surpass. The hybrids are excellent, especially when well grown. The color pink is somewhat unusual.

Berberis: This mounding sp. is covered with its yellow pea flowers for several weeks in Spring. It looks nice with rocks on a slope.

Lavandula: The cultivar named 'Hidcote' is very floriferous and slender stemmed. The hedge shears will be used here after the blooming season.

Papaver: Here is a solid bed of the Poppy grown as an annual for its long season of Spring and Summer bloom. Through hybridization, wonderful colors have been developed.

Cynoglossum: Resown and planted out fresh each year, this Hound's Tongue makes sheets of blue. It can be used for a carpet, as here in a rose bed.

Campanula: Many trailers which can be used as ground covers in part shade. The lavender bloom here accentuates the purple cast in the fern fronds.

Centaurea: Several dwarf spp. are more frilly than their relative, Bachelor's Button. Here in the shade, the small mauve flowers brighten the green mass of *Patrinia*.

SOME PARTICULARLY ATTRACTIVE PERENNIALS

V. conspersa: **The American Dog Violet.** N. Am.; woodlands & meadows, Nova Scotia to Mo., U.S. Flowers on slender stalks. Pale violet with dark veins.

V. pedata: **Bird's Foot Violet.** N. Am.; dry acid infertile soils in sunny fields & open woodlands, Me. to Tex., U.S. Tufts. Leaflets divided into linear segments. Flowers flat to 1½ in. across; upper 2 petals velvety dark violet, lower 3 pale lilac with darker veins; gold center. Beardless. Pansy-like. Var. *alba* rare. April to June.

V. p. var. *lineariloba* (V. p. var. *concolor*): Name sometimes given to those with a single color. Much admired. Not easy to grow.

Sev. W. spp. of which 23 from Calif., U.S. A few examples:

V. sempervirens: Stolon-like stems. Purple spots on round leaves. Flowers pale lavender or yellow.

V. sheltonii: Wooded areas, Orange Co. to Wash., U.S., 2500–8000 ft. Leaves divided. Flowers yellow with brownish purple streaks on 2 of the petals. April.

V. pedunculata: Calif., U.S. Below 2500 ft., Sonoma Co. to lower Calif. Deep rooted. More or less decumbent stems to 2 ft. long. Leaves coarsely-toothed. Flowers pansy-like. Side petals bearded. Orange-yellow with brown on the backsides, stripes on lower petals & purple-veined at the centers.

V. lobata: **Yellow Wood Violet.** Oreg. & Calif., U.S. Stems leafy to 1 ft. Leaves palmate, 3 to 7 lobes. Petals yellow, purple outside, veined at base.

V. nutallii: **Yellow Prairie Violet.** N. Am.; Brit. Col. to Calif. & east to Rockies. 4 varieties with slight differences. Stems leafy to 5 in. Leaves lanceolate. Flowers yellow-brown, veins on 3 lower petals ½ in. long. Spur short.

For a few other *Violas* see Outdoor Room Plant Descriptions.

Watsonia: IRIDACEAE **Bugle Lily**
S. Afr.

Herb. About 60 spp. Fibrous tunicate corms. Sun. Soil loamy. Division.
Leaves sword shaped, strong.

W. meriana: Less than 3 ft. Flowers rose red to salmon to pink. Look for preferred color.

W. marginata: To 5 ft. Very strong. Basal leaves several. Flowers small, magenta-pink fragrant. Early summer. See Large Site.

Watsonia

18. The Sample Layouts

INTRODUCTION

Would model paper plans be a help or hindrance? The layouts which follow are merely suggestive and, of course, come nowhere near to covering all of the conceivable species gardeners must deal with nor all the solutions possible. A large number of species will be found in Plant Descriptions which have not been assigned to any layout. If a plant sounds good to you, you will look for it and put it in your own plan.

I recommend strongly your own paper plan even if you do not expect to follow it. It will be helpful in a number of ways. You will be able to observe whether you have chosen the right proportions of broad leaves and narrow leaves. A paper plan provides not only good guidance when visiting nurseries to purchase plants to implement it; but more importantly, the plant list derived from your plan will help to bridle that besetting sin of every dedicated gardener—spur-of-the-moment purchase of plants which have no place to go when you get them home. I am not suggesting that you observe calvinistic puritanism, only a little bit of restraint to keep you closer to the mark.

None of the sample layouts are meant to be models as to size and shape: some had to be curtailed in length in order to fit the page. Some may contain too many different species of plants; do you think perhaps a few were tucked in in order to have a reason to describe them? Perhaps your space allows you to have only a single border; the double border is just a further challenge if you have the space.

These sample paper plans are very simple in structure. The most complicated is the double border which occupies rising tiers. No border has been drawn for a raised bed although this is an excellent situation for a mixed planting, both for appearance and for maintenance. However, you may use any of the plans or parts of them for a raised area; those with curving front edges need a curving wall. Again, the purpose of making the various layouts is to suggest plant combinations which you could adopt for your own garden.

In order to study any layout, compare the names of plants more or less in order of their appearance beginning in the left hand upper corner; you will be referred to the list on which the species description occurs. Many of the perennials you will have met already in a previous chapter. I hope all the cross references will not make you dizzy.

The layouts all have the same scale, one quarter inch to one foot but liberties have been taken. No one of them is such an exact model that you can transpose it to your garden. You can follow it but it is not intended that you copy. Each one has been put in a typical situation, however. In order that they may seem a part of a garden, they have been given backgrounds and paths and a few subshrubs, shrubs and trees. All of these model plans face south, unless otherwise indicated. When you imitate some combinations from a sunny layout, place it in your own plan in a site which has sufficient light; when you choose plants from a shady place in a layout transpose them to a corner with established shade. There is a climate mean as well as a temperature mean. These plans are for an area not too hot and not too cold; you will know how to adjust to the place you live, and the several different exposures in your garden.

One good principle to guide you in making your plan is repetition. If you believe you have found a pleasing association between two or three kinds of plants, do the same combination further along, either copying the relation of the drifts or changing it a little. You can take just a piece of one of these layouts, if you wish, in case a special combination fits both your site and your preference, and meld it and modify it and multiply it.

The materials indicated for paths and walls can be replaced with anything you like better. Perhaps you will think of something quite different.

A legend follows to help you interpret these paper plans.

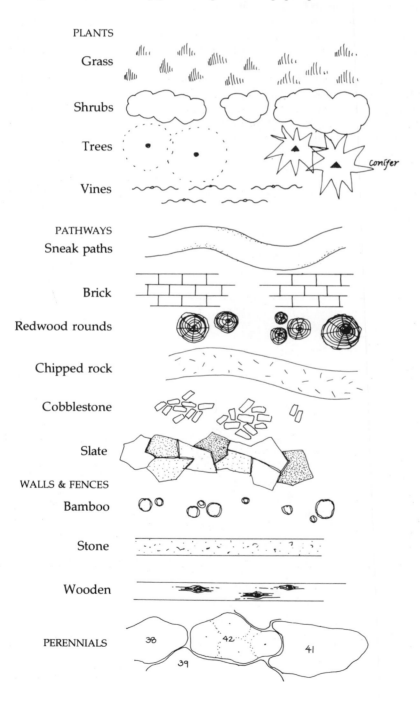

PLANTS

Grass

Shrubs

Trees

Conifer

Vines

PATHWAYS
Sneak paths

Brick

Redwood rounds

Chipped rock

Cobblestone

Slate

WALLS & FENCES
Bamboo

Stone

Wooden

PERENNIALS

LAYOUT 1
SUN: AGAINST A HEDGE

This planting is in sun and in medium soil. Some spp. are drought tolerant but all will grow better with water on a schedule.

Shapes of the plants are various—pillar, round and arching. The textures are from heavy, the *Canna,* to dainty, the *Gypsophilia.* Shapes of foliage add to the design factor, e.g. the small, narrow leaves of the Lavender and the lobed leaves of the *Pelargonium* with fragrant foliage. The "true" *Geranium* on the forward edge makes a mound of quite curly-shaped leaves.

The blade-shaped leaves of the *Iris* stay in good condition into autumn after the flower stems have been cut to the ground. Since the leaves are numerous and erect, they make a sturdy clump of medium green in the background. The leaves of the *Aubrieta* are small and soft; they must be sheared after the first blooming period. For a short time the remainder of the short stems will look ragged but new growth will follow soon and be fresh-looking.

The *Pelargonium* foliage looks exceedingly fresh almost every month of the year. *P. graveolens* is a darker green than *P. crispum.* Both give solidity to the overall plan.

There are some drifts of greyish foliage which play their part in melding, e.g. the Lavender and the *Dianthus.* The *Gypsophila* has a similar function. Although not actually grey, its little leaves and blossoms make a large mound which appears "misty". The *Baptisia* has a decided shade of grey in its leaves, and seed pods, a dusky, blue-grey hue. The foliage of this cv. of *Achillea* is feathery and greyer than in some other *Achilleas.*

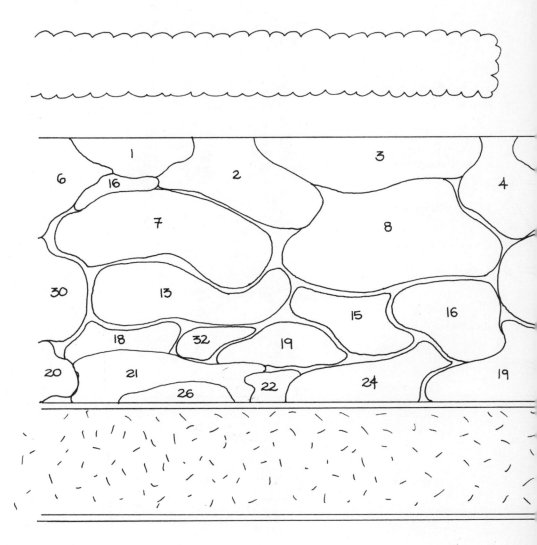

There are some noticeable clear greens. The leaves of this *Penstemon* cv. are shiny and quite dark. *Iberis* cvs. are probably the greenest edging plants to be found. After the bloom of the first period has been sheared off, new leaves quickly appear. Several plants of *Iberis* are placed together in the foreground to produce some very good masses of dark green; they make a year-around contribution.

The *Canna* is a cv. with dark leaves; this was used to produce a strong vertical line against the green of the back-ground hedge.

Most of the bloom occurs in summer; *Iris monnieri* and *Aubrieta deltoidea,* one at the back and one at the front, start to bloom in early spring. The mixture's predominant flower color is lavender; there are several shades with two almost blue, i.e. the *Salvias.* The deep-purple of the *Penstemon* is intense, good for an accent. Yellow is the companion color, with at least three shades introduced. There is a little pink and a few bright spots of bright-pink to red. There are not many whites but the drift of *Gypsophila* and *Iberis* and the spikes of *Veronica* 'Icicle' act as coolers together with the greens and greys of the foliage.

Substitutes could be found for all the spp. suggested, keeping in mind the relationships of color and form.

This hedge is clipped to six feet and not allowed to get more than a little higher. Some of the tallest perennials reach almost to this height, but these do not make a solid bank against the green background. The strongest forms are of middle height and build a wavy line stretching both backwards and forwards. The edging plants are of varying heights, mostly low but high enough in some parts to tie into the central range. This is a mixture of perennials with foliage interest most of the year with no attempt to make a blaze of color in any one week even in summer when a majority of its perennials bloom.

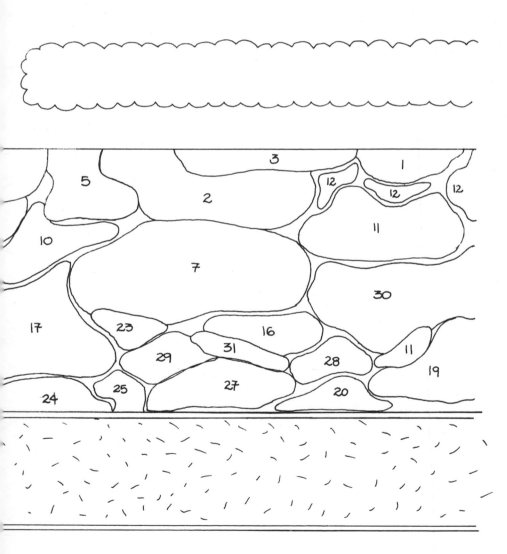

1. Canna hyb. 'Wyoming' (General P.D.)
2. Aster tongolensis (General P.D.)
3. Iris monnieri (General P.D.)
4. Echinacea purpurea 'Bright Star' (General P.D.)
5. Rudbeckia fulgida 'Goldsturm' (General P.D.)
6. Coreopsis verticillata (General P.D.)
7. Pelargonium graveolens 'Grey Lady Plymouth' (General P.D.)
8. Lavandula angustifolia 'Hidcote' (Subshrub P.D.)
9. Baptisia australis (General P.D.)
10. Thermopsis caroliniana (General P.D.)
11. Veronica hybs. 'Blue Charm' & 'Icicle' (General P.D.)
12. Salvia azurea var. pitcheri (General P.D.)
13. Aquilegia, Spring Song Strain & × Biedermeier Strain (General P.D.)
14. Gypsophila paniculata 'Perfecta' (General P.D.)
15. Catananche caerulea 'Blue Giant' (General P.D.)
16. Penstemon hybs. 'Midnight' & 'Rose Elf' (General P.D.)
17. Salvia patens (General P.D.)
18. Jasione perennis (General P.D.)
19. Achillea hyb. 'Moonshine' (General P.D.)
20. Dianthus chinensis (General P.D.)
21. Aster hyb. 'Winston Churchill' (General P.D.)
22. Aubrieta deltoidea (General P.D.)
23. Nicotiana "Sensation Strain"—chartreuse & red (Annual P.D.)
24. Chrysanthemum cv., border type (General P.D.)
25. Iberis sempervirens 'Snow Flake' (General P.D.)
26. Linum flavum 'Compactum' (General P.D.)
27. Geranium sanquineum 'Lancastriensis' ('Prostratum') (Slope P.D.)
28. Mimulus hyb.—muted color (General P.D.)
29. Viola pubescens var. eriocarpa (General P.D.)
30. Lobelia siphilitica (General P.D.)
31. Stokesia laevis (General P.D.)
32. Erodium pelargoniflorum (General P.D.)

LAYOUT 2
SUN: AGAINST A WALL

This border is composed of a number of forms, the vertical line predominating. There are a variety of different spike-like stems but only a portion of them are stiff. The *Boltonia* and the *Cephalaria* are tall but they branch at the top. The flower stems of the hybrid *Penstemon* curve. *Campanula primulifolia* has an erect stem which comes to a point but it has a softer look than *Campanula persicifolia* because of its open trumpets and its numerous stem leaves. The *Eremurus,* if it will grow for you, will make a strong, bold vertical line; it is not only towering but fat and full. The spikes of the *Kniphofia* might be as many as a dozen to a clump; they emphasize the vertical form.

In the middle section, look for other spike forms. *Physostegia* 'Summer Snow' is less rigid than *Physostegia* 'Vivid'. *Phlox* is upright but has a rounded top. The *Digitalis* is stiffly erect. *Scabiosa* is upright but it has a loose look because of slender stems and branches. *Scabiosa* introduces the round form with its pincushion flowers; the heads of *Knautia* are only a little smaller. The flowers of *Cosmos* make a circle with evenly spaced petals. The cv. of *Campanula carpatica* on the forward level produces many flowers with

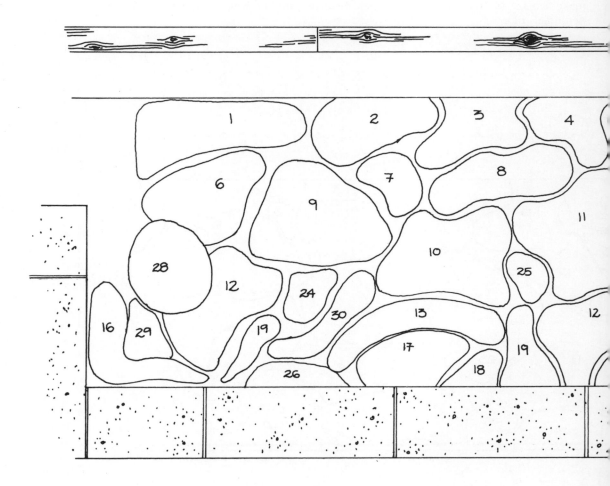

a perfect circle, quite unlike the stars and bells of its cousins. The most prominent example of the round form is of course the *Paeonia*.

Bloom is mostly early summer. White or light colors predominate; eight selections are white or cream; there are three yellow. Towards the foreground white is repeated on the edge with lavender interwoven and there is quite a bit of lavender in some smaller spaces. Green is not emphasized but it contributes to the finished product. *Yuccas* make a decided period at either end. This border is situated against a wall; there is a "sneak" path between it and the planting and on either end there are paths, one going to a doorway, the other to the vegetable garden. The wall is made of wood, stained not painted; the paths are finished with a brownish-grey chipped rock. Around the corner out of sight is a potting shed; some of the species included will need renewal and this owner will grow his own *Cosmos* from seed and will divide and multiply these perennials as needed.

The color of the fence and the path is muted and allows the color and form of the flowers to stand out strongly and make a decided statement in their season. There are a number of old-fashioned border plants here but the majority have foliage ample enough to tie plants together in a drift and to meld the drifts together.

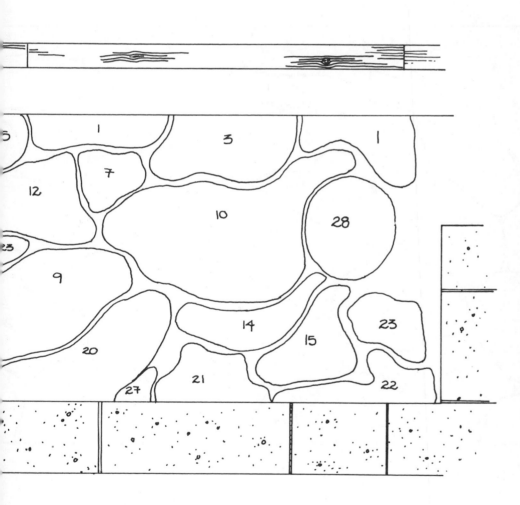

1. Digitalis mertonensis (Woodland P.D.)
2. Boltonia asteroides 'Snow Bank' (General P.D.)
3. Cephalaria gigantea (General P.D.)
4. Penstemon hyb. 'Apple Blossom' (General P.D.)
5. Eremurus Shelford hybs. (General P.D.)
6. Kniphofia hyb. 'Vanilla' (General P.D.)
7. Cosmos diversifolia (General P.D.)
7. Digitalis lutea var. australis (Woodland P.D.)
9. Paeonia, herb. hyb. (General P.D.)
10. Phlox carolina 'Miss Lingard' (General P.D.)
11. Eryngium × zabelii (General P.D.)
12. Campanula primulifolia (Slope P.D.)
13. Scabiosa hyb. (General P.D.)
14. Knautia macedonica (General P.D.)
15. Verbascum chaixii (General P.D.)
16. Alchemilla conjuncta (Slope P.D.)
17. Arabis sturii (General P.D.)
18. Campanula carpatica 'White Star' (Slope P.D.)
19. Silene schafta (Slope P.D.)
20. Penstemon heterophyllus (General P.D.)
21. Erigeron speciosus (General P.D.)
22. Achillea argentea (General P.D.)
23. Physostegia virginiana 'Summer Snow' (General P.D.)
24. Dictamnus fraxinella var. albus (General P.D.)
25. Platycodon grandiflora (General P.D.)
26. Houstonia caerulea 'Millard's Variety' (Outdoor Room P.D.)
27. Aethionema × warleyense (General P.D.)
28. Yucca recurvifolia (or Y. smalliana) (Site For A Large Perennial P.D.)
29. Rehmannia elata (General P.D.)
30. Adenophora tashiroi (General P.D.)

LAYOUT 3
RECTANGLE

In this garden, an area has been selected for a perennial garden which might have been designated for a lawn in an old-fashioned design. It is free standing; a path runs around all four sides and it is seen from all directions. There is no immediate specific background and no trees or shrubs in the immediate vicinity. It is a modified "island bed", modified because no island is oblong. It might be called a panel because of its geometric shape except that it is wider than the usual panel and it is surrounded by a path. It is a hybrid. Some of the principles for an island bed are followed, i.e. the plants on the outside edges are low and the heights graduate toward the center; the species are planted very close together—they hold each other up; and there is a large proportion of species dependant to a considerable extent on interesting foliage. This

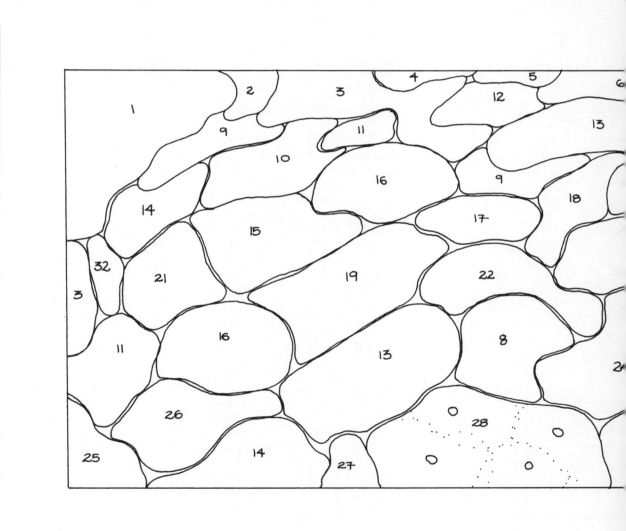

same space could use a plan with dwarf shrubs through the center to create the body of the composition. The strong tall perennials in this plan are adequate. The edge is soft; some of the edging perennials are allowed to spill over the path. This type of space can be bordered with a low hedge; with such a treatment the number of species would be reduced.

This plan should have the appearance of a tapestry. Some 30 kinds of perennials are dispersed in a manner which should appear casual and crowded but always guided by the relationships of form and character of the various parts.

The time of maximum bloom is summer but some begins in spring and several species keep going into fall. The foliage of *Hemerocallis, Potentilla* and *Teucrium* contributes to the picture all through the seasons. The groups of species selected for this rectangular interweave. Although the heights from all angles increase toward the center, the progression is not in tiers but rather in uneven waves.

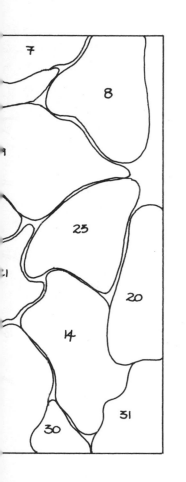

1. Felicia amelloides (Subshrubs P. D.)
2. Anacyclus depressus (General P.D.)
3. Potentilla nepalensis 'Willmottiae' ('Miss Willmott') (Slope P.D.)
4. Chrysanthemum mawii (General P.D.)
5. Verbena canadensis (General P.D.)
6. Iberis gibraltarica (General P.D.)
7. Geranium pratense (Slope P.D.)
8. Pelargonium crispum (General P.D.)
9. Helenium autumnale 'Peregrinum' (General P.D.)
10. Gaura lindheimeri (Site for Large Perennial P.D.)
11. Salvia leucantha (General P.D.)
12. Scabiosa columbaria (General P.D.)
13. Kniphofia cv. (General P.D.)
14. Achillea tomentosa 'King George' (General P.D.)
15. Baptisia australis (General P.D.)
16. Hemerocallis cv. (Site for Large Perennial P.D.)
17. Phlomis russeliana (Subshrubs P.D.)
18. Thermopsis caroliniana (General P.D.)
19. Veronica longifolia var. subsessilis (General P.D.)
20. Bellis perennis (Ground Covering list)
21. Potentilla fruticosa (Subshrubs P.D.)
22. Artemisia lactiflora (Site for a Large Perennial P.D.)
23. Santolina chamaecyparissus (General P.D.)
24. Chrysanthemum anethifolium (General P.D.)
25. Nepeta faassenii (General P.D.)
26. Scabiosa caucasica (General P.D.)
27. Geum chiloense (General P.D.)
28. Teucrium chamaedrys (General P.D.)
29. Campanula glomerata (General P.D.)
30. Stokesia laevis (General P.D.)
31. Chrysanthemum parthenium (General P.D.)
32. Digitalis grandiflora (D. ambigua) (Woodland P.D.)

LAYOUT 4
CORNER: WITH ORIENTAL FEELING.

This is a corner site. The wide path leads from the house (out of sight), to the swimming pool. It is edged with a low stone wall on the one side and wooden header-boards on the other. The surface of the path is earthen covered with a thin layer of large river rock and studded with large flat type stones placed casually. There is a minor path on the two sides of the triangle; back of this path is a fence made of bamboo poles placed to leave wide spaces between them.

Five medium-sized trees and two groups of shrubs shade the planting area while a large tree

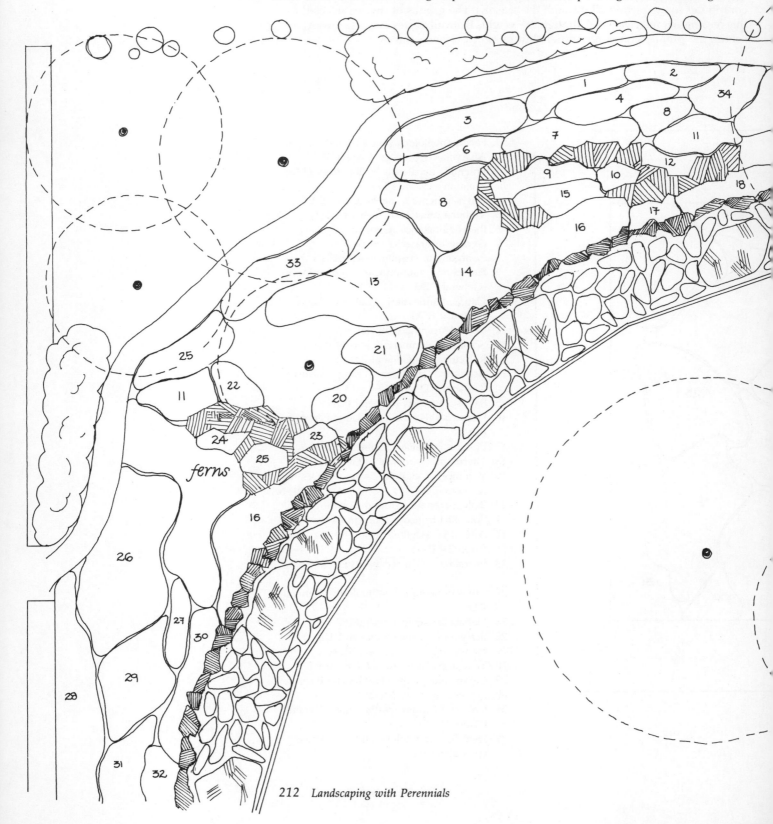

across the path adds more shade. This site could be called "part shade".

There are three clusters of low rocks to create a setting for several perennials especially suitable for a small rock garden. *Rhodohypoxis* is given a pocket in a prominent position. It stays underground seemingly forever; shortly after spring comes, clumps of very small sword-shaped leaves emerge; soon the clump is studded with small, delightful starry flowers.

Convallaria forms a patch above the next group of rocks. Its foliage is easily recognized amongst its neighbors; the oval leaves grow in a sort of sheath. See #5. The leaves of its cousin, *Maianthemum*, are quite different.

Kirengeshoma has a place of honor. Here is another herbaceous perennial very slow to appear in spring. But then it speedily develops into a most charming small bushlet; the green of its uniquely shaped leaves is very fresh looking.

Some bold accents are provided by *Dietes, Diplarhenia, Arthropodium* and *Bulbinella.* The leaves of these four make vertical lines but those of *Arthropodium* and Bulbinella are curvaceous. Each has a different shade of green.

Several plants have a soft, delicate appearance, two especially, *Boykinia* and *Patrinia*. There is contrast in this planting but there are traits common to many of the subjects which establish a personality for the whole.

This mixed border has a trace of Oriental influence by virtue of its bamboo fence and its river stones. The rocks as they are placed are accompaniment to the personality of certain plants as in the Eastern tradition. The area has a somewhat woodsy look but is not strictly casual; the plants, the tree trunks, the rocks, all contribute to its architectural form.

1. Dietes vegeta 'Johnsonii' (Site for Large Perennial P.D.)
2. Boltonia asteroides var. latisquama (General P.D.)
3. Diplarrhena moraea (Site for Large Perennial P.D.)
4. Pasithea caerulea (Woodland P.D.)
5. Maianthemum kamtschaticum (Bog P.D.)
6. Arthropodium cirrhatum (Woodland P.D.)
7. Convallaria majalis (or C. montana) (Outdoor Room P.D.)
8. Paradisea liliastrum (General P.D.)
9. Hepatica acutiloba (Woodland P.D.)
10. Epigaea repens (Woodland P.D.)
11. Gillenia trifoliata (Woodland P.D.)
12. Disporum hookeri var. oreganum (Woodland P.D.)
13. Patrinia gibbosa (Woodland P.D.)
14. Aquilegia ecalcarata (Woodland P.D.)
14. Cheiranthus linifolius (Slope P.D.)
16. Boykinia elata (Woodland P.D.)
17. Edraianthus graminiifolius (Woodland P.D.)
18. × Heucherella tiarelloides forma Baldaccii (Woodland P.D.)
19. Kirengeshoma palmata (Bog P.D.)
20. Podophyllum peltatum 'Splendens' (Woodland P.D.)
21. Rhodohypoxis baurii (Woodland P.D.)
22. Sanguisorba canadensis (Woodland P.D.)
23. Saxifraga × arendsii (Woodland P.D.)
24. Shortia galacifolia (Woodland P.D.)
25. Sanguinaria canadensis 'Multiplex' (Woodland P.D.)
26. Actaea alba (A. pachypoda) (Woodland P.D.)
27. Eucomis punctata (Woodland P.D.)
28. Francoa sonchifolia (Woodland P.D.)
29. Bulbinella robusta (General P.D.)
30. Campanula × haylodgensis (Slope P.D.)
31. Asarum shuttleworthii (Woodland P.D.)
32. Astrantia maxima (Woodland P.D.)
33. Brunnera macrophylla (Woodland P.D.)
34. Elmera racemosa (Woodland P.D.)

LAYOUT 5
NORTH SHADE

This site is on the north side of the house. It is carved out of the center of five trees and the same number of shrubs. It is mostly shady but not deep shade. Many of the perennials are evergreen—almost a third; ten are herbaceous. The remainder are without foliage for only a short time.

The strongest motif is greenery of various forms. The Japanese herbaceous fern, *Athyrium nipponicum* 'Pictum' is a stunning fountain of muted colors. The *Arum* is grown mostly for foliage; the leaves are plentiful, excellent for picking. *Helleborus foetidus, Bergenia cordifolia* and *Asarum caudatum* have striking foliage—leathery and shiny.

Heights are mostly low to medium except for the delicate flower sprays of *Thalictrum, Cimicifuga* and *Aruncus*. There are several foliage forms—sword-shaped, rounded and delicately branched.

As for color, a large proportion of the flowers are white or cream and several bloom together in the summer. White cultivars have been selected in *Astilbe, Bergenia* and *Digitalis* in order to itensify the muted scheme. (Red or lavender could be used in these genera together with a rose species of *Helleborus* by the person who likes a brighter scheme.) There is at one end a good-sized drift of

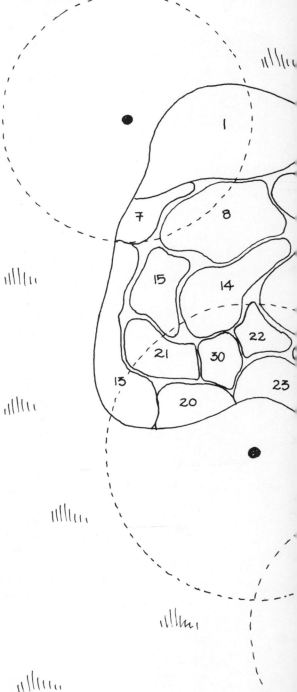

1. Athyrium nipponicum 'Pictum' (Woodland P.D.)
2. Pulmonaria lutea (Woodland P.D.)
3. Ceterach officinarum (Woodland P.D.)
4. Astilbe × arendsii cv. (Woodland P.D.)
5. Arum italicum (Woodland P.D.)
6. Actaea rubra (Woodland P.D.)
7. Tanakaea radicans (Woodland P.D.)
8. Anemone blanda (Woodland P.D.)
9. Helleborus lividus var. corsicus (Woodland P.D.)
10. Arthropodium cirrhatum (Woodland P.D.)
11. Aristea eclonis (Site for a Large Perennial P.D.)
12. Agapanthus inapertus (Site for a Large Perennial P.D.)
13. Bergenia cordifolia (Woodland P.D.)
14. Heuchera sanguinea (Woodland P.D.)
15. Thalictrum rugosum (Woodland P.D.)
16. Cimicifuga simplex (Woodland P.D.)
17. Aruncus dioicus (A. sylvester) (Woodland P.D.)
18. Liriope muscari 'Silvery Sunproof' (Woodland P. D.)
19. Doronicum caucasicum (General P.D.)
20. Asarum caudatum (Woodland P.D.)
21. Francoa ramosa (Woodland P.D.)
22. Digitalis ferruginea (Woodland P.D.)
23. Boykinia elata (Woodland P.D.)
24. Corydalis cheilanthifolia (Woodland P.D.)
25. Dicentra spectabile (Woodland P.D.)
26. Eucomis undulata (Woodland P. D.)
27. Saxifraga umbrosa (Woodland P.D.)
28. Tellima grandiflora 'Rubra' (Woodland P.D.)
29. Tradescantia cv. (Woodland P.D.)
30. Omphalodes verna (Woodland P.D.)

Doronicum to produce a mass of bright yellow in earliest spring. Both the *Pulmonaria* and the *Thalictrum* are yellow species; they are pale and bloom in spring early or late according to climate. The flower spike of *Eucomis* is a pillar; it is a feature of late summer, cream with palest overtones. Look for the tuft of foliage which tops the *Eucomis*; it is hat-like.

The *Agapanthus* is the herbaceous species. The all new leaves are shiny green and the lavender color of the flower is clear also, deeper than many flowers of other species. The tubular flowers grow in a cluster; they hang in maturity, a form which differentiates this species from its cousins.

Lapeirousia has been naturalized. There is a white one as well as the nice coral one. Other bulbs can be added, small species which are self-reliant and increase over the years.

Most of the species used in this design are what you may call woodsy. When light comes through the upper branches of the trees, it makes patterns upon the surfaces of the several kinds of foliage.

This treatment of shade, both dense and filtered, has more the look of a natural copse than the more studied planting of #4. Several of the species are ground covering and the base of the planting has a full mass of greenery in certain stretches; however, the foliage of a number of species gives height, form and solidity to this base. Several other species have been chosen for contrast—to create vertical lines.

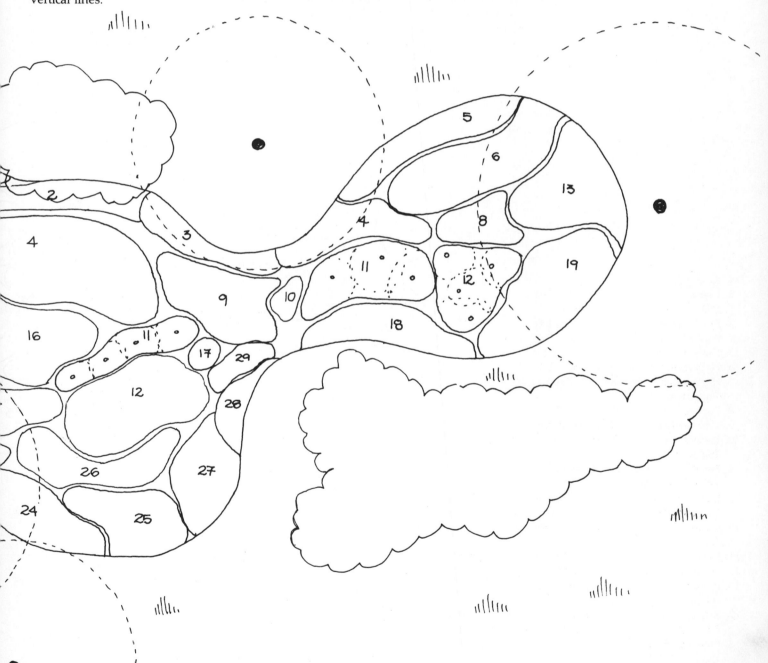

LAYOUT 6
LONG, WAVY, NARROW

This is a narrow border surrounded by paving, more or less the shape of an island bed. The space around it is wide and open so that the bed appears to be an independent unit. The covering is a chipped rock of a soft wood-brown color. The bed sits on a raised portion of the garden, in the foreground with a backdrop of trees and some shrubs on the fringes. One small tree stands at one end of the bed where it casts light shade. The rest of the longitudinal center space is in the sun. This narrow perennial border winds in gentle fashion, having indentations on either side. Two "bays" are opposite each other so that there is a Victorian waistline. This raised portion of the garden is glimpsed from below before you mount five steps. Having gained the upper level, there is an overall view from either end of the bed, whence you can see both sides and the manner in which the horizontal and vertical lines of the plants make a unique design.

There are a few subshrubs to lend weight; the woody *Potentilla* 'Mt. Everest' with white flowers punctuates one of the central ovals. The low rose bushes give weight to the sunny end. At that end also the *Euphorbia* is an important finishing plant not only for its color of green but for the flattened circles of its flowers which remain decorative when in the seed-making stage. At the other end, with shade from the tree, are placed a few perennials with foliage of distinctive form. The single plant of *Hosta plantaginea* has a strong rosette, the *Heuchera* leaves grow in a full clump and are dark green;

1. Rosa 'Margot Koster'
2. Dianthus 'Helen', or 'Doris' (General P.D.)
3. Brachycome iberidifolia (Annual P.D.)
4. Aurinia saxatile 'Luteum' (Slope P.D.)
5. Dianthus hyb. 'Parfait' (General P.D.)
6. Hypericum cerastoides (Slope P.D.)
7. Hemerocallis lilio-asphodelus hyb. (Site For A Large Perennial P.D.)
8. Papaver atlanticum (General P.D.)
9. Chrysanthemum cv. (General P.D.)
10. Helianthemum nummularium 'Apricot' (Slope P.D.)
11. Heuchera sanguinea cv. (white) (Woodland P.D.)
12. Euphorbia epithymoides (E. polychroma) (General P.D.)
13. Cosmos bipinnatus, "Sensation Strain" (General P.D.)
14. Lavandula pinnata (Subshrub P.D.)
15. Delphinium ajacis (General P.D.)
16. Physostegia virginiana 'Summer Snow' (General P.D.)
17. Salvia grandiflora var. pitcheri (General P.D.)
18. Potentilla fruticosa 'Mt. Everest' (Subshrub P.D.)

Francoa finishes the bed with a curving sweep.

Several annuals are incorporated for color: *Nigella* (left after blooming for its curious seed heads), *Nicotiana* which comes in wonderful shades, this one the greenish cultivar. *Lobelia,* the blue edger, is tucked between other edgers to give bright spots here and there. *Cosmos* stands high in two central positions; what a good long season it has!

Several small patches of the South African Gladiolus, *G. callianthus* make distinctive pale accents. *Physostegia* makes a tall line, a straight upthrust.

Now there is to be noted a pleasing motif in the color scheme, copper, apricot, bronze and salmon; even burnt-orange, provided by *Papaver atlantica.* The larger units in these tones are made by two *Daylilies* and two clumps of *Telephinum* 'Autumn Joy'. The *Phlox* cv., 'Sandra', is "scarlet-orange". The cvs. of the low *Potentillas* and those of the Sunrose pick up the tints in the larger units. The cvs. of the *Mimulus* and the *Chrysanthemum* are muted shades of the same colors.

There are several yellows in the foreground to add to this spectrum: the *Aurinia,* the *Onosma,* the *Linum,* the *Hypericum.* They do not bloom all at once, in fact, the first is gone before the second starts, but there is always a bit of yellow somewhere. Lavender (the color) has a minor part but white much more than minor. The bulges of the bed are raised a bit; through the center two clumps of rocks are carefully buried.

The square footage of this perennial border is less than the average but over 30 varieties fit into it in a comfortable manner.

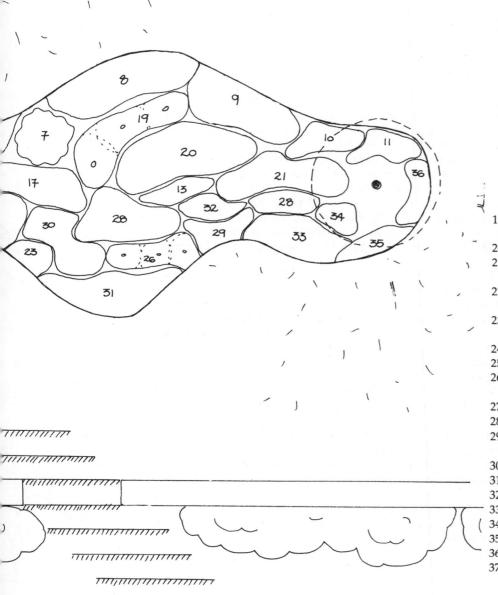

19. Telephium spectabile (See Sedum in General P.D.)
20. Pelargonium crispum (General P.D.)
21. Physostegia virginiana 'Vivid' (General P.D.)
22. Fragaria vesca 'Rugen's Improved' (General P.D.)
23. Lobelia erinus 'Cambridge Blue' (General P.D.)
24. Nigella damascena (Annual P.D.)
25. Rocks
26. Onosma stellulatum var. tauricum (Slope P.D.)
27. Nicotiana cv. (General P.D.)
28. Potentilla nepalensis (Slope P.D.)
29. Tanecetum haradjanii (Chrysanthemum) (General P.D.)
30. Linum flavum (General P.D.)
31. Erigeron speciosus (General P.D.)
32. Phlox paniculata 'Sandra' (General P.D.)
33. Aquilegia flabellata 'Nana' (General P.D.)
34. Hosta plantaginea (General P.D.)
35. Viola pedata (General P.D.)
36. Francoa ramosa (Woodland P.D.)
37. Mimulus hyb., M. lewisii × M. cardinalis (General P.D.)

LAYOUT 7
ISLAND IN THE SUN

Here is an island bed right out in the open, right out in the full sun. It has a bulge and two smaller projections; in an area where lawn is easy, these would abut straight onto grass. The center of the bed is slightly mounded through a large portion of its length.

The taller plants are placed more or less along this center line. These are stylish plants: *Delphinium, Lupinus, Paeonia, Phlox.* All are herbaceous so the soil in their area can be refurbished in winter. *Aristea* and *Libertia* are evergreen and therefore their positions will be left undisturbed. Both provide the upthrust of the sword-shaped leaf.

At #11, you will see the two positions for Lilies. Lilies can be started in pots and set in the bed when in bloom but these were planted directly in the soil and are established. (The bulbs will be lifted during the annual renovation.) The four drifts of *Delphinium* may be replaced with new plants next spring if the *Delphinium* cvs. have not held over well.

The long edge gives a wide opportunity to combine foliage of various character. Note the bronze *Sedum* next to the grey of *Stachys* and the round leaf of *Alchemilla* next to the narrow form of the *Veronica.* You will see some of my favorites, i.e. *Erysimum, Fragaria* and *Lavandula stoechas.* Note the name change for the dwarf *Globularia (G. meridionalis).*

You will probably grow some of the other perennials from seed, e.g. the *Iberis gibraltarica,* the *Linaria* 'Canon Went' and the *Dianthus barbatus;* and from cuttings, some of those hard to find in the market, e.g. the *Knautia,* the *Aster yunnanensis* and *Veronica* 'Minuet'.

I have included some clumps of *Cyrtanthus,* a reliable South African bulbous plant. I grow it in pots and it multiplies well enough so that I have extra for the garden.

The edges are trimmed with some mats including *Alchemilla* which you will see occur in other layouts because I like it so much. The *A. mollis* leaf has such a wonderfully round shape, with delicate embroidery around the edges; they are numerous and grow from the stems at pleasing angles. The color is a light green, a shade I want to call "apple-green". The wood-strawberry is more upright and higher; the leaves are somewhat lacey—much indented on the edges. (The old ones should be removed often.) The little white flowers hardly show, nor do the red berries. The birds and bugs find them soon enough. *Stachys lanata* is best placed in a wide sweep and its flower stems cut back continually; then the foliage is improved. The thick, grey, rich oval leaves are more velvety. I wanted a repetition of the color lavender along the edges, so I used the lavender species of *Iberis, I. gibraltica* as well as a lavender *Veronica* and *Globularias* used twice in positions #6 and #23. *Veronica* 'Minuet' and *Linaria* 'Canon Went' have greyish foliage and pale pink flowers.

This is not a pink and blue border but there is a large amount of both. One of the Peonies is single white and *Phlox* is white at the other end. The Peony is a beautiful mature "bush" with numerous leaves oval and lobed; they provide a wide area of strong handsome foliage from spring into fall. The *Phlox* is the species to which 'Miss Lingard' belongs and its foliage is typically more green and lush.

Bright colors are introduced for sparkle and the species are chosen partly for interesting foliage. *Dianthus* 'Little Joe' is crimson-red on greyish green mounds. *Dianthus barbatus* makes a high mat of green foliage nice to look at if the snails don't nibble too much; the plants have been raised from seed (apt to be true from seed) of a cv. called 'Copper Red'. It may have to be replaced after its second year. *Knautia* shows its relationship to *Scabiosa;* the stems are often leafier, the leaves are usually smaller and more finely cut, the clump is quite full, producing dark greenery in an oval shape to about two feet at maturity. Its flower is considerably smaller than that of *Scabiosa;* it is a compact pincushion of deep red. Keep new plants coming along from cuttings.

You will see a few drifts of yellow: *Oenothera, Erysimum* and *Asphodeline.* The latter is selected for its curious, almost wispy foliage; two or more plants are enough to make their introduction eye-catching.

Relatives are often used for purposes of recognition and comparison; they are not placed next to each other but near enough to discover a common characteristic. Find two *Asters,* two *Campanulas* and four *Veronicas.* Repetition is carried out by designating more than one position for *Paeonia, Delphinium, Phlox* and the Lilies. Their foliage is decorative during the periods before and after bloom.

A winding traffic lane surrounds the border, widening on the curves. It is paved with brick since brick has been used for the terrace and steps of the house. In some gardens, turf could be brought up to the edge obviating a traffic lane.

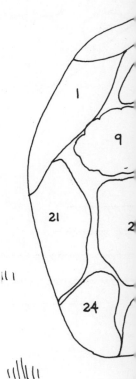

1. Alchemilla mollis (General P.D.)
2. Veronica spicata 'Icicle' (General P.D.)
3. Veronica spicata 'Minuet' (General P.D.)
4. Iberis gibraltarica (General P.D.)
5. Erysimum kotschyanum (General P.D.)
6. Globularia meriodionalis (G. bellidifolia) (Woodland P.D.)
7. Thymus drucei (General P. D.)
8. Veronica grandis var. holophylla (General P.D.)
9. Libertia formosa (Site For A Large Perennial P.D.)
10. Linaria purpurea 'Canon Went' (General P.D.)
11. Linaria triornothophyros (General P.D.)
12. Platycodon grandiflorus (General P. D.)
13. Asphodeline lutea (Slope P.D.)
14. Scabiosa caucasica (General P.D.)
15. Knautia macedonica (General P.D.)
16. Aster yunnanensis 'Napsbury' (General P.D.)
17. Paeonia, herb. cv. (General P.D.)
18. Phlox paniculata cv. (Woodland P.D.)
19. Delphinium hyb. cv. (General P.D.)
20. Aristea eclonis (Site For A Large Perennial P.D.)
21. Veronica pectinata (General P.D.)
22. Campanula persicifolia (General P.D.)
23. Globularia repens (Woodland P.D.)
24. Sedum stahlii (Slope P.D.)
25. Stachys lanata (General P.D.)
26. Oenothera tetragona (General P.D.)
27. Campanula carpatica cv. (Slope P.D.)
28. Dianthus barbatus: selected form (General P.D.)
29. Aster × frikartii (General P.D.)
30. Dianthus hyb. 'Little Joe' (General P.D.)
31. Fragaria vesca 'Baron Solemacher' (General P.D.)
32. Lupinus polyphyllus 'Little Lulu' (General P.D.)
33. Linum narbonense (General P.D.)
34. Cyrtanthus mackenii (Outdoor Room P.D.)
35. Lavandula stoechas (Subshrub P.D.)
36. Mitchella repens (Woodland P.D.)

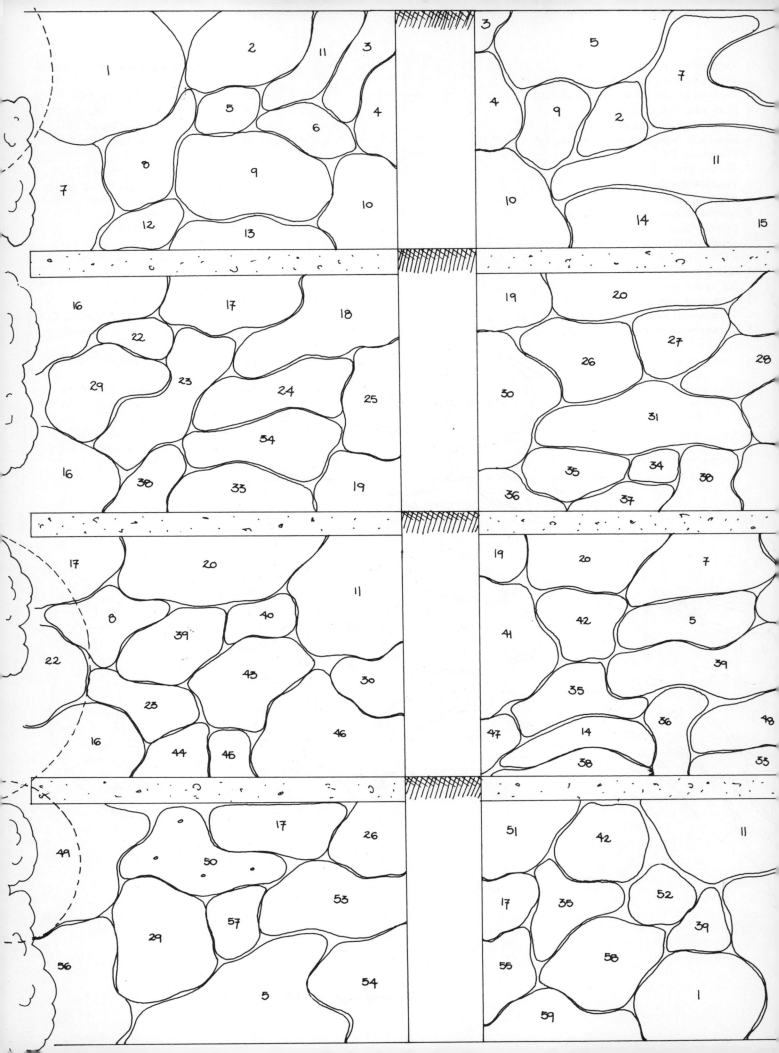

LAYOUT 8
DOUBLE, RISING

This double border rises almost ten feet from its base to a platform at the top ornamented by a gazebo in the center. There are antique benches on either side with espaliered *Sasanquas* on the wall behind them. There are four levels each with a two foot stone wall. The path is stepped at the points of the walls. The soil is raised to meet the top of the wall in each section.

The design has two parts. Each bed is a separate section with a composition of various heights and forms; all beds are tied together with an overall design. To accomplish these connections, there is considerable repetition; there is also a placement of the tallest growth subjects in like places in each. To give examples: *Paeonia, Delphinium, Iris, Campanula, Lavandula, Penstemon,* and *Salvia*; all are repeated. *Delphinium, Iris* and Tree peonies which link the beds, have positions in several sections, more or less in the center of the retaining walls as well as at the back looking either way from the wall.

Two terminal bushes, *Euryops pectinata*, create a solid period, one in a high position, one in a low position, upper right and lower left. This is asymmetrical balance.

Mostly low species are planted along the path and on the lower edge of each bed. Grey foliage is used generously to associate with the grey in the stone. E.g. *Senecio, Lavandula, Dianthus, Origanum, Chrysanthemum haradjanii (Tanacetum haradjanii.)* Some of the trailers which drape over the wall are *Convolvulus mauritanicus, Helianthemum* and Thyme.

As for color, there is blue and bluish lavender, ample white, a little yellow and some vivid accents, e.g. *Dahlia, Penstemon, Clivia* and the dark *Pelargonium* 'Black Knight'. The Peony cvs. were selected for their rich color.

The background of the left side, looking up, is shaded by trees and shrubs but the aspect of the greater proportion of the site is almost full sun.

This is a large border with many plants; it requires many hours of care but even the smallest ministration is evident.

The landscape architecture here is quite formal with the twin spaces again divided into equal rectangles and with the steps and walls and decorative viewing station, placed as they are at uniform points. As you see, the planting is natural rather than matched or measured. It is an achievement to rise above the precise outlines of the setting and at the same time incorporate meandering lines in the design of the planting.

1. Euryops pectinata (Site For A Large Perennial P.D.)
2. Digitalis mertonensis (Woodland P.D.)
3. Primula polyantha (Woodland P.D.)
4. Geranium wallichianum (Slope P.D.)
5. Paeonia herb. hyb. 'Tria' (General P.D.)
6. Gonospermum canariensis (Site For A Large Perennial P.D.)
7. Iris pallida 'Alba' and/or I. siberica 'Skywing' (General P.D.)
8. Thalictrum dipterocarpum 'Flore-plena' (Woodland P.D.)
9. Dahlia cv. (General P.D.)
10. Iberis sempervirens (General P.D.)
11. Penstemon hyb., cv. 'Firebird' (P. hartwegii) (General P.D.)
12. Campanula carpatica var. turbinata (Slope P.D.)
13. Galium odoratum (Woodland P. D.)
14. Helianthemum cv. (Slope P.D.)
15. Gerbera cv. (General P.D.)
16. Aruncus dioicus (A. sylvester) (Woodland P.D.)
17. Iris siberica 'White Swirl' (General P.D.)
18. Senecio cineraria (General P.D.)
19. Lavendula stoechas (Subshrub P.D.)
20. Delphinium bellamosum, D. belladonna hyb. (General P.D.)

21. Iris hyb. (I. germanica) 'Sunset' (General P.D.)
22. Cimicifuga racemosa (Woodland P.D.)
23. Filipendula palmata (General P.D.)
24. Aquilegia hyb., "Spring Song Strain" (General P.D.)
25. Tanacetum haradjanii (Chrysanthemum haradjanii) (General P.D.)
26. Lavandula spica (Subshrub P.D.)
27. Campanula persicifolia (General P.D.)
28. Achillea taygetea (General P.D.)
29. Aconitum carmichaelii (A. fischeri) (Woodland P.D.)
30. Jasione perennis (General P.D.)
31. Salvia guaranitica (General P.D.)
32. Aster × frikarkii (General P.D.)
33. Convolvulus mauritanicus (General P.D.)
34. Hemerocallis hyb. 'Katherine Woodbury' (Site For A Large Perennial P.D.)
35. Veronica spicata 'Icicle' (General P.D.)
36. Origanum dictamnus (Slope P.D.)
37. Pelargonium domesticum 'Black Knight' (General P.D.)
38. Thymus drucei (General P. D.)
39. Phlox paniculata 'Bright Eyes' (General P.D.)
40. Eucomis punctata (Woodland P.D.)
41. Salvia hyb. 'Victoria' (General P.D.)

42. Chrysanthemum coccineum (General P.D.)
43. Campanula glomerata (General P.D.)
44. Campanula carpatica 'Dark Star' (Slope P.D.)
45. Ceratostigma plumbaginoides (Woodland P.D.)
46. Salvia patens (General P.D.)
47. Achillea tomentosum 'King George' (General P.D.)
48. Macleaya cordata (General P.D.)
49. Astilbe × arendsii 'Fanal' (Woodland P.D.)
50. Clivia miniata (Outdoor Room P. D.)
51. Linum flavum (General P.D.)
52. Diplarrhena moraea (Site For A Large Perennial P.D.)
53. Genista × kewensis (Subshrubs P.D.)
54. Campanula rotundifolia or C. pilosa var. dasyantha (General P.D.)
55. Calceolaria hyb. cv. 'John Innes' (Outdoor Room P.D.)
56. Franco ramosa (Woodland P.D.)
57. Potentilla × tonguei (Slope P.D.)
58. Dianthus hyb. 'Zing Rose' (General P.D.)
59. Liriope spicata (Woodland P.D.)

There are many old trees in this little garden. One is a large *Magnolia grandiflora*, casting almost 50 feet of shade all year long. Another is a Live Oak which has been sending its branches wide for many, many years. Another is a younger tree *Melaleuca linariifolia* which has grown five feet a year since released from its gallon container six years ago; it stands to the northwest to break the wind and it blocks the sun toward evening from reaching its portion of the garden. There are smaller trees as well, evergreen, as *Azara* and *Cornus capitata* and several deciduous trees, for instance *Acer palmatum, Styrax japonicum, Nyssa* for fall color, and *Stewartia,* three species, and some flowering fruits. All add to the shade.

You can readily see that this garden needs subjects that do not require much sun. I will name only two or three of the large number of shrubs which not only prefer shade but also disperse shade for their accompanying perennials. Examples are *Trochodendron araloides, Rhododendron lutea, Viburnum.* The perennials selected must thrive in shade, light shade, part shade, overhead shade in places but deep shade in others where only momentary shafts of light reach the earth; there is optimum opportunity to grow perennials with surfaces which glimmer when reached by an occasional ray of sun. There are a few spots, of course, which receive more light than that received by most of the area.

There are four places where low rocks are buried. They project only enough to balance the small plants in their vicinity.

The perennials: several species are herbaceous. Their foliage is present for many months and changes appearance over the long season. The foliage of both herbaceous and evergreen selections must harmonize with the adjacent shrubs. *Macleaya* has a fantastic leaf with interesting indentations and unique color; the backside is partly visible, of a muted shade too difficult to name. *Macleaya* is tall enough to be placed in the rear of the bed but it must have some light behind it to bring out the character of the foliage. It is seen through a gap in the shrubbery. In front of it is a group of *Cimicifuga* with stems not much less tall, set well enough apart to view the *Macleaya.* The leaves of *Cimicifuga* are finely cut; they curve horizontally below the flower stems. The wand-like flower spikes are silhouetted against the background.

Several plants have been placed to clamber or drape over the rocks. The *Gentiana* and *Campanula* are herbaceous; the *Metrosideros* and the *Leptospermum* are evergreen. *Metrosideros* has shiny, tiny round leaves and the dwarf *Leptospermum* has very fine needle-like leaves.

In order to intersperse a vertical line, some blade-shaped leaves are placed in strategic places. There are two prominent drifts of Pacific Coast Iris, on the front edge where light comes down the path. The leaves of *Liriope* echo the blade shape. The leafy stems of *Polygonatum* and *Uvalaria* contribute a curving vertical line.

There is feathery foliage in *Dicentra, Rupicapnos, Thalictrum* and *Astilbe.* The species of the latter two are dwarf. However, the site chosen for them is in a clearly visible position, in a niche provided by rocks and with no overhanging foliage to screen them.

On first observing this small, simple garden, you might wonder how to include plantings of flowering perennials. If the garden seems overplanted with trees, there are none you would want to remove; they establish the personality of the garden as well as its special climate. The site is in a valley, where in spring and summer the temperatures are high and the air dry. The foliage of the trees both makes an umbrella from the sun's strongest rays and makes the air beneath cooler by its respiration. There are several small spaces throughout the garden in between the trees and shrubs for a bit of a bed or border or strip in which to plant one or two or a combination of several perennials.

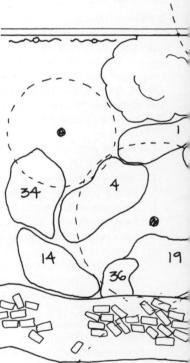

1. Maclaeya cordata (General P.D.)
2. Aruncus dioicus 'Kneiffii' (Woodland P.D.)
3. Metrosideros carmineus (Woodland P.D.)
4. Cimicifuga cordifolia (Woodland P.D.)
5. Polygonatum odoratum (Woodland P.D.)
6. Pulsatilla alpina var. apiifolia (P. thunbergii) (Woodland P.D.)
7. Dicentra eximia 'Snow Drift' (Woodland P.D.)
8. Rupicapnos africana (Woodland P.D.)
9. Gentiana septemfida hyb. 'Hascombensis' (Woodland P.D.)
10. Gentiana asclepiadea (Woodland P.D.)
11. Trillium ovatum (Woodland P.D.)
12. Paris polyphylla (Woodland P.D.)
13. Polemonium carneum 'Album' (Woodland P.D.)
14. Pulmonaria angustifolia (Woodland P.D.)
15. Campanula isophylla (Outdoor Room P.D.)
16. Liriope muscari 'Silver Midget' (Woodland P.D.)
17. Ophiopogon planiscepus 'Arabicus' (Woodland P.D.)
18. Thalictrum kuisianum (Woodland P.D.)
19. Selaginella rupestris (Woodland P.D.)
20. Tanakaea radicans (Woodland P.D.)
21. Anemone sylvestris 'Grandiflora' (Woodland P.D.)
22. Uvularia caroliniana (Woodland P.D.)
23. Cornus canadensis (Woodland P.D.
24. Convallaria majalis (Outdoor Room P.D.)
25. Cyclamen coum (Woodland P.D.)
26. Houstonia caerulea (Outdoor Room P.D.)
27. Globularia cerastioides (Woodland P.D.)
28. Disporum sessile var. variegatum (Woodland P.D.)
29. Rhodohypoxis baurii (Woodland P.D.)
30. Astilbe microphylla (Woodland P.D.)
31. Aruncus aethusifolius (Woodland P.D.)
32. Primula juliae hyb. (Woodland P.D.)
33. Tiarella wherryi (Woodland P.D.)
34. Iris innominata (General P.D.)
35. Leptospermum humisifusa (Subshrub P.D.)
36. Maianthemum canadense (Woodland P.D.)

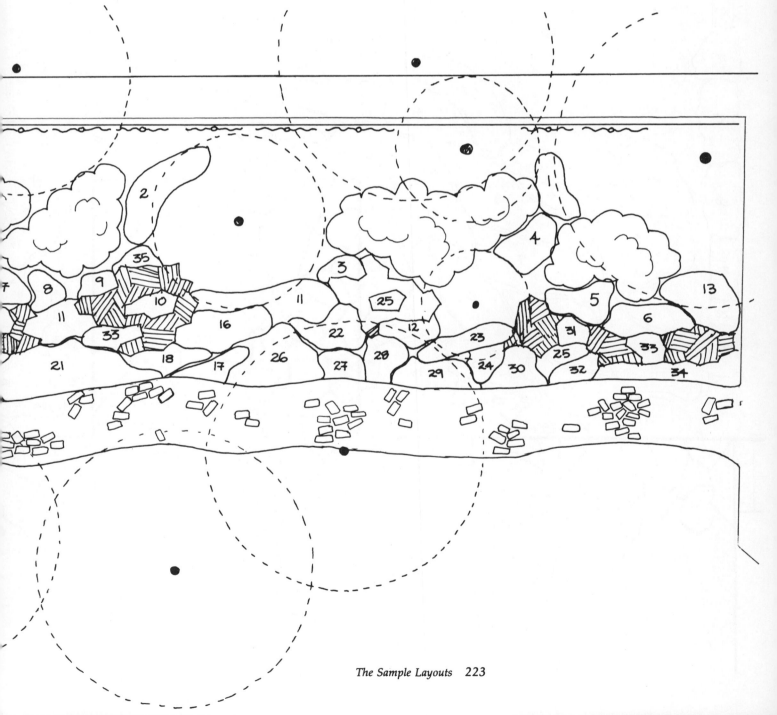

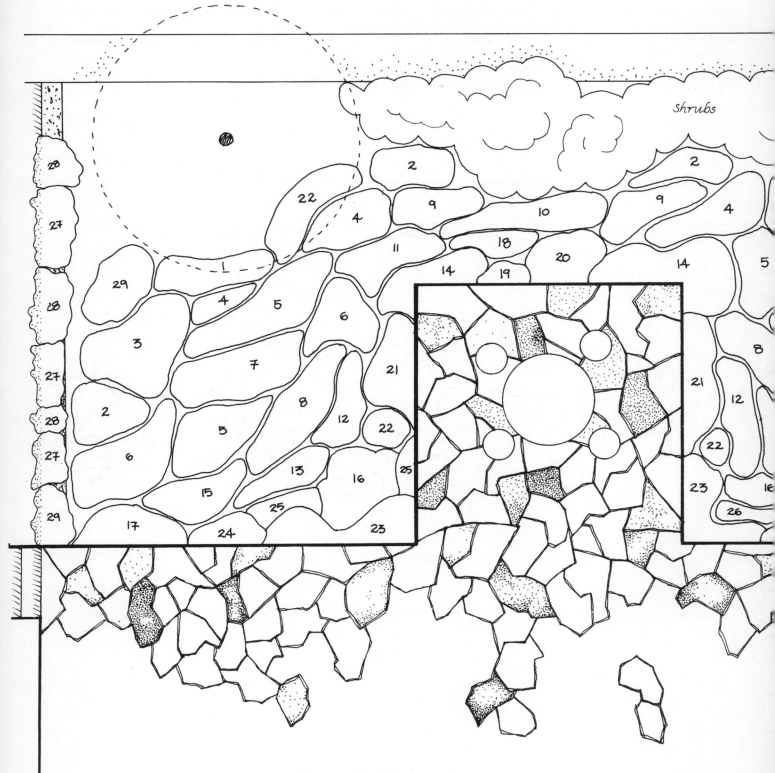

Shrubs

LAYOUT 10
PATIO

A small patio adjoins a small house. The paving is slate of a warm beige color. A portion of the paving makes a square indentation into the flower border. This is big enough to hold a small table and chairs.

The beds either side of the square are treated with drifts of similar perennials augmented by annuals in their seasons. Two or three trees are in the background towards the northwest whence comes the prevailing wind. A wall borders the property beyond the path which separates wall and border. A wide path on the south side leads to doors of the house. From the path's level two steps rise to the higher level of the patio and the south side of the bed is held up by a low wall. A wing of the house is across the patio and a wall closes it in to the north.

The style of this little garden is quite traditional. The two sides contain the same species but their positions are not exactly the same. They are twins but not identical twins. Height is established on the sides as well as at the back. Just above the south retaining wall is an edging of *Artemisia canescens, Ballota nigra, Origanum dictamnus* and prostrate Thyme. These provide greyish foliage and are suitable for the warm exposure of this part of the site.

Many of the spp. planted to give bloom in the summer have ample basal and stem leaves. The *Dahlia* cvs. were obtained for the color and quality of the flowers but their foliage is good also. They will be lifted for winter storage although the modern cvs. are often excellent the second year without lifting. The *Lupine* makes a handsome clump center stage; we will have to see whether it is reliably perennial.

The edges are treated with some plants attractive out of bloom as well as at the height of the bloom, especially *Penstemon heterophyllus* and *Centaurea montana*. Some annuals are inserted in conspicuous places in early spring to augment the summer flowering. *Mignonette* in particular forms a full, low mound when it does well.

You will note in this fully packed little border a few out-of-the-ordinary spp. or cvs. The unusual is eyecatching when used in an important position; e.g. *Gladiolus callianthus* and *Anthericum liliago* both with slender, graceful stalks.

As for color, you have noted that the motif is pastel. There is considerable blue and nearly blue. Yellow is in several areas especially from the flowers of *Oenothera* and *Achillea*. There is pink in both tall and short spp., e.g. the Hollyhocks, the *Chrysanthemum* and the *Dianthus*.

The owner of this little garden takes pride in the fullness of bloom. She will "tuck in" a pot or two of annuals if any small section is lacking in color temporarily. The plants are well-grown because they are constantly cared for.

The patio is in almost constant use for sitting or sunning or visiting. You are actually in the garden while you are outdoors since the perennial borders are in direct proximity. From the house windows, however, you will see from either direction the architectural form. The proportion of the two levels, the geometric form of the flower borders and the relationships of the various heights and types of foliage, all are pleasing.

1. Anemone vitifolia 'Robustissima' (General P.D.)
2. Digitalis cvs. (Woodland P.D.)
3. Alcea rosea (Althaea cannabina) (Annual P.D.)
4. Salvia cacaliaefolia (General P.D.)
5. Dahlia cvs. (General P.D.)
6. Phlox carolina 'Miss Willmott' (General P.D.)
7. Penstemon hyb. 'Pink Gem' (General P.D.)
8. Cynoglossum nervosum (Woodland P.D.)
9. Salvia uliginosa (General P.D.)
10. Lupinus hyb. (General P.D.)
11. Geranium grandiflorum (Slope P.D.)
12. Achillea hyb. 'Moonshine' (from 2 garden clones) (General P.D.)
13. Chrysanthemum coccineum (Pyrethrum) (General P.D.)
14. Penstemon heterophyllus (General P.D.)
15. Oenothera tetragona (General P.D.)
16. Dianthus hyb. 'Beatrix' (General P.D.)
17. Petunia (Annual P.D.)
18. Liriope muscari 'Munroe #1' (Woodland P. D.) (L. m. 'Munroe White')
19. Acorus gramineus 'Variegatus' (Bog P.D.)
20. Reseda odorata (Annual P.D.)
21. Centaurea montana (General P.D.)
22. Anthericum liliago var. major (General P.D.)
23. Allium moly (overplanted with purple Hesperis) (bulb)
24. Aethionema warleyense (General P.D.)
25. Clematis × eriostemon 'Hendersonii' (General P.D.)
26. Gladiolus tristus var. concolor (corm)
27. Thymus quinquecostus 'Albus' (General P.D.)
28. Ballota nigra (General P.D.)
29. Origanum dictamnus (Slope P.D.)
30. Artemisia canescens (Slope P.D.)

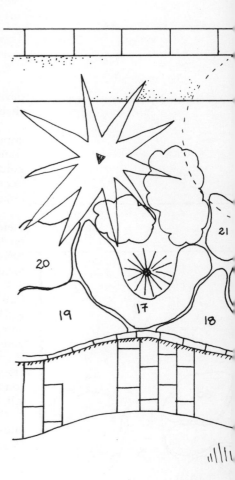

LAYOUT 11
PERENNIALS WITH SHRUBBERY

This is a shrubbery border accompanied by perennials. It backs up to a brick wall and has a brick curbing on its curving front edge. The background trees cast a little shade but the two conifers are somewhat columnar and the deciduous trees are open rather than dense. The border faces south.

This border continues on almost twice as far as this part shown and while some of the plants are of different spp., the design is created in the same manner.

Two shrubs make a wonderful combination, *Cotinus* and *Perovskia*, one dark plum-red, the other white-grey and bright lavender. The grey is reflected in the foliage of the perennials on the forward edge, in *Zauschneria, Dorycnium, Origanum,* and *Androsace*. The plum-red is carried out in the leaves of *Hesperaloe*, False Yucca. Note the foliage of the out-of-the-ordinary spp. of *Teucrium, Foeniculum* and *Cheiranthus*.

Two unusual *Scillas* are permanent residents of the border.

The annual, *Brachycome,* will hopefully set seed. The white form of *Stokesia* must be increased by cuttings.

Several other dwarf spp. are placed in the foreground. Two drifts of *Cyclamen* are planted between rocks.

The *Trillium* is not selected so much for its spectacular flowers as for the aspect of the whole plant. Nothing is allowed to encroach upon its space. Its cousin, *Paris,* is perhaps the Chef d'oevre of the whole piece—what a miracle of nature's art!

Shrubbery does not play a dominating role in this border. The species have been chosen to give a special restrained form for their positions. This is not a case where bushes were planted for a boundary and thereafter perennials added wherever there appeared a little space. The composition was made with trees, shrubs and low-growing plants all relating to one another and creating an architectural design.

Only a portion of this shady garden is pictured but this is a portion where some of the most choice perennials are assembled.

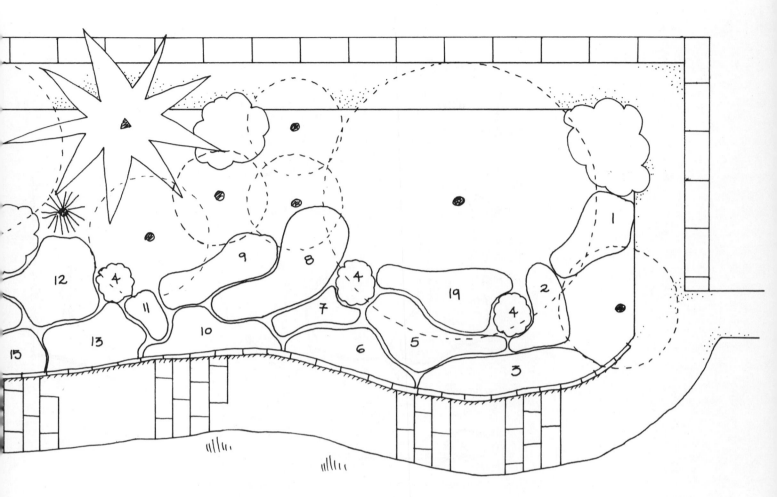

1. Erysimum capitatum (General P.D.)
2. Potentilla oweriana (Slope P.D.)
3. Androsace lanuginosa (Woodlnd P.D.)
4. Hesperaloe parviflora (General P.D.)
5. Stokesia laevis 'Silver Moon' (General P.D.)
6. Origanum × hybridum (O. dictamnus × O. sipyleum) (Slope P.D.)
7. Salvia guaranitica (General P.D.)
8. Eucomis comosa (Woodland P.D.) (bulb)
9. Cheiranthus linifolius (Slope P.D.)
10. Cheiranthus linifolius 'Variegatus' (Slope P.D.) (Erysimum)
11. Endymion hispanicus 'Album' (bulb)
12. Penstemon digitalis (General P.D.)
13. Zauschneria arizonica (Z. californica subsp. latifolia) (Slope P.D.)
14. Foeniculum vulgare cv.(General P.D.)
15. Teucrium scorodonia 'Crispum' (Slope P.D.)
16. Scilla peruviana 'Alba' (bulb)
17. Dorycnium hirsutum (General P.D.)
18. Brachycome iberidifolia (Annual P.D.)
19. Dianthus petraeus subsp. noeanus (General P.D.)
20. × Solidaster luteus (Aster × Solidago) (General P.D.)
21. Phyllodoce empetriformis (Woodland P.D.)
22. Calocephalus brownii (Slope P.D.)

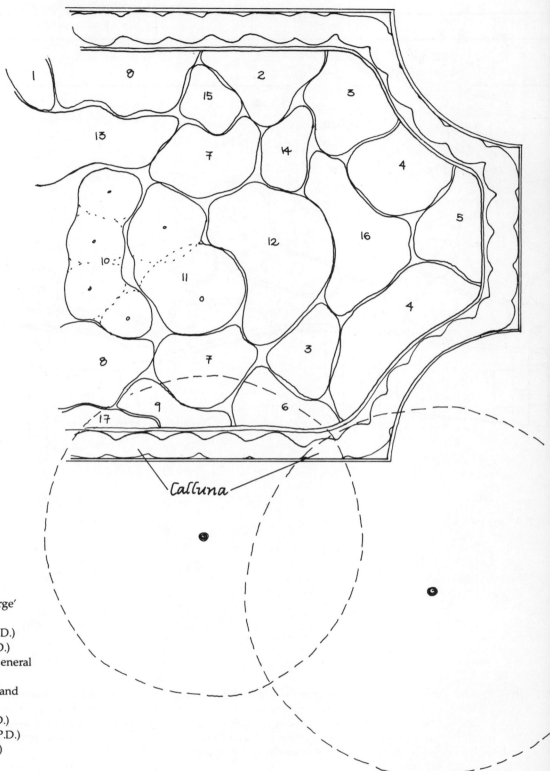

Calluna

A Panel & a Herb Garden

1. Achillea tomentosum 'King George' (General P.D.)
2. Erodium cervifolium (General P.D.)
3. Veronica spicata cv. (General P.D.)
4. Salvia farinacea 'Blue Bedder' (General P.D.)
5. Cynoglossum nervosum (Woodland P.D.)
6. Geum georgenberg (General P.D.)
7. Chrysanthemum hyb. (General P.D.)
8. Scabiosa caucasica (General P.D.)
9. Aquilegia cv. (General P.D.)
10. Kniphofia hyb. (Genereal P.D.)
11. Gaura lindheimeri (Site For A Large Perennial P.D.)
12. Baptisia australis (General P.D.)
13. Thermopsis caroliniana (General P. D.)
14. Chrysanthemum mawii (General P.D.)
15. Bulbinella hookeri (General P.D.)
16. Echinops tournefortii (General P.D.)
17. Muscari cv. (bulb)

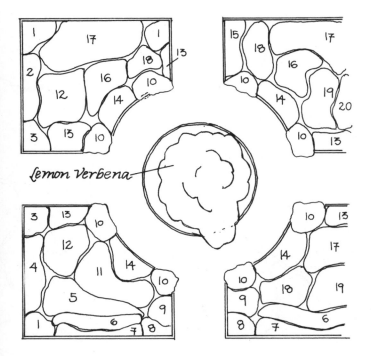

Lemon Verbena

1. Rosmarinus cv. (Subshrub P.D.)
2. Lavandula dentata (Subshrub P.D.)
3. Pelargonium fragrans (General P.D.)
4. Lavandula stoechas (Subshrub P.D.)
5. Thymus (General P.D.)
6. Lettuce
7. Parsley
8. Ballota nigra (General P.D.)
9. Santolina neapolitana (General P.D.)
10. Lavandula angustifolia 'Hidcote' (Subshrub P.D.)
11. Anethum graveolens (General P.D.)
12. Beta vulgaris (Site For A Large Perennial P.D.)
13. Satureja montana (General P.D.)
14. Allium ampeloprasum (bulb)
15. Allium schoenoprasum (bulb)
16. Origanum vulgare (Slope P.D.)
17. Salvia sp. (Lemon sage) (General P.D.)
18. Origanum dictamnus (Slope P.D.)
19. Helianthus tuberosus (General P.D.)
20. Rumex scutatus (General P.D.)

Alternatives or additions

1. Melissa
2. Mentha
3. Symphytum officinale (General P.D.)
4. Fragaria (General P.D.)

LAYOUT 12
RELATED, ADJACENT, GEOMETRIC

Here are portions of two gardens which can be planned in combination with each other or may be used separately in a site for which one or the other is suitable. The plants used in both are informal but are spaced in a more or less balanced fashion relating to the geometric outline by a selection of foliage which melds together all the plant material into the site restriction. Either or both gardens could be features of a terrace or just a yard. The rectangle may be called a panel since it is longer than wide and stands free in a space unrelated to any architectural form.

Only part of it has been sketched since its length will depend on the measurements of the space available. It could be a simple rectangle but you will find that some design which modifies the corners may be decorative in your setting. I have edged the panel with a solid row of a *Calluna* which grows in a ball shape. You could select the most dwarf Holly or the most dwarf *Azalea* or Boxwood, *Buxus*, according to your tastes.

The perennials in the center of the panel are taller and sturdier. An alternate treatment would be a combination of perennials all of the same height. You could change the scheme once or even twice a year and could include annuals in order to make a solid cover of plants.

This is the only flower bed in the garden so some pickables have been included. There is a small patch of *Gypsophila* from which panicles may be cut to soften mixed bouquets and many flowers may be cut from *Achillea* and *Scabiosa*. The colors of the *Scabiosa* are mixed but there is a preponderance of white.

Upkeep of this panel is not too arduous except for dead-heading, of course. How do you get to the center? You must thread your way and walk gently, cultivator in hand, on all the occasions when you wish to pick. Heavier walking necessary for general maintenance will wait until all is cut back in the fall.

The little herb garden has a traditional design. The plants in the corners accentuate the pattern. This layout contains some herbs which are favorites not only for looks but for use.

The angles of the herb garden are marked with permanent substantial species. They are kept clipped to a point so that the outline of the beds is not obliterated. Some alternatives were added in a list which was abbreviated since there is no other field in which the preference of the owner will play a greater part.

Add these two individual, useful-plus-ornamental gardens in a longitudinal line or a parallel line and both the form and the contents may be related. You may be able to intensify the relationship by using in both some species of the same genus.

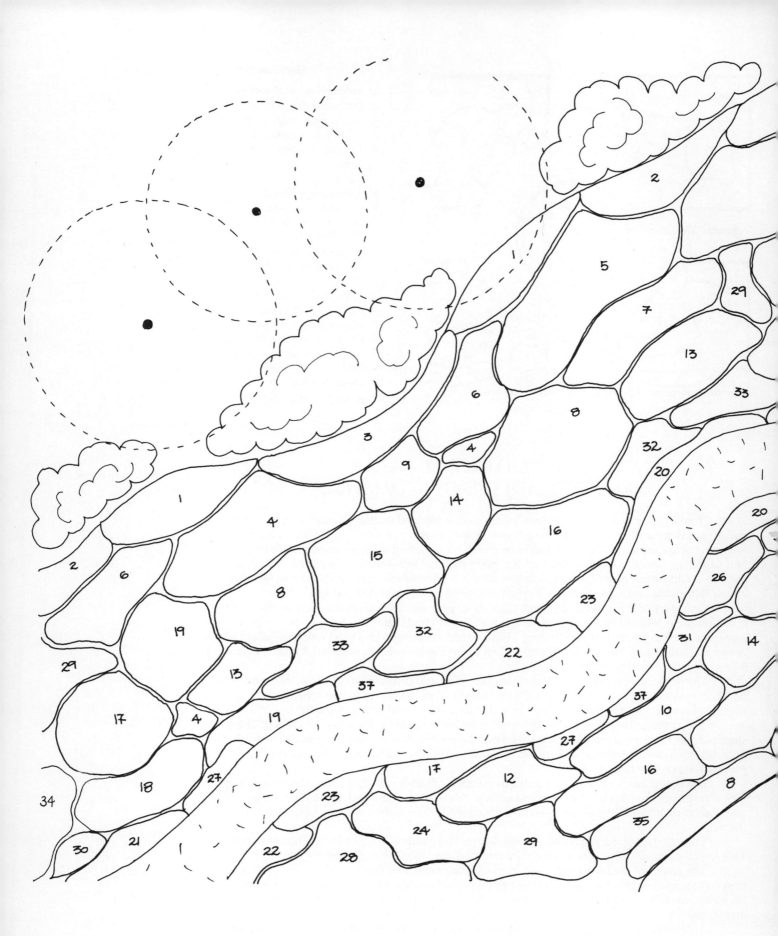

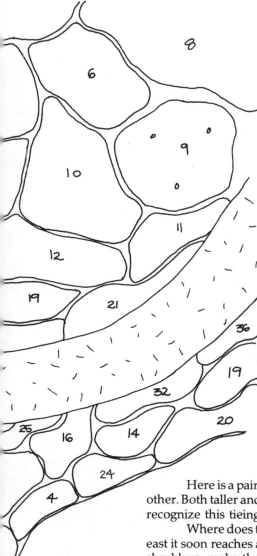

1. Gaura lindheimeri (Site For A Large Perennial P.D.)
2. Artemisia lactiflora (Site For A Large Perennial P.D.)
3. Kniphofia hyb. (General P.D.)
4. Helenium autumnale 'Rubrum' (General P.D.)
5. Baptisia australis (General P.D.)
6. Phlomis fruticosa (Subshrub P.D.)
7. Thermopsis caroliniana (General P.D.)
8. Hemerocallis cv. (Site For A Large Perennial P.D.)
9. Euphorbia epithymoides (General P.D.)
10. Lavandula angustifolia cv. (Subshrub P.D.)
11. Stokesia laevis (General P.D.)
12. Scabiosa columbaria (General P.D.)
13. Campanula glomerata General P.D.)
14. Pelargonium fragrans (General P.D.)
15. Echinacea purpurea 'White Lustre' (General P.D.)
16. Echinops ritro (General P.D.)
17. Felicia amelloides 'Santa Anita' (Subshrub P.D.)
18. Aster dumosus (General P.D.)
19. Veronica grandis var. holophylla (General P.D.)
20. Santolina chamaecyparissus (General P.D.)
21. Nepeta faassenii (General P.D.)
22. Erodium cheilanthefolium 'David Crocker' (General P.D.)
23. Verbena tenera var. maonettii (General P.D.)
24. Teucrium chamaedrys 'Prostratum' (General P.D.)
25. Anacyclus depressus (General P.D.)
26. Chrysanthemum mawii (General P.D.)
27. Achillea tomentosa cv. (General P.D.)
28. Salvia farinacea 'Blue Bedder' (General P.D.)
29. Potentilla fruticosa 'Snow Flake' (Subshrub P.D.)
30. Eupatorium coelestinum (Woodland P.D.)
31. Geranium andressii (Slope P.D.)
32. Geum chiloensis 'Princess Juliana' (General P.D.)
33. Eryngium amethystinum (General P.D.)
34. Lychnis chalcedonica (General P.D.)
35. Anchusa azurea 'Loddon Royalist' (General P.D.)
36. Cerastium tomentosum (General P.D.)
37. Potentilla nepalensis 'Willmottiae' (Miss Willmott') (Slope P.D.)

LAYOUT 13
UNEQUAL PAIR

Here is a pair of wavy unequal borders along a winding path one side half again as broad as the other. Both taller and shorter plants are often repeated in the opposite panel near enough so that you recognize this tieing action which makes the two sides join to become a whole.

Where does the path go? Down the way a bit to the west it goes to the vegetable garden. To the east it soon reaches a terrace bordering the house. A few trees flank the biggest curve and some low shrubbery make the southeast boundary.

This planting scheme is carried out with somewhat tough perennials. All need some attention, however, in order to present an attractive scene. The evergreen spp. must be trimmed, e.g. *Felicia*, *Lavandula*, *Teucrium* and *Santolina*. Some spp. receive a pruning deeper than a trim, e.g. *Echinops*, *Eryngium*, *Scabiosa* and *Thermopsis*. The herbaceous spp. must be cut to ground level, e.g. *Geum*, *Campanula*, *Helenium*, *Artemisia*.

The background woody plants are of medium height so that only a little shade touches the farthest back corners. The tallest perennials add a little also. Those in this back position are seldom staked but are held up by their neighbors. Lower spp. in the middle range are sturdy growers. Along the edges a number of trailers are repeated and take turns showing color along the path.

Phlomis, in a center position, has a sturdy personality due in great part to the rugose texture of the leaves. *Gaura*, on the other hand, is light and airy, an effect brought about by the willowy stems and the dainty flowers.

Many of the spp. are old-fashioned, for instance, *Nepeta*, *Iberis*, *Geranium* and *Geum*. You will note some newcomers perhaps as *Chrysanthemum mawii*, *Anacyclus*, *Thermopsis* and *Artemisia ludoviciana* var. *albula* 'Silver King'. The latter is used to create the tallest and most upright line along the backbone of the composition. Many of the spp. around the boundary are familiars. You will see that those chosen for the corners are planted to wrap around the triangles, thus softening the geometry.

As for color, yellow occurs in several different shades. Lavender and purple are used as counterparts shading into a bit of magenta for spark. On either end the foliage color tapers off into minor patches of grey.

The form of these borders would be termed "natural". It is all the more important that the various perennials be placed with a plan in mind. Curving lines must sweep in a graceful fashion and the plants must mount and proceed in a clear if ungeometric pattern.

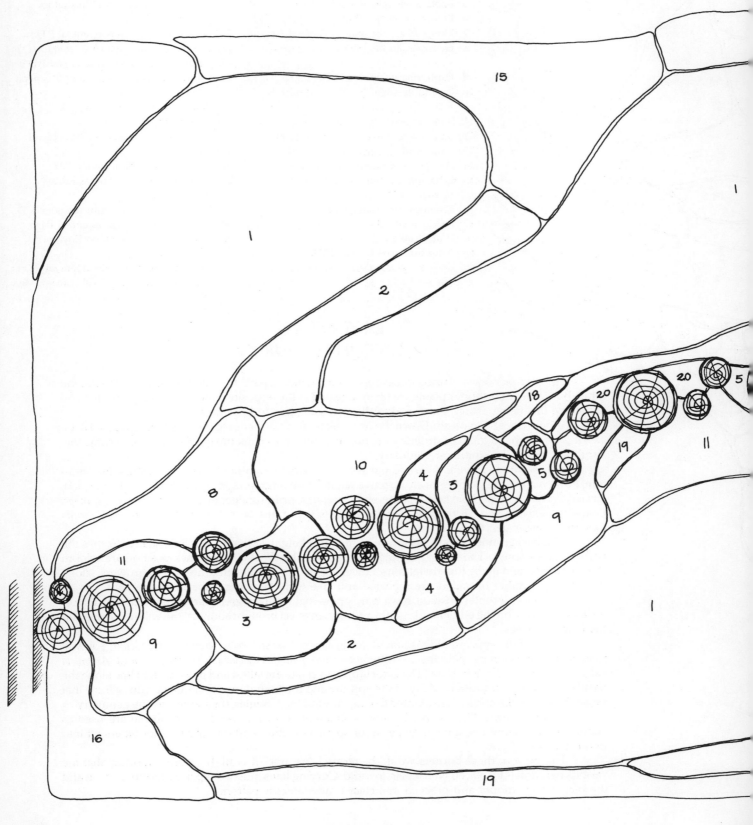

A more or less flat place in your garden lends itself to a planting of ground covers. I have chosen for this model carpet mostly spp. which lie very flat; some of them flower but the flowers are either very tiny or they grow on very short stems. Except in a few small corners, this whole carpet can be mowed. Stepping "stones", here redwood rounds, lead from a set of steps from the upper terrace to two other steps leading into a small building. Between and around the rounds you will see small drifts; these are spp. of either a dainty nature or of a rarity which might be lost among the coarser more rampant spp. The plants which make up these small patches may have to be trimmed by hand. Only two spp. are really herbaceous; their absence is hardly discernible since such a large proportion of the carpet stays green. *Parochetus* sometimes disappears for no obvious reason but almost always a bit on the edge remains alive; from this remainder, you can make divisions to get its appointed place full again. *Paronychia serpyllifolia* Whitlowwort, Nailwort, is a charming mat but suits better a slope on which its tiny procumbent stems can trail. Camomile is the base, the ground of the rug design. It is cut often enough to prevent flowering as well as to remove loose and shaggy stems. The Wooly Thyme is no trouble since it hugs the ground and its flowers are minute; the other Thymes need a little attention for neatness but they are allowed to bloom, especially the bright ones. For a carpet, it is best to choose the smallest *Potentilla* you can find. Some of them like to roam. The *Campanula* here is really a rock garden sp.; it may have to be replaced by a sturdier one.

Adjacent to the small gazebo there is some shade. The fern in any case will take some sun; on the other side, the *Viola* prefers part shade. At the other end a little shade is available for the *Waldsteinia fragariodes*. But on the whole this is an open sunny place.

You are thinking that this is not a border, not even a garden? True, it is built almost entirely on one plane. The nuances of shape and color in the small foliage are important in order to keep the carpet from being dull. The carpet must be more than a bypass from architectural steps to architectural summerhouse. It must be good to look at as well as good to walk upon for its fragrance and to sit upon for a picnic.

1. Chamaemelum nobile (Ground Covers P.D.)
2. Laurentia fluviatilis (Woodland P.D.)
3. Thymus hybs. & cvs. (General P.D.)
4. Neirembergia rivularis (Ground Covers P.D.)
5. Pratia angulata (Ground Covers P.D.)
6. Potentilla tridentata (Slope P.D.)
7. Sedum anglicum (Outdoor Room P.D. & Slope P.D.)
8. Erinus alpinus 'Albus' & 'Dr. Hanele' (Ground Covers P.D.)
9. Thymus lanuginosus (General P.D.)
10. Parochetus communis (Ground Covers P.D.)
11. Saxifraga paniculata (Woodland P.D.)
12. Viola hederaceae (General P.D.)
13. Veronica pectinata (General P.D.)
14. Blechnum penna-marina (Woodland P.D.)
15. Waldsteinia fragarioides (Ground Covers P.D.)
16. Myoporum parviflorum (Subshrub P.D.)
17. Parahebe decora (Subshrub P.D.)
18. Raoulia australis (Woodland P.D.)
19. Arenaria balearica (Ground Covers P.D.)
20. Rubus calycinoides (General P.D.)
21. Paronychia kapela subsp. serpyllifolia (Slope P.D.)

Appendices

1. Culture: General Principles with Special Application to Perennials

PRUNING

I hope you took to heart my advice about not walking on soil; there are exceptions, however, in order to carry out jobs which necessitate walking into the heart of the bed. The first of these is pruning.

Pruning of woody materials

Most of the pruning should be finished in November. When it is clear that the flowering season is over, we must remember that the stems of perennials having no basal leaves can then be cut to the ground and we mean to stop right then and do it. As we have seen though, the leafy stems of some species still contribute to the design; these are left for later because there are other jobs more pressing.

Take for example the Matiliya Poppy. Its leaves have a most artistic shape and quite a few remain on the green colored trunks. The pods were removed not because they were unsightly but for health's sake; the brown tips were also cut off, but the six-foot stems were left all fall after the bloom was finished. Now this poppy must be pruned for next season; of the two methods of pruning this plant, one must be chosen. I alternate. Every other year I removed the tall stems all the way to the soil surface. This year is the odd year so I will only trim back part way. I will cut back two-thirds of the heavier trunks just above new leaves already breaking out from a healthy node, and I will cut back the younger ones less than one-third. Of course, anything broken or injured will be removed. The clumps of Matiliya are continually increasing by underground roots but sideways fortunately; the stand does in time get too thick in the center and when it does, some of the oldest stems should be removed.

This big poppy was chosen first, as an example of perennials with somewhat woody stems and second, because it responds to special variations in general pruning methods. I am sure you have recognized that this herbaceous plant is treated more or less as if it were a choice shrub.

Most woody perennials should be pruned in winter or earliest spring. The standard methods for shrub pruning are applicable to most perennials with woody stems. You do not need to be reminded, except to emphasize, that some perennials are really miniature shrubs needing pruning to stimulate growth.

Cleaning out the dead and dying is most important for perennials. Many have a thick, even congested, habit of growth or others grow new twigs constantly while an older generation of twigs dies. For example, *Dimorphotheca*, which may have fresh green tops and buds among the leaves, will probably be messy in the center. This is an example of a subshrub. You will have several others like it in your garden. They all require: 1) cleaning up and 2) opening up.

A few others: *Felicia, Doronicum,* the bushy *Chrysanthemums, Eriogonum.*

Euryops is an exception: it is pruned the lazy way—merely sheering the outside. When the inside of any plant becomes too cluttered and woody—a situation which inhibits the lushness of new growth—the bushlet is discarded to be replaced with a fresh specimen. Religious pruning and/or shearing will insure longer life for this type of perennial and also for the herbaceous species.

Let us now consider the soft stemmed perennials more specifically.

All perennials respond to dead-heading. Some require constant flower-stem removal in order to make new flower stems. Some perennials can be dead-headed in one fell swoop when the blooming is over or nearly over. In other species, you must cut every individual flowering stem. However, shearing is a time saver. To shear or not to shear, as well as how deep to shear, depends on the species. A few examples will give you guide lines.

To shear lightly leaving most of the foliage: *Achillea, Cerastium, Myosotis, Origanum, Teucrium, Thermopsis, Santolina.*

To shear even more lightly, taking only a few leaves below the flower stemline: *Ajuga, Aquilegia,* some *Chrysanthemum, Dianthus, Euryops, Felicia, Lavandula, Nepeta, Scabiosa, Teucrium.*

To shear deeply but leaving a few leaves: *Aethionema, Arabis, Aubrieta, Aurinia, Geranium, Mimulus, Phlox, Silene, Thymus.*

To shear merely to shape: *Artemisia* (e.g. 'Silver Mound'), *Aster, Centaurea, Chrysanthemum* (e.g.*C. anethifolium* and *C. ptarmicifolium*), *Liriope, Iberis, Lavandula.*

To shear all the way to the ground: a number of matting and tufting perennials and those which are herbaceous in a cold climate. If there is need to remove all last year's foliage, you will find the hedge shears both time-saving and efficient. Examples: *Euphorbia, Filipendula, Francoa, Gaura, Geum, Helenium, Penstemon* (some), *Primula, Salvia, Astilbe, Solidago.* There are probably hundreds in this group; use the hedge shears for speed and thoroughness unless the stems are too heavy and tough for a clean cut. Carry the hedge shears to the garden in winter or earliest spring. You may find tag-ends of old stems which for cleanliness and looks can be sheared off so that new growth will spring up unhandicapped.

A few other species which need either cutting or shearing to the level of the ground are: *Achillea* (cooler climates), *Cerastium, Chrysanthemum* X *superbum, Hypericum* (trailing sorts), *Iris unguicularis, Physostegia* (at least to its basal tufts), *Platycodon, Salvia* (most spp.), *Thalictrum, Veronica, Vinca.*

Some tender species, both herbaceous and shrubby, must wait to be cut back until danger of frost is over because the frosted tops protect the lower parts and the roots. In the freeze of '31 in California, we learned the value of this practice. If some subshrubs look, after a very cold winter, as if damage is total, wait a while. In another month, look beneath the bedraggled tops and discover at what point there is life. *Chrysanthemum anethifolium* may look completely finished, the *Artemisias* may have several limbs appearing quite dead, *Ceratostigma* is completely brown, the twigs are covered with small brown leaves, the whole mound appearing to be a complete loss; but leave everything untouched to act as an umbrella for the future weeks of low temperatures. The most tender plants which have been given extra mulch to protect the roots, *Asarum, Crinum, Hedychium, Reinwardtia, Oxypetalum, Parochetis, Anacyclus,* and the like might keep their top growth in a warm year yet in another year lose it completely; but we know that underground they are in good shape. Mounding over the whole plant with a mulch does not burn the remaining foliage and this is the approved method of protection for tender plants. If you decide to use any kind of a cloth or plastic over your tender plants, be sure that it does not touch any part.

Some herbaceous perennials never die back completely in the temperate zones; some have a basal rosette which is almost permanent. Others start their new basal leaves with almost no pause when last year's die. Most of these clumps of leaves need cleaning up—periodically but especially in earliest spring after rains have made old leaves soggy.

Take, for instance, Columbine—weeks ago its flowering stems were cut off, but not all the way. Now new leaves are springing out from the crown amidst a clutter of dry brownish grey sticklets from last year. Most of these can be pulled out, some must be cut. It looks unbelievably better, amd the fresh foliage can now develop unhindered. Many of the dwarfer kinds make basal leaves with attractive pattern, texture and color which decorate the earth while awaiting the blossoming time.

All the species of perennial Foxglove need checking—the rosettes of *Digitalis lutea* will be found to be in the best condition of any of this genus.

Removing old, decayed, or spent leaves is a continuing pruning job, but especially timely, after the resting period during cold and wet weather. On woody plants, last year's leaves can often be rubbed off. Just rub the stem upward and the stipules snap easily from the nodes. Sometimes just a thorough shake or even slap will do. However, some old brown leaves usually hang on and must be cut. Once in a while, a sword-shaped leaf can be pulled, if it is old enough. But those of a strong plant like Louisiana Iris must be cut. Another type of leaf will just lie on the ground attached to the root indefinitely, with a firm connection. These ragged, or rotted leaves must be cut away.

I can hear you saying why not leave them. Do they not become organic compost? Usually, their integration with the soil takes too long. But the chief reason is to remove the home of insects and diseases.

Often the fruit or seed head after flowering is colorful and handsome. I am thinking of a calyx which remains after the flower, often changes color and becomes enlarged. *Silene* and Love-in-the-mist are examples.

The head of a *Salvia* is in a whorl, and the old calyx holds the seed. *Salvia, Ballota, Phlomis, Helleborus* are examples of perennials in which the form of the calyx is important. We do not deadhead these until the "last minute". But by late winter the stem will have died and needs to be removed.

Plants which have seed heads of beauty are those in which the head is a whirl of winged seeds. Examples are *Clematis* and *Anemone.* I could not cut these silky, clever contrivances before new growth is ready to take their place in the landscape.

WATER

Some like it wet, some like it almost dry, none like it altogether dry all the time. Again and again you hear people talking about "drought resistant" plants and often in the posture of being a proper conservationist. I suspect that some are hoping to save work rather than water. Certainly, some plants like less moisture at their roots than do others. Naturally it is best to plant members of this group together. Some plants like a lot of water in one season and then less or none in another.

Let us take a garden of perennials with average needs. How to devise a system best for them. Best for you is a sprinkler system on an automatic timer. Like a computer you have to feed it the right information. No sprinkler system can be built which can prophesy the growth of the plants in its wake. The normal growth of some perennials in its yearly development may completely block the passage of water to smaller plants the other side of it. Change the sprinkler head? Prune the taller plant? Put the sprinkler heads down the middle so the water will go in all directions? (Good idea but it will be blocked nevertheless.) Put in a lot more heads and expect each to cover just a few plants in its vicinity? If pipes are thoroughly hidden so as not to detract from the overall design—no doubt the tops—the head which emits the water will be hidden too. How about a drip system? There would be a better chance that water would reach the roots. Or a mist system? If left on long enough, it might properly drench everything in the area. It is excellent for plants which like water on their leaves. Watering the earth is, however, an important priority. Then how about perforated hoses which lie along the ground? What a maze you would have to make in a garden with any depth or width. All these methods have their faults and inadequacies so probably a mixture is the answer. Mechanics for watering are difficult, never perfect, certainly always temporary. A combination will still require checking and hand-watering spots the system misses.

But the solution is not drought tolerant plants. They may live longer with no water but not much longer. A better solution is to create a garden small enough to be able to watch and tend it and give all its members as much as they like to drink as well as satisfying their wants. But this solution is impossible also; because a true gardener is never satisfied! He adds more to care for everytime he finds himself successful with the first attempt. He really knows that care is essential but he seldom knows how much he is getting himself in for. Nothing is too much trouble however for a garden which you really enjoy and admire.

What to do? First of all, plan to take extra, really extra, care of the newly planted perennials— the first week and the first month and then the first year. It is an infant and can only stand neglect when it is truly on its feet, if then. You are rewarded. Your plant is now a strong adult and a happy one.

How much water then? You have added "Superthrive" to the watering on the first day. Do this again in two to five days depending on the weather. Then water "as needed" twice a week for the first three months. Then water once a week if you think the roots have begun to grow and your soil is a type which can absorb water. If it is sandy, and water runs through it quickly, it probably needs humus; if it is clay and water won't penetrate, it better be improved; if it is part of a steep slope it may need retaining walls or props of rocks or if it is in a hollow it may need better drainage. What any soil needs most is for you to ascertain its moisture content. Feel of its dampness—feel below the surface to the depth of six inches or more (with a dry finger). And then spend the time needed to get water to your plants properly.

SOIL

You are all familiar with all the exhortations to improve your soil. Or have you inherited a garden in which the preparation has been so thoroughly carried out that you can ignore such advice. Even so, amendments wear or wash away—soil improvement can never stop.

What is special in care of soil for perennials? It should be friable and rich at least two feet and preferably three feet down. You will find a note in the Plant Descriptions to tell you when a perennial needs soil especially good or when it will grow and bloom quite well with ordinary soil. But only a few genera prefer lean soil so you run little risk of making the soil too good. If you are making a new space for perennials, you will be well repaid if you do a superb job. Mix and add and mix and add. You have a choice of what to add—manure, compost, rotted sawdust, rotted leaves, peat moss and ground bark. Several kinds of amendments are better than just one. Some people buy a package which is supposed to be all-purpose with fertilizer included. Others prefer to make their own decision of how much of what. To make the condition right—break up and completely mix—it is not so much what, but your skill and brawn with the fork and cultivator.

After-care is most important, especially for perennials. More than for annuals, because annuals have a short life and more than for shrubs and trees because the roots of perennials are usually finer and closer to the surface. The conclusion is no doubt evident—the condition of the soil in the area of those perennial roots should be kept as rich and well-aerated as possible. The way to bring this about is to keep adding mulch to the surface, a little at a time and scratching it in. Remember not to pile it up over the crown. Good watering practices are essential in order to keep the soil moist down to the depth of roots but by means gentle enough so that the soil does not pack or run away.

Did I hear someone ask, "What kind of mulch?" Perhaps you have plenty of well-made, home-made compost; perhaps you have a source of mushroom compost; or "mulch" in the package made from bark. Peat?—too fine. Leaf mold? Like compost but lacking in some of the ingredients of a good compost but useful for loosening. Firbark is especially beneficial around clumps of fine roots where there is no chance to fork in the mulch.

Since a mulch helps to keep the surface from drying out, perennials which especially need moisture require a generous layer. You will find a list of those which like it wet. I will give you here only one example: *Filipendula* may be grown in the ordinary moisture of a mixed planting but to bloom well must have abundant water during its growing period. *Iris ensata* is an example of a plant which requires extra water and likes to *stand* in water while growing. Even this Iris should be given a period of rest on drier ground. The great majority of genera do not like wet feet. Always keep in mind that the great majority of plants must be in soil with good to excellent drainage. The condition of the soil under the root area of a perennial must be as permeable as possible, perhaps broken with pick or the road mender's jack. For a time, at least, excess water will find an exit route. Meanwhile, the perennial need never be overwatered (exception, rainy season) because its pocket of soil retains for long intervals sufficient water for the needs of the plant. Two methods to insure conservation of moisture: 1) water retentive material in the medium, and 2) mulch over the surface to decrease evaporation from the soil around the roots.

So the point of your endeavor is to provide a beneficial soil for perennials, to allow the penetration of water evenly throughout, dispersing nutrition in the process, and to allow excess water which the soil can not absorb to run away. At the same time the soil must be sufficiently friable so that air can circulate and fine roots can find a medium easily penetrated.

FEEDING

I know I do not have to remind you about feeding on a regular basis. Keep a calender. Supplemental feeding is important also. What needs food specifically and what? Any of those plants which are in bud or are setting buds would welcome a boost, say of fish emulsion, as would those which have a reputation for not blooming to their fullest, and those which would prefer more sun than they receive in their situation. I give an extra boost to any of those liking extra nutrition which are growing on the steepest banks where some of the food in the soil is routinely washed away.

When planting in a woodland, there are almost no plants which resent food; most trees are greedy. There are a number of plants which prefer an acid soil. I mix extra conifer needles in the compost used for mulch in their vicinity.

Only a very few plants need a lean diet but a number of plants which seem to be growing very well indeed get nothing at all, except mulch and whatever it contains. I use hoof and horn, cottonseed, blood, or bone meal and "spoon it" on the side; you can see that I favor the organics. You can make the soil *too* rich for maximum health by using commercial mixes with manure included.

Pots are another matter, of course; much of their food is regularly leached away. So we go the rounds with a watering pot (instead of the hose) to which a spoonful or two of chemical fertilizer (20-20-20) has been added every other time with fish emulsion.

Some gardeners use slow release "pills" for all feeding and swear by them. When you buy a tree from a nursery don't think that those round gelatin blops are eggs of an insect. This is your slow release fertilizer, a balanced nutrition additive. The best opportunity for application is at transplanting time—a pinch to a pot. Your plants will be stronger and reach maturity more quickly. Slow feeding is a good practice for the growers and nursery people. Good for you, too.

WEEDING

This interminable job which breaks our backs, literally and figuratively, is necessary the year round. Why not use a weed killer? Perhaps apply something like "Roundup" in a place where you are preparing a new garden (not to be planted for two or three weeks)? If you can apply weed killer without "drifting" some onto a plant you do not wish to kill, you are most uncommon. Besides the birds and the wind will resow the very next day. In my garden the weeds are pulled, but if they are in open space they may be hoed. Every weed is quickly gotton rid of; the smallest piece left on the ground, even overnight, will root even if upside down. If the heads are loaded with seed, a paper bag for disposal should be carried into the bed to prevent a number of the flying seeds from getting away.

Of course, the principle "get the infants" is the wisest, but we are all human. Despite human frailty we really need to get some before they reach adulthood and have thrown their seed. Most are precocious. In earliest spring, it is best to first take the weeds which are ahead of others in their life cycle. Do not cater to your principle of being "thorough"; do not try to completely clear any area of the garden. Ahead of you are weeds developing seed overnight. Take one kind at a time—before they set seed.

You ask again—why not a pre-emergent eradicator? I use one sometimes on the paths—never in beds because I value the chance seedlings of many flowers which I have planted.

I hope to keep all the earth so full of desirables that there is no room for the undesirables—but this is dreaming. (Sometimes the weeds grow out of the center of a plant.) So if we are to have a nice garden, we must face arduous hand work.

Some of the weeds are charming and it is easy to start a debate entitled "What is a weed?" In one part of the world we try hard to grow some kinds of plants which in other parts are considered obnoxious. A few plants are obnoxious anywhere. Concientious surveillance is the answer.

PEST CONTROL, INSECTS AND DISEASES

They are always with us; a sterile garden is not possible.

Insects hatch unbelievably fast; they hatch every minute from the onset of warm weather till the days grow short again. We can get predators which help. Five dollars worth of ladybugs can clean up 500 aphis overnight but when surfeited they fly away. They don't eat all the eggs and in a few weeks there is another batch. If we are alert we can get the young in infancy. Spraying? With systemics? A few people can measure exactly, apply as stated on the label and stay with the work for as many applications as necessary, but most can't.

Controlling the eggs is a good idea. (1) Destroy as many ants as possible. They act as dairymen carrying the eggs to places conducive to hatching, since they relish the juices prepared for the infants. (2) Keep the lower story of the garden cleaned up. Dead leaves, twigs and all excess soil around roots make for ideal insect nesting places.

Slugs and snails: Keeping the garden tidy and clean is the #1 control for snails and slugs. Hand picking is of course the surest method and a hunt especially at dawn is always rewarding. Not enough, however, for some are too well hidden. A pest bait should be laid around in little piles; it is less potent if scattered. The slugs and snails are attracted to it by an odor which is released as the bait gets damp. If it gets thoroughly wet, it is less palatable and the poison washes away. When I have to protect foliage which is both my favorite and theirs as well, I make a thin track all the way around the plant. I alternate with different makes; slugs' tastes may change. Sometimes I try an all-purpose meal which is supposed to attract sow bugs, those vicious earwigs which live in the soil, and everything else the label says. Slugs are probably the hardest to eradicate, they must multiply at an horrendous rate. Try a circle of wood ashes placed like a moat around the enticing plant. Or better, make the moat of some flour; they don't like the feel when it sticks to their slimy bodies.

Worms: Their appetite is prodigious. They hide so well between two leaves. If you have plants attractive to worms (such as Geraniums) watch for leaves pressed together. "Hunting" is the surest method of control. They may have done an amazing amount of eating before your hunt bears fruit. They are camouflaged, of course. Try *Dipel*. It works at least to some extent. It is reputedly absolutely safe.

Sow bugs: Yes they are harmful; their diet includes plant material, common opinion to the contrary. There is a stomach poison to put under pots where no cat or dog or bird can reach but the sow bugs can.

Soil insects: Perish the thought. A new garden may be drenched ahead of the planting date with a sterilizing agent. Weed seed is destroyed also. The surest method is a gas. But you get to do that only once. In an established garden, you have to depend as did the Romans on repeated counter-attack.

Mealy-bug: Alcohol drenched cotton on the end of a Q-tip. Again, watchfulness is the first step. You know where they live—in the nodes and along the midribs of leaves.

Beetles: Not common except the green speckled one which chews out a perfect moon-shaped bite. If you get one of the bad beetles you need help from a professional. There are small but hungry beetles inside that spittle.

White flies: Some years much worse than others. "Sticky-fly-paper" helps—and a dog's flea collar around the plant.

Rabbits: Can you plant enough young stuff with soft, green leaves so they can eat and still leave some for you? "Have a heart" traps, they soon recognize, no matter what the bait.

These are the most common enemies. And the only answer is constant surveillance. Except, select perennials not very susceptible, i.e. not delicious from their point of view.

PLANTING

Everybody knows how to plant! Everybody thinks his way is the best. Hardly anybody is patient enough to do the job the way he knows it should be done. Let us remind ourself of the best way step by step.

1. Preparing the entire area if perennials are to be planted for the first time or replanted. (We used to "double dig" in the year when perennials were divided and their place renewed.)
2. Preparing a wheelbarrow full of "mix", an ideal mixture of soil with ingredients good for the soil. (See section on soil.) In the wheelbarrow or on a bench the mixing can be done as for a cake.
3. Make a hole for the plant or plants; make it big—space at bottom and sides for mix. Put mix in the bottom of the hole.
4. Push a fork into soil all around the circle of the hole. Move it back and forth a few times to loosen boundaries.
5. Prepare the ball of the plant after tapping it out of its container; if it will not come out by tapping, cut the container down to the bottom on both sides. Pull the roots apart gently around the top, scratching them apart on the bottom with a fork. Cut four slits in the sides of the ball with a knife if the roots are very congested.
6. Test the depth of the hole to be sure that the top of the ball will be at soil level when placed firmly on its base of mix. Then place, with slight pressure applied to the top of the ball.
7. Tuck the mix in around the ball. Use hands to push the mix well down around the sides. In a crowded area of the garden where a smaller hole is necessary and only two or three inches around the ball's circumference can be provided, push the mix down to the bottom with a stake or other straight tool.
8. Press top of mix gently; do not *stamp* down mix or soil in the area.
9. Water thoroughly. If the ball is the size of a five gallon container, water when the circle is half full of mix to settle it. Then fill to the top with mix. Water slowly again. If mix sinks a bit as a result of the wetting, fill with more mix, just enough to keep the surface of the ball level with the surrounding soil. (The crown of the plant must not be smothered.)
10. Top off with lukewarm water in a watering can in which a dilution of growth starter has been prepared. (I use "Superthrive". I aim to follow with a second dose in three to seven days.)

When to plant? When the soil is right. When a rain can be expected. For most perennials fall or winter. For those which bloom in later summer, early spring is preferred. Tender plants—later spring.

Transplanting instead of planting. Translate the rules to suite a different shaped ball.

Another principle must be emphasized. Do not walk on the soil when it is wet and walk on it as little as possible when it has been aerated. If you must walk to reach the planting spot, walk only on one path instead of stamping down the whole area. If you have a wide plank, lay it as a path; it somewhat relieves the pressure on the earth. Go back to repair the path only after the soil has had time to dry out somewhat.

I do not follow the practice of leaving a trench for catching water (except temporarily while planting). I believe those who make catch-basins intend to come back soon but then forget it to the detriment of the plant. Some people always water the tops as well as the roots, a practice beneficial most of the time for that all important start. However in cold weather, it is not good to water leaves which will hold the water on their surface; sometimes they are shaped in such a way that there is a sort of cup at their base, nor is it good to water leaves which have crevices in which the water will be held. It is not good to water soft foliage into which the water may penetrate; think of some of the plants with soft grey foliage. Don't water the tops of succulents; if you do by mistake, blow the excess water off.

What else do we do for the newly planted perennial? Often I cover it with a cone made out of fine mesh "hardware cloth"; such a roof breaks the cold air and also the sun. Mostly, it advertises the presence of the new plant and thus keeps not only rabbits and birds away but spades and feet as well.

PROPAGATION

Do you want to grow your own? No doubt you all know how to plant seeds and "stick" cuttings. If you have any kind of a work bench, home propagation is a temptation. It is a way to increase your plants and a way, often necessary, when you want more of a species not easily found in the market place. I believe some species you will find difficult from both seed and cuttings—a challenge.

You will see in the Plant Descriptions, notes to indicate that some species are easy from seed.

When a species is not easy, there will be pleasure in any success. Here are a few extra tips which apply in particular to the normal perennial. Of course there are many details you may or may not forget but the following are the most often neglected.

By Seed

Timing: Give seed plenty of time. Some seed will not germinate for a year or more. Have patience. Sometimes, a few germinate. Wait, the rest may germinate days or weeks later. That pot or flat must be guarded even after you are certain that there is no chance. Sometimes moss grows over the top; don't touch it. Will it germinate faster if sown at a particular time of the year? Perhaps; for a few species early spring but others not all that predictable. Try again if you have no luck. Your seed may like a particular month or it may be a waiter by nature.

Collect seeds from perennials you like in your garden and in those of your friends. Sow it soon; some seed needs to be sown when fresh. Leave it on the plant if you suspect it is not quite ripe but collect before it falls or the rains come or the birds find it. After you collect, store in a cool dry place. If you clean as you collect, you will be more apt to sow at an auspicious time—because it is ready.

Choice of container: If you are sowing small amount of several kinds of seed you can use a separate pot for each or a flat divided into sections. Place parallel sticks to mark divisions and label rows. Be certain to constantly inspect and pot on seedlings as they become ready. Almost certainly they will germinate at different times making your pricking out more difficult. But a wooden flat has one advantage over separate pots: moisture is more easily controlled.

You may want to use the tent method; the construction of individual greenhouses made of polyethylene. I prefer to make the tent over the top of the pot held above the rim by bamboo "poles" and then tied around the pot half way down with an elastic band or plant tie (twist). This method allows watering from the bottom by soaking with the tent still in place. Another method uses the bag as a container: the pot sitting within it and the open end of the bag tied above the top of the pot. In this second method also stakes are used to hold the bag upright above the pot.

Preparation of seed: It is worthwhile to prepare the seed of some species by stratification. In simplest terms, to stratify is to crack or soften the seed cover. (a) Hot water is the easiest treatment; boil a cup of water, remove from heat, put seeds in the water and allow them to soak until the water cools. (b) Cold followed by heat induces a natural change in the seed coating: refrigerator for a period prescribed for the specific seed by scientific experiment—from three days to three months. Then remove and stand in a warm place for three hours to three days. (c) Filing or nicking of one side edge of the coating is recommended for some seeds with very hard shells. Which ones? If you have no reference work in which to learn the best method, a good rule of thumb is that any seed with a hard coating will germinate more easily if the coating is treated. When you obtain seed from a shop, a seedsman or a plant society like the Rock Garden Soc., you will usually receive information concerning any special germinating requirements.

Important details: Here are a few reminders which apply to seed of any kind.
1. Dampen planting medium before sowing.
2. Don't cover seed too deeply. If seed becomes exposed another layer of medium can be sifted over the top.
3. Protect the surface from drying out and from molestations by bugs, birds, mice, etc.
4. Label.

Transplanting

The seedlings are up. Hopefully not weeds—this stage is risky. You transplant 12 and two might live, unless you are growing an easy or a tough species. Plant the seedlings in individual containers or several, four to six, in a large pot or box.

Again, reminders are in order. Have their new home and the tools ready. Loosen the seedlings with a fork so that no roots break. If the seedlings are small or dense in the medium take up a section with your fork. Raise it eight to ten inches above your work bench and drop it. The medium will fall apart a bit. Clip off the tips of any roots which are straggling. Lay a seedling in a slot or slit in the soil opened up to the depth of the root. Spread the root out against one side of the slot with neck at soil level (only exceptionally can the stem be slightly covered with soil). Do not touch the root; instead hold the plant by its leaves. Push the soil from the other side of the slot toward the slot opening until the slot is closed.

Water? Mist is best if the seedling is delicate. Otherwise, water gently applying in a circle around the plant. The water should contain your favorite transplant "medicine".

How long before the young plant can go in the ground? Depending on the kind and the season: a wide range, the average is six months.

By Cuttings

Propagation by cuttings is quicker. A few perennials will root in water. Roots started in water often resent the move to earth. A helpful precaution is to use a soft and moist medium when transplanting.

There are various schools of propagation by cuttings. Recipes for mediums abound; however, all of them seem to work equally well from a mixture of different ingredients provided one part is moisture holding (like peat) and one is rough (like sand or perlite). You may get faster rooting if the cutting is near the side of a clay pot; stick them in a circle as wide as possible. A professional rooting hormone is better than those bought over the counter in the retail nursery.

Short lengths are better than long. Use both node and tip cuttings. Remove any growth on the part of the stem which will be buried in the medium. For cuttings worthy of extra precautions, clean the stems in a solution of soap and water with a fungicide added. Tips should not be so wet that excess rooting powder will not shake off; more than a thin coating of the tip is detrimental to rooting. A species may have its favorite day of the month and year to root but you must find it by trial and error. Don't fail to label. It is useful to put the date of planting on the marker also.

How soon will there be roots? A fresh bit of vigor on the tops may indicate rooting. Pull gently on the stem; if it resists, roots may have started. If it pulls easily, raise it from the medium in order to look. It may only have begun to callous: you can be optimistic but it must be reinserted with another thin layer of rooting power on the tip. At this time, remove any drooping stems and resettle your medium; if too few have begun to "take" you can add some new plant material. If you enjoy the craft of propagation, always have one or more containers full of cuttings in progress. Any extras which develop into plants will be good for a "swap" or a give-away.

Division

The quickest method of plant multiplication is by division. I have noted in the Plant Descriptions those species which can be propagated by division—when? Fall or early spring according to your climate and renovation schedule. Save the best parts which will be found on the outside of the clump; the oldest part will be in the center and can be discarded. Put in containers a few parts you do not need; perhaps these will be welcomed by someone whose perennial garden is in the building stage. Beware of giving away a root with nematodes, mealy-bug or the like. Plant encyclopedias should be consulted; you should not be without a major plant reference. It's always a source of proper information. The natural time to divide is when you are renovating the bed or border or whatever. But you may dig up and divide any perennial as it needs division at any time except when the earth is too wet or too dry. Good division requires proper tools: you will need saws, forks or two sharp spades depending on the toughness and thickness of the crown. Some perennials need careful hand disentanglement of the separate root crowns. Readiness of the immediate planting place whether ground or container is important. Two prerequisites: a good plan and good weather.

See the 1984 Handbook of the Brooklyn Botanic Garden, "Propagation for the Home Gardener", Plants & Gardens, Brooklyn Botanic Garden Record, Vol. 40, #1, #103.

2. Lists by Flower Color

WHITE

Achillea
Aconitum
Actaea
Allium
Anchusa
Androsace
Anemone
Anthericum
Aquilegia
Arabis
Arenaria
Armeria
Artemisia
Aruncus
Aster
Astilbe
Baptisia
Begonia
Bellis
Bergenia
Boltonia
Boykinia
Calluna
Camassia
Campanula
Cassiope
Catananche
Centaurea
Cerastium
Chaenostoma
Chrysanthemum
Cimicifuga

Clematis
Convallaria
Convolvulus
Cornus
Cyclamen
Daboecia
Delphinium
Dianthus
Dicentra
Dictamnus
Digitalis
Dodecatheon
Draba
Epimedium
Erica
Erinus
Erodium
Eryngium
Erysimum
Eupatorium
Filipendula
Fragaria
Gaultheria
Gentiana
Geranium
Gerbera
Gysophila
Helianthemum
Helleborus
Heuchera
Hibiscus
Hosta

Iberis
Iris
Kniphofia
Lantana
Lathyrus
Lavandula
Linnaea
Linum
Lobelia
Lupinus
Lychnis
Maianthemum
Malva
Mitchella
Nierembergia
Omphalodes
Pachysandra
Paeonia
Papaver
Paradisea
Pelargonium
Penstemon
Phlox
Phyllodoce
Physostegia
Platycodon
Polemonium
Potentilla
Pratia
Primula
Pulmonaria
Ranunculus

Rehmannia
Romneya
Salvia
Satureja
Saxifraga
Scabiosa
Sedum
Shortia
Silene
Sisyrinchium
Soldanella
Statice
Stokesia
Tanakaea
Thalictrum
Thymus
Tiarella
Tradescantia
Trillium
Tunica
Verbena
Veronica
Vinca
Viola
Watsonia
Waldsteinia
Yucca
Zauschneria
Zenobia

BLUE OR ALMOST BLUE

Anagallis
Anchusa
Amsonia
Aquilegia
Aster
Brunnera
Ceratostigma
Clematis heracleifolia var. davidii
Cynoglossum
Delphinium 'Cambridge
   Blue', 'Azure Fairy', 'Blue
   Jay' 'Blue Bird',
Echinops
Eryngium
Felicia
Gentiana
Linum

Lobelia
Meconopsis
Mertensia
Myosotis scorpioides
   'Victoria'
Omphalodes
Pasithea
Penstemon heterophyllus
Polemonium
Primula
Pulmonaria
Rhazya
Rosmarinus
Salvia
Scabiosa
Veronica

LAVENDER

Aethionema
Agapanthus
Ajuga
Aquilegia
Aster amellus, A. alpinus, A. dumosus, A. subcoeruleus, A. × frikartii, A. yunnanensis 'Napsbury', 'Nancy', 'Goliath', 'Victor', 'Blue Bouquet' 'Prof. Kuppenberg', 'Royal Opal', 'Star of Eisenach'
Aubrieta eyrei 'Purple Knoll'
Baptisia
Campanula bononensis C. haylogensis, C. carpatica 'Cullinore' C. glomerata, C. isophylla 'Mayii', C. persicifolia, C. primulifolia, C. thessala, etc.
Clematis
Convovulus mauritanicus
Cymbalaria
Dianthus 'Loveliness'
Erigeron
Eupatorium
Geranium
Heliotropum
Hosta

Iberis gibraltica
Iris
Lavandula
Limonium
Nepeta
Origanum
Pelargonium
Penstemon
Phlox
Platycodon
Polemonium
Primula obconica, P. polyantha, P. sinensis, P sieboldii, P. juliae 'Roberta', 'Wanda', etc.
Rosmarinus
Salvia
Satureya
Stokesia
Thalictrum
Tradescantia
Verbena rigida (V. venosa)
Veronica armena, V. hybrida, V. holyphylla
Vinca minor 'Alpina', V.m. 'Atropurpurea', V.m. 'Bowlesii', V.m. 'Double Purple'
Viola

LAVENDER, CALLED BLUE

Anemone
Aquilegia
Aster
Babiana
Baptisia
Campanula

Clematis
Delphinium
Echinops
Meconopsis
Phacelia
Primula
Veronica

YELLOW

Achillea
Aconitum
Adonis
Alstroemeria
Anigozanthus
Anthemis
Aquilegia
Aurinia
Begonia
Canna
Centaurea
Cephalaria
Cheiranthus
Chelidonium
Chrysanthemum
Chrysogonum
Clintonia

Coreopsis
Corydalis
Delphinium
Digitalis
Diplacus
Doronicum
Eranthis
Erysimum
Euphorbia
Euryops
Gazania
Gerbera
Geum
Glaucium
Halimium
Hedychium
Helenium

Helianthemum
Helianthus
Heliopsis
Hemerocallis
Hermannia
Iris
Kirengeshoma
Kniphofia
Linum
Lotus
Lupinus
Mimulus
Odontospermum
Oenothera
Onosma
Paeonia
Papaver

Potentilla
Ranunculus
Reinwardia
Rudbeckia
Ruta
Sedum
Senecio
Solidago
Solidaster
Stylophorum
Sisyrinchium
Thalictrum
Thermopsis
Trollius
Uvularia
Verbascum
Viola

ORANGE

Begonia
Canna
Cheiranthus
Chrysanthemum
Crocosmia
Fuchsia procumbens
Gazania
Geum 'Fire Opal'
Glaucium

Helenium
Helianthmum 'Burnt
    Orange', 'Apricot'
Hemerocallis
Malvastrum
Mimulus
Lychnis
Papaver orientale, P.
    pilosum, P. rupifragum, P.
    atlanticum

Pelargonium hortorum
    'Madam Aurore', 'Irma',
    'Madam Kovalesky'
Potentilla
Trollius
Zauschneria

PINK

Achillea
Aethionema
Androsace
Anemone
Aquilegia
Arabis
Armeria
Aster. cvs. 'Adorable', 'Little
    Pink Lady', 'Countess of
    Dudley', 'Daphne', Aster
    dumosus 'Marjorie'
Astilbe
Bellis
Bergenia
Boltonia
Campanula
Chrysanthemum spp. &
    hybs.
Chrysanthemum coccineum
Chrysanthemum mawii
Coreopsis
Delphinium
Dianthus
Dicentra

Digitalis
Echinacea
Erigeron
Eriogonum
Felicia
Filipendula
Francoa
Geranium
Gerbera
Gypsophila
Helianthemum 'Wendel's
    Rose'
Hemerocallis 'Rosalind'
Heuchera
Iris
Lantana
Limonium
Linaria 'Canon Went'
Lupin
Lychnis
Lythrum
Malvastrum
Paeonia
Papaver

Pelargonium
Penstemon
Phlox divaricata
Phlox subulata
Phlox hybs.
Physostegia
Platycodon
Polygonum
Primula
Saponaria
Saxifraga
Sedum
Silene
Stachys
Teucrium
Thymus
Tradescantia
Trillium
Verbena pulchella 'Oxford
    Pride'
Verbena tenera maonettii
Veronica
Vinca minor var. rosea

RED & SCARLET

Alstroemeria pulchella
Aquilegia 'Crimson Star'
Aster 'Beechwood
    Challenger'
Aster 'Winston Churchill'
Astilbe 'Fanal'
Canna
Centranthus
Cheiranthus
Chrysanthemum
Delphinium
Dianthus 'Will Rogers'
Dianthus 'American Beauty'
Dictamnus var. rubra
Digitalis
Erinus
Gazania 'Firestone,
Gazania 'Fiesta'

Geum
Glaucium
Helianthemum 'Ben Ledi',
    'Boule de Feu' 'Brunette',
    'Jock Scott' 'Mitchell's Red'
Helleborus
Hemerocallis 'Kennedy Red'
Heuchera
Knautia
Kniphofia 'Bressingham
    Flame'
Lilium
Lobelia cardinalis
Lobelia tupa
Lychnis
Mimulus
Monarda

Paeonia
Papaver
Pelargonium 'Pygmy' , 'Mrs.
    Taylor', 'Hal Cain', 'Nevit
    Pointevine', 'Pride of
    Camden'
Pelargonium peltatum 'Old
    Mexico'
Penstemon 'Firebird',
    'Garnet', 'Southgate Gem'
Phlox
Potentilla
Primula juliae
Primula polyantha hybs.
Primula seiboldii 'Kokanor',
    'Marie Louise'
Verbena hortensis 'Red
    Firefly'
Zauschneria

MAROON

| Asarum | Cheiranthus | Dianthus | Iris | Papaver |
| Aquilegia | Chrysanthemum | Helenium | Paeonia | |

3. Lists by Habit

FLOWERING STEMS OVER TWO, NOT FOUR FEET

Achillea
Amsonia
Anchusa
Anemone
Aquilegia
Asclepias
Aster
Baptisia
Belamcanda
Campanula
Centaurea
Chrysanthemum
Clematis
Coreopsis
Dicentra
Dictamnus
Digitalis
Doronicum
Echinops
Eryngium
Eupatorium
Filipendula
Helenium
Hemerocallis

Hesperis
Hosta
Iris
Kniphofia
Liatris
Lilium
Lobelia
Lupinus
Lychnis
Lythrum
Paeonia
Papaver
Penstemon
Phlox
Platycodon
Polemonium
Polygonatum
Ranunculus
Rudbeckia
Salvia
Saxifraga
Solidago
Thalictrum
Veronica

FLOWERING STEMS FOUR FEET AND OVER

Acanthus
Achillea
Aconitum
Agapanthus
Alcea (Althaea)
Alpinia
Amarcrinum
Anemone
Anigozanthus
Aralia
Artemisia
Aruncus
Aster
Baptisia
Boltonia
Campanula pyramidalis
Celsia
Cimicifuga
Crinum
Delphinium
Dianella
Digitalis
Doranthes
Eremurus

Eupatorium
Filipendula
Fritillaria imperialis
Gypsophila
Hedychium
Helenium
Helianthus
Heliconia
Heliopsis
Liatris
Ligularia
Lobelia cardinalis
Macleaya
Phlomis
Phormium
Physostegia
Puya
Rudbeckia
Salvia
Solidago
Strelitzia
Thalictrum
Thermopsis
Verbascum
Veronica
Watsonia
Yucca

FOLIAGE HEIGHTS

Below 8 inches		8 inches to under 2 feet	2 feet & over
Ajuga	Mimulus	Acorus	Acanthus
Anemone	Mitchella	Allium	Aqapanthus
Arabis	Myosotis	Aquilegia	Alocasia
Arenaria	Nepeta	Aster	Alpinia
Asarum	Nierembergia	Campanula	Amarcrinum
Bellium	Oenothera	Cheiranthus	Arthropodium
Campanula	Papaver	Clintonia	Clivia
Chrysanthemum	Parochetus	Coreopsis	Crinum
Convallaria	Phlox	Dianthus	Dianella
Convolvulus	Potentilla	Doronicum	Doryanthes
Coptis	Ranunculus	Euphorbia	Gaura
Cornus	Saponaria	Festuca	Hedychium
Dianthus	Sedum	Gonolium	Heliconia
Dicentra	Sempervivum	Hosta	Hemerocallis
Duchesnea	Silene	Iberis	Macleaya
Fragaria	Thymus	Jasione	Phormium
Galium	Tricyrtis	Limonium	Puya
Gentiana	Veronica	Pachysandra	Strelitzia
Geranium	Vinca	Phlox	Thalictrum
Globularia	Viola	Platycodon	Watsonia
Hernaria		Satureja	Yucca
Iberis		Smilacina	
Linaria		Stachys	
Lithodora		Stokesia	
Lithospermum		Teucrium	
Lotus		Thymus	
Lysimachia		Trillium	
Maianthemum		Uvularia	
Mentha			

FOLIAGE, COLORS

Blue-green	Grey-green	Grey	
Allium	Achillea	Achillea	Origanum
Arthropodium	Aquilegia	Androsace	Paronychia
Aquilegia	Aubrieta	Anthyllis	Potentilla
Arundo	Lavandula	Artemisia	Salvia
Dianthus	Nepeta	Aurinia	Santolina
Eryngium	Primula auricula	Ballota	Sedum
Festuca	Pulsatilla	Calocephalus	Senecio
Glaucium	Ruta	Cerastium	Stachys lanata
Helleborus foetidus	Sanguinaria	Chrysanthemum 'Silver Leaf'	Teucrium
Hosta	Santolina	Convolvulus cneorum	Thymus
Iris	Thymus	Echinops	Veronica incana
Linaria		Elymus	Zauschneria
Linum		Eriocephalus	
Mertensia		Geranium	
Rodgersia		Glaucus	
Rosmarinus		Kochia 'Acapulco Silver'	
Saxifraga		Lavandula	
Sedum		Lychnis	
Silene		Macleaya	
		Onosma	

FOLIAGE, VARIEGATED

Acanthus
Acorus
Adiantum raddianum
  'Variegatum Tasselatum'
Agapanthus
Agave
Arrhenatherum elatius var.
  tuberosum 'Nanum'
Arrhenatherum elatius var.
  bulbosum 'Variegatum'
Arundinaria var. viride stricta
Arundo
Athyrium nipponicum
  'Pictum'
Begonia
Canna
Carex conica 'Variegata'
Crassula
Disporum sessile
  'Variegatum'
Echeveria
Equisetum
Erysimum linifolium
Eucomis
Hemerocallis
Heuchera americana
Hieracium maculatum
Hieracium waldsteinii
Hosta

Houttuynia cordata
Imperata
Iris kaempferi, I.k. var. rotunda
Iris pallida
Iris pseudoacoris
Lamium
Libertia peregrinus
Ligularia
Liriope
Melissa
Milium effusum 'Aureum'
Ophiopogon planiscarpus
  'Kokurga' or 'Nigrescens'
Origanum vulgare 'Aureum'
Pennisetum
Phormium tenax cvs.
Phylostachys
Pleione
Pteris
Pulmonaria
Rheum
Sauromatum guttatum
Sisyrinchium striatum
  'Variegatum'
Synnotia villosa var. variegata
Trillium
Tulbaghia
Zingiber darceyi

FOLIAGE, CHARACTER

Bold

Acanthus
Arundinaria
Arundo
Cynara
Eryngium
Gunnera
Haplopappus
Hosta
Iris
Ligularia
Macleaya
Papaver
Phlomis
Phormium
Rheum
Rodgersia
Rumex
Yucca

Finely cut, delicate or compound

Achillea
Adiantum
Adonis
Anemone
Artemisia
Aruncus
Asparagus
Asperula
Astilbe
Chrysanthemum
Cimicifuga
Dicentra
Epimedium
Filipendula
Paeonia
Polemonium
Thalictrum
Vancouveria

FOLIAGE, AROMATIC

Achillea
Allium
Anthemis
Arabis
Artemisia
Cedronella
Centaurea
Chaenostoma
Chamaemelum
Cheiranthus
Chrysanthemum
Convolvulus
Dianthus
Dicentra
Dictamnus
Erysimum
Foeniculum
Galium
Hedychium
Heliotropum
Hemerocallis
Hermannia

Lavandula
Mentha
Melissa
Mitchella
Monarda
Narcissus
Nepeta
Onosma
Origanum
Pelargonium
Perovskia
Rosmarinus
Ruta
Salvia
Satureja
Santolina
Tanacetum
Teucrium
Thymus
Verbena

BLOOM BY SEASON

January and February

Aconite, Bergenia, Calluna, Clivia, Erica, Erysimum, Helleborus niger, Iris unguicularis, Narcissus, Petasites, Primula, Pulmonaria, Reinwardtia, Vinca, Viola

March and April

Adonis, Aethionema, Androsace, Arabis, Armeria, Arum, Bellis, Calluna, Cheiranthus, Claytonia, Daboecia, Dicentra, Draba, Erica, Erysimum, Euphorbia, Fragaria, Fritillaria, Fuchsia procumbens, Gentiana, Helleborus, Hepatica, Iris, Narcissus, Omphalodes, Papaver, Pelargonium, Phlox, Primula, Veronica, Viola

May and June

Actaea, Aethionema, Agapanthus, Ajuga, Alchemilla, Alstroemeria, Anchusa, Anemone, Anigozanthos, Aquilegia, Arabis, Arenaria, Aubrieta, Aurinia, Baptisia, Bellis, Caltha, Campanula, Cerastium, Cheiranthus, Chelidonium, Clintonia, Convallaria, Convolvulus, Cornus, Corydalis, Cymbalaria, Cynoglossum, Dianthus, Dicentra, Digitalis, Doronicum, Draba, Epimedium, Erigeron, Erysimum, Erythronium, Eupatorium, Euphorbia, Felicia, Fragaria, Francoa, Galium, Gentiana, Geranium, Glaucium, Helianthemum, Helleborus, Hemerocallis, Hepatica, Heuchera, Hypericum, Iris, Lantana, Lavandula, Lewisia, Linaria, Linum, Lupinus, Lychnis, Maianthemum, Malvastrum, Mertensia, Mimulus, Muscari, Myosotis, Narcissus, Nepeta, Odontospermum, Ornithogalum, Pachysandra, Paeonia, Papaver, Pasithea, Penstemon, Phlomis, Phlox, Pratia, Primula, Pulmonaria, Ranunculus, Rehmannia, Romneya, Salvia, Saxifraga, Scilla, Silene, Sisyrinchium, Stylophorum, Teucrium, Thalictrum, Tiarella, Thymus, Trillium, Trollius, Tulipa, Uvularia, Vancouveria, Verbascum, Vinca. Some Saponaria bloom in June.

July and August

Achillea, Aconiyum, Alcea (Althea), Alstroemeria, Anchusa, Anemone, Anigozanthos, Anthemis, Anthericum, Aquilegia, Arabis, Armeria, Aruncus, Asclepias, Aster, Astilbe, Astrantia, Begonia, Belamcanda, Boltonia, Boykinia, Brunnera, Callirhoe, Campanula, Canna, Catananche, Centaurea, Cephalaria, Cerastium, Ceratostigma, Chaenostoma, Chrysanthemum, Clematis, Coreopsis, Corydalis, Cosmos, Dahlia, Delphinium, Dianthus, Dicentra, Dictamnus, Echinacea, Echinops, Eremurus, Eryngium, Eupatorium, Filipendula, Gaillardia, Galium, Gazania, Geranium, Gerbera, Geum, Glaucium, Goodyera, Gypsophila, Helenium, Helianthus, Heliopsis, Hemerocallis, Heuchera, Hosta, Iberis, Iris, Jasione, Kirengeshoma, Kniphofia, Lamium, Lilium, Limonium, Linum, Lobelia, Lychnis, Lythrum, Macleaya, Malvastrum, Meconopsis, Monarda, Nepeta, Nierembergia, Oenothera, Omphalodes, Onosma, Papaver, Pasithea, Pelargonium, Penstemon, Phlox, Phormium, Physostegia, Platycodon, Polianthes, Pulsatilla, Rehmannia, Rudbeckia, Salvia, Satureya, Scabiosa, Scutellaria, Sedum, Solidago, Solidaster, Stachys, Stokesia, Symphytum, Thalictrum, Thermopsis, Thymus, Tigridia, Tradescantia, Trillium, Trollius, Tunica, Uvularia, Verbascum, Verbena, Veronica, Viola, Yucca, Zephyranthes, Zauschneria

September, October, and November

Achillea, Aconiyum, Alpinia, Alstroemeria, Anemone, Artemisia, Aruncus, Aster, Begonia, Boltonia, Callirhoe, Campanula, Canna, Centaureum, Cerastium, Ceratostigma, Chrysanthemum, Chrysogonum, Cimicifuga, Clematis, Convolvulus, Coreopsis, Crinum, Dimorphotheca, Echinacea, Eryngium, Eucomis, Eupatorium, Fragaria, Gaillardia, Galium, Gentiana, Geranium, Gerbera, Hedychium, Helenium, Helianthus, Heliopsis, Hosta, Kirengeshoma, Kniphofia, Liatris, Limonium, Lobelia, Lotus, Nepeta, Nerine, Oenothera, Origanum, Papaver, Penstemon, Phlox, Physostegia, Platycodon, Pratia, Primula, Rudbeckia, Salvia, Saponaria, Satureja, Schizostylis, Sedum, Silene, Solidago, Solidaster, Stokesia, Tradescantia, Verbascum, Vinca, Viola. Some repeats and some carryovers from summer.

December: A few very late and a few very early.

LONG BLOOMERS

Usually at least six weeks (esp. if dead-headed)
Starred species are floriferous

*Achillea
*Allium
Althaea
*Anemone
Anthemis
Aquilegia
*Anchusa
Bellis
Campanula
Chrysanthemum
*Coreopsis
Delphinium
*Dianthus
Dicentra
*Digitalis
*Doronicum
Echinacea
Gaillardia
Geranium
Glaucium

*Gypsophila
*Hemerocallis
Heuchera
Hypericum
Lathyrus
Linaria
Linum
Lychnis
Monarda
*Myosotis
Phlox
Platycodon
*Physostegia
Rudbeckia
Salvia
Saxifraga
Scabiosa
*Sedum
Veronica
Viola
Yucca

LONG LIVED

Achillea
Aconitum
Actaea
Amsonia
Anemone
Anthericum
Aralia
Artemisia
Asclepias
Aster
Astilbe
Baptisia
Belamcanda
Boltonia
Campanula
Catananche
Centaurea
Chelone
Chrysanthemum
Cimicifuga
Clematis
Convallaria
Coreopsis
Cornus
Delphinium (some)
Dianthus (some)
Dicentra
Dictamnus
Digitalis
Doronicum
Echinacea

Echinops
Eremurus
Erigeron
Eupatorium
Euphorbia
Filipendula
Gaillardia
Galium
Gentiana (some)
Geranium
Helianthus
Heliopsis
Hemerocallis
Hepatica
Hosta
Iris, many
Liatris
Lilium
Linaria
Lupinus
Lychnis
Lythrum
Oenothera
Pachysandra
Paeionia
Papaver
Phlox
Platycodon
Polemonium
Polygonatum
Potentilla

Rudbeckia
Saponaria
Smilicina
Solidago
Thalictrum
Tradescantia
Trillium
Uvularia
Veronica
Vinca
Viola
Yucca

4. Lists by Preference

PERENNIALS WHICH PREFER MOISTURE

Sun

Arundinaria
Aster puniceus
Astilbe
Brunnera
Bulbinella
Chrysanthemum
Erigeron
Filipendula rubra
Gentiana andrewsii
Geum
Helianthus
Hibiscus
Hieracium
Houstonia
Iris
Ligularia
Lilium
Lobelia
Lythrum
Monarda
Myosotis
Paeonia
Phlox
Ranunculus
Rudbeckia
Sisyrinchium
Solidago
Teucrium
Tradescantia
Trollius
Veronica

Shade

Actaea
Adiantum
Anemone
Aralia
Ardisia
Asarum
Astilbe
Brunnera
Cimicifuga
Clintonia
Cornus
Cypripedium
Dicentra
Epimedium
Equisetum
Erythronium
Eupatorium
Filipendula
Gaultheria
Gentiana
Geranium
Habenaria
Helleborus
Heuchera
Hydrocotyle
Inula
Kirengeshoma
Ligularia
Lilium
Linnaea
Lysichiton

Lysimachia
Lythrum
Maianthemum
Meconopsis
Mitchella
Monarda
Omphalodes
Oxalis
Parochetus
Peltiphyllum
Phlox divaricata
Podophyllum
Polygonatum
Primula
Rheum
Rhodohypoxis
Rodgersia
Sanguinaria
Sanguisorba
Thalictrum
Tiarella
Tradescantia
Trollius
Vaccinium

PERENNIALS WHICH DO BEST ON MARGINS OF WATER

Acorus
Arundo
Arundinaria
Carex
Iris
Lilium
Lobelia

Lythrum
Monarda
Myosotis
Phyllostachys
Polygonum
Ranunculus
Rudbeckia

Saxifraga
Tradescantia

Aquatics   See encyclopedias
Bogs   See List

PERENNIALS WHICH TOLERATE DENSE SHADE

Actaea
Adiantum
Aruncus
Asarum
Boykinia
Cimicifuga
Convallaria

Dicentra
Dryopteris
Gillenia
Hosta
Osmunda
Pachysandra
Polygonatum

Polystichum
Sanguinaria
Tiarella
Trillium
Vinca
Viola (some)

PERENNIALS WHICH ARE DROUGHT TOLERANT

Artemisia
Campanula (some)
Centaurea
Cerastium
Chaenostoma
Convolvulus
Dianthus (some)
Eriogonum
Glaucium

Halimium
Hypericum
Lavandula
Limonium
Lotus
Rosmarinus
Senecio
Stachys
Statice

PERENNIALS FOR POOR SOIL, FULL SUN

Achillea
Amsonia
Anthemis
Arabis
Arenaria
Artemisia
Asclepias
Aster
Aurinia
Centaurea
Coreopsis
Eupatorium
Euphorbia
Gaillardia
Hemerocallis

Liatris
Linum
Lotus
Lupinus
Origanum
Papaver nudicaule
Potentilla
Rudbeckia
Santolina
Saponaria
Sedum
Thymus
Verbena
Yucca

TOUGH PERENNIALS (OR FOR EASY MAINTENANCE)

Acanthus
Achillea
Agapanthus
Anchusa
Anemone
Anthemis
Artemisia
Aster
Bergenia
Brunnera
Campanula glomerata
Catananche
Centaurea spp.
Chrysanthemum spp.
Crocosmia
Coreopsis verticillata
Doronicum
Echinops
Erigeron
Echinacea
Eryngium
Erysimum
Euphorbia
Felicia
Filipendula
Gaura
Gazania
Geranium
Geum

Grasses & sedges
Gypsophila
Helenium
Helleborus
Hemerocallis
Heuchera
Iris pallida
I. foetidissima
Kniphofia
Limonium
Liriope
Lythrum
Lychnis
Macleaya
Nepeta
Oenothera
Omphalodes
Penstemon
Physostegia
Potentilla
Putoria
Rudbeckia
Salvia
Satureja
Scabiosa
Sedum
Silene
Solidago
Stachys

Stokesia
Thalictrum
Thermopsis
Verbascum
Veronica
Yucca
Zantedeschia

5. Annuals

ANNUALS TO USE WITH PERENNIALS

Ageratum	Hunnemannia
Alcea	Iberis
Alonsoa	Lobelia
Althaea cannabina	Lonopsidium
Anagallis	Lunaria
Antirrhinum	Lupinus
Argemone	Nemesia
Brachycome	Nemophila
Browallia	Nicotiana
Campanula	Nigella
Centaurea	Papaver
Centaurium	Petunia
Cosmos	Phacelia
Cymbalaria	Rehmannia
Daucus	Reseda
Diascia	Salpiglossis
Dianthus	Silene
Erysimum	Stylomecon
Eschscholtzia	Tagetes
Eustoma	Trachymene
Gilia	Tropaeolum
Gypsophila	Verbena
Hesperis	Zinnia

Annuals
Plant Descriptions

Antirrhinum: SCROPHULARIACEAE. Snapdragon. Mediterranean & W. N. Am.
Herb. Wide range of colors & shapes.
Sun.
Select newest cv. for size, flower shape & resistance to mildew. Garden varieties of common snapdragon are divided into 3 groups: tall, intermediate & dwarf or Tom Thumb (this last 9 in.). Obtain from A-1 nursery. One of the very best anns. to mix with pers. Cutting.
A. molle: S. France. Leaves woolly; flowers whitish to soft yellow in loose leafy spikes.
A. glutinosum: Spain 8–14 in. Prostrate. Tender. Flowers yellowish white, lip striped red. Related to *Asarina* (See Outdoor Room).

Argemone: PAPAVERACEAE. Prickly Poppy.
N; Cent. & S. Am.,
Best treated as an ann. since it comes easily from seed.
Sun. Drainage. Moisture.

Brachycome COMPOSITAE. Swan River Daisy.
W. to N. S. Australia.
Plant in quantity.
B. iberidifolia: Seed. Combines well with pers.

Centaurea: COMPOSITAE. Knapweed, Basket Flower, Cornflower, Dusty Miller, Mountain Bluet, Sweet Sultan.
Eur. & No. & S. Am. (1 in Aust.) Armenia, Caucasus.
Herb. & evgrn. 600 spp. ½ hdy. Bracts in sev. overlapping rows, often fringed, sometimes prickly. No true ray florets, but marginal florets often enlarged & frilled.
Sun. Soil less than rich. Water 4 times during long dry spell. Grey group prefers water at roots & porous soil.
C. moschata, Sweet Sultan, *C. cyanus,* Bachelor's Button, *C. montana,* Mountain Bluet, excel. to mix with pers.
C. montana: Mountain Bluet or Perennial Cornflower. Grown as an ann. To 1½ feet. Leaves oval, pointed, plentiful. Florets petal-like, fringed; bright-blue, white or rosy-red. All summer. Wide drifts. Prefers light shade. Feed early spring. Remove worst portion of mat formed by spread of underground roots. *C. m.* 'Parkman': Flower clear-purple.

Centaurium: GENTIANACEAE. Mountain-Pink.
Warm & temp. regions, widely.
Ann. or bien; seeds prolifically.
Sun or shade.
Leaves in neat, small rosettes. Pull whole plant as bloom finishes. Best in natural mixed planting.
C. pulchellum: Europe; naturalized in dampish soils in N. Am.

Cymbalaria: SCROPHULARIACEAE
Herb. Trailer gc. or Hanging basket. Shade. Moisture. Seed.
C. muralis: Seen on old walls in Europe & Asia. Naturalized in N. Am.
C. hepaticaefolia: Corsica. Tiny lilac-blue, flowers

snapdragon-shape. This a little larger than *C. muralis*. Tender.

C. globosa: Europe & *c. g.* var. *nana*. The dwarf, compact, in neat clumps. Flowers tiny lavender-pink.

C. aequitriloba: S. Europe. Carpet. Leaves ½ in. across. Flowers mauve-purple. Close to foliage. Tender. A white form.

Daucus: UMBELLIFERAE. Carrot.
N. Am., Europe, Asia, Africa.
Herb. Bien.
Esp. good for a "wild garden".
D. carota: Queen Anne's Lace. Erect bien. which seeds itself, hopefully. To 3 ft. Leaves finely dissected. Flowers tiny in flat umbels; white or faintly purple.

Diascia: SCROPHULARIACEAE S. Afr.
Ann. or per. About 50 spp. Low, Slender.
Sun. Soil rich. Reg. water. Ample seed. Easy germination
A barberae: Twinspur. To 1 ft. Lvs. ovate to 1½ in long. Flowers erect delicate spikes. Bloom for a long period, at least 2 mos. Corolla 2-lipped, lower lip 2-spurred. Two-toned coral-pink and pink.
A. cordifolia (cordata): Another sp. which grows easily from seed.
A. rigescens: Uncommon per. Excel. for the "bedding" look. All stems upright & of like height. Leaves small & soft, plentiful. Flowers, dainty, coral, 6 in. spikes, all summer. Seed available.

Eschscholtzia: PAPAVERACEAE California Poppy
Numerous poppies with waxy texture.
E. caespitosa: Foothill Poppy. Leaves much dissected. Flower yellow, slightly folded; looks square. Big seed pods.
E. hypecoides: Rare in cultivation. Leafy. Leaves much dissected. Yellow petals often spotted orange.
E. lobbii: Frying-pans. Leaves twisted, divided into linear segments. Flowers solitary. Clearest butter-yellow.

Gilia (Linanthus): POLEMONIACEAE
G. nuttalli var. *floribunda*: Nutalli Gilia. Might broadcast.

Hesperis: CRUCIFERAE. Sweet Rocket, Dame's Rocket or Dame's Violet.
S. Europe, Siberia.
Sun or part shade. Easy. Might be invasive.
Fragrance strongest in the evening.
H. matronalis: 1–3 ft. tall; naturalized near old N. Am. gardens. Invasive but easy to pull. Flowers in terminal racemes; purple or white.
H. m. var. *flore-plena*: Dble. Flowers look like *Phlox*.

Hunnemannia: PAPAVERACEAE. Mexican Tulip Poppy or Golden Cup.
Mexico.
Herb. Best grown as an ann. Comes readily from seed.
Delicate foliage. Clumps to 18 in.
Sun. Seed. Sow in plant bands.
H. 'Sunlight': A selected form. Poppies—clear yellow.
Cut in bud.

Lunaria: CRUCIFERAE. Honesty, Moonwort or Satin Flower.
Europe.
Herb. 1–3 ft. Noted for papary white septum.
Part shade or part sunny. Ordinary cult. Seed.
Plant in order to cut the seed pod stems.
L. annua: Grown for the circular, papery seed-pods. *L. rediviva*: Elliptical-shaped seed pods. Per.

Lupinus: LEGUMINOSAE. *L. densiflorus* 'Ed Gekling': Elegant spires; 12-plus whorls, very even. Golden-yellow; May.

Nemophila: HYDROPHYLLACEAE. Baby Blue Eyes, Five Spot.
Delicate anns. seen at various altitudes. Will grow anywhere. 6–10 in. Waterleaf family.
N. menziesii: Flowers cup-shaped, sky-blue, whitish center; bloom spring for short period. Stems branch from base.
N. maculata: Seldom higher than 6 in. Flowers white with fine purple lines, small dots and 1 large dot on each of 5 lobes.
Sow seed. In a wild flower mix. As a low cover for a bulb bed. Will adapt to gardens at sea level.

Nigella: RANUNCULACEAE. Fennel Flower or Love-in-the-Mist.
Mediterranean region & W. Asia.
Easy from seed. Good filler with pers. Good dried.
N. damascena: To 2 ft. Leaves fine, lacy. Powder-blue or white. Shread-like bracts. Conspicuous stamens to 1½ in.; rose-pink or bright red. Delicate spidery appearance. Native habitat almost pure sand but appear to tolerate a mix with sand included. Invasive?

Phacelia: HYDROPHYLLACEAE. California Bluebell, Wild Canterbury-Bell, Wild Heliotrope.
Mostly W. N. Am.
Mostly ann. Blue list.
P. viscida: Seed is available. *P. campanularia*: Ann. from S. Calif., U.S. Bell-shaped corolla tube twice as long as petals. Good dark-blue. Good over lilies.
P. bolanderi: Scalloped. Seed available of this sp. & *P. purshii*? Occasional volunteers from this & other anns.

Rehmannia: SCROPHULARIACEAE.. China. U.S. Outdoors in Calif. & Pacific NW.
Herb. Not reliably per. ½ hdy. Partial shade. Soil moist. Ordinary cult.
Propagate from seed, cuttings or root cuttings.
R. elata: (In gardens sometimes misidentified as *R. angulata*.) To 4 ft., usually less. Flowers bright rosy-purple with red-spotted yellow throats.
R. angulata: To 3 ft., more often 1 ft. Leaves with only a few toothed lobes along margins. Bracts narrow abruptly. Flowers purplish-red with scarlet margin to upper petals, orange spots on lower petals. Hybs. between sev. spp. produce various colors.
R. kewensis: *R. glutinosa* × *R. henryi*. Creamy-yellow marked with dark-red blotch. More difficult to find & to grow.

Salpiglossis: SOLANACEA. Painted-Tongue.
Chile.
S. sinuata: A good ann. to mix with pers. About 2 ft. ½ hdy. Good to pick.

Trachymene (Didiscus coerulea; now obsolete): UMBELLIFERA. Blue Lace Flower.
Sun, ½ shade. Ordinary cult. Easy from seed.
T. coerulea: Australia. Very good for cutting. Good with pers.

Tropaeolum: TROPAEOLACEAE. Nasturtium.
Mexico to Chile.
Mostly anns. or vines. Many soft or bright colors developed by breeders. Pleasing in containers especially "hanging baskets."
Sun. Good drainage. Not hdy. Only mild & dryish climates.

T. polyphyllum & *T. speciosum:* Chile & Argentina. Fleshy-rooted pers., prostrate or climbing. Leaves roundish, deeply divided into 5 to 7 ovate lobes. Flowers yellow or orange-red with notched upper petals.

ANNUALS, BIENNIALS AND PERENNIALS TO GROW ANNUALLY

Ageratum
Alcea (Althaea)
Anagallis
Anemone
Antirrhinum
Argemone
Brachycome
Browallia
Callirhoe
Campanula (some spp.)
Centaurea
Centaurium
Chrysanthemum, Korean hybrids
Cosmos
Cymbalaria
Daucus
Delphinium ajacis
Diascia
Dianthus
Erysimum
Eschscholtzia caespitosa, E. hypecoides, E. lobbii
Gilia (Linanthus)
Gypsophila elegans, G. muralis
Hesperis
Hunnemania 'Sunlight'

Iberis
Lobelia
Lonopsidium acaule
Lunaria
Lupinus
Myosotis
Nemesia
Nemophila
Nicotiana
Nigella
Papaver, P. 'Summer Promise'
Petunia
Phacelia
Rehmannia
Reseda odorata
Salpiglossis
Saponaria
Schizanthus
Silene, S. pendula var. compacta
Stylomecon heterophylla
Tagetes tenuifolia
Trachymene (Didiscus) caerulea
Tropaeolium
Verbena
Viola
Zinnia

6. Perennials which Self Sow

Althaea rosea
Anchusa italica
Anthemis tinctoria
Aquilegia caerulea
A. canadensis
A. vulgaris
Aster novae-angliae
Claytonia virginica
Coreopsis grandiflora, C.
    lanceolata
Delphinium grandiflora, D.
    elatum
Dianthus barbatus
Dicentra eximia, D. formosa
Gaillardia aristatum
Geranium maculatum

Gypsophila acutifolia
Heliopsis scabra
Helleborus
Hesperis matronalis
Lathyrus latifolius
Liatris
Linaria
Linum
Lychnis
Lythrum
Penstemon
Rudbeckia
Stokesia
Verbascum
Viola

7. Bulbs to Combine

A FEW SUGGESTIONS
FOR BULBOUS AND CORMOUS PLANTS

Many bulbous or cormous plants suit containers very well indeed. They should be raised to combine with pots containing herbaceous and evergreen perennials, usually contributing both form and color. Tulips and Daffodils are naturals for spring display but there are many other less known genera from which to choose for different seasons and for different values.

Many bulbous plants are tender or semi-tender. These can be grown within a greenhouse or under shelter until such time as they are ready, and safe, to display. Usually several pots should be made ready containing the same species since the best use of most bulbous plants is as extra decoration at the base of or in front of larger plants in containers especially those which depend on fine foliage as their major contribution.

All schemes of decorating with pots are more interesting if changes are planned three or four times a year. A discussion of general principles will be found in "Outdoor Room".

There follows a list of bulbous and cormous plants both for containers and to mix with perennials in the garden. Those especially great in containers are marked with a "c".

BULBS TO COMBINE WITH PERENNIALS INCLUDING CORMS

Allium	Iris unguicularis
Amaryllis c	Ixia
Anemone	Lachenalia c
Anthurium c	Leucocoryne
Arum	Leucojum
Babiana c	Lilium c
Belamcanda	Liriope
Bletilla c	Lycoris
Brachycome	Muscari c
Brodiaea	Narcissus c
Brunsvigia c	Nerine c
Camassia	Ornithogalum
Colchicum c	Oxalis c
Crocus	Pleione c
Cyclamen c	Polianthes c
Cyrtanthus c	Polygonatum c
Dahlia	Ranunculus c
Dichelostemina	Schizostylis
Endymion c	Scilla
Eranthis	Sparaxis
Erythronium c	Spathiphyllum c
Eucharis c	Sprekelia c
Eucomis	Sternbergia
Freesia c	Strelitzia c
Fritillaria c	Streptanthera c
Gladiolus	Tigridia c
Haemanthus c	Tritonia
Hesperantha c	Tulbaghia
Hippeastrum c	Tulipa c
Homeria c	Vallota c
Hyacinthus c	Watsonia
Hymenocallis c	Zephyranthes
Iris reticulata	

8. Neat Growers

GOOD FOR BEDS

Anemone, Tecolite strain
Asarum europeum
Asarum caudatum
Aster sobcoeruleus
 'Wartburg Star'
Begonia spp.
Campanula persicifolia cvs.
Corydalis spp.
Chrysanthemum coccineum
 'Helen'
Chrysanthemum maximum
 'Snowcloud'
Chrysanthemum roseum
 "Robinson's Hybrids"
Chrysanthemum rubellum
 'Clara Curtis'
Felicia amelloides
Gerbera jamesonii
Iberis
Lupinus cvs.
Paeonia spp.
Papaver nudicaule
 "Champagne Bubbles"
Pelargonium domesticum
Pelargonium hortorum cvs.
Pelargonium spp.
Primula anisodore
Primula aurantiacum
Primula beesiana
Primula bulleyana
Primula capitata
Primula denticulata
Primula japonica
Primula polyneura
Primula pulverulenta
Primula seiboldii
Tiarella
Viola odorata cvs.

9. Grasses
A Brief Selection

The slender vertical of grasses offers a special line in mixed planting. The flower heads often have most graceful and intriguing shapes. Some other genera can be found with grass-like foliage, e.g., *Sisyrinchium*, Blue-eyed Grass and *Leucocrinum*, Sand Lily.

Here is a very short list of my favorite grasses and grass-like sedges: *Acorus, Acyphylla, Arrhenatherum, Arundinaria, Arundo, Avena, Carex, Elymus, Ferula, Festuca, Foeniculum, Hakonechloa, Helictotrichon, Imperata, Luzula, Miscanthus, Molina caerulea* var. *zebrinus, Ophiopogon, Pennisetum, Phyllostachys, Selaginella, Uniola.* Read a good book, such as *Ornamental Grasses for the Home and Garden* by Mary and Robert Mower, for other examples (Hackenberry-Meyer).

Grasses
Plant Descriptions

Acorus: ARACEAE.
N. hemis., India, Ceylon. Marshy places.
Evgrn. G.c., bog. Low & clumping. Leaves *Iris*-like or grass-like. Flowers minute, greenish in a spadix.
Shade & ½ shade. Spreads slowly. Division.
A. calumus: Common Sweet Flag. Creeping rhizomes. Best in water with mud bottom.
A. gramineus: Grassy-leaved Sweet Flag. India to Japan. Better known sp. Useful for boggy ground, edges of streams or areas permanently damp. Flowers inconspicuous.
   A. g. pusillus: Smaller & more tufted.
   A. g. 'Variegatus': Cream stripes on the grassy leaves.

Arrhenatherum: GRAMINEAE. Oat Grass.
A. elatius 'Variegatum': Variegated Oat Grass. Blades flat, soft, erect, slender. Cv. less tall than sp. Small flowers in panicles, pale green, much incised. See also *A. elatius* var. *bulbosum.*

Avena: GRAMINACEAE. Oat.
Temp. regions of Old World & New World.
A. sterilis: Animated Oats. Differs from *A. fatua,* Wild Oat, in spikelets almost 2 in. long with awns to nearly 3 in. Awns twist on a wet surface.
A. fatua: Wild Oat. Like *A. sterilis.* Leaves used for cutting.

Briza: GRAMINEAE. Quaking Grass.
Eurasia, naturalized temp. regions.
B. minor: Little Quaking Grass. Ann. Stems to 16 in., erect.

Carex: CYPERACEAE. Sedge.
Throughout the world.
A sedge with clumps of grass-like foliage.
Shade or ½ sun. Mostly wet soils.
Carex from Greek "keiro", to cut, in reference to saw-toothed edges of leaves.
C. riparia. var. *variegata:* Eur., 3 to 4 ft. tall. Striped with white. Watersides.
C. buchanini: One of the most ornamental.

Ferula: UMBELLIFERAE. Giant Fennel.
N. Afr.
Familiar in vacant lots & sidewalk fringes of the city.
F. tingitana & F. communis: Colossal weeds in Calif., U.S. The tap root is so strong that it can penetrate concrete. To 7 ft. Flowers like those of huge parsley.

Festuca: GRAMINACEAE.
F. ovina var. *glauca (F. glauca):* Blue Fescue. Compact tufts.

Foeniculum: UMBELLIFERAE.
Herb.
Sun or shade. Ordinary cult. Control. Grown in the vegetable garden. Seeds prolifically.
Look for the dark one. Interesting for cutting.
F. vulgare: To 6 ft. Leaves green, very finely divided, like hair. Fragrant, pungent.

Imperata: GRAMINEAE.
I. cylindrica 'Rubra': Japanese Blood Grass. A small grass with some leaves unbelievably red. Short clumps of slender blades stained scarlet most of the length. (See: Short Introduction to Grasses, Pamela Harper, Summer, 1983, *Pacific Horticulture;* or, *Ornamental Grasses,* Roger Grounds.)

Luzula: JUNCACEAE. Wood-Rush.
Widespread N. & S. hemis.
L. maxima (L. sylvatica): Interesting heads. Rampageous surface spreader.
L. campestris: To 1½ ft. Leaves soft, flat. Flowers small brown in graceful clusters.

Miscanthus: GRAMINEAE.
Asia.
Sev. ornamental pers. Stems to 10 ft. Leaf blades mostly basal. Panicles; feathery. Robust.
Division. Seed.
M. sinensis 'Variegatus': Eulalia, Zebra Grass. Leaf blades striped—white or yellowish. Large clumps.

Phyllostachys: GRAMINEAE. Bamboo.
Himalaya.
Big.
An important genus.
P. niger: Black Bamboo. Running rhizomes somewhat contained. Stems valuable.

Uniola: GRAMINEAE. Sea Oats.
N. Am. to S. Am.
U. paniculata: To 8 ft. Much smaller in the garden since old stems are cut to ground. Graceful, wavy stems. Will tolerate shade. Interesting flowers.

10. Subshrubs

SUBSHRUBS PLANT LIST

Acantholimum
Actaea
Amsonia
Anacyclus
Andromeda
Aralia
Arctostaphylos
Artemisia
Aster
Astilbe
Baptisia
Baueria
Calluna
Calocephalus
Caryopteris
Ceratostigma
Chaenostoma
Chamaedaphne
Chelidonium
Chrysanthemum
Clematis
Convolvulus cneorum
Coprosma
Correa
Cotoneaster dammeri
Cyathodes
Daboecia cantabrica
Daphne blagayana
    & other dwarves

Dendromecon
Dictamnus
Dimorphotheca (See
    Osteospermum)
Diplopappus
Erica
Eriogonum
Euryops
Felicia
Gaultheria
Genista
Haplopappus
Hebe
Heliotropium
Helichrysum
Hermannia
Hypericum
Indigofera
Jasminum
Kalmia
Lavandula
Leptospermum humisifusa
Leucothoe davisii
Ligularia
Linum
Lupinus
Lythrum
Metrosideros
Mimulus
Myoporum
Nandina
Olearia

Pachystegia
Paeonia suffruticosa
Parahebe
Pernettya
Perovskia
Phlomis
Phyllodoce
Pieris
Pimelea
Potentilla fruticosa
Prunus pumila
Purshia
Putoria
Reinwardtia
Rosa 'Margot Koster' & other
    dwarfs
Rosmarinus
Salix glacialis
Salvia
Scutellaria
Senecio petasitis
Teucrium
Thymus
Vaccinium
Whipplea
Yucca
Zenobia

Subshrubs Plant Descriptions

A Few Examples of Genera Good to Grow With Perennials

Acantholimun: PLUMBAGINACEAE. Prickly Thrift. Greece, Crete, E. Eur., Cent. Asia to W. Tibet.
Requires Sandy place, sun and warmth. Cuttings.
A. androsaceum: Dense cushion-like calyx, heavy corolla, purple.

Andromeda: ERICACEAE. Bog Rosemary.
N. Am., Eur., Asia.
Evgrn. Low, compact. Leaves narrow-oblong, tapering both ends, dark green, tomentose beneath.
Shade or ½ shade. Moisture. Soil humusy.
Named for the daughter of Cepheus & Cassiope, rescued by Perseus from the sea.
A. polifolia: To 1 × 1 ft. Leaves linear to 1½ in. long. Flowers pendant in umbels. Sev. cvs. of 4 varieties of 1 sp.

Arctostaphylos: ERICACEAE. Bearberry or Manzanita.
Widespread.
Evgrn. Attractive branching habit. Low to high. Many low & compact spp. & cvs. Foliage small, leathery. Flower a closed bell; clusters.
Sun & shade. Soil humusy. Protect foliage from mud splash. Trailers are flat g.c. to 6 ft. long × 4 ft. w.
A. uva-ursi: Excel., in combination with a number of pers. Look for 'Wood's Red'. 'Wood's Compactum', trailing. 'Miniature', upright.

Bauera: SAXIFRAGACEAE.
New S. Wales, Aust., N. Zealand.
Evgrn. Small. 18 in. w. Leaves 3 partite. Flowers solitary in leaf axils. Bloom nearly all year.
Sun or shade. Soil sandy, loamy, peaty. Greenhouse

in cold climates.

B. rubioides: Evgrn. subshrub. Open habit. Said to reach 2 ft. but behavior in Calif., U.S. appears more prostrate. Looks like members of the heath family. Neat, clean growth. Leaves dark green, opposite, very small, sessile. Flowers small, solitary closed cups. Winter & spring.

Calluna: ERICACEAE.
Evgrn. Many fine small shrubs, as well as larger shrubs.
Sun & shade. Soil with acidity.
C. vulgaris 'Foxii': Heather. A dwarf white. Forms a tight dense, round cushion. 18 × 18 in.

Caryopteris: VERBENACEAE. Bluebeard.
A deciduous, small shrub to cut back annually.
Sun or part shade. Soil fert., water retentive.
C. × *clandonensis: C. incana* × *C. mongholica.* To 3 × 2 ft. Leaves only slightly toothed. Flowers blue-lavender in many flowered cymes.

Chaenostoma: SCROPHULARIACEAE.
S. Afr.
Evgrn. 30 spp. Leaves small, usually toothed. Flowers num. for long period.
C. hispidum (Sutera hispida): Perhaps this subshrub is not permanent because it will suffer from poor drainage, frost, & an excessively wet winter. It is worth growing from cuttings, however, in order to have plants on hand for replacement. It is evgrn., low, and hardly 2 ft.; compact & spreads to 18 in., with an aromatic fragrance. It is sim. to a bushy thyme but more brittle. Leaves are numerous on stiff upright, massed stems, dark green, hairy, 1 in. long, sticky to touch. In summer, there should be profuse bloom from tiny white flowers.

Chelidonium: PAPAVERACEAE. Greater Celandine or Swallow Wort.
Eur., Asia.
Herb. Bushlet. 2 ft. × 18 in. Invasive. Interesting leaves.
Sun. Ordinary cult. Seed or division.
Greek: a swallow=folklore.
C. majus: Seen on mid-Atlantic coast. Related to Celandine-Poppy *(Stylophorum diphyllum).* Seeds itself freely. Weeks of summer.
C. franchetianum: Grow for leaves which hold the dew. Don't allow to bloom.

Convolvulus:
C. cneorum: A subshrub sp., with silvery, silky foliage. 2 × 2 ft. See general Plant Descriptions.

Coprosma: RUBIACEAE.
N. Zealand.
Evgrn. Shrubs & subshrubs. Foliage glossy.
Sun or shade. Ordinary cult. Soil med. Semi-tender. Cuttings.
Small spp. tough. Grow at a good pace. Not invasive.
C. petriei var. *petriei:* Creeping mat. Branches slender. Leaves linear, leathery, to ¼ in. Flowers solitary. Fruit globose, purplish red or pale blue, translucent. Useful in r.g.
C. pumila: N. Zealand. Prostrate. To 2 ft. w. Creeping. Leaves often in clusters—elliptic, leathery, somewhat fleshy. Fruits red.

Correa: RUTACEAE. Australian Fuchsia.
Aust., Tasmania.
Evgrn. Leaves opposite, stellarly downy on many branches forming a bush usually low, usually dense.

Sun or ½ shade. Soil peaty, good drainage. Semi-hdy.
Plant against a south wall or under protection. Bloom long period.
C. reflexa: Prostrate evgrn. subshrub to 1 ft. with small, leathery leaves. Flowers are narrow funnels green at the base & red at the tips. Good with pers. on the raised edge of a mixed border.

Daphne: THYMELAEACEAE. Garland Flower.
Eur. & Asia.
Herb. & evgrn. Some semi-evgrn. in mild climate. Subshrubs as well as shrubs. Fragrant. Bloom winter.
Part sun. Soil somewhat moist. Excel. drainage. Those from alkaline areas will tolerate some acidity. Semi-hdy. Cuttings.
The smallest *Daphne* are excel. for woodland or r.g. Seek *D. bluohi* (sometimes spelled "bholua"). This sp. is described as a synonym of *D. cannabina* & *D. papyracea.* Seek the latter for its remarkable bark. Jan. bloom. Not the smallest.
D. cneorum: Hdy. through Mass., U.S.; from dry rocky places, Spain to the Ukraine. 12 × 8 in. Leaves very small; flowers in clusters, pink, sometimes white. *D. c.* var. *pygmaea:* Very dwarf.
D. 'Somerset' & *D.* 'Alfred Burkwood': *D. caucasica* × *D. cneorum;* 2 good cvs. of the hyb.; deciduous. 2 × 2 ft.
D. alpina: Hdy. to S. New England, U.S. Deciduous. A somewhat crowded shrublet sometimes only 6 in. high. Flowers white, sweet-scented. Fruits orange-red.
D. blagayana: Mtns. of Balkan Peninsula. Evgrn. Creeping to 1 ft. tall. Open branched. Flower stems to 15 in., heads 2 in. wide, pinkish or yellowish white. Fruit pinkish.
D. collina: To 1 ft. Forms fat mound. Masses of purple flowers with excel. scent. Subject to scale.

Dendromecon: PAPAVERACEAE. Bush-Poppy.
Calif., U.S.; Baja California, Mex.
Evgrn. Grow on a slope with *Eriogonum* & *Penstemon.* Not easy. 6 × 3 ft.
Greek: mekon=poppy, dendron=tree.

Diplopappus: COMPOSITAE.
S. Afr.
Genus used to be included in *Aster* & at least 1 sp. in *Cassinia.* Deciduous.
D. filifolius (Aster fruticosus): Much branched. To 2½ × 1½ ft. Leaves crowded, linear to ½ in.; flowers usually purple. See *Felicia.*
D. canus & *Cassinia retorta:* With shoots white with down.

Eriogonum: POLYGONACEAE. Wild-Buckwheat or California Buckwheat.
W. Am. & one on the E. Coast.
Anns., biens., herb. pers., evgrn. subshrubs, some from high altitudes, some from the sea-coast. The dwarfer, kinds are decorative in a sunny r.g. on the dry side, often looking best with siblings or cousins. A slope in which rocks have been incorporated is a suitable situation for *Eriogonum* & other W. natives of sim. character. Many spp.
Sun. Perfect drainage. Associate with rocks. Groom. Leaves leathery, some grey, some green. Semi-hdy. Division or seed.
Greek: erion=wood, gony=a joint or knee; alludes to jointed stems & pubescence of many kinds.
E. crocatum: Saffron Buckwheat. Easy; suffruticose; with almost white foliage.
E. fasciculatum: California Buckwheat. 3 subspp.

Leaves inrolled. Flowers small, white to pink.
E. latifolium: Low much-branched shrub, 9 in. to 2 × 2
ft. Sev. forms.
   E. l. rubescens (sometimes *E. latifolium* subsp. *grande*
   var. *rubescens*): Flowers rosy red.
   E. l. var. *sulphureum:* Yellowish.
E. umbellatum: Sulphur Flower. Low & spreading to
form a dense mat as wide as 3 ft. Leaves smooth
green above. More or less white-hairy beneath.
Flowers in full clusters, cream-colored. A cv. with
excel. habit is being raised by Saratoga
Horticultural Foundation, Ca. USA.
E. subalpinum: Very low & tight with very small
leaves; to 1 ft. Flowers soft yellow. Can be difficult.
E. ovalifolium: Another mtn. sp. from high altitudes
has flourished in the r.g. of the New York Botanic
Garden in the U.S. Cushions to 3 in. tall × 1 ft. w.,
silvery-white-hairy. Flowers on slender stalks to
10 in., spherical heads, cream first, fading to
purple.

Felicia: COMPOSITAE. Blue-Marguerite, Blue-Daisy,
King Fisher Daisy.
Species described here are from S. Afr.
Related to *Aster.* Shrubby. Stems slender & brittle.
Either the horizonal or the upright shape may be
emphasized by strategic pruning.
Sun. Drainage. Soil of average fertility & moisture.
Semi-tender. Hdy. to N.Y., U.S. Cuttings.
For Herr Felix, a German offical. Seen sometimes
grown in pots or hanging baskets. Massed flowers
at height of bloom. Very tedious to dead-head. Ray
florets of many spp. roll up in dull light.
F. amelloides: Subshrub, erect to 2 × 2 ft. w. Leaves
mostly elliptic. Numerous. Daisy: petals blue,
center yellow, on 6 in. stems. Cvs. offered by most
retail nurseries, e.g., 'Santa Anita'.

Genista: LEGUMINOSAE Broom.
Eur., N. Afr., W. Asia.
Evgrn. Choose procumbent spp. for sunny slopes. 1
ft. × 3 ft. Sev. dwarf. Good as companions for pers.
Cuttings. Try *G. tournefortia, G.* × *kewensis, G. lydia,
G. tinctoria, G. hispanica.*

Hebe: SCOPHULARIACEAE.
N. Zealand.
Evgrn. 100 spp. Shrubs as well as subshrubs. Leaves
leathery many, oval on superimposed branches.
Sun. Semi-tender. Cuttings.
Formerly included in *Veronica*
H. chathamica: Stems prostrate or trailing on a much
branched shrub to 1½'. × 2½ ft. For mild climates.
H. glaucophylla: Lower, blue-grey with white flowers.
H. hulkeana: Procumbent, leafy. To 3 ft. Flowers on
the tips of branches. Soft lavender.
H. hartiei: Recommended.

Hermannia (Mahernia): BYTTNERIACEAE. Honey-
bells.
Warm parts of S. Am., Arabia & Aust.
A twiggy trailer; stems well clothed with very small,
incised leaves. Curly.
Sun. Tender. Cuttings.
H. verticillata (Mahernia verticillata): Sandy flats in S.
Afr. Stems slender, "straggling", woody at base to
3 ft. long, longer on a bank or in hanging basket.
Flowers in pairs, bell-shaped, yellow, honey-
scented.

Indigofera: LEGUMINOSAE. Indigo.
China, Japan, Himalaya.
Deciduous. May be treated as if herbaceous.
Sun. Ordinary cult. Soil med. Cuttings.

Speedy growth of branches when the woody structure has been cut to ground. Semi-Tender.
I. gerardiana: India. Leafy shrub to 3 ft. Leaves pinnate.
Flowers rosy purple, & white, in racemes. Early
summer to fall. One of sev. shrubby plants which
benefit from being cut clear to the ground in early
spring. (This treatment for renewal is sometimes
used for such shrubs as *Fuchsia, Cestrum* &
Phygelius.)

Jasminum: OLEACEAE.
Evgrn. & deciduous. 200 spp. climbing, trailing or
erect.
Sun or ½ shade. Drainage. Hdy. to tender.
J. parkeri: N.W. India. Hdy. Tufted prostrate subshrub
to 1 ft. which has a most pleasing way of spreading,
esp. when planted at the top of a wall. To 3 ft. w.
Small pinnate leaves to 1 in. long on green stems
make a pattern. Flowers solitary yellow.

Kalmia: ERICACEAE.
N. Am. & Cuba.
Good in a container. Neat growth with shiny, green
foliage.
Shade & ½ sun. Soil porous, fert. Cuttings.
Evergreen. Semi-tender.
Flowers in clusters; distinctive shape.
K. latifolia & *K. hirsuta:* Shrubs which combine well
with pers. 3 × 3 ft.

Lavandula: LABIATAE. Lavender.
Chiefly Mediterranean. Also Canary Islands.
Semi-evgrn. Aromatic, both leaves & flowers. From
1–3ft. & almost as wide. Leaves usually toothed,
various shades of grey.
Sun. Soil med. Groom. Cuttings.
Many uses: strips, beds, borders, containers. Place
for fragrance. Seek the uncommon spp. in an
Arboretum sale.
L. angustifolia (L. officianalis, L. spica, L. vera):
Common English Lavender. To 3 ft. Leaves grey,
narrow with turned under margins to 2 in. long.
Stalks of flower spikes to 8 in.
   L. a. 'Hidcote', excel. habit; *L. a.* var. *alba,* white; *L. a.*
   'Nana', more dwarf; *L. a.* var. *atropurpurea,* early,
   almost purple.
   L. a. 'Munstead': Early, lavender-blue.
   L. a. var. *rosea:* With pink flowers. (Also *L. a.* 'Jean
   Davis', pink.)
   L. a. 'Twickel Purple': Flowers purple in long
   spikes, fanlike clusters. Very good
L. multifida (L. pubescens): To 2 ft. Compact. Leaves
greyish green, dissected. Lacy design. Flowers in
dense, pointed spikes, with collar of light violet.
Likes moisture. Semi-tender. Excel. for a
container.
L. stoechas: Spanish, French or Portuguese Lavender.
Mediterranean. Canary Islands & Madeira. Shrub
to 3 ft., only 2 ft. if kept pruned. Equally wide.
Many stems. Leaves linear to 1 in., revolute,
clothed with hairs. A curly look. Flowers in
compact spikes crowned with sev. flaring purple-
veined bracts, wavy. Blooms dark purple only
partially exposed from between the folds of the
spikes. Plentiful bloom. Dead head.
L. dentata: French Lavender. W. Mediterranean.
Different. Compact subshrub. Leaves linear to 1½
in., green. Toothed like a comb on both margins.
Flowers on long stalks, dense spikes to 2 ft. Purple.
A crown of bracts, lavender-blue.

Mimulus:
The shrubby spp. might be listed as *Diplacus.*
M. cardinalis: Scarlet flowers. A woody bush to 2 × 2 ft.

Myoporum: MYOPORACEAE. Bastard Sandalwood.
Aust.; N. Zealand; Hawaii, U.S.
Sev. spp. large shrubs or trees. Some used for windbreaks in warm climates. Some low & trailing as *M. debile:* good for banks.
M. parvifolium: Trailing stems, with evgrn., glossy, small leaves. Tender. Good g.c.

Olearia: COMPOSITAE. Daisy Bush, Daisy Tree, Tree-Aster.
Mostly N. Zealand & Aust. Tender.
A shrub, but mixes well with other woody pers. Borders & banks.
O. haastii: Natural hyb. between *O. avicenniifolia* & *O. moschata.* To 10 × 2 ft. Pruning decreases size & increases bloom clusters of small white "asters". Also a sp. with purple flowers. The bloom looks like typical per. bloom. Good to cut.

Osteospermum (Dimorphotheca): COMPOSITAE.
E. Cape & Natal.
Many clones & hybs. Shrubby, evgrn., to 1 ft. with masses of daisies, summer & fall. Tolerant of seaside conditions.
Not tolerant of cold. Cuttings. Division.
O. jucundum: Hairy, herb. to 1½ ft. Ray flowers cerise with dark purple disk.
O. ecklonis (Dimorphotheca eclonis): One of the tallest & widest. 2 × 2 ft. unpruned. Flowers bluish white with dark blue centers. Prune & groom.

Pachystegia: COMPOSITAE.
N. Zealand.
Evgrn. Robust. Spreading. Soft grey backsides.
Sun. Drainage. Semi-hdy. Cuttings.
P. insignis (Olearia insignis): To 6 ft. when unpruned. To 3 ft. in cultivation. Wider than high. Leaves thick, leathery, blades over 6 in. long. Beneath, dense white to yellow soft hairs. Leaves felted beneath. Flower heads to 3 in. across, May. Noted for large leaf & large flower head.
P. i. var. *minor:* Smaller in all parts.

Paeonia: See General Plant Descriptions.
P. suffruticosa: Deciduous shrub to 6 ft. Leaves twice-pinnated with lobed leaflets, hairy on undersides. Flowers to 6 in. wide, with 8 or more concave petals, rose-pink to white. Horticultural vars., all shades of red & pink as well as white & dbles. as well as singles. Many cvs. one or two nearly yellow.

Parahebe: SCROPHULARIACEAE.
N. Zealand.
Between *Hebe* and *Veronica.* Semi-woody. Leathery. Flowers solitary. Good for r.g.
Sun. Soil med. Drainage. Semi-hdy. Cuttings.
Warm winters, cool summers. Flourishes in Northwest, U.S.
P. catarractae: Low mounds, bright green. To 2 × 2 ft. Stems decumbent. One form with blue flowers. Mostly flowers white with purplish veins. Stems purplish. *P. c.* var. *diffusa:* Dense mat with flowers white, veined rose-pink.
P. lyallii: Shrublet. Pale mauve flowers. Prostrate rooting stems 2½ ft. w.
P. decora: Creeping subshrub forming low hummocks to 1 ft. Flowers white or pink.

Perovskia: LABIATAE. Russian Sage.
Himalayas to NE. Iran.
Deciduous shrub. To be pruned drastically. Aromatic.
Sun. Soil med., on the dry side. Good drainage. Cuttings.
Noted for white stems white-grey undersides leaves & overall grey look.
Flower looks like the flower of *Lavandula.*
P. atriplicifolia & *P. abrotanoides:* To 3–4 ft. × 2–3 ft. Widely branching with many slender stems. Leaves twice pinnately cut about 1 in. long. Inflorescence narrowly paniculate, bluish lavender. Cut back all branches, at least ⅓ up to ⅔ of total bush.
P. hyb. 'Blue Spire' & 'Blue Haze', *P. abrotanoides* × *P. atriplicifolia:* To 4 ft., more likely less. A shrub more woody than *Lavandula* but branches more slender & more limber. In winter, when leafless, the almost white stems make a distinctive pattern in a per. border. Leaves bluish, finely dissected. Flowers in slender spires, clear, blue-lavender; although resembling Lavender, the placement of the flowers on the spike is more open & the color brighter. Late summer. Many branches, many flower stems.

Phlomis: LABIATAE. Jerusalem Sage.
Temp. parts of Eur. & Asia.
Evgrn. Noted for whorls.
Sun. Soil ordinary. Somewhat drought resistant. Cuttings.
Handsome planted in a wide strip, instead of a hedge.
P. fruticosa: Evgrn. Shrubby to 4 × 3 ft. wide. Cut back ⅓ in the fall. New shoots grow from green buds on last year's wood. Densely hairy shoots. Leaves to 5 in., hairy & wrinkled, white hairy beneath. Flowers pale yellow, in dense whorls with flaring bracts under the clusters. Blooms sev. mos.
P. russeliana (misnamed *P. viscosa*): Shrubby & pubescent. 3 × 2 ft. Leaves to 4 in. Wrinkled, rough, green above, hairy beneath. A mat to 6 in. of dense sessile leaves below flower stems. Width of mat doubles the second year. Flowers hooded, yellow, superimposed whorls of 40–50 flowers. Bracts awl-shaped. Early summer bloom continues if deadheaded.

Phyllodoce: ERICACEAE. Mountain Heather.
N. hemis. Mostly high altitudes.
Evgrn. Small shrublet with very small, heath-like leaves. 1 × 1 ft.
Part shade. Soil moist, air cool. Cuttings.
For r.g. or woodland. Plant with other ERICACEAE.
P. caerulea: To 6 in. Dense. Leaves ¼ in. Flowers urn-shaped, rose-purple.
P. empetriformis: U.S., Alaska to Calif. Stems upright to 6 in. Flowers bell-shaped, corolla tube longer than lobes. Rosy purple.
P. glanduliflora: Alaska to Oreg., U.S. To 1 ft. Flowers sulphur-yellow, urn-shaped. Will not tolerate hot summers. Will not transplant.
P. breweri: Calif., U.S. Semi-procumbent to 12 in. w. Flowers in terminal racemes to 6 in. Corolla basin-shaped, rich pink; May & June.
P. tsugifolia: N. Japan. To 6 in. White. Available.

Pieris (Arcteria): ERICACEAE. Japanese Andromeda or Mountain Andromeda.
N. Am., Cuba, E. Asia.
Evgrn. Shrubs & dwarf shrubs. Leaves exceedingly narrow & delicate; numerous.

Shade or ½ shade. Moist, fert., acid soil. Contained. Cuttings. Semi-hardy

P. japonica 'Pygmaea': A treasure for a r.g. Leaves tiny. Flowers closed-bells, white, fragrant, in clusters of 2 or 3 along tops of 4 in. stems. Slow-growing dwarf. 1 × 1 ft.

P. 'Valley Valentine': One of current cvs. Colorful. Larger than the dwarf.

Pimelea: THYMELAEACEAE. Rice Flower.
Aust., N. Zealand, Timor, & Lord Howe Island.
Evgrn. 100 plus spp. Erect to prostrate shrubs & shrublets. R.g.
Flowers on points of shoots made the previous year. Shade. Good drainage. Semi-tender.

P. ferruginea: To 4 ft.; best known; flowers rose-pink, hairy in pincushion-like heads.

P. prostrata (P. coarctica): For a shady bank, sturdy branches trail somewhat. Wide grey-green carpet, 1 in. or so high. 3 ft. w. Flowers tiny, white. Spring, fragrant, in clusters of 10 to 20. Berries white.

Potentilla: For genus description see Slope Plant Descriptions. Also, see General Plant Descriptions for certain other spp.
Subshrubs. The woody species keep a number of leaves through the winter in mild climates.
Sun. Prune to shape & groom. Cuttings.

P. fruticosa: Golden Hardtack or Widdy. Sp. from which many cvs. descend. To 5 ft. but often 1 ft. As wide as tall. Leaves divided into 3–7 leaflets & fully clothe the twigs. Flowers numerous, white, shades of yellow, and tangerine. Many cvs., e.g.:

P. f. 'Longacre': Dwarf, dense, spreads to 1½ ft. Flowers sulphur-yellow. June–Oct.

P. f. 'Gold Drop', 'Sutter's Gold', 'Tangerine', 'Snowflake', 'Mt. Everest': With numerous flowers.

P. davurica: A less known sp. with white flowers.

Prunus: ROSACEAE.
Some prostrate spp. good for r.g.

P. pumila var. *depressa:* Deciduous. Radiating branches. Brilliant red fall color. Flowers white. Perhaps only 8 in. high; may spread 4 ft.

Purshia: ROSACEAE. Antelope Bush.
W. N. Am.
Native to Calif., U.S. 1 sp. Uncommon. Frederick Pursh a German wrote about N. Am. plants.
Sun. Semi-hdy. Root from layers.

P. tridentata: To 10 ft. but usually to 3 ft. Arches. Downy young shoots. Leaves to 1 in., wedge-shaped & 3-toothed at apex, pubescent above & with white hairs underneath. Flowers small, creamy yellow. Bloom Mar. Grow for a woody accent in a grey combination.

Putoria: RUBIACEAE.
Mediterranean.
Evgrn. Spreading, slightly woody. One sp. not higher than 6 in. to 2 ft. w. Flowers & fruits at same time.
Sun. Ordinary cult. Semi-tender. Cuttings.

P. calabrica: Shrubby ground-hugging evgrn. Rather tender. Requires sun. Tap-like root. Stems branch horizontally, approximately in a circle, rooting as they spread. Leaves to 1 in. with recurved margins. Dense, forming a mat. Flowers small, pink, in terminal clusters, but partly hidden. Fruits round, light red. Spring & through summer. Foliage when crushed has a slightly unpleasant odor.

Reinwardtia: LINACEAE. Yellow Flax (not like true flaxes).
Mtns. of India & China.

Evgrn. To 3 × 3 ft., usually less as a result of pruning.
Sun or shade. Soil med. Top will freeze in cold winter. Pinch to make compact.
Bloom in winter or late fall. Grow several plants to form a group. Sometimes both flowers & fruit together.

R. indica (*R. tetragyna* or *R. trigyna*): Subshrub to 4 ft. Leaves toothless to 3 in. Bright dark green. Flowers bright yellow in few-flowered clusters, nearly round, to 2 in. across.

Rosmarinus: LABIATAE. Rosemary.
Seacliffs & nearby in S. Eur. & Asia Minor.
Aromatic. Dry the leaves by hanging the branches or strip leaves from branches while fresh & spread to dry. Prune lightly carrying out artistic form. When very young, tip-pinch the branches directing growth.
Sun. Soil somewhat dry, somewhat lean. Semi-hardy.

R. offinalis: Wide shrub to 6 ft. with leafy branches. Grey-green. Stiffly erect in the typical form. Leaves narrow-linear about 1 in. long with rolled under margins. Flowers light blue in clusters of 2 or 3 in leaf axils. Cvs., e.g.:

'Collinwood Ingram' (*R. ingramii*): Branches arch forming a shrub twice as wide as tall. Color of flowers deeper than the sp.

'Prostratus': Height 2 ft., breadth 8 ft. Branches sturdy. From the top of a wall, branches descend in a perpendicular cascade.

'Lockwood de Forrest': Prostrate but branching, woody stems arch & angle. Leaves light & bright. Flowers clear blue-violet. Good for a bank.

R. angustifolia: Worth seeking. Strong branches stiffly erect. Width may be kept to 3 ft. Flowers excel color.

Scutellaria: LABIATAE. Skullcap (from shape of calyx in seeding stage).
Wide distribution. esp Eur. & Cent. Asia. About 80 spp.
All spp. have snapdragon-shaped flowers; upper lip of 2 lobes, lower lip of 3; with leafy bracts. Calyx closes when flower fades. Bracts colored.
Sun or ½ shade. Soil not too rich; prefer alkalinity. Need drainage.
Good on a bank. Some spp. to 3 ft.

S. alpina: Somewhat subshrubby. To 1 ft. or somewhat procumbent. Stems many, semi-prostrate, hairy, leafy. Leaves ovale, dark green with coarse, rounded teeth cordate at base. Four angled spikes. Calyx bell-shaped. Flowers in oblong, terminal crowded racemes to 3 in. with conspicuous purple-flushed bracts. Bloom Aug. Blue-violet with white lower lips (or all purple, all yellowish or white). *S. orientalis,* sim. but flowers yellow with pink lower lips.

S. canescens (S. incana): Ohio, U.S. Erect. To 3 × 2 ft. Leaves sage-grey. Spikes branching, num.; flowers small, dark lavender; summer.

Senecio: See General Plant Descriptions.

S. petasitis: Velvet Groundsel. Becomes a large, 8 × 3 ft. shrub in 1 season; is cut all the way to ground in fall. Sun. Moisture. Spreads. Division. Stunning very velvety, large leaves.

Vaccinium: ERICACEAE. Bilberry, Blueberry, Cranberry, Deerberry, Farkleberry, Lingonberry, Whortleberry.
N. hemis., mtns. of tropics, S. Afr., Madascar & the Andes.

Herb. or evgrn. Creeping, trailing, or upright. Leaves small with decorative placement.

Shade & ½ shade. Soil moist, porous. Acid. Humus. Division or cuttings.

V. macrocarpon: American Cranberry or "Large Cranberry".

V. oxycoccus: Small Cranberry. A carpeter to 1 ft. w. Long, limp trailing stems. Tiny in all parts, leaves & pink bells & red fruits. Edible.

V. vitis-idaea var. *minus:* Mountain Cranberry or Mountain Cowberry. American variant of European & Asian Lingonberry, *V. vitis-idaea.* Labrador & Brit. Col., Can.; Alaska & Mass., U.S. Creeping rhizomes. Dense mats with shiny evgrn. foliage. To 6 in. × 2 ft. w. Leaves small, neat to ½ in. long. Flowers dark pink to red. Fruits for jellies. Only thrives in soil with high acidity. Grow with *Gaultherias* & other plants of ERICACEAE.

Whipplea: SAXIFRAGACEAE. Modesty or Yerba de Selva.

Shaded slopes, Oreg. to Calif., U.S.

Evgrn. Related to currents & gooseberries but unlike them. Only one sp.

Shade. Soil moist. Drainage. Cuttings.

W. modesta: Stems slender, trailing, somewhat woody. To 3 ft. Stems root at nodes which touch soil. Called deciduous but never without leaves in Calif., U.S. Leaves small, ovate, slightly toothed to 1¼ in., clothed with stiff short hairs. Flowers small, cream-colored, fragrant. Graceful cascading habit.

Zenobia: ERICACEAE.

Coastal plain, Va. to S.C., U.S.

Single sp. Deciduous or partly evgrn. small shrub.

Sun or light shade. Soil acid, somewhat moist. Hdy. to S: NE. Muted fall color.

Flowers in clusters. Each flower looks like a flower of Lily-of-the-valley.

Z. pulverulenta: To 6 ft. Very slow growing. Wide graceful habit. Leaves to 3 ft. elliptic, bluish green & on the undersides almost white. Flowers white, fragrant, bell-shaped. A feature with perennials in a mixed woodland planting.

11. Perennials for Ground Covering

PERENNIALS FOR GROUND COVERING PLANT LIST

(b=both sun & shade)

Sun

Acaena
Achillea
Aethionema
Alchemilla
Anacyclus
Anaphalis
Androsace b
Antennaria
Arabis
Arctostaphylos
Armeria
Artemisia
Asarina
Aster b
Aubrieta
Aurinia
Bellis
Campanula b
Cerastium
Ceterach b
Chamaemelum
Chrysanthemum
Chrysogonum
Convolvulus
Coreopsis
Cotula b
Crucianella
Dalibarda b
Dampieri
Delosperma
Dianthus
Draba b
Duchesnea b
Elymus
Erigeron
Erinus b
Erodium
Erysimum
Euphorbia
Festuca
Fragaria b
Gazania
Geranium
Geum
Globularia
Gypsophila
Hebe
Helianthemum
Herniaria
Helichrysum
Hieracium
Hypericum
Iberis
Iris
Lamiastrum

Lamium
Lantana
Laurentia
Leontopodium
Limonium
Lippia
Lotus
Lupinus
Lycopodium
Lysimachia
Malvastrum
Mazus
Melissa
Mentha
Mesembryanthemum
Muehlenbeckia
Nepeta
Nierembergia
Oenothera
Onosma
Origanum
Osteospermum
Pachyveria
Phlomis
Phlox
Phyla
Pelargonia
Penstemon
Potentilla
Pratia
Prunella
Rubus b
Ruta
Sagina
Santolina
Saponaria b
Satureya
Scaevola
Schizocentron
Sedum
Sempervirum
Silene
Stachys
Tanacetum
Thymus
Teucrium
Trifolium b
Tripleurospermum
Tunica
Verbena
Veronica
Viola b
Vitaliana
Zauschneria b

Shade

Acantholimum
Acorus
Adiantum
Ajuga
Anemone
Ardisia
Arenaria
Aruncus
Asarum
Asperula
Azederach
Bergenia
Blechnum
Brunnera
Ceratostigma
Convallaria
Cornus
Corydalis
Cymbalaria
Dicentra
Elmera
Epigaea
Epimedium
Erica
Fuschia
Galium
Gaultheria
Gunnera
Hedera
Helleborus
Hepatica
Heuchera X Heucherella
Heuchera
Hosta
Hydrocotyle
Linnaea
Liriope
Lysimachia
Maianthemum
Mentha
Mertensia
Micromeria
Mimulus
Mitchella
Mitella
Myosotis
Nephrolepis
Omphalodes
Ophiopogon
Oxalis
Pachysandra

Parochetus b
Patrinia
Pellaea
Pimelea
Polemonium
Polygonatum
Polygonum b
Polypodium
Polystichum
Primula
Pulmonaria
Raoulia
Ramonda
Ranunculus
Sanguinaria
Saxifraga
Selaginella
Smilacina
Tellima
Tiarella
Tolmeia
Vancouveria
Vinca
Waldsteinia b

Acantholimum: PLUMBAGINACEAE. Prickly Thrift. Greece & Crete thru E. Eur. & Cent. Asia to Tibet, mostly in mts. & rocky places.
Slow growing. Suitable for r.g. Sun. Warmth, soil sandy.
A. echinus (A. androsaceum) Dense. Cushion-like. Some shade. Var. *creticum* pubescent.

Achillea: COMPOSITAE. Yarrow.
Spreading mats or low clumps.
No. temp. zone. Some spp. with grey foliage; some white flowers, some yellow. Sun. Easy.
A. ageratifolia, A. chrysocoma, A. clavennae, A. × *kelleri, A. myrtifolia* (not listed).
A. ageratifolia: Tufted to 8 in, silvery pubescent, Ray flowers, white.
A. umbellata: Tufted to 6 in, white-wooly leaves, silvery-tomentose, pinnately-toothed, white flowers in terminal corymbs.
A. tomentosa: Spreading clumps of green foliage, flowers yellow, mostly spring—clipping of spent flowers essential.

Acorus: ARACEAE. Grassy-leaved Sweet Flag.
Tufted herbs of marshy places. Leaves narrow, shiny in small clumps.
A. gramineus: A spreading grass not more than 1 ft. × 1 ft. *A. g. 'Pusillus'* is a dwarf form, *A. g. 'Variegatus'* is less vigorous but highly ornamental.

Adiantum: POLYPODIACEAE. Maidenhair Fern.
Full shade, moisture.
Several species.
A. pedatum var. *aleuticum:* one of several choice maidenhairs, only for those suitable situations where their needs may be met.

Aethionema: CRUCIFERA. Stone Cress.
Borders or rock gardens.
Flowers, mostly in spring.
A. × *warleyense. (A. 'Warley Rose'):* A compact hybrid. Leaves pinnately dissected. Spreads slowly to 1 ft.

Anaphalis margaritacea: COMPOSITAE. Pearly Everlasting. Dark green mat of very small leaves. Flower stems to 3 ft. Sometimes persists, sometimes seeds itself.

Androsace: PRIMULACEAE. Rock Jasmine.
Alpines which prefer sand, limestone and chips.
A. alpina, A. sarmentosa and *A. primuloides 'Chumbyï':* The first tufted, the other two stoloniferous; the dense rosettes of small leaves make a cushion.
A. lanuginosa: Prostrate covered with silky-white hairs; stems trailing. To 1 ft.

Antennaria: COMPOSITAE. Everlasting, Cat's Ear, Pussytoes. Ladies' Tobacco. No. Hemisphere. Mainly for rock gardens or edge with poor soil. Greyish foliage forming a close carpet 1 in. × 10 in. Flowers, small white heads mid-summer.
A. plantaginifolia var. *dioica:* No. Am. Foliage dark-green, broad, bronzed in winter. Stoloniferous. Rosette leaves tomentose. Many small heads, white with pale-green or purplish bracts.

Arabis: CRUCIFERA. Rock Cress. No. Am. and Eurasia.
Some spp. alpine, for a r.g. Others form mats, to 6 in. high and at least 12 in. across. White flowers in spring. Need sun and heat.
A. alpina: Mountain Rock Cress. Plants grown under this name are perhaps *A. caucasica,* to 12 in., tufted, procumbent. Flowers in loose recemes, fragrant, petals white.
A. albida 'Variegata': 4 in by 1 ft. Listed sometimes under *A. alpina,* but it may be a form of *A. caucasica.* In any case, there are pleasing markings on soft foliage; groom once a year.
A. aubrietioides: Turkey Mts. Grows to 6 in. tufted. Leaves toothed, greenish-grey. Flowers purplish-pink. Somewhat tender.
A. sturii: A low compact plant. Increases by rosettes slowly. Leaves small blue-green. Flowers, white. Hot dry areas are suitable.

Ardisia japonica: MYRSINACEAE. Marlberry.
Grown outdoors in warm climates, for shady, moist places. Spreads by underground roots to form a 3 ft. wide cover. Stems are nearly erect to 1 ft. tall. Foliage is leathery and bronze. Flowers pinkish-white, not conspicuous. Red berries, ¼ in. in diameter, lasting.

Arenaria: CARYOPHYLLACEAE.
N. hemis. & from Chile to S. tip of S. Am.
Evgrn.
Mostly in moss-like patches or in mounds or mats, ½ in. to 12 in. Sun or part shade. Soil moist & fert. Division.
A. balearica: Corsican Sandwort. From shady, rocky slopes. Stems. 2½ in.
A. verna var. *caespitosa:* Irish Moss (name also applied to *Sagina subulata*) & *A. v.* var. *aurea,* Scotch Moss, sometimes used instead of lawn; also between flagstones. If mounds become bulging, strips may be cut out to allow flattening. Leaves tiny. Part shade. Dilute fertilizer.
A. montana: Sandwort. W. & SW. Eur. Flowers white cups to 1 in. R.g. pocket or rock over which to trail. Likes water. Easy.
A. kingii: From dry sagebrush hills & alpine slopes. Flowers white in loose clusters. Useful in crevices.
A. gyposphiloides: One to seek.

Armeria: PLUMBAGINACEAE. Thrift Sea Pink.
Border, r.g. or as edger.
A. maritima: Very variable, most cultivated plants are forms of this sp. Narrow stiff leaves in compact tufts or basal rosettes. 5 in. × 18 in. Long-lived with good drainage. Sun. Flowers rose-pink and other pinks and white. *A. m. 'Laucheana':* Very compact, flowers deeper color.
A. juniperifolia: (*A. caespitosa*) Densely tufted with many rosettes to 6 in. Resembles *A. maritima* but leaves shorter and plant as low or lower. Sun, light soil, good drainage.

Artemisia: COMPOSITAE. Sagebrush, Mugwort, Wormwood.
Mostly grey to white foliage. Mats to 6 in. Sun. Hardy. Drainage.
A. caucasica: A silvery spreader to 6 in., silky hairy.
A. pycnocephalus: Sandhill Sage. From West Coast of No. Am. Sprawls to cover the ground. Wooly, almost white foliage on somewhat woody branches. Flowers greenish yellow in narrow panicles. Cut off to keep the plant low and compact. Seek a dwarf cv.
A. schmidtiana: Foliage very finely cut, soft, silky. Spreads slowly by underground roots. To 2 ft. The species is variable.
'Silver Mound', 12 in. tall, grows in a sort of dome.
'Silver Frost. a selection sometimes available.
'Nana' a dwarf form perhaps only 2 in. high.
'Angels' Hair' is a name used; perhaps for a distinctive plant.
A. reptans: Pendant stems with leaves short, white-grey. Looks like a Sagebrush.
A. canescens (A versicolor, a listed name only) Chainlink. A very spreading mound about 10 in. tall, with interlocked, slender, narrow woody stems in a fascinating pattern.

Asarum: ARISTOLOCHIACEAE. Wild Ginger, Asarabacca.
Shiny extensive cover for shade. Spreads by overground and underground runners, to 3 ft. Round, glossy, evergreen leaves. Flowers hidden by foliage. Housing for snails & slugs.
A. europeum with leaves to 3 in. across. Flowers greenish purple. Used in E. No. Am.
A. caudatum, A. hartwegii, A. lemmonii, spp. native in W. U.S.A. *caudatum* more commonly planted.

Asperula: RUBIACEAE. Eur., Asia.
The best known sp. now found in *Galium.* Some spp. remaining in *Asperula,* one follows:
A. cynanchica: To 16 in. Decumbent. Stems sprawling, leaves in whorls. Cymes panicled.

Astilbe: SAXIFRAGACEAE. Meadow Sweet. See Woodlands and Shady Places.
Clumps 1 ft. across, more or less according to sp. or cv. Leaves palmate & notched. Begins growth in March; buds remain unopened for 2 mos. plus; flowers plumy sprays, June & July.
A. × arendsii: Hybrid race. Clumps multiply & can be divided for increase in order to create wide drifts in the shade. Explore spp.

Aubrieta deltoidea: CRUCIFERAE. Aubrietia.
Best used on edges. Sprawls & hangs to 8 in. After shearing, foliage ragged looking. Sun.

Aurinia: CRUCIFERAE (Alyssum).
Edges or r.g. Mat forming to 3 ft. Sun. Several forms of *A. saxitile.*

Bellis perennis: COMPOSITAE. Dresden China good. Grown as annual.

Bellium bellidioides: COMPOSITAE.
Creeping by stolons. Short-lived. Tiniest daisies.

Bergenia: SAXIFRAGACEAE.
Several spp.; see Woodland. Wide spreading. Leaves glossy, bold, roundish. Groom. Control slugs & snails. Roots will usually stay alive even if tops are winter killed.

Blechnum: POLYPODIACEA.
Several spp. low enough for g.c.
B. spicant, Deer Fern grows fast to make a full cover.

B. penna-marina makes a tight carpet. Excel. pattern.

Brunnera: BORAGINACEAE. Siberian Bugloss.
Good under shrubs. Low-lying stems make a colony. Flower sprays like miniature forget-me-nots. Summer. See Woodland.
B. macrophylla best known.

Calluna: ERICACEAE. Heather.
Several dwarves make dense cushions.

Calocephalus brownii: COMPOSITAE. Cushionbush.
White-grey. Crinkled-look. Plant several close together to form a grey mass, 2 × 4 ft.

Campanula: CAMPANULACEAE. Bellflower.
Select the smaller spp. which are tufted or creeping. See Woodland.
C. caespitosa: Stems many; slender, erect to 8 in. *C.c.* 'Alba'.
C. carpatica: Tussock Bellflower. Fine white form 'Alba'. Many cvs. Dense, compact, upright tufts, 8 in. w. Leaves small, fresh green. Popular for r.g.
C. × pseudoraineri: C. carpatica × C. raineri: Greyer foliage than *C. carpatica.* Tight leafage.
C. cephallenica: Spreading. Leaves pointed, notched. Uncommon. (Star-shaped flowers).
C. cochleariifolia: (*C. pusilla*). Spreading (not tufted). Slowly forms a carpet to 3 ft. *C.c.* 'Alba' is choice. Cv. Miranda especially dwarf. (The latter sometimes listed as a sp.)
C. warleyensis 'Alba': properly the cv. 'Warley White' of a hyb., × *haylodgensis,* a cross between *C. carpatica* & *C. cochlearifolia.* Close mat with 4 in. stems; stems slender & sprawling. Leaves sharply serrate.
C. elantines, Adriatic Bellflower. *C.e.* var. *garganica,* sometimes considered a sp. Restrained spread. Leaves basal, mostly oval, green with minute pubescence. Semi-sh.
C. portenschlagiana: Sim. to *C. elantines.* Continuous flowers.
C. poscharskyana: More rampant, more lax.
C. raddeana: Foliage "soft". Leaves ovate, coarsely serrate.
C. pulla 'Bakeri': A dwarf. Leaves glossy, crenate to 1 in.

Cerastium: CARYOPHYLLACEAE. Mouse-ear.
Makes a carpet cover to 3 ft. or more. Remove flower buds for fresher foliage.
C. bierbersteinii: A white woolly mat to 1 ft. plus.
C. tomentosum: width can be contained. Leaves small, rather ragged; on slim stems to 6 in.

Ceratostigma: PLUMBGINACEAE
C. plumbaginoides (P. larpentae). Dense herbaceous cover widely spreading. Stems to 20 in. usually less. Leaves rough, green in spring, reddish bronze in fall.
C. abyssinicus: a similar ground-covering sp., has flowers pale blue instead of intense blue. Semi-hdy. See Woodland.

Chamaemelum: COMPOSITAE *C. nobile* is one of the plants called Chamomile. Resembles a moss, pleasant to walk upon. Shear off flowers. Plant with small pieces; spaces will fill in.

Chrysanthemum: COMPOSITAE.
C. ptarmiciflorum: Dusty Miller; Silver Lace (Cineraria candicans). Tomentose.
Keep to 8 in. Leaves finely cut almost white-grey.

Cornus: CORNACEAE. *C. canadensis* is the dwarf Dogwood. Spreads by underground roots in auspicious site to form a colony. Stems to 9 in. from small woody rhizomes. Difficult without rough, humusy soil containing decayed wood. Charming miniature. See Woodland.

Corydalis: FUMARIACEAE. Related to *Dicentra.*
A few spp. contained enough. Leaves lacey, compound, dainty.
C. cheilanthifolia: Chinese Corydalis. Fern-like foliage in a dense rosette. 8 × 8 in.
C. lutea: Sim. in habit. Delicate in character.

Cotula atrata: (*C. squalida*) COMPOSITAE. Brass Buttons.
Carpeting 2 in × 3 ft. Slender stems creeping & rooting. Leaves fern-like, bronze & tiny. Sun or shade; damp or dry soil.

Cyclamen: PRIMULACEAE.
Makes a colony by seeding itself as well as by bulblets. Good under trees & shrubs. See Woodland.

Cymbalaria: SCROPHULARIACEAE. Several spp. were formerly classed as *Linaria.*
Two or 3 spp. will creep over the ground as easily as up the bark of a tree or other support.
C. muralis: Kenilworth Ivy is the best known; *C. aequitriloba* & *C. hepaticifolia* are also seen. All are tender. All seed themselves freely in woodsy soil in a shady site. Rampant but not very invasive. A white form is the more compact.

Cyrtomium falcatum: POLYPODIACEAE. Holly Fern.
Each clump 1 ft. wide in maturity.
Plant in quantity in moist shade.

Dampieri: GOODENIACEAE. Trailing or spreading with slender stems to 1 ft. or more. Stems and branches grow at angles producing a spritely look.

Delosperma: AIZOACEAE. Mesembryanthemum.
D. pruinosum 'Alba' (*D. echinatum* 'Alba'). One of the useful "Iceplants". Spread unlimited in rich, porous soil.

Dianthus: CARYOPHYLLACEAE. Hardy Pink.
Many spp. make dense tufts of grass-like foliage. Many described as "cespitose". Foliage mostly grey but often green. Some trailers & some spreaders. See General Plant Descriptions for a number of spp. including cvs. sometimes named 'Compactus'. *D. winteri,* a name with no botanical standing but often used for forms of *D. plumarius* with apricot or yellow flowers.

Dicentra: FUMARICAEA. Bleeding Heart.
Several spp; see Woodland. Leaves dissected, delicate; the white forms especially fern-like. Very pleasing in shade, especially with the daintier types of ferns.

Draba aizoides: CRUCIFERAE.
Tufted. 4 in. × 4 in. Leaves in basal rosettes. Many spp.; best in alpine garden or r.g.

Drosanthum floribundum: AIZOACEAE. Segregated from the mesembryanthemums. Branches short, somewhat decumbent.

Dryopteris: POLYPODIACEAE. Wood Fern.
Many spp. A number grow well in peaty soil near water, most to 2 feet.

Duchesnea indica: ROSACEAE. Indian Strawberry or Mock Strawberry.
Unlimited spread, by runners. Leaves oval, coarsely toothed, shiny. (Flowers yellow).

Echeveria: CRASSULACEAE.
Many spp; spread varies. For tropical or semi-tropical climates.

Elmera racemosa: SAXIFRAGACEAE. Mts. of Washington. Related to *Tellima* & *Heuchera.* Low, pubescent. Slender, horizontal rootstocks, 4 in. to 10 in. Leaves mostly basal; long-stalked, kidney-shaped, double-toothed, more or less hairy. One sp. herb.

Elymus glaucus: GRAMINACEAE. Blue Wild Rye. Stems to 4 ft.; needs therefore a large site. Spreads to wide clumps of flat blades of excel. blue-grey color.

Epimedium: BERBERIDACEAE.
Several spp. will spread to make wide drifts, to 10 ft. Airy effect of soft green with bronze highlights. May be sheared for renewal. Undercover for shrubs or along shady paths. See Woodland.

Erica: ERICACEAE. Heath.
See subshrubs. Spreaders or in tight cushions. Excel. on a bank. *E. thunbergii* is probably the smallest of many So. Afr. heaths.

Erigeron: COMPOSITAE. Fleabane. Beach Aster.
Sev spp. Some sprawl to 3 ft., 6–12 in. high.
E. glaucus, w. No. Am. *E. karvinskiana,* Mexico; avoid.

Eriogonum: POLYGONACEAE. Wild Buckwheat.
Several low spp. See subshrubs. Alpine forms are choice.

Erysimum: CRUCIFERAE. Wallflower.
Closely related to *Cheiranthus.* Some spp. cespitose.
E. pumilum is probably the most fussy, preferring scree.

Festuca glauca: GRAMINACEAE. Blue Sheep Fescue.
"Glauca" is a variety of *F. ovina.* Stems densely clustered to 1–2 ft. Blades very slender. Spreads to make a continuous mat.

Fragaria: ROSACEAE. Strawberry.
Spreads mostly by runners.
F. californica is rampant & can become a pest.
F. chiloensis is another W. U.S. native, but better behaved. Becoming an endangered sp. One of the parents of garden strawberry. Many glossy green leaves well spaced on runners a foot or more long. Make a close mat. #25 is an ornamental strawberry which makes an attractive g.c.

Fuchsia procumbens: ONAGRACEAE.
From New Zealand, but fairly hdy. Slender, branched, prostrate. Subshrub.

Galax: DIAPENSIACEAE. Evgrn.
Tufted with very shiny rounded leaves. Good g.c. in acid humus, in shade; colonize in woods but not easy without natural conditions.
G. urceolata (G. aphylla). Excel. reddish bronze color in leaves.

Galium: RUBIACEAE. Bedstraw; Cleavers.
G. odoratum to 1 ft., usually less. Many erect stems make a wide mat easily penetrating neighboring g.c. Bristle tipped leaves. This is Sweet Woodruff.
G. baldense; More trailing. Leaves in whorls. Shear once a year.

Gaultheria: ERICACEAE.
Many spp., mostly shrubs; some low or prostrate.
G. procumbens, with dark glossy leaves in a dense carpet; the easiest; try others in moist, lime-free, humusy soil in woods. See Woodland.

Gazania: COMPOSITAE.
Several spp. for g.c., tough & somewhat coarse. Tender.
G. ringens var. *leucolaena* has somewhat tomentose grey foliage on trailing stems spreading widely, rapidly, rooting freely. Withstands poor soil & drought.

Gentiana: GENTIANACEAE.
A few spp. are easier to grow than is reputed, but only in a cool, moist situation with adequate acidity. Basal leaves may spread slowly into a neat green clump. See Woodland.

Geranium: GERANIACEAE. Cranesbill.
Several spp. spread well with leafy stems more or less prostrate making colonies to 3 ft. or more. Some moisture.
G. pratense has a double form; does not overspread by seeding. *G. sanguineum* has compact and refined cvs: e.g., 'Album', 'Alpinum', 'Nanum'.

Globularia: GLOBULARIACEAE.
Decorative dense mats for small areas.
C. cordifolia 'Alba' is a nice subject for a sunny r.g.
G. aphyllanthes has leaves noticeably spoon-shaped.

Gunnera: GUNNERACEAE.
From cool, moist, frost-free climates e.g. Patagonia, Falkland Is.
G. magellanica probably the most hardy & perhaps the smallest. Rich green, rough, scalloped leaves form a carpet about 3 in. high by 3 ft. across. Rich, water-retentive soil for all spp.

Gypsophila: CARYOPHYLLACEAE.
Trailing forms spread to almost 4 ft. in breadth. Leaves green or greyish green; on wiry stems intertwining. Delicate look.

Hebe: SCOPHULARIACEAE.
At least 4 spp. subshrubs which are trailing or prostrate & much branched. For mild climates. See subshrubs.
H. glaucophylla is low & blue-grey.

Hedera: ARALIACEAE. Ivy.
Even the most dwarf need control.

Helianthemum: CISTACEAE. Sunrose.
Especially good for steep banks. See Slope P.D. Trails or spreads to 2 ft. or more. Tolerant; but limestone in the soil suits them. Leaves mostly green, some grey, small, crinkled on many stems. Straw or branches to protect in winter in the colder regions.

Helichrysum: COMPOSITAE. Dwarf subshrub.
See Subshrubs. 1 sp., *H. bellidioides*, grows to 3 in. with grey-green tiny leaves. Leaves in some spp. spatula-shaped. Hdy. to Philadelphia, Penn. U.S. Interesting.

Helleborus: RANUNCULACEAE. Hellebore. See Woodland. Several spp. make a complete cover when they have developed a colony.
H. foetidus probably makes the most uniform and dense mass. Very fresh & crisp with attractive leaf design & dark color. Find seedlings.

Helzine soleirolii: A pest without compare.

Hepatica: RANUNCULACEAE. Liverleaf.
Closely related to *Anemone.* Naturalize in rich, well-drained soil in shade in suitable climates. Tufts increase to form a clump to 1 ft. or more w. Leaves 3 to 5 lobed. 3 or more spp. suitable for half-shady woods.

Hermannia: BYTTNERIACEAE. (Mahernia) Honey Bells.
A tender, twiggy trailer from So. Afr. See subshrubs.

Herniaria: CARYOPHYLLACEAE. Herniary.
A thick green carpet. Persists even in poor, dry soil but greener with some moisture.
H. glabra & *H. rotundifolia*—possible grass substitutes.

Heuchera: SAXIFRAGACEAE. Alumroot.
Good foliage in several spp. Leaves wavy-edged; excel. texture. More sun than shade. Moisture in Spring.

× *Heucherella, Heuchera* × *Tiarella.* Stoloniferous. Tufted. 4 in. × 12 in.

Hosta: LILIACEAE. Funkia. Plantain Lily.
Herb. Many kinds. Clumps of medium to large leaves with interesting texture, veinage & markings. Slug control. Spreads.

Hydrocotyle: UMBELLIFERAE. Marsh Pennywort, Navelwort. Waterside plants. See Bog. Glossy peltate leaves. 1 sp. inv.

Hypericum: HYPERICACEAE. St. John's Wort.
Some excel. dwarf spp. e.g., *H. cerastoides (H. rhodopeum), H. yakusimanum.* Avoid the tough invasive spp.

Iberis: CRUCIFERAE. Candytuft.
Spp. low & compact, attractive as foliage mats.
I. gibraltarica, quite tight.

Iris: IRIDACEAE. Flag, Fleur-de-lis.
Of some 200 spp., a few have qualities which make them desirable for g.c.
I. unguicularis has low tufts of leaves, which multiply to form a colony.
I. innominata is the lowest of the natives of western U.S. The leaves fan sideways; they are dark green, narrow & glossy.

Laurentia fluviatilis (Isotoma fluviatilis): LOBELIACEAE. So. Aus., Tasmania, New Zealand.
The height of the mat can hardly be measured in a fraction of an inch; the spread can be limitless in a suitable site. Sometimes seems to die out but often comes back again. Flat lying stems root as they creep. The miniscule carpet can be covered with taller ground covers, and when discovered it is often persistently growing. Sun or part shade. Soil fair & needs regular watering.

Leontopodium: COMPOSITAE.
L. alpinum: Edelweiss.
Whitish wool on the flat foliage rosettes compliments the color of rocks. Needs limestone, sand, part shade, water. Not easy in captivity.

Limonium: PLUMBAGINACEAE. Sea Lavender, Marsh Rosemary or Statice.
Several spp. with leathery leaves, forming tufts or rosettes. Usually spreads to 2 ft. A few rare spp. only suitable for r.g.

Linnaea: CAPRIFOLIACEAE. Twinflower.
Evgrn., creeping, forming broad, leafy patches in moist, peaty soil & shade. Leaves nearly round & closely placed on trailing stems; prostrate, warm brown, branching. Spill over rocks.

Liriope: LILIACEAE. Lily Turf. Related to *Ophiopogon.* Clumps enlarge moderately slowly to 1 ft. Leaves narrow & quite erect. Older leaves should be removed often to give the plant a groomed appearance.

Lysimachia: PRIMULACEAE.

L. nummularia: Creeping Jenny.

Fragile stems to 1 ft. long; trail twice as far on a slope. Needs moisture. Can be invasive.

Maianthemum: LILIACEAE. False Lily-of-the-Valley. Related to Smilacina.

Stems form a wide mat to 3 ft. (or more) when grown in cool, shady & moist places. Leaves waxy, thick, upright from underground 4 to 6 in. high. Control snails. Improves with age.

Mazus: SCROPHULARIACEAE. Himalayas. Related to Mimulus.

M. reptans & *M. japonicus.* Sun, warmth, good drainage. Tufted or trailing; to 2 in. Mat-forming. Found in waste places or lawns.

Melissa officinalis: LABIATAE. Herb.

Upright to 2 ft. Lemon fragrance. Spreads to form clumps. Cut back.

Mentha: LABIATAE. Mint.

Several upright spp. spread widely. Some too widely & hard to eradicate; some spp variegated. E.g., *M. rotundifolia* var. *variegata.* Cut back; control.

M. pulegium: Pennyroyal. Aromatic. Spread limitless. Flat stems except for those which bear the flowers. Inv. *M.p.* var *gibraltarica,* more dwarf, better carpet.

M. requienii: Corsican Mint. A miniature carpet with tiny, closely spaced leaves. Peppermint scent when rubbed. Spreads slowly in moist, shady corners, as a grass substitute. (It looks like Baby Tears at first glance.)

Mertensia virginica: BORAGINACEAE. Virginia Cowslip.

Best known sp. Only easy in habitat sim. to moist woods of Virginia. Foliage turns yellow soon after Spring blooming season & dies soon after that.

Mesembryanthemum: AIZOACEAE. Ice Plant.

Large group of succulent spreaders. (Group divided into smaller genera.) A few "magic carpet" coloring with small leaves, but form & size of foliage & color of flowers differ in various spp. Need good drainage & temperate climate.

Micromeria chamissonis now *Satureja douglasii.*

Mimulus: SCROPHULARIACEAE. Monkey Musk.

Perhaps *M. luteus* var. *alpinus,* from Chile, is the most decumbent. Densely matted stolons spread widely; if too widely they are easy to pull.

Myoporum: See subshrubs.

Myosotis scorpioides (M. palustris): BORAGINACAEAE. Marsh Forget-me-Not.

Creeping stems persistent for several years on a cool, moist site. Naturalize along shady walks. Modern cvs.

Nepeta hederacea (Glechoma hederaceae): LABIATAE. Ground Ivy, Gill Over-the Ground.

Will grow widely in shade & in poor soil; could become a pest. Leaves small, round, heart-shaped at the base.

Nephrolepis: POLYPODIACEAE.

N. exaltata: One of the most rapid growing ferns, when planted in warm climates.

Nierembergia repens (N. rivularis): SOLONACEAE. Cupflower. Herb. mat in moist, shady places. Slender stems root & creep; hardly over 8 in. at tallest.

Oenothera: ONAGRACEAE. Evening Primrose. Sundrops.

Sev. spp. may become weeds; others make restrained low ground covers. Running underground root stocks. See General.

Omphalodes: BORAGINACEAE. Blue-Eyed Mary. Navelwort. Creeping Forget-me-not. Asia Minor.

Increases by runners to make patches 1 ft. or more wide in humusy, light woodland.

O. cappadocica spreads the most rapidly.

O. verna: With a neater pattern of foliage. Leaves ovate-lanceolate, rugose with veins prominent.

Onosma: BORAGINACEAE. Herb, but evgrn. in warm climate.

Needs sun, good drainage & rich, sandy soil.

O. nanum: 5 in. high. Not common.

O. alboroseum: A grey low mat made up of tight, silky, woolly rosettes. Perfect drainage; slope best. Control slugs. Other spp. grow in mats but taller.

Ophiopogon: LILIACEAE. Mondo Grass.

Related to *Liriope.* Growth in tight clumps. Leaves narrow, curved.

O. japonicus, one of the lowest; increases rapidly.

O. planiscapus 'Arabicus' distinctive; spreads slowly. See Woodland.

Origanum: LABIATAE. Marjorum. Oregano.

Good on a slope. Some spp. may become invasive.

O. dictamnus: Dittany of Crete: Contained & procumbent. Stems, perhaps to 1 ft. growing from a central point horizontally. Grey, velvety.

Osteospermum fruticosum: COMPOSITAE. Trailing African Daisy.

Half-hdy. subshrub. Vigorous.

Oxalis: OXALIDACEAE: Very weedy ones & useful g.c.'s.

O. oregano: Redwood Sorrel since it is the lush g.c. under West Coast U.S. redwoods. A rich green carpet; the three lobed, patterned leaves forming a beautiful drift. The leaves of Oxalis fold esp. when exposed to sun. Several other spp. are hdy. according to their country of origin & not too invasive.

O. variabilis var. 'Alba': Num. small white flowers.

O. hirta: Small succulent leaves on procumbent stems.

Pachysandra: BUXACEAE. Spurge.

A well-known g.c. with patterned foliage. Filtered light, good soil & adequate water required for a healthy look.

P. procumbens: From rich woods E. U.S.

P. terminalis: Japan; *P.t.* 'Variegata', much slower than the sp. and very attractive.

Pachyveria: CRASSULACEAE (Hybs. between spp. of *Echeveria* & *Pachyphytum*).

Multiplying rosettes spreading well in warm climates.

Patrinia: VALERIANACEAE.

Clumps spread 1 ft. wide & join to form a colony. Rhizomatous or stoloniferous. Leaves usually pinnate or palmately lobed & clear-green color. Full & lush in light rich soil in semi-shade.

P. triloba is one of more dwarf spp.

Pelargonium: GERANIACEAE.

Several spp. & hybs. spread or trail.

P. peltatum will cascade down a bank or hang to 6 ft. Seek new hybs. Some scented-leaved species make sprawling ground covers; will come up from roots even though foliage is killed by cold or cut back to the ground.

P. tomentosum is tender, peppermint-scented with very velvety leaves on stems as long as 4 ft., hanging or lying close to the ground. (As stems lengthen, they become prostrate.)

Pellaea: POLYPODIACEAE. Cliff Brake.
Clumps of this fern spread, though slowly, to 1 ft. or more in suitable situations. It does not require moisture on the leaves, but it must not become dry at the roots.

P. atropurpurea, P. falcata, P. rotundifolia are more or less hdy.

Penstemon: SCROPHULARIACEAE.
P. heterophyllus subsp. *purdyi* is decumbent & mat-forming 1 ft. × 1 ft.

Phyla: VERBENACEAE. Frogfruit. Carpet Grass. (*Lippia*) Creeping, rooting at the nodes.
P. nodiflora var. *canescens* makes a flat, solid mat in warm climates. Plant small sods a few ft. apart.

Pimelea prostrata: THYMELICACEAE. Riceflower. New Zealand.
2 in. tall with tiny leaves, glaucus, grey-green on slender stems. Slowly spreading to 1 ft. Also, *P. coarctica.* (Or this may be a synonym.)

Polygonatum: LILIACEAE. Solomon's Seal.
Herb; spreads by underground root stocks to form colonies to 3 ft. or more. Several stems close together in full or part shade in loamy, woodsy soil.

Polygonum: POLYGONACEAE. Fleeceflower.
Most spp. become very inv. Appearance not refined. Need moist soil.
P. affine: Quite dwarf & mat-forming.
P. capitatum roots from runners. Tender. (Flowers pink balls.)
P. vaccinifolium: Evrgn, prostrate & mat-forming. Much branched stems & leaves sometimes tinged red.

Polypodium: POLYPODIACEAE.
Many spp. of this fern. Plant with roots just barely underground in a shady, cool & damp situation. See Woodland.

Polystichum: POLYPODIACEAE. Shield Fern.
Many spp. need greenhouse culture. Fronds usually leathery.
P. lonchitis: Holly Fern. Hdy & not difficult.
P. munitum & *P. lemmonii*, natives of the U.S. West Coast, grow freely with ample water in a shady site & in temperatures sim. to that of their native habitat.

Potentilla: ROSACEAE. Cinquefoil.
About 350 spp. & a number of hybs. The majority are herbaceous; many are low & spreading; almost all hdy. The leaves look like strawberry leaves esp. in the green-leaved kinds. A few are too invasive; a few are somewhat weedy looking; more than a few make excel. ground covers. All require sun and some water all year around. In order to obtain a carpet, plant small clumps about 2 in. wide at distances apart of about 3 in. these bits will connect.
P. cinerea is quite dwarf, hardly more than 2 in. high with very small palmate leaves. Tufted.
P. nitida forms mats & is silky-hairy.
P. alchemilloides is whitish-silky & one of the most refined.
P. tabernaemontani & *P. crantzii* are 2 spp. previously

known as *P. verna:* Mat forming & somewhat downy.
P. alba has grey-green leaves deeply divided.
P. fragiformis: Foliage handsome in shape & texture; a soft down makes it look velvety. the palmate leaves lie quite flat & overlap one another.
P. magalantha has a resemblance, sparsely hairy above, greyish long-hairy beneath. To 6 in. Both spread slowly to 1 ft; both dislike excess water on the leaves.
P. tridentata: Spreads by underground shoots. Dark green; leaves turn wine-red in colder climates.
P. reptans is too invasive. Consider the above merely a sampling.

Pratia treadwellii: LOBELIACEAE.
This is known as *P. angulata*—a mat-forming sp. from New Zealand. If it will establish itself, it looks well especially between paving stones. Stems rooting at nodes (*Hortus III* gives precedent to *P. angulata.*)

Primula: PRIMULACEAE.
Several spp. naturalize in damp, suitable soil. Dwarves will make very good drifts, although slowly.
P. × pruhoniciana (*P. × juliana*) is a race of hybs. from crosses between *P. juliae* & other spp. of the section Vernales. Modern hybs. variable. See Woodland for names of cvs.

Prunella: LABIATAE. Self-heal.
Can become a troublesome weed. Roots are tough & anchor strongly from a creeping stem. Several spp. make tight carpets or mats to 2 ft. or more.
P. grandiflora subsp. *pyrenaica* with hastate leaves the most decorative. (*P. vulgaris* is widely naturalized.)

Ramonda myconi (*Ramonda pyrenaica*): GESNARIACEAE.
A basal rosette to 6 in. across. Leaves crinkled, with soft, reddish hairs. Variable; the best forms beautiful. An alpine plant which needs a shady, cool exposure & perfect drainage. Best in a r.g.

Ranunculus repens: RANUNCULACEAE. Creeping Buttercup.
The double form is not as rampant as the single-flowered form. Leaves dark green, roundish, shiny. Hdy.

Rubus: ROSACEAE. Bramble, Raspberry. Two or more spp. for ground covering.
R. calycinoides will cover a large area to 6 ft. & more when given good soil & moisture. Stems tight to the ground, rooting as they creep. Leaves, small, round, wavy-edged & crinkled, overlapping on the stems. Greener in some shade. Good for edging & for steps—it will cling to step risers. Invasive.
R. arcticus: Herbaceous rather than evergreen. Leaves light green instead of dark. Spreads by creeping root stocks, but slowly. Shy fruits are edible. Difficult.

Ruta graveolens: RUTACEAE. Rue, Herb of Grace.
Several plants together form a striking drift of unusual blue-green, 1 ft. × 3 ft. Cvs. of this acrid herb have been developed with interesting colored foliage. E.g.'Blue Mound'.

Sagina subulata 'Aurea': CARYOPHYLLACEAE. Scotch Moss. The mossy foliage will stand light traffic. Sun or part shade. Fairly hdy.

Sanguinaria canadensis: PAPAVERACEAE. Bloodroot.

Clump 1 ft. × 1 ft. Basal leaves palmately lobed. Part shade. See Woodland.

Santolina: COMPOSITAE.
Two or more spp., to 2 ft. in height may be used in mass plantings & kept low by periodic trimming.
S. chamaecyparissus is grey-green.
S. virens is bright' green. Needs sun & heat.

Saponaria ocymoides: CARYOPHYLLACEAE. Soapwort.
To 10 in. procumbent, much branched. Stems branch from the base, trailing further on a slope. Open, sunny site.

Satureya (Satureja): LABIATAE.
Trailers or clumpers.
S. douglasii (Micromeria chamissoni): Yerba Buena. Tracery over the ground, not very thick. Down a slope, the stems will trail 2 ft. or more. Likes moisture & some shade, esp. in hot areas.
S. montana: Winter Savory. Semi-evergreen subshrub with somewhat pendant stems. Clumps increase in size & several together make an aromatic g.c. to 3 ft. across.

Saxifraga: SAXIFRAGACEAE. Saxifrage, Rocktoil.
Of some 200 spp., several are r.g. pers. and most somewhat difficult. Two are easy, however, spreading rapidly in shade & with moisture.
S. sarmentosa (S. stolonifera), Strawberry Saxifrage, has round, deeply-veined leaves, the undersides red. In flat rosettes. Pendulous runners root as they touch earth. It is easy to pull if it becomes invasive. Tender.
S. umbrosa: London Pride. The rosettes grow close together in clumps which gradually widen to 2 ft. or more. Leaves round, toothed & leathery. If older foliage dies out in the center, lift the clump & replant the fresher parts.

Scaevola: GOODENACEAE.
Ground-hugging mat; many stems with very small leaves. Cvs. e.g. 'Mauve Clusters'.

Schizocentron elegans (now *Heterocentron*): MELASTOMATACEAE.
Stems which root at the nodes creep to form a dense mat; leaves small, reddish. Likes shade & loose soil. Tender.

Sedum: CRASSULACEAE. Stonecrop.
Many spp.; the search for some as yet unknown far from exhausted. Several root readily & spread quickly even in poor soil. Several resent constant watering in summer. Place plants 6 in. apart to acquire a quick cover.
S. acre: mat-forming, evgrn, hdy. Can become inv.
S. anglicum: mat-forming, evgrn. Restrained, esp. 'Minus'.
S. amecamecanum: Spreads well on a slope but not where soil is too poor or dry. Leaves yellowish green. Tender.
S. brevifolium: Creeping stems & chalky grey leaves.
S. spathulifolium: Nor. U.S. Runner-like branches with small, round leaves tinged red. 'Capo-Blanco', a fine form with grey leaves.
S. stahlii: Coral Beads. Leaves with purplish brown tones.
S. sieboldii: Herb but tiny basal rosettes persistent. Flowering stems trail—decorated with neat rows of round leaves, blue-green in Spring, striking pinkish red in fall. Only a few of many spp. & dvs.

Sempervivum: CRASSULACEAE. Houseleek.
Tight rosettes increase slowly by offsets. Leaves many. Will fill a container, beginning with a small plant, in 3 to 5 years.
S. tectorum: The sp. most commonly seen in gardens.

Silene: CARYOPHYLLACEAE. Catchfly.
Several spp. are low, wide-spreading but not rampant. Sun & ½ shade; year around moisture.
S. acaulis: Cushion Pink. Contained creeper; moss-like.
S. hookeri: Oregon. Small grey tufts.
S. ingramii: Oregon. Hairy foliage.
S. ocymoides (S. italica): Grey-green leaves on slender stems. Good trailing down a steep slope.
S. schafta: Unusual, showy dwarf. Tufted. 6 in. × 8 in.

Smilacina racemosa: LILIACEAE. False Spikenard. Herb.
Upright, sometimes over 2 ft. Many leafy stems hide the ground. Spreads to 10 ft. or so.

Stachys: LABIATAE. Betony.
Some procumbent kinds; well-drained soil & sun.
S. byzantina (S. lanata): Leaves white woolly, thick, close to the ground. Remove flowering stems as they start to grow. Sun. Spreads rapidly; could become invasive.

Tanacetum: COMPOSITAE. Tansy.
T. camphoratum: Native around San Francisco.
T. vulgare var. *crispum:* Garnish. Pungent. Very leafy, fern-like.
T. haradjanii: Foliage grey, crinkled.

Teucrium: LABIATAE.
Edges or hedges; 1 to 2 ft.; can be sheared. Leaves small & numerous. Heat, ½ hdy., drought tolerant.
T. chamaedrys var. *prostratum:* Prostrate Germander, good for a bank. See Slope.

Thymus: LABIATAE. Thyme.
Many spp. See Slope. Several tight to the ground. Some with green leaves, some with grey & some variegated.
T. pseudolanuginosus: looks like woolly moss.
Seek *T. praecox* subsp. *arcticus* 'Coccineus': esp. good on a slope—low creeping.

Tiarella: SAXIFRAGACEAE. False Mitrewort.
Erect but low growing. Use in shady woodland.
T. cordifolia: Foamflower, spreads by slender stolons to form a wide mass.
T. wherryi: without stolons, is compact. Leaves triangular, thin texture patterned, dainty. Several spp. from the NW coast of No. Am. worth seeking.

Tolmeia: SAXIFRAGACEAE.
T. menziesii: Pickaback Plant; known as a house plant but useful as a g.c. in shade.

Tripleurospermum: COMPOSITAE.
Leaves dissected. Related to Chrysanthemum.
T. tchihatchewii, formerly found under *Matricaria:* seen in old gardens, spread to 1 ft. Seeds itself too readily; noted for tiny pink daisies. Called Turfing Daisy.

Vancouveria: BERBERIDACEAE (Related to *Epimedium*).
Creeping plants with beautiful glossy foliage. See Woodland.
V. planipetalum (V. parviflora): very refined.
V. hexandra: substance of the leaflets is less leathery than that of *V. planipetala.* Shear off stems in autumn.

Verbena: VERVAIN.

Many spp., some prostrate.

V. peruviana: Dense, low carpet of dark green foliage often half-hidden by flowers. Grows strongly; unlimited spread. ½ hdy.

Veronica: SCROPHULATIACEAE. Speedwell.

Several low spp. *V. filiformis* can become a pernicious weed.

V. incana: a white-pubescent, leafy mat; restrained.

V. prostrata: mat-forming. Garden forms usually go by the name *V. rupestris.*

V. gentianoides: A clump—4 in. × 15 in. Leaves small, green, glossy.

V. repens: Forms flat, wide & close mats which will take a little traffic. But it is quite inv.

Vinca: APOCYNACEAE. Periwinkle.

Spreads widely; stems prostrate, rooting & trailing, esp. when on a slope. It is hard to remove if once established. See Slope. Foliage leathery, dark green, darker in some varieties.

V. major: too agressive & does not lie flat.

V. minor var. *alba* & *V. minor* var. *punicea* both have good habits.

Viola: VIOLACEAE.

Many spp.; see General. Impossible to choose one or two as best for ground covers. (Those which cover the ground most rapidly are sure to be inv.)

V. odorata, Sweet Violet, has many forms; usually chosen for fragrance. A few are chosen for their flowers. The wild Sweet Violet spreads by long, prostrate, rooting stolons.

V. hederacea, Australian Violet, forms a tight carpet. Leaves rounded & overlapping. Tender.

V. saxatile (V. alpestris): Quite small & low. Seeds itself.

V. pedata, Bird's Foot Violet: Tricky in the garden. Add both sand & leafmold to the soil.

Waldsteinia: ROSACEAE. Related to Strawberry.

Creeping rhizomes near surface of the ground. Mat-forming. Not rampant. Sometimes planted in a rock garden. Easily grown but needs considerable light.

W. fragaroides, Barren Strawberry, is the most common.

12. *Culture of Chrysanthemums for Flowers*

Preparation of Beds
1. Location: sun, but with shade in the afternoon in order to provide a shortened day.
2. Soil: work in ample compost or rotted manure; maintain a slightly acid pH.
3. Support: six-foot stakes at least two by two; place two at every 12 feet, two feet apart (or at the end of the row, if the row is a little less or a little more than 12 feet).

Planting
1. Place plants one foot to one and a half feet apart with similar heights adjacent to each other.

Support
1. String a double row of strong twine from post to post on at least two levels, at one foot apart (more if needed for tallest growing spp.)
2. Tie stems as needed with double twine, (or if stems are numerous, they may simply lean for support). Use soft material to tie.

Feeding
1. Add extra food with superphosphate, small amounts at a time.
2. Feed (with anything) twice a week in summer; stop when buds show color.
3. Mulch with rotted manure, or equivalent, one inch deep, once in each of three months—June, July and August.
4. Water with a solution of ammonium sulphate at least once a summer; one handful in two and a half gallons of water, applying when the soil is damp.

Pests (Aphids, Caterpillars, Cabbageworms, Grasshoppers)
1. Hand hunt *early* in the morning.
2. Leave on the stem one extra bud for grasshoppers (if disbudding).
3. Use your own system of control early before any insect begins to multiply.

Pinching and Disbudding
(Only if extra quality or quantity is desired)
1. When eight inches high, thin out to keep five or less best stems and pinch off laterals.
2. Disbud about August 20 (for one flower to a stem).
   a. "Crown" bud=first or middle bud—with grasslike leaf—leave this for most early types.
   b. "Terminal" bud=bud with clusters of smaller buds—with true leaf—leave this for most late types.
   c. Choose well-rounded, healthy bud to keep.

Covering (Glass or Cloth)
1. Hastens bud formation.
2. Protects from wind and weather.
3. Improves color—clearer and stronger.

Winter Care
1. Don't mulch (covering crowns induces rot).
2. Store under overhead protection one or more of best kinds.
3. Make cuttings to increase stock.

Water
1. Use wilting of leaves as a guide. Keep on dry side while divisions or rooted shoots are being held, but not beyond sign of wilt.
2. Water about twice a week in season. (Weather, climate, situation in garden modify.) Caution: Rot may occur if too wet near crown.

13. Herbs for Decoration as well as Culinary

Allium (Chives)
Allium (Leek)
Aloysia (Lemon verbena)
Anethum graveolens (Dill)
Angelica
Artemisia (Tarragon)
Beta vulgaris (Chard)
Borago (Borage)
Chamaemelum nobile (Camomile)
Foeniculum (Fennel)
Galium (Asperula) (Sweet Woodruff)
Helianthus tuberosus (Jerusalem artichoke)
Marjorana (Marjorum)
Marrubium (Hoarhound)
Melissa (Lemon balm)
Mentha
Ocimum (Basil)
Origanum
Rosmarinus
Rumex scutatus (Sorrel)
Ruta (Rue)
Salvia (Sage)
Santolina (Lavender Cotton)
Satureja montana (Winter Savory)
Symphytum (Comfrey)
Tanacetum (Tansy)
Teucrium (Germander)
Thymus (Thyme)

14. Glossary

albus	white
anther	tip of the stamen, pollen bearing part
apex	tip
arboreus	tree-like
argenteus	silver
australis	southern
barbatus	bearded
bicolor, discolor	of more than one color
blade	expanded part of the leaf
bract	modified leaves below flower
calyx	circle of sepals
capitatus	head-like
carneus	flesh colored
citrinus	yellow
coccineus	scarlet
coeruleus	blue
coma	tuft of soft hairs on a seed. Tuft of leaves or bracts on apex of inflorescence; a leafy crown or head
concolor	of one color
cordatus	heart-shaped
corm	thickened underground stem
corolla	collection of petals
corona	appendage on inner side of corolla in some flowers
corymb	inflorescence, short & broad, more or less flat, outer flowers first
cyme	inflorescence, usually broad, more or less flat, central flowers first
decumbent	lying down
edulis	edible
emarginate	notched (shallow) at apex
fastigiate	column-like
foetidus	unpleasant scented
formosus	beautiful
fruticosus	shrubby
glabrous	without hairs
glaucus	as if sprinkled with light powder
gracilis	slender
hortensis	of gardens
imbricated	overlapping
incanus	grey, hoary
labiate	two lipped
laciniatus	fringed
laevigatus	smooth
latifolius	broad leaved
littoralis	of the seashore
loose (soil)	open, humusy and friable
luteus	yellow
minimus	small
mollis	soft, hairy
montanus	of the mountains
nanus	dwarf
niger	black
node	growing point on a stem
officinalis	medicinal
palmate	divided, radiating fanwise
panicle	branching inflorescence
papilionaceous	butterfly-like
pedicle	stalk of individual flower

peduncle	stalk of flower cluster
pinnate	feather-like, arranged both sides of an axis
procumbent	lying flat, but not rooting
prostrate	lying flat
pubescent	bearing hairs, wooly
pumilus	dwarfish
raceme	inflorescence, unbranched, elongated
rachis	the axis of an inflorescence or compound leaf
repens, reptans	creeping
reticulate	veined
rhizome	rootstock, on or under the ground, leaves or stem at apex
rivularis	of streams
rugosus	wrinkled or rough
saxatilis	inhabiting rocks
scabrus	rough feeling
scandens	climbing
scree	fragmented rocks
sessile	without stem
spicata	spike-like
stolon	stem running along, taking root at nodes
triloba	leaves in threes
triphylla	leaves in threes
truss	cluster of flowers closely spaced
tuber	short thick stem, bearing buds & acting as food storage
villous	with hairs, long, soft, shaggy, not matted
whorl	three or more leaves or flowers circling a node

15. Common Names

Adder's Tongue	Erythronium	Brown-Eyed Susan	Rudbeckia
Agrimony	Eupatorium	Buckwheat	Eriogonum
Alumroot	Heuchera	Bugbane	Cimicifuga
Angel's Hair	Artemisia schmidtiana	Bugloss, Italian	Anchusa
Angel's Tears	Narcissus triandrus	Bugloss, Siberian	Brunnera
Apache Plume	Falluga paradoxa	Bugle Weed	Ajuga
Apostles Plant	Neomarica	Bunchberry	Cornus canadensis
Artichoke	Cynara	Burning Bush	Dictamnus
Asphodel	Asphodeline	Bush Germander	Teucrium
Aster, Tree	Olearia	Bush Morning Glory	Convolvulus cneorum
Autumn Crocus	Colchicum	Butterbur	Petasites
Avens	Geum	Buttercup	Ranunculus
Baboon Flower	Babiana	Butterfly Silkweed	Asclepias
Baby's Breath	Gypsophila elegans	Calla, Black	Arum palaestinum
Balloon Flower	Platycodon	Calla Lily	Zantedeschia
Balm, Lemon	Melissa	Camass	Camassia
Bamboo	Arundinaria	Campion	Lychnis or Silene
Baneberry	Actaea	Candytuft	Iberis
Basil	Ocimum	Canterbury Bell	Campanula medium
Basket Flower	Hymenocallis	Cardinal Flower	Lobelia cardinalis
Basket-Of-Gold	Aurinia	Cardoon	Cynara
Bastard Sandalwood	Myoporum	Carnation	Dianthus
Beard-Tongue	Penstemon	Carpet Bugle	Ajuga reptans
Bear's Breech	Acanthus	Catchfly	Silene pendula
Bear's Foot	Aconitum	Catmint	Nepeta × faassenii
Bellflower, Willow	Campanula persicifolia	Cats' Ears	Calochortus
Bellwort	Uvularia perfoliata	Century Plant	Agave
Betony	Stachys	Chamomile	Chamaemelum nobile
Bird's Bill	Dodecatheon	Checkerberry	Gaultheria procumbens
Bird's Foot Violet	Viola pedata	Checkerbloom or Prairie	Sidalcea maniflora
Bird-of-Paradise Flower	Strelitzia	Mallow	
Birthroot	Trillium erectum	Chia	Salvia columbariae
Bishop's Cap	Mitella diphylla	Chilean Lily	Alstroemeria
Bishop's Hat	Epimedium	Chincherinchee	Ornithogalum thyrsoides
Bitter-Sweet	Solanum	Chinese Ground Orchid	Bletilla striata
Black-Eyed Susan	Rudbeckia	Chive	Allium schoenoprasum
Black Hoarhound	Ballota nigra	Christmas Rose	Helleborus niger
Blazing Star	Liatris	Cinquefoil	Potentilla
Bleeding Heart	Dicentra	Clary, Meadow	Salvia pratensis
Blood Leaf	Iresine	Cliff Brake	Pellaea
Bloodroot	Sanguinaria	Cobweb Houseleek	Sempervivum
Bluebeads	Clintonia	Coffee Fern	Pellaea andromedifolia
Bluebell	Campanula rotundifolia	Cohosh	Actaea
Bluebells	Mertensia	Cohosh, Black	Cimicifuga
Blue Bells	Hosta ventricosa	Cohosh, Blue	Caulophyllum
Blue Cowslip	Pulmonaria	Coltsfoot, Western	Petasites
Blue Cupidone	Catananche	Columbine	Aquilegia
Blue Dicks	Brodiaea or Dichelostemma	Comfrey	Symphytum
Blue-Eyed Grass	Sisyrinchium	Common Sneezeweed	Helenium
Blue-Eyed Mary	Omphalodes	Coneflower	Echinacea & Rudbeckia
Blue Lace Flower	Trachymene caerulea	Coral Bells	Heuchera
Blue Oxalis	Parochetus	Cornflower	Centaurea
Bluets, Mountain	Centaurea montana	Cowberry	Vaccinium vitis-idaea
Bocconia	Macleaya	Cow Poison	Zygadenus
Bowman's Root	Gillenia	Cowslip	Primula
Bridal Wreath	Francoa	Cowslip, Lungwort	Pulmonaria

Cowslip Virginia	Mertensia	Fennel	Ferula or Foeniculum
Crane's Bill	Geranium	Fescue	Festuca
Creeping Forget-me-not	Omphalodes	Feverfue	Chrysanthemum parthenium
Crete Dittany	Origanum dictamnus		
Crimson Flag	Schizostylis	Flag, Blue	Iris
Crowfoot	Ranunculus	Flag, Crimson	Schizostylis
Crowfoot Violet	Viola pedata	Flame Freesia	Tritonia
Crown Imperial	Fritillaria	Flamingo Flower	Anthurium
Cuckoo Pint	Arum maculatum	Flax	Linum
Cupid's Dart or Cupidone	Catananche	Flax, Bronze	Phormium colensoi
Cushion Bush	Calocephalus brownii	Flax, New Zealand	Phormium tenax
Daffodil	Narcissus	Flax, Yellow	Reinwardtia indica
Daisy, African	Arctotis	Fleabane	Erigeron
Daisy, Blue	Felicia	Foam-Flower	Tiarella
Daisy, Bush	Olearia	Foolish Maids	Galanthus nivalis
Daisy, Gloriosa	Rudbeckia hirta	Forget-Me-Not	Myosotis
Daisy, Michaelmas	Aster	Fortnight Lily	Moraea
Daisy, Paris	Chrysanthemum frutescens	Fountain Grass	Pennisetum rupelii
Daisy, Shasta	Chrysanthemum maximum	Foxglove	Digitalis
Daisy, Transvaal or Barberton	Gerbera	Freesia, Flame	Tritonia
Daisy, Yellow	Rudbeckia	Fritillary	Fritillaria
Dame's Pocket	Hesperis	Fuchsia, Ca.	Zauschneria
David's Harp	Polygonatum	Fumitory	Corydalis
Daylily	Hemerocallis	Funkia	Hosta
Death Camas	Zygadenus	Garlic, False or Crow Poison	Nothoscordum bivalve
Desert Bitterbrush	Purshia	Garlic, Society	Tulbaghia violacea
Desert Candle	Eremurus	Garlic, Sweet	Tulbaghia fragrans
Desert Mountain Bitterroot	Lewisia rediviva	Geranium, Applescented	Pelargonium odoratissimum
Didiscus	Trachymene	Geranium, Garden	Pelargonium hortorum
Disappearing Fern	Polystichum californicum	Geranium, Ivy	Pelargonium peltatum
Dittany of Crete	Origanum dictamnus	Geranium, Lemon Scented	Pelargonium crispum
Dock	Rumex	Geranium, Martha Washington	Pelargonium domesticum
Dog's Tooth Violet	Erythronium		
Dogwood	Cornus	Geranium, Nutmeg Scented	Pelargonium fragrans
Dolls' Eyes	Actaea	Geranium, Rose	Pelargonium graveolens
Donkey Tails	Sedum morganianum	Gentian, Alpine	Gentiana andrewsii
Dragonhead, False	Physostegia	Gentian Sage	Salvia patens
Dropwort	Filipendula hexapetala	Gentian, Spring	Gentiana
Drumstick Allium	Allium sphaerocephalum	Gentian, Willow	Gentiana asclepiadea
Dusty Miller	Artemisia stellariana	Germander, Bush	Teucrium fruticans
	Centaurea cineraria	Gill-Over-The-Hill	Nepeta hederacea
	Centaurea gymnocarpa	Gilliflower	Dianthus or Clove Carnation
	Chrysanthemum ptarmiciflorum	Ginger (Tame)	Hedychium
		Ginger (Wild)	Asarum
	Senecio cineraria	Globe Flower	Echinops
	Senecio leucostachys	Globe Thistle	Trollius
Dutchman's Breeches	Dicentra cucullaria	Globe Tulip	Calochortus
Elephants Ear	Colocasia	Glory Lily	Gloriosa
Eryngo	Eryngium	Glory-of-The-Snow	Chionodoxa
Evening Primrose	Oenothera	Goatbeard	Aruncus
Everlasting	Helichrysum or Anaphalis margaritacea	Gold Moss	Sedum acre
		Goldback Fern	Pityrogramma
Fairy Bells	Disporum	Golden-Drop	Onosma
Fairy Candles	Cimicifuga	Golden Eardrops	Dicentra chrysantha
Fairy Lily	Zephyranthes	Golden Marguerite	Anthemis tinctoria
Fairy Wand	Dierama	Goldenrod	Solidago
False Dragonhead	Physostegia	Grape Hyacinth	Muscari
False Indigo	Baptisia	Grass, Ruby	Tricholena rosea
False Solomon's Seal	Smilacina	Grass Widow	Sisyrinchium douglasi
Farfugium	Ligularia	Grecian Windflower	Anemone blanda
Fawn Lily	Erythronium	Green Brier	Smilax
Felt Plant	Kalanchoe beharensis	Guinea Hen Flower	Fritillaria meleagris

Harebell	Campanula	Lady, Our Lady In A Boat	Dicentra
Harlequin Flower	Sparaxis	Ladybells	Adenophora
Harvest Brodiaea	Brodiaea coronaria	Ladys' Fingers & Thumbs	Lotus corniculatus
Heal-All	Prunella	Lady's Locket	Dicentra
Heart's Ease	Viola lutea	Lady's Mantle	Alchemilla
Heath	Erica	Lamb's Ears or Lamb's	Stachys byzantina
Heath Irish	Daboecia	Tongue	
Heather	Calluna	Larkspur	Consolida ambigua
Heliotrope	Heliotropium	Lavender	Lavandula
Hellebore	Helleborus	Lavender Cotton	Santolina
Helmet Flower	Aconitum	Leadwort	Ceratostigma
Herb-of-Grace	Ruta graveolens	Leek	Allium porrum
Heron's Bill	Erodium	Lenten Rose	Helleborus orientalis
Holly, Sea	Eryngium	Leopard Plant	Ligularia kaemferi 'Aureo-
Hollyhock	Althea rosea		maculata'
Honesty	Lunaria	Leopard's Bane	Doronicum
Honeybells	Hermannia (Mahernia)	Lily, Abyssinian Sword	Gladiolus callianthus
Hoop Petticoat	Narcissus bulbicodium	Lily, African	Agapanthus
Horned Poppy	Glaucium	Lily, African Blood	Haemanthus
Horned Rampion	Phyteuma	Lily, African Corn	Ixia or Sparaxis
Horse Mint	Monarda	Lily, Alpine	Erythronium or L. parvum
Horsetail	Equisetum	Lily, Amazon	Eucharis
Horsetail, Giant	Equisetum	Lily, Avalanche	Erythronium
Hound's Tongue	Cynoglossum	Lily, Aztec (Jacobean or St.	Sprekelia
Houseleek	Sempervivum	James)	
Huckleberry	Vaccinium	Lily, Blackberry	Belamcanda
Hyacinth	Hyacinthus	Lily, Blood	Haemanthus
Hyacinth, California	Brodiaea	Lily, Bluebead	Clintonia
Hyacinth, Grape	Muscari	Lily, Bugle	Watsonia
Indian Paintbrush	Castilleja	Lily, Butterfly	Hedychium
Indian Physic	Gillenia	Lily, Calla	Zantedeschia
Indian Warrior	Pedicularis densiflora	Lily, Checker	Fritillaria
Indigo, False	Baptisia	Lily, Chilean	Alstroemeria
Indigo, Wild	Baptisia	Lily, Coral	Lilium pumilum
Inside-Out-Flower	Epimedium or Vancouveria	Lily, Corn	Clintonia, Ixia, Sparaxis,
Iris, African	Dietes		Veratrum
Iris, Butterfly	Moraea	Lily, Cuban	Scilla peruviana
Iris, Mourning	Iris susiana	Lily, Eucharist	Eucharis
Iris, Orchid	Iris japonica	Lily, Fairy or Zephyr Flower	Zephyranthes
Iris, Roof	Iris tectorum	Lily, Fawn	Erythronium
Iris, Shatu or Iris, Japanese	Iris kaempferi	Lily, Fire	Cyrtanthus
Iris, Walking	Neomarica	Lily, Fortnight	Dietes
Iris, Winter or Algerian	Iris unguicularis	Lily, Foxtail	Eremurus
Ithuriel's Spear	Triteleia laxa	Lily, Ginger	Alpinia, Hedychium
Ivy	Hedera	Lily, Glacier	Erythronium
Jacob's Ladder	Polemonium	Lily, Gladwin	Iris foetidissima
Jacob's Rod	Asphodeline	Lily, Globe	Calochortus
Jerusalem Artichoke	Helianthus tuberosa	Lily, Glory	Gloriosa
Jerusalem Sage	Phlomis	Lily, Guernsey	Nerine
Jewel of Tibet	Allium giganteum	Lily, Ifafa	Cyrtanthus
Joe Pye Weed	Eupatorium purpureum	Lily, Kaffir	Clivia or Schizostylis
Johnny-Jump-Up	Viola tricolor	Lily, Mariposa	Calochortus
Jonquil	Narcissus	Lily, Natal	Moraea
Kaffir Lily	Clivia	Lily, New Zealand Rock	Arthropodium cirrhatum
Kaffir Lily	Schizostylis coccinea	Lily, Paradise	Paradisea
Kamchatka	Cimicifuga simplex	Lily, Perfumed Fairy	Chlidanthus
Kangaroo Paw	Anigozanthos	Lily, Peruvian	Alstroemeria
Katherine Wheel Flower	Haemanthus katherinae	Lily, Pineapple	Eucomis
Kennelworth Ivy	Cymbalaria muralis	Lily, Plantain	Hosta
King's Spear	Asphodeline	Lily, Rain	Zephyranthes
Knapweed	Centaurea	Lily, Sacred Lily of China	Rohdea japonica
Knotweed	Polygonum	Lily, Sand	Leucocrinum

Lily, Scarborough	Vallota	Mourning Widow	Geranium phaeum
Lily, Solomon's	Arum	Mt. Atlas Daisy	Anacyclus
Lily, South African	Anthericum	Mugwort, White	Artemisia lactiflora
Lily, Spider	Lycoris or Hymenocallis	Mullein	Verbascum or Celsia
Lily, Star	Zigadenus	Muskrat Weed	Thalictrum polygamum
Lily, St. Bernard's	Anthericum liliago	Myrtle, Running	Vinca
Lily, St. Bruno's	Paradisea	Naked Lady	Amaryllis belladonna
Lily, Sword	Gladiolus	Nap-At-Noon or Dove's	Ornithogalum lactum
Lily, Toad	Tricyrtis	Dung	
Lily, Torch	Kniphofia	Nasturtium	Tropaeolum
Lily, Trout	Erythronium	Navelwort	Hydrocotyle
Lily, Water	Nymphaea	New Zealand Bur	Acaena microphylla
Lily-of-China	Rohdea	New Zealand Flax	Phormium tenax
Lily-of-The-Amazon	Eucharis	New Zealand Rock Lily	Arthropodium cirrhatum
Lily-of-The-Incas	Alstroemeria	Oats	Avena
Lily-of-The-Nile	Agapanthus	Oats, Sea	Uniola paniculata
Lily-of-The-Valley	Convallaria	Obedient Plant	Physostegia
Lily-of-The-Valley False or	Maianthemun	Oconee-Bells	Shortia galacifolia
Wild		Old Man	Artemisia abrotanum
Lilyturf	Liriope	Old Woman	Artemisia stelleriana
Lingonberry	Vaccinium vitis-idaea	Onion, Flowering	Allium
Lion's Tail	Leonotis leonorus	Onion, Pregnant	Ornithogalum caudatum
Liverleaf or Liverwort	Hepatica	Oregano	Origanum
London Pride	Saxifraga × umbrosa	Oswega Tea	Monarda
Loose-Strife	Lysimachia or Lythrum	Our-Lady-In-A-Boat	Dicentra
Lords-And-Ladies	Arum	Painted Tongue	Salpiglossis sinuatus
Love-In-A-Mist	Nigella damascena	Palm Lily	Yucca
Lungwort	Pulmonaria	Panda Plant	Kalanchoe tomentosa
Lupin, Carolina or Lupin,	Thermopsis	Pasque Flower	Pulsatilla
False		Patate Della Madonna	Cyclamen hederifolium
Lyre Flower	Dicentra	Patridge Berry	Mitchella
Madwort	Allyssum	Pennyroyal	Mentha pulegium
Maidenhair Fern	Adiantum	Peony	Paeonia
Maiden's Wreath	Francoa	Periwinkle	Vinca
Mallow	Hibiscus or Malva	Persian Candytuft	Aethionema
Marguerite	Chrysanthemum frutescens	Pimpernel	Anagallis
Marigold	Tagetes	Pincushion Flower	Scabiosa
Marjorum, Sweet	Majorana	Pineapple Flower	Eucomis
Marjorum, Wild	Origanum	Pink	Dianthus plumarius
Marsh Rosemary	Limonium perezii	Pink, Rainbow	Dianthus chinensis
Martha Washington Plume	Filipendula rubra	Pink, Sea	Armeria
May Apple	Podophyllum	Plumbago	Ceratostigma
Mayflower	Epigea repens	Poker, Red-Hot	Kniphofia
Meadow Clary	Salvia	Poor Man's Orchid	Schizanthus
Meadow Rue	Thalictrum	Poppy, Alpine	Papaver alpina
Meadow Saffron	Colchicum	Poppy, Anemone	Hybrid anemones de Caen or
Meadow Sweet	Filipendula or Astilbe		St. Brigid
Megasea	Bergenia	Poppy, Blue Tibetan	Meconopsis
Mexican Star	Milla	Poppy, California or Foothill	Eschscholtzia
Mignonette	Reseda odorata	Poppy, Himalayan	Meconopsis
Milkweed	Asclepias or Euphorbia	Poppy, Horned	Glaucium
Mint	Mentha	Poppy, Iceland	Papaver nudicaule
Mission Bells	Eschscholtzia	Poppy, Little Golden	Eschscholtzia minutiflora
Mock Strawberry	Duchesnea	Poppy,Mallow	Callirhoe
Mondo Grass	Liriope	Poppy, Matilija	Romneya
Monkey Musk	Mimulus	Poppy, Mexican Tulip	Hunnemania
Monkshood	Aconitum	Poppy, Oriental	Papaver orientalis
Montbretia	Crocosmia	Poppy, Plume	Macleaya
Moonwort	Lunaria	Poppy, Shirley or Corn	Papaver rhoeas
Morning Glory	Convolvulus	Poppy, Welsh	Meconopsis cambrica
Mosquito-Bills	Dodecatheon hendersonii	Preacher-In-The-Pulpit	Arum
Moss Pink	Phlox subulata	Pretty Face or Golden	Triteleia ixioides
		Brodiaea	

Primrose	Primula	Spotted Dog	Pulmonaria
Primrose, Evening	Oenothera	Spring Star Flower	Ipheion uniflora
Purple-Eyed-Grass	Sisyrinchium	Spurge	Euphorbia
Quamash	Camassia	Squill	Scilla
Queen Ann's Lace	Daucus carota	St. Catherine's Lace	Eriogonum
Queen-of-The-Meadow or Meadows	Eupatorium or Filipendula	St. John's Wort	Hypericum
		St. John's Wort, Creeping	Hypericum calycinum
Queen-of-The-Prairies	Filipendula rubra	Star of Bethlehem	Ornithogalum
Ragged Robin	Lychnis	Statice	Limonium
Rain-of-Fire	Heuchera	Stoke's Aster	Stokesia
Reed, Giant	Arunda	Stonecress	Aethionema
Rhubarb	Rheum	Stonecrop	Sedum
Rockcress	Arabis or Aubrieta	Strawberry	Fragaria
Rockfoil	Saxifraga	Strawberry, Beach	Fragaria chiloensis
Rock Jasmine	Androsace	Strawflower	Helichrysum
Rose, Christmas	Helleborus niger	Sulphur Flower	Eriogonum umbellatum
Rose, Lenten	Helleborus orientalis	Summer Hyacinth	Galtonia
Rosebay Willow Herb	Epilobium	Sundrops	Oenothera
Rosemary	Rosmarinus	Sunflower, False	Heliopsis
Ruby Grass	Tricholaena rosea	Sunrose	Helianthemum
Rue	Ruta	Sweet Cicely	Myrrhis
Sage	Salvia	Sweet Coltsfoot	Petasites
Sage, Clary	Salvia sclarea	Sweet Flag	Acorus
Sage, Jerusalem	Phlomis	Sweet Rocket	Hesperis
Sage, Meadow	Salvia pratensis	Sweet William	Dianthis barbatus
Sage, Mealy-Cup	Salvia farinacea	Sweet Woodruff	Galium odoratum
Sage, Vatican	Salvia sclarea var. turketsanica	Tailflower	Anthurium
Sailor-caps	Dodecatheon	Tansy	Tanacetum
Sandwort	Arenaria	Tarragon	Artemisia dracunculus
Satin Flower	Sisyrinchium douglasi	Three-Birds-Flying	Linaria
Savory	Satureja	Thrift	Armeria
Saxifrage	Saxifraga or Bergenia	Throatwort	Trachelium
Sea Holly	Eryngium	Thyme	Thymus
Sea Lavender	Limonium	Tickseed	Coreopsis verticillata
Sedge	Carex	Tiger Flower	Tigridia
Self-Heal	Prunella	Toadflax	Linaria
Shamrock Pea	Parochetus	Tobacco Plant	Nicotiana
Sheep's Bit	Jasione	Torch Lily	Kniphofia
Shooting Star	Dodecatheon	Tree Daisy	Olearia stellulata
Signet Marigold	Tagetes tenuifolia	Tritoma	Kniphofia
Silverbush	Convolvulus cneorum	Trout Lily	Erythronium
Snake-Head	Fritillaria	Tuberose	Polianthes
Snake Plant	Sansevieria	Tulip	Tulipa
Snakeroot, Black	Cimicifuga	Turkey Mullein	Eremocarpus
Snakeroot, White	Eupatorium	Twinflower	Linnaea borealis
Snapdragon	Antirrhinum	Umbrella Plant	Peltiphyllum peltatum
Sneezeweed	Helenium	Venus's Fishing Rod	Dierama
Snowdrop	Galanthus	Violet	Viola
Snowflake	Leucojum	Violet, Australian	Hederacea
Snow-In-Summer	Cerastium	Violet, Sweet	Viola odorata
Soap Plant	Chlorophytum	Wake Robin	Trillium
Soapwort	Saponaria	Wallcress	Arabis
Soldiers and Sailors	Pulmonaria	Wallflower	Cheiranthus or Erysimum
Solomon's Seal (also King Solomon)	Polygonatum	Wandflower	Galax or Sparaxis or Dierama
		Water Pennyworth	Hydrocotyle
Solomon's Seal, False	Smilacina	White Cup	Nierembergia repens
Sowbread	Cyclamen	Windflower	Anemone or Pulsatilla
Speargrass	Aciphylla	Wind Poppy	Stylomecon heterophylla
Speedwell	Veronica	Wing Head	Pterocephalus
Spider Plant	Anthericum	Wintergreen	Gaultheria
Spiderwort	Tradescantia	Wolf's Bane	Aconitum
Spiraea, False	Astilbe	Wonder of Stafa	Aster frikartii

Wood Sorrel	Oxalis oregana
Wormwood	Artemisia
Yarrow	Achillea
Yerba buena	Satureja douglasii
Yerba de pescado	Eremocarpus
Yerba de selva	Whipplea modesta
Yerba mansa	Anemopsis californica
Yucca, Red	Hesperaloe

Index

Asparagus 88, 133, 250
Asperula = Galium 53, 54, 58,
  58B, 140, 143, 250, 268, 270
Asperula bryoides var. olympica
  51, 58
Asperula cynanchica 270
Asperula gussonii 141
Asperula nitida 58
Asperula odorata See Galium
  odorata
Asphodeline 88, 89–90, **89C,** 122,
  218, 281, 283
Asphodeline liburnica 90
Asphodeline lutea 90, 219
  var. flore-pleno 90
Asphodeline taurica 90
Asphodelus 88, 90, 122, 170
Asphodelus aestivus 90
Asphodelus albus 90
Aspidistra 16, **16B,** 53, 120, 122,
  132, 140, 143
Aspidistra elatior 143
  var. variegata 143
Asplenium 134
Astilbe × 'Gloria Superba' 58
Astartea 13, 122
Aster **12,** 14, 30, **30B,** 33, 38, 122,
  152, 155, 165, 171–172,
  172A, 179, 180, 188, 198,
  218, 237, 245, 246, 248, 249,
  251, 252, 254, 262, 268, 282
  'Beechwood Challenger' 247
  'Lucida' 38
  'Winston Churchill' 247
Aster alpinus 84, 172, 246
  var. albus 172
Aster amellus 172, 246
Aster cordifolius 172
Aster cvs 33, 172, 247
  'Adorable' 247
  'Blue Bouquet' 246
  'Climax' 172
  'Countess of Dudley' 247
  'Crimson Brocade' 172
  'Daphne' 247
  'Goliath' 246
  'Harrington's Pink' 172
  'Little Pink Lady' 247
  'Prof. Kuppenberg' 246
  'Royal Opal' 246
  'Star of Eisenach' 246
  'Victor' 246
  'White Lady' 172
Aster dumosus (dwarves) 172,
  207, 231, 246
  'Marjorie' 172, 247
  'Nancy' 172, 246
  'Ronald' 172
  'Twinkle' 172
  'Winston Churchill' 172
Aster farreri 172
Aster 'Finalist' 172
Aster × frikartii 14, 172, 219, 221,
  246, 285
  'Monch' 172
  'Wonder of Staffa' 172
Aster hybridus
  "Gay Border Blue" 172

'Harrington's Pink' 172
'Mt. Everest' 172
'Nanus' 172
'Niobe' 172
Aster novae-angliae 172, 258
Aster nova-belgii 172
Aster Oregon semi-dwarf:
  'Adorable' 172
Aster puniceus 253
Aster subcoeruleus 246
  'Wartburg Star' 260
Aster thompsonii var. nana 172
  'Little Red' 172
Aster tongolensis (A.
  subcaeruleus) 172, 207
  A.t. 'Berggarten' 172
  A.t. 'Napsbury' (A.
    yunnanensis 'Napsbury' of
    gardens) 172
Aster yunnanensis 218
  A.y. 'Napsbury' 172, 219, 246
Asteriscus See Odontospermum
Asteriscus maritimus 38
Astilbe 9, 17, 27, **32C,** 48, 51, 53,
  54, 55, 56, 58, **58C,** 66, 78,
  99, 122, 131, 136, 140, **150C,**
  151, 184, 214, 222, 238, 245,
  247, 250, 251, 252, 253, 262,
  270, 284, 285
  'Fanal' 247
Astilbe × arendsii hybs. (A.
  chinensis var. davidii, A.
  astilboides, A. japonica, A.
  thunbergii) 33, 58, 214, 270
  'Bridal Veil' 58
  'Crispa' 58
  'Deutschland' 58
  'Fanal' 33, 58, 221
  'Peach' 58
  'Peach Blossom' 58
Astilbe astilboides Parents: A.
  chinensis var. davidii
  A. japonica, A. thunbergii 58
Astilbe biternata 58
Astilbe chinensis (A. sinensis) 58
Astilbe chinensis var. pumila 32,
  58, 141
  'Gnome' 58
Astilbe dwarf garden hyb. (A.
  arendsii × A. simplicifolia)
  58
Astilbe microphylla 223
Astilbe taquetii 'Superba' 58
Astrantia 17, 53, 58, 122, 172, 251
Astrantia biebersteinia 58
Astrantia involucrata See A. major
Astrantia major 58, 172
  'Shaggy' 58
  var. involucrata 172
Astrantia maxima 58, 172, 213
Athyrium 20, **42–43,** 53, 58, 157
Athyrium nipponicum 'Pictum'
  (A. goeringianum, A.
  japonicum) 20, 47, 58, 214
  'Pictum' 20, 47, 58, 214, 250
Aubrieta 54, 86, 152, 155, 172, 206,
  237, 249, 251, 268, 285
Aubrieta deltoidea 172, 207, 270

'Pink Parachute' 172
'Vindictive' 172
Aubrieta eyrei
  'Purple Knoll' 246
Aubrieta novalis 38
  'Blue' 38
Aurinia 54, 88, 90, 155, 165, 172,
  217, 237, 246, 249, 251, 254,
  268, 270, 281
Aurinia petraea 90
Aurinia saxatile 270
  'Luteum' 90, 216
  'Tom Thumb' 141
  var. citrina 90
  var. compactum 90
  var. plenum 90
  (var. sulphureum, A.s. var.
    lutea) 90
Avena 261, 284
Avena fatua 261
Avena sterilis 17, 261
Azalea 229
Azara 222
Azederach 86, 268
Azederach officinale 47
Azorella See Glebaria 143

Babiana 14, 18, 122, 141, 172,
  172B, 246, 259, 281
Baccharis 86
  'Pidgeon Point' 86
Ballota 24, 30, 121, 122, **123A,** 168,
  172, **173A,** 238, 249
Ballota nigra 14, 172, 225, 229, 281
Ballota pseudodictamnus 172
Baptisia 13, **13B,** 29, 122, 165, 167,
  172, **173B,** 206, 245, 246,
  248, 251, 252, 262, 282, 283
Baptisia australis 172, 207, 211,
  228, 231
  'Madam Mason' 172
  var. 'Exaltata' 172
Bauera 17, 262–263
Bauera rubioides 263
Begonia 17, 132, **134C,** 135, 140,
  142C, 143, **143A,** 151, 155,
  162, 245, 246, 247, 250, 251,
  260
Begonia foliosa 135, 143
Begonia semperflorens-cultorum
  (Hort. derivative of B.
  cucullata var. hookeri) 143
Belamcanda 24, 122, 172, **172C,**
  248, 251, 252, 259, 283
Bellis 122, 245, 247, 251, 252, 268
Bellis perennis 211, 270
Bellium 54, 141, 249
Bellium bellidioides 51, 270
Bellium minutum 51
Bergenia 17, 30, 48, **48B,** 53, 58–
  59, 119, **119C,** 122, 153, 167,
  214, 245, 247, 251, 254, 268,
  270, 284, 285
Bergenia cordifolia 59, 153, 214
  'Alba' 153
Bergenia crassifolia (B.c. var.
  purpurea) 59
Bergenia hybs. 59

carpatica × C. raineri 270
Campanula pulla 91, 270
  'Bakeri' 270
Campanula pulloides 91
Campanula pyramidalis 27, 144, 248
Campanula raddeana 91, 270
Campanula raineri 90
Campanula rapunculoides 173
Campanula rotundifolia (C. hondoensis or C. pilosa var. dasyantha) 173, 221, 281
Campanula thessala 246
Campanula vidalii 173
Campanula warleyensis
  'Alba' 270
  'Warley White' 270
Campion 96
Canarina 88, 91
Canarina campanula 91
Canarina canariensis 91
Canna 16, 20, 108, 155, 174, 206, 207, 246, 247, 250, 251
Canna cretica 174
Canna hybrids 174
Canna 'Wyoming' 174, 207
Cardamine 54
Carex 54, 100, **139B,** 144, 155, 253, 261, 285
Carex buchanini 261
Carex conica
  'Variegata' 250
Carex morrowii var. variegata 139
Carex riparia 'Variegata' 261
Caryopteris 262, 263
  × clandonensis 263
Caryopteris incana 263
Caryopteris mongholica 263
Cassinia retorta 263
Cassiope 25, 50, **50C,** 51, 53, 54, 60, 245
Cassiope lycopoidioides 60
Castilleja 283
Catananche 122, 140, 174, 245, 251, 252, 254, 281, 282
Catananche caerulea 32, 174, 207
  'Bicolor' 174
  'Blue Giant' 207
  'Major' 174
  'Perry's White' 174
Caulophyllum 281
Cedronella 250
Celsia 29, 109, 112, 248, 284
Celsia acaulis × Verbascum phoenicium 38
  'Golden Wings' 38
Celsia arcturus 38
Celsia cretica 112
Celsioverbascum (Celsia × Verbascum) 29, **36A,** 38, 112
  'Golden Wings' 38
Centaurea 174, 237, 245, 246, 248, 250, 251, 252, 254, 255, 257, 281, 283
Centaurea cineraria (C. candidissima) 140, 174, 282
Centaurea dealbata 'Sternbergii' 174

Centaurea gymnocarpa 174, 282
Centaurea hypoleuca 174
  'John Coutts' 174
Centaurea macrocephala 174
Centaurea montana 174, 225, 255, 281
  'Parkman' 174, 255
Centaurea moschata (C. cyanus) 174, 255
Centaurea ragusina 174
Centaurea ruthenica 174
Centaurea simplicicaulis 174
Centaurium 255, 257
Centaurium pulchellum 255
Centranthus 109, 112, **112A,** 247
Centranthus ruber (Valeriana rubra, Valeriana coccinea) 112
Cephalaria 122, 174, 208, 246, 251
Cephalaria alpina 174
Cephalaria flava (C. leucantha) 174
Cephalaria gigantea 174, 209
Cephalaria leucantha 174
Cephalaria tatarica 174
Cerastium 86, 88, 174, **174B,** 237, 238, 245, 249, 251, 254, 268, 270, 285
Cerastium biebersteinii 174, 270
Cerastium tomentosum 174, 231, 270
Ceratostigma 53, 54, 60, 86, **87A,** 88, 238, 245, 251, 262, 268, 270, 283, 284
Ceratostigma abyssinicus 60, 270
Ceratostigma griffithii 60
Ceratostigma plumbaginoides (Plumbago larpentae) 32, 60, 221, 270
Ceratostigma willmottianum ('Miss Willmott') 60
Cestrum 264
Ceterach 53, 60, **60A,** 134, 268
Ceterach officianarum 60, 214
Chaenostoma 245, 250, 251, 254, 262, 263
Chaenostoma hispidum (Sutera hispida) 263
Chamaecyparis obtusa 151
  'Juniperoides' 151
Chamaedaphne 262
Chamaemelum 20, 250, 268, 270
Chamaemelum nobile 233, 278, 281
Cheiranthus 54, 88, 91, **91A,** 181, 226, 246, 247, 249, 250, 251, 271, 285
Cheiranthus × allionii (Erysimum hieracifolium) 91
Cheiranthus capitatum 91
Cheiranthus cheirii 91
Cheiranthus coccineum 91
Cheiranthus linifolius (Erysimum linifolium) 50, 91, 213, 227
  'Bowles Mauve' (E. H. Bowles) 91
  'Variegata' 91, 227
Cheiranthus mutabilis 91

Cheiranthus semperflorens (C. mutabilis) 'Wenlock Beauty' 91
Cheiranthus suffruticosum (Erysimum suffruticosum) 91
Chelidonium 174, **175A,** 246, 251, 262, 263
Chelidonium franchetianum 263
Chelidonium majus 174, 263
Chelone 100, 252
Chelone glabra See Penstemon
Chionodoxa 282
Chlidanthus 137, 283
Chlidanthus fragrans 137
Chlorogalum 109, 112
Chlorogalum pomeridianum 112
Chlorophytum 285
Chrysanthemum 24, 33, 88, 120, **121A & B,** 122, 131, 132, 140, 151, 155, 165, 174–175, 199, 216, 217, 225, 237, 245, 246, 247, 248, 249, 250, 251, 252, 253, 254, 262, 268, 270, 277
  "Cushion" 140
  "Large flowered" 140
  'Silver Leaf' 249
Chrysanthemum anethifolium 140, 161, 175, 211, 237, 238
Chrysanthemum, border type cvs. 207, 216
  'Emperor of China' 120
  'Red Rover' 120
  'Silver Lace' 120
  'Waikiki' 120
Chrysanthemum coccineum (Pyrethrum roseum) 120, 175, 221, 225, 247, 260
  'Evenglow' 120, 175
  'Helen' 260
  'Kelway's Glorious' 175
  'Robinson's Hybrids' 175, 260
Chrysanthemum coreanum 175
Chrysanthemum frutescens 140, 175, 282, 284
  'Kayo Watanake' 140, 175
  'Maxine' 140, 175
  'Pink Lady' 140
  'Snow Cap' 140, 175
Chrysanthemum, garden hybrids 120, 175
Chrysanthemum haradjanii (Tanacetum haradjanii) 175, 221
Chrysanthemum, hybrid moderns 175, 228, 247
  'Clara Curtis' 175
  'Emerald Isle' 175
  'Emperor of China' 175
  'Red Rover' 175
  'Royal Command' 175
  'Shodoshina' 175
  'Silver Lace' 175
  'Waikiki' 175
Chrysanthemum "Korean hybrids" 120, 175, 257
Chrysanthemum leucanthemum 175

Geranium sessiliflorum 92
  'Nigrum' 92
Geranium stapfianum 92
Geranium tuberosum 92
Geranium wallichianum 92, 221
  'Buxton's variety' 92
·Geranium wlassovianum 92
Gerbera 25, **37A**, 38, 119, 122, 162,
  182, 221, 245, 246, 247, 251,
  282
  'Black Heart' 38
  'Happipot' 38
  'Frisbee' 38
Gerbera × cantabrigiensis (G.
  viridifolia × G. jamesonii)
  182
Gerbera jamesonii 260
Geum 14, 33, 54, 121, 122, 136,
  136C, 145, 182–183, 231,
  238, 246, 247, 251, 253, 254,
  268, 281
  'Fire Opal' 247
Geum × borisii (G. reptans × G.
  bulgaricum plus ? G.
  coccineum) 183
Geum bulgaricum 183
Geum chiloense (G. quellyon)
  183, 211
  'Dolly North' 183
  'Fire Opal' 183
  'Lady Stratheden' 183
  'Mrs. Bradshaw' 183
  'Princess Juliana' 183, 231
  'Red Wings' 183
  'Rubin' 183
Geum coccineum (of gardens) (G.
  chiloense, G. quellyon) 183
Geum 'Georgenberg' 14, 17, 145,
  183, 228
Geum quellyon (G. chilense)
  (Geum coccineum of
  gardens) See above. 183
Geum reptans 183
Geum rivale 183
  'Leonards Variety' 183
Geum rossii 183
Geum triflora var. campanulatum
  183
Gilia 255, 256, 257
Gilia nuttalii 256
  var. floribunda 256
Gillenia 53, 68, 253, 281, 283
Gillenia trifoliata 68, 213
Gladiolus 25, **26B**, 54, 121, 122,
  259, 284
Gladiolus callianthus 121, 217,
  225, 283
  (Acidanthera bicolor, A.
  murielae)
Gladiolus tristus var. concolor 25,
  121, 225
Glaucium 183, **183A**, 246, 247,
  249, 251, 252, 254, 283, 284
Glaucium phoeniceum 183
Globularia 51, 53, 54, 69, **69A**, 140,
  141, 145, **145B**, 186, 249,
  268, 272
Globularia aphyllanthus 69, 145,
  272

Globularia cerastioides 69, 145,
  223
Globularia cordifolia 69
  var. alba 69, 272
  var. bellidifolia 69
  var. rosea 69
Globularia incanescens 69, 145
Globularia meridionalis (G.
  bellidifolia) 16, 69, 218, 219
Globularia repens 69, 145, 219
Globularia trichosantha 69, 145
Globularia vulgaris 69
Gloriosa 122, 133, **133B**, 140, 145,
  282, 283
Gloriosa rothschildiana 145
  var. citrina 145
Gloriosa superba 145
Godetia **157B**
Goniolimon 24, 88, 92, 249
Goniolimon tataricum 92
Gonospermum 17, 109, 114, **114B**
Gonospermum canariensis 114,
  221
Goodyera 109, 114, 251
Goodyera decipiens (Sprianthes
  decipiens, Epipactus
  decipiens) 114
Goodyera oblongifolia (G.
  menziesii) 114
Grevillea 86
Grevillea humisifusa 87
Grevillea tripetala 85
Gunnera 17, 92, 99, 100, 108, 109,
  114, **117**, 140, 145, 250, 268,
  272
Gunnera chilensis 114
Gunnera dentata 145
Gunnera hamiltonii 145
Gunnera magellanica 92, 272
Gunnera manicata 114
Gypsophila 14, 51, 54, 122, 155,
  183, **183B**, 206, 207, 229,
  245, 247, 248, 251, 252, 254,
  255, 268, 272
Gypsophila acutifulia 183, 258
Gypsophila aretioides 141, 183
Gypsophila × bodgeri (G. repens
  var. rosea × G. paniculata
  var. flore-pleno) 183
Gypsophila cerastioides 183
Gypsophila elegans 38, 257, 281
  'Giant white' 38
Gypsophila muralis 257
Gypsophila paniculata 183, 207
  'Bristol Fairy'
  'Perfecta' 183, 207
  'Rosy Veil' 183
  var. ehrlei
  var. flore-pleno 183
Gypsophila petraea 183
Gypsophila repens 183
  var. rosea 183

Habenaria 100, 253
Haberlea 14, 51, 54, 69
Haberlea ferdinandi-coburgi 69
Hacquetia 69
Hacquetia epipactus 69

Haemanthus 122, 138, 141, 259,
  283
Haemanthus katherinae 283
Hakonechloa 140, 261
Hakonechloa macra 145
  var. albo-variegata 145
  var. aureola 145
Halimium 246, 254
Haplopappus 109, 250, 262
Hawarthia 152
Hebe 54, 262, 264, 265, 268, 272
Hebe chathamica 264
Hebe glaucophylla 264, 272
Hebe hartiei 264
Hebe hulkeana 264
Hedeoma pulegioides 189
Hedera 140, 268, 272, 283
Hedera helix 62
Hederacea 285
Hedychium 13, 106, **106A**, 109,
  110, 114, **114C**, 122, 238,
  246, 248, 249, 250, 251, 282,
  283
Hedychium coronarium 114
Hedychium flavescens 114
Hedychium gardnerianum 114
Helenium 33, 121, 122, 179, 183,
  231, 238, 246, 247, 248, 251,
  254, 281, 285
  'Copper Spray' 183
Helenium autumnale 183, 211
  'Bruno' 183
  'Coppelia' 33, 183
  'Gold Fox' 183
  'Peregrinum' 183, 211
  'Pumilum Magnificum' 183
  'Riverton Beauty' 183
  'Rubrum' 231
Helenium bigelovii 183
Helenium hoopesii 183
Helianthemum 14, **14A**, 54, 85, 87,
  88, 92, **92C**, 140, 161, **161E**,
  221, 245, 246, 251, 268, 272,
  285
  'Ben Ledi' 247
  'Brunette' 247
  'Burnt Orange' 247
  'Jock Scott' 247
  'Mitchell's Red' 247
  'Wendel's Rose' 247
Helianthemum apenninum 92
  var. roseum (H. rhodanthum)
  92
Helianthemum canum 92
  var. scardicum 92
Helianthemum croceum 92
Helianthemum cv. 85, 92, 221
  'Apricot' 92, 247
  'Ball of Gold' 92
  'Boule de Feu' 92, 247
  'Butterpat' 92
  'Dazzler' 92
  'Flame' 92
  'Goldilocks' 92
  'Peach' 92
  'Snowball' 92
  'St. Mary's' 92
  'Sun Fleck' 92